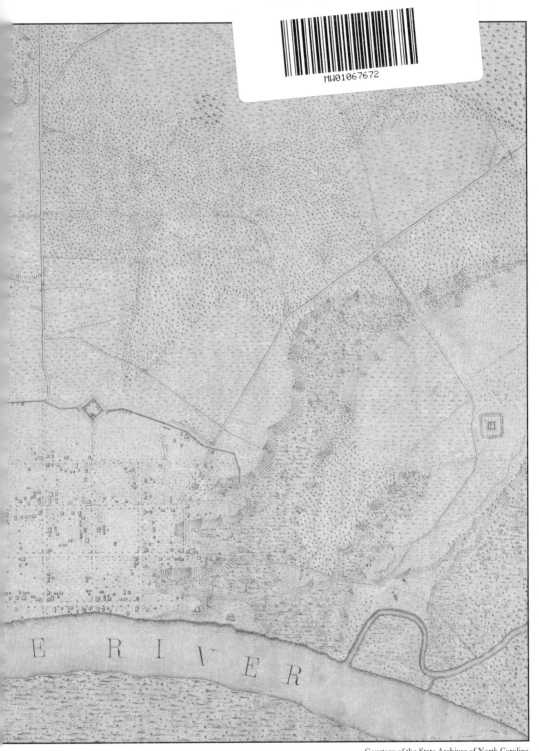

E RIVER

The Fight for
the Old North State

MODERN WAR STUDIES

Theodore A. Wilson
General Editor

The Fight for the Old North State

THE CIVIL WAR IN NORTH CAROLINA, JANUARY–MAY 1864

Hampton Newsome

 University Press of Kansas

Published by the University Press of Kansas (Lawrence, Kansas 66045), which was organized by the Kansas Board of Regents and is operated and funded by Emporia State University, Fort Hays State University, Kansas State University, Pittsburg State University, the University of Kansas, and Wichita State University

Library of Congress Cataloging-in-Publication Data

Names: Newsome, Hampton, author.
Title: The fight for the Old North State : the Civil War in North Carolina, January–May 1864 / Hampton Newsome.
Description: Lawrence, Kansas : University Press of Kansas, [2019] | Includes bibliographical references and index. | Series: Modern war studies
Identifiers: LCCN 2018046927
  ISBN 9780700627462 (cloth : alk. paper)
  ISBN 9780700627479 (ebook)
Subjects: LCSH: North Carolina—History—Civil War, 1861–1865. | New Bern (N.C.)—History—19th century. | Plymouth, Battle of, Plymouth, N.C., 1864.
Classification: LCC E476.2 .N49 2019 | DDC 975.6/03—dc23.
LC record available at https://lccn.loc.gov/2018046927.

British Library Cataloguing-in-Publication Data is available.

Printed in the United States of America

10 9 8 7 6 5 4 3 2 1

The paper used in this publication is recycled and contains 30 percent postconsumer waste. It is acid free and meets the minimum requirements of the American National Standard for Permanence of Paper for Printed Library Materials Z39.48-1992.

Contents

Illustrations and Maps

Illustrations

Maps

Preface

"The Time Is at Hand"

On January 2, 1864, a stinging cold seeped over the pastures and forests of central Virginia. Outside Union camps north of the Rapidan River, sentinels trotted along their beats to stay warm in the frigid air.[1] Several miles to the south, the chilly Saturday found Robert E. Lee in his headquarters at Middle Hill, a farm just east of Orange. With the help of his small staff, the Confederate general juggled piles of reports, requests, and other correspondence, tackling the mundane along with the consequential. In the midst of this endless paperwork, he turned his attention to conditions in North Carolina and offered a proposal to President Jefferson Davis. "The time is at hand when, if an attempt can be made to capture the enemy's forces at New Berne, it should be done," the Virginian wrote. "I can now spare troops for the purpose, which will not be the case as spring approaches."[2]

Lee had good reason to focus on North Carolina. Two years earlier, combined Union army and naval forces had captured much of the state's coast. The victorious Federals set up their principal base at New Bern and occupied other posts along the sounds and rivers at Plymouth, Washington, and Roanoke Island, as well as on the coast at Hatteras, Fort Macon, Beaufort, and Morehead City. The Northern triumph, orchestrated in large part by Ambrose Burnside, established a toehold deep in the Confederacy complete with several good ports and a rail line stretching into North Carolina's interior. In support of these bases, Union naval superiority cemented control of the region and allowed army commanders to move troops and supplies at will between the various posts. The Union occupation also created a persistent threat to rebel supply lines serving General Lee's forces in Virginia and closed several agriculturally rich counties to the Confederate Subsistence Department. But despite the potential benefits of this early lodgment, Union leaders took little advantage of their gains. With the exception of the occasional raid, Federal forces remained mostly stationary, and the region soon became a backwater during the war's first years.

Despite the lack of significant offensives, the Federal presence in the state made a substantial impact, producing immense social transformation as slaves fled their owners for the Yankee lines and strong Unionist sentiment fueled internal resistance to Confederate rule. Social instability spread throughout the region, affecting slaves as well as wealthy planters, yeoman farmers, free blacks, and white laborers. The existing economic and social fabric in the coastal plain began to crumble as the grip of the slaveholding class loosened. In addition, opponents of secession directly aided the Union cause by joining Federal regiments at recruiting stations such as New Bern, while others resisted the Confederacy through more subtle means.

As the war extended into 1864, Confederate leaders faced many challenges in the wake of a year that saw their fortunes decline dramatically. In the west, Union columns under Ulysses S. Grant had captured Vicksburg and, with it, gained full control over the Mississippi River. In the fall, Grant took Chattanooga and his legions coiled to march south toward Atlanta. In the east, Lee's summer foray into Pennsylvania ended poorly at Gettysburg. All the while, Federal troops maintained their presence along the mid-Atlantic coast in Virginia and the Carolinas. Aside from these broad military developments, new issues transformed the war. By 1864, matters of race and slavery undergirding the struggle began to manifest themselves directly on the battlefield. As African Americans joined the Union ranks in 1863 following President Lincoln's Emancipation Proclamation, Confederate troops began to meet black Federal soldiers in combat.

At the beginning of 1864, matters in North Carolina had not changed significantly since the initial Union victories earlier in the war. The previous year, Confederate forces had conducted unsuccessful operations against Washington on the Pamlico River. In addition, the rebels sought to construct powerful ironclads far upriver from the Federal bases. However, while the Confederates schemed, Union commanders launched several raids, both large and small, from their bases and aggressively recruited local white Unionists and former slaves into Federal regiments.

As this low-intensity conflict smoldered, a burgeoning peace movement materialized, led by newspaper editor and politician William W. Holden. At community meetings and in editorials, Holden and his supporters broadcast dissatisfaction with the Confederate war effort and called for immediate yet ill-defined negotiations to end the conflict. Holden himself, however, remained supportive of the rebellion's goals, particularly the preservation of slavery, believing that a settlement with the Lincoln administration could still leave the institution intact. Holden and other dissenters posed a serious threat not only to the state's secessionist leadership—namely, Governor Zebulon Vance—but also to the Confederacy as a whole.

In planning an expedition against New Bern in the first days of 1864, Lee and other Confederate leaders understood that military victory would buoy Confederate morale, help Governor Vance win reelection, and quell political dissent in North Carolina. The proposed offensive also promised to ease supply problems plaguing Lee's army. Lack of food, forage, equipment, and men had become a principal focus for the general, and he rarely missed the opportunity to raise the issue with Richmond officials. The Union provisions, armament, and ammunition at New Bern would greatly support his army. In addition, success would open the surrounding countryside to the Confederate commissary, erase the Federal threat to rail lines supplying armies in Virginia, and eliminate the Union springboard into the interior.

Over the next few months, Lee's January 2 dispatch to President Davis would precipitate a string of momentous events. Using rail lines to consolidate their forces rapidly, the Confederates would attack New Bern in February, raid the northeastern counties in March, and hit the Union garrisons at Plymouth, Washington, and New Bern once again in late April and early May. The expeditions would involve joint-service operations, a rarity for the Confederates during the war. Such efforts typically raised complex issues of timing, command, and communication. Nevertheless, the Southerners would attempt to coordinate their army columns with their limited naval resources, especially the deadly ironclads.

The Confederate offensives in early 1864 would witness the failures and successes of Southern commanders, including George E. Pickett, John Taylor Wood, James W. Cooke, and a young, aggressive North Carolinian named Robert F. Hoke. The operations would also challenge the leadership of Union army and navy officers such as Benjamin F. Butler, John J. Peck, Innis N. Palmer, Samuel Phillips Lee, and Charles W. Flusser. These rebel strikes would call into question the wisdom of a Union defensive strategy that spread forces among several small, isolated posts instead of concentrating them in one citadel. They would also highlight, in stark relief, the contributions of former slaves and white Unionists in the state to the Federal war effort, as well as the secessionists' reaction to these opponents of the rebellion.

To be sure, events elsewhere in the summer of 1864 would soon overshadow the fighting in North Carolina. Grant and Lee's titanic struggle in Virginia and Sherman's steady march toward Atlanta would consume the attention of commanders on both sides. Nevertheless, Lee's January proposal triggered one of the last successful Confederate offensives. It aided rebel officials and Lee's Army of Northern Virginia by increasing supply for the troops, improving civilian morale, lifting the spirits of Richmond officials, and assisting Governor Vance in maintaining political control over the state. This is the story of those operations—the late-war Confederate resurgence in the Old North State.

PART ONE

The War in North Carolina

In the war's first year, Union forces attacked the North Carolina coast and captured the forts at Hatteras Inlet on the Outer Banks. In early 1862, the Federals struck again, seizing key points at New Bern (often spelled "New Berne" or "Newbern" in the nineteenth century), Washington, and Plymouth in a campaign led by Brigadier General Ambrose Burnside. Over the next two years, Confederate and Union forces conducted a series of raids and small offensives while a guerrilla struggle emerged to plague much of the region. In this swirl of war, social and political factors impacted the state's eastern counties. Slaves freed themselves from their owners and took refuge at Union bases. Federal officials organized North Carolina natives, both black and white, into fighting regiments. Confederate leaders struggled with desertion and Unionist dissent. In addition, a peace movement emerged in the state, endangering Governor Zebulon Vance's administration and, more importantly, threatening to pull North Carolina out of the Confederacy.

CHAPTER ONE

Taking the Coast

"United as If by Magic"

On January 10, 1861, Thomas N. Crumpler, a young legislator and attorney from Ashe County, stood up to speak in the House of Commons in Raleigh. The secession crisis was exploding throughout the South. South Carolina had left the Union several weeks before, and other states would soon follow. In the midst of these events, North Carolina lawmakers weighed their state's future. During his lengthy address, Crumpler spoke of slavery, union, and his home. "She is a modest and conservative State," he explained, "but in the memorable days of 1775, she led in the race of glory, and let her now . . . add the honor of making the first movement for its preservation. I think the Union can yet be preserved." But Crumpler assured his audience that, should "the bosom of my country . . . be bared to the ploughshare of civil war," he would join the fray against his state's foes. He was true to his word. A few months later, the twenty-six-year-old lawmaker enlisted in a cavalry regiment, and in a year he would be dead of wounds suffered east of Richmond.[1]

As Crumpler's words attest, North Carolina did not rush to join the rebellion in the turbulence of 1861. Like its sister states in the Upper South, the Old North State was lukewarm about leaving the Union. After Abraham Lincoln's victory at the polls, the majority of the state's electorate rejected a secession ordinance in February 1861. To be sure, strong pockets of secessionists mottled the state. But when radicals attempted to seize Federal installations in the name of rebellion, Governor John Ellis swiftly blocked their efforts. Most North Carolinians stuck to the Union, at least for the time being.[2]

Antebellum North Carolina displayed a striking contrast of social and economic interests. The state's eastern third held a rich band of agricultural lands where plantation slavery dominated and the planter class ruled.[3] In addition to the slave owners and their slaves, the region contained yeoman farmers, some free blacks, white laborers, and merchants. Elsewhere in the state, the slave economy was less prevalent. Coastal communities relied heavily on maritime commerce, and the western mountainous region contained few large plantations. Many citizens in these areas held little stake in slavery's survival and expressed an open hostility to calls for secession.[4] The same was true for large portions of the central Piedmont, where small farmers and abolitionist-leaning Quakers were common. Nevertheless, despite the ambivalence and even hostility toward the South's defining institution in some areas, the majority of voting whites in the state strongly supported slavery.[5]

Even as secessionists gained momentum following Lincoln's election, support for the status quo remained strong. For most, though, this sentiment was a heavily qualified "conditional Unionism." In other words, many North Carolinians were willing to keep the country intact only if Northern interests did not threaten slavery or otherwise coerce the Southern states. For the most part, these people—sometimes called "watch-and-wait" conservatives—agreed with secessionists on the fundamental issues underlying the conflict. They supported slavery, opposed Lincoln, and despised abolitionists, and if war came to their state, they planned to align with the South. In fact, secessionists and conditional Unionists differed more on matters of strategy than on underlying goals. Secessionists believed the best course lay with independence and even war, while those in the conditional camp held out hope for a negotiated settlement that would leave the country and slavery intact and avoid a ruinous war.[6]

In the first months of 1861, the conditional Unionists held sway, sustaining a delicate balance that prevented the state from seceding. However, the scales tipped in mid-April following the seizure of Fort Sumter and Lincoln's call for troops to quell the rebellion. That request signaled the coercion so many watch-and-wait conservatives had feared. Governor Ellis rejected the president's demand with a curt, categorical "you can get no troops from North Carolina," and he immediately directed state soldiers to seize key Federal installations, including Fort Macon, Fort Caswell, Fort Johnson, and the Fayetteville Arsenal.[7] As the governor took aggressive action, those on the fence fell to the side of rebellion, and soon the state's quiet equivocation became a full-throated belligerent roar. With the argument ended and the sword drawn, many in the state, as former Unionist Zebulon Vance put it, "united as if by magic, as only a common danger could unite them," and embraced secession. "I died last night a Union man. I am resurrected today a Secession man," proclaimed an enthusiastic Vance to an impassioned audience.[8]

Despite secession's wide support, not all North Carolinians firmly united around the Confederacy. Indeed, support for the rebellion was never universal. Dissent endured throughout the conflict in the form of die-hard "unconditional" Unionists spread thinly across the state who chose to remain loyal to the United States despite Lincoln's actions or because of them. Joined solely by their desire to keep the country intact, Unionists included a wide variety of groups, including blacks set on slavery's demise, whites who feared that secession would jeopardize slavery, people who were simply loyal to the Union, and a small number of white abolitionists. Though this diffuse collection lacked any central organization, its numbers were not trivial. One recent study estimates that about 5 percent of the state's male population (about 20,000 men) eventually either enlisted in Union regiments or actively supported anti-Confederate organizations.[9]

From the outset, Confederate North Carolina dove into the war effort. Mobilization began immediately. Governor Ellis sought to enlist 30,000 volunteers, and thousands, both young and old, answered the call. Training camps teeming with volunteers mushroomed throughout the state. Officials began to supply the new troops with uniforms, arms, equipment, rations, and every other conceivable good. Though manufacturing facilities were few, mills, tanneries, and machine shops geared up to produce all manner of things from harnesses to percussion caps. These efforts yielded results quickly, and eventually the state raised more than seventy regiments comprising about 110,000 men. During the conflict's early months, the first six such formations headed to Virginia to support Confederate forces there. Other regiments embarked to protect coastal points, including Wilmington, New Bern, and Hatteras.[10]

"That Troublesome Coast"

The coast constituted North Carolina's front line against Union forces. Its defense created immense challenges. In reflecting on coastal protection early in the war, Robert E. Lee observed, "There are so many points of attack, and so little means to meet them on the water, that there is but little rest."[11] Indeed, several inlets, numerous ports, dozens of small harbors, and many accessible beaches flecked the sandy shores of the thin barrier islands and inland waterways that made up the state's coastline. Some of these locations connected to the rebel interior via rail lines, making them ideal staging areas for large offensive operations. Others were more isolated and less suited for such ventures.

The state's shoreline offered multiple targets to Northern invaders. To the south, Wilmington served as the state's primary port; its capture would eliminate a vital source of foreign shipments for the Confederacy. Beaufort and Morehead City, up the coast, offered another haven for oceangoing vessels. Still farther north, the Outer Banks framed much of the state with a long band of sandy barrier islands covered in sea oats and stubby maritime forests. Inlets punctuated this chain at irregular intervals, opening westward toward shallow sounds that led to three major rivers meandering through a flat coastal plain covered with farms, pine groves, hardwood forests, and swamps.[12] To the north, the Albemarle Sound stretched west from Roanoke Island, narrowing and splitting into the Chowan and Roanoke Rivers, which ran by the towns of Winton and Plymouth. In the region's center, the Pamlico River flowed past the town of Washington, often referred to as "Little Washington," and

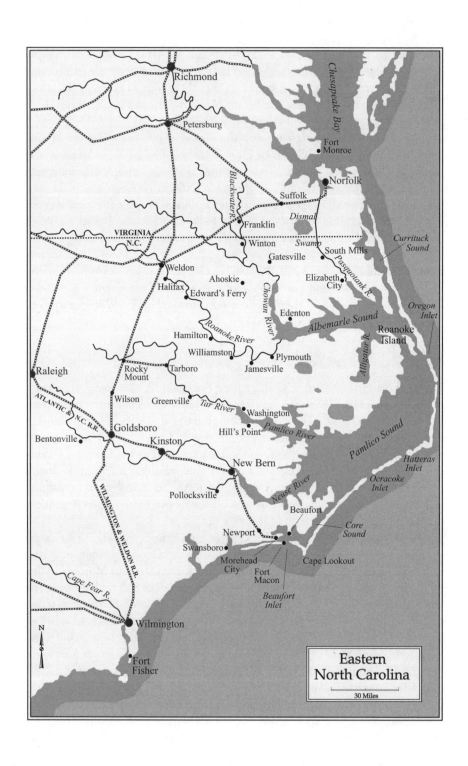

Eastern
North Carolina

30 Miles

into the Pamlico Sound. Finally, to the south, the Neuse River—the third and south-ernmost major watercourse—surged by Goldsboro, Kinston, and New Bern before also emptying into the Pamlico Sound.

Union leaders understood the geographic challenges they faced in North Carolina. In Washington, DC, during the summer of 1861, Secretary of the Navy Gideon Welles convened a commission to study the southern coast. The Blockade Strategy Board, as the four-member body came to be known, met infrequently at the Smithsonian Institution over a four-month period, generating much discussion, several published reports, and a stack of internal notes, memos, and maps. To aid their deliberations, the board members divided the Atlantic coast into different segments. North Carolina fell within the portion bracketed by Cape Henry in Virginia and Cape Romain in South Carolina, encompassing the Oregon, Loggerhead, Hatteras, Ocracoke, Beaufort, Bogue, and Cape Fear Inlets. In its initial July 16, 1861, report, the board concluded that "the sterile or half drowned shores of North Carolina might be neglected," but for its vast importance to the rebels. It recommended that Union forces block these inlets with sunken vessels.[13] However, events soon overtook this recommendation.

As the board deliberated, the state's inlets caught the attention of other Union military leaders. From the war's first days, Confederate privateers had slipped out of Hatteras Inlet to capture, sink, or plunder dozens of Union merchant vessels sailing up and down the coast. One steamer, the *Winslow*, enjoyed particular success, capturing sixteen prizes in less than two months. These raids soon created concern in Washington, DC, as complaints piled up at the Navy Department. As early as June, General Benjamin F. Butler recommended that something be done to neutralize the threat posed by rebel raiders. Secretary Welles took action, directing Silas H. Stringham, commander of the North Atlantic Blockading Squadron, to tend to the privateer problem and close "the ports and inlets on that troublesome coast." In late August, a combined navy and army expedition, led by Butler and Stringham, captured the Confederate fortifications at Hatteras. This modest victory boosted Northern spirits, which had dipped following battlefield reverses at Manassas and elsewhere. With Stringham's consent, Butler established a strong garrison at Hatteras, leaving open the possibility of further operations in the state's interior. Butler's prescience would prove a boon to future Federal military efforts.[14]

"A Most Gallant Charge"

In the wake of the Hatteras success, the Blockade Strategy Board changed its recommendations. In a September 2, 1861, memorandum to Secretary Welles, the board suggested an incursion into the Pamlico Sound by a six-vessel flotilla to disrupt the state's "interior trade and communication." In a separate report, it also urged the seizure and occupation of Fort Macon and Beaufort Harbor. With these recommendations, the board placed the possibility of a Union invasion of the state on the table.[15] However, the autumn passed without further operations in the region.

With the arrival of 1862, though, Union commanders sought greater results consistent with the board's advice. The War Department assembled a "coast" division under the affable Ambrose Burnside, an arms inventor, carbine manufacturer, railroad officer, and Mexican War veteran. In early January, Major General George B. McClellan drafted orders directing Burnside to work with the navy to seize positions in coastal North Carolina, including Roanoke Island, New Bern, Beaufort, and Fort Macon. Once Burnside was in possession of these locations, McClellan's directive urged him to seize the key rail junction at Goldsboro "should circumstances favor such a movement," destroy the Wilmington and Weldon Railroad, and then to turn his sights on the port at Wilmington. McClellan suggested that Burnside consider establishing a persistent presence inland and occupy portions of the railroad to the extent allowed by the "temper of the people, the rebel force at hand, &c."[16]

Burnside initiated the operation a few weeks later. In tandem with naval forces ably led by Captain Louis M. Goldsborough, Union forces shoved over the Hatteras bar in late January and steered north to Roanoke Island, the key gateway to the agriculturally rich northeastern portions of the state. On February 8 they made quick work of the rebel defenders there. The Confederates stood little chance against the Union flotilla of transports, packets, and formidable gunboats such as the *Southfield*, *Underwriter*, and *Commodore Perry*.[17]

After this initial victory, Burnside's force regrouped for its next move, a thrust against the city of New Bern at the forks of the Trent and Neuse Rivers. Once again, navy gunboats, now led by Commander Stephen C. Rowan, covered Burnside's infantry as it landed on the banks of the Neuse several miles from the city. After some sharp fighting on March 12, the Federal troops routed the defenders with, in Burnside's words, "a most gallant charge" and captured New Bern. In the chaos of the battle, some Confederates—notably, future governor Zebulon Vance and a young lieutenant colonel named Robert F. Hoke—were forced to escape the advancing bluecoats by boat over a stream known as Brice's Creek, which would become important in future efforts to recapture the city.[18]

In late April, Burnside's final blow fell on Fort Macon, a pentagonal brick casemate installation at Beaufort Inlet guarding Morehead City and Beaufort. In late March, Brigadier General John G. Parke landed men and mortars at Hoop Hole Creek and constructed strong batteries in the high dunes within range of the fort. In conjunction with a squadron of four ships plying the inlet, Parke's guns opened fire on April 25, and the fort soon fell.[19]

Fort Macon's capture largely completed the Federal conquest of eastern North Carolina. Using their newly won foothold, Union forces began to conduct operations against other locations. In late March, they visited Washington on the Pamlico

River, seeking to recover lenses pilfered by rebels from the Hatteras lighthouse. Finding abundant Union sentiment there, Burnside ordered a regiment to occupy the town.[20] In addition to Washington, Union gunboats visited Plymouth on the Roanoke River. Later, after additional trips in May and June, a company of the 9th New York set up a small garrison there.[21] With these acquisitions, Union commanders had established a military presence at three of the region's principal towns: New Bern, Washington, and Plymouth. Though the new Federal reach was broad, Union forces did not install permanent garrisons everywhere. Other notable coastal towns, such as Winton on the Chowan and Elizabeth City on the Pasquotank, would receive occasional attention from the Federals but would never be permanently occupied.[22]

"A Dagger Always Poised"

The Union victories of 1862 bred discontent among North Carolina's Confederate leaders. Many bristled at the lack of urgency with which Richmond officials reacted to Burnside's offensive and accused the War Department of failing to shift troops south to help the Tar Heels, even though units in Virginia were mostly idle at the time.[23] Some critics simply viewed the Confederate government's response as feeble. The people "saw plainly," D. H. Hill explained, "that the Richmond authorities had been far too slow in realizing the State's condition and the importance of the territory being lost."[24]

Eventually, Confederate military leaders would demonstrate genuine concern about the enemy bases, particularly their impact on efforts to supply troops in Virginia. Over time, the Confederates would shuttle large numbers of troops to Wilmington, Kinston, Goldsboro, and Weldon to ward off Union operations. Despite these efforts, the Federal threat in the eastern portion of the state would persist, in the words of historian Glenn Tucker, like "a dagger always poised at the heart of the Confederacy."[25] This was no exaggeration. The Wilmington and Weldon Railroad connected Lee's army to the vital port at Wilmington and the rest of the South. The Union presence at New Bern posed a constant danger to that artery, forcing Confederate officials to divert precious troops to guard against Federal incursions. As Robert E. Lee explained later, Union possession of the rail line would "cut off our communication with the south" and lead to "hopeless disaster."[26]

For the Union cause, the 1862 campaign gave reason for cheer and reason to praise Ambrose Burnside. Later that year, the Rhode Islander would fail in front of Fredericksburg at the head of the Army of the Potomac. In 1864 he would lose his corps command after the disastrously managed Battle of the Crater at Petersburg. During the war and well beyond, he would suffer the criticism and ridicule of comrades and historians, but his North Carolina campaign gave his detractors little ammunition.[27] The victory brought a welcome boost to Northern morale at a time when good news was sorely needed. It created a host of serious problems for Confederate leaders. It snagged nearly every port and inlet in the state, with the exception of Wilmington. These captured coastal bases, most notably New Bern, created a standing threat to Confederate supply lines and tied down rebel manpower needed elsewhere. The new Federal positions also provided ideal points from which to launch raids and larger operations. As noted by the energetic assistant secretary of the Union navy, Gustavus Fox, possession of the coast furnished "a fine base to push any number of troops into the interior, so that with North Carolina and Tennessee in our possession, or nearly so, we divide them." The new positions also hampered Confederate efforts to extract supplies from some of the state's most productive agricultural counties, where immense quantities of pork, fish, corn, and other foodstuffs were located.[28]

Despite the well-deserved adulation for Burnside and the army, the ground forces did not accomplish the victory alone. The navy deserved praise as well. The campaign would qualify as one of the war's more successful joint-service (army-navy) operations. From beginning to end, the navy's sailing and fighting formed part and parcel of the Union success. Despite the navy's contribution, the army received most of the credit in the press, a slight not lost on naval officers. In the midst of the campaign, Commander Rowan reported to his superiors that "the affair at New Bern was well managed, but, as usual, the army with its corps of reporters monopolized the credit."[29] Rowan and his fellow naval officers had good reason to complain. With the countryside full of Confederate units and guerrillas, the navy furnished the logistical support necessary for the army to reach its targets and, once there, receive reinforcements and supplies. Navy ships and gunboats provided essential support during the campaign and would continue to do so during Union occupation of the region.

Following Fort Macon's capture, Burnside wanted to achieve more. Consistent with McClellan's suggestion, he hoped to stretch beyond the sounds, drive into the interior, and hit the Goldsboro railroad junction, a mere 60 miles west of New Bern. McClellan's plan contemplated permanent possession of the railroad, if circumstances warranted. In June, Burnside began to devise such a strike, but just as his column prepared to leave New Bern, a series of urgent dispatches from Washington, DC, directed him to shelve the operation and transfer many of his troops north to McClellan's Army of the Potomac, east of Richmond. Alas, priorities and plans elsewhere would starve Burnside's command of men and resources, preventing substantial operations in the state. The lost opportunity would fit an emerging pattern in North Carolina. In lieu of pursuing further gains in the state, the Union high command chose to concentrate troop strength at other points, especially in Virginia. With his force drained in the summer of 1862, Burnside could not conduct any significant operations into the interior. He soon received orders to head north himself, leaving only a small force to tend to the newly won positions.[30]

With Burnside gone, Major General John G. Foster remained at New Bern to oversee a diminished force and attend the occupation of the state's eastern region. July troop inspections revealed only about 6,000 men present for duty in the region.[31] Competing needs elsewhere would continue to constrain Federal efforts to exploit the foothold gained by Burnside's triumph. Foster, remaining at New Bern, focused on improving the fortifications and protecting Union positions. The work proceeded for several months, and by late August, New Bern had become a heavily fortified position.[32]

Foster's troops did not remain passive during the summer and fall of 1862. Army and navy forces conducted several small raids. In July, Lieutenant Commander Charles W. Flusser led three gunboats up the Roanoke River to reconnoiter Confederate defenses there, capturing a small steamer in the process. In addition, Foster's men ventured into the countryside to snatch supplies from local farms and Confederate depots. Not to be outdone, the Confederates conducted operations of their own. In September 1862 a small force led by Lieutenant Colonel Stephen D. Pool attacked the Federals in Washington. During the scuffle, the powder magazine on the US gunboat *Picket* exploded. Nevertheless, the Union garrison held. Confederates also attacked and ransacked Plymouth, drawing fire from Union gunboats that managed to ignite much of the town. Similar low-intensity operations would occur again and again in the coastal region.[33]

In addition to these raids and skirmishes, the Union occupation brought other changes to the state's eastern half. On May 26, 1862, the Lincoln administration installed North Carolina native Edward Stanly as military governor at New Bern to oversee the newly captured territory and help mobilize the Unionists in the state. Stanly quickly found himself at odds with nearly everyone. Predictably, given his alignment with Union forces, he drew nothing but disdain in Confederate circles. He also ran crossways with Union officials. To him, the war served as a means to repair the Union and little else.[34] He helped slave owners retrieve escaped slaves, and he closed schools that had recently opened to educate freed people. His actions quickly alienated Union soldiers and officers in New Bern and administration officials in Washington, DC.[35]

Governor Stanly aside, Union officials took other, more successful steps to increase their hold in the state. Shortly after their victories, they began enlisting white North Carolinians in combat units.[36] In May 1862, Burnside authorized the formation of the 1st North Carolina Union Volunteers (NCUV).[37] On June 12, Colonel Rush C. Hawkins of the 9th New York held a community meeting in Plymouth and began to draw local citizens into this unit. These and other efforts snowballed. By January 1863, the 1st NCUV numbered more than 500 men, and its companies served in garrisons throughout the state's eastern portion. Four hundred more men joined the regiment in 1863. Many hailed from eastern counties such as Beaufort, Bertie, and Washington. Several months later, officials formed an additional regiment, designated the 2nd NCUV. Eventually, about 1,400 in total served in these two regiments. Similar regiments were formed elsewhere in the state.[38]

Early on, native North Carolinians in Union units earned the nickname "Buffaloes," a term with murky origins that may have reflected Confederate partisans' disdain for them. Not surprisingly, these Union regiments triggered more than name-calling, and the ill feelings lingered long after the war. Confederate supporters viewed the Buffaloes not as members of legitimate military units but as bushwhackers, thieves, and traitors. In addition, some members of the 1st and 2nd NCUV had seen Confederate service prior to their Union enlistment. As Federal soldiers, they occasionally participated in operations between and behind the lines, taking advantage of their intimate knowledge of local terrain. By and large, though, Union commanders used loyal North Carolinians for garrison duty at various Federal positions across the region. These posts often accommodated the soldiers' families.[39]

"Inequality of Numbers May Be Compensated by Invulnerability"

In the face of the Union presence in North Carolina's coastal region and elsewhere, Confederate officials searched for countermeasures, particularly on the water. From the war's first days, Confederate navy officials in Richmond strained to compete with an enemy naval force superior to theirs in almost every respect. The burden of developing the rebel navy fell primarily on the shoulders of the unflappable, clear-minded Stephen Mallory, a Floridian and former chairman of the US Senate Naval Affairs Committee who was well acquainted with maritime matters. Navy Secretary Mallory understood the challenges ahead. The Confederacy had no real navy to speak of and, afflicted by financial and material deficits, did not have the means to create one. It also lacked construction facilities and experienced personnel. Dealt this hand, Mallory knew that conventional approaches would prove inadequate, so he devised a multifaceted strategy to wring the most out of limited resources. Mallory set his sights on the deployment of fast steam cruisers to wreak havoc on the enemy's commerce, the installation of powerful rifled cannon in Confederate gunboats and ships, and the development of unconventional weapons such as submarines and mines. Finally, and perhaps most famously, he focused on the design and construction of armored gunboats, arguing that the "inequality of numbers may be compensated by invulnerability." His department's efforts would result in the creation of several dozen ironclads that would, in some cases, go toe-to-toe with the much larger and better equipped Union navy.[40]

In eastern North Carolina, Mallory initiated efforts to construct heavily plated, shallow-draft vessels that could challenge any Union gunboat afloat in the state's waters. Beginning in the spring of 1862, Mallory entered into several contracts to build such ironclads at Elizabeth City. When Union victories made that location untenable, the builders shifted west, away from Federal control. These efforts eventually spawned three separate projects: one near Kinston on the Neuse River, conducted by the shipbuilding firm of Howard and Ellis; another at Tarboro, upstream from Washington, under the supervision of nineteen-year-old naval architect Gilbert Elliott; and a third, also overseen by Elliott, in a cornfield on the banks of the Roanoke River near Halifax. Beset by a shortage of labor and material—symptoms of the Confederacy's anemic industrial capability—these projects crawled along, and their completion was still far away in 1862.[41]

"It Is Best to Push On to Charleston"

As the Confederates worked on their ironclads, Union commanders looked to expand their gains in North Carolina. In late 1862, Major General John G. Foster planned a large-scale push into the state.[42] In early December, Foster's men prepared to march on the Goldsboro rail junction and destroy the rail bridges there. After completing the raid, Foster hoped to conduct a much larger attack on Wilmington with the cooperation of naval forces under Rear Admiral Samuel Phillips Lee, the new commander of the North Atlantic Blockading Squadron. Foster floated his plan with Major General Henry W. Halleck, Lincoln's general in chief in Washington, DC, who approved the venture but noted that no additional troops were on hand to support it.[43]

With a force of more than 10,000, Foster struck out toward Goldsboro, timing his move to coincide with Burnside's attack on Fredericksburg, Virginia. Foster understood that destruction of the rail bridges near Goldsboro would impede Confederate efforts to reinforce Wilmington in response to his upcoming attack there. From December 11 through 17, he dueled with an outnumbered Confederate force in engagements at Kinston, White Hall, and Goldsboro. Near White Hall on the Neuse, his troops discovered an unfinished ironclad resting on stocks and guarded by a small force. From across the river, Union gunners fired rounds at the vessel but failed to destroy it. The Federal troops also managed to burn the rail bridge and tear up some track, but the Confederates repaired the damage within days after Foster returned to New Bern. Foster's effort represented the deepest Union incursion into the state up to that point and spread alarm among North Carolina's politicians and citizens.[44] With the expedition over, Foster informed Halleck in Washington, DC, that the move had been a "perfect success."[45]

Back in New Bern, Foster looked toward Wilmington, but he needed reinforcements to attempt the assault and contacted the War Department for assistance.[46] Halleck continued to see merit in the operation and, after calling Foster north for consultations, reversed his earlier position and authorized an additional 12,000 men from Virginia to augment the Wilmington offensive.[47] Foster planned the strike in close cooperation with Admiral Lee, who gathered ironclads and other vessels for the fight.[48] The offensive would be the largest attack launched by Union army forces from its bases in North Carolina. By initiating this attack, Federal commanders would finally take advantage of the foothold they had gained months before.

But Foster's planned operation never materialized. Days before the offensive kicked off, a naval reconnaissance revealed that the ironclads could not enter the Cape Fear River due to the shoals and Confederate obstructions there. In addition, two of the ironclads, so important to the navy's participation, failed to arrive. On the voyage south, the *Passaic* broke down and the *Monitor* sank in a storm off Cape Hatteras. Following these setbacks, Halleck canceled the effort, and the focus shifted to Charleston Harbor.[49] Secretary Welles wrote in his diary, "it is best . . . to push on to Charleston," and Assistant Secretary Fox later observed, "we are inclined to skip [Wilmington] . . . for the fall of Charleston is the fall of Satan's kingdom." Admiral Lee disagreed, however, and continued to advocate for operations against Wilmington, believing the port had "much more importance in a military and naval point of view."[50]

Notwithstanding Admiral Lee's misgivings, the administration stuck with the idea of concentrating operations at Charleston. Foster took two divisions and embarked for South Carolina in February.[51] He did not stay long, though, and returned, bitter and frustrated, to North Carolina after disagreements arose about his command responsibilities. His troops, however, remained to support a campaign at Charleston that would grind along for much of 1863. This strange turn of events drained the North Carolina district of its Union manpower and effectively destroyed any real possibility of large-scale Federal operations there for the foreseeable future. For the second time, a major Union offensive in the state had been scratched to feed the need for troops elsewhere.[52]

"Get Out Immense Supplies"

As Union troops shifted south to Charleston at the beginning of 1863, the Confederates grasped the initiative in North Carolina. With large-scale campaigning suspended in Virginia, Robert E. Lee put his idle forces to good use during the colder months. He understood that, with no naval force to speak of, the Confederates could not hope to make permanent gains in the state. However, he also knew that valuable supplies could be drawn from the coastal region if his men could bottle up the depleted Federals in their bases, if only for a few weeks. To effect this plan, Lee ordered Generals James Longstreet and D. H. Hill to move against enemy positions and extract stores from agriculturally rich areas of southeastern Virginia and North Carolina.[53] Hill, assigned to operate in the Old North State, hoped the effort would "drive the enemy to his strongholds, and get out immense supplies of corn and bacon from the rich eastern counties." He also predicted the campaign "would secure confidence to the planters and protect that planting interest so essential to our very existence another year."[54]

In March, Hill began with a diversion against New Bern and then marched on Washington and besieged the garrison there. But the operation ended after only a few weeks when the Union steamer *Escort* slipped past the Confederate batteries on the Pamlico River and delivered much-needed supplies. With the Federals amply provisioned, Hill abandoned his designs and withdrew from the town. In departing, a member of the 32nd North Carolina left the following note in the vacated siege lines: "Yankees we leave you, not because we cannot take Washington but because it is not worth taking; and besides, the climate is not agreeable. A man should be amphibious to inhabit it."[55]

As Hill's siege at Washington ended, Longstreet operated outside Suffolk, Virginia, with a similar conclusion. With spring campaigning in Virginia already begun, Longstreet and Hill made their way back to Lee's army. Though devoid of dramatic results, their operations in the spring of 1863 had bought breathing room for Confederate supply efforts, allowing commissary agents to comb the countryside unimpeded for several weeks. Lee recognized the benefits garnered by Hill. "I am much gratified to learn that the enemy has been so harassed and punished during the past months," he wrote, "and wish that your force was sufficient to drive them from the State." However, as Lee had understood early on, without an effective naval presence, the Confederates would have trouble seizing and holding the Federal enclaves at New Bern, Washington, and Plymouth.[56]

"A Fine Iron-Clad"

In the following months, John G. Foster, with his diminished Union force, did not conduct or plan any large offensives. However, his force did not remain completely idle. In July he unleashed a cavalry raid led by Brigadier General Edward E. Potter into the counties north of New Bern. The blue column moved swiftly and wreaked havoc in several towns, including Greenville, Rocky Mount, and Tarboro. Official reports from the raid cataloged a long list of destroyed items, including a railroad bridge at Rocky Mount, a cotton mill, a machine shop and armory packed with munitions, a flouring mill, a large train depot, 25 wagons, and 800 bales of cotton. But buried in these tallies of wrecked property was a particularly notable item at Tarboro: "a fine iron-clad, in process of construction." Potter's men had found the incomplete gunboat on the stocks, and it had a "heavy and solid" frame of the "Merrimac model."[57] The Union cavalrymen promptly burned or dismantled the nascent vessel, one of three ironclads then under construction in the region. Adding to this tangible destruction, the rebel defenders found another aspect of the raid particularly troublesome. Reports indicated that one of the units involved in the Yankee raid included native North Carolinians, members of Company L, 1st NCUV. One Confederate remarked, "Let everybody remember this, and they will know how to treat the members of company [L], if they are captured."[58]

Throughout 1863, the Federals refrained from conducting large-scale operations aimed at permanently capturing the enemy's key positions. For the high command, priorities elsewhere dominated, tying up both army and navy resources. Even during the Confederate offensive against Washington that spring, Halleck informed Union commanders that no men were available for North Carolina and no offensives were planned there. He grumbled that "every general is pressing for more troops as though we had a cornucopia of men from which to supply their wants." He also confirmed that no offensive movements were planned and emphasized that any operations in the state should be "strictly defensive and the troops concentrated as much as possible." Officials in Washington, DC, trained their attention on the upcoming conflict in Virginia and active operations at Charleston. There was simply no significant interest in pushing the Federal advantage in North Carolina.[59]

In addition to Foster's raid and Hill's short siege, dozens of smaller clashes took place throughout 1862 and 1863. Union patrols routinely left the relative safety of their garrisons to seize supplies and attack Confederate outposts. Gunboats, often guided by the aggressive Lieutenant Commander Charles Flusser, ascended the rivers to shell rebel positions and conduct reconnaissance. The Confederates conducted movements of their own. On both sides, the objectives varied but often included bridges, salt works, lighthouses, commissary supplies, and picket posts. In addition, numerous guerrilla-type actions occurred throughout the region as part of a continuous low-level conflict. Fighting between Confederate partisan rangers and Unionists was common. All this combat, both the formal military operations and the irregular clashes, greatly affected the lives of those who called the region home and would sow the seeds for profound social changes, liberating some, demoralizing others, and disrupting everyone.

CHAPTER TWO

Liberation, Discontent, and the Friends of Peace

"Overthrown the Whole Fabric of Society"

Her name was Juno, and she lived on a plantation somewhere along the Neuse River between Kinston and New Bern. When one of her children died, her owner refused to help bury the little one's body. The owner's wife, distraught by the tragedy, stepped in to build a rude coffin and dig the grave. Afterward, the kind woman enjoined, "Juno, this place is horrid; if you can make your way to the Yankees, do it. . . . Take this basket of eggs as a present to General Burnside, from me, and tell him if he can rescue a Union woman, for God's sake do it." Juno followed the advice. The journey was not an easy one. At dark, she bundled her remaining children into a canoe at the riverbank and pushed off into the night "to come to the Yankees." She made steady progress, paddling with the current until gusts threatened to tip her precious cargo. To avoid disaster, she steered to shore, climbed out, and guided the craft on foot. After trudging through the shallows for 12 miles, Juno and her children, "dripping wet, hungry and tired," reached New Bern and found the doorstep of Vincent Colyer, the superintendent of the poor in that city. Juno began her life anew as a free person, but she did not forget her former mistress's kindness. Indeed, for weeks she pleaded with Colyer to rescue the woman. Finally, a Union gunboat steamed up to the plantation for provisions, took the woman on board, and brought her back to New Bern.[1]

Beyond the raids and minor clashes, Union military control in eastern North Carolina triggered a profound social upheaval.[2] The changes destabilized the existing social order and created tension and even violence in many communities. While the changes affected nearly everyone, including yeoman farmers, merchants, free blacks, landless whites, and slaveholders, it impacted the region's enslaved people the most.[3] Well before the issuance of Lincoln's Emancipation Proclamation, thousands seized the opportunity opened by the Federal occupation to flee their owners and head for the safety of Union garrisons. At first, the former slaves traveled in small boats bulging with men, women, and children, floating down the Albemarle Sound to Union-controlled Roanoke Island.[4] Then they began to arrive at New Bern and other Federal enclaves from all directions. For the most part, Union commanders protected these freed people from former owners seeking to reenslave them.[5] At the same time, Union officers attempted to mollify local whites. In February, General Burnside issued a proclamation assuring white citizens that the "mission of our joint expedition is not to invade any of your rights" nor "liberate your slaves."[6] Such statements did not deter the slaves from aggressively seeking their own freedom. Moreover, Burnside's officers did not discourage such self-emancipation, and once the refugees reached the protection of the Federal bases, they remained there and immediately began to aid Union forces. By March, Burnside began paying wages to the "contrabands" on Roanoke Island, employing them to the "best possible advantage" by putting them to work on fortifications.[7]

At New Bern, Vincent Colyer managed the deluge. "Freed people came into my yard from the neighboring plantations," he recalled, "sometimes as many as one hundred at a time, leaving with joy their plows in the field, and their old homes, to follow our soldiers when returning from their frequent raids."[8] By late 1862, thousands inhabited the city and continued to arrive by the "boat loads." The former slaves conducted "most of the business done in the city," washing and mending clothes, selling food and other items. According to one soldier, the men in the ranks preferred the goods produced by these new residents over those peddled by the sutlers, at least as far as "gingerbread and pies and roasted potatoes" were concerned.[9] The number of African Americans in the city continued to swell over time. A census conducted by a regimental chaplain at the beginning of 1864 counted more than 17,000 blacks living in New Bern and protected by Union forces, reflecting a significant increase over the city's population of approximately 3,000 blacks in 1860.[10]

The profound change was hard to ignore. The head of a New Bern school noted that the Union military victories had perhaps "unintentionally . . . overthrown the whole fabric of society, founded as it was, on the institution of negro Slavery."[11] Having faced substantial danger to gain their liberty, the freed people cemented their new role through employment with the US government or local private interests, hoping to pitch in and take part in the war effort against their former owners. Confederates lamented the transformation.[12] A Raleigh paper informed its readers that the "Newbern of old—is not there: the people who gave a respectability and refinement to the ancient town; far in advance of any other in the State, are scattered throughout the country,—homeless, hopeful, and determined."[13]

Many former slaves, as many as fifty of the "best and most courageous" in New Bern, served the US Army invaluably as spies, scouts, and guides. These men employed their knowledge of the surrounding country to penetrate rebel picket lines, observe enemy military camps, and gather crucial information about Confederate dispositions and movements. Colyer marveled at the bravery of these men, who worked for little pay and viewed their activities almost as a "religious duty." The devotion and perseverance of the black scouts reflected their strong desire for social and political change. One of the chief spies at New Bern was a young man named Abraham H. Galloway, an individual of unusual influence and bravery who frequently traveled into enemy territory and worked closely with Union officials on his return. As the war continued, Galloway shifted his focus away from the spy business and became heavily engaged in black recruitment and advocacy for black political rights, including suffrage.[14]

"In Danger of Being Ruined If These Things Continue"

The conflict brought other transformations. The chaos of war in the eastern counties eroded existing social boundaries and fueled the growth of guerrilla forces.[15] Conditions varied from area to area. In Washington County, which included the Federal base at Plymouth, conflict and division dominated. As chronicled by historian Wayne Durrill, planters saw their firm hold on power rapidly disintegrate and their slaves flee into Yankee lines. Confederate deserters, yeoman farmers, and landless Unionists entered the void. The deserters formed lawless bands in the woods that harassed and stole from locals; Unionists seized land from slaveholders. Eventually, conditions devolved into a vicious guerrilla conflict that would last for much of the war.[16] In Pasquotank County and other areas north of the Albemarle Sound, events followed a similar course. Though Union gunboats plied the region's waters and could deposit Union troops anywhere at will, there were no permanent Federal bases there. This left a vacuum of political control, which bred fear and lawlessness.[17] But conditions were not the same everywhere. In Craven County, which surrounded Federally controlled New Bern, internal divisions among local whites did not boil over. There, according to historian Judkin Browning, white planters, laborers, and yeoman farmers tended to resist Federal occupation, despite their sometimes conflicting interests.[18]

Planters in the eastern counties found that Union military successes had substantially diminished their power. With more and more of their slaves escaping into the Union lines, owners rented many of their remaining slaves to other whites far away from the Union garrisons, in the Piedmont and elsewhere. In October 1862, a slaveholder in Goldsboro reported that he was "advising my particular friends to remove [their slaves] up the country, and many of them are doing so—the blood & thunder fellows have long since done so."[19] At Goldsboro, Confederate General Thomas Clingman warned, "Negroes are escaping rapidly, probably a million of dollars' worth weekly in all." According to Clingman, slave owners and other Confederate supporters fretted that the eastern section of the state "is in danger of being ruined if these things continue." The general urged that "negroes and movable property" be taken out of the state's eastern region.[20] In some cases, the owners themselves fled, and their former slaves remained to occupy and operate the abandoned plantations.[21]

Social changes accelerated with the issuance of Lincoln's draft Emancipation Proclamation in September 1862 and the release of the final version on January 1, 1863. For most parts of the South, the document had the curious effect of emancipating slaves where the US government had no troops to enforce the proclamation. In North Carolina, however, it freed slaves in areas under firm Union military control, such as New Bern and Plymouth.[22] The proclamation sped the exodus that had already begun following Union victories the previous spring. More slaves fled from bondage, and more planters pulled their slaves into the interior.[23] Many Union soldiers stationed in the state took a favorable view of these developments. One Connecticut infantryman in New Bern predicted that the decree "will encourage our arms and weaken the Rebels equal to three hundred thousand Soldiers in our favor."[24]

The proclamation also served as a tipping point for many whites native to the state, leading some to discard their Unionist leanings and firmly align with the Confederates.[25] In October 1862, a Massachusetts soldier noted significant support for the Union "before the proclamation, but now it is the other way."[26] The proclamation spurred unpopular Union governor Edward Stanly to resign. Stanly predicted the document would cause "infinite mischief," crush any hope of peace, "fill the hearts of Union men with despair," strengthen the "traitors," and bring "direful calamities" to former slaves.[27] Others expressed similar views. In Raleigh, newspaper editor William W. Holden branded it "one of the most monstrously wicked documents that ever emanated from human authority."[28] For its detractors, the proclamation also clearly revealed the consequences of military defeat for the South. With abolition firmly established as one of Lincoln's war aims, the rebels now clearly understood that failure in the contest would bring slavery's demise.

The Emancipation Proclamation also stoked deep-seated fears. For decades, the specter of slave insurrection had haunted white Southerners. In 1831, Nat Turner's brief uprising in Southampton County, Virginia, on the North Carolina border left more than sixty dead. Similar revolts had occurred earlier in Virginia and South Carolina. Most recently, John Brown's 1859 raid on the Harpers Ferry arsenal had reinforced the already heightened anxiety.[29] In 1863, the proclamation fed dismay and rumor. After the defeat at Gettysburg in July, Major General D. H. Hill informed state officials of a possible slave uprising within the month.[30] And on July 25, 1863, plantation owner John Pool warned Governor Vance that black regiments planned to incite a "servile insurrection" in Bertie and Hertford Counties.[31] Following the proclamation's issuance, the Confederates met the few instances of black crime with a swift, unmerciful response. The attention paid to these cases underscored the concern felt by the white populace.[32] Catherine Edmondston of Halifax, whose extensive diary amply captured the views of the state's slaveholding class, worried about the institution's prospects and wondered "what is to become of the country when our slaves are free."[33]

Lincoln's proclamation also impelled the Federal recruitment of African Americans in North Carolina and elsewhere. Some such recruitment had already begun in the Union-controlled areas of the South. However, with the edict's formal issuance, the effort began in earnest and would constitute, in Lincoln's words, "the heaviest blow yet dealt to the rebellion."[34] At New Bern, former slaves began to enlist as early as January 1863.[35] A Connecticut soldier predicted that these men "would fight like Tigers to defend their rights as they now enjoy them."[36] Freedmen participated in their first combat during a Confederate attack on Washington, North Carolina, in late April. As the Union garrison's white soldiers raced to fill the town's defenses, officers plugged the gaps in the line with "every able-bodied" black man they could find. At first, some of the white soldiers expressed skepticism about the arrangement, but as one Massachusetts veteran later recalled, "the exploding shells, the bullet tz-z-zps, were wonderfully persuasive arguments on such a question, and settled it once [and] for all with the garrison of Washington."[37]

Such ad hoc soldiering was soon replaced by a more systematic effort to arm North Carolina's former slaves. On the national level, Massachusetts led the way when energetic, abolitionist Governor John Andrew authorized the first black regiments in March. The governor did not limit his thinking to the Bay State. Heeding recommendations from Massachusetts officers, Andrew wrote to Secretary of War Edwin Stanton on April 1, 1863, to suggest "some able, brave, tried, and believing man . . . undertake in North Carolina the organization of the colored troops."[38] The War Department pressed ahead with the proposal, and by April 13, Colonel Edward Augustus Wild had received orders to raise a brigade of four regiments in the Old North State.[39]

Wild, an abolitionist-leaning physician educated at Harvard and Jefferson Medical College in Philadelphia, proved a fitting choice for such an effort. Brave and aggressive, he had lost an arm in combat at South Mountain the year before. With recruiting orders in hand, he went to work at New Bern gathering officers for a new regiment. At first, the effort lagged. Leaders of the African American community in New Bern feared recruits would be underpaid, ill treated, and misused. However, this changed when a recruiting official held a meeting with Abraham Galloway and other black leaders. With pistols clearly visible under their belts, the audacious young spymaster and his companions dictated conditions for black recruitment in New Bern.[40]

Following that encounter, the pace of enlistment accelerated dramatically. Placards appeared around town "calling for four thousand men for 'Wild's colored Brigade.'" Processions of freed persons coursed through the streets singing, "We'll hang Jeff Davis to a sour-apple tree."[41] By June 15, 1863, Wild had filled the first regiment, the 1st North Carolina Colored Volunteers (NCCV) led by Lieutenant Colonel James C. Beecher, and had already enlisted 150 for another regiment, later designated the 2nd NCCV under Colonel Alonzo Draper. An additional unit, the 3rd NCCV, would eventually form, commanded by Captain John Wilder. The army would later designate these three regiments the 35th, 36th, and 37th United States Colored Troops (USCT), respectively. Training progressed rapidly, much to the satisfaction of the officers. Lieutenant Colonel Beecher, son of Congregationalist minister Lyman Beecher and half brother of Harriet Beecher Stowe, wrote home: "My regiment is a 'buster,' improves every day; and such a line of battle as we form! It would make your eyes shine to see these six weeks' soldiers going through a dress parade."[42] Beecher's unit would spend much of the war in South Carolina and Florida, participating in the Battle of Olustee and other engagements. The other two regiments, fully organized much later, would serve in the bloody campaigns outside Richmond and Petersburg in 1864.[43]

"The Sternest Punishment"

While the Federals filled their units with former slaves eager to fight, Confederates struggled to keep many of their men in the field. By 1863, desertion had become a serious problem, not only for Confederate commanders on the battlefield but also for people on the home front. Although North Carolina contributed more soldiers than any other state to the Confederate cause, it also lost more to desertion. Many of these demoralized absentees made their way home, where they stirred dissent and fed the guerrilla bands roaming the state. Deserters tended to flock to the counties of the Quaker Belt west of Raleigh, where Unionist sentiment was strong. State officials in Raleigh and Confederate officers took steps to combat the issue. In January 1863, Governor Vance issued a proclamation urging absconders to return to their units. He followed with another in April calling on "all good citizens and true patriots" to assist in rounding up these men, to "frown down [on] all those who aid and assist them," and to "place the brand upon them" so they would "feel the scorn and contempt of an outraged people."[44]

Despite the governor's efforts, the problem did not go away. North Carolina desertions spiked following Gettysburg. Robert E. Lee urged President Davis to address the problem with a dose of executions for malefactors and furloughs for loyal men still in the ranks.[45] The crisis also spurred Vance to action. In August, the governor complained about dissatisfaction among North Carolina troops in Lee's army. A week later, he informed Richmond officials that deserters in the western counties had overwhelmed the home guard's efforts to control them. These men "have so accumulated lately," he warned, "as to . . . exert a very injurious effect upon the community in many respects." The governor also admitted that his home guards were "poorly armed, inefficient, and rendered timid by fear of secret vengeance from the deserters." The exasperated Vance then asked whether the army could send "one of our diminished brigades" or a strong regiment to help.[46] General Lee, who was well aware of the state's desertion problem, responded to the governor's plea and detached young Brigadier General Robert F. Hoke, a favorite of Lee's, for this service.[47] In early September, Hoke made his way home to tackle the problem; accompanying him were two regiments, the 21st and 56th North Carolina, and a squadron of cavalry.[48] In Raleigh, he received instructions from the governor to proceed west to the Quaker Belt and capture deserters, break up "bands of lawless men," and arrest anyone aiding these men.[49]

Over the next two months, Hoke's men hunted down deserters in Randolph, Wilkes, and Yadkin Counties, where war disaffection was high. Even though it was successful in snaring men and depositing them back in the army, Hoke's mission carried more than a hint of political repression. Indeed, the endeavor generated reports of harassment of locals, particularly those with Unionist leanings. Accusations of rough treatment of civilians and voter intimidation during the fall congressional elections followed in Hoke's wake. In Wilkes County, one witness complained, "There has been a great deal of property destroyed or taken in Wilkes by the troops employed to catch deserters, such as horses, saddles, wagons, work steers, &c." Another asserted, "instead of arresting deserters in a proper way," the troops plundered houses, taking stock, grain, and provisions from women and children.[50] A Confederate supporter in Wilkes protested to Vance that Hoke's men had paid "very little for the articles" they took, and "for a large portion paying nothing"; in addition, they had killed at least seven deserters in cold blood. In Yadkin County, editor William W. Holden's brother-in-law, Josiah Cowles, reported that the families of deserters had been mistreated.[51]

While Hoke was in North Carolina, his own brigade suffered disaster at Rappahannock Station in Virginia when Union forces overran a bridgehead there on November 7 and delivered an embarrassing defeat for Lee and his army. Three of Hoke's regiments, the 6th, 54th, and 57th North Carolina, suffered an astounding 928 casualties (all captured, save 3), paring these regiments down to a mere shell of 30 officers and 321 men.[52] Several days later, Lee personally relayed the devastating news to Hoke and sought to soften the blow, suggesting that many of the missing would likely turn up later. He urged Hoke to continue to focus on his mission in North Carolina and "arrest any stragglers you can find."[53]

As Hoke conducted his hunt, Lee directly addressed the deserter crisis. In late October, he reaffirmed his intention to deal with the problem firmly, through execution if necessary. In discussing the matter with Confederate Secretary of War James Seddon, he noted that a lenient policy toward deserters had been "ruinous to the army." In his view, the army needed to address desertion "with the sternest punishment, and leave the offender without hope of escape, by making the penalty inevitable." He emphasized that execution "almost exclusively" served as a warning to others and that the "slightest prospect of escape" from punishment would be readily embraced by potential offenders. Lee tempered his position by recommending clemency for those who voluntarily returned to the ranks.[54]

"Tired of War and Desire Peace"

Desertion was not Governor Vance's only challenge as he headed into 1864. Many citizens throughout North Carolina continued to oppose, and in some cases actively resist, Confederate rule. The scattered Unionism extant at the war's start began to sink shallow roots as Confederates lost their grip on the eastern region and as unhappiness with the war's course increased. Unionists could be found nearly everywhere, although concentrated pockets existed in the mountains, the Piedmont's Quaker Belt, and some coastal communities. Despite their numbers and widespread presence, these dissenters generally did not coordinate activities or plan strategy. For much of the war, they remained diffuse and largely ineffective. In fact, nearly all the state's political leaders gravitated to the Confederacy at the war's outset, regardless of their pre-secession opinions. Opponents of the Confederacy remained a minority, and many would pay a tremendous price during and after the war for their continued loyalty to the United States. They would suffer intimidation at the polls, arbitrary arrests, restrictions on travel, and imprisonment, among other things. In Craven County, before the Federal capture of New Bern, Confederate soldiers and officers harassed local Unionists with threats of arson and death. In May 1861, secessionists tarred and feathered one elderly laborer for his "unsound sentiments" and later publicly shaved the head of an African American who spoke out for the Union. More intimidation and violence occurred elsewhere, particularly in western counties, where opposition to Confederate rule was high and deserters were numerous.[55]

Despite these obstacles, many did their best to bring down the Confederacy. From the beginning, the largely powerless foes of the rebellion demonstrated their opposition by avoiding rebel conscription and aiding deserters. They also expressed themselves through more subtle means, such as refusing to fly the Confederate flag or use Confederate currency. Confederate conscription, instituted on a wide scale in April 1862, was particularly vexing to Unionists, breeding even more dissent and violence as it forced men to fight for a cause they opposed. Rebel officials employed various means to bring such dissenters into line. Political intimidation, property confiscation, arrest, and violence were common tactics. Still, opposition persisted, although it remained ineffective.[56]

In 1863, the disaffection took a new form. Under the informal leadership of William W. Holden, editor of the *North Carolina Standard* in Raleigh, a peace movement emerged. Holden, a secession supporter in 1861, had been instrumental in forming the Conservative Party, a coalition of former Whigs and former conditional Unionists. In 1862, the Conservatives challenged the Confederate Party for the governorship, and their candidate, Zebulon Vance, won the race. In fact, Vance and Holden had been friends and political collaborators. But with Vance in office and the war grinding along, the two gradually parted ways. Holden became increasingly disenchanted with Confederate policies, and in the summer of 1863 he began to call for a negotiated peace. He explained that "the people of both sections are tired of war and desire peace. We desire it on terms honorable to our own section, and we cannot expect it on terms dishonorable to the other section." Though he continued to support the Confederacy, he urged advocates of peace to speak up and "pave the way for negotiations." Holden, however, was vague about where such negotiations would lead.[57]

Though Holden and like-minded citizens had grown disillusioned with the conflict, they had little desire to do away with slavery.[58] For the most part, peace advocates sought to keep slavery intact. To them, the institution's survival depended on securing a settlement before battlefield losses evaporated any remaining Confederate leverage.[59] Holden himself was clear about this. In January 1864, he warned that slavery would "be utterly and finally destroyed" after another year of war, and "it will be impossible to reestablish the institution." He insisted that one of his primary goals was to "prevent the sudden abolition of slavery."[60] Following the losses at Gettysburg and Vicksburg in the summer of 1863, another Raleigh editor, John Pennington, urged negotiations because "peace now would save slavery."[61]

Throughout the state, citizens met and drafted resolutions calling for "an honorable and lasting peace."[62] Holden's paper published these resolutions. In the fall congressional elections, North Carolina sent several peace-leaning representatives to Richmond. Some dissenters even formed a clandestine group known as the Heroes of America (or the Red Strings), a loose, decentralized coalition firmly opposed to the Confederacy. Holden sought to distance himself from this group and vigorously denied membership in it or even knowledge of it, although evidence suggests that his bodyguard and some of his other associates were active members.[63]

Holden's agitation represented more than just a curious anecdote in Civil War history. The North Carolina peace movement posed a grave danger to the Confederacy's viability, representing, in the view of historian James M. McPherson, "the most serious internal threat to the Confederacy" up to that point.[64] Many feared that peace negotiations would take the state out of the Confederacy. Holden was never clear on the subject, but his statements strongly implied support for unilateral action by North Carolina should the Confederate government fail to seek a negotiated end to the war.[65] The state's exit from the conflict would potentially constitute a death blow to the rebellion. Its departure would virtually isolate Virginia from the rest of the South and deprive the Confederacy of much supply, its last major port, and tens of thousands of soldiers. Without North Carolina, the Confederacy's prospects would dim significantly.

The call for negotiations from members of the peace movement created confusion and uncertainty. Holden provided few specifics, and other peace advocates shared no consistent position. For instance, some sought an independent North Carolina, while others focused on helping the Confederate government negotiate a way out of the war that left slavery intact. The precise results of any negotiation were nearly impossible to predict, particularly if North Carolina chose to act unilaterally. Holden's opponents seized on this uncertainty as the peace movement took hold. There were many questions. Would North Carolina become a neutral party in the conflict? Would the state actively participate in the struggle, with Tar Heel troops donning blue uniforms and joining Federal ranks? Finally, and most important, what would become of slavery in the state? These various uncertainties strongly suggested that any effort by North Carolinians to remove themselves from the war would set in motion a chain of chaotic, unpredictable events that might not achieve the desired result.

Governor Vance warned President Davis of the growing dissatisfaction and agitation in his state. In July, a few weeks after Gettysburg, he pointed to the "bad feeling" harbored by many North Carolinians toward the Confederate government. The governor expressed a desire to work with the president on the issue. Davis was concerned and, in response, took aim at Holden. He asked Vance whether the editor was "engaged in the treasonable purpose of exciting the people of North Carolina to resistance against their government and cooperation with the enemy." Vance, believing that Holden's motives coincided with Confederate goals, sought to allay the president's concerns, and Richmond officials backed off.[66]

Though Holden escaped punishment, his views triggered a sharp response from soldiers in the army. In June, General D. H. Hill had warned the War Department that Holden and his supporters would rush "to meet the Yankees and welcome them to the State" should the Federals capture the railroad junction at Goldsboro. In August, Major John T. Jones of the 26th North Carolina wrote that Holden's words "certainly had a bad effect on some of our troops," and some Tar Heel officers in Lee's army formally called for an end to Holden's newspaper and the peace movement.[67] In September, the blowback spread beyond threats and decrees when Georgians from H. L. Benning's brigade, temporarily stationed in Raleigh, stormed Holden's offices and destroyed papers and other property.[68] Holden fled the scene and found refuge at the Governor's Palace—Vance's official residence—of all places, while the governor raced to break up the mob. The incident demonstrated that, despite their growing political differences, the two men remained on civil terms. However, more violence was at hand. The next day Holden's supporters ransacked the offices and printing equipment of the Vance-leaning State Journal. Again, the governor hurried to the scene but failed to arrive before significant, irreparable damage had been done.[69]

"Fight the Yankees and Fuss with the Confederacy"

At the helm of North Carolina's war effort throughout 1863, Zebulon Baird Vance had managed to weather a long string of challenges. He was a strong, charismatic leader and a significant asset to the Confederacy. At six feet tall and 200 pounds, with a tuft of thick black hair, he cut an imposing figure. He was also a natural, engaging politician and a commanding speaker whose charm and wit were difficult to match.[70] A soldier who met the governor in 1864 noted that the "intelligent humor that sparkles in his dark bright eye would impress you at once with the idea that he is a *jolly old fellow*, yet the mouth indicates a firmness and decision of character."[71] Vance proved to be a flexible, pragmatic, and highly skilled politician. A conditional Unionist before the war, he strongly embraced the Confederate cause following Fort Sumter's capture. As a war governor, he often quarreled with authorities in Richmond. His frequent clashes with President Davis led some to label him an obstructionist, but such characterizations do not ring true.

Vance certainly argued with officials in Richmond, often taking issue with Confederate policies limiting individual rights, as well as measures that hamstrung his own administration's efforts to promote the war. His frequent clashes with Davis demonstrated Vance's refusal to blindly follow policies emanating from Richmond. But at the heart of it, Vance remained an indefatigable Confederate nationalist who was focused on preserving the Confederacy's defining institution. In an unpublished autobiography prepared after the war, he candidly explained, "I concluded therefore to go with my state and to fight—not for secession—not for the Confederate States [as] an object desirable in itself—but to avert the consequences—the abolition of Slavery." Thus, broadly speaking, his many disagreements with Davis most likely reflected a conflict over tactics rather than overall goals. In fact, observers sometimes referred to his platform as "fight the Yankees and fuss with the Confederacy."[72]

As 1863 came to a close, there was much to fuss about. The growing distrust between North Carolina and Virginia, a situation that predated the Civil War, remained a source of tension.[73] The discord between the two states stemmed, in part, from Virginians' predominance in the Confederate high command, particularly in Lee's army.[74] In the summer of 1863, Lee did not help matters when he filled vacancies at corps command with two Virginians, A. P. Hill and Richard Ewell. North Carolinians were not alone in noticing the pattern. Lafayette McLaws, a division commander from Georgia, identified a strong feeling among troops from other states that "no matter how trifling the deed may be which a Virginian performs it is heralded and at once as the most glorious of modern times."[75]

The results at Gettysburg only exacerbated the tension. The ruinous assault on the battle's third day stoked the interstate rivalry to a rolling boil. In the campaign's aftermath, Richmond newspapers pointed fingers at the North Carolina brigades in Johnston Pettigrew's division, claiming they had performed poorly and exposed George Pickett's Virginians. A widely reprinted account in the *Richmond Enquirer* delivered a particular sting. In it, correspondent Jonathon Albertson accused the Tar Heels of breaking and running, leaving Pickett alone "to contend with the hordes of the enemy now pouring in upon him on every side."[76] North Carolinians fired back. A contributor to the *Raleigh Register* wrote of the "grossest injustice to Gen. Pettigrew's brigade."[77] Others chimed in, and the controversy dragged on. In fact, the acrimony would continue well beyond the Confederacy's collapse and would be rehashed again and again in historical society papers and regimental histories. However, in 1863, the slights and perceived slights were still fresh and provided an uncomfortable backdrop to the events of 1864.[78]

As the post-Gettysburg controversy festered, Governor Vance wrote to the War Department in late August 1863 to complain about dissatisfaction among the North Carolina troops in Lee's army, the Gettysburg controversy, and the appointment of officers. In a lengthy reply on September 9, 1863, Lee explained that he regretted "exceedingly the jealousies, heart-burnings, and other evil consequences resulting from the crude misstatements of newspaper correspondents, who have, necessarily, a very limited acquaintance with the facts . . . and who magnify the deeds of troops from their own States at the expense of others." Lee emphasized that the official reports had done "justice" to the brave North Carolina soldiers "whose heroism and devotion have illustrated the name of their State on every battle-field in which the Army of Northern Virginia has been engaged."[79] After receiving the general's reply, Vance let the issue go for the time being. Over the coming months, he would have bigger problems.

"An Instructive Turn of the Tables"

In November 1863, Vance's troubles swelled with the appointment of Major General Benjamin F. Butler to replace John Foster as head of the Union's Department of Virginia and North Carolina, a command that included New Bern and other points in the state.[80] Butler, hated by the rebels and disliked by many Northerners, was a skilled attorney with scant military experience. His views on the issues underlying the war had evolved over the years. Before secession, he had supported pro-slavery advocates in the Kansas conflict, spoken favorably of the *Dred Scott* decision, and, at the 1860 Democratic Convention, backed none other than Jefferson Davis. However, his experiences in the war's early stages convinced him that Union forces had to target slavery to win.[81] In Virginia, he gained notoriety by coining the term "contraband of war" in 1861 to describe the slaves who escaped into Union lines. By July 1862, he confessed to his wife, "I am changing my opinions. There is nothing of the people [the white Southerners] worth saving. I am inclined to give it all up to the blacks."[82] Energetic, intelligent, and fearless with the pen, Butler would become one of the most creative and vociferous advocates of hard, abolitionist military policies. His brash, unpolished style ruffled feathers, particularly during his tenure as Union commander of New Orleans in 1862. He would gain a reputation for pomposity, corruption, and military incompetence. Although some criticism was overblown, his bluster often worked against him, generating detractors in the army and the administration.[83]

As the new chief of Federal operations in the region, Butler conducted an inspection tour of North Carolina with Brigadier General John Peck, in command of the District of North Carolina, and Rear Admiral Samuel Phillips Lee in November 1863. Accompanied by his wife and daughter, Butler landed at Morehead City, visited Fort Macon, and took the train to New Bern, where crowds, including many freed people, lined the streets in anticipation of his arrival. From New Bern, Butler traveled to Little Washington, Plymouth, Roanoke Island, and Hatteras. Sarah Hildreth Butler, the general's wife, was not particularly impressed by what she saw. "North Carolina seems to be all water," she concluded. She observed that every town had a long main street draped with elms and lined with "some few good-looking houses."[84]

New York Herald reporter William H. Stiner accompanied the Butlers and provided a detailed description of the trip to Northern readers.[85] General Butler himself left few impressions of the tour. Later he would claim the inspection convinced him to recommend that the War Department abandon Plymouth and Washington, although no record of this communication has been found. However, Sarah Butler may have been echoing the general's opinions when she informed her sister that "the little towns we have taken and fortified at great labour and expense . . . are of no earthly use but oblige us to feed and take care of the inhabitants." She insinuated that Union forces had seized these positions only to boost the reputation of General Foster, her husband's predecessor. She viewed Wilmington as the only position in the state worth having. It is possible that the general communicated similar views to the War Department during subsequent in-person meetings, but if he shared such opinions, he left no trail in his correspondence and reports.[86]

As part of his new responsibilities, Butler paid special attention to putting the black units under his command into active service. Following a small raid in November by two African American regiments in southeastern Virginia to gather supplies, free slaves, and hunt down rebel irregulars, Butler approved a much more ambitious operation out of Norfolk aimed at recruiting slaves from northeastern North Carolina. For this task, he tapped Colonel Edward Wild, the officer who had organized recruits at New Bern. Wild gathered a force of 2,000 black troops for the mission. In addition to bringing slaves into the ranks, Wild hoped to clear the region of guerrillas, men for whom he harbored a particular distaste, and to encourage those Unionist-leaning civilians who were tired of the war.[87] The raid would also capture provisions otherwise destined for Confederate commissaries from a region described by a Fayetteville paper as "one of the most important sources of meat supplies that is now accessible to [Confederate] armies," amounting to about 3 million pounds of pork and beef.[88]

On December 5, 1863, Wild's units left their camps and marched south toward the Albemarle Sound, the start of a three-week expedition through several counties that ended with the temporary occupation of Elizabeth City.[89] The Confederates scrambled to organize a decisive response but managed to muster only weak resistance from militia and irregular units. In many ways, Wild's jaunt was a success. During the raid, his men liberated about 2,500 slaves, seized property, captured guerrillas, and burned their camps. However, as a recruiting effort, the operation was not particularly fruitful. Most of the freed people were women, children, and elderly men. In fact, fewer than 100 men who joined the column proved fit to shoulder a rifle. Union officers transported many of the former slaves to the Federal base at Roanoke Island, where a large community of refugees had formed.[90]

Despite the mixed results, Wild's raid stood out as particularly noteworthy for its aggressive conduct. In a December 17, 1863, dispatch to Captain John T. Elliott, Wild warned that he would treat guerrillas as "pirates" and tell them, "you will never have rest until you renounce your present course or join the regular Confederate Army."[91] At one point during the raid, Wild captured and executed Daniel Bright, "a man of about thirty, a rough stout fellow . . . dressed in butternut homespun [who] looked the very ideal of a guerrilla." Bright died at the end of a rope, but not until he had dangled for twenty agonizing minutes. A slip of paper pinned to his back bore the message: "This guerrilla hanged by order of Brig.-Gen. Wild, Daniel Bright, of Pasquotank County." Union soldiers left his body where it hung as a warning to "bushwhackers."[92]

In his official report, Wild candidly admitted he had "adopted a more rigorous style of warfare" that included burning houses and barns, consuming livestock, and taking hostages from the families of suspected guerrillas.[93] The hostage taking, particularly the seizure of white women, struck a raw nerve among Confederates. The symbolism conjured by the operation caught the attention of many. Dr. William Porter Ray, a correspondent for the *New York Times* writing under the pen name "Tewksbury," accompanied Wild and prepared a lengthy account of the raid that was published in early January 1864.[94] Ray reminded readers that Wild's expedition ranked as one of the war's first large-scale operations conducted solely by black troops. The reporter recognized the revolutionary nature of the event: "It is an instructive turn of the tables that the men who have been accustomed to hunt runaway slaves hiding in the swamps of the South, should now, hiding there themselves, be hunted by them."[95]

The raid ignited outrage among Confederate officials and North Carolina politicians. Major General George E. Pickett, head of the North Carolina Department and the scion of an established slaveholding family in Virginia, was beside himself.

"Butler's plan, evidently, is to let loose his swarm of blacks upon our ladies and defenseless families, plunder and devastate the country," Pickett complained. "I will not stand upon terms with these fellows any longer," he fumed, and "against such a warfare there is but one resource—to hang at once every one captured belonging to the expedition, and afterward any one caught who belongs to Butler's department." He understood that the Lincoln administration's efforts to arm former slaves would strengthen the Union army while weakening the rebel labor force, and he urged the War Department to transfer all slaves in exposed areas into Confederate lines. He passed on his correspondence to his subordinates in the Albemarle region, and in turn, these men acted.[96] On January 12, 1864, state troops under Captain John T. Elliott seized Private Samuel Jordon of the 5th USCT from his confinement in northern Pasquotank and promptly hung him from the same beam used to execute Daniel Bright weeks before. In an effort to quell this escalating violence, Butler wrote to Confederate Colonel James Hinton, a prominent lawyer in Pasquotank who commanded a unit in the region. Butler announced that he did not wish "to conduct the war like a fishwoman in Billingsgate by calling hard names, such as 'brute,' 'beast,' &c." and affirmed his intent "to carry on this war according to the rules of civilized warfare." However, Butler's word did little to reduce the bitterness.[97]

Wild's expedition also rattled the Southern press. Newspapers gathered reports of the raid and passed them on to horrified readers. The *Daily State Journal* in Raleigh claimed that white women in Elizabeth City had been "jostled by the negro troops and had to permit them to walk by their side and converse with them, on pain of arrest." "The negro," the story concluded, "ran riot during the Yankee stay in Albemarle country."[98] The *Richmond Examiner* remarked that the "fiat seems to have gone forth for stern and terrible work on the North Carolina frontier, in this dark and melancholy country of swamps, overrun with negro banditti, and now the especial theatre of the war's vengeance."[99]

Wild's raid had other repercussions. Citizens in Pasquotank County petitioned Governor Vance to remove state troops from the area because their presence only invited more Federal raids. The resolution highlighted the failure of Confederate efforts in the northeastern counties and, most assuredly, embarrassed Vance and other officials. In fact, the governor had organized some of these troops himself, including a company led by Colonel Hinton.[100] Like other Confederate officials, the governor became deeply troubled by the entire episode. However, he appeared to direct much of his venom at the Confederate War Department in Richmond. A livid Vance fired off a menu of objections to Robert Ould, the Confederate official responsible for prisoner exchanges. The governor groused about the failure of Wild's men to treat the North Carolina militiamen as legitimate prisoners of war, as well as the black troops' hostage taking. He demanded a response to "this horrible, cowardly, and damnable disposition on the part of the enemy to put women in irons as hostages for negro soldiers!" He concluded, "If it is not done and these outrages upon defenseless females continue I shall retaliate upon Yankee soldiers to the full extent of my ability and let the consequences rest with the damnable barbarians who began it."[101]

"A Bad State of Feeling Here toward the Confederate Government"

Vance's note to Ould added to the parade of complaints he had submitted to Richmond officials throughout 1863. In July, he reminded President Davis of "a bad state of feeling here toward the Confederate Government" and followed up with additional correspondence throughout the fall.[102] A few days before Christmas, he wrote to James Seddon to complain about the misdeeds of detached Confederate troops; by Vance's reckoning, their primary activities appeared to involve stealing, pilfering, and burning citizens' property, particularly in the western portion of the state. Vance's epistle included this extraordinary morsel of hyperbole: "If God Almighty had yet in store another plague worse than all others which he intended to have let loose on the Egyptians in case Pharaoh still hardened his heart, I am sure it must have been a regiment or so of half-armed, half-disciplined Confederate cavalry."[103] This statement met with some derision in Richmond. Seddon forwarded Vance's letter to Adjutant General Samuel Cooper with the following endorsement: "Can you suggest, or do you advise, a general order to avert the threatened disasters which so affect Governor Vance's imagination?"[104] On Christmas Day, when War Department clerk John Beauchamp Jones mentioned the letter to Senator Robert Hunter, the latter remarked that many North Carolinians were "prone to act in opposition to the Confederate States Government."[105]

Vance continued his late-year salvo against Richmond. On December 29, he complained about the "crying evil and injustice" of overzealous impressment agents and their tendency to strip too much from North Carolina farmers, leaving families with inadequate supplies. On the last day of the year, he wrote again, grousing about War Department distilleries operating in the western part of the state.[106] Seddon and his subordinates struggled with Vance's volleys, diplomatically batting them away. For example, in response to his colorful concerns about the undisciplined cavalry, Seddon responded with a sober, evenhanded note asking for more information about the units involved.[107]

Amid Vance's constant badgering, one letter stood out. On December 30, 1863, the governor penned a dispatch directly to President Davis, broaching the issue of war and peace. Vance began his letter by recommending "some efforts" to conduct peace negotiations with the enemy to help remove "the sources of discontent in North Carolina." In short, Vance urged the president to use peace overtures as a tactic to strengthen Southern resolve. Under his plan, he expected Lincoln to promptly reject any suggestion of a negotiated peace. With the possibility of peace eliminated, the governor hoped those clamoring for negotiations would close ranks with the Confederate government. Though Vance explained his strategy in the wordy letter, his point was a subtle one.[108]

In raising this suggestion, tactics, not principles, drove Vance. In reality, he had no intention of seriously seeking a negotiated peace. In fact, his scheme to use peace talks to rally the disaffected into supporting the war masked his growing anger with Holden and other peace proponents. Two days after his letter to President Davis, Vance told his political ally William Graham, "I will see the Conservative party blown into a thousand atoms and Holden and his understrappers in hell . . . before I will consent to a course which I think would bring dishonor and ruin upon both the State & the Confederacy!" The next day, in a private letter to University of North Carolina president David Swain, the governor added that, in his view, Holden's policy was to "take N.C. back to the United States," a course that would "steep the name of North Carolina in infamy and make her memory a reproach among the nations."[109] But Vance kept such statements among his friends and would not speak out publicly against Holden's peace efforts for several weeks.

Vance's December 30 letter to the president backfired. Davis missed, or chose to miss, the subtlety behind the governor's arguments. In his January 8, 1864, response, Davis simply argued against the proposal for a negotiated peace, citing a host of practical problems and substantive concerns. He did not engage Vance's main proposal to use peace negotiations as a vehicle to bring peace advocates back into the fold. Instead, the president argued that a settlement with Lincoln would strip the Confederacy of all it had fought for, including slavery.[110]

Unofficial Richmond greeted Vance's epistle as nothing short of a call for surrender. Diarist Mary Chesnut, whose husband James served as an aide to Davis, recorded that North Carolina "wants to offer terms of peace." "We only need a break of that kind to finish us," Chesnut lamented. "I really shivered nervously as one does when the first handful of earth, comes rattling down on the coffin in the grave of one we cared for more than all who are left."[111] Davis complicated matters by sharing the letter with some officials in North Carolina.[112] The exchange of correspondence would eventually make its way into the newspapers later that spring, generating much discussion in the press.[113] Given his true feelings on the subject, the governor must have felt dismayed by President Davis's misapprehension. In the coming months, Vance would clarify his views on the issues of peace and war and firmly reject negotiations with the Lincoln administration. But as 1864 began, his letter stood out as a significant misstep.

Vance's frantic letters to Richmond ended a darkening year for Confederate North Carolina. Dissatisfaction was building. The sources of unhappiness were many. The ongoing Union occupation of the coastal zone continued to vex state officials, Confederate commanders, and citizens supportive of the rebellion. Wild's raid, with its spectacle of black men in blue uniforms operating unfettered in the agriculturally rich northeastern counties, added to the despondency. Forty years later, Walter Montgomery, a state supreme court justice and former Confederate officer, would sum up conditions as follows: "A great majority of the people . . . thought that the time had arrived when the question of peace with the United States government should be considered. It was thought that the contest was hopeless after the surrender of Vicksburg and the defeat . . . at Gettysburg, and that the further effusion of blood and destruction of property should cease."[114] At the beginning of 1864, support for the Confederate war in North Carolina was diminishing. Governor Vance understood this. Richmond officials did as well, and so did Robert E. Lee.

PART TWO

Military Plans for North Carolina in 1864

By the end of 1863, a host of problems plagued the Confederates. Union forces had made substantial gains in the west, including a significant victory at Vicksburg in July. In the east, a supply crisis, exacerbated by the Union presence in North Carolina, threatened Robert E. Lee's troops in Virginia. In Raleigh, editor William Holden and other peace advocates continued to clamor for a negotiated end to the war, thus posing a tangible threat to Governor Zebulon Vance and Confederate control of the state. In an effort to improve supply and quell the peace movement, General Lee proposed military action in North Carolina. He hoped a victory in the Old North State would improve the morale of the Confederates there and help feed his men. As Lee schemed, Union commanders, most notably Ulysses S. Grant, also cast their eyes toward North Carolina, seeking to unleash a large offensive there. However, when officials in Washington, DC, pushed aside Grant's proposal, the initiative remained with the Confederates in the state.

CHAPTER THREE

Lee's Design for North Carolina

"I Fear the Army Cannot Be Kept Together"

As 1864 arrived, the Confederates hoped for better results in North Carolina. The previous year had been a challenging one for the rebellion. Over the summer, Robert E. Lee's ambitious offensive into Pennsylvania stumbled at Gettysburg, bleeding men, depressing morale, and sending his army back into Virginia. More reverses occurred elsewhere. In July, Ulysses S. Grant captured Vicksburg and seized control of the Mississippi River for the Federals. In November, Grant struck again, taking Chattanooga, Tennessee, and opening the gateway to Atlanta and the Lower South. As they licked their wounds and looked toward 1864, rebel leaders hoped their efforts in the coming year would exhaust Union morale and turn the Northern populace against the war. They focused on the upcoming presidential election in the North. Lee, in particular, hoped Confederate military success would demoralize Republicans in the North and usher the "friends of peace" into office in the fall.[1]

Confederate problems extended beyond military setbacks. The Southern economy was flagging. Shortages of arms, manpower, and subsistence continued, with meager hope of improvement. As John Beauchamp Jones recorded from his War Department desk, "It is getting to be the general belief among men capable of reflection that no jugglery can save the Confederate States currency." At Christmas, the clerk noted the exorbitant prices in Richmond and remarked that such "is the scarcity of provisions, that rats and mice have mostly disappeared, and the cats can hardly be kept off the table."[2] For certain, the Confederacy's shaky foundations were crumbling. Limited resources at home, highly restricted access to markets abroad, and a shortage of financial expertise in the government all combined to doom any hope of a well-functioning economy. Confederate officials exacerbated matters by failing to raise revenue through either taxation or bond sales. The government had relied on Treasury notes to finance the war, a policy that raised commodity prices. When taxes were finally increased in 1863, dissatisfaction among the populace rose as well.[3] The unhappiness persisted. Robert Kean, an official in the War Department, explained that "the irretrievable bankruptcy of the national finances, the tenacity with which the President holds to men in whom the country has lost all confidence, the scarcity of means to support . . . are producing deep disgust."[4]

These economic woes manifested in one overarching problem for officials in the War Department and commanders in the field: supply. As 1864 approached, units in Lee's Army of Northern Virginia suffered from shortages of nearly everything—shoes, blankets, meat, grain, horses, and hay. Concerns about supply consumed much ink in government correspondence. Confederate and state leaders argued over the impressment of crops and other items needed for the war effort.[5] With all manner of goods nearly exhausted in the army camps, officials sought to obtain items through the ever-tightening blockade and the overencumbered, inadequate rail system.[6] Despite these efforts, administrators estimated in early December 1863 that only a twenty-five-day meat supply was on hand for the forces east of the Mississippi. In Virginia, the meat ration was "nearly exhausted."[7]

Predictably, supply became a nagging obsession for Robert E. Lee and expended much of his energy. In October, he wrote to Quartermaster General Alexander Lawton about the lack of shoes and blankets for the men. He even went into the details of shoemaking, going so far as to advise Lawton about the proper facing for shoe leather.[8] On January 5, the general complained to commissary chief Lucius B. Northrop about having to cut rations to "a quarter of a pound of salt and three-quarters of a pound of fresh meat," in addition to "half rations of sugar and coffee, one day's issue of fruit, and some lard."[9] Several days later, he informed President Davis that meat invoiced to his army was not reaching his men. This hint of fraud triggered a flurry of letters from Northrop's office and elsewhere.[10]

As the first days of 1864 arrived, Lee remained in the thick of the crisis. He sought to collect supplies for his own army by sending troops to forage at the "front of our line of operations." His own commissary officers bought all the cattle and provisions within their reach.[11] Lee's cavalry units also spread throughout the Virginia countryside to ensure adequate fodder for their mounts.[12] He advised the War Department that "short rations are having a bad effect upon the men, both morally and physically," and were encouraging desertions to the enemy. "I fear the Army cannot be kept together," he warned.[13]

"The Key to a Large and Productive Country"

With supply challenges mounting, Lee concluded it was time to strike a blow against Federal positions in North Carolina and open up the agriculturally rich coastal plain. On January 2, a freezing Saturday, Lee wrote to President Davis from his headquarters outside Orange, Virginia, and declared that the "time is at hand" for military operations in the beleaguered state. Although the proposed campaign fell outside of Lee's formal sphere of authority as chief of the Army of Northern Virginia, the general showed no hesitancy in recommending the operation to Davis. He also proposed to send men from his own army to augment the attacking force. Lee understood that a successful offensive to retake key positions in the state would do more than solve the supply problem. It would also address the effects of Wild's demoralizing raid in December, the continual threat of Federal operations, Governor Vance's unhappiness with Confederate policies, and, perhaps most important, the growing peace movement threatening the Confederacy's viability.[14]

In forming the plan to capture New Bern, Lee no doubt remained mindful of the host of issues afflicting North Carolinians, including the skyrocketing desertion rates in the state's regiments. The general was certainly aware that Union military control of the coastal region had emboldened Unionists, forced planters to send their slaves west, and caused disruption in these counties. He surely knew about Wild's raid and its impact, as well as Governor Vance's numerous complaints to officials in Richmond about conscription and other policies impacting the state's citizens.[15]

In his note to the president, Lee identified New Bern as the target. He believed the city was ripe for the taking, and his proposal reflected a firm conviction that its fortifications were vulnerable, despite the stout network of trenches and forts built during two years of Union occupation. Indeed, Lee indicated that, according to Confederate intelligence reports, the city's garrison had "been so long unmolested, and experiences such a feeling of security, that it is represented as careless."[16]

Lee's plan for New Bern also reflected an expectation that the ironclads under construction on the Roanoke and Neuse Rivers would soon be completed. These boats promised dramatic benefits. But without them, some other means would have to be found to counter the Union naval presence there. To meet this need, Lee recommended a surprise night assault led by a "bold naval officer" to seize the enemy's vessels and turn them on Union defenses. Should the Confederates take New Bern, the captured gunboats, along with the completed ironclads, would eventually clear out the state's rivers and sounds.[17]

New Bern was a large prize. It was the main Federal base in North Carolina, and its possession was crucial to control of the state's eastern region. The railroad connected the city to both the coast and points inland, including Kinston, the Goldsboro rail junction, and the capital at Raleigh. In addition, New Bern's natural strength and location provided an excellent point from which to launch Union offensives. Confederate success there would reduce the pressure on Wilmington and open the way for more operations against Federal positions at Plymouth, Washington, Roanoke Island, Morehead City, and Beaufort.

Established in 1710 by Swiss immigrants, New Bern had served as the seat of co-

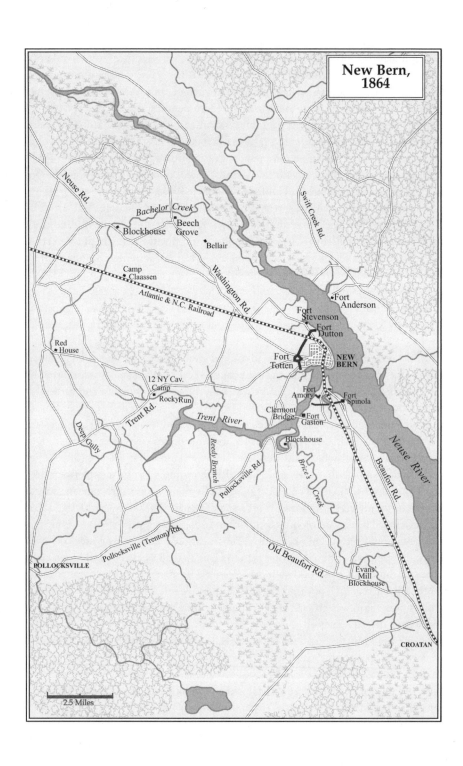

New Bern, 1864

Neuse Rd.

Bachelor Creek
Beech Grove
Blockhouse
Bellair

Swift Creek Rd.

Camp Claassen

Atlantic & N.C. Railroad

Washington Rd.

Fort Anderson

Fort Stevenson
Fort Dutton

Red House

Fort Totten

NEW BERN

12 NY Cav. Camp
RockyRun

Trent Rd.

Deep Gully

Trent River

Reedy Branch

Fort Amory
Clermont Bridge
Fort Gaston

Fort Spinola

Blockhouse

Neuse River

Beaufort Rd.

Brice's Creek

Pollocksville Rd.

Pollocksville (Trenton) Rd.

POLLOCKSVILLE

Old Beaufort Rd.

Evans' Mill Blockhouse

CROATAN

2.5 Miles

lonial government and as the state capital after independence. Its economy thrived in the nineteenth century through vibrant trade with Caribbean and northeastern markets.[18] Decades before the Civil War, New Bern contained a large free black population of artisans and merchants who contributed greatly to the city's economy.[19] In the late 1850s New Bern received a boost when it became a stop on the Atlantic and North Carolina Railroad, and by the time of the Civil War, it had grown to more than 5,000 residents and ranked as one of the state's largest cities.[20]

A Confederate military victory at New Bern would capture the arms and equipment stored there and open the region to rebel subsistence officers. In his note to Davis, Lee reported that New Bern and the surrounding countryside held large quantities of food and other supplies "which are much wanted for this army."[21] One Confederate correspondent identified the city as "the key to a large and productive country," as well as a "rendezvous of a large number of fugitive slaves, and the most important depot of supplies which the enemy has in eastern North-Carolina."[22] Another source noted that, prior to Union victories, the Albemarle and Pamlico Sounds had provided nearly all the provisions consumed by Confederate soldiers in Virginia.[23]

In addition to capturing vital supplies, victory would help secure the transportation network serving Confederate forces, primarily the vital Wilmington and Weldon Railroad, one of the few links between Lee's army and the rest of the South. According to Confederate commissary of subsistence Frank G. Ruffin, in early 1864, nearly all the provisions for Lee's army depended on the railroad connection to North Carolina.[24] A break in the rail line at Goldsboro or at some other spot would force Confederate officials to ship supplies arriving at Wilmington through a meandering, circuitous route into South Carolina and then north on tracks of varying gauges.[25] A gap at Weldon would be even worse. In fact, at the beginning of 1864, only a single connection existed between North Carolina and Virginia—a line joining Petersburg and Weldon. Confederate and state officials would eventually open a second junction later in 1864, the 45-mile Piedmont line connecting Danville to Greensboro. But in January, that connection was still under construction. Accordingly, should Union forces occupy Weldon, Virginia would become completely isolated.[26] Lee and his generals appreciated the importance of protecting approaches to the railroad, particularly the crucial position at Kinston, near Goldsboro. As George Pickett explained in early January, "Kinston must be held if possible, as it is the key to that whole country. No movement can be made upon Wilmington from New Berne without first clearing us out of Kinston."[27]

In addition to military considerations, Lee's proposal had a clear political angle, a fact he expressly acknowledged. In subsequent communications detailing the plan, he predicted that victory would "have the happiest effect in North Carolina and inspire the people." Although his correspondence over the previous months had revealed little awareness of the discontent in the state, this brief line clearly demonstrated that, in recommending the enterprise, Lee had more than supply in mind.[28] He knew victory would serve as a welcome tonic for Confederate morale in a region that had seen limited success throughout the war. Moreover, New Bern itself had become a symbol for everything the Confederates despised about the Union occupation of the state. As one rebel supporter put it: "The regiments stationed [in New Bern] have been composed principally of men from Massachusetts and New York, the blackest of abolitionists, full of schemes and plans for negro emancipation, equalization and education; negro regiments have been organized; companies of disloyal Carolinians put in service against us; the most tyrannical rule established; and both men and officers have been guilty of the greatest outrages and atrocities."[29]

This political goal behind the New Bern operation was widely understood. Thomas Kenan, an officer in the 43rd North Carolina who served as attorney general long after the war, recalled that, given increasing disaffection in 1864, "it was determined to make an effort to allay it by an attempt to change the military situation."[30] D. H. Hill Jr., son of the Confederate general, also later reflected that Lee's North Carolina plan represented "an effort to alleviate" the "gloomy" state of affairs among the state's citizens.[31]

"Your Suggestion Is Approved"

Lee did not have to wait long for a response to his proposal. "Your suggestion is approved," Davis wrote two days later in a letter conveying high hopes for the venture. The president clearly viewed the expedition as much more than a routine operation. To begin with, he suggested that Lee himself lead the attack to "give it form" and "insure success." Without the general's personal attention, Davis feared the scheme would fail, as similar attempts had elsewhere. If Lee was not available, the president offered to lead the operation himself, "though it could only be for a very few days." This extraordinary proposal demonstrated the president's inclination to immerse himself in details well outside his role as the Confederacy's chief executive. It also revealed a distrust of other officers—namely, George E. Pickett, the man in charge of the Department of North Carolina.[32]

Ultimately, Davis did not leave his desk in Richmond to command the expedition. He did, however, attend personally to the operation's naval component. He knew progress on the ironclads had slowed, and a completion date was uncertain. Like Lee, he understood the expedition required strong naval support to counteract the Union navy and augment the ground attack. To fill this role, the president did not look far. He turned to his thirty-three-year-old aide and nephew John Taylor Wood, who enjoyed both an army and a navy rank (colonel and commander, respectively). Wood was a logical choice to lead the expedition's naval arm. The grandson of President Zachary Taylor, Wood was much more than a paper-pushing clerk. He was a fearless, experienced naval commander who had conducted several successful military operations during the war.

In the first week of January 1864, President Davis discussed the New Bern offensive with Wood. In fact, the pair may have talked about such an effort earlier. According to a postwar account, the Confederates had for some time "entertained the idea" of seizing one of the gunboats at the Federal base to add to the slim Confederate navy in North Carolina; another story even suggested that Wood had "visited Gen. Lee's headquarters and induced him to make an attack upon New Berne."[33] Whether Wood ever made such a proposal is unclear. In any case, on January 6, 1864, the president handed him written orders and sent him to North Carolina "without unnecessary delay" to carry out "the verbal instructions which have been given to you" and then return "to this city and report to me in person."[34] With that, Wood boarded a train in Richmond and headed south to gather information.

"The Gunboat Has Been Towed up to Halifax"

As Wood traveled to North Carolina, work continued on the ironclads there. At Halifax, construction crawled along on the boat that would eventually be named the *Albemarle*.[35] Over the past several months, it had often been unclear whether the vessel would ever go anywhere. Although the causes of delay were many, the scarcity of armor plating stood above the rest. The South's fledging railroads had imposed severe challenges on Confederate officials, including shortages of stock, limited lines, inconsistent gauges, and simple wear and tear. The soft iron rails of the 1860s did not stand up to frequent use. To maintain the vital, well-used routes during the war, rail companies often cannibalized lesser-used lines. This left little iron available for building gunboats.[36] Iron shortages impacted naval construction efforts throughout the state, including the projects at Wilmington, Kinston, and Halifax. To move these endeavors along, Confederate officials were forced to search for plating. Native North Carolinian James W. Cooke, an experienced naval officer assigned to the projects in 1863, complained to Governor Vance and pointed to the state's unused railroads as the best source for such material, but shortages continued. The search would continue into 1864 and would eventually involve Confederate and state officials at many levels.[37]

After much effort, the Confederates eventually obtained more iron. In February 1863, Secretary Mallory informed the ranking naval officer in the state, William F. Lynch, that more than 700 tons of railroad iron was available from an abandoned extension in Lawrenceburg. In addition, the Atlantic and North Carolina Railroad agreed to sell the rails from portions of the line east of Kinston, abandoned after New Bern's fall in 1862. Once harvested, much of the iron made its way to Richmond to be smelted and rolled. The finished plates eventually arrived in Halifax (for the *Albemarle*), Kinston (for the gunboat *Neuse*), and Wilmington. Despite this progress, at the time of Wood's trip in early January 1864, the *Albemarle*'s plating remained far from complete.[38]

Iron was not the only problem. Acrimony and charges of mismanagement plagued the projects in Halifax and Kinston. Lynch had made several questionable decisions, and he proved difficult to deal with. His actions and correspondence angered the men managing the work on the *Albemarle*, most notably Gilbert Elliott and James Cooke. In October, Lynch had assumed overall supervision of the projects, writing to Governor Vance, "I have seized and taken possession of . . . the Iron Clad Gun Boat 'Albemarle.'"[39] Concerned that the *Albemarle*'s construction site, the cornfield near Edward's Ferry, was vulnerable to Union attack, Lynch had ordered the unfinished vessel launched and towed upstream to Halifax. However, the launch on October 6, 1863, caused the vessel to "hog," or bend, leaving the stern several inches higher than the boat's center point.[40] Meanwhile, at Kinston, Lynch ordered iron plating attached to the *Neuse* before any of its internal machinery had been installed, a maneuver that later required some of the armor to be removed before the gunboat's completion.[41] Lynch also peppered Cooke and Elliott with numerous contract issues, a distraction that hampered progress. The two men bristled at Lynch's meddling, and when relations with Lynch deteriorated, they complained to Governor Vance. They also discussed the matter at a dinner with Catherine Edmondston in late October. "They told us that the Gunboat had been towed up to Halifax to be finished at a heavy expense to government," she wrote, "but that little great man Com Lynch could not get a house large enough for his dignity short of the town."[42] Despite the quarreling, work crews had made real progress on the gunboats by the time Commander Wood visited in January.[43] The *Albemarle* at the Halifax shipyard was shaping into a formidable weapon. Its hull was about 150 feet long and 35 feet wide at the extreme; it had a remarkably shallow draft of 6½ feet when unloaded and unarmored. A solid oak, iron-plated prow, which doubled as a ram, jutted out from its bow. An octagonal casemate would hold its guns and crew.[44] And its engines were on board already.[45]

It is not clear whether Wood actually inspected the two vessels during his January 1864 visit. Undoubtedly, he had a good idea of what was happening before arriving in North Carolina. Wood likely explored whether a flotilla of rowboats could materially aid a ground assault on the Union stronghold at New Bern. From Kinston, Wood no doubt gathered as much information as possible on the subject. One postwar recollection suggested that a "meeting of the officers was held in a spur of pine woods some miles distant" from New Bern to discuss operations against the Federal base there. One of the men reportedly visited the city, disguised as an "up-country farmer," and examined the New Bern wharf. There, the spy found a 170-foot side-wheel steamer and ascertained the size of its crew, the number of guns, security routines, and "all particulars relative to discipline and routine duties."[46] The vessel turned out to be the USS *Underwriter*, the largest of three gunboats guarding New Bern.

"The Complexion of Affairs"

During the first weeks of January, neither Lee nor Davis shared plans for the upcoming offensive with the commanders overseeing matters in the state. This included George Pickett, in charge of the Department of North Carolina. As part of his command, Pickett supervised three brigades in the region: Seth Barton's Virginians (about 1,600 men) at Kinston, Matt Ransom's North Carolinians (2,600 men) spread throughout the northeastern part of the state, and Thomas Clingman's North Carolinians (2,500 men) at Petersburg.[47] In overseeing his department, Pickett juggled many issues, including Union threats to North Carolina and southeastern Virginia. He also gave some thought to the supply situation. On January 12, he informed Secretary of War Seddon about plans for an expedition into northeastern counties, including Pasquotank, to collect bacon and other supplies. According to War Department clerk Jones, "several million pounds of bacon and pork" were reportedly in the Chowan region, in the hands of farmers who were reluctant to leave their land in the enemy's presence.[48]

While Pickett focused on his military duties, he remained mindful of political conditions.[49] In the midst of a dispute about troop transfers, he expressed concern about sending more North Carolina troops into that state, fearing they would not provide dependable service in the event of "internal trouble" there. "The complexion of affairs there now is very threatening," he warned the War Department.[50] Instead of Tar Heel troops, Pickett recommended Kemper's Virginia brigade (commanded at that time by Colonel William Terry) for duty in the state. Samuel Cooper in Richmond agreed.[51] This brief exchange revealed much about how Confederate officials viewed conditions in January 1864. Pickett and Seddon, both Virginians, were clearly concerned about civilian morale and the possibility of serious disturbances in North Carolina. The antipathy stirred by William W. Holden and others was well known to Confederate officials. Robert E. Lee was not pleased about transferring troops there either, albeit for different reasons. He questioned the need to send men south and noted the growing strength of the Army of the Potomac in Virginia, warning that "the spring will open upon us and find us without an army."[52]

Throughout January, Lee continued to devote attention to the North Carolina offensive. Around the second week of the month, John Taylor Wood completed his visit south and returned to Virginia to help plan the operation, which was still apparently unknown to most. He traveled north to Lee's headquarters to discuss the mission and the naval component of the upcoming operation. At that time, Wood no doubt reported to Lee that completion of the ironclads was many weeks, if not months, away. Given these delays, Lee and Wood understood that the Union gunboats at New Bern posed a substantial obstacle to the success of any operation there. In the face of this Federal naval power, a Confederate attack would have to be a strong one. Using information from Wood and other knowledgeable officers, Lee began to assemble a detailed plan designed to deliver New Bern into Confederate hands.[53]

CHAPTER FOUR

Grant's Suffolk Plan

"An Abandonment of All Previously Attempted Lines"

By coincidence, while the Confederate high command discussed plans for the Old North State, Union military leaders thought along the same lines. In early January, Henry W. Halleck, Lincoln's general in chief in Washington, DC, sought Ulysses S. Grant's ideas for the upcoming spring campaign, hoping that "an interchange of views on the present condition of affairs and the coming campaign will be advantageous."[1] From his headquarters at Nashville, Grant considered the request and consulted with two of his subordinates, Lieutenant Colonel Cyrus Comstock and Brigadier General William "Baldy" Smith. In a memorandum, the pair fleshed out a proposal Smith had developed earlier in the war. It called for an operation in North Carolina, specifically, a large raid into the heart of the state to sever rail lines, capture supplies, and generally disrupt Confederate operations.[2] On January 18, 1864, Comstock recorded in his diary: "Gen W. F. Smith & I submitted Mem. To Gen. as to landing 60,000 men at Norfolk or Newbern & operating against Rail R. south of Richmond & alternatively against Raleigh & Wilmington."[3]

Armed with Comstock and Smith's input, Grant submitted his proposal to Halleck the next day. In his direct, efficient prose, the general described a new approach to the war in the east. "I would respectfully suggest," he wrote, "whether an abandonment of all previously attempted lines to Richmond is not advisable, and in lieu of these one be taken farther south." Under Grant's plan, a large force of 60,000 would steam to Suffolk, Virginia, and march to Raleigh, without regard for its own lines of communication. After destroying railroads and capturing the capital, the column would head south and take Wilmington in reverse, using New Bern as its supply base. Grant recommended the operation's immediate implementation, noting that the southern climate would eliminate the need for months of "inactivity in winter quarters."[4]

The plan was aggressive and unconventional. Throughout the war, although

Union commanders had clung to their hard-won positions in eastern North Carolina, they had never devoted the troops or resources necessary to conduct large-scale offensive operations there. Instead, such energy had been targeted elsewhere, in grueling, often static campaigns at Charleston Harbor, around Fredericksburg, and in the Virginia Tidewater. Grant's approach would change all that. It would bypass Lee's strong position in Virginia, avoid direct attacks, and drive straight at the heart of the Confederate logistical network. If successful, the movement would cut the Confederacy at its neck, lopping off Virginia and opening the Deep South to further operations. The raid would also flush Confederate troops out of Virginia, away from their chosen defensive positions. As Grant explained, "this would virtually force an evacuation of Virginia and indirectly of East Tennessee." He expected these "new fields" would allow the Union armies to live off the land while reducing enemy stores. In addition, perhaps alluding to the growing unhappiness in the state, he predicted the operation would "cause thousands of the North Carolina troops to desert and return to their homes." Acknowledging the weapon that emancipation had become for the Union, he expected the expedition to "give us possession of many Negroes who are now indirectly aiding the rebellion."[5]

Grant's plan demonstrated much about his evolving approach to the war. It was consistent with the large-scale raiding strategy he and William T. Sherman would develop and employ on several occasions throughout 1864 and 1865. This innovation would unleash large attacking forces deep into the rebel interior, without regard for maintaining supply lines. Once in the state, his unencumbered columns would destroy railroad lines, break up Confederate communications, and draw enemy forces away from strong positions. Grant's proposal also reflected an inclination, often implemented in the coming months, to conduct indirect maneuvers that forced the enemy to react and conduct its own costly offensive operations. The offensive would yield important results. It would close the port at Wilmington and block all direct rail communication into Virginia. It would also require Jefferson Davis and Robert E. Lee to choose between sending a substantial force south to defend the railroads and launching another strike to threaten Washington, DC, and other points north. After providing his recommendation to Halleck, Grant received feedback on the plan from Major General John G. Foster, recently in command of Union troops in North Carolina, as well as Major General George H. Thomas, a native Virginian and commander of the Army of the Cumberland in the west.[6]

Despite its promise, Grant's plan never saw the light of day. After several weeks of reflection, Halleck politely rejected it, warning that the proposed operation would expose the Northern capital and other key points, a risk that leaders in Washington, DC, simply found unacceptable. His reply to Grant, however, was a study in confusion. In prefacing his response, Halleck announced that he had "never considered Richmond as the necessary objective point of the Army of the Potomac; that point is Lee's army." This statement was odd, for nowhere in the brief proposal did Grant mention Richmond as a target. Halleck's dispatch also wandered into a discussion of operations against Charleston Harbor and Savannah. He explained that he had always been opposed to "isolated expeditions on the sea and Gulf coast" because the troops necessary for such movements would be better used against "some important line of military operations." He concluded, "We have given too much attention to cutting the toe nails of our enemy instead of grasping his throat." These comments were consistent with Halleck's tendency to seek concentrations in force and avoid small, detached efforts. But in making this point, Halleck did not indicate whether he lumped Grant's proposed expedition together with these activities farther down the coast.[7]

In the course of its wandering, Halleck's letter expressed his most direct argument against Grant's plan. In essence, he did not believe the expedition would force Lee to abandon Virginia. Instead, he predicted the Confederate general would collect all the forces available and advance north. In turn, "popular sentiment will compel the Government to bring back the army in North Carolina to defend Washington, D.C., Baltimore, Harrisburg, and Philadelphia." In Halleck's view, Lee would gladly swap queens by exchanging "Richmond, Raleigh, and Wilmington for the possession of either of the aforementioned cities." Accordingly, Halleck preferred to mass Union forces in Virginia and directly confront the Confederates there. He also worried about the limited resources available for a North Carolina raid. If he had more troops, he would "not hesitate to" back Grant's proposal. But without sufficient numbers, he believed it should not be attempted. Even so, Halleck planned to share Grant's remarks with Lincoln and, striking a note of collaboration, explained, "I write to you plainly and frankly, for between us there should be no reserve or concealment of opinions."[8]

Following Halleck's response, Grant abandoned the North Carolina plan. In the coming months, he would develop a different scheme for the east, one that pitted the Army of the Potomac against Lee's veterans north of Richmond and hit other rebel positions simultaneously. Grant's blueprint would lead to the colossal struggles of the Overland Campaign in Virginia during the spring and summer of 1864. By turning down Grant's North Carolina scheme, Halleck ensured that the initiative in the state would belong to the Confederates.

"Expensive, Insecure, and Subjecting Us to Attack in Detail"

With Grant's plan shelved, John Peck and his forces in the District of North Carolina continued to focus on defense. Following Burnside's victories in 1862, the Federals had strengthened their key positions throughout the region. As they solidified their posts, Union commanders in both the army and the navy discussed the wisdom behind manning multiple positions in the state, an approach that spread limited troops and gunboats all over the region.[9] To support the main base at New Bern, the Federals had established fortified positions along the rail line connecting the city to the railhead at Morehead City on Bogue Sound. They also occupied nearby Beaufort, which served as a navy coaling station, and Fort Macon, which guarded Beaufort Inlet. Federal units continued to garrison Washington on the Pamlico River, as well as Plymouth to the north on the Roanoke. The latter post furnished a convenient base for raids along the Chowan River and placed Federal troops within reach of the rail bridge at Weldon. In addition, Union troops continued to man Roanoke Island, gateway to the Albemarle Sound.

Early on, this Federal strategy for eastern North Carolina raised concerns, particularly in the navy. Rear Admiral Samuel Phillips Lee, commander of the North Atlantic Blockading Squadron, argued that the "scattered occupation is certainly bad and can not too soon be abandoned," for it was "expensive, insecure, and subjecting us to attack in detail." On several occasions in 1863, Admiral Lee urged the army to cease "the occupation of so many points in the sounds." He recommended instead that Union forces concentrate at one "good position."[10] John Foster, in command of army forces in North Carolina during most of 1863, held a different view. In response to the admiral's concerns, he argued that the multiple positions were too important to disregard and vowed to hold them "as long as I am strong enough." Foster emphasized the fertile region's importance to Confederate supply efforts and noted that the different enclaves gave Union gunboats control of the rivers, providing ideal "landing places" to concentrate Union forces. He also worried the Confederates, if left unmolested, would use spots such as Washington and Plymouth "as yards and arsenals" for gunboat construction.[11]

In response to Foster's arguments, Admiral Lee conceded that Union forces should hold firmly to key locations at Fort Macon, Beaufort, Hatteras, and Roanoke Island. He recommended that the land defenses and garrisons at those locations be "complete as practicable in itself" to minimize reliance on naval support. He also recognized the potential advantage offered by other posts, such as Washington and Plymouth. But he questioned whether the benefits of their retention were worth the costs. He asserted that these positions were "sickly places," particularly Plymouth, and required "considerable military defenses" to guard against enemy threats, especially gunboats. Instead of manning so many posts, Admiral Lee urged the army to retain only those locations of particular "military importance" and abandon the rest after leveling any works there. In the end, Lee failed to convince Foster, and despite the admiral's continued misgivings and recommendations, the army held on to the positions at Plymouth and Washington.[12]

"To Shelter the Garrison"

Army and navy officers discussed the need to garrison the smaller posts, but there was little debate about New Bern, the region's principal Federal base. Located at the junction of the Neuse and Trent Rivers, the city was well suited to defense. The Neuse, a mile wide, ran along the city's entire eastern flank, effectively shielding a large portion of the perimeter, while the narrow Trent River wrapped along the southern and western outskirts. Beyond the two rivers, the only solid ground abutting the city lay to the west and northwest. Even in this quadrant, the swampy, sluggish streams crisscrossing the landscape provided a substantial screen. About 5 miles to the west, Bachelor Creek formed a moat of sorts running south to north for several miles, studded with blockhouses and strung with picket posts.[13]

Adding to New Bern's inherent strength, Union troops had steadily improved the defenses since 1862. Much of the initial design came from Foster and his staff, and much of the actual work was performed by newly arrived freedmen flooding in from surrounding plantations. The hard work continued on and off throughout 1862 and 1863. A soldier in the 46th Massachusetts, which also toiled on the forts, noted that the soil around New Bern was "sandy and easy digging but not the best material for building steep banks." To help the works maintain their shape, the men topped parapets and curtains with turf.[14]

The defenses covered all approaches to New Bern. On the city's western edge, engineers traced out a long, continuous inner line. Along these works, they positioned a particularly massive complex, Fort Totten, at the spot where the Trent and Neuse Roads entered the city from the west. Foster's men also inserted several smaller fortifications north along this western line, including the four-bastioned Fort Rowan, which nestled next to the railroad, and Fort Dutton, located at the north end of the line on the banks of the Neuse. The small, detached Fort Stevenson sat outside the main line, several hundred yards upriver from Fort Dutton.[15]

The Federals also built strongholds protecting other approaches. Across the Neuse near Barrington's Ferry, Fort Anderson sat with its back to the river; it contained six guns, four of which were 32-pounders, and had a traverse to protect its large interior. The fort, flanked on the left by a creek and on the right by a swamp, covered the northern bank and deterred attackers from establishing batteries there to enfilade the city at long range. A smaller work, Fort Chase, was sited downriver on the same (northern) bank and served the same purpose.[16] On the right bank of the Trent River, across from New Bern, three works protected approaches from the south and east: Fort Gaston, Fort Amory, and Fort Spinola. In addition to covering the fields to the south, these fortifications protected the Clermont Bridge, spanning the Trent 2 miles south of the city, as well as the Trent railroad bridge, which ran directly into New Bern and had been widened by Union engineers to carry wagon traffic.[17]

Of all the works shielding the city, Fort Totten was the most impressive. Its massive footprint spread over seven acres. Its parapets rose 8 feet high and were 12 feet thick, all revetted with layers of sod. Its bastions occupied points of a pentagon; each bastion held five guns, which pointed through embrasures made of sand-filled wicker gabions.[18] The guns commanded an "extensive plain" to the west, the site of a former cotton plantation. A ditch backed by a steep embankment covered the front and, according to a Massachusetts soldier, presented an impossible obstacle to attackers.[19] A huge traverse stood out as the fort's most impressive feature. Thirty-five feet high, 28 feet thick, 400 feet long, and topped with rifle pits for sharpshooters, the huge mound stretched across the fort's center "to shelter the garrison" from bombardment. "This great traverse was a landmark to the country for miles around," a Rhode Island veteran recalled. Additional traverses shielded other portions of the fort from enfilading fire. The fort held twenty-eight guns in all, including several naval 32-pounders on ship carriages, a 64-pounder Columbiad, two 100-pounder rifled Parrotts, and several 8-inch mortars.[20]

A sophisticated communications system augmented New Bern's defense network. A line of signal stations connected headquarters in town with Fort Anderson across the Neuse, Fort Gaston across the Trent, and picket posts to the west at Bachelor Creek. After capturing the city in 1862, the Federals built a 70-foot tower downtown that rose directly from the roof of headquarters and allowed the Signal Corps to communicate with the various posts using flags and torches. A telegraph line, constructed in June 1863 and running from downtown out to Bachelor Creek, cut through dense swamp and added to the visual system. From Bachelor Creek, Signal Corps officers extended the wire to separate outposts north to the Neuse River and south to the Trent Road at the Harrison House, near Camp Palmer, headquarters of the 12th New York Cavalry.[21]

In addition to the many forts, trenches, and signal stations, New Bern's defenses relied heavily on the navy gunboats stationed there. These vessels provided mobile firing platforms, which greatly strengthened the city's defenses. However, unlike the rebel craft under construction in the state, all the Union gunboats in the North Carolina sounds had wooden sides, a vulnerability recognized by the commanders there. As early as October 1862, Admiral Lee had warned Assistant Navy Secretary Gustavus Fox that supremacy in the sounds could be maintained only by "iron clads adapted to the navigation there."[22] Admiral Lee, a Virginian and a cousin of Robert E. Lee, had chosen to remain with the Union when the war began and had reportedly remarked that he would join the Confederacy only when he found the word "Virginia" in his commission.[23] The admiral understood all too well the threat posed by rebel ironclads. In August, he informed Secretary Gideon Welles about a rebel boat up the Roanoke River. According to Lee, whose information was based on intelligence reports, the vessel promised to be "a formidable affair." He warned that Confederate defenses along the river, particularly at Rainbow Bluff, rendered

Key Federal Forts at New Bern

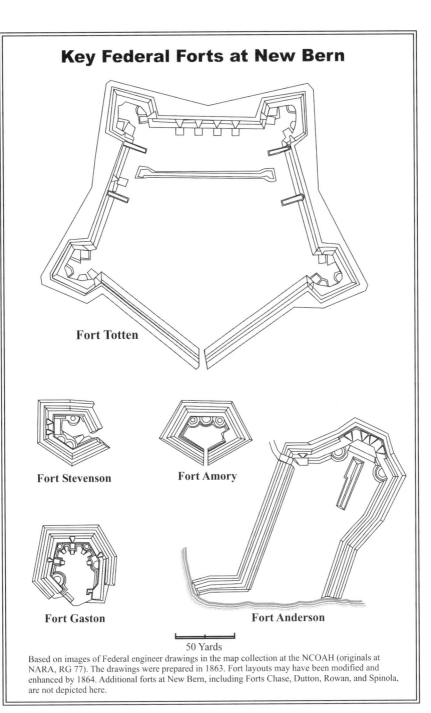

Fort Totten

Fort Stevenson

Fort Amory

Fort Gaston

Fort Anderson

50 Yards

Based on images of Federal engineer drawings in the map collection at the NCOAH (originals at NARA, RG 77). The drawings were prepared in 1863. Fort layouts may have been modified and enhanced by 1864. Additional forts at New Bern, including Forts Chase, Dutton, Rowan, and Spinola, are not depicted here.

any naval effort to destroy the menacing craft "impractical" and concluded that the navy would need ironclads to avoid disaster. But the Union navy had no iron-plated craft with a draft shallow enough to float across the Hatteras bar and navigate the sounds. Navy officials moved to address this vulnerability by ordering twenty shallow-draft ironclads in early 1863—vessels later dubbed *Casco*-class boats. But design and construction problems plagued this effort and delayed these armored craft until the middle of 1864.[24]

In 1864, Major General John Peck presided over army affairs in the District of North Carolina from his headquarters at New Bern. Over the course of the war, Peck, a New Yorker, had performed with inconspicuous reliability. In 1862 he commanded a brigade and then an entire division during the Peninsula Campaign, where he earned the rank of major general for his performance at Malvern Hill. He then received command of Union forces in southeastern Virginia and successfully defended Suffolk against James Longstreet's efforts there in 1863. During that campaign, Peck suffered a serious injury to his right arm, which was slow to heal and afflicted him into the next year.[25] Over the course of these events, Peck proved to be a steady, competent commander and was described by one soldier as a "most pains-taking and deserving officer."[26] Other aspects of his performance, however, did not make a positive impression. For instance, he was not an enthusiastic advocate of employing freedmen for the army's work; nor was he an energetic recruiter of black troops.[27] In addition, most found his personality less than sparkling. Cautious and dour, Peck, who was in his early forties, gave the impression of being old beyond his years. One young officer described him "as thorough an old woman as ever wore petticoats." Another found him overly anxious and not much of a combat leader.[28]

Whatever his failings, Peck paid close attention to improving the defenses of the Union posts in North Carolina. Shortly after taking charge at New Bern in 1863, he began to reevaluate and improve the network of fortifications there.[29] Generally, he found the works "extensive, very complete, and admirably arranged." But Peck and his engineers sought to cover every contingency. He expected that any serious attack would approach the forts along the Trent River opposite New Bern, so he improved the defenses there by clearing the forests in front of Forts Gaston and Amory.[30] Throughout the fall of 1863 and into 1864, Peck tinkered with the city's defenses. His efforts, combined with the works in place before his arrival, yielded a robust system. Indeed, the blockhouses and signal stations of the outer lines, the sturdy forts and trench of the inner works, and the gunboats circling the waters offshore posed a formidable obstacle to any offensive operation. For two long years, New Bern's defenses had never been seriously challenged. That would soon change.

PART THREE

The New Bern Expedition

In early 1864, Robert E. Lee's plan for military operations in North Carolina took shape in the form of an offensive against New Bern led by Major General George E. Pickett. The expedition faced many hurdles. The New Bern defenses were stout, the product of many months of Union planning and construction. To attack them successfully, Pickett would have to coordinate multiple columns separated by large distances. Communications would be challenging. In addition, Commander John Taylor Wood's naval force, with its odd collection of rowboats, would be severely tested in its attempt to nullify Federal naval superiority in the Neuse River. Despite all the obstacles, a successful operation would reap far-reaching benefits, and Confederate leaders pushed ahead, eager to put the plan into action.

CHAPTER FIVE

On to New Bern

"The General Plan"

By Wednesday, January 20, 1864, Robert E. Lee had completed his deliberations and concluded that it was time to launch the campaign. He sent off a flurry of dispatches from his headquarters near Orange. Letters went out to Jefferson Davis, Robert F. Hoke, George Pickett, and others. In his note to the president, Lee expressed optimism about the upcoming offensive. At the same time, he voiced regret that the ironclads were not ready. "Without them," he predicted, "the fruits of the expedition will be lessened and our maintenance of the command of the waters in North Carolina uncertain." Nevertheless, he predicted New Bern would fall if Colonel Wood could capture the Union gunboats. Lee also clarified the operation's command arrangement. In responding to the president's earlier suggestion, he declined to direct the expedition himself; instead, he chose to remain in Orange to continue his "struggle to keep the army fed and clothed."[1]

In place of Lee, Major General Pickett, head of the North Carolina Department, would lead the effort. Though Pickett assumed formal command, much of the credit for the planning went to Hoke, the young Tar Heel brigadier who had spent the fall hunting deserters in the Quaker Belt.[2] Hoke had risen rapidly in the Army of Northern Virginia before suffering a wound in the spring of 1863. He had become a favorite of Robert E. Lee and had been lauded by Thomas "Stonewall" Jackson in 1862 as an "officer of great promise."[3]

Hoke was well acquainted with New Bern. While serving there as an officer in the 33rd North Carolina in early 1862, he had conducted a tour of the city's defenses for a staffer from the North Carolina adjutant general's office. Armed with this knowledge, Hoke helped plan Lee's strike on New Bern. Although the extent of his role is not clear, some accounts suggest it was quite extensive.[4] During discussions with Lee in January, Hoke offered suggestions about the planned expedition.[5]

According to one story, Lee considered Hoke "the actual leader" of the offensive but put a major general (Pickett) "in nominal command."[6]

The operation presented a complicated puzzle involving five widely separated columns arriving from different locations. According to Lee's plan, the first and strongest column, led by Brigadier General Seth Barton, would approach New Bern from the southwest along the Trent River, attack the enemy works at Brice's Creek, and then turn to New Bern itself. Pickett viewed Barton's as the main or, as he noted later, "real" attack. The second column, commanded by Hoke, would approach from the west and hit the Bachelor Creek line between the Trent and Neuse Rivers. A third column, led by Colonel James G. Dearing Jr., would push down the north bank of the Neuse, seize Fort Anderson across the river from New Bern, and "endeavor to take in flank with the batteries the line south of the Neuse, so as to lighten Hoke's work." Finally, Brigadier General James Martin's force from Wilmington would threaten Swansboro and strike New Bern's rail communications to the coast, "so as to fix the attention of the enemy at Morehead City, &c, and to co-operate otherwise in the general plan."[7] The expedition's force would include four brigades from Pickett's department (Barton's and Montgomery Corse's Virginians, as well as Thomas Clingman's and Matt Ransom's North Carolinians), one brigade from the Department of Richmond (Colonel William Terry's Virginians), and one brigade (Hoke's) from Lee's army.[8] Two artillery battalions (James R. Branch's and John Read's) would join the columns as well and would include several 20-pounder Parrott rifles, among the heaviest field pieces in service at the time.[9]

To add to the four land attacks, Colonel John Taylor Wood would row down the Neuse with 200 men in small craft, seeking to "surprise and capture" the Union gunboats and use them against enemy land batteries.[10] Robert E. Lee hoped Wood's party would at least "create a diversion, draw off the enemy, and if the chance offered go in the town."[11] After the city's capture, Lee advised Wood to gather all "water transportation" to move troops and supplies and encourage the ironclads' rapid completion.[12]

The success of the New Bern operation was by no means certain. In fact, the whole enterprise was a long shot. The plan called for Confederate commanders to coordinate several widely separated columns, a difficult task for any military endeavor even under ideal conditions. It also depended on joint operations between army and navy forces. Such combined efforts were not common during the Civil War and were almost unheard of on the Confederate side. Even without the plan's naval component, its complexity was high. The four prongs of the ground attack would converge from different directions separated by large distances. Victory depended on several contingencies, a few key assumptions, and much luck. On the city's far side, success relied on Barton's attacks against the fortifications arrayed along Brice's Creek and the south bank of the Trent River. North of the Neuse River, Dearing's small force would have to contend with the high walls of Fort

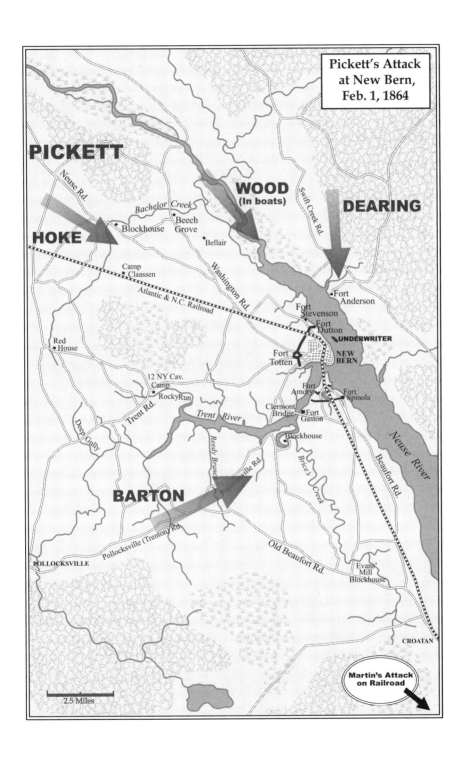

Pickett's Attack
at New Bern,
Feb. 1, 1864

PICKETT

WOOD
(In boats)

DEARING

HOKE

Neuse Rd.

Bachelor Creek
Blockhouse
Beech Grove
Bellair

Swift Creek Rd.

Washington Rd.

Camp
Claassen

Atlantic & N.C. Railroad

Fort
Anderson

Fort
Stevenson

Fort
Dutton

UNDERWRITER

Red
House

Fort
Totten

NEW
BERN

12 NY Cav.
Camp
RockyRun

Trent Rd.

Trent River

Reedy Branch

Fort
Amory

Fort
Spinola

Clermont
Bridge

Fort
Gaston

Deep Gully

Blockhouse

Pollocksville Rd.

Brice's Creek

Neuse River

BARTON

Beaufort Rd.

Pollocksville (Trenton) Rd.

POLLOCKSVILLE

Old Beaufort Rd.

Evans
Mill
Blockhouse

CROATAN

2.5 Miles

Martin's Attack
on Railroad

Anderson. West of the city, Hoke's attacking column would have to break through the Federal forces arrayed in the blockhouses and works behind Bachelor Creek. Once they were through these, the men would face formidable works along the Fort Totten line at New Bern's edge. And finally, Martin would have to confront a series of blockhouses and detached fortifications protecting the various Federal positions southeast of New Bern.

Given the stout nature of New Bern's land defenses, the fifth column, Wood's water-borne attempt to capture the gunboats and gain naval supremacy, stood out as crucial to the expedition's success. It was a hopeful design, perhaps even a harebrained scheme. Because the Union naval presence on the Neuse changed frequently, it was difficult to predict the number and size of the vessels guarding the base there. Surely, Wood's collection of small craft would struggle to match the Federal gunboats. However, if he managed to succeed, the prospects for an attacking force would increase dramatically. Federal engineers had not designed the New Bern defenses to repel substantial attacks from the water. Should Wood gain control even temporarily, he could easily enfilade the Federal lines and aid Pickett's assault by transporting infantry behind the city's main line.

In his instructions to Pickett, Lee set out the operation's general framework, but he also gave Pickett the flexibility to modify the plan "according to circumstances developed by investigation and your good judgment."[13] Lee stressed the need for "secrecy, expedition, and boldness." He urged Pickett to conceal the operation's purpose and avoid communicating details over the telegraph. In coordinating with Wilmington, he advised Pickett to transmit only the day of the planned attack to Whiting and nothing more. Lee also furnished cover stories for the mobilization, urging Pickett to say that his troops had come south to repel an expected assault and telling Hoke to claim that he was headed home to arrest more deserters and recruit for his diminished regiments.[14] Lee looked beyond a New Bern victory. Should the city fall, he instructed Pickett to seize Washington and Plymouth as well, with Wood's aid.[15]

For Lee, the operation's potential benefits justified the risks involved. His orders identified the two important goals that impelled the offensive. First, Lee hoped to capture large quantities of materiel and free the surrounding countryside so that Confederate commissary agents could gather crops and livestock. He noted that successful operations would obtain "much subsistence" for the army. Second, Lee expected that victory would tamp down the state's peace agitators. He predicted such a result would have a positive impact and inspire the people of North Carolina. Although his letters and reports revealed little about his awareness of the animosity brewing in the state, this acknowledgment in his orders clearly demonstrated that such matters were an important factor for him.[16]

In aiming for New Bern, the Confederates headed into well-known country. They had defended the city, albeit unsuccessfully, in 1862 and marched to its outskirts in 1863 before laying siege to Washington. In addition, several officers in Pickett's command were natives of the New Bern area and had extensive knowledge of the city's environs. Additional information about the defenses leaked out from deserters and other sources. A catalog of rumors appeared in a Raleigh newspaper in mid-January, including reports of a rise in Unionist sentiment and word that the Federal garrison included men who had deserted from a Confederate partisan ranger unit known as "Nethercutt's Battalion."[17] Despite this knowledge, the Confederates needed more information. John Peck's continual improvements to the works ringing the city had rendered much of the rebel intelligence obsolete. To improve their understanding of the task ahead, the Confederates sent several men to infiltrate enemy lines.

One such mission fell to Captain John G. Smith, a Georgia cavalryman stationed at an outer picket post 10 miles northwest of New Bern. After months of field duty around Kinston, Captain Smith possessed a solid familiarity with the local roads and terrain. In mid-January he received instructions to penetrate Union lines outside New Bern and "look well into the location of the surrounding blockhouses and forts and get as far as possible the number and location of the Federal troops." His orders, as he recalled, also directed him to "pay special attention to the location of the camp of Confederate deserters," members of the 2nd North Carolina Union Volunteer Regiment.[18] After slipping past the picket posts west of the city, Smith tramped through enemy territory for several days, roaming among enemy positions and collecting intelligence about Union fortifications, troop strength, and even the location of the "deserter" camp.[19]

Smith was not the only rebel to catch a glimpse of the New Bern defenses. General Barton sent William G. Morton and several other members of the 53rd Virginia to escort three civilians through the lines into New Bern, ordering them to make note of the fortifications there. When he returned, Morton sketched a diagram of the works, pinpointing the post manned by the Buffaloes from the 2nd NCUV.[20] In addition to Smith and Morton, Barton employed at least one additional scout, a county surveyor who sketched the defenses along the Trent River south of New Bern. He assured Barton that "there were no other fortifications than those abandoned by our troops at the capture of New Berne, and that these were constructed to meet an advance from the east and south." He also reported that Brice's Creek, which lay across Barton's path, was a viable approach for an attacking force.[21] The surveyor's reports, along with those of the other scouts, were crucial to the upcoming Confederate offensive. Much would depend on them.

"General Pickett Is to Attack"

During the last days of January, Confederate commanders scrambled to bring their forces together. It was not a simple exercise. John Taylor Wood collected sailors from Richmond, Wilmington, and Charleston. James Martin gathered his column at Wilmington.[22] The task of collecting the troops for Pickett's force fell mostly to Robert Hoke, who went to work gathering the components of the strike force—the better part of six infantry brigades—from their various winter quarters. Seth Barton's Virginia brigade and Matt Ransom's regiments were already in North Carolina. However, the other units, including those of Hoke, Montgomery Corse,[23] Thomas Clingman, and William Terry, were far flung, stationed throughout Virginia and even west in Tennessee.[24] To shore up his own brigade following the losses at Rappahannock Station, Hoke added the 21st Georgia from George Doles's command and the 43rd North Carolina from Junius Daniel's.[25]

These various units made their way south. Judging from official returns at the time, the offensive would include most of the units in the North Carolina Department, augmented by forces from Virginia. This would leave few troops to guard Kinston, Weldon, and other key points. The entire expedition probably involved about 13,000 men, including the infantry gathering at Kinston; various artillery, cavalry, and naval units; as well as troops marching from Wilmington.[26] The movement of so many men did not escape notice. In Richmond, War Department clerk John Beauchamp Jones observed the railcars hauling troops through downtown and guessed they were headed to check an enemy threat against the Wilmington and Weldon Railroad.[27]

Kinston, the last rebel-controlled stop on the Atlantic and North Carolina Railroad, served as the offensive's staging area. A vital outpost on the front lines facing the Union strongholds at New Bern and Washington, Kinston's garrison in January consisted mostly of Barton's brigade, along with 600 cavalrymen and a complement of artillery.[28] The Virginians enjoyed the region's relative warmth and the plentiful, inexpensive food, especially potatoes, turnips, and pork. But a mutual enmity developed between Barton's soldiers and local citizens following a rash of thefts from nearby farms.[29]

On Friday, January 29, the town bustled as train after train huffed into the depot, depositing hundreds of travel-weary soldiers. With all the activity, even the dullest observer understood that something was afoot. Nevertheless, Confederate officials tried to shield the operation's nature from prying eyes. Barton dispatched several companies from the 3rd North Carolina and 62nd Georgia Cavalry to strengthen the picket line between the Neuse and the Trent and "cover all the roads and paths south and east of Kinston."[30] But despite these and other efforts, the expedition became somewhat of an open secret, at least to some.[31] James Randall, a poet, newspaper editor, and shipping merchant, wrote from Wilmington on Saturday, January 30: "General Pickett is to attack Newberne in this state, next week, with 12,000 men." Randall hoped for success but noted that victory was "generally doubted."[32] Adolphus W. Mangum, a Methodist minister from Goldsboro, informed his sister on February

1: "About 20,000 of our troops are to surprise + attack Newbern today or tonight probably. Isn't that exciting?"[33] Such stories occupied a crowded field of rumors. In fact, while Pickett and Hoke gathered men for the strike, reports of an impending Federal attack arose, perhaps the product of Confederate misdirection.[34]

With the plan hatched, orders issued, and units gathered, the various columns set off for New Bern. Most of Pickett's force departed from Kinston on Saturday morning, January 30. Martin's command, marching up from the south along the coast, had left Wilmington two days earlier.[35] Wood's force would descend the Neuse in their small boats on Sunday. As the various columns began their journey, Pickett hoped for a simultaneous attack on Monday morning, February 1, but the logistical complexities presented much potential for error. Most of the component columns would take widely different routes separated by dozens of miles.[36] Even with the most diligent couriers, communication would be challenging, and the confusion inherent in any operation threatened much mischief.

Barton's wing departed Kinston early on Saturday with Barton's own brigade (led by Colonel William R. Aylett), Terry's brigade, most of Ransom's brigade, twelve pieces of artillery, and twelve companies of cavalry. With four days of rations stuffed in their haversacks, the men headed southeast. On Sunday, they crossed the Trent over a pontoon bridge and marched to Trenton and then toward Pollocksville.[37] As Barton advanced, his cavalry swept the countryside of potential informants, detaining "negroes and every other person likely to be friendly to the enemy."[38]

Dearing waited until late Saturday to depart from Kinston with his command. The young officer led two of Corse's regiments, the 15th and 17th Virginia, totaling about 600, along with John N. Whitford's 67th North Carolina, which numbered about 500.[39] Dearing's force took a northeasterly route from Kinston, passing over difficult sandy roads and threading through swamps.[40] By Sunday, after nearly twenty-four hours on the march, Dearing's exhausted men approached Fort Anderson, ready to attack the next day.

Pickett and Hoke's force, the center column, left Kinston on Saturday evening with the three other regiments of Corse's brigade (18th, 29th, and 30th Virginia), two regiments of Clingman's brigade (8th and 51st North Carolina), 56th North Carolina of Ransom's brigade, and Hoke's own brigade (augmented by 21st Georgia and 43rd North Carolina), along with four Napoleons, eight rifled pieces, and some cavalry.[41] After marching a few miles, the troops stopped at Wise's Fork. On Sunday morning, the column fell in and marched along the Dover Road, heading east for Bachelor Creek and New Bern.[42] Early that morning Hoke pushed his own North Carolina brigade ahead, "arresting all persons who saw us," while Corse's and Clingman's two regiments followed close behind.[43] The road narrowed as it passed through the vast Dover Swamp, an inhospitable morass "alive with creeping things" and "heavy with moisture and foul odors."[44]

"A Very Dashing Officer"

Major General George Pickett, the expedition's commander, chose to accompany Hoke's column. Later, Pickett would claim he had not been enthusiastic about Lee's plan, which Hoke had handed him in late January.[45] In addition, the command arrangement for the operation lacked clarity, or, as W. G. Lewis explained after the war, the "thing seemed somewhat mixed."[46] Pickett was in charge of the entire expedition, while Hoke apparently exercised direct command over the center column. It is unclear why Pickett chose to join Hoke instead of Barton, who was assigned the important task of attacking defenses along the Trent River. Perhaps Pickett wanted to remain in a central position between the wings of the operation.[47]

The venture represented the major general's first stint at independent field command. Born to an old Virginia family, Pickett was a colorful figure, "a very dashing officer [who] was very foppish in his dress and wore his hair in long ringlets." He "was what would be called a dapper little fellow but brave as they ever make men," according to one observer.[48] His wife described him as "not tall, and rather slender, but very graceful," with "very small hands and feet."[49] Others noted that Pickett stood straight and erect and often donned a "well-fitting uniform," presenting a "distinguished and striking" appearance. He often carried a riding whip. But his hair usually garnered the most comment. It "flowed loosely over [his] shoulders, trimmed and highly perfumed; his beard likewise was curling and giving out the scents of Araby."[50] Pickett attended West Point and served in the Mexican War. In 1859 he ably commanded a diminutive US force in the San Juan Islands against British troops during a bitter border dispute, where he showed great pluck standing firm against a superior force. At the height of danger, he reportedly quipped, "We'll make a Bunker Hill of it." However, that heated conflict in the Pacific Northwest fizzled out before any blood was shed.[51]

The Civil War had been a mixed affair for Pickett. In 1862, he commanded a brigade at Williamsburg, Seven Pines, and Gaines' Mill, where he suffered a shoulder wound. That fall, with James Longstreet's support, he rose to major general and commanded a division in Longstreet's corps. Spared combat at Fredericksburg and Chancellorsville, Pickett led his division into the teeth of the Union line at Gettysburg, in a tragic charge that would forever bear his name. The horrific losses in Pennsylvania drove Pickett to despair, and he "seemed to lose his snap." In his battle report, which is lost to history, he reportedly indulged in bitter finger-pointing, which raised the ire of Robert E. Lee and damaged relations between the two, perhaps irreparably. The extent to which the Gettysburg debacle affected Pickett is difficult to determine. In fact, a fog obscures many aspects of his career, due to the lack of reliable records. After Pickett's death in the 1870s, his widow, LaSalle "Sallie" Corbell Pickett, served as custodian of his papers. For fifty-five years, she worked tirelessly to manufacture her husband's legacy by publishing his correspondence and her reminiscences of his war service. However, modern historians suspect that she often bent and embroidered the record, and thus they have called into question the reliability of what she left behind.[52]

Following the Gettysburg campaign, the Confederate high command spread Pickett's division far and wide and deposited Pickett himself in Petersburg as head of the department covering North Carolina and southern Virginia. In September, he married twenty-year-old Sallie Corbell at St. Paul's Church in Petersburg; the ceremony was followed by a twelve-gun salute from batteries on Dunn's Hill, north of the Appomattox River. That afternoon, the couple boarded a train for Richmond to enjoy a short honeymoon. The marriage followed a long courtship that, in the eyes of some of his peers, had distracted the general and eroded his effectiveness as a soldier.[53]

From his headquarters at Petersburg, Pickett shouldered the difficult burden of managing his department during the latter half of 1863. The position saddled him with competing priorities from two distinct fronts. In North Carolina, threats constantly arose from the Federal enclaves at New Bern, Plymouth, and Washington. In Virginia, Union forces endangered the vital rail hub at Petersburg, as well as the Blackwater River line guarding the overland routes into southern Virginia.[54]

"All Is a Wasted and Desolate Country"

On the march to New Bern, Pickett's men traveled through a war-torn countryside. In eastern North Carolina, the roads sometimes passed "through high and dry lands" full of "loose, white sand," which made marching a chore; at other times, they cut through forests crowded with longleaf pines, which supported the local turpentine distilleries; still other paths wound through impossibly difficult swamps.[55] Trudging along these routes toward New Bern, the soldiers observed the war's impact firsthand. Captain Henry Chambers, with the 49th North Carolina in Barton's column south of the Trent River, witnessed "farms lying untilled and unattended, deserted negro quarters, dilapidated fences and out houses, and occasionally the charred vestiges of some residences where the vandal invaders had wreaked their vengeance upon some secessionist."[56] Hoke's men found that many landowners, without their slaves and worn down by the conflict all around them, had simply abandoned their plantations. "Nothing can properly picture the desolation of the country between the Trent river and Newbern," wrote one soldier. "The dwellings in [the] entire neighborhood have been burned, and for miles not a habitation or sign of life can be seen. All is a wasted and desolated country."[57] Another soldier with Barton recalled that the region had once been "one of the most beautiful farming countries," with elegant dwellings housing a "wealthy, prosperous, and refined society." But after four years of conflict, he found the homes "deserted, the fields uncultivated, fences burnt, and every moveable gone."[58]

As darkness fell on Sunday evening, January 31, Hoke's men remained on the march, having already covered 23 miles along the Dover and Neuse Roads. They had passed through a seemingly interminable swamp, marched along the railroad for some 6 miles, and then climbed a slight rise called Sandy Ridge. Eight miles beyond that, they finally halted. Ahead of the column, General Hoke, accompanied by Lieutenant Colonel Henry T. Guion, located a dry field at Stevens' (now called Jasper's) Fork about 3 miles from the enemy picket lines.[59] The infantry, ordered to stay quiet and to light no fires, lay down to get some rest, while the artillery remained in the road with the horses still hitched to their traces.[60] Most of the men remained ignorant of the expedition's goal or even "what was in front of them."[61] But not everyone was uninformed. A member of Clingman's brigade learned that New Bern was the target and wrote that the men "anticipated a jolly time pitching into the negro troops there."[62]

"Such a Sense of Security"

As the gray lines snaked toward New Bern on Sunday, the Federals defending the city went about their business. With Major General John Peck away on leave, Brigadier General Innis Palmer, commander of the New Bern subdistrict, filled in temporarily as district chief.[63] The thirty-nine-year-old Palmer, a native of Buffalo, New York, had spent his entire professional career in the army. An 1843 graduate of West Point, he had served with distinction during the Mexican War. At Bull Run he led a cavalry battalion, and in 1862 he commanded an infantry brigade during the Peninsula Campaign. Afterward, he held a series of posts in eastern Virginia and North Carolina.[64] At New Bern, Palmer counted on a force of about 3,500 men, including the better part of five infantry regiments (92nd, 99th, and 132nd New York; 17th Massachusetts; 19th Wisconsin), a few artillery units (3rd New York Light, 5th Rhode Island Heavy, 2nd Massachusetts Heavy), and several cavalry companies of the 12th New York. The North Carolina Department contained other units totaling about 10,000, but these were spread throughout the region at Beaufort, Washington, Plymouth, and Roanoke Island.[65]

The Federals received no clear warning about the Confederate columns converging on New Bern. To be sure, various rumors of rebel threats had been circulating for weeks, but that was nothing new.[66] The repeated alarms over the past months may have dulled the city's inhabitants to the danger of a rebel attack. According to one correspondent in New Bern, the people there "had felt such a sense of security, that the civilians, at least, gave them little heed."[67] During January, Union forces in the region remained busy, staging several raids out of Newport Barracks and the stronghold at Plymouth. In the last days of the month, Union commanders occupied themselves with routine matters, including the distribution of new army regulations, surveys of army property, disciplinary matters, and supplies.[68] Although

New Bern's defenders were not expecting an imminent attack, they kept up their guard. To the west, they manned the picket posts, blockhouses, and detached works along Bachelor Creek, the first obstacle to any attacking force approaching from the west. Closer to the city, infantry and artillery units filled the forts in the interior line. The soundness of this defensive arrangement would soon be tested.

CHAPTER SIX

Bachelor Creek

"The Fight Began"

The Confederates' first obstacle on the way to New Bern was Bachelor (or Batchelder's) Creek, "a narrow, marshy bordered and [in] some places impassable little stream" several miles west of the city. Running north for nearly 9 miles and emptying into the Neuse, the watercourse had divided the combatants since 1862, framing a treacherous no-man's-land of swamp, forest, and farmland. Early on, soldiers who strayed over the stream would find "most certain capture or death."[1] However, over time, the foes in this sector began to conduct informal, unauthorized exchanges, and by 1863, pickets regularly traded newspapers, coffee, brandy, and gossip. One Northerner described the area as a "wild kind of place" speckled by "gum swamp" and cluttered with oak, pine, hickory, cedar, and beech trees.[2] "Winding as it does through forests of pine and cedar," wrote one observer in 1864, the creek resembled "to some extent the bayous of Louisiana."[3] The region teemed with snakes and insects, including tiny gnats that bit "like thunder." Wildlife roamed the forests, and the creek itself brimmed with eels, catfish, and pickerel, which frequently snapped at the makeshift hooks fashioned by Union soldiers. In the warm months, the men enjoyed fresh mulberries and strawberries.[4] Since Burnside's campaign, the region had served as a comparatively tranquil post for the Northern soldiers stationed there. Beyond the occasional picket fire, this sector had seen limited combat. That all changed on the morning of February 1.

At 1:00 a.m., Robert Hoke roused his men and formed them up on the Neuse Road in a heavy fog. The young general, accompanied by Lieutenant Colonel William G. Lewis, rode out near the head of the column where the 43rd North Carolina took the lead. After crossing a small stream name Core Creek, officers nudged sharpshooters ahead into the murky gloom. At about 2:30 a.m., they approached the Union outposts. Yankee pickets attempted to hail the dark forms in the road, but when they received no friendly reply, they emptied their rifles into the blackness, and "the fight began."[5] Balls zipped through the air, some passing over Hoke's head and whistling into the blackness. Unhindered by the fusillade, the Confederates rushed forward and captured most of the pickets, but not before several managed to scamper back east to raise the alarm.[6]

Following this initial exchange, the Confederates continued their push to Bachelor Creek with "all possible speed." Along the Neuse Road, the North Carolinians soon approached the narrow bridge spanning the stream. Within 100 yards, Lieutenant Colonel Lewis dismounted and ordered members of the 43rd North Carolina to advance. They did not get far. The Tar Heels encountered a "strong force" of the enemy, which announced its presence with several well-directed volleys. They also found the 75-foot bridge over the creek barren of its planks, and the narrow, steep-banked stream was too deep and difficult to cross.[7] According to Lewis, "the enemy were so near the smoke of their guns came in our faces." He soon pulled his men back after losing several and called on the pioneers to bring planks and bridging equipment up from the rear.[8] The Confederates had come to a dead stop. A soldier-correspondent from the 43rd North Carolina explained: "Here we were, between 2 and 3 o'clock, with a bridge destroyed in front of us and the point guarded by a strong picket, under a hot fire of musketry, and knowing that every moment was giving the enemy time for reinforcements."[9] The rebels believed they had met insurmountable resistance, an extensive line manned by a substantial force. They were wrong.

"Every Man to His Post"

Remarkably, instead of the powerful defense perceived by the Confederates, only a tiny party, numbering about a dozen men, stood in their way. This force, a detachment of New Yorkers led by First Lieutenant Abram Pye Haring, unleashed an intimidating and deceptively heavy fusillade from the east side of the stream. The small group crouched along a short line of breastworks and poked their rifles out from a stout blockhouse just north of the road. Just minutes before, the retreating pickets had brought news of the enemy's approach, and Haring and his men had quickly removed the bridge planks and used them to reinforce their "small but strong breastwork."[10]

The appearance of the Confederates early Monday came as a surprise to the defenders. Colonel Peter J. Claassen, in charge of this sector, commanded about 1,500 men, a force that included the 132nd New York Infantry, a large portion of the 12th New York Cavalry, some companies of the 99th New York Infantry, and a company from the 2nd North Carolina Union Volunteers.[11] Claassen had arrayed his men to cover various road and rail crossings in his sector, including, from north to south, the Washington Road, the Neuse Road, the Atlantic and North Carolina Railroad, and the Trent Road. On the right of this line near the Neuse River, a company of

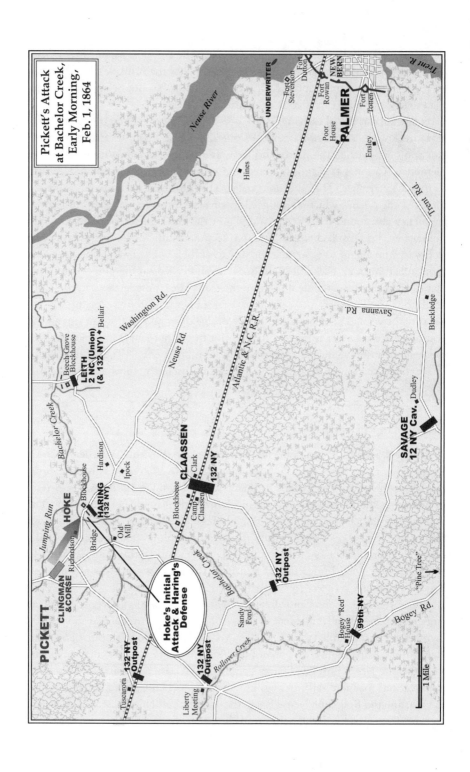

Pickett's Attack
at Bachelor Creek,
Early Morning,
Feb. 1, 1864

Neuse River

UNDERWRITER

Fort
Stevenson
Fort
Dutton

NEW
BERN

Fort
Rowan

PALMER

Fort
Totten

Trent R.

Poor
House

Ensley

Hines

Trent Rd.

Washington Rd.

Savanna Rd.

Blackledge

Neuse Rd.

Beech Grove
Blockhouse

Bellair

LEITH
2 NC (Union)
(& 132 NY)

Atlantic & N.C.R.R.

Bachelor Creek

Hardison

Ipock

CLAASSEN

Clark

132 NY

Dudley

SAVAGE
12 NY Cav.

Jumping Run

HOKE

Blockhouse

HARING
(132 NY)

Blockhouse

Camp
Claassen

PICKETT

CLINGMAN
&CORSE

Richardson

Bridge

Old
Mill

Hoke's Initial
Attack & Haring's
Defense

Bachelor Creek

132 NY
Outpost

Bogey "Red"
House

"Pine Tree"

99th NY

Bogey Rd.

Sandy
Ford

132 NY
Outpost

Tuscarora

132 NY
Outpost

Rollover Creek

Liberty
Meeting

1 Mile

the 2nd North Carolina Union Volunteers manned a blockhouse guarding the east bank at a spot called Beech Grove. These were the Buffaloes who had attracted attention from Confederate commanders and their scouts over the previous weeks. In the center, the 132nd New York protected the perimeter outposts where the Neuse Road and the rail line crossed the creek. This regiment, also known as the Hillhouse Light Infantry, had spent much of its war on garrison duty in New Bern and had seen little fighting.[12] To the left of the 132nd, several companies of the 99th New York covered the approaches from the southwest along the Trent Road at picket posts named Red House and Pine Tree. Nearby, six companies of the 12th New York Cavalry manned the lines at Deep Gully, near the Trent River.[13]

The Federals had no inkling of an attack. Throughout the previous day, the signal station at Claassen's headquarters had clicked routine messages back to New Bern. That afternoon, General Innis Palmer had stepped away from his headquarters in the city and visited the outer line to conduct an informal inspection of the quarters and defenses along Bachelor Creek.[14] He had found no reason for concern. On Sunday evening, Captain Charles G. Smith of the 132nd New York inspected all the posts stretching from Red House to Beech Grove and found "all quiet and everything satisfactory."[15] That evening, a scouting party returned to camp and reported no sign of the enemy in front. Most of the New Yorkers turned in for the night, expecting to wake up to another routine day. But the rebel attack at the Neuse Road bridge shattered the tedium. As one New Yorker explained, "eight months of uninterrupted quiet had lulled the department into a full-spirit of security, and our little regiment alone was charged with the duty."[16]

As the attack commenced, Haring's men fended off the Confederate spearhead. Up to that point, the young lieutenant, a man of average height with dark hair and hazel eyes, had enjoyed a relatively quiet war. On a late summer day in 1862, he had stepped out of his clerk's office at Otis & Company, a wholesale millinery on Broadway, to enlist in the 132nd New York. Described as "modest" and "brave," Haring was promoted to first lieutenant of Company G by March 1863.[17] The action at Bachelor Creek marked his first real combat experience, and he made the most of it. His small command met the initial Confederate advance at close range. The "rebels came in a hurry," wrote one defender, "and their ear-splitting yell brought every man to his post."[18] Haring's men fired their weapons at the forms across the creek, reloaded, and fired again as fast as they could. Haring sought to convey an impression of strength, urging his men to discharge their rifles in small groups and thus stagger their fire. "One to six fire, seven to eleven fire!" he called. As the rebels recoiled, Haring hurried a messenger to Claassen's headquarters, about a mile and a half to the south at the railroad.[19]

Soon, however, the Confederates made a second attempt. Once again, Haring and his men kept up a steady fire, which threatened to deplete their ammunition.[20] The lieutenant continued his efforts to conceal the size of his force. He bellowed,

"Come on! Come on cowardly cut throats! Come on with your bull dogs!" And he cried out to imaginary reinforcements behind him to "hurry up."[21] The Southerners, crowding the west bank, attempted to breach the creek several times. But Haring's men, protected by the stream and the blockhouse, stymied the advance again and again.[22]

As the Federals held on, the Confederates brought artillery forward. The gun crews had guided their teams along the Neuse Road behind the infantry that morning. After halting and unlimbering, they received orders to roll the pieces into position by hand near the ruins of Rigdon Richardson's house. After a short distance, they reached the crest of a gradual slope leading down to the creek. The crews dug shells out of their limbers, loaded their guns, and opened on Haring's blockhouse, which "could barely be distinguished, owing to the fog." The artillerists worked with determination, "discharging shell and grape shot," which rattled through the trees and sprayed the Union position.[23] However, much of the iron sailed too high to inflict much damage.[24] Lieutenant Colonel Henry T. Guion of the 10th North Carolina (also known as the 1st North Carolina Artillery) recorded that the guns opened "briskly upon the Block house with no effect," for it was "too dark to see the object."[25] Responding to the artillery fire, Haring ordered his two best marksmen to take a position in the blockhouse from which they had "complete range of the rebel battery." The riflemen successfully picked off several gunners, despite the fog and darkness, compelling the crews to switch positions several times.[26]

The Confederate attackers found themselves in an unpleasant spot as the Union rifles let fly from the front and their own shells whistled overhead from behind. One skirmisher secreted himself behind a large stump and tried to survive the ordeal. From his position, "the whole heavens seemed on fire, and the thunder of two cannon almost uprooted the stump." Hoke's men replied from the high ground behind the skirmishers, sending "volley after volley" over the creek. The exchange continued for about an hour and then ceased. Concluding there was no use in prolonging the attack, Hoke ordered the men in front to stay put and protect themselves.[27]

As Hoke's vanguard pressed against Haring's barricade, the regiments of Thomas Clingman's brigade remained on the Neuse Road to the rear.[28] Around 4:00 a.m., the 8th North Carolina, led by Colonel Henry M. Shaw, rested beside the road only a few hundred yards west of the blockhouse. As the men sat on the ground, bullets zipped through the air. Colonel Shaw, a physician, congressman, and enthusiastic secessionist before the war, remained on his horse in the road's center conferring with General Clingman and his staff, oblivious to the danger. In an instant, one of the bullets spinning through the fog split his cheek and drove into his skull, killing him immediately.[29] After the incident, a story emerged that an African American soldier had shot Shaw while the officer was laying the bridge. However, a member of the 43rd North Carolina scoffed at the claim, noting it was "certainly a mistake" because Shaw "was in [the] rear of our brigade and was struck by an accidental shot at least a quarter of a mile (if not a half), from the bridge."[30]

"Distant Rumbling, Like Thunder".

When word of the Confederate assault arrived at Colonel Claassen's regimental headquarters near the railroad, he organized a response. A native of Holland, the thirty-two-year-old Claassen had attended university in Germany before moving to New York, where he began a lucrative career as a prominent banker. During the war, he organized two New York units—the 9th and the 132nd.[31] Of "robust health" and "sober and regular habits," Claassen was an impartial but strict disciplinarian who quickly won the confidence of his officers and men.[32] Early in the morning of February 1, he rushed reinforcements to Haring, including Company D, a unit that contained German immigrants from New York and Native Americans recruited from the Six Nations, including members of the Tuscarora, Cattaraugus, Allegany, Tonawanda, and Onondaga tribes.[33] Major John B. Honstain also arrived, leading Companies E and G.[34] With these additions, the thin force at the bridge had become a bulwark.

By the time the reinforcements arrived, Haring had managed to hold the entire Confederate column at bay for more than an hour. It was a remarkable feat—one that would earn him the Medal of Honor years later. A New Yorker speculated that the Confederate "ignorance of the country," coupled with the Federals' intimate knowledge of the terrain, gave the defenders a significant advantage. Other factors worked in Haring's favor as well. The deep creek, the hollow bridge, the darkness, and the fog all combined to thwart rebel designs. After the fight, rumors spread that Pickett later refused to believe such a small force had frustrated his advance. But some rebel soldiers supposedly confessed that Haring's men were the "d—dst Yankees they'd ever seen to fight."[35]

Back in New Bern, Union defenders knew something was afoot when the "distant rumbling, like thunder" began drifting in from the west even before the first frantic reports arrived from the front. Officers initially assumed the cracks and booms signaled a mere "conflict of pickets." But it soon became clear there was much more to it. In the New Bern camps, buglers sounded "boots and saddles," and the long roll roused the infantry. "There was mustering of regiments, and hitching of horses, and standing to guns," according to one witness, and in "less than ten minutes, Newbern was under arms."[36] By daybreak, the city vibrated with activity. General Palmer pushed every available man into the inner defense line stretching from the Neuse River to the Trent. Infantrymen rushed to their posts, artillery crews manned the batteries, and the gunboats took up their stations in the river.[37] The streets echoed with "the clattering of horse's feet everywhere" as aides and orderlies shuttled messages "like mad" in all directions. Rumors whirled through the camps and quarters. Members of the 17th Massachusetts, on provost duty in town, rushed to the works on either side of Fort Totten, while clerks and civil government employees grabbed rifles and stood at the ready.[38] Freedmen shouldered rifles and relieved the guards in the city; some of the former slaves immediately volunteered, while others required "a polite invitation to do so." By one reporter's estimate, Palmer's informal muster added 1,000 men to the garrison, bringing the total men under arms to well over 4,000.[39]

Palmer then went to work reinforcing the outer line. At 5:30 a.m., from his headquarters in New Bern, Palmer telegraphed Claassen that a section of artillery was on the way and urged him to hold out as long as possible. However, Palmer noted that "any persistent defense" must be made in the city's fortifications and not along the outer posts at Bachelor Creek.[40]

The telegraph wires hummed between the Signal Corps stations at Fort Totten, Bachelor Creek, and Fort Gaston across the Trent River. Gunboats in the rivers kept in continual communication with the army in New Bern.[41] Colonel Claassen maintained a steady stream of dispatches back to Palmer in the city.[42] According to Palmer, the "attack had scarcely commenced when the telegraph had . . . informed me of all that was going on in front," allowing him to alert all the posts between New Bern and Beaufort of the attack.[43] In addition, the signal stations began to share information as the fog dissipated.[44]

After 6:00 a.m., Claassen looked to manage his forces. He understood that the main enemy threat emanated from the center at the Neuse Road bridge, where his regiment had been fending off Hoke's advance all morning. To support his immediate front, he dispatched Company K (132nd New York) to the railroad crossing to guard against any rebel advance over Bachelor Creek.[45] He also sent warning dispatches to Colonel James W. Savage south on the Trent Road, where men from the 12th New York Cavalry and 99th New York Infantry had seen no sign of the enemy.[46]

Quiet also prevailed to the north near the Neuse River, where the Buffaloes of Company F, 2nd NCUV, and several dozen New Yorkers guarded the isolated blockhouse at Beech Grove on the Washington Road. Concerned about this position, Claassen asked Palmer for another artillery section to bolster the Beech Grove outpost. Throughout the morning, Claassen had tried to reach the commander there, First Lieutenant Samuel Leith of the 137th New York, and order a withdrawal along the Washington Road. But the fog frustrated signal officers, and a series of couriers sent to the beleaguered position had all been killed or captured. Thus, unknown to the colonel, the men at Beech Grove remained at their post, ignorant of their plight.[47] The position quickly became a problem. If the Confederates managed to overrun the center and take the railroad, their advance would neatly isolate Beech Grove and doom the men there.

As he arranged his forces for defense, Claassen remained optimistic. Writing to

Palmer in New Bern, he boasted, "I think at daylight we will have some fun here." Around 7:00 a.m., Claassen began to contemplate a counterattack after concluding that the Confederates "have had about enough."[48] Sensing an opportunity at the railroad bridge upstream from Haring's position, he sought to gain the initiative or at least throw the Confederates off balance. The enemy had made no appearance there, and if a Union force could get across, it could descend on the right flank of the Confederate force confronting Haring. Claassen ordered Captain Charles Smith and his aide-de-camp, Lieutenant William W. Wells, to probe west over the railroad bridge and test the Confederate right with three companies of the 132nd New York (F, H, and I).[49] Smith's small force pushed out and turned north on the Mill Road, but it achieved little and tumbled back after encountering Corse's regiments advancing under Pickett's orders.[50]

"The Plan and Execution Was Most Admirably Done"

Back at the Neuse Road, dawn greeted the combatants along Bachelor Creek, and shapes began to emerge in the mist. "By degrees we were able to distinguish the strong line of fortifications along the edge of the creek on both flanks of a powerful block-house which commanded the approach to the bridge," wrote one Tar Heel. Soon, many of the rebels realized they lay within several dozen yards of the enemy's position. However, the fog lingered, making it difficult for the men to see out to the front.[51] For several hours, Hoke's brigade had remained static at Bachelor Creek, while Union troops in New Bern manned their defenses.

But Hoke did not give up. He searched for a way around the unplanked bridge and Haring's strongpoint. To that end, he devised a flanking maneuver. At a point downstream and north of the Neuse Road bridge, he directed two regiments under Colonel John T. Mercer to cross the swampy creek and press against the flank and rear of the Federal position.[52] To aid the flanking maneuver, the 43rd North Carolina, led by Lieutenant Colonel Lewis, would resume its frontal attack, replanking the bridge if possible and hitting Haring's position.[53] Mercer, a West Point graduate and veteran of prewar frontier service, bore a reputation as both a tyrant and a drunk. Nevertheless, he was known to be "splendid in a fight." He also enjoyed Hoke's confidence.[54] Around 7:00 a.m., his force waded through the mucky ground north of the Neuse Road. Threatened by a "galling fire," the rebels felled trees under the direction of Georgia Colonel T. C. Glover, their axe blows audible to the defenders at the blockhouse, and placed the trunks over the deep, narrow creek.[55] When Glover mounted the logs and shouted to his men to follow, the Georgians and North Carolinians responded, pouring over the stream.[56]

The rebel yell rent the air, signaling the end of Haring's tenacious defense at Bachelor Creek. The Confederates scrambled over their makeshift bridge and sprang into action just as the fog began to lift. With Mercer's infantrymen pressing

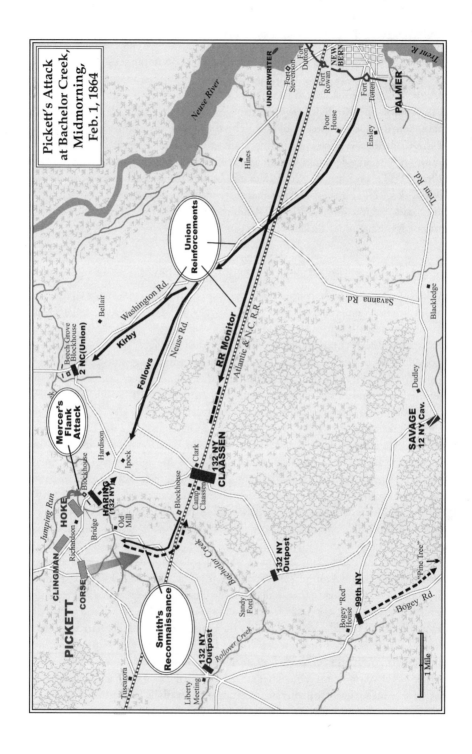

Pickett's Attack
at Bachelor Creek,
Midmorning,
Feb. 1, 1864

forward, the rebel cannon at the creek "belched forth," and minié balls whipped the air.[57] The Confederates swarmed toward the Union position. The defenders at the blockhouse stole nervous glances rearward and soon began to withdraw.[58] As rebel cheers penetrated the mist, the 43rd North Carolina, still on the west side of the creek, attacked from the front. Lieutenant Colonel Lewis had armed three of his regiment's companies with wooden planks, borrowed from the pontoon train wagon. When Mercer's guns signaled the flanking attack, Lewis's men rushed the bridge, "laid their planks and crossed over in the face of a hot fire."[59] With the span covered, Hoke crossed the remainder of the command, adding the skirmishers and the balance of the brigade to the fight.[60]

The Confederate infantry bounded forward, "charging with a yell," and several guns followed across the bridge. One witness recalled years later that the artillerists also "charged" the position, "moving the guns down the incline and across the creek by hand, stopping occasionally to fire a shot at the fort and loading as they advanced."[61] The results were decisive. "We broke the line of cowardly skunks, who mizzled from their cover," reported a member of the 43rd North Carolina.[62] Mercer's flank attack made all the difference, and the Federals gave way in confusion.[63] As the Union men at the blockhouse withdrew, they fought through Confederates spilling into their rear. Sprinting through Mercer's skirmishers, the New Yorkers turned, emptied a volley into the Confederates, and continued east toward New Bern.[64]

Challenged from the flank and front, the Neuse Road bridge position had finally collapsed at around 9:00 a.m., after hours of dogged resistance.[65] The Confederates were pleased. A member of the 43rd North Carolina concluded that "praise and partiality aside, both the plan and execution was most admirably done."[66] The results of the fighting along the Neuse Road were visible all around. The widow Hardison's house, a few hundred yards east of the blockhouse, had been riddled by "shot and shell," as was the nearby home of Julia Adams.[67]

The fighting continued after the blockhouse fell. The rebel cannoneers at the creek retrieved their horses and led the pursuit.[68] Virginia Captain William H. Caskie of the Hampden Artillery, wrapped in a blue Union overcoat and topped with a slouched hat, bawled out, "Pieces to the front!" and the teams thundered past the foot soldiers.[69] One Tar Heel remembered that "Caskie's splendid battery was with us, and no one can say that they left their part undone. They galloped to the front even to the sharpshooters, unlimbered their pieces, fired, and were ready for another gallop ahead."[70]

"Like a Tidal Wave"

As Hoke breached the Bachelor Creek defenses, Colonel Claassen prepared for the worst. Around 8:00 a.m., a train from New Bern arrived at his camp just east of the creek. In a short time, Claassen's men loaded the cars with "commissary stores and all the ammunition, together with the sick, the non-combatants, such as laundresses, &c." An assistant quartermaster returned to New Bern on the rails with orders to have another train "sent up at once."[71] Such help would need to arrive soon, for the size of the attacking column became apparent when the fog cleared. At 8:25 a.m., Claassen reported that Pickett's entire division was in his front, and he requested even more support.[72]

In response to Claassen's pleas, Palmer sent 125 members of the 17th Massachusetts, commanded by Lieutenant Colonel John F. Fellows, and an artillery section from the New Bern garrison.[73] In the city, Fellows gathered men and directed a junior officer to lead them to the front. But the young man, who had been promoted only days before, uttered a string of excuses. He had no horse and then, when given a horse, he refused to ride it, not knowing "anything about it." Exasperated, Fellows scrambled onto his own mount and led the detachment himself, not even pausing to grab his sword.[74] Hurrying along the Neuse Road, Fellows's infantrymen, along with a section of Battery K from the 3rd New York Artillery under Lieutenant Thomas J. Mersereau, arrived at the front around 9:00 a.m., as Claassen's New Yorkers were withdrawing from the blockhouse.[75] About a mile from Bachelor Creek, Fellows encountered men from the 132nd New York "falling back in some confusion across the fields" and pursued by "long ranks of men in gray, reaching as far as the woods would permit one to see to the right and left."[76]

The Confederate assault had punched a hole in the Federal perimeter, opening a gap through which the rebels now poured, flooding the roads and paths leading eastward. Claassen's entire position began to fold. What followed was a chaotic mix of events, as various Union companies and squads tangled with the advancing Southerners and tried their best to avoid capture. By 9:20 a.m., Claassen's earlier bravado had dissolved, and his dispatch to Palmer betrayed a hint of panic. "They are pushing us very hard," he observed. "They are advancing regularly on us on the Neuse road. They are now coming down the railroad."[77] Claassen and his officers sought to get their men back to New Bern safely. Amid the confusion, Captain Smith asked the newly arrived Lieutenant Colonel Fellows and his Bay Staters to stand as skirmishers on the crossroads leading from the Neuse Road to Claassen's camp near the railroad. After speaking with Fellows, Smith received orders for a general retreat. For those who received the command, the withdrawal to New Bern began.[78]

However, before the full retreat was on, the Federals made one more stand. To confront the advancing gray columns on the Neuse Road, a few companies of the 132nd New York formed in the open, joined by Fellows's infantrymen and Mersereau's guns, near the Ipock Farm, about a mile and a half east of the creek. The battle line held about three companies and had the look of a determined defense.[79] Soon, the North Carolinians, advancing from the west, arrived and likewise arrayed in a battle line. For a moment, the two forces stood facing each other in neat rows. Lieutenant Haring, fresh from his prolonged stand at Bachelor Creek, joined in, but he was familiar with the ground and informed an officer "that the position was indefensible."[80] He was correct.

The standoff near the Ipock Farm was short-lived. Mersereau's guns "opened hotly with shot and shell" and checked the Confederate advance momentarily, but according to a New York veteran, the rebels "were in strong force, and they swept forward again, like a tidal wave, loading and firing and cheering, and rolled everything back before them."[81] A Federal soldier noted, "It would be worse than madness to engage the avalanche of rebels," calling it a "hopeless encounter with a vastly superior force."[82] With its overwhelming numbers, the rebel line overlapped the Federal force. In the face of certain defeat, the men in blue quickly broke and withdrew through the woods in their rear, firing as they went.[83] The Confederates saw panic and sensed victory and, according to Hoke, "soon drove them before us and completely routed them."[84]

Following the short fight at the Ipock Farm, the Confederates pushed forward, seeping onto the roads leading toward New Bern. Most of the attacking units, including Hoke's brigade, proceeded directly along the Neuse Road, bypassing Claassen's headquarters and main campsites to the south. Others, including Corse's brigade and elements of Clingman's, swung south and pressed along the railroad in pursuit.[85] As Hoke surged ahead on the Neuse Road with two of Clingman's regiments in support, Corse attacked from the west across the railroad bridge and captured the camp of the 132nd New York, "with all its furniture and stores, except one house, which they burned before leaving."[86]

Along the Neuse Road, the guns continued to lead the Confederate advance. An infantryman who struggled to keep up with the artillerists recalled that "position after position was selected, but after a few shots each was abandoned, and onward dashed our artillery after them."[87] Captain William I. Clopton, commanding the Fayette Artillery, wrote, "We had a magnificent chase on our road. My guns were in the extreme van all the time. I 'charged' a battery with my two rifle guns & drove it off the field. When I say 'charged' I literally mean it, although it is very unusual in our arm of the service."[88] With the Confederate guns advancing, Union Lieutenant Mersereau gradually withdrew his pieces back to New Bern along the Neuse Road, stopping from time to time to hurl the odd round at the advancing gray coats. "He was the last to leave the field," wrote the battery's historian. "He served his guns gallantly in the action and all admitted that he saved our troops a total capture."[89] To be sure, the delaying action allowed many men in Claassen's command at the railroad to escape.

With their positions abandoned, the Union soldiers all along the Bachelor Creek line struggled to reach New Bern. They withdrew from the center along the railroad, from the outposts of the 99th New York at Red House and Pine Tree, and from the cavalry pickets posts farther south near the Trent Road. But on the right, the Buffaloes and other troops at Beech Grove remained in place. The speed of the rebel advance along the Neuse Road and the breakdown in Union communications sealed the small squad in place, a fact the Confederates would not realize until later. The Confederates also overran other pockets of retreating Union troops. One of these unlucky groups included Lieutenant Colonel Fellows and about seventy other members of the 17th Massachusetts Volunteers who had become separated from Claassen's main column.[90] Fellows and most of his small command had withdrawn east along the Neuse Road, where Mersereau's gunners conducted their fighting withdrawal. However, in the confusion, the order to leave did not reach Fellows. Unable to keep pace with the horse-drawn batteries, he found his command completely surrounded by the advancing rebels and ordered his men to do their best to escape. Many succeeded, but Fellows and several dozen members of this regiment were taken prisoner.[91]

"As the Train Sped Past"

In the midst of the Federal collapse, trains from New Bern chugged into Claassen's camp, very near the fighting. This rail traffic would create an unusual twist to the morning's action. One locomotive arrived at 8:00 a.m. to ferry supplies back to the city. A second pulled up from New Bern at around 9:00 a.m.[92] Unlike the earlier train, this one was a weapon of war that included "an iron-plated gunboat on wheels, mounted with two Wiard pivot-guns, and kept always in readiness to run up or down the railroad wherever it might be needed."[93] Similar trains had been used earlier in the war, notably by the Confederates at Seven Pines and by Union forces at Vicksburg. At New Bern, Union commanders referred to the machine simply as the "railroad monitor." The long-range Wiard guns, named after Canadian designer Norman Wiard, were highly accurate with low recoil.[94] When the train arrived, its guns, under the direction of First Lieutenant John Walker, opened with deadly effect on Corse's rebels advancing on the railroad.[95] The train also shelled the woods to the west, providing Claassen with some cover to withdraw his forces. Soon, Confederate artillery, with the aid of spotters atop a captured Union signal station west of the creek, returned fire with plunging shot, which arced over the dense woods screening the camps.[96]

With the armored train lingering at the front, Hoke developed an audacious scheme. Initially, the young general had expected the monitor not only to shell his men but also to race west and deposit Union soldiers on the opposite bank and outflank the Confederates. Hoke welcomed such a move, for he hoped to capture the train in the process, load it with men, and drive it into the New Bern fortifications. However, when the train did not advance, Hoke devised a different approach. He sought to push his men well east to where the Neuse Road intersected the rail line. There, he hoped to halt and capture the train. "It was my intention," Hoke later explained, "to place my men upon it and go into New Berne."[97] To this end, his own brigade pressed forward to reach the intersection before the train did. If successful, he planned to capture and load the train with the 43rd North Carolina and 21st Georgia, roll into New Bern, and empty his men behind the fortifications.[98] It was an inventive, ambitious plan that promised decisive results. But before Hoke could attempt the gambit, there was more marching to do. His exhausted men strained to reach the intersection of the Neuse Road and the rail line.[99] Lieutenant Colonel Lewis pushed his command "at quick and double-quick time" along the Neuse Road.[100] The Confederates advanced over the flat farmland, getting closer and closer to the rail line. Clingman's command followed behind.[101]

It was a close thing. Lieutenant Mersereau's New Yorkers reached the intersection ahead of the pursuing rebels. There, just south of the railroad, they unlimbered their guns and began to fire northwest at the approaching Southerners.[102] The railroad monitor, racing back to the city, had yet to reach the crossing. According to one Confederate, the superior condition of the Union artillery horses gave these batteries a distinct advantage in the race toward the rail line. The rebel gunners eventually reached the intersection. However, in the triangular space framed by the Neuse Road and the railroad, a jumble of tightly packed stumps remaining from a recent timber harvest impeded deployment of the gun teams. Nevertheless, the rebel crews unlimbered their weapons where they could and trained them on the rail line. Minutes later, the winded Confederate infantry arrived and formed a line of battle facing the rails. Soon, the monitor train approached from the west, speeding toward New Bern. According to artillerist E. W. Gaines, the Confederates opened fire as soon as the train came into sight, but an embankment shielded the engine and cars from damage. Henry Guion from the 10th North Carolina recalled that "our artillery at full gallop reaches within 600 or few yards at the crossing when the train under full headway passes—they unlimber and fire."[103] The Wiard guns fired back from the rearmost car "as the train sped past."[104] Union infantry also discharged their rifles from the cars, and the bullets flew "thick and fast," although not much damage was done.[105]

Though the rebel artillerymen managed to fire a few ineffective rounds toward the train, the Confederate infantry missed the opportunity by just a hair. Lieutenant Colonel Lewis's men reached within 20 yards of the track as the train sped by "loaded with troops running for New Berne at the rate of sixty miles per hour." He estimated that if the train had been a half minute later, his men could have torn up the tracks and captured the cars and their contents.[106] Others recalled things a little differently. William H. S. Burgwyn, one of Clingman's aides, noted in his diary, "The troops being very much exhausted they only came in view of the train so it passed with the iron clad car and about four hundred Yankees."[107] "We were only foot cavalry," another soldier wrote shortly after the event, "and as we came in about one hundred and fifty yards of the road, the train passed."[108] In

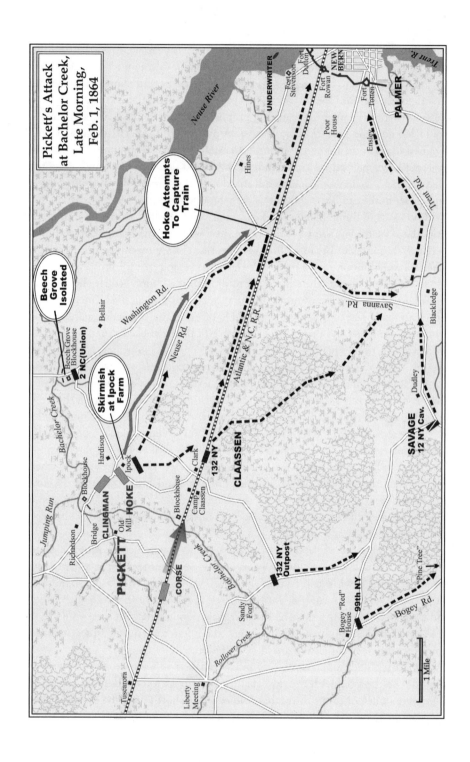

Pickett's Attack
at Bachelor Creek,
Late Morning,
Feb. 1, 1864

Beech
Grove
Isolated

Hoke Attempts
To Capture
Train

Skirmish
at Ipock
Farm

1 Mile

any event, the train clattered on to New Bern, and Lieutenant Mersereau, having expended seventy-five rounds "of good Union iron," hitched up his section and hurried back to the city, where he arrived around noon.[109] Hoke's golden opportunity had slipped away.

"For Richmond! Was the Universal Thought"

As the train sped back toward New Bern, most of Claassen's men continued their withdrawal on foot, taking several different routes. Some used the Neuse Road and stayed just ahead of the enemy's pursuing column. Some trekked across the countryside through the fields and into the forests, and others shuffled along the railroad. It was a harrowing journey. One soldier, fearing capture, remarked, "For Richmond! was the universal thought."[110] Whatever their route, most of them made it back to the fortifications. Some, however, failed to find their way back and became prisoners. One large group of infantrymen tramping along the rail line fell captive to an eight-man squad from the 21st Georgia, led by Captain W. B. Kimbrough.[111]

The men on the Union left, along the Trent Road, had their own difficulties. Although the Confederates had not appeared in this sector, the rapid penetration in the center threatened to cut the Yankees off. During the morning, fog prevented Colonel James Savage of the 12th New York Cavalry from discerning the signals transmitted from Claassen's headquarters. Eventually, though, messages arrived, and Savage began to pull his men back.[112] With his wagons already loaded, he burned his tents and ordered his troops to withdraw. On the retreat along the Trent Road, Savage reached Camp Palmer, where he met Colonel Claassen and men from the 132nd New York, and the group headed to New Bern.[113] As the Federals withdrew to their fortifications, the Confederates cautiously approached the main line. Hoke halted his brigade to "meet any advance of the enemy from the town." Pickett ordered Clingman across to the Trent Road to block Union troops retreating from Deep Gully. But Clingman did not advance in time to achieve this.[114]

"Retreated to Newbern"

Union forces had successfully delayed Pickett's attack at Bachelor Creek, allowing most of the men to reach New Bern's interior line. However, the withdrawal had not been perfect. The capture of Lieutenant Colonel John F. Fellows, who had volunteered to lead a small detachment into the fight, stood out as an embarrassment for General Innis Palmer and Colonel Peter Claassen. Claassen later offered a convoluted explanation of the incident and managed to cast blame on Fellows, while professing no "desire to impugn the abilities nor bravery of this re-enforcement." Claassen's words and deeds would not endear him to the men of the 17th Massachusetts.[115] Henry Splaine, a veteran of that regiment, placed the fault for

Fellows's capture squarely on Claassen's shoulders. At "a critical moment [Fellows's men] were neglected, deceived and deserted by Colonel Classon [*sic*], who hurried his men on to the steam-cars, and retreated to Newbern, leaving Colonel Fellows and his handful of men to their fate."[116]

Other than Fellows's loss, the engagement's most far-reaching impact would stem from the isolation of the Beech Grove blockhouse on the Washington Road. In fact, the failure to evacuate the Union men from that post would trigger a tragic string of events in the coming weeks. However, throughout Monday, the garrison there remained intact. That force under First Lieutenant Samuel Leith contained a full company of North Carolina Unionists from the 2nd NCUV, along with New York infantry and some artillery. After the Confederates blocked their path back to the city, the men at Beech Grove kept their heads low and hunkered down.[117]

In all likelihood, the Beech Grove detachment never received orders to withdraw. Claassen's couriers failed to get through, all of them captured or killed in the morning's chaos. Later, the colonel would point to the fog and the messengers' troubles as the root causes of the position's isolation.[118] He was also more than willing to point the finger at Leith. In Claassen's mind, the lieutenant "should have had himself informed of events occurring" south on the Neuse Road and "shaped his course accordingly." Claassen's criticism was unfair. Given the boom of cannon and crack of rifles discernible from the Neuse Road for most of the morning, Leith surely understood that something serious was afoot. But in the absence of positive orders to abandon his post, he had little choice but to remain at the blockhouse and prepare to repel all attackers.[119]

CHAPTER SEVEN

Fort Anderson and Brice's Creek

"A Ditch from 4 to 6 Feet Deep and 12 Feet Wide"

Even though Hoke had broken the outer Union line, the Confederate offensive would need to accomplish much more to capture New Bern. The city's defenders were fully alert. Pickett and Hoke understood that the fortifications on the western side were probably too strong to attack directly. Pickett looked for good news elsewhere. He expected that ultimate success would depend on Barton's actions south of the Trent River and Wood's efforts in the Neuse against the Union gunboats. However, by Monday afternoon, Pickett had heard nothing hopeful from these two. Wood's men had left Kinston Sunday and descended the Neuse in their launches, but for reasons that would become apparent to Pickett later, they had not initiated an attack. In addition, no news had arrived from Barton south of the Trent River or, for that matter, from Martin approaching from Wilmington.

Pickett also hoped for word about Colonel James Dearing's effort to seize Fort Anderson near Barrington's Ferry across the Neuse River. The twenty-three-year-old Dearing, a Virginian who had ranked first in his class at West Point, had resigned his commission shortly before graduation to fight for the Confederacy. He began the war as an artillery lieutenant and soon became somewhat of a phenomenon in the Confederate army. By early 1863, he had risen to chief of artillery in Pickett's division. Just a few weeks before the New Bern operation, he earned the temporary rank of colonel and received command of a small unit designated the 8th Confederate Cavalry but more commonly known as Dearing's regiment. In recommending the promotion, Pickett had praised Dearing as "a young officer of daring and coolness," as well as "a good disciplinarian, and at the same time generally beloved by his men." Another Virginian who served with Dearing during this period recalled that the colonel's "temper was sunny and bright, his courage of the highest order, in fact he was absolutely fearless."[1]

Dearing hoped to take Fort Anderson and lay a direct fire across the Neuse onto

New Bern, enfilading the Federal works there. If successful, his efforts would also prevent the fort's garrison from assisting New Bern's defense and help block any reinforcements arriving from Washington on the Pamlico River.[2] Around midday, after struggling over Craven County's sandy roads, Dearing reached the fort with his force, which included his own cavalry regiment, two regiments from Corse's Virginia brigade, and Colonel John Whitford's 67th North Carolina. The fort, commanded by Lieutenant Colonel Hiram Anderson, contained several companies of the 99th New York totaling about 300 men, along with five 32-pounder pieces (three smoothbore, one rifled, and one carronade), two howitzers, and a band, which greeted Dearing's men with "Dixie" as they formed for the attack.[3] Flanked on the left by a creek and on the right by a swamp, the fort covered the river's north bank and deterred attackers from establishing batteries there.[4]

After Dearing's men surrounded the work on Monday, the defenders in the garrison remained under arms, anticipating an assault. However, as Dearing quickly discovered, a successful attack was nearly impossible. The fort was formidable, lined with 14-foot-high walls and encircled by "a ditch from 4 to 6 feet deep and 12 feet wide." As a rebel correspondent explained, the "most that could be done was to keep this force engaged, and at the same time to threaten the Washington road to prevent reinforcements."[5] Concluding that nothing more could be done, Dearing halted and placed Whitford's regiment near the fort and the Virginia regiments in reserve. He then reported his situation to Pickett.[6]

"Important and Delicate Business"

With Dearing stalled, Pickett hoped to hear from Seth Barton, but no word arrived on Monday. The thirty-three-year-old Barton, captured at Vicksburg the previous summer and later exchanged, had received command of the late Lewis Armistead's brigade in the latter part of 1863. The six-foot-tall Barton had blue eyes, sandy hair, and an ample beard. Early in the war, he had served under Robert E. Lee in West Virginia, Stonewall Jackson in the Shenandoah Valley, and Kirby Smith at Cumberland Gap. His assignment during the New Bern expedition provided a rare opportunity to operate largely on his own. Monday morning, his column crossed south of the Trent River and marched east along the Pollocksville (or Trenton) Road. Barton's instructions from Lee were simple: "attack the forces said to be stationed behind Brice's Creek."[7] To accomplish this, Barton had to take several steps. Specifically, his mission required him to approach New Bern from the southwest, cross Brice's Creek, take the forts there, cut the railroad, and plant guns on the banks of the Trent River. Pickett expected Barton to then "pass across the railroad bridge," presumably into downtown New Bern, take the enemy's forts there in reverse, cutting off reinforcements.[8]

Difficulties plagued Barton's march along the Pollocksville Road. Confronted with a blanketing darkness on Sunday evening, he waited until the moon rose at 1:30 a.m. to leave his bivouac, putting the 24th North Carolina from Ransom's brigade in the lead.[9] On the march, the vanguard encountered a "broken bridge" at a creek across the route. Barton estimated that repairs would take up to eight hours, but William J. Clarke, the colonel of the 24th, stepped in with some of his men and fixed the bridge in an hour, using only a few axes. The column moved on, and soon word circulated that New Bern—that "already hated place"—was their target.[10] As Barton headed for the city, he detached Colonel John Baker's 3rd North Carolina Cavalry to swing south along the Old Beaufort Road and destroy the track and telegraph lines near Evans' Mill and Croatan Station. Baker's riders set off early Monday morning, passing the infantrymen, as Barton's main force continued on the Pollocksville Road toward New Bern.[11]

Barton's men made contact with the enemy at around 8:00 a.m. As the column closed in on New Bern, the lead elements encountered Union outposts west of Brice's Creek, well outside the Union fortifications. The Federal pickets, suspecting the disturbance signaled only a minor raid, stepped into the road and called out, "Here's your mule," a common taunt during the war. Men in the rebel vanguard replied, "Here's your rider" and "pitched into them with a will." The brief melee produced a volley of musketry, cries, and shouts audible in the rear of Barton's column. A "lively chase of the fugitive Yankees" ensued as the rebels pressed forward. In a moment, three blue-clad men lay dead, and five more had become prisoners. Several escaped and sprinted rearward to the swamps. Barton's advance resumed.[12]

As the morning light grew, the Confederates peered to the north and could make out a flag flying on the distant horizon. At first, some thought it was a hospital banner, but they soon identified it as the "Stars and Stripes" waving over New Bern's fortifications. Immediately, the mission became clear to all.[13] Shortly after daylight, the men received the order to "load at will," and the ordnance wagons rolled to the front of the column.[14] As his force prepared to fight, Barton conducted a reconnaissance toward Brice's Creek with Brigadier General Matt W. Ransom and Colonel William R. Aylett.[15]

Barton found that this spot was a bad place for an attack. Inching forward, he came upon an open plain "from 1 to 2 miles in breadth," cut by a few narrow streams. In the distance, he could see Brice's Creek, nearly 80 yards wide—much wider than the 30 yards they had been told to expect. In this area, the creek formed a large hairpin curve, bulging to the west. In the hairpin's neck, a temporary bridge spanned the creek, offering the only direct approach to the Union position on the other side. Just across the bridge sat a blockhouse, breastworks, and a cavalry camp. Beyond, there were several works. Closest was Fort Gaston, which mounted ten guns and fronted the Clermont Bridge. Several hundred yards to the northeast, also on the south bank of the Trent, sat Fort Amory, bearing eight more guns. Barton also learned that farther east, about 3 miles from his position, was Fort Spinola, a "very large fort for land and river defense" that was connected to the railroad by a line of breastworks.[16]

This imposing array of Federal works was more than Barton had bargained for. Once he was in sight of these defenses, his resolve eroded and he lost momentum. During the march, he had caught wind of unforeseen challenges ahead. Several local citizens informed him "that the fortifications on the south of the Trent were of the most formidable character, deemed by the enemy impregnable." The locals were correct. The Union defenses on the south bank of the Trent were robust and manned.[17]

Barton formed his men for battle, placing Ransom's North Carolina regiments to the left of the Pollocksville Road and his own Virginians to the right. Skirmishers, a company's worth from each regiment, pushed forward, along with some cavalrymen. On the left, Henry Chambers, captain of Company C in the 49th North Carolina, volunteered for this "important and delicate business." Chambers, who had a reputation for "prudence, vigor, and courage," received instructions to advance cautiously half a mile to the front and conceal his men there. As the sounds of artillery rolled in from Bachelor Creek and the men prepared for the assault, anxiety coursed through Barton's ranks. In Terry's brigade, a rumor circulated that Barton wanted to be in New Bern by 1:00.[18] Expecting the worst, some men pulled personal letters from their haversacks and tore them up or burned them. It was "a point of honor," explained one soldier, to ensure that the "characters traced by the hand of affection shall never be gazed upon by the rude and vulgar eye of Yankee curiosity."[19]

But Barton's attack never occurred. Instead, his guns opened a "vigorous fire" on the blockhouse while the skirmish line pushed ahead half a mile but no more.[20] On the right, Virginia skirmishers advanced 200 to 300 yards in front, "their heads bobbing up and down among the cornstalks."[21] On the left, Captain Cicero Durham took charge of the North Carolina skirmishers in Ransom's line. From their advanced positions, the men could clearly see the Federal fortifications, as well as New Bern's church spires and houses beyond. They also noticed the obstacles barring their way—the Trent to their left, nearly half a mile wide, Brice's Creek in front, and "formidable earthen works" cramming the space between the creek and the railroad.

The infantrymen ducked as the shells from Barton's artillery passed above them. "The shot and shell now went screaming and shrieking through the air over our heads," wrote Chambers. But the Federals were ready and responded. At the first sign of Barton and his force, Colonel Thomas Amory had hurried a section of Battery I, 3rd New York Light Artillery, to the Brice's Creek blockhouse, along with some men from the 19th Wisconsin.[22] The New York gunners loaded their ordnance with case shot and shell and fired at Barton's column; they would continue to do so throughout the day. "The aim of the enemy was pretty good," Chambers admitted, "many of their shells bursting and scattering their destructive contents and fragments in liberal profusion and in rather unpleasant proximity to our position." Nevertheless, the men on both sides suffered only a few casualties.[23] Later, more guns from the New York battery rolled into position, pressing the Southerners away from the creek and disabling one of the rebel guns. Barton's efforts largely ended there. In the words of one New York veteran, "the rebels had no stomach for charging on those unerring guns." Behind the skirmish line, the Confederates lay in line of battle, mostly undisturbed, for the rest of Monday.[24]

"Insurmountable by Any Means at My Disposal"

Met with the tangle of fortifications and this violent greeting, Barton concluded that his appointed task was simply impractical. This decision spelled doom for his mission and placed the success of the entire expedition in doubt. In his view, the Union fortifications along the Trent River were "insurmountable by any means at my disposal," and even if he managed to capture them, they would have been "useless for the accomplishment of our object." The brigade commanders with Barton "fully coincided" with his conclusion.[25]

Rebel intelligence efforts had failed Barton. Reports from scouts and spies had downplayed the strength of the works along the Trent River. The county surveyor, who undertook a special reconnaissance and drafted sketches and maps for the expedition, failed to note Federal improvements to the works and did not identify Brice's Creek as the obstacle it turned out to be. Barton, who later recounted his efforts to gather a clear picture of the defenses before the expedition, was deeply disappointed. "I had made every exertion consistent with secrecy to arrive at accurate information as to this part of the enemy's position, having entertained doubts as to its not being fortified."[26]

With his preferred approach blocked, Barton considered other options. He could march south to the headwaters of Brice's Creek, cross at Evans' Mill, and head north along the rail line. But this approach held no appeal, for it "would have brought me in front of the same and other fortifications." Already separated from Pickett by a march of more than 20 miles, Barton saw little value in attempting the Evans' Mill gambit, which would extend the distance another 11 miles. Furthermore, his cavalry had experienced trouble in that direction. Around noon on Monday, Colonel Baker returned, having failed to cross the upper reaches of Brice's Creek and seize the railroad. The colonel blamed his "incompetent" guide as well as rain and darkness. Later that day he tried again, unsuccessfully.[27]

In the afternoon, Barton could hear the Federal guns playing on Pickett's force opposite New Bern. Hoping to reduce this pressure, he opened six rifled guns on the blockhouse at Brice's Creek and the nearby works. But achieving little, he soon gave up. Later, the Federals threw a force across the creek, but Barton's skirmishers pushed them back easily. In the meantime, Barton dispatched several couriers and scouts to inform Pickett. But throughout Monday at least, these communications failed, and Barton and Pickett remained out of contact.[28]

"Successful Resistance"

West of New Bern, Pickett remained ignorant of Barton's status. He expected little from the troops in his own column west of the city. Hoke's, Clingman's, and Corse's men were weary after hours of combat at Bachelor Creek and more hours of marching and skirmishing.[29] By the afternoon, the Confederates, led by Clingman's regiments, reached New Bern's strong inner fortifications. There, Union fire belched from the guns of Fort Totten and other positions along the line, including two howitzers sited outside the works and serviced by Colonel Savage's New York cavalry.[30] A Southern journalist described the landscape: "For two miles around Newbern the forest had been cleared, and the guns of three large forts, together with two parks of field artillery stationed in the town, had a clear sweep, and would have played havoc with our advance."[31] Outside the fortifications, the Southerners soon gained an appreciation for the strength of the works, as well as the difficulty of the canal, filled by recent rains, framing much of the defense line.[32]

As Hoke looked into New Bern, he was dismayed to hear two trains arriving from across the Trent River, revealing that the line to Morehead City was clear and Barton had not advanced.[33] Other matters occupied the attention of the young Tar Heel officer. From New Bern's ramparts, the Union guns played on the newly arrived rebels. At one point, a shell fragment hit the sandy ground and ricocheted into General Clingman, who shrugged off the bruise and ordered his men to hug the ground behind a swell, where they endured the fire largely unscathed. The gunnery did not impress Clingman. "Had their practice been good we must have sustained serious injury; in point of fact, however, their fire proved nearly harmless," he recalled.[34] While the Confederates huddled in the woods, Union troops harassed them, venturing outside the trenches several times. But in each instance, the Yankees shrank back whenever the Confederate line "rose to its feet." Clingman was eventually ordered to withdraw to a less exposed position.[35] Ultimately, Pickett and Hoke did not challenge the Union works any further, and "the sun went down without any attempt to assault the lines."[36] The Federals stood firm at their posts. One New York veteran later recalled the "gallant sight" of the flags, muskets, infantrymen, and cannon frowning down on the Confederates. Union officers crowded Fort Totten's huge traverse, peering out at the enemy through their field glasses. A feeling of resolve prevailed. The defenders expected that they would annihilate any attack.[37] That afternoon, accompanied by his staff, several officers, and a journalist, General Innis Palmer ascended the parapet at Fort Totten to observe Pickett's men. According to the reporter, the rebels "could be seen with a glass, and sometimes with the naked eye, passing back and forth in the edge of the woods skirting the plain on the west." Major S. C. Oliver, in direct command of the fort, ordered shells fired into "their midst, soon scattering them into the woods for safety."[38]

With the Confederates threatening, Union officials looked to protect the occupants of the three freedmen's camps scattered about the New Bern area. The largest, which would come to be known as James City, sat on the south bank of the Trent River near the rail line, within the Union works between Forts Gaston and Spinola. The other two camps, which contained about 2,000 refugees, fell outside the protection of the forts. One was located west of the city, just in front of Fort Totten.[39] The arrival of Confederate soldiers endangered the camps' residents. In the midst of the fighting, Horace James, the superintendent of Negro affairs, gathered the refugees and brought them within the city's works at the fairgrounds.[40] But even James's best efforts failed to save all the freed persons from the Confederates. "A number of them were captured within two miles," he recounted, "some were killed, and all were driven from their homes."[41] A *New York Times* reporter on the Fort Totten ramparts witnessed the danger posed by the rebels firsthand. Surveying the front, the correspondent spied a black family coming from the west, struggling to reach the safety of the garrison. The father shepherded the children while the mother "came up as a rear-guard." A Confederate soldier fired at her several times. When his bullets failed to hit their mark, he debouched from his position and sought to block her way and capture her. According to the account, "She met him, wrested his gun from him, knocked him down, and came into the city with the musket as a trophy, and a dislocated forefinger as an evidence of the contest."[42]

Throughout Monday, Palmer maintained contact with the forces at Beaufort and Morehead City. Early that morning, he ordered Colonel James Jourdan, commanding the subdistrict at Beaufort, to send the 158th New York to New Bern. The regiment, loaded with rations, traveled by rail accompanied by its commander, Lieutenant Colonel William McNary. This transfer nearly emptied the Morehead City garrison, leaving only a company of the 2nd Massachusetts Heavy Artillery and about 200 new, unarmed recruits from the 158th New York. Jourdan also warned Colonel Valentine Barney, commanding a force at the Newport Barracks up the railroad, to prepare for an attack and to maintain communication with other posts along the line, including Croatan.[43]

During the night, the New Bern defenses remained alive as the men in the forts sipped hot coffee and waited for the Confederate attack. Rumors spread that the rebels planned to lob incendiary rounds into the city. Firemen and other citizens mobilized to stand guard in case that danger materialized.[44] Late in the evening, a detachment from the 5th Rhode Island Heavy Artillery, stationed at Croatan southeast of the city, entered New Bern, much to the relief of others in the regiment. On their way, the artillerymen gathered about 250 black refugees and led them to safety.[45]

In the city that evening, as the Union troops pressed against the walls of Fort Totten and the adjacent earthworks, their commanders weighed their options for the next day. Palmer relayed news of the situation to General Butler in Virginia, projecting confidence and predicting a "successful resistance," even though his force was small relative to the enemy's.[46] Palmer and his men understood that more danger lay ahead. The Federals' effort throughout the morning at Bachelor Creek, particularly the plucky defense by Haring's band, had stymied the Confederate advance and bought precious time. Now they waited to see what else the enemy had in store for them.

"Listened Anxiously for the Sound of His Guns"

At his field headquarters on Monday evening, Pickett waited in vain for news of Barton's progress. The day had ended with Pickett's men holding the woods in front of Fort Totten and the other works covering New Bern's western face.[47] Many things had occupied Pickett's mind over the last few months: the disaster at Gettysburg, his new marriage, the responsibility of the North Carolina Department, and the anger triggered by Edward Wild's December raid. Now, trusted to lead the New Bern expedition, Pickett surely felt the weight of this independent command. Without news from Barton, the entire complicated operation appeared to be in jeopardy. The uncertainty ate at Pickett. According to one observer, he "listened anxiously for the sound of his guns, expecting every moment to hear [Barton] open upon the town in the rear; but the day wore away and nothing was heard from him."[48] "Great disappointment evinced on this account," recorded Henry Guion.[49]

The general was joined that evening by veteran reporter Dr. William G. Shepardson, who wrote for the *Richmond Daily Dispatch* under the pen name "Bohemian." Shepardson, an Alabama native who had traveled extensively in Europe, routinely placed himself at the scene of danger to gather war news for his eager readers. A fervent Confederate nationalist, he enjoyed cigars, history, and Shakespeare. Driven by his extensive literary interest, he published a book of Confederate anthems in 1862 titled *Songs of the South*.[50] He had filed stories from many battlefields, beginning with Manassas. In 1863, he accompanied John Taylor Wood on his cutting-out expeditions in the Chesapeake Bay, setting aside his reporter's pen to employ his surgeon's skills on the wounded. From Richmond, he had traveled south with Wood's sailors. Outside New Bern on Monday evening, he had already put in a full day, having floated down the Neuse from Kinston with Wood.[51]

On Monday afternoon, Shepardson left the sailors and somehow made his way to Pickett's headquarters. There, he joined the Confederate officers in sizing up the Union defenses and waiting for news from Barton. He was struck by Pickett's anxiety and described the general "standing under a tree; in full sight of the town and its fortifications . . . looking anxiously towards the Trent, twirling his sword knot around his small white hand, or, as if in perplexity, fastidiously biting his finger nails." Once the day was over, Shepardson observed that the lack of news from Barton had made a visible imprint: "Gen. P looks more perplexed than ever, and twists his sword knot more rapidly, and bites his nails persistently. Presently he disposes of the troops for the night and turns away from the field."[52] Pickett was truly baffled. In a letter to his wife, he confessed that "hour after hour of restless anxiety and impatience went by and yet no sound of a gun—and no message came to tell me why. The torture and suspense was unbearable."[53]

Later, in his official report, Pickett complained about the lack of cooperation: "the other parties having failed to attack . . . I found we were making the fight single-handed." This was true. By Monday evening, Barton remained stationary, Wood had done nothing, Dearing had found Fort Anderson too strong to attack, and Martin had not appeared.[54] As one Union veteran accurately noted, Pickett "sat down before the city and only gazed longingly at the grand prize he coveted."[55]

While Pickett fretted on Monday night, news of the operation began to spread throughout the state, breeding an optimism among the secessionists that would increase over the coming days. By Tuesday, the North Carolina papers contained hints of the expedition. The *Daily Progress* reported, "We . . . know that the air is filled with rumors, and that everybody expects that something is about to turn up." The editors discussed the "feverish excitement" the offensive had generated among the Confederate citizens in eastern North Carolina. The paper explained that New Bern natives, flushed out by the Union occupation earlier in the war, had traveled to the city's outskirts, hoping to return to their homes. "We only have to request that they will save us a place at the feast," implored the editors.[56] The *Weekly Standard* echoed that sentiment, noting that the "public mind has been excited by the" developments and that "possession of Newbern, and the permanent occupation of that region of that State by our forces would result most beneficially to our people and to the Confederate cause."[57]

CHAPTER EIGHT

The *Underwriter*

"Never Saw Such a Circus Before"

Much depended on John Taylor Wood. With Confederate infantry columns stalemated in front of New Bern on Monday, the young colonel had yet to make his mark on the operation. Lieutenant George W. Gift, one of Wood's officers, explained that "our part of the programme was to board and carry the enemy's gun boats, whilst the army carried the works that defended the town, thus we would make a joint victory, beat the reprobate, by land and sea."[1] The men knew Wood was well suited for the job. Born in Minnesota, where his father served in the army, Wood grew up on the frontier with all the freedom and danger it entailed. In 1847, he joined the navy and then attended the Naval Academy in the early 1850s. He served in the Mexican War and then on the West Coast during the California gold rush. He also participated in naval operations against the African slave trade, gaining his first command at the helm of a seized slave ship. At the outbreak of the Civil War, he was teaching gunnery at the Naval Academy. In those chaotic days, Wood wrote in his diary, "war, that terrible calamity, is upon us, and worst of all, among us."[2] Though his parents remained loyal to the Union, Wood resigned his commission. After a short, unsuccessful attempt to sit out the war as a neutral citizen, he aligned with the Confederate cause, following his uncle, Jefferson Davis, and his younger brother.[3]

Wood had already earned a reputation as an able fighter. Early in the conflict, he manned batteries on the Potomac and commanded a gun on the famous ironclad *Virginia* in 1862. But he gained the most attention in a series of successful cutting-out expeditions, revealing his innovation and daring. With Secretary Mallory's hearty approval, Wood proposed, planned, and executed several operations against Union vessels. Using custom launches built under his supervision in the Rocketts Navy Yard at Richmond and transported over land, he surprised unsuspecting Union vessels anchored near shore. He conducted his first raid in October 1862, when he captured two merchant vessels in the Chesapeake Bay near the Rappahannock River. On January 26, 1863, Davis appointed Wood as a liaison between the army and navy to conduct inspections of coastal installations and the ironclad construction efforts. However, Wood did not remain fastened to a desk in Richmond.[4] In August, he conducted another expedition with his "navy on wheels," this time capturing the USS *Satellite* and USS *Reliance* near the mouth of the Piankatank River.[5]

The New Bern expedition provided Wood with his next combat opportunity. But, like Pickett and Hoke, Wood faced logistical challenges in assembling his force. At Richmond, he drew the bulk of his crew from the James River Squadron, a command that had remained mostly idle since notable engagements at Hampton Roads and Drewry's Bluff in 1862. For the most part, the men of the squadron had spent their days tending to the handful of ironclads and gunboats holed up at Richmond. When news of a North Carolina mission arrived, the sailors welcomed the opportunity to participate in active campaigning. As the men prepared to move south, Wood issued rifles, cutlasses, and revolvers, as well as blankets, peacoats, utensils, and a few axes. He also secured two decent boats, originally from the Gosport Yard at Norfolk, and an additional eight skiffs fitted out to meet the mission's requirements.[6]

Wood did not find everything he needed at Richmond. To make up the deficit, he sent Lieutenant Gift to Wilmington to gather more. Gift, a Naval Academy graduate who had spent his prewar years in California, had served on the Confederate ironclads *Louisiana* and *Arkansas*. With an order from President Davis directing all persons to aid him, Gift immediately boarded a southbound train. Once in Wilmington, the naval personnel there obliged his requests, for the most part. However, the army—in the person of General William Whiting—did not, a rebuff that earned Gift's lasting enmity. Despite the friction, Gift managed to acquire two launches from the navy, each with space for twenty-four oars and a 12-pounder howitzer fitted with both a field and a boat carriage. Eventually, Gift also pried a few smaller boats away from the unaccommodating Whiting.[7] On Saturday, January 30, the lieutenant received orders to proceed north. Strengthened with additional hands from Charleston, he boarded a train to Goldsboro and Kinston loaded with the two heavy launches and two large rowboats, 125 men, and 12 officers.[8] "We had an abundance of fighting material," Gift recalled, "all eager to go wherever Wood would lead."[9]

Back in Richmond, Wood also got under way. Several days before the scheduled New Bern attack, his men left their berths on the *Patrick Henry*, the Confederacy's floating naval academy, and rowed their small boats down the James River and up the Appomattox into Petersburg. Wood shared the plan's details with Lieutenant B. P. Loyall, the executive officer for the operation, and Lieutenant William H. Parker. Among the crew, though, ignorance prevailed. The next morning in downtown Petersburg, the men dragged their boats to the train depot and loaded them onto waiting flatcars.[10] As the cars headed south, the sailors sat inside their boats and waved their hats, smiling "to the astonished natives, who never saw such a circus before."[11] The odd show also proved quite a curiosity for the locals at other stations along the line.[12]

"The Narrow Lonesome River"

As the various elements converged on Kinston, timing became an issue. Confederate planners had hoped for a simultaneous attack on Monday. Specifically, Pickett expected Wood to attack the Union gunboats in conjunction with the ground assault. Wood was cutting it close. His train arrived in Kinston at 2:00 a.m. on Sunday, and Gift's party did not appear from Wilmington until nine hours later, laboring into town behind a "wheezy old engine with a leaky boiler," compliments of the indifferent Whiting. Wood met Gift at the depot, clearly anxious to launch the boats into the Neuse and get under way. With the sailors tugging on their ropes, Gift's smaller boats scraped through the town and slid into the river. However, the bulky launches procured at Wilmington presented a stiffer challenge. Not willing to delay any further, Wood cast off with about ten boats, leaving Gift and eighty-two men to devise a way to get the larger vessels into the water.[13]

About 2 miles down the river, every man received a white cotton band to fasten on his left arm, and officers designated "Sumter" as the watchword.[14] South of Kinston, the Neuse flowed through a deep, 50-yard-wide channel framed by low banks. Cypress and juniper trees curtained the shore, interrupted here and there by swampy lowlands crowded with fallen logs and dead branches. Before the approaching boats, ducks rose from eddies in the river's sharp turns, and muskrats and otters skittered to cover. With strict orders enforcing silence, the steady cadence of the oars dipping into the frigid water offered the only sound.[15] At sunset, Wood halted on a small island for supper and a short rest. He gathered the men to explain the mission, identifying the small Union flotilla at New Bern as the target. After capturing one of the enemy vessels, Wood planned "to get up steam and cruise after other gunboats."[16]

Back at Kinston, Gift wrestled the launches off the flatcars, lashed them to wagon axles, and dragged them through the streets and into the river with the help of twenty mules and dozens of citizens. He managed to get under way at about 3:00 p.m., a few hours behind Wood. "We left the landing cheered by a great many pretty ladies," recalled Gift. Ten miles down the Neuse, his men pulled to the bank for a quick meal and then returned to their oars. With eighty men rowing, Gift's two boats moved down "the narrow lonesome river" at about 7 miles per hour. However, the boats progressed cautiously, for no pilot could be found among the crew, and not a soul on board had ever navigated the Neuse.[17] The men, still ignorant of their mission, pulled throughout the freezing night. It was rough work. The boats ran aground several times, causing collisions and forcing some men to wade up to their armpits to coax the boats into deeper water. Back in the launches, the men shifted uncomfortably on their freezing seats. As the night stretched on, fog obscured the banks, adding to the challenges. With his men thoroughly tired, cold, and hungry, Gift halted at about 3:00 a.m., several miles short of New Bern, and pulled the boats up onto a small island.[18]

"We Pulled for the Lights of the City"

Downriver, Wood pressed forward Monday morning and reached the point on the Neuse where it widened above New Bern.[19] At 3:30 a.m., the line of boats closed up in double column and "pulled for the lights of the city," according to surgeon Daniel Conrad.[20] Battling through a thick fog, Wood's men headed straight for New Bern's wharfs. The plan was an ambitious one. It "was Captain Wood's idea," one sailor wrote, "that we would probably find two U.S. Gunboats at New Bern, these he expected to capture, probably get their signal book, and run down with the captured crafts at once to Morehead City and capture the rest of the U.S. fleet in those waters."[21] But during the early hours of Monday, they found nothing. Wood's men searched the harbor "from one end to the other" and even ventured into the Trent for a stretch, but they encountered only the sound of Union voices floating from shore through the mist.[22] They rowed around for nearly an hour but failed to locate any prey and, astonishingly, managed to avoid detection by the enemy picket posts. Nevertheless, with no target found, Wood abandoned the search, ensuring that no naval attack would accompany Pickett's operations, at least on Monday. Wood's inability to find a suitable target left the infantry to confront the New Bern lines alone. As daylight approached, Wood's boats struck back up the river and pulled for a small island. There, tall grass and low shrubs shielded the launches and the men as they slept on the damp ground.[23]

As Wood's men hunkered down Monday morning, "a heavy and sharp cannon-ading" drifted over their hideout, heralding Pickett's and Hoke's arrival at Bachelor Creek. Throughout the day, as Hoke pushed toward the city, Wood's boats remained nestled in the "tall sedge and grass" along the bank, hidden from Union lookouts. The men lit smoldering fires, large enough to generate a little warmth without producing much smoke. The sailors swallowed cold rations and waited for darkness to cloak their next sortie. The idle hours invited reflection. One popular midshipman, Palmer Saunders, wondered aloud, "Fellows, where will we be this time tomorrow?" Others surely thought the same. Peering from the reeds and bushes, the men could see a Union signal post on the opposite bank, a crow's nest out near the enemy picket line. The sentinel put them on edge. It gave one sailor a "creepy, uneasy feeling to think that our whole movement and intention might be discovered."[24] Throughout the day, the men listened to sounds of combat rolling eastward toward New Bern. By afternoon, the rumble of cannon came from farther to the southeast, signaling Pickett's arrival outside the city's fortifications.[25]

Upstream from Wood, Gift's crew remained at their own island camp. The men unloaded the guns, posted guards, built fires, rested, and chewed on broiled bacon and hardtack. During the day, a messenger arrived from James Dearing, who reported a gunboat lying under the works across the river at New Bern. In a few hours, Dearing arrived in person, imploring Gift to attack Fort Anderson from the river. But Gift was obliged to support Wood. Earlier that morning, the lieutenant had probed south hunting for Wood's flotilla, with no luck. During his search, he encountered an agitated white woman at a shanty on the riverbank who mistook him for a Union officer. Frantically "swinging an old sun bonnet," the woman yelled, "Haven't yer been up here stealin' often enough for me to know yer?" Retreating, Gift drifted on and soon came upon a black man who, also mistaking Gift's allegiance, implored him to rush back into the forts, for the woods were full of rebels "worse than pigeons in pigeon time." In the evening, Gift finally found what he was looking for when his men observed a boat laboring up Swift's Creek. After a signalman dipped his lantern three times, the craft approached and delivered messages from Wood. Soon, Gift's vessels floated down on the ebb tide for the reunion, the men "highly delighted" to learn the mission had not been conducted without them.[26]

"Picture to Yourself a Steamer"

Indeed, a target was at hand. Earlier, in the daylight, Wood's lookouts had spied smoke from a Union gunboat churning upriver. The vessel halted near the New Bern shore only a few hundred yards from the Federal battery at Fort Stevenson. The ship's crew dropped the starboard anchor and fastened a line to the wharf. Looking on, Wood and his men sized up the vessel and concluded they could seize it. However, the craft's location, so close to the big guns on shore, promised to complicate matters. As Gift explained, the raiding party "would have to thread our way between these formidable land defenses."[27]

Wood's lookouts had found the *Underwriter*, a large side-wheel steamer that had served the Union cause well in Carolina waters. In 1861, the navy had bought the former New York harbor tug for $18,500. The following year, the craft fired the first gun at Roanoke Island and supported New Bern's capture. At 170 feet long, 24 feet wide, 341 tons, and 800 horsepower, its armament in 1864 included four guns in all—two large 8-inch smoothbores, one 12-pounder rifle, and one 12-pounder howitzer.[28] With its shallow draft of 8 feet, it could navigate many of the region's waterways with ease. It also sat unusually low, its sides barely clearing the water's surface. Lieutenant Loyall left the following description: "Picture to yourself a steamer . . .

with very low guards and stripped of her sides or bulwarks, except a wooden rail with rope netting from that to her deck."[29] At the time of the Confederate attack, the *Underwriter*'s watch bill listed seventy-two hands, although the actual number on board was probably lower.[30] Its commander, Acting Master Jacob Westervelt, had been a merchant captain and had run a schooner between New Bern and New York before the war, work that made him well acquainted with the local waters. His decision to remain loyal to the Union, however, earned the scorn of some rebels, who labeled him a "grand rascal." By the same token, his roots raised doubts among Northerners about his fidelity to the United States.[31]

The *Underwriter*'s movements observed by Confederate lookouts were part of the navy's efforts to protect New Bern on Monday. Early that day, General Palmer urged Lieutenant George W. Graves, acting commander of the base's naval force, to position his gunboats to repel the Confederate land assault. Graves relied on three side-wheel gunboats: the 114-foot *Lockwood*, the 141-foot *Commodore Hull*, and the *Underwriter*. A fourth gunboat, the *Hetzel*, was away at Ocracoke Inlet with New Bern's absent naval leader, Commander Henry K. Davenport.[32] As the Confederates arrived at the defenses, the *Underwriter* was preparing to resume its duties at Hatteras Inlet. However, with the danger to New Bern clearly identified, Graves directed Westervelt to helm the *Underwriter* up the Neuse to cover the open ground outside the Union works. Graves also ordered the *Commodore Hull* to anchor farther upstream, but it quickly ran aground and remained stuck for the next two days, despite best efforts to wrench it free. Lieutenant Graves himself steered the diminutive *Lockwood* up the Trent River to help counter Barton's incursion at Brice's Creek and cover the railroad bridge.[33] The *Underwriter* found its spot at around 9:00 a.m. and moored about 100 yards off Foster's Wharf, near Fort Stevenson. The crew shifted all its guns to the port side and trained them on the plains beyond fieldworks on the shore, away from the open river.[34]

"Give Way!"

As Graves deployed his gunboats, Wood prepared his command for the cutting-out mission after a day of watching and waiting. The men were anxious for close action and felt lucky to have Woods as their commander for the task ahead. He was a natural leader, "retiring and modest in his disposition, quiet and easy in his manners, but in action a lion."[35] "His hair and eyes were dark" and his "complexion swarthy, with a muscular frame, possessing, in fact, a physique far above the average allotted to man." He often wore a simple gray suit and a slouch hat, and he carried an old navy sword and a naval Colt at his side.[36] On Monday evening, Wood developed his plan of attack.[37] Lee's orders directed him to "endeavor to surprise and capture the gun-boats in the river, and by their aid drive the enemy from their guns."[38] However, since his arrival, he had only found one vessel, the *Underwriter*. Gift, writing immediately after the events, recorded that the "intent was to have attacked 5 gunboats but we found only one."[39] Nevertheless, with Pickett and Barton stalled before New Bern, Wood could not afford to delay and resolved to go after the *Underwriter* that night.

Wood and his officers, numbering 35 or so, furnished detailed instructions to the force of 250 seaman, 25 marines, and an exhausted journalist, the omnipresent William Shepardson, who had spent the day ashore at Pickett's headquarters.[40] Wood divided the men into three groups: two large divisions of five boats each, with the port led by Wood and the starboard by Loyall, and one division of four boats in reserve, handled by Gift. The two attacking columns would head straight for the Union vessel. At the point of contact, the oarsman in each boat's bow would leap onto the *Underwriter* with a grapnel and fasten his craft tight.[41]

As they pulled away into the Neuse, Wood called out, "Hats off for prayers!" and asked for "the Divine blessing" on the expedition. Following the entreaty, the boats glided toward New Bern, a phosphorescent wake trailing behind them. At one point, when Gift's two massive launches in the reserve column grounded, Wood reversed the entire flotilla and encouraged the men to free the craft in "his peculiar, cheery, good-natured way." But there was no need. Gift's crews leaped out and dragged the vessels into deeper water.[42]

Out in the middle of the river, a "dark and gloomy" night cloaked the boats, but New Bern's twinkling lights glowed in the distance, and a rising moon threatened to reveal the attackers. The brush of the oars through the inky water provided the only sound. Soon, the *Underwriter*'s outlines emerged from the darkness. Breaking the tranquility, five sharp pings rang out from a bell on the Union vessel signaling 2:30 a.m. The rebel column "turned its head and struck out steadily and noiselessly for [its] victim," looking, in Gift's estimation, like a "naval funeral procession."[43] With the distance closing, an alert lookout aboard the *Underwriter* saw the oncoming boats and shouted three times, "Boat ahoy!" before sounding the alarm rattle. Union sailors raced from their hammocks and scrambled to their stations.[44] On board Loyall's boat, the report woke Shepardson, who had been recovering from his long day.[45] Wood stood up and ordered his men to "give way." The men yanked on their oars, and the attack accelerated as the "boats nearly sprang out [of] the water."[46]

Aboard the *Underwriter*, the crew struggled unsuccessfully to shift the larger guns from port to starboard and then grabbed all the muskets and pistols they could gather.[47] With 200 yards separating the combatants, the decks of the Union craft opened with a bristling fire. The rebels returned the favor. Confederate marines, under Captain Thomas Wilson, stood in the bows of their boats firing at the *Underwriter*. Through the hail of bullets, the attackers closed the distance to the gunboat in forty-five seconds.[48] Wood remained standing, swaying from side to side with anticipation. From their whaleboats and launches, the Confederates could see the heads and shoulders of the enemy rising above the *Underwriter*'s railing.[49] The

Union sailors crowded near the wheelhouse and discharged their rifles and revolv-ers at close range. The flash of small-arms fire lit up the combatants' faces, and a sulfurous aroma soon filled the air.[50]

Under Wood's plan, one division would board at the stern and another at the bow. However, due to a misunderstanding, most of the boats arrived in front of the *Underwriter*. Only Loyall's craft ended up near the stern, just aft of the wheelhouse, losing its course a bit after tangling with a line in the water.[51] From the bow of Loy-all's boat, oarsman James Wilson swung a grapnel over the *Underwriter*'s rails and tied it fast, allowing the men to hoist themselves on board.[52]

Wood's own boat ended up amidships. His coxswain, "a burly, gamy English-man," steered with his knees while he fired his pistols at the enemy. Then a bullet pierced his forehead and he slumped forward, leaving the boat careening away from the gangway and toward the wheelhouse, touching soon after Loyall's boat.[53] At the *Underwriter*'s bow, the other boats arrived, and "in quick succession" the men tumbled "on board as soon as the grapnel was made fast."[54] The low sides proved a boon to the attackers, and soon the Confederates had winched themselves onto the deck in the face of a wicked fire.[55] "A dozen six-shooters at once" sprayed the quarterdeck. Confederate engineer Emmet Gill raised his head above the deck and received seven bullets in his skull. His brother, close behind, immediately killed one of the men responsible. In Shepardson's estimation, the fire was hotter than any he had witnessed during the war. Wiping the blood trickling from a slight head wound, the journalist boarded the *Underwriter* just as a marine who had been shot through the chest collapsed on top of him. Others gave a yell and rushed onto the deck.[56]

The combat was most fierce at the gunboat's center and toward the rear, where Wood and Loyall had touched. "The cracking of firearms and the rattle of cutlasses made a deafening din," recalled Loyall. As he scrambled on board, Loyall lost his glasses and stumbled onto the deck as injured men fell over him. He then climbed on the wheelhouse. All the while, the sound of Wood's bellowed orders rose above the clash. The Union sailors continued to resist. From the *Underwriter*'s armory just underneath the hurricane deck, they maintained a rapid fire, using loaded weapons handed up by comrades behind them. To Loyall, the fire "seemed like a sheet of flame, and the very jaws of death."[57] From the shore, members of the 99th New York in the trenches could hear the "heavy discharge of small-arms and the clashing of steel."[58]

The fight lasted about ten minutes, but it surely seemed much longer to the com-batants. Throughout the turmoil, Gift remained in reserve about 70 yards behind the lead boats as they pulled for their quarry. Witnessing the intense fire from the *Underwriter*, he feared much damage would be done. But, from his post, he could see his comrades gain ground and heard "the sharp quick reports of the pistols, and the clash of cutlasses," along with a cloud of oaths. Gift could hardly restrain his eighty-two men, watching from their launches bobbing in the river. At one point, his marines picked off a solitary figure on the wheelhouse. The man crumpled and rolled off into the water. At one point, Gift fired his howitzer when he feared the *Underwriter* would get under way.[59]

As Gift looked on from his whaleboat, the Confederates swarming over the *Underwriter*'s bow gradually gained ground, the fire slackened, and the cry of "We surrender!" rose from the gunboat's crew.[60] However, the fight was not over yet. Some of the officers continued to resist from below the hurricane deck. They dug in their heels and would not yield until several had been shot at close range.[61] Rebel surgeon Daniel Conrad heard "a strange synchronous roar, but did not understand what it meant at first though it soon became plain: 'She's ours.'"[62]

Wood had won. He now had the formidable gunboat in his hands and the rest of the Union's naval force at New Bern within his grasp. Before he could do anything else, though, he would have to get his new command under way. Immediately after the cheering died down, the rebel sailors "commenced plundering & much confusion ensued."[63] To the *Underwriter*'s crew, the victors appeared to be "strapping big men and desperate looking characters." Captives later recalled that some of the rebels "wanted to cut and slash at us after we had surrendered," but Wood's officers gained control and gathered the prisoners on the quarterdeck, tied their hands, and assigned marines to guard them at the gangways. Although a few Union sailors escaped in a boat to the shore, all the *Underwriter*'s officers and most of the crew were either captured or killed.[64] Westervelt, the boat's acting master, had been wounded in the leg and carried below for treatment. A rumor began to circulate that Westervelt had shied away from combat during the engagement. While the rebel surgeons were attending to others, Westervelt snuck back on deck and managed to reach the stern. He stepped over the side and grabbed the rope mooring the gunboat. However, before he could escape, a rebel guard on the quarterdeck sent a bullet into his head, dropping him into the murky Neuse.[65]

In the wardroom, surgeon Conrad found half a dozen men slightly wounded by "shots from revolvers." On deck, he located the severely injured midshipman Palmer Saunders, cradled in the lap of a comrade. Only hours before, Saunders had wondered who would be "up in the stars" after the fight. Now, his own life was ebbing away. Conrad recalled his examination of the injured man: "In feeling his head I felt my hand slip down between his ears, and to my horror, discovered that his head had been cleft in two by a boarding sword in the hands of some giant of the forecastle." Yet, despite this certainly fatal wound, Saunders continued to breathe. At Conrad's direction, the men laid the midshipman, along with other casualties, on the quarterdeck.[66]

With his prisoners and the wounded attended to, Wood focused on getting the *Underwriter* in motion. As long as the vessel remained tethered to its moorings, it could serve only as a stationary, floating battery and would be vulnerable to several

Union gun positions only a few hundred yards away. Under the circumstances, it would be of little use to the Confederates. Wood sought to convert the craft "at once into a Confederate man-of-war, and . . . take and destroy as many of the vessels of the enemy as possible." If Wood could achieve this, he would rule the Neuse, at least until Federal naval reinforcements arrived. Rebel engineers and firemen scurried to the engine room to get up steam. A captured Union engineer gladly explained the workings of the pipes and pumps. On deck, Lieutenant Loyall and several seamen attempted to raise the anchor and cast loose the cable that secured the ship to the wharf.[67]

Half an hour later, Wood gathered the officers to receive reports on the vessel's condition. The news was not good. The anchor was stuck. Using the tackle on deck, Wood's men had strained to raise it but found "the ends of the two chains shackled together after a turn around the keelson [a wooden structure parallel to the keel] had been taken." The tools to fix this problem had been mislaid.[68] Loyall tried unsuccessfully to unshackle the chains that moored the vessel to a buoy. He reported, "it [was] useless to spend any more time . . . unless he could have hours in which to perform the work."[69]

The Union gunners on shore soon brought a halt to Wood's tribulations. As the rebel officers discussed boilers and chains, the gunners in Fort Stevenson "opened fire . . . with small arms, grape and solid shot."[70] Gun crews had rushed to Fort Stevenson after escapees from the *Underwriter*'s crew reported its capture. The men in the batteries reluctantly executed this agonizing assignment. Captain Henry B. Landers of the 5th Rhode Island recalled: "It seemed hard to fire into her when our wounded were groaning and crying for help but it was my duty to shell the rebels out, and burn and sink her."[71] A shower of iron soon hammered the gunboat. Grape, canister, and solid shot plowed the water around the vessel. The first shell to hit the boat smashed into the port wheelhouse and signal box, wounding several Confederates sailors. According to one soldier observing from shore, the second shell set the boat on fire. Artillerists riddled the gunboat's hull. Within fifteen minutes, shot had disabled the walking beam, the lever perched high above the deck connecting the engine to the paddle wheels. Another boat appeared, rounding New Bern from the Trent. With the Union shells hitting home, it became evident that Wood and his men had captured a death trap.[72]

Wood understood that the *Underwriter* had no chance and ordered it abandoned. His men first transferred the prisoners and wounded to the boats that were lined up in a double row on the gunboat's lee side, shielded from the shore fire. Saunders, close to death from his shocking head wound, was carried off the gunboat in a blanket. According to some accounts, Wood's men left the bodies of Union seamen on board, including three or four dead black sailors stuffed into the coal bunkers. Wood ordered four lieutenants to head below and fire the ship, directing them to remain until the decks had ignited. W. F. Clayton and others tore up mattresses and other combustibles and soaked them in oil. Loyall ordered Lieutenant Francis Hoge to set the fire. Hoge gathered turpentine and a stack of kindling, lit the pyre, and left the *Underwriter*, believing it would soon be engulfed in flames.[73]

Wood's men scrambled into the boats, grabbed their oars, and pulled away. They crammed about eighteen prisoners into one of the *Underwriter*'s small launches. The crowded vessel took a slow, erratic course and soon fell behind the other boats as their crews worked to distance themselves from the doomed gunboat. Outnumbered and isolated, the Confederate guards in the launch hailed others ahead for assistance, but it was too late. Some of the prisoners dove into the Neuse and swam for shore. Others remained. One of them, engineer Edgar Allen, overpowered a guard, throwing the rebel's cutlass overboard and urging his comrades to take the oars and pull for shore.[74]

When his flotilla had pulled several hundred yards away from the *Underwriter*, Wood glanced behind and saw no flames in the distance. Approaching Loyall's boat, Wood asked what was amiss. A distraught Loyall replied that he had given the order to fire the craft, and Lieutenant Hoge assured them that he had put the torch to the *Underwriter*. However, the effort had clearly failed, and Wood ordered the lieutenant back to finish the job. Soon, from his position upriver, Loyall could see flames pouring out of the forward wheelhouse and Hoge pulling away. As Wood's boats resumed their withdrawal, a heavy squall burst over them, soaking the men and shielding the flotilla from the Union shore batteries. Despite the storm, the *Underwriter* continued to burn. The loaded guns on board discharged in the flames, emitting loud reports that echoed over the water.[75] Conrad recalled, "We saw great columns of red flames shoot upward out of the forward hatch and ward-room."[76] The gunboat eventually erupted. The "explosion & light . . . was plainly heard & seen from where we were," reported William Pfohl, who had a full view from the New Bern ramparts.[77] Years later, one New York veteran wrote, "A writhing, crackling, rolling column of brilliant flame rose from the doomed boat, bearing aloft a torrent of burning sparks and clouds of dense black smoke." The spectacle lit up New Bern and the surrounding countryside for miles. The rebel boats glided safely out of sight, their mission only partially successful.[78]

By sunrise Tuesday, Wood's party reached an island upriver at Swift Creek. Saunders, the wounded midshipman, died as his friends carried his body to shore. At 3:00 p.m., the men washed and dressed the dead. Loyall read a burial service as two officers and several men were interred in a long pit dug in the sand. Gift transported the wounded, both Confederate and Federal, to the village of Swift Creek (modern-day Vanceboro) and the house of Mr. E. Cleve, where a Dr. Southerland tended to them. Afterward, reports of actual casualties varied. Loyall later put the Confederate total at "six killed and twenty-two wounded." He estimated Federal losses at nine killed, eighteen wounded, and nineteen prisoners, with thirty prisoners escaping.[79]

"Light of Battle"

After transporting the wounded to Swift Creek, George Gift received orders to proceed to James Dearing's field headquarters near Fort Anderson. Gift met with Dearing, and together they surveyed the Confederate deployment outside the fort. According to Gift, they discussed the possibility of transporting men by boat to attack the fort. John N. Whitford's unit, the 67th North Carolina, had surrounded the Union position, with the Virginia regiments in reserve. Most of Whitford's men had spent the war in eastern North Carolina and had not fought much, save for a short stint in the works during the Union attack on New Bern in 1862.[80] Gift detected unease among the men deployed so close to the Union guns. Throughout the day, Whitford "sent many messages and pressing reports" to Dearing, but the Virginian seemed unperturbed. However, in the afternoon, a report arrived that the Yankees were spilling out of the sally port. Soon, shots began to fall around Dearing and Gift as they lay under a pine tree that served as the field headquarters. Dearing pulled out his spyglass and confirmed that the Federals were indeed pouring from the fort. He and his staff scrambled to get their men in line, rushing to the field in the rear that held the Virginia regiments.

Gift moved forward as well. He had spent much of the war with the navy and harbored a curiosity about land fighting. When he reached the field where the Virginia regiments were located, he beheld a motley lot. Some men had jackets and caps; others did not. They lay in "all sorts of positions, playing, romping, and amusing themselves," with their muskets stacked at the ready nearby. But when the drums began to beat, the scene transformed. Leaving their blanket rolls on the ground, the Virginians "threw on their cartridge boxes, seized their arms," and formed within seconds. In a column of fours, they stepped out toward the fort with Gift in tow, looking like one of the boys who keep "up with the procession . . . on muster days." Gift noted the "light of battle" in the infantrymen's eyes as they passed him. When the Virginians drew even with the North Carolinians, Whitford's men raised a yell and pushed forward. The show of strength proved too much for the Federals, who had barely ventured outside the fort. They hurried back behind its protective walls. The Confederates reversed course, and in no time they had resumed their comfortable postures in the open field.[81]

Dearing did not attack either. Later, Gift reported that the planned operation had been abandoned but did not identify the cause.[82] That afternoon, he remained at Dearing's headquarters, partly to enjoy dinner with him and his staff. However, when mealtime came and went with no sign of food, a mortified Dearing confessed: "I have made a diligent search and inquiry throughout the whole brigade, and there is not enough grub in our camp to feed a mouse." He had even asked local citizens for food and found nothing except a complaint from one that they had "spored [spared] and spored until they can't spore another bite." When Gift returned to

Wood's flotilla that evening, he sent Dearing a side of bacon and a bag of bread. But the lack of food in Dearing's command did not bode well for the long-term prospects of the New Bern operation. Time was running out.[83]

"Utterly Inexcusable"

The *Underwriter*'s destruction weighed on the Union command. On Tuesday morning, Innis Palmer and George Graves struggled to boost New Bern's naval defenses in the wake of the debacle. The Union troops in the city felt more vulnerable than ever, at least from the water. With the *Hetzel* still away in the east, only the *Lockwood* and *Commodore Hull* patrolled the shore. To support these two vessels, Palmer placed guns aboard the dispatch boat *Allison* and the ferry *Eagle*. In addition, larger gunboats raced from the Plymouth garrison, dispatched by Lieutenant Commander Charles Flusser there.[84] During the day, Lieutenant Graves piloted the *Lockwood* to the *Underwriter*'s position and found the gunboat's wreck burned down to the waterline. Later, Commander Henry Davenport reported that he had managed to extract a 12-pounder howitzer, an anchor, and a chain from the Neuse. Across the river on Tuesday, George Gift, who was still with Dearing, spied the *Lockwood* taking up its position. Seeing no crew on board, Gift suspected a trap and guessed that Union sailors were hiding in the vessel, ready to spring should Wood return that evening. But the Confederates made no such effort.[85]

The *Underwriter*'s capture and destruction marked a discreditable episode for the Union navy. Days after the vessel's demise, naval commanders would revamp their procedures for protecting gunboats at night.[86] Though improvements would be made, the surprise capture of one of the largest gunboats in the Carolina sounds resulted in a black eye. Palmer did not hesitate to voice his dissatisfaction with his colleagues in the naval arm. On Tuesday, he informed officials in Virginia, "without venturing to fix the responsibility for her capture, I may say it appears to me utterly inexcusable." Several days later, he amplified his criticism: "This shows a lamentable lack of vigilance, I conceive, on the part of the gun-boats, and I hope the lesson will be a profitable one."[87] The press broadcast concern as well. "The loss of this gunboat caused more anxiety than anything which had thus far taken place," relayed a *New York Times* correspondent. Echoing this, a writer from New Bern complained about the "sad lack of gunboats in these waters." Over the next several weeks, Union naval commanders would seek reinforcements in light of the *Underwriter*'s loss, the increased Confederate activity, and the ongoing construction of rebel ironclads.[88]

In the days following the gunboat's sinking, some trained their ire on Jacob Westervelt, the *Underwriter*'s acting master. Rumors emerged that Westervelt's Southern connections had compromised his commitment to the United States.[89] However, these accusations died down when Westervelt's corpse turned up in the river in late February. On February 29, the Union garrison at New Bern buried the native Carolinian with full honors.[90] Despite the gunboat's capture and destruction, about fifty members of the *Underwriter*'s crew managed to escape the disaster.[91] Included were the men saved by engineer Edgar Allen's heroics in seizing the *Underwriter*'s whaleboat from its rebel captors. In the midst of the losses, Allen's bravery stood out as a hopeful sign. In reflecting on the episode, one Union naval commander, John S. Barnes, noted, "So there is a little leaven to the loaf."[92]

The Confederates were mostly pleased with the results. Some, however, understood that a single sunken Union gunboat would do little to help Pickett capture New Bern. Gift provided perhaps the most accurate assessment, written several hours after the fight: "On account of not finding the vessels where we expected, the expedition has not proven so great a success as was anticipated." He added that, with the Union forces on alert, another attack would not be "feasible or prudent." Similarly, Shepardson concluded in his report to the *Richmond Dispatch*: "Although the navy did not accomplish all it anticipated, enough was done, in cutting out a gunboat under Yankee batteries." Nevertheless, Wood's effort served as a dramatic interlude to what had been, up to that point, an unproductive Confederate operation. In time, Wood's accomplishment expanded in the minds of Confederate partisans. Gift, in his later correspondence home, also began to change his tune. "The attempt of the army was a failure, but our effort for once was a complete and thorough success and the whole country here-abouts is congratulating 'our gallant little navy,'" he wrote.[93] Over the years, the *Underwriter*'s capture swelled in importance and lost its context at times, as former Confederates recalled bright spots in the struggle for their lost cause. In the end, Wood failed, yet perhaps he achieved more success than he had any right to expect.[94]

CHAPTER NINE

Beech Grove and Newport Barracks

"They Did Excellent Service"

As the *Underwriter's* hulk smoldered in the shallows of the Neuse on Tuesday morning, a quiet dawn broke over the Confederates ringing New Bern. Pickett's offensive was not going well. Hoke's column remained fixed west of Fort Totten. To the southeast, no word had arrived from Martin. Along the Trent River, Barton's soldiers woke early on Tuesday morning, expecting to launch an attack across Brice's Creek at dawn.[1] But nothing happened, so the men resumed their slumber and arose much later, "greatly refreshed from the labor and fatigue of the day before." The soldiers assembled their breakfast from the stores as commissary officers ventured out to local farms to augment the dwindling rations.[2] Throughout the day, the Confederates sat immobile. "The Yanks did not trouble us," wrote a member of Hoke's brigade, "only bombed us some, but then they only killed 11 men." Likewise, the Confederates showed no inclination to attack. It was clear that Pickett's time at New Bern was slipping away.[3]

During the day, Union artillery shelled the rebels west of the city. The cannoneers kept a close eye on the plain in front and opened up on anything that moved. "The firing was excellent," Palmer noted, "and whenever [the enemy] appeared they were forced to retire immediately."[4] The Southerners traded occasional shots with the pickets "but showed no fight."[5] More than artillery fire disturbed Tuesday's relative tranquility. Eager for information on the enemy's dispositions, Palmer ordered some of his men to probe the Confederate positions. Around 9:00 a.m., a detachment of Savage's 12th New York Cavalry ventured out on the Trent Road about a mile past the Ensley house. They did not get far. As they trotted west, a "severe fire" burst from the rifles of Clingman's North Carolina brigade tucked in the woods near the road, killing one cavalryman and wounding another. The cavalcade reversed course and reentered Fort Totten with the body of the deceased draped across one of the mounts.[6]

Taking advantage of the lull, Palmer also looked to improve his defenses and boost his force. He ordered fatigue parties to strengthen the earthworks and placed rifles in the hands of white civilians within New Bern.[7] Later, he noted that "the citizens turned out nobly and took the place of the provost guard, thus liberating an additional force for duty in the intrenchments." African American residents helped out as well. By Tuesday, Captain George Bartlett of the 27th Massachusetts had armed 900 freedmen and organized them into companies. "They did excellent service," concluded Palmer.[8] In addition, British-born Frederic Greenhalge, the chief clerk in the commissary department and future Massachusetts governor, organized a group of civil employees, procured uniforms, and marched them into the trenches north of Fort Totten.[9]

"Close within Their Works"

With no hope of progress west of New Bern, Pickett and Hoke yearned for good news from Barton. The silence was disappointing. West of Brice's Creek, Barton remained mostly idle throughout the "fair and pleasant" Tuesday, doubling his skirmishers but doing little else. On the main line, the men rested on ground made soggy by the previous evening's rain.[10] The Federals south of the Trent kept "close within their works," though gunners remained active.[11] During an exchange with Barton's batteries, Edward Eastham of the 3rd New York (Battery I) lost his hand when a piece went off prematurely.[12] Aside from this unfortunate event, the artillery duel did not amount to much.

Barton's inaction angered Pickett. In his report he would criticize his fellow Virginian for failing "to cut the railroad and telegraph to Morehead City." On Tuesday, he had hoped Barton would drive into the city's underbelly. But eventually a courier arrived at Pickett's camp that day to report that Barton had "found the work laid out for him impracticable."[13] But the displeased Pickett wanted to know more. Hoke, also eager to regain the momentum, volunteered to take his brigade and open communication with Barton's column. Guided by New Bern native and confidant Lieutenant Colonel Henry T. Guion of the 10th North Carolina, Hoke's regiments marched south over the Trent Road and cross-country to the banks of the Trent River. Hoke eventually managed to get one of Pickett's staffers, Captain Robert A. Bright, across the river on a skiff. The captain made his way to Barton's field headquarters.[14]

Barton explained that "he had been entirely misinformed as to the strength of the place, and that he pronounced the works as too strong to attack." He had not conducted an assault and had no plans to do so. Furthermore, despite two attempts, his cavalry under Colonel Baker had failed to cut the railroad, although Baker would finally manage to do so that evening, but only after "very great labor." Given the lack of progress, Bright ordered Barton to abandon the Brice's Creek approach, cross the Trent upstream, and join Pickett in an assault against the city's western defenses. Barton warned that he would not arrive until late that night or even the next day. Nevertheless, he began his return "a little before dark" on Tuesday.[15]

"Rose Right up out of the Brush"

Blunting the disappointment of Barton's failure, Tuesday yielded some good news for the Confederates. That morning, the small detachment of Union soldiers remained stranded at Beech Grove west of New Bern, well behind Confederate lines. The outpost contained a full company from the 2nd NCUV (fifty-seven men), two companies of the 99th New York (about sixty men), fourteen members of the 132nd New York, and Lieutenant William Kirby's gun section from the 3rd New York (about sixty men).[16] Most of the North Carolina Unionists defending the position had enlisted at New Bern in the previous months, drawn in by aggressive recruiting efforts. Some, in fact, had served earlier in a local rebel defense unit known as Nethercutt's Battalion. Service in that irregular unit allowed them to avoid Confederate conscription and remain near their homes. But when Confederate officials formerly assigned the unit to the 66th North Carolina in 1863, many deserted and headed to the Union lines, where they joined the 2nd NCUV. Union commanders generally assigned these men to relatively safe posts and spread them among the various garrisons in the region. However, for some reason, Company F had been inserted into the front lines along Bachelor Creek.[17]

Following Monday's fighting, the soldiers at Beech Grove understood their predicament and chose to remain in place, lying low and "hoping not to attract attention." They also prepared for an attack. Lieutenant Kirby, who had arrived with his artillery section during the fighting on Monday morning, placed his two guns in breastworks near the blockhouse, and Captain Bailey threw a picket line out around the position.[18] In New Bern, Union commanders had worked to rescue the isolated garrison. Late Monday evening, Giles F. Ward, General Palmer's aide-de-camp, volunteered to lead a breakout attempt. With five armed crew, he climbed into the *Underwriter*'s gig (hours before John Taylor Wood's attack) and rowed out to make contact with the beleaguered force. Under a severe deluge, the boat glided up the Neuse and into Bachelor Creek through the Confederate lines, passing close enough to pickets to hear rebels conversing. However, after several fruitless attempts to reach the blockhouse, Ward concluded that the swampy reaches of Bachelor Creek were simply "impossible."[19] While he tried to reach the isolated position by water, William H. Ingram of the 99th New York attempted a more conventional effort over land. But he failed too.[20]

As the Federals tried to save their comrades, the Confederates resolved to capture the isolated position. The Beech Grove blockhouse sat just south of the Washington Road facing west, about 100 yards east of the Bachelor Creek crossing. Two short trench segments fronted the structure, one on either side of the road. East of the blockhouse stood a small rural church. On Monday night, General Montgomery Corse posted men east on the Washington Road to observe the position. That force, led by Captain Robert D. Graham, included two companies (D and K) of the 56th North Carolina, along with the guns of Stribling's Battery and the Fayette Artillery.[21]

On Tuesday morning, the Confederates descended on Beech Grove from the east. Two more regiments, the 29th and 30th Virginia from Corse's brigade, joined Graham's force. Most of the attacking force advanced along the south side of the Washington Road, while the 30th Virginia moved along the road to the north.[22] The gunners raced straight down the road looking for suitable firing positions. To the north stood Bellair, a handsome Georgian manor built in the late 1770s and owned by the Richardson family. The estate's driveway angled away from the Washington Road, and an immense lawn adorned the several acres surrounding the brick mansion. The crews of the Richmond Fayette Artillery turned their teams onto the lawn near the house, a move that brought the Union blockhouse into view to the west. There, Union soldiers could be seen rushing about preparing to meet the impending attack. After finding an ideal position on the Bellair lawn, the rebels deployed their guns and sighted them toward the blockhouse. The Confederate infantrymen moved in as well.[23]

The defenders knew they had little chance. With the gray cordon tightening, Lieutenant Kirby emerged from the blockhouse carrying a flag. As he paced forward, two rebel regiments rose from the brush not 200 yards away, and Lieutenant William I. Clopton and Sergeant Major Robert I. Fleming of the Fayette Artillery stepped forward to greet him. Captain David J. Bailey, the ranking officer at the Union outpost, formally surrendered.

It had been a bloodless affair. In fact, not a shot had been fired. The parties agreed to terms, which allowed the Union officers to keep their sidearms.[24] Union reports claim that some members of the garrison escaped the Confederate net, but their numbers are unclear. According to a Confederate account, the rebels scooped up some blue-clad North Carolinians in the woods after the surrender.[25] They also seized Kirby's 3-inch steel rifled guns, a "valuable prize," as Hoke would state later, as well as "100 stand of small arms, and a supply of ammunition."[26] Lieutenant Clopton's company drove the captured cannon to the camp of the Fayette Artillery, where Pickett formally presented them to the unit. Much pleased, Clopton joked later, "I think I should send in a requisition on some yankee ordnance officer for two more parrotts."[27]

Though the captured guns gained immediate attention, the much darker repercussions of the engagement would become apparent later. For good reason, the episode struck terror among the members of the 2nd NCUV, many of whom had served in Confederate units and now found themselves prisoners of their former comrades. Postwar accounts suggest that Confederate commanders specifically targeted Beech Grove, hoping to snag these men.[28] However, no official reports reveal any concerted effort to do so. Nevertheless, the capture of these North Carolinians in blue would trigger events that spawned controversy for years to come.[29]

"Nothing but Sand and Stunted Pine"

For Pickett, Beech Grove's capture provided a silver lining in the cloud of an otherwise bleak Tuesday. The various prongs of his operation had not yielded much. Hoke remained outside New Bern, Barton was stalled at Brice's Creek, Dearing had not progressed at Fort Anderson, and Wood had captured and then lost the *Underwriter*. On top of these setbacks, James Martin had not made an appearance south of New Bern to cut off rail communications with Morehead City.[30]

Martin was running a day behind Pickett's main columns. The brigadier general, a native of Elizabeth City, had fought in the Mexican War, where he lost an arm and gained acclaim. For much of the Civil War, though, he had served inside North Carolina and proved to be a capable administrator, carrying out duties that provided him little opportunity to lead on the battlefield. The New Bern expedition gave him a chance to distinguish himself in combat. Under the plan, Martin's role was to sever all land communications between New Bern and the Union positions at Beaufort and Morehead City. His success would block reinforcements and supplies to the city along the Atlantic and North Carolina Railroad and severely hamper Palmer's ability to mount a prolonged defense.

Martin's march from Wilmington had dragged on longer than expected, a delay stemming in part from the difficult river crossings in his path, but perhaps mostly from the fact that General Whiting had not handed Martin his orders until January 28. In any case, Martin's force departed that day with portions of the 17th and 42nd North Carolina Regiments, an artillery battery (Staunton Hill Artillery), and a small cavalry force (a company of the 5th North Carolina). The route ahead covered about 100 miles over two large rivers. By Friday evening, January 29, Martin had traveled 30 miles over "heavy sandy roads."[31] During the march, he was joined by troops stationed outside Wilmington led by Colonel George Jackson, including a cavalry company under Captain Joseph Harlan (Company K, 5th South Carolina), another artillery battery, several companies of the 17th North Carolina, and the remainder of the 42nd Regiment, bringing his total force to about 2,000.[32]

At noon on Saturday, Martin reached Jacksonville and crossed his wagons and artillery over the New River on a single flatboat, consuming much of the afternoon and evening. On Sunday morning, his column continued the march as his pickets swept out ahead to arrest "every person moving about." Couriers, spreading north to open communications with Barton, learned that Pickett's attack would commence the next day and that Martin was to "push on and reach there as quickly as possible."[33]

Martin did push on. However, north of Swansboro on Sunday, a destroyed bridge over the White Oak River at Smith's Mill caused more delays. Acting brigade inspector Captain Lucien Starke and others spent much of the night constructing a "sort of dam" out of pine trees using a few tools and no nails.[34] Martin's force finally crossed this makeshift structure early on Monday morning (February 1), with more than 20 miles still ahead of them. At 8:00 a.m., Martin relayed another report to Barton, seeking news and expressing concern that his "rear is entirely uncovered except by your force." Throughout Monday, Martin's men marched along Bogue Sound toward Newport Barracks, making it about halfway there. During the day, he scooped up a deserter who volunteered details about "the position, strength, and condition" of the Union forces ahead. That evening, with rain pelting his column, Martin sent some of his wagons back over the White Oak River, fearing the roads ahead would become impassable. But his force continued to close in on the Federals.[35]

The Union troops in Martin's path fell under the command of Colonel James Jourdan, a New Yorker who had been a builder and musician before the war.[36] The colonel's area of command, known as the Beaufort subdistrict, encompassed Morehead City, Beaufort, Fort Macon, and Newport Barracks and was connected to New Bern by the main road through Carteret County; the railroad through Newport, Croatan, and Evans' Mill; and a shallow, roundabout water route up Core Sound, into Pamlico Sound, and up the Neuse River.[37] The primary posts in the subdistrict clustered near Beaufort Inlet. Morehead City, a small town of a few hundred people, had been occupied by Union forces in 1862.[38] Beaufort, a precolonial harbor town just a few miles to the east, had also been captured by the Federals early on; it sat at the blunt end of a peninsula framed by rivers and served as an important coaling station for the North Atlantic Blockading Squadron.[39] The countryside around Morehead City and Beaufort did not impress the Union men who had pulled garrison duty there. They complained about the insects, the swamps, the locals, and the poor soil. Upon arriving, a Massachusetts soldier described his surroundings as "nothing but sand and stunted pine and scrub oak and laurel brush. I thought the rebels had not ought to be blamed much for Seceding if they had to live on such soil."[40]

By Tuesday, Jourdan had received plenty of warning about the coordinated Confederate offensive.[41] Martin's late arrival and the failure of Barton's cavalry to cut the rail line had given Union commanders ample time to exchange information and much more. In fact, with a full day to shuttle troops, Jourdan had loaded most of the 158th New York on cars Monday and shipped them to New Bern along the unblocked railroad. "Vigilant and energetic," Jourdan had managed his command well over the last few days. However, some feared his force would be too small "to compete with the enemy successfully." Tuesday's events would test that notion.[42]

"We Will, We Will"

Early on Tuesday, February 2, with the *Underwriter* sunk and Pickett stalled at New Bern, Martin closed in. Under a steady rain, Colonel George Jackson led the advance along Bogue Sound. Lieutenant Colonel Robert J. Jeffords led the cavalry, joined by three infantry companies and Captain Andrew Ellis's battery (the Northampton Artillery). The balance of the infantry, artillery, and train followed, and a rear guard trailed in back under Martin's immediate command.[43] Throughout the morning, the men struggled through an "endless succession of dark, dreary swamps" that crowded the road with bamboo briar and laurel.[44] As they neared the Federal outposts, General Martin rode to the head of the column, drew up his horse, and delivered a brief, inspiring, if somewhat inaccurate address: "Soldiers, you hear the Guns of Gen'l Lee. He has come to take Newberne and he has sent you down here to take this camp and cart off supplies and he expects you will do it." "We will, we will," thundered the response.[45]

Late in the morning, while muscling over the soggy path near Bogue Sound, Martin's van encountered an enemy picket post near Gale's Creek manned by Company H of the 9th Vermont under Captain James T. Gorham. Jeffords's cavalry immediately charged the position, led by Lieutenant Noah Muse of the 5th North Carolina Cavalry (Company E). The Federal pickets fell back, and one of their officers suffered a long saber gash across his shoulder. The Yankees managed to land blows of their own. Oberon Payne, a greenhorn, reportedly brought down Lieutenant Muse and captured his riderless horse. Nevertheless, the rebels thundered on in pursuit of the retreating Federals. Many of the horses slipped in the muddy road, and some turned "somersaults," bruising the riders and breaking one horse's neck.[46]

Near Gale's Creek, Captain Gorham deployed forty armed Vermonters to meet the rebel column, while some new, unarmed recruits stood by helplessly. The defenders fired deliberately and slowly fell back to a line of trees choked with undergrowth. Martin's artillery responded, igniting the barracks, a former meetinghouse. According to Union reports, the small force twice repulsed the rebels but soon yielded to "their vastly superior numbers" and withdrew, leaving nearly a dozen of their own in rebel hands.[47]

After sweeping aside the picket post at Gale's Creek, Martin's men passed a Federal trading post and encountered a small blockhouse about half a mile away. The Confederates prepared to storm the position but found that the defenders had fled, leaving provisions, books, and personal letters behind.[48] Two and a half miles beyond the abandoned position, Martin's force reached an intersection containing yet another blockhouse. This one, known as the Bogue Sound block-house, was a "well-built, thick walled structure, surrounded by a circumvallation of earth works" and defended by sixty-two men from Company B of the 9th Vermont, led by Lieutenant Alfred Ballard, along with an old howitzer mounted on a navy carriage. In front, the Confederate cavalry reined up and waited for the infantry. When the foot soldiers arrived, they fell into line. Like the defenders at Gale's Creek, half of Ballard's men were green, most having received their muskets and cartridge boxes that morning. Against the odds, the defenders brought Martin's advance to a dead halt at about 11:00 a.m., sending solid shot from their howitzer "whizzing" over the Confederates' heads. Ellis's battery unlimbered and sent a few shells in reply.[49]

Undaunted, Martin's men attacked. Company A of the 17th North Carolina, led by Captain William Biggs and filled with men who were "well instructed as skirmishers," rushed forward to take the position. Two hundred yards from the block-house, Biggs directed his men to charge. From the rifle pits, the Vermonters "gave them a very warm reception," bringing down several, but the Tar Heels responded with a yell and bounded forward as the Union men "fled in disorder."[50] By Martin's recollection, the blockhouse "was hurriedly left by the enemy after a few discharges from our artillery." But a Union report painted a different picture, recalling "a brisk fight of about half an hour with artillery and infantry." In any event, there was no dispute about the engagement's result.[51] At the captured position, the victors found "rifles, knapsacks, clothing, and commissary stores," as well as a few wounded soldiers in blue. After this brief pause, the Confederate column continued, shifting north toward New Bern along the railroad. Martin and his men would soon encounter a more formidable obstacle at Newport Barracks. There, several companies from the 9th Vermont Infantry, two cavalry companies, and a company of the 2nd Massachusetts Heavy Artillery stood ready to greet them.[52]

When news of the Confederate advance arrived Tuesday morning, Colonel Jourdan left his headquarters at Morehead City and hopped a train for Newport Barracks. Lieutenant Colonel Valentine G. Barney had taken charge of the entire garrison there, in place of Colonel Edward Ripley, who was at Fort Monroe. Consequently, command of the 9th Vermont shifted from Barney to Captain Samuel H. Kelley.[53] Jourdan ordered Barney "to fight as long as possible, and if driven back to do so slowly, falling back on Morehead City," but only after burning the stores and throwing the guns into the Newport River. If the enemy cut the retreat to Morehead City, Barney was to proceed to Beaufort on a roundabout route passing through Newport village. After discussing matters with Barney, Jourdan loaded the sick men and quartermaster's stores on the train and headed back to Morehead City, somehow managing to complete his trip before Martin's column progressed beyond the Bogue Sound blockhouse. Back at his headquarters, Jourdan wired the news to

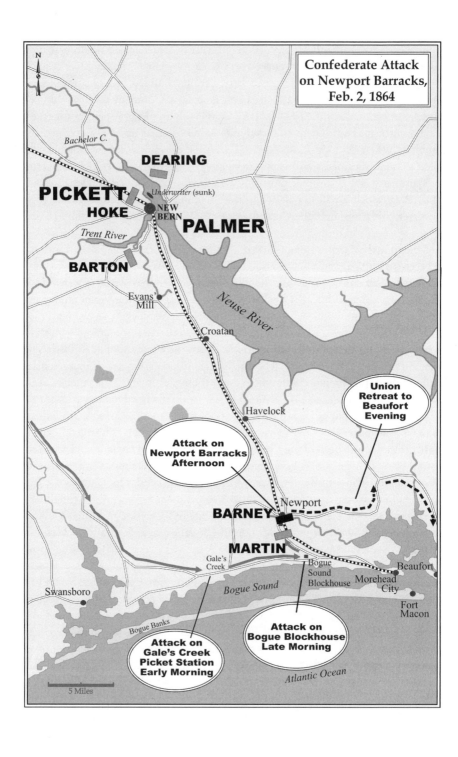

N

Confederate Attack
on Newport Barracks,
Feb. 2, 1864

Bachelor C.

DEARING

PICKETT   *Underwriter (sunk)*
HOKE   NEW
BERN   PALMER

Trent River

BARTON

Evans'
Mill

Neuse River

Croatan

Union
Retreat to
Beaufort
Evening

Attack on
Newport Barracks
Afternoon

Havelock

Newport

BARNEY

MARTIN

Gale's
Creek

Bogue
Sound
Blockhouse   Morehead
City   Beaufort

Swansboro   *Bogue Sound*

Fort
Macon

Bogue Banks

Attack on
Bogue Blockhouse
Late Morning

Attack on
Gale's Creek
Picket Station
Early Morning

Atlantic Ocean

5 Miles

Palmer. He did not despair, though, reporting, "I am confident in my ability to hold the Morehead line."[54]

Causing "the Very Ground to Quake"

As Jourdan and Barney hastily prepared, General Martin's column turned for Newport Barracks, about 3 miles distant, and marched north, "throwing their right flank across the railroad."[55] Newport Barracks offered a substantial target. If Martin could seize it, he could easily destroy the rail and road bridges across the Newport River and sever an important communication line between New Bern and the coast. The barracks themselves and a fort lay south of a small village variously called Newport, Shepardsville, or Lucknow, which contained about fifteen houses, three stores, and a small church. "Bad and marshy" ground dominated the area around the town—"a pretty miserably poor country," in one Northerner's opinion. The landscape was sprinkled here and there with small corn or sweet potato patches, as well as stands of pine trees harvested for their pitch. South of town beyond the Newport River, between the railroad and the county road, the Federals had sited their log barracks in a "pleasant" spot on sandy soil.[56] Edward Ripley, who arrived in November to command the post, found the camp "intolerably dirty" and "the Forts, wretchedly constructed in a shifting soil . . . rapidly going to destruction."[57]

With the rebels approaching, Barney readied his men. The 9th Vermont could not boast of a particularly distinguished wartime record. During the Maryland Campaign in 1862, the entire regiment was surrendered at Harpers Ferry and then spent several months as prisoners in Chicago's Camp Douglas. Throughout much of 1863, they served in southeastern Virginia and then transferred to New Bern in the fall. As Martin's column approached, the Vermonters likewise had many inexperienced men in their ranks. On January 27, 350 raw recruits arrived from the north, nearly doubling the regiment's size to 844 men and most certainly diluting its combat readiness. Nevertheless, Barney sought to challenge Martin in the field. Accordingly, Captain Kelley gathered the regiment, delivered a short speech, and marched his men south to meet the enemy.[58]

Around 3:00 p.m., Martin's force appeared about 2 miles away from Barney's position. As the Confederates closed, the Federal gunners opened fire. "Just as our forces were emerging from a dense wood into an open field," one Southerner recalled, "they were admonished by a shell from a six-pounder Parrott gun that the enemy were about to contest their further advance." According to one of the attackers, the Union shelling was by "no means lazy or childlike" but nevertheless "poorly directed."[59] As the rounds whistled toward him, Martin deployed his command in a large clearing and formed his lines perpendicular to the main road on his left, with the rail line on his right.[60] Ahead lay an open field about 600 yards long with a swamp at the end. Martin placed the 17th North Carolina under Lieutenant Colonel John E. Lamb on the right and Colonel John E. Brown's 42nd North Carolina on the left. Still farther to the left, Colonel George Jackson ventured ahead with a detachment from the 17th. Captain Ellis's crews unlimbered their guns between the two wings. The cavalry and the remaining guns, the Staunton Hill Artillery under Captain Andrew Paris, remained in reserve. Ellis's battery replied to the Union fire, causing "the very ground to quake with its deafening thunder" and filling "the air with the whizzing noise and loud screams of its shot and shell."[61]

Waiting to greet the Confederates, the Vermonters formed a line on rising ground south of the fort, beyond the swamp and open field. To augment the infantry rifles, Lieutenant Eugene Viele had rolled a cannon forward from the works by hand, and this piece sent the initial rounds toward the Southerners. Captain Kelley stretched his Vermonters across part of the clearing and nudged skirmishers out to the front, some taking positions in the swamp. The skirmishers, led by twenty-year-old Lieutenant Thomas S. Peck, crept through the trees and observed the Confederates on the other side forming for battle. Given the shortage of staff officers, the regiment's surgeon, Walter Carpenter, stepped in to observe the enemy's advance and shuttle orders to different portions of the field.[62]

The 17th and 42nd North Carolina formed up, still straddling the road. Two companies from each regiment edged forward as skirmishers. Soon, the order to charge rang along the Confederate battle line.[63] Unseen in the distant woods, Federal riflemen fired their first volley, and immediately the "musketry became animated on both sides."[64] The Vermont skirmishers in the brush emptied several rounds into the rebels while gradually edging rearward.[65] Lieutenant Viele's cannon continued to fire, scoring a direct hit on a Confederate caisson and then showering the rebels with grapeshot.[66] William A. James, a private in the 17th North Carolina, wrote: "I was in front rite facen the artilrey and sharpe shooters, their was two cannon balls that cum near taken me A way and meney balls whisken close."[67] The Confederate fire was just as dangerous. During the engagement, a bullet zipped two inches past Barney's head.[68]

The Federals stubbornly gave ground, eating up daylight as they unleashed volley after volley. Viele's single gun provided effective service, with little help from the Massachusetts artillerymen back in the fort. But Captain Paris pushed his rebel crews forward and "poured a storm of canister and shell through thickets . . . almost impenetrable to a musket ball." This seemed to make the difference, and the Union defenders finally withdrew toward the fort. Barney and Kelley's men stepped back from the thick strip of trees, firing as they did.[69] The fight continued for perhaps an hour as the Confederates pushed the Vermonters backward. In the minds of some Federals, their stand lasted much longer.[70] But Confederates remembered it differently. According to Captain John L. Swain of the 17th North Carolina, "the enemy showed a bold front but soon broke in confusion before the reckless impetuosity of our boys."[71]

With the clash in the open ground at an end, the Vermonters trudged back to the works at Newport Barracks with the rebels on their heels. Once past the bushes and trees, Martin sent his men in for a final rush, throwing skirmishers out ahead of the ranks. But a final assault was unnecessary, and the defenders abandoned the position altogether.[72] The cannons in the fort, manned by Company D, 2nd Massachusetts Heavy Artillery, proved ineffective. One Vermonter insinuated that the gunners "showed the white feather generally, not a gun being fired from the fort."[73] Colonel Jourdan agreed, later complaining that the artillerymen "rendered but little assistance as a company, having failed to properly work their guns." Their commander, Captain Russell Conwell, had inexplicably stepped away from the fort early in the morning, leaving inexperienced officers in charge.[74]

According to General Martin, the Federal soldiers fled past the barracks; set fire to the storehouses and stables, with some horses trapped inside; and crossed the road and rail bridges over the Newport River.[75] One rebel witness recalled that the Yankees "offered us but feeble resistance, flying before us like chaff before the wind." He believed the Federals could have stood firm at the fort, but, he sneered, such a "course their unparalleled cowardice would not allow." While the New Englanders fled, the Stars and Stripes remained flapping over the deserted stronghold. "This was soon hauled down," recounted another Confederate. It was then trampled in the dust and ripped to pieces, like a "slice of bloody meat, when thrown to a pack of starving wolves."[76]

"Great Danger of All Retreat Being Cut Off"

The Confederates advanced to the bridges stretching over the sluggish, deep, 100-foot-wide Newport River. To impede Martin's force, the Vermonters set about destroying the spans. A detail under Lieutenant Theodore S. Peck tended to the highway bridge to the west, ripping up the planks there. With no tar or turpentine at hand, they fired the pine stringers using dried grass torn from the ground nearby. At the railroad trestle just to the east, about seventy men from Company K, led by Lieutenant Erastus W. Jewett, directed a continuous fire at the rebels while Lieutenant Josiah O. Livingstone and surgeon W. S. Vincent set the structure alight. Jewett and Peck would receive the Medal of Honor for their efforts. The bridge burners gained valuable time for their comrades and helped their regiment escape from the village. However, in doing so, they isolated more than the rebels. A few of their comrades who were trapped on the southern bank threw themselves into the Newport River in desperation and drowned.[77] Mary Phinney, a nurse stationed in Morehead City, identified these unfortunate men as members of the 2nd Massachusetts Heavy Artillery. Phinney, who had served at a Union hospital in Alexandria, Virginia, earlier in the war, was not an admirer of the 9th Vermont and blamed that unit for leaving the others behind.[78]

North of the river stood a small redoubt in the village itself, which remained un-touched. However, Barney found that the Massachusetts men had spiked the guns there without firing a shot. In the end, he decided to leave and "retired under cover of the darkness in the direction of Beaufort," taking one of the guns with him, losing another that became mired in the mud, and disabling the rest.[79] The entire engagement consumed only a few hours of the afternoon. Faced with the "great danger of all retreat being cut off," Colonel Barney abandoned the post, concluding there was little "use wasting the lives of our men to oppose so large a force."[80] With night approaching, the Confederates chose not to pursue.[81] Barney's force reached Beaufort at sunrise the next morning, "hungry, faint, and exhausted" and having lost several dozen men during the engagement.[82]

At about 8:00 p.m., the Confederates made camp at the captured barracks, where they found mounds of commissary stores, many small arms, and eight pieces of artillery. They also gathered about ninety prisoners. The captured supplies would feed Martin's entire force for the expedition's duration. The Confederates also de-stroyed a thousand barrels of turpentine.[83] The stores impressed the rebels. One Tar Heel quipped that the "poor fellows there were living so well any thing a man wanted they had it—the people [back home] never lived so well as the yankee soldiers did in [Newport]."[84] That evening, dinner included ham, eggs, bacon, strawberry preserves, molasses, biscuits, butter, crackers, tea, and coffee with white sugar.[85] Martin would catalog the spoils, which included "1 flag, 10 pieces of artillery, 20 barrels of powder, several hundred small-arms, 200 boxes fixed ammunition for artillery, a considerable quantity of forage and other stores." Martin also mentioned the capture of six African Americans. His men destroyed the railroad bridge as well as some track and trestlework. His command lost six killed, including Captain Leith of the 17th North Carolina and Lieutenant Muse of the cavalry, and about fifteen wounded. For want of transportation, the Tar Heels buried the dead men.[86]

"Done the Very Best That Possibly Could Be"

The Newport Barracks victory furnished some good news for the Confederates of the Old North State and some rare accolades for James Martin. His performance answered lingering questions in the eyes of some. "Gen. Martin has at last done something," wrote a civilian several weeks later.[87] A letter in the *Wilmington Journal* explained that no one had ever questioned the general's "ability to organize, drill, and discipline troops," but with the victory at Newport, "his courage in the field" had "been amply vindicated." The same correspondent ranked Martin's achieve-ment "among the most brilliant ever won upon the soil of the old North State," an assessment that was probably accurate, given the Confederates' track record up to that point in the war.[88] From Wilmington, General Whiting informed Martin that he had "done all and more than General Lee directed."[89]

While the Confederates celebrated the small victory, the fight raised a host of questions for Federal commanders. With the better part of a regiment protected by fortifications, the defenders might have done more to hold the post. In their reports and reminiscences, Northerners pointed to two root problems: the many raw recruits at the garrison, and the poor performance of the 2nd Massachusetts Heavy Artillery, particularly Captain Russell Conwell.[90]

Captain Conwell's absence would lead to a guilty verdict at his court-martial and dismissal from the service. It would also produce a long trail of ink over the next several decades, in part because Conwell became a well-known public figure in the late nineteenth century. After the war, he enjoyed significant success as an orator, minister, philanthropist, and founder of Temple University. The reasons for Conwell's absence on February 2 were unclear at the time and remain so. The court did not find a clear explanation for his absence. However, after the verdict, general orders from Butler's headquarters stated, "There would seem upon the evidence to be but two causes for his desertion: one was fear, and other insanity."[91]

Contemporary accounts underscore the curious nature of the case. For example, two months after the battle, Lieutenant Colonel Barney from the 9th Vermont wrote home: "I have been up here at Newbern as a witness in the case of Capt Conwell who was in Commd of the heavy Artilery at Newport Bks at the time or just before the Attack by the Rebs on that place. I dont know what will be done in his case but I fear he will be dismissed [from] the service. His case is a very misterious one and no one knows why he left Newport at the time he did, as yet." Conwell would eventually concoct his own story, which prominently featured a subordinate named "Johnnie Ring," who had supposedly died while retrieving Conwell's sword from the barracks and crossing the burning bridge. The Johnnie Ring story and other representations about his war service have eluded substantiation. Conwell would rehash the account again and again in the postwar years to receptive audiences.[92]

Blame for the loss spread well beyond Conwell. Some Confederates thought the Vermonters had given up their post too easily.[93] Others agreed. Nurse Mary Phinney at Morehead City asserted that the Vermonters' lack of grit and experience had doomed the position. "Had I really believed the Ninth and Cavalry made a good stand and had really lost many men," she wrote, "I might have felt different; but as they once passed six months in Chicago as paroled prisoners, and Harper's Ferry was all the fight they ever were in, I believed they would skedaddle ingloriously, as I believe they did."[94] Another account, from a Vermonter serving in the Signal Corps, echoed the contempt for the defenders, asserting that members of the 9th "all ran like sheep they never stopt to fire a shot but ran for the woods."[95]

Such criticism seems excessive, for the battle's result was not really surprising. Barney's force, with about 900 men, fought at a significant disadvantage against Martin's larger column. Colonel Jourdan, the district commander, certainly thought so and assured Barney that he had "done the very best that possibly could be" accomplished under the circumstances. In his report, Jourdan commended Barney and Captain Kelley "for the faithful manner in which they executed [their] orders." Barney wrote home that he had lost eight killed, fifteen wounded, and thirty missing.[96] He estimated the enemy had lost one captain, two lieutenants, and fifteen men killed and as many as thirty wounded.[97]

"I Am Very Much Embarrassed to Know What to Do"

On Tuesday evening, Martin's next move was unclear. He still had not heard from Barton or Pickett. He sent messengers north to New Bern but received nothing in return. At 8:00 p.m., he wrote to Whiting and explained, "I am very much embarrassed to know what to do on account of my entire ignorance of the state of affairs at New Berne." At 9:30 p.m., he sent a similar note to Barton seeking news and instructions. Although he felt isolated and exposed, he did not plan to sit and wait. Martin believed that "only a few organized commands" remained in the vicinity, and he planned to move on Morehead City and occupy it Wednesday morning.[98]

To the east, Colonel Jourdan prepared to defend Morehead City and Beaufort. With most of the 158th New York away at New Bern, his remaining force consisted of only a detachment of the 2nd North Carolina Union Volunteers and 200 recently arrived recruits assigned to the 158th New York, along with two artillery pieces, a 12-pounder Wiard, and a 24-pounder howitzer. With the help of civilians, Jourdan's men dug a line of earthworks to protect the town and advanced pickets toward the Bogue Sound blockhouse and Newport Barracks.[99] Jourdan's strength increased dramatically early Wednesday morning when Colonel Barney and his Vermonters arrived from Newport, dejected and exhausted after the previous day's defeat. He also received help from the navy in the form of several small gunboats.[100]

As Jourdan organized his men on Tuesday evening, the news of the rebel offensive alarmed Morehead City's inhabitants. Nurse Mary Phinney wrote that such "a scurrying time you never saw." She observed men loading the regimental and company stores onto boats and complained that everything "seemed to be thought of except the patients." The citizens in town were in a panic, and anxious refugees streamed in from the countryside. After packing her own bags, Phinney ventured out to the defenses. By her estimate, 300 men had gathered to repulse the expected attack behind the hastily constructed trenches. Across Bogue Sound, she caught the streaks of the signal flares and could see the newly arrived gunboats.[101] With the defensive preparations complete, Phinney and her fellow Unionists watched and waited to see what the rebels would do next.

CHAPTER TEN

Decisions at New Bern

"I Deemed It Prudent . . . to Withdraw"

By Tuesday evening, February 2, Pickett considered the future of his expedition. It was not promising. West of New Bern, his forces sat immobile, pinned by Union gunners. To the north and south, Dearing and Barton had accomplished nothing. Union gunboats continued to ply the Neuse, and reinforcements were undoubtedly on their way. Martin's victory that afternoon at Newport Barracks would bring heartening news, but it meant little in light of the other failures. Most importantly, Pickett's troops were running out of rations. Faced with these conditions, the general convened a council of war on Tuesday evening to consider the next steps. At the meeting, he received contradictory advice. Hoke strongly recommended an attack, a grand assault against New Bern's ramparts. The young general did not expect Union reinforcements to arrive anytime soon and believed success was still possible.[1] Similarly, Clingman urged Pickett to demand the garrison's unconditional surrender and conduct an "immediate assault" should the demand be refused.[2] Not everyone concurred. Ransom argued that an attack would be "madness," but he "would go wherever ordered."[3] Ultimately, Pickett rejected Hoke and Clingman's advice and chose to end the offensive. Later, he would explain his decision this way: "The enemy having had ample time to re-enforce both by water and railroad, the trains running in constantly night and day from Morehead City, and in fact the whole plan by which the place was to be reduced having failed, I deemed it prudent, after consultation with my officers, to withdraw, which we did at our leisure."[4] Accordingly, Pickett halted further operations at New Bern and ordered his men back to Kinston.[5]

In Hoke's camp late Tuesday night, Lieutenant Colonel Guion received orders to pack up and leave in a few hours. Curious about these instructions, he caught up with Hoke shortly after 11:00 p.m. and found "despair depicted on his countenance." Hoke identified Barton's failure as the driving force behind the decision. "Pickett is uneasy for fear the enemy [is] reinforcing," Hoke explained, "and we are ordered to move back at half past 2 o'clock. I bring up the rear." Pickett's orders left the young general visibly embittered. "Too bad, too bad," Hoke complained. "The place is ours if only I could make General Pickett believe it but it does no good, no good, he won't listen to me." Referring to his improvised plan to capture the Union train on Monday, Hoke told Guion, "Oh Colonel I wish we had carried out [that] plan, we would now be in New Bern." In the wake of the war council, however, Hoke had thoroughly abandoned any hope of success. "Too late now," he concluded. "I must be up at 2 o'clock and will take a short nap."[6]

To mask the withdrawal on Tuesday night, the Confederates deployed their musicians. "After dark the rebel bands serenaded us," wrote General Palmer. The Confederate ensemble played "Bonnie Blue Flag" and other Southern standards, much to the enjoyment of the Federals. Not "to be outdone in politeness," a band in Fort Totten "gave some patriotic airs from the top of the traverse," including "Rally Round the Flag," according to Palmer.[7] The Confederates replied with "Dixie." Palmer's official dispatch painted the impromptu concert as a rare instance of mutual goodwill. However, the amiable feelings were apparently short-lived. According to one account, Lieutenant Charles F. Gladding, a Rhode Islander in Fort Rowan, "thought the serenade would not be complete unless he joined in with some music of his own." He aimed a 100-pounder Parrott toward the rebel band out near the railroad and fired, halting the musical exchange. Even before the tunes ended, though, Captain Henry Splaine of the 17th Massachusetts suspected the rebels had put on more than a musical performance. Speaking to Lieutenant Phil Mason, he speculated that the enemy was retreating, and their music was "only throwing dust in our eyes to cover their retrograde movements."[8] He was right.

With the music hanging in the air, Pickett's forces prepared to leave the front and return to Kinston. Most of the men began their trek sometime after midnight. Many units would not reach Kinston until Friday afternoon (February 5).[9] North of the Neuse River, Dearing's column withdrew shortly after noon on Wednesday and began a 40-mile trek back to Kinston, camping at Swift Creek that evening. Barton's men departed Tuesday night to join Pickett west of New Bern, leaving large fires to mask their withdrawal.[10] At Pollocksville, they placed a pontoon bridge over the Trent. However, when they received Pickett's orders canceling the entire operation, Barton's pioneers disassembled the bridge and headed for Kinston, crossing the river farther upstream.[11]

The journey back was not easy. "I never have seen such muddy roads in all my life," recalled a member of Ransom's brigade, "and some of our men had not eat anything that day."[12] The mud "was everywhere over our shoes, often up to your knees, and sometimes waist deep," wrote one Virginian. Some became so glued in the mire that they "had to be pulled out like a cow in the spring of the year." One unlucky soul sank to his waist and cried out, "Well, if I just had three days rations, I'd lie here til it sorter dried out."[13] Henry Chambers of the 49th North Carolina recalled that briar-choked swamps funneled traffic onto the mired road. During the retreat, some of the Virginians torched pine orchards to illuminate the route, along with the faces of the weary, mud-caked soldiers.[14] When Barton's men finally arrived in Kinston on Thursday, they stretched out and sunned themselves on the "broom sedge" and boiled their pork rations "over their hot fires, recounting their adventures over the last few days."[15]

John Taylor Wood's sailors also withdrew. After consulting with Pickett on Tuesday evening, his flotilla began the long pull back up the Neuse to Kinston. Touching the shore, the men dragged the boats up the hill to the train depot, where a string of gondola cars waited for the trip north. In two days they reached Petersburg, where they portaged their vessels to the Appomattox and rowed them back to the James River Squadron. Back home, the men proudly displayed their craft to their comrades, scarred by the rounds fired from the *Underwriter* and the New Bern shore batteries.[16]

South of New Bern, Martin also pulled back. After the Newport Barracks victory, he had received no clear direction from anyone. However, on Wednesday, messages arrived from Barton announcing the expedition's termination and directing Martin to withdraw. Martin departed Thursday morning, eventually reaching Wilmington on February 10. For several days, Jeffords's cavalry remained behind to harass the Federals, doing damage along the railroad and to the deserted outposts at Havelock, Croatan, and Evans' Mill.[17]

The lingering Confederate cavalry made the Union soldiers and civilians at Morehead City anxious.[18] Writing on February 4, Mary Phinney noted that black refugees "began to flock in; they came by hundreds, such frightened beings, leaving everything except their children behind them." Citizens in town took up arms, and many pitched in to improve the defenses.[19] Colonel Jourdan kept his forces active, ensuring that Martin's men no longer posed a threat. He pushed up the railroad and reoccupied Newport Barracks with the 9th Vermont and the newly arrived 21st Connecticut.[20] Over the next few days, the Federals continued to chase reports of rebel cavalry activity.[21] Finally, on February 9, Jourdan's men ventured southwest along Bogue Sound past Gale's Creek to the White Oak River near Pelletier's Mills and found no rebels to speak of. By that time, Martin had nearly reached Wilmington.[22]

"Co-operation with General Butler"

Early on Wednesday, February 3, Palmer at New Bern learned from soldiers along the line that Pickett had evacuated the front.[23] "All was quiet" when Palmer rode the lines at 3:00 a.m. "I was not surprised when I discovered they had retired," he wrote, "although I certainly thought with their large force they would make a strong effort to capture this place." However, he "never had any fears as to [his command's] ability to hold the position." Now that the danger had passed, Palmer turned his attention to reopening communications with Morehead City and Beaufort. He also sent out cavalry out toward Kinston to track the rebel withdrawal. Wednesday brought news that naval support was headed Palmer's way. By the afternoon of February 4, several gunboats arrived from Plymouth, including the *Miami, South-field,* and *Whitehead.* For the Federals, the immediate crisis in North Carolina was over. With the Confederate force gone, about a hundred deserters emerged from the brush and the woods and gave themselves up to Union pickets. Most of the exhausted rebels belonged to North Carolina regiments, with some hailing from Virginia and Georgia. The demoralized men provided Union officers with a good picture of Pickett's order of battle.[24]

In Virginia, news of the Confederate offensive had triggered notable events at the hands of the energetic, ever-scheming Benjamin Butler. Concerned about the rebel threat in North Carolina, and sensing an opportunity for himself, Butler proposed two operations to relieve pressure on the New Bern garrison. First, he urged Henry Halleck to approve a large raid against Richmond by his own troops on the peninsula. With the aid of intelligence gathered by Union spymaster Elizabeth Van Lew, he hoped to dash into the city and free Union prisoners confined at Libby Prison. Second, he recommended that Major General George G. Meade's Army of the Potomac conduct a demonstration against Robert E. Lee's army west of Fredericksburg to prevent Lee from reinforcing Richmond and North Carolina.[25]

Although Halleck signed off on Butler's scheme, it was greeted with hostility by Major General John Sedgwick, temporarily commanding the Army of the Potomac in place of the ailing Meade.[26] But after a testy exchange with Butler, Sedgwick reluctantly agreed to help "as far as I can by vigorous demonstrations, and take advantage of such chances as may occur."[27] On Saturday, February 6, Sedgwick conducted an advance along the Rapidan River, where his men became embroiled in some bloody fighting. At Morton's Ford, a Second Corps division crossed the river and clashed with Richard Ewell's corps, costing the Federals 262 casualties. In a bitter note drafted after the engagement, Sedgwick did not hide his unhappiness with Butler's scheme. "One result of the co-operation with General Butler," he jabbed, "has been to prove that it has spoilt the best chance we had for a successful attack on the Rapidan."[28]

Butler's operation to liberate Union prisoners at Richmond similarly failed. In fact, his raid fizzled before it began. The column left Williamsburg and arrived at Bottom's Bridge on the Chickahominy River well before sunrise Sunday morning. However, acting on a deserter's tip, Confederate troops completely blocked the passage to Richmond and abruptly ended the raid.[29] As it turned out, Butler's machinations accomplished little. His efforts did not materially aid the North Carolina district, which was already free of immediate danger when these events occurred in Virginia. At the same time, Butler's push harmed the main Union army in Virginia and undoubtedly decreased his stock in the eyes of many.

"The Great Valor Displayed by a Handful of Union Troops"

After Pickett's men left New Bern, the Union and Confederate commanders assessed the expedition's results. Despite the number of troops involved, casualties were quite low. With the exception of the fight at Bachelor Creek (326 Union casualties, 302 of them prisoners) and the capture of Newport Barracks (about 60 Union casualties), the operation had been largely devoid of substantial combat. It certainly would not rank as one of the war's more significant or decisive campaigns, by any means. Nevertheless, it had been full of close calls, including the attack on the *Underwriter* and Hoke's near seizure of the Union train. Broadly speaking, the number of men and resources devoted to the operation heralded a strong Confederate resolve to achieve lasting gains in North Carolina. For the Federals, the offensive raised the alarm and demonstrated that, even with Union forces poised to go on the offensive in other theaters, Federal posts in the Old North State remained vulnerable.[30]

For New Bern's defenders, it had been an exhausting several days. Palmer and his staff "were incessantly active during the attack," observed a *New York Times* correspondent.[31] Giles Ward, Palmer's aide-de-camp, did not sleep for forty-five hours during the crisis. Only after Palmer received additional confirmation of the Confederates' complete withdrawal did the general and his men stand down.[32] By Sunday, February 7, Palmer, still in temporary command for the absent John Peck, had ordered his forces back to their original positions on the Bachelor Creek line.[33] Three days later and a full week after Pickett's departure, Peck returned to New Bern and issued general orders announcing that he had given "up his leave of absence" and returned to his post after "learning of the desperate advance of the rebel hordes upon his lines in quest of bread, meat, clothing, and plunder." He had come back "not so much from doubt of the ability of the troops to hurl back the enemy as to share with them the honors, toils, and privations of the opening campaign." Along with this bombast he expressed appreciation to Palmer, Jourdan, Amory, and Claassen for orchestrating Pickett's repulse and to the garrison for earning "fresh laurels."[34]

Peck's pronouncements aside, there was time for sound reflection and analysis. From the mouths of deserters and prisoners, Union officers obtained an excellent grasp of the enemy's operation and the reasons for its failure. Many puzzled over Pickett's reluctance to assault the city's fortifications. "I certainly thought with their large force they would make a strong effort to capture this place," Palmer later stated.[35] A member of the 132nd New York agreed and noted that the "great query here in military circles is why did the enemy abandon the enterprise." Some believed the Federals could not have concentrated sufficient troops at any one point to oppose a determined attack.[36] Palmer also recognized that General Barton, despite having arrived in good time, had failed because he "could not cross Brice's Creek without bridging it" and retired "without effecting anything."[37]

The New Bern battle produced some reason for Federal cheer. The popular *Leslie's Illustrated* celebrated the victory and featured a brief account of the successful defense. A large engraving of African American volunteers passing through the city's streets adorned the newspaper's cover. Noting that both black and white citizens had pitched in to protect the city, the article added that "the city was loud in its exultation" after Pickett's withdrawal, and "one of the strange sights was the negro volunteers marching down Broad Street, singing the John Brown song and other melodies of the kind, not at all to the satisfaction of some original secessionists still residing in the town."[38]

Union commanders also pointed out the bright spots. Palmer pegged his men's "stout resistance" and the successful stand at the Neuse Road bridge as crucial in thwarting Pickett's design. Certainly, Abram Haring's performance at Bachelor Creek stood out. Haring and his men had been instrumental in delaying Pickett's column and giving precious time to the New Bern defenders.[39] Peter Claassen related, without exaggeration, Haring's feat: "With eleven men [he] heroically held that all-important point for hours, against thousands of the enemy." In congratulatory orders, Claassen asserted that the lieutenant's efforts stood "foremost in the action."[40] An anonymous writer from New Bern agreed. "If it had not been for the great valor displayed by a handful of Union troops," he recorded, "the affair would have been a very unpleasant thing."[41]

Haring's accomplishment would later gain him the Medal of Honor, a decoration he requested himself in a letter that began, "I beg to call your attention to the following statement and if consistent for the award of a Medal of Merit I should be pleased to be put in the way of getting it."[42] Using Claassen's report as corroboration, the War Department accepted the petition, and the medal was issued in 1890.[43] Haring would also attain notoriety in the press. In 1897, the *New York Sun* featured Haring in a novelty story after his doctor discovered a tooth lodged inside his tongue, the relic of an old war wound. When the reporter asked about his exploits at Bachelor Creek, Haring simply said, "None of us ever knew how many were there. We just knew that the bridge was there for us to hold and we held it."[44] In 1901, a colorful and surely embellished account of his deeds appeared in *Everybody's Magazine.*[45]

Colonel Claassen, the commander in Haring's sector, had managed the battle and the withdrawal at Bachelor Creek adequately. Afterward, however, his report teemed with awkward attempts to avoid responsibility for the morning's low points. He sought to distance himself from Lieutenant Colonel Fellows's capture as well as the rebel seizure of the Beech Grove blockhouse. At the same time, he did not miss an opportunity to emphasize his own role during the day. He pointed out the personal risk he ran in withdrawing his men and claimed that his presence prevented them "from rushing pell-mell into camp endeavoring to save their" personal belong-ings.[46] Claassen nevertheless complimented "the brave, calm, and implicit obedient conduct of all my officers."[47] The Bachelor Creek fight would mark Claassen's most important battlefield command of the war. After the conflict, he returned to a suc-cessful career in banking. Unfortunately, in his twilight years he failed spectacularly, becoming ensnared in an embezzlement scandal that landed him in prison before his frailty led to a presidential pardon from Grover Cleveland.[48]

Beyond the individual performances, the overall Union effort was largely suc-cessful. The defenses performed true to their design. The network of picket posts, blockhouses, and modest trenches at Bachelor Creek delayed the attackers long enough for Federal commanders to fill the city's main fortifications. Those strong inner defenses, especially Fort Totten, discouraged any further attack by Pickett from that direction. To the south, the works constructed on the Trent River and the defenses arrayed behind Brice's Creek quelled any enthusiasm for an attack by Barton. Other infantry and artillery units performed well, including the garrison at Fort Anderson across the Neuse, which held out against Dearing's force. The Signal Corps also rendered highly effective service, advising headquarters "of the smallest movement of the enemy at any point of the line." In his report, Palmer doled out ample praise for the telegraphers and signalmen. "At no time, I suspect, during the present war has the utility of the military telegraph and the signal corps been more fully demonstrated than during this late attack."[49]

Next to these bright spots, several shadows fell on the Union efforts. Palmer focused his disappointment on the *Underwriter* affair, contending the gunboat's loss demonstrated "a lamentable lack of vigilance . . . and I hope the lesson will be a profitable one." He complained about the navy, noting that only two or three small gunboats were present at New Bern at the time of the *Underwriter*'s demise. As for additional naval support, Palmer wrote, "I have no idea of the locality of the others."[50] The gunboat's loss was not the only problem. The seizure of Newport Bar-racks, the capture of Colonel Fellows of the 17th Massachusetts, and the wholesale capitulation of the Beech Grove garrison provided stings of their own.[51]

"Too Vital to Be Exposed to the Possibility of Recapture"

In the pause following Pickett's withdrawal, Union officers, soldiers, and the North-ern press took note of the political component behind the Confederate offensive and looked to the future. The *New York Times* correctly concluded that, in conducting the expedition, the Confederates sought to check "the growing disaffection in North Car-olina with the Confederate Government." The editors expected that Pickett's failure would damage efforts to keep North Carolina firmly in the Confederacy.[52] Charles Flusser, the naval commander at Plymouth, agreed and surmised that many North

Carolina citizens were primed to rejoin the Union, but only if slavery remained intact.[53] General Peck predicted that President Davis "would scourge [the state's] people with his armies until the last knell of the revolution shall be sounded."[54] But Confederate partisans took issue with reports of unhappiness. "Too many false tales are circulated about growing dissatisfaction," reported William Shepardson after his return from the expedition. "Wherever I went, the people, without exception, were loyal and true to our government." He concluded that the action of "a few traitors alone has brought this general accusation against the State."[55]

Despite the Confederate setback, many Federals suspected the offensive augured more of the same in the coming weeks. Anticipating further trouble, General Peck sought reinforcements from Butler, including a regiment of cavalry and an infantry brigade, to defend the Union positions.[56] The navy recognized weaknesses too. On February 4, 1864, Rear Admiral Phillips Lee urged Secretary Welles to send several heavy-gunned, double-ended boats with drafts of no more than 8½ feet to manage the shallow waters.[57] Less than a week later, the 1,173-ton *Eutaw* steamed from Baltimore, and after grounding on the Hatteras bar, it eventually made its way into the North Carolina sounds.[58]

The Northern press also viewed the New Bern attack as a warning. The *New York Times* emphasized the city's importance to "the campaigns yet to be carried on in the Coast States," particularly if Union success in Virginia pushed Confederate forces southward. New Bern, the center of operations in North Carolina, was "too vital to be exposed to the possibility of recapture." The editors questioned the wisdom behind the army's seemingly half-hearted efforts to protect Union positions in the state. "We hope that few men, citizens and undisciplined negroes, however willing they may be to act, will not be called into service again to enable us to feel any degree of safety."[59] The *New York Tribune* observed that "the garden of North Carolina, with all its extensive water communications," had cost much in blood and treasure and that control of the eastern waterways was "morally equivalent to the possession of the whole state." The paper argued that the lack of an adequate defense made a "mockery" of Union "military pretensions."[60]

Pickett's operation also pointed out the potential weaknesses in Federal strategy. Since 1862, Union commanders had dispersed their forces among multiple posts, operating under the assumption that their fortifications and naval superiority would repel any threat. The Confederate attempt against New Bern called that long-standing approach into question. Had Wood captured the *Underwriter* or had Hoke taken the train and ridden his men into the city, the Confederate offensive might have ended much differently. Since gaining these positions early in the war, Union commanders from both the army and the navy had debated whether to concentrate their forces in the state. To be sure, the multiple garrisons allowed them to project power into the surrounding countryside and furnished a platform for large operations. But up to this point, Union officials had largely declined to take advantage of such benefits. The rebel attack on New Bern, following on the heels of the Washington siege the year before, demonstrated the risk of dispersing Union strength among multiple posts. Looking forward, perhaps it was time for Federal commanders to reassess their approach.

"Our Well-Formed Plans . . . Miscarried"

The Federal missteps at New Bern were small compared with the rebel failures. Nevertheless, many Southerners sought to put a good face on the effort. Back in Richmond, Robert E. Lee tried to find an upside. In a dispatch to Robert Hoke, the general stated that "much was accomplished," and he hoped "the information obtained will secure future success." He also acknowledged the problems involved in a combined attack, particularly the difficulties in harmonizing all operations on "an extensive field."[61] Lee's role in proposing and planning the operation remained somewhat of a secret. Several days after the expedition, his aide, Walter Taylor, traded a little a gossip with his fiancée. "How do you know where such movements have their origin," he mused. "But I mustn't claim too much for our chief. I fear I am already too proud of him."[62]

The Confederate press also sought to splash some sunshine on the results. The peace-leaning *Daily Progress* in Raleigh proclaimed the operation "a brilliant success" and concluded that it was "folly to sacrifice good men to take Newbern" before an adequate defense of the post could be arranged. The *Staunton Spectator* labeled the New Bern reconnaissance "very successful."[63] D. K. McRae, an injured veteran who had accompanied the expedition, contended that the "'Yankee brethren' about Newbern have had a sound thrashing and a most awful scare."[64]

Many accounts focused on the supplies captured from the outer camps and Pickett's low casualty count (about 100 killed and wounded). In his official report, Pickett noted the expedition's material gains, which totaled more than 300 prisoners (including 14 African Americans), 2 cannon, 300 muskets, 4 ambulances, 3 wagons, 103 livestock, "a quantity of clothing, camp and garrison equipage, and 2 flags."[65] A member of the 49th North Carolina noted the capture of hundreds of Yankees, several black refugees, and 20,000 pounds of bacon, as well as the destroyed gunboat.[66] W. R. Burwell of the 43rd North Carolina explained to his brother: "On our raid, I got almost any thing I wanted. I got into a cavalry camp (12th New York) and you never saw anything like it. . . . We got fifteen horses and as many blankets, saddles and bridles as we wanted and a few yankees & negroes."[67] The bounty represented the contents of only a few camps near the outer line. Captain Clopton wrote that there was no telling "what booty the men would have gotten" had New Bern been captured outright.[68]

In addition to these immediate gains, the Confederates hoped for more. The *Daily Progress* in Raleigh recognized that a continued Confederate offensive could isolate the enemy troops in their garrisons and "produce large supplies."[69] According to a correspondent for the *Petersburg Register*, the Confederates could "get large supplies from a country still abundant, to prevent raids on points westward, and keep tories in check, and hang them when caught."[70]

Many inside and outside the army brushed aside the silver linings and looked to divine the underlying reason for the operation's failure. At this point in the war, troops from the Army of Northern Virginia had won on the battlefield more often than they had lost. The Confederate press and citizenry had grown accustomed to good news following a campaign. Thus, the New Bern setback drew significant attention. Pickett had no delusions about the operation's overall results. "Our well-formed plans for the capture of Newbern miscarried," he confessed to his wife.[71] In his official report he wrote, "I am sorry nothing more was done, but the surprise being over, and no co-operation, it would have been a desperate matter to attempt an attack in front."[72]

Others cast about for the failure's root cause and, more important, someone to blame. The newspapers were quick to pounce. A writer for the *Richmond Sentinel* explained, "the key to the position was not properly represented to those in command, either from ignorance on the part of the scouts, or else because very recent fortifications had been thrown up."[73] The *Wilmington Journal* was more direct: "Somebody is to blame! It is time these failures in Eastern North Carolina were put a stop to."[74] "We cannot divest ourselves of the impression that 'somebody blundered,'" the *Journal* continued in a separate article, "although we are in doubt whether any good can be accomplished by any further remarks that we might feel disposed to make."[75]

But the remarks persisted, and blame was cast. The criticism focused on the most obvious targets: Pickett and Barton. The plan's real architects, Hoke and Lee, escaped much of the discussion and scrutiny, perhaps because their involvement was not widely known. Accusations first fell on Seth Barton, and they were tossed there by his commanding officer, George Pickett. Pickett did not hesitate to complain in both private and official correspondence. He did not mince words in his official report: "I have but little doubt that had Barton pushed on we might have been successful." He also asserted that New Bern would have fallen if Barton had attacked simultaneously with Hoke. To his wife, Pickett explained that he had ordered Barton to "cross at once to me and let me try a coup de main" should the crossing of Brice's Creek prove "impracticable." In the same letter, he twice emphasized that Barton was supposed to make the "real attack" and that Hoke's and Dearing's efforts were merely feints. "Newbern was ours—ours—if—well—hope died out and the dejection and despair of the men, with their hopes dashed, cannot be told," he wrote. The disappointed commander did more than complain. Pickett requested an investigation into the matter.[76]

Others shared Pickett's assessment.[77] According to Captain Henry Chambers, officers and men shared the belief that Barton should have pushed early to surprise the pickets on Monday morning because the "enemy was not dreaming of our approach."[78] "The works could have been taken easily" if the cavalry had only dismounted and joined the skirmishers in storming Brice's Creek, concluded another.[79] Some New Bern defenders agreed with these assessments.[80]

Other participants and observers commended Barton's caution. John Lane Stuart of the 49th North Carolina recalled feeling great relief when he learned the charge had been scrubbed because the "Generals found it was too strongly fortified."[81] Later, in response to editorials criticizing the expedition, the *Daily Progress* wrote, "If those who have seen the works tell the truth, it is one of the best fortified places in America."[82] Before the withdrawal, a soldier with Barton's force caught a glimpse of New Bern and Fort Gaston from a high tree limb near the picket line and concluded that the "river defenses are quite strong."[83] When asked whether Barton was to blame, William Izard Clopton, captain of the Fayette Artillery, noted that "Genl B. met with such heavy works that nothing but fatuous temerity would attempt to escalade."[84]

The controversy angered Barton. In his official correspondence, he complained that the "press and common rumor have been kept busy in casting censure upon my course." He hoped to erase the negative impressions generated by the official and not-so-official accounts and requested a court of inquiry to consider the matter. After reading Pickett's damning report, Barton again demanded an opportunity to clear his name, and a court-martial was convened.[85] However, for some reason, the War Department canceled the inquiry, and nothing came of the matter.[86] After the war, the general consensus would label Barton's performance at New Bern a failure.[87]

"There Were Too Many Contingencies"

Despite the criticism heaped on Barton, blame for the entire operation's failure eventually stuck to an unhappy George Pickett. Artillerist Henry Guion, a New Bern native and Hoke confidant, found no mystery behind the results. In his journal, he wrote of his dissatisfaction with Pickett and Barton and asserted that "events conclusively proved that Hoke was right, that town was ours, one sharp brief struggle would no doubt have been required and they would have yielded." According to Guion, the men were "disappointed, grieved, and mortified" that they were not allowed to attack the town.[88] Hoke and Clingman certainly shared this view; the former, in particular, believed Pickett should have been more aggressive throughout the operation. But some observers complimented Pickett for refusing to launch an all-out assault against the New Bern defenses on the last day. A soldier writing to a Richmond paper observed that Pickett had "prudently retired," and he expected his comrades would have enough to deal with in the coming year without fighting "at such disadvantages."[89]

The New Bern operation had played havoc on Pickett's strained nerves. The pressures of independent command, the scars of Gettysburg, and the disruption of Wild's recent raid surely weighed on his mind. To his wife, he described the hours of "restless anxiety and impatience" in waiting for news from Barton.[90] His unease was no secret, and unflattering assessments appeared in the press. William Shepardson's report to the *Daily Dispatch* in Richmond dwelled on Pickett's agitation, highlighting the general's nail-biting and his habit of "twirling his sword knot around his small white hand."[91] In Ohio, the unsympathetic editors of the *Western Reserve Chronicle* piled on, warning, "if the Yankees do not quit perplexing this General, it is evident that he may be driven to fastidiously eating all the nails of his small white hands, and that would be a pity."[92]

What is to be made of the Confederate operation at New Bern? It was an unusual, complicated operation, requiring the coordination of navy and army elements and multiple land-based columns as well. The defenses presented difficult obstacles to an attacking force. Against the Union naval strength, chances for success were slim, no matter the plan or its execution. Furthermore, without an ironclad to overcome or at least nullify the Union naval presence in the sounds, there was little chance that a victory could be sustained. Nevertheless, even the temporary occupation of the city would have yielded significant benefits—namely, supplying Lee's army in Virginia from the garrison's stores as well as the surrounding countryside.

But there was more to it than Union naval power. Additional factors hindered the operation's chances for success. First, the faulty intelligence about the Trent River defenses, a point widely noted by observers, sorely complicated Barton's efforts. The incorrect reports led Pickett to devote a large portion of his strength to Barton's column. Had the intelligence been different, Pickett might have used those troops for a more effective purpose. Furthermore, although Martin's achievement at Newport Barracks qualified as a Confederate victory, it added little to the overall expedition. Martin was simply too late. By the time he cut the railroad at Newport late Tuesday afternoon, Federal commanders had already shuttled men and supplies, including an entire regiment, to face off against Pickett's attack. Later, Palmer would correctly paint the loss at Newport Barracks as "trifling."[93]

It is not clear that the criticism of Pickett and Barton hit the mark. The complaints directed at the two were straightforward: if Pickett had pushed against the New Bern forts, or if Barton had challenged the defenses across Brice's Creek, the Confederates would have discovered the brittle defenses there and the paucity of troops manning them. But the fortifications were, in fact, formidable, surely dooming all but the most fortuitous attack. On the city's western face, Fort Totten and the adjoining fortifications posed a particularly difficult obstacle. Constructed over the course of years, these extensive works provided the defenders with clear, interlocking fields of fire, deep ditches, and high parapets. Natural obstacles, such as the swamps south of Fort Totten, added to the difficulties. Finally, devastating fire from Union naval support in the river would no doubt have smothered any attacking force in this sector.

Surely, Barton could have been more aggressive and pushed his men to attack without hesitation at Brice's Creek. The casualty returns attest to his inactivity. During the entire expedition, he lost one killed and four wounded. But it is far from certain that a more aggressive effort would have yielded anything but additional casualties. Near the Trent River, the creek was wider and deeper than Barton had been led to believe. It is not clear whether Barton was instructed to approach that particular point of the creek or whether he simply lacked detailed directions. Lee's orders merely directed him to "attack the forces said to be stationed behind Brice's Creek." Given that Hoke had been forced to cross the small creek in a boat during the hasty retreat from New Bern in 1862, it is curious that Barton was not made more familiar with this waterway. Nevertheless, once they were over this obstacle, Barton's men would have had to take Fort Gaston, Fort Amory, and several nearby trench lines and then cross the railroad bridge into New Bern. Such movements would not have been easy. Although the New Bern garrison was not huge (about 4,000, counting the civilian "volunteers"), it was not trivial either, and Palmer was able to fill the works with his men. Perhaps Barton could have marched upstream to the headwaters of Brice's Creek, stormed the Union outpost at Evans' Mill, and approached from the south. Barton considered this alternative and rejected it. Such a move would have consumed more time, separated him even farther from Hoke's column, and, most important, brought him into an open plain facing the strong Union works astride the railroad.[94]

Even if Barton had taken these obstacles, Pickett wanted him to cross the Trent railroad bridge, which had been widened by Union forces to accommodate wagons, and march right into downtown.[95] How Pickett expected Barton to do this is unclear. Surely the Federals, tightly packed into the defenses, would train their substantial firepower on the long, narrow bridge. Instead of attempting to ease his way across the river on the railroad bridge, Barton could have planted his artillery on the south bank and bombarded the city. However, reducing the garrison would have taken time, allowing the Union navy to concentrate its vessels from other posts. Clearly, there were abundant reasons for caution. But Barton's critics did not dwell on such details.

Other important factors contributing to the expedition's failure had little to do with Barton or Pickett. The limited results of Wood's naval expedition hamstrung one of Pickett's best chances to take the town. If Wood's men had managed to capture the *Underwriter* intact, that might have tipped the scales. By all accounts, the Union fortifications were well conceived, well built, and strongly held. However, they were not designed to repel a naval threat. With the *Underwriter*'s powerful guns enfilading the defenses either at New Bern or on the south bank of the Trent, a land assault might have been successful. Over the years, Wood's daring feat received much attention in naval histories of the war, and it was often served up as an example of Confederate pluck. But less attention has been paid to how the mission's failure contributed to the outcome at New Bern.[96]

Whatever the weaknesses in the scheme, the best chance for victory at New Bern had nothing to do with poor planning or with Barton's and Pickett's questionable performance. Hoke's improvised lunge at the Union train headed into the city's defenses offered an unexpected opportunity, and the young general lamented its failure. Had he managed to load his men onto the cars and enter the defenses, he was certain the garrison would have fallen.[97]

The chances of success were also perhaps diminished by the plan's complexity. The staging alone was complex, involving multiple columns arriving from different locations and directions. Combined operations were notoriously difficult, and New Bern's defenses and geography presented unique challenges.[98] Without naval superiority, Pickett believed he could not overcome these obstacles. He recognized the plan's difficulties when he candidly remarked in his report that the "present operation I was afraid of from the first, as there were too many contingencies." He wrote, "I should have wished more concentration, but still hope the effect produced by the expedition may prove beneficial."[99] In making this statement, Pickett, whether intentionally or not, was taking a jab at the operation's underlying architects: Robert E. Lee and Robert Hoke. Indeed, if the plan itself was the root cause of the failure, perhaps less blame should have been directed toward Pickett and Barton.[100] Pickett had not become aware of the expedition until January 20, when Hoke handed him Lee's nearly finished blueprint only a few days before the offensive's commencement. In any case, neither Hoke nor Lee were criticized, a fact that surely irritated an already unhappy Pickett.[101]

"Had All Parties Done Their Duty"

The first crack at New Bern may have failed, but Confederate leaders did not give up on the 1864 offensive. Many of the units involved in the expedition, including those of Hoke, Ransom, and Corse, remained in North Carolina. In the operation's aftermath, Hoke emerged with his reputation enhanced. "Indeed, the execution by Gen Hoke of the difficult task of clearing the road at Bachelor's Bridge, was skillful and brilliant," wrote a correspondent to a Raleigh paper. "His rout of the enemy—the pursuit of the fugitives, and the advance of these brigades to within range of the fortifications . . . were successful exemplifications of the ardor and courage of our troops when well handled, and of their superiority over the foe."[102] A member of the 43rd North Carolina, W. R. Burwell, claimed the operation would have been a success if Hoke had been in overall command.[103] According to a rumor circulated years later, John Taylor Wood offered the same opinion to President Davis.[104]

Hoke, who stayed in North Carolina during February, remained frustrated with

the expedition's results.[105] Straying from matters involving his immediate command, Hoke criticized Barton indirectly, asserting in his official report, "Had all
parties done their duty our hopes would have been more than realized." He also
claimed, somewhat coyly, "Being [a] junior officer it does not become me to speak
my thoughts of this move." Looking ahead, he saw cause for optimism. In his native
state, he hoped to gather recruits for his brigade, which had been sorely depleted
after the disaster at Rappahannock Station. The young Tar Heel believed the effort
to capture the Federal positions "could have been done, and still can be accomplished." Hoke also reported that his men were "in good health and fine spirits."
By his reckoning, the soldiers in the ranks did not view the campaign as a "failure,"
perhaps mainly due to their ignorance of its real purpose.[106] Like Hoke, the men expected more. "I think it is quite probable that another attempt will be made before
long to capture Newbern," wrote William Pfohl of the 21st North Carolina, who
also feared a "golden opportunity" had passed.[107]

With the New Bern expedition over, talk of the ironclads resumed. Still incubating upriver from New Bern and Plymouth, the leviathans would be the key to further operations. To aid the boatbuilding efforts, Hoke put his brigade's carpenters
and blacksmiths to work, 200 men in all.[108] He expected the task to be completed in
six weeks. "They are going to try it again soon," wrote an observer, "and the enemy
know it already—this time they will have the ironclad to go down with them."[109] The
Union commanders also continued to pay attention to the ironclads, monitoring a
parade of intelligence from prisoners and deserters. From one loose-lipped captive,
General Palmer learned that Confederate officials hoped to complete the gunboat
on the Roanoke River soon. The man reported that the vessel, modeled after the
Virginia, had four embrasures, carried several heavy guns, and was jacketed in four-
inch iron plating. Palmer feared such a monster would do "incalculable damage"
should it get into the New Bern harbor.[110] Pickett, still in command of the North
Carolina Department, also remained mindful of the ironclads' progress. Understanding that success depended on these vessels, he cautioned Confederate officials
in Richmond to delay any further military operations in the state "till the iron-clads
are done."[111] However, Pickett had some very unpleasant business to attend to, a
matter that would haunt him long after the conflict.

PART FOUR
Carolina Winter

Following the failure of George Pickett's New Bern offensive, the Confederates settled into their quarters at Kinston and other posts. At Beech Grove, the capture of North Carolinians in Union uniforms, many of whom had served in Confederate units, would lead to grim results over the next few weeks. In late February, Matt Ransom would conduct a protracted expedition into the northeastern portion of the state, an operation that ended in fighting at Suffolk, Virginia. As Ransom raided, Governor Zebulon Vance began campaigning in earnest against William W. Holden in the state's upcoming gubernatorial contest. All the while, officers and men rushed to complete the ironclads on the Roanoke and Neuse Rivers as Pickett and Robert Hoke waited eagerly for another chance to attack Union bases in the state.

CHAPTER ELEVEN

The Kinston Hangings

"I'll Have You Shot, and All Other Damned Rascals
Who Desert"

On their return from New Bern, Pickett's troops halted at sunset on Wednesday, February 3, and made camp near the small town of Dover, about 15 miles east of Kinston. Not far from General Pickett's wall tent, several members of the 10th North Carolina gathered around a fire as a pair of Union prisoners captured at Beech Grove idled nearby. To some of the men huddled over the flames, the pair of Yankees bore a striking resemblance to soldiers they had served with earlier in the war. Lieutenant H. M. Whitehead mentioned this to Blunt King, a forty-six-year-old veteran of the Mexican War. Accompanied by a few comrades, King approached the two captives. "Good evening, boys," he said. "Good evening, Mr. King," they replied. As King returned to his seat at the fire, General Pickett emerged from his tent, with Generals Hoke and Corse trailing behind. Pickett spoke a few words with Lieutenant Whitehead, who confirmed the duo's identity. The general then approached the two men and demanded, "What are you doing here; where have you been?" Their responses were inaudible to King and the others who witnessed the exchange. But Pickett's reply was clear. "God damn you," he snapped, "I reckon you will hardly ever go back there again, you damned rascals; I'll have you shot, and all other damned rascals who desert." The general then ordered the prisoners away.[1]

These two unlucky men, David Jones and J. L. Haskett, had deserted their North Carolina unit on November 15, 1863, then headed to New Bern and enlisted in a Federal regiment, the 2nd North Carolina Union Volunteers. During Pickett's attack, they had fallen into Confederate hands at the Beech Grove blockhouse, along with dozens of comrades from their regiment. After Jones and Haskett had been whisked away from the campfire outside Dover, King heard Pickett exclaim: "We'll have to have a court-martial on these fellows pretty soon, and after some are shot the rest will stop deserting." General Corse chimed in, "The sooner the better."[2] Pickett moved quickly. That evening, he convened a general court-martial to arraign and try the pair. The tribunal, headed by artillery captain James R. Branch, found the two guilty of deserting and taking up arms "in the service of the United States forces."[3] By Friday evening, Jones and Haskett were dead, strangled by a hangman's noose.

After discovering the pair of turncoats, the Confederates looked for more of the same among the prisoners. The dragnet's effectiveness greatly increased when a captured sergeant from the 2nd NCUV stepped forward with a company roster.[4] About twenty more men were fingered, most of them natives of the region with families nearby. Many, but not all, had volunteered early in the war with Nethercutt's battalion (8th Battalion, North Carolina Partisan Rangers), a local defense unit.[5] Like similar outfits, the battalion had been organized under state law, and many of its members had joined to avoid conscription in the regular service. There was much confusion regarding the status of these men in the regular army.[6] One observer noted that "it was a loose arrangement." The men had no regular camp, and many lived at home.[7] It seemed that few of Nethercutt's men felt a deep connection to either the Confederate or the Union cause. Federal officers generally had a low opinion of these soldiers. For instance, Edward Ripley, commanding Union troops at Newport Barracks, wrote that North Carolina conscripts arriving at his post "never intend to keep their oaths . . . I assure you they are as strongly Secesh in their sympathies as the Virginians."[8]

It is likely that many of Nethercutt's men would have served out the war in their local unit, participating in occasional operations and remaining comfortably close to their families. However, near the end of 1863, Confederate and state officials combined the battalion with several local units and bridge guard companies and formed the 66th North Carolina.[9] When the 66th swallowed Nethercutt's outfit, many of the men protested, claiming they had been misled and unfairly treated. In their minds, they had joined the local unit "on a distinct promise . . . that they were never to be sent above the Wilmington and Weldon railroad."[10] Governor Vance would later agree, saying, "I am inclined to think the confederate government did not keep faith with those local troops."[11] In responding to the change, the men chose different paths. Some filed writs in state supreme court and received discharges from sympathetic justices. Others refused to remain in the ranks and melted into the woods.[12] Still more headed for Union-controlled New Bern, where recruiting officers swept them into Federal service, in some cases using intimidation and threats, according to some accounts. In this roundabout fashion, these individuals found themselves in Union uniforms at the beginning of 1864.[13]

"Marched to the Gallows"

After returning to Kinston, Pickett's expeditionary force disbanded, at least for the time being. Some units settled into camp there, while others boarded trains for Virginia. Those troops remaining in town enjoyed the pleasant weather, which "was so fine" it discouraged some men from building chimneys for their tents and huts. They quickly regretted that decision, however, when chilly, rainy conditions returned. Chimneys or no, the soldiers hunkered down in their camps.[14]

Kinston drew mixed reviews. Some soldiers found the small town appealing. "A charming little place situated on the Neuse River [and] beautifully laid out," penned Henry Kennon, a Georgian stationed there in 1863. The wide streets "with beautiful shade trees on either side" and the cottage-style houses "with large flowering gardens in front" were pleasing to Kennon.[15] Others did not share his enthusiasm. In October 1863, a Virginian complained that the locals were under Holden's influence and "quite disloyal."[16] In addition, an unnamed correspondent for the *Charleston Courier* described Kinston as "the soberest, dullest, bluest collection of modern antiquities on the continent." Its streets, in his impression, were mostly deserted, except for officers shuttling in and out of Confederate headquarters, and the townspeople sat on their doorsteps watching the world, their cheeks packed with tobacco. Dining options were poor, and entertainment was nonexistent. According to the correspondent, the arrival of the mail train from Goldsboro was the "event of the day."[17]

Unfortunately, February would bring trouble to the sleepy borough. With the weather deteriorating, the prisoner controversy continued as more Union soldiers captured at Beech Grove faced charges of desertion from the Confederate service. In hearings held at Kinston and at Goldsboro, Captain Branch's tribunal presided over the trials of more than twenty-five men. Branch was joined on the board by fellow Virginian Lieutenant William I. Clopton and several others whose identities have never been firmly established. One North Carolina soldier stationed at Kinston later recalled that the board consisted mainly of Virginians, a rumor that undoubtedly raised the ire of Tar Heel soldiers and citizens.[18]

The court-martial quickly reviewed the cases and passed judgment. A few of the prisoners escaped with their lives. One was transferred to civil authorities; another, described as mentally and physically impaired, received a year of hard labor; and three more were branded with a four-inch "D" (for deserter), shackled with a ball and chain, and confined to hard labor for the rest of the war.[19] But most of the accused were not so lucky. Jones and Haskett, the men identified at the Dover Road camp, were hung first, almost immediately after Pickett's return to Kinston, on Friday, February 5. The pair struck one witness as illiterate, hardened men who readily "admitted they had deserted, but insisted that the Yankees compelled them to take the oath and enlist." The condemned reportedly expressed little concern for their own plight and "marched to the gallows with apparent indifference."[20] King, who had helped identify Jones and Haskett, furnished ropes borrowed from Hoke's pontoon train and personally placed a noose over one of the prisoners.[21] "A large portion of the army" witnessed the execution "without exciting the sympathy of a single individual," according to Henry Guion.[22]

Several more executions followed, carried out on gallows constructed of "rude" material in a field behind the Kinston jail. After the initial hangings, another set of executions took place on Friday, February 12.[23] In anticipation of more, workers erected additional scaffolds on Saturday.[24] On Monday, the largest execution took place when thirteen men swung from the noose.[25] Once again, Confederate troops tramped out of camp to witness the spectacle. According to one soldier, nearly the entire force at Kinston gathered to see Jones and Haskett hanged. Hoke's brigade attended at least two more hangings.[26] Some of the officers found that these unpleasant events furnished an example to the "weak-kneed among the North Carolina soldiers." Others were not so sure. Lieutenant Samuel Tate of the 6th North Carolina recalled, "[there] were so many executions that I was considerably worried at having to take my men over so often."[27]

All the executions followed a similar pattern. The troops formed a square around the scaffold as local citizens, including the prisoners' families, watched. Officers read aloud the charges, findings, and orders. Regimental chaplains uttered a public prayer. The prisoners then climbed the scaffold steps and shuffled along, standing in a single row while the hangmen eased the ropes over their heads. In some cases, the men delivered their own remarks. On February 12, when five succumbed to the noose, the men "ascended the scaffold with a firm and elastic step, and seemed to bear up under their trials with much fortitude," recorded one witness. A few of the condemned peered out into the crowd and uttered their last words, some touching on the circumstances that had brought them to this ignoble end. "I went to Newbern and they (the Yankees) told me if I did not go in their service I should be taken through the lines and shot," declared Mitchel Busick minutes before his death.[28] "Oh, that I was never born," uttered another.[29] After their last words were spoken, the platform's trap swung open and the men plummeted, their falls arrested by the ropes fastened to the crossbeam. "They were in eternity in a few moments. The scene was truly appalling," explained one observer.[30] The soldiers remained in line, gaping at the twitching forms, until surgeons pronounced the condemned men dead. Writing home several weeks later, W. R. Burwell, who had attended the first set of executions, confessed that these were "the first men I ever saw hung in my life + the last I ever intend to see if I can help it."[31] The hangings ended on February 22, when the last two prisoners were executed.[32]

Throughout the ordeal, Confederate officials treated the prisoners poorly, undoubtedly reflecting the bitterness Pickett and his officers harbored for these men. Stories of neglect and abuse welled up from families and acquaintances. During their confinement in the Kinston jail, the condemned received little food. In the first four days of John F. Brock's imprisonment, he had "but four crackers to eat." After the hangings, the men's bodies were carelessly handled. Brock's wife received her husband's remains dressed in "old cast-off clothing." The executioners stripped the bodies nearly bare and tossed them out on the open ground. After much searching, the wife of one prisoner found his lifeless form "in an old loft," naked except for his socks. A mother of five, she could find no one to help with her husband's remains because the locals feared being called out as Unionists.[33] One man approached General Hoke, seeking to retrieve his brother-in-law's body, which still bore the Union uniform he had been captured in. Echoing Pickett's disdain, Hoke expressed surprise that the man would want his relative buried in a Yankee uniform.[34]

"Unheard of Barbarity"

The hangings triggered swift and widespread condemnation in the Northern press. "At this unheard of barbarity our native troops are exasperated beyond all bounds," proclaimed one correspondent in a typical reaction.[35] The *New Berne Times*, a pro-Union paper, dwelled on the mistreatment of the prisoners' dead bodies and described the hangings as one of the "most infamous . . . and inhuman acts perpetuated since this bloody rebellion commenced."[36] Some painted the events as part of a Confederate effort to repress political dissent in the state. In an article widely reprinted in the North, a *New York Times* reporter writing from New Bern described the executions "as part of a system of terrorism" designed to keep North Carolina in the Confederacy. The piece also passed along rumors of a large riot at Raleigh in response to the hangings, forcing Pickett to dispatch troops to "quell the outbreak in that city." However, there is no evidence that such events occurred. The account also claimed that the government in Raleigh had suppressed newspaper coverage of the executions, a more believable assertion, given the scant attention the hangings received in North Carolina papers.[37]

In the Union lines at New Bern, anxiety and talk of retaliation boiled up from the Buffaloes.[38] Lieutenant Colonel Charles Henry Foster, a North Carolina Unionist and commander of the 2nd NCUV, labeled the hangings an "inexcusable massacre" and argued that the Confederate government lacked "the rights of a separate and independent sovereignty" necessary for such action.[39] His men reacted even more vehemently. Those who had fled rebel units fully expected "to be hung if caught by the enemy." In response to the executions, they announced plans to show the black flag in future combat and urged their officers to resign if they could not commit to such a course. They also vowed to kill any officer who surrendered to the enemy or asked for quarter in future operations. The Kinston hangings dampened enthusiasm for Union service and damaged recruiting efforts in the 1st and 2nd NCUV.[40] After the war, Benjamin Butler remarked that, after the Kinston hangings, "it is needless to say that recruiting for our forces in North Carolina ceased."[41]

The hangings also generated concern behind Confederate lines. Some North Carolinians, particularly Kinston locals, viewed Pickett's actions as unreasonably harsh or even cruel. The dead were local men, with families and relatives from the surrounding area. Most had no education, no means to speak of, and limited allegiance to either side in the conflict. Furthermore, the circumstances leading to their conviction remained murky. John Neathery, an assistant in the North Carolina adjutant general's office, later recalled that the "people expressed great regret at the execution, feeling that it was for a small offence."[42] George Quinn, a Confederate courier, asserted that Kinston citizens believed "these men ought not to have been hung," for they had been assured their service would not pull them away from their homes. As such, many of these men, as well as those observing the proceedings, did not believe their actions amounted to desertion.[43]

Though some expressed unhappiness with Pickett and his officers, many others approved of the executions. John Paris, a chaplain with the 54th North Carolina who had administered to the prisoners, expressed hearty support for the hangings in a widely reprinted article from a Fayetteville paper. "The knell of vengeance has sounded," waxed Paris. "The right man is here in the right place . . . and deserters in North Carolina must now open their eyes, from the mountains to the seaboard." Consistent with the opinion of his commanding officers, Paris concluded that desertion had become a desperate disease in the army that required drastic remedies.[44] Leonidas L. Polk, an officer in the 43rd North Carolina and a populist reformer after the war, added his view that the "criminals" were deserving of "this awful penalty," although he was "not fond of seeing the execution of fellow men."[45]

The Confederate press looked for a cause behind these unfortunate events and found one in the peace movement. With a thinly veiled jab at William W. Holden and the conservative newspapers, the *Raleigh Weekly Confederate* asked, "Did no newspaper take also the ground, that the Government had committed towards them a breach of faith?" It further alleged that the peace-leaning newspapers had "instigated the crime" and were responsible for the consequences. The *Daily Progress*, whose editor John L. Pennington had urged peace negotiations, fired back several days later, vigorously denying the allegations.[46]

"The Sternest Punishment"

Whatever the causes, few could disagree that the events evoked a deep, angry reaction from George Pickett. His statements at the Dover camp and subsequent correspondence betrayed an intense animus toward the Beech Grove prisoners. During the war, officials rarely executed men for desertion, even though, under military law, it was punishable by death. However, the Beech Grove prisoners were not typical deserters. They had fled their units and joined the enemy, taking up arms against the Confederacy. Under the circumstances, an unhappy Pickett apparently did not hesitate to condemn these men to death.[47]

The previous months had given the general much to be bitter about. His tenure as commander of the North Carolina Department had produced little success.

Wild's raid, with its hostage taking and aggressive operations by African American troops, marked a low point, and the execution of Daniel Bright had struck Pickett as barbarous and wholly unjustified. On top of these events, the failed advance on New Bern opened another sore. Pickett carried the weight of these disappointments and setbacks when he approached Jones and Haskett by the campfire on the Dover Road.

But there was more to the Kinston hangings than the impulsive decision of a frustrated officer. Indeed, Pickett's actions fell in line with opinions expressed by Robert E. Lee only months before. As the war progressed, desertion ate away at Confederate forces and stoked public disaffection. Many units in Lee's force were bleeding men, and he expressed particular concern about absentees from North Carolina units; he had even released Hoke to deal with the problem months earlier.[48] In Lee's view, a soft policy toward desertion was ruinous. The previous fall, he had recommended the "sternest punishment," even execution, for men who had not voluntarily returned to their units.[49] Lee would repeat his position in the spring, once again advocating harsh consequences except where mitigating circumstances existed. In April, he would write to President Davis, "Notwithstanding the executions that have recently taken place, I fear that the number of those who have escaped punishment . . . has had a bad effect already."[50]

In light of Lee's guidance and the seriousness of the offense, Pickett's actions were not particularly shocking. Unlike typical deserters, the Beech Grove prisoners had not left their units for a short recuperative break or fled to the hills to sit out the war. Instead, they had switched sides and, in doing so, directly aided the Union war effort. For Pickett, a man who had cultivated a deep antipathy toward the enemy, the decision to press forward with capital punishment was not a difficult one. Apparently, he saw no choice but to deal with these men harshly. His subsequent correspondence on the matter betrayed little reluctance, a demeanor that would infuriate his enemies.

"For Every Man You Hang I Will Hang 10"

The hangings did not escape the attention of Union commanders. Even before news of the Kinston executions reached New Bern, John Peck found himself engaged with George Pickett on prisoner issues. It began on February 11, when Peck read in the newspaper that Confederates had captured and hung a black soldier suspected of shooting Colonel Henry Shaw at Bachelor Creek. Peck wrote to Pickett about the alleged incident and urged his counterpart to "disavow this violation of the usages of war," adding that he planned to execute a rebel prisoner in retaliation.[51] Two days later, Pickett replied, labeling the story "ridiculous." Although Pickett did not bother to apprise Peck of the details, he knew that a stray bullet fired in the dark morning hours had hit Shaw and that the colonel's death was not the result of a deliberate shot by an identified marksman. Pickett did not stop there, though. He could not help adding, "Had I caught any negro who had killed [an] officer, soldier, or citizen of the Confederate States I should have caused him to be immediately executed."[52] Responding to Peck's threat of retaliation, Pickett warned, "I have merely to say that I have in my hands . . . some 450 officers and men of the U.S. Army, and for every man you hang I will hang 10 of the U.S. Army."[53]

As the two men traded threats, Peck caught wind of the executions in Kinston. On February 13, he sent Pickett a list of fifty-three Union men captured "on your late hasty retreat from before New Berne." These men were "loyal and true North Carolinians," Peck explained, "and duly enlisted in the Second North Carolina Infantry." He demanded that Pickett treat them as he would other prisoners of war.[54] After obtaining newspaper reports of the executions several days later, Peck demanded an explanation and, backed by a directive from Benjamin Butler, threatened retaliation against Confederate prisoners held in Virginia.[55] In a reply several days later, a truculent Pickett taunted Peck, pointing out that the list "so kindly furnished . . . will enable me to bring to justice many who have up to this time escaped their just desserts." He also provided the names of the men who had already been convicted of desertion and executed and noted that the information provided by Peck would "prevent any mercy being shown any" other men identified as deserters.[56]

Pickett's letter triggered a fierce response. From Fort Monroe, Butler instructed Peck to "enforce the strictest retaliation" should the rebels fail to treat the captured men as prisoners of war. Butler also planned to hold eight Confederate officers as "hostages."[57] Peck then responded to Pickett, arguing that a "merciless conscription" had driven these loyal men into the Confederate service and that the US government would quickly counter "these outrages upon humanity." In a harbinger of future troubles, Peck declared that "the blood of these unfortunates will rest upon you and your associates." For him, Pickett's correspondence evinced "a most extraordinary thirst for life and blood," and the hangings offered the best evidence of a "weak and crumbling" Confederacy. "This wicked rebellion," fumed Peck, "has now attained that desperate state which history shows is always the shortest of revolutionary stages," and "the friends of the Union everywhere truly interpret these signs of madness and recklessness."[58]

The poisonous exchange eventually ceased. The threatened retaliation did not occur on either side. Nevertheless, Pickett's tart, callous tone made him a marked man. Butler did not drop the matter and pursued the controversy with his accustomed zeal in his role as commissioner of exchange for prisoner affairs. After digesting reports of the Kinston hangings, the congenitally fractious general fired off a letter of protest on March 3, 1864, to his Confederate counterpart, Robert Ould. Butler acknowledged that the execution of Confederate deserters captured from the Union ranks represented an issue "worthy of careful consideration and discussion."

However, he also took a direct shot at Pickett, noting the Virginian had "deserted his own flag" in 1861 and knew all too well the fate of a deserter "found in arms against his Government." Butler threatened retaliation unless "some period is put to such acts and such threats," and he called on Ould to declare whether Pickett's acts were "sanctioned and authorized." The Confederate official never responded.[59]

A month later, Butler referred the matter to General Grant, including the various letters exchanged between Peck and Pickett. Butler offered his own theory of the Kinston case. "I do not recognize any right in the rebels to execute a United States soldier," he argued, "because either by force or fraud, or by voluntary enlistment even, he has been once brought into their ranks and has escaped therefrom." The Massachusetts general agreed that the Confederates could execute men who deserted from their army. However, once such individuals claimed the protection of the Union army, the rebels, in his view, lost "any power over him other than to treat him as a prisoner of war if captured."[60]

Grant did not share Butler's legal opinion on the matter. In fact, he had addressed a similar issue only a few weeks earlier in a letter to Confederate general Joseph Johnston. In that communication, Grant did not sanction retaliation in cases in which the Confederates punished deserters "who had actually been mustered into the Confederate army and afterward deserted and joined ours." However, in his opinion, the same rule should not apply to men who had joined the Union ranks before formally entering Confederate service. In taking this position, Grant simply echoed a stance consistently held by the US government throughout the struggle.[61] Eventually, the legality of the Kinston executions would become the rub for those examining the matter. For many, the question boiled down to whether the individual prisoners had, in fact, formally entered Confederate service before leaving the ranks and heading for Union lines. However, in the spring of 1864, Union officials had no access to such details, and with more pressing matters occupying their time, they shunted the issue aside.[62]

"The Guilty Party"

The controversy reemerged after the war. Several weeks after the Confederate surrender, George Pickett learned of his exclusion from the list of paroled officers. To rectify this, on June 1, 1865, he sent a letter to President Andrew Johnson expressing willingness to renew his allegiance to the United States. However, officials still refused to parole him.[63] Several weeks later, Pickett took the loyalty oath in Richmond but found that he remained under investigation for "the unlawful hanging" of citizens in North Carolina.[64] Concerned about where such charges might lead, Pickett hurried off to Canada with his wife and children. During his absence, in late 1865, Federal officials convened a full investigation of his actions at Kinston.

Several rounds of inquiry took place over the following months. Two separate boards interviewed dozens of witnesses, pored over correspondence between Union and Confederate officials, examined newspaper reports, and delved into the complicated facts and legal issues involved in the case. On March 29, 1866, the second board issued its conclusions, finding that some of the executions had been justified, at least for the men who had voluntarily enlisted in Confederate service and then joined the Union army. In those cases, "there would seem to be little doubt" that Confederate officials were justified in punishing the desertion capitally. However, the board also found that rebel officials had wrongly executed the men from Nethercutt's battalion and the bridge guard companies who had left their local units before being conscripted in the Confederate service.[65] Under this interpretation, the Confederate court-martial had no jurisdiction to try men who had merely served in local militia units and never formally entered the Confederate army. The board identified Pickett as "the guilty party by whom or by whose order the sufferers were arrested and prosecuted, and by whose order executed." However, it was unable to determine exactly how many men fell into this category, thus frustrating any firm conclusions.[66]

As the wolves circled that spring, Pickett reached for a lifeline. On March 12, 1866, he wrote to his prewar friend Ulysses S. Grant, seeking "favorable consideration" in his case. Pickett asserted "that certain evil-disposed persons are attempting to reopen the troubles of the past, and embroil" him for actions taken during the war. He argued that the executions had been conducted in accordance with the accepted rules of war.[67] Grant was sympathetic to Pickett's plight and acted immediately, furnishing a pass that exempted Pickett from arrest by military authorities, "except as directed by the President . . . Secretary of War, or from these Hd. Qrs."[68] Grant forwarded Pickett's request to President Johnson several days later and recommended clemency, or at least an assurance that no trial would take place. In Grant's view, Pickett's action, though harsh, was one the Confederates considered necessary to keep men in the ranks. Although Grant vaguely criticized the Virginian for doing "what cannot well be sustained," he believed a trial would suggest to some that the US government did not intend to honor the surrender terms.[69]

Despite Grant's intervention, Pickett's problems remained. Calls for a hearing continued through 1866. On July 21, the judge advocate general recommended Pickett's arrest. Nothing happened. On December 3, 1866, a frustrated House of Representatives sought additional information on Pickett's case from the Johnson administration.[70] However, the matter largely disintegrated over the next few months, reemerging only briefly during President Johnson's impeachment hearings the next summer. Eventually, it all faded away, and on Christmas Day 1868, a universal amnesty announced by Johnson rendered Pickett's case moot.[71]

For some, though, the bitterness remained. Colonel Rush Hawkins, who had served in North Carolina at the head of the 9th New York, prepared an account of the hangings shortly after the war and published it decades later. In his view, the episode represented "a wanton and cruel assassination . . . by the order of an inhuman monster who had been placed beyond the reach of the power to punish." Hawkins seethed at the terms Grant had extended to Confederate officers at Appomattox, as well as the leniency afforded former Confederate leaders. He devoted much thought and energy to the legal issues underlying the executions. Hawkins argued that Pickett had executed the men for the crime of "constructive desertion." As the boards of inquiry found in 1865 and 1866, many of the condemned men had deserted before being conscripted into the 66th North Carolina. "There can be no desertion," Hawkins argued, "unless the deserter has been regularly mustered into some branch of the service before the act of desertion takes place."[72] Hawkins was not the only one to dwell on the events in Kinston. Colonel James Savage, who had led the 12th New York Cavalry at New Bern, drafted a paper in 1866 that conveyed his resentment. In his concluding remarks, he touched on the men hung at Kinston in 1864. After Union forces overran the town in 1865, Savage, apparently unaware that the hangings had taken place on a scaffold, remarked, "[the] trees of North Carolina never bore nobler or more spotless fruit."[73]

"The Happiest Effect"

The larger impacts of the hangings in eastern North Carolina are not clear. The executions appear to have dissuaded many local men from joining the Federal ranks, an important goal for Confederate military leaders. However, the Confederates also aimed to quell the growing unhappiness among North Carolinians, particularly those who were threatening to pull the state out of the Confederacy. Lee aptly described this objective when he predicted that victory at New Bern would "have the happiest effect in North Carolina and inspire the people."[74] Ultimately, Pickett's decision to execute the deserters did not advance this political goal. Indeed, some North Carolina soldiers and citizens doubted the guilt of the condemned men, and even among those who found them culpable, there was a feeling that the punishment did not fit the crime. This impression was undoubtedly aggravated by the fact that a Virginian (Pickett) had orchestrated the executions, and the tribunal itself was reportedly staffed exclusively by Virginians. The incident may have deepened tensions between the two states throughout the war. Viewed in this light, the Kinston hangings added to the cluster of setbacks and disappointments suffered by North Carolinians over the previous months. Confederate leaders had failed to protect them from Wild's marauders, botched the attack on New Bern, and then executed poor, uneducated locals under murky circumstances. For those wavering between support of the Confederate war effort and withdrawal from the war on honorable terms, Pickett's actions may not have had the impact Confederate officials desired.

CHAPTER TWELVE

The Politics of Peace

"New Bern Was a Fizzle"

The setback at New Bern in early February did not douse Confederate ambitions. As the winter of 1864 wore on, additional operations in North Carolina remained viable. Robert E. Lee still looked for supplies to feed his army, and other rebel leaders still hoped for military victories to reduce the unhappiness threatening to wrench the Old North State from the Confederacy. With spring campaigning in Virginia still months away, Lee was willing to keep some of his troops in the state. Accordingly, Robert Hoke remained in Kinston with his brigade, once again poised to strike Union forces as soon as the ironclads were complete. While the rebel generals waited, political matters continued to churn. Zebulon Vance, with an eye on the August gubernatorial election, developed a strategy to suppress the peace movement and neutralize its leader, William W. Holden.[1]

Vance was not happy about Pickett's failure in February. "The expedition to New Bern was a fizzle, as most expeditions in N.C. are," he complained to his close ally E. J. Hale, editor of the *Fayetteville Observer*.[2] With this remark, Vance lumped the New Bern expedition with past rebel setbacks in the region, including the previous year's operations against Washington. However, Vance did not dwell on the disappointment; other issues fixed his attention in February. He struggled with low spirits and personal health problems. In December, he had been "sick and quite gloomy." Around this time, doctors removed a large tumor from his neck. On top of these ailments, he strove to manage affairs in his state.[3] Throughout January and February, he continued to joust with Richmond officials over Confederate policies and to manage North Carolina's state-owned blockade-runners.[4]

"Treasonable Designs"

In the first months of 1864, dissatisfaction with Richmond's policies endured. The grumbling was not limited to North Carolina. Voices from other states, particularly Georgia, rose in opposition to Confederate policies for conscription, taxation, and the impressment of property and slaves. In turn, officials in the rebel capital became concerned about the groundswell of resistance. In February, alarmed by the growing unhappiness and perceived disloyalty in North Carolina and elsewhere, Jefferson Davis urged the Confederate Congress to suspend the writ of habeas corpus to curb the release of jailed dissenters. Implemented twice before as a temporary measure, the suspension was viewed as a vital tool for rebel officials. In its absence, to the dismay of Richmond officials, sympathetic state judges had freed men who had been confined for desertion and other crimes. In North Carolina, state supreme court justice Richmond M. Pearson routinely issued writs to release men jailed for violations of the conscription laws.[5]

In a February 3 letter to Congress, Davis warned that "discontent, disaffection, and disloyalty are manifested among those who . . . have enjoyed quiet and safety at home." In an unmistakable reference to conditions in North Carolina, he complained of public meetings held with "treasonable designs" and masked by "a pretended devotion to State sovereignty." He also targeted calls for state conventions designed to accomplish what he considered treason. The president expressed frustration over the frequent release of alleged spies and other disloyal persons due to the lack of sufficient evidence, even though their guilt was beyond question, in his opinion.[6] He believed suspension of the writ would improve matters. Not everyone in the Confederate Congress agreed. Nevertheless, Davis garnered enough support to get the measure passed. The legislation, set to expire after ninety days, listed thirteen specific circumstances or conditions under which habeas corpus requests could be denied.

Mostly, the new law targeted dissent. Its ninth condition specifically applied to "persons advising or inciting others to abandon the Confederate cause or to resist the Confederate States, or to adhere to the enemy."[7] This struck a raw nerve for many North Carolinians, especially Holden and others seeking a peace convention. They understood that, in pushing to pass the legislation, Davis and his government had taken aim at them. Holden was livid. He viewed the new law as another link in a long chain of measures hostile to his home state. A few weeks before, he had warned that the suspension "would silence our Judges, silence the press, deprive our people of the freedom of speech, and destroy personal liberty."[8] Now he understood that the legislation could effectively muzzle any candidates running on a peace platform, including himself, for it was clear that any public discussion of peace would draw attention from Confederate authorities. To protest the measure and avoid legal troubles with Richmond, Holden halted publication of his newspaper, the *North Carolina Standard*. He later explained, "If I could not continue to print as a freeman I would not print at all, and I could not bear the idea of lowering or changing my tone."[9]

Governor Vance was not pleased either. When word reached him of the pending legislation, he fired off a complaint to Davis on February 9. It was one of his typical long-winded epistles. He urged Davis to "be chary of exercising" the power extended by the bill. He hoped "the morale effect of holding this power over the heads of discontented men" would suffice and eliminate the need to shock the entire citizenry by "hurling freemen into sheriffless dungeons." He assured Davis that many were working hard to tamp down calls for a peace convention. Indeed, Vance himself planned to "take to the field" and campaign against the movement, anticipating that people would listen to "right and reason." He asserted that the "potent weapons" of persuasion would be preferable to "bayonets and dungeons" to tap into the "zeal and affection" of supporters. He also argued that the peace advocates' chances were weak, and the prospects for a successful peace convention extremely low. In his view, Holden and his colleagues could not corral the necessary two-thirds majority in the legislature. In light of this assessment, Vance assured the president that no convention would be assembled in the state that year.[10]

Vance probably should have ended his February 9 letter there. Instead, as was his tendency with Davis, he added other complaints. He groused about demoralization stemming from Union military gains in the state, general Confederate policies, and economic conditions. He also devoted substantial ink to the perceived mistreatment of North Carolinians by Richmond officials. Repeating a theme sounded in earlier exchanges, he claimed the government doubted Tar Heels' loyalty because of the state's late decision to secede. He then complained of a "studied exclusion of the anti-secessionists" from important government posts and army promotions.[11] Vance's letter offended Davis, who delayed his response until February 29. The first few lines of the president's reply revealed the harm done. "I regret that you have deemed proper . . . to make unjust reflections upon my official conduct," he chirped, explaining that Vance's accusations of bias were "unjust to my conduct, my feelings, and my character." He then sought to refute Vance's assertions at length.[12]

The exchange did not advance the relations between North Carolina and the Confederate government. Nor did it improve the rapport between the two men. But Davis understood that the governor was his best ally in combating unhappiness in the vital state. As such, he knew that a Vance victory in the summer election was crucial to the Confederacy's viability. Accordingly, instead of burning his bridge with the governor, he took pains to punctuate his letter with assurances of support for the "good people" of North Carolina.[13] But friction between the two continued. Later in March, Vance complained about the conscription law, currency reforms, and regulations for blockade-running.[14] He continued this pattern of protest through the spring and beyond. There was no end in sight to his fussing.[15]

"Fight It out Now"

Beyond his tangles with Richmond, Vance struggled to maintain support for the Confederacy and for himself in his home state. Disaffection had become one of the principal issues for the upcoming election. Throughout the winter months, the peace movement gained steam, buoyed by Holden's ongoing call for a state convention and negotiations to end the war before slavery's irreversible demise. Beginning in December, the Raleigh editor predicted the election would turn on these questions, and before halting his newspaper's publication, he filled his columns with calls for a May convention.[16] In doing so, he was careful to moderate his advocacy. To ensure he was not mistaken for a "reconstructionist," Holden stressed that negotiations offered the best means "to prevent the sudden abolition of slavery," preserve human life, and "prevent the extinction of State sovereignties."[17] In pressing for a peace that left slavery intact, Holden's views mirrored those of the Northern Copperheads, Democrats who urged an end to the war that kept "the Union as it was, and the Constitution as it is."[18]

As Vance fretted about Richmond's policies, he prepared for the August election and developed his plan to deal with Holden. Back in December, he had told Hale that the election would turn on the convention question.[19] And in early January, he sensed support building for Holden's positions, which he flatly opposed. To Vance, a separate negotiated peace for North Carolina would bring shame and infamy to the state. He vowed that, if such a course became inevitable, he would "quietly retire to the army and find a death which will enable my children to say that their father was not consenting to their degradation."[20]

As the peace advocates continued to broadcast their message, Vance understood that he was losing ground by not confronting Holden head-on. Support for the editor remained high among many voters, and from the camps in Virginia, some North Carolina soldiers reported significant backing for Holden in the ranks.[21] Over the previous months, the editor's message had resonated with those weary of the war. "A few days ago we held a secret ballot in our brigade," wrote a member of the 57th North Carolina to Holden's paper in the fall of 1863, "and all our regiment but eleven endorsed your course." In January 1864, a member of the 45th North Carolina Infantry, which included many men from the Quaker Belt, told family back home that "all the N.C. boys wish that old N.C. would go back into the union."[22] Another reported incidents of intimidation against those supporting Holden. One soldier in Kinston wrote, "if our officers knew that I had written such a letter to you, they would punish me for it; but I have written the truth."[23]

Vance believed the situation was headed for a crisis, a view reinforced by his allies. Writing to the governor from Hendersonville on February 17, John D. Hyman warned Vance, by "your silence you are daily losing friends," and the "secession party allege that Holden [is] your spokesman & that you are in favor of a convention." Vance understood that he was slipping while Holden was gaining ground. His own supporters were becoming restless with his reluctance to publicly challenge his opponent. They hoped he would step forward and clear the air.[24]

Despite Vance's lack of public statements on the matter, he had devoted much thought to the upcoming campaign. Back in December, he had developed plans to visit the camps of Lee's army in Virginia, where the Tar Heel troops represented a large voting bloc.[25] He also sensed an opportunity with the civilian electorate. He knew Holden's drift toward Confederate opposition created the possibility of gar-nering votes from the hard-core secessionists (the "destructives"), who were unlikely to field a candidate of their own.[26] "They are dead as a door nail," wrote Vance. "They will be obliged to vote for me, and the danger is in pushing off too big a slice of the old union men with Holden."[27] By appealing to the middle, Vance expected to maximize his support.

In late February, he kicked off the campaign with his first speech. On the twenty-second, he traveled to Wilkesboro, the seat of Wilkes County and a hotbed of peace agitation at the edge of the state's Quaker Belt. The stump provided an ideal environment for the governor. He was an exceptionally talented speaker who could keep audiences engaged for hours as he followed nothing but a simple outline. He deftly wove humor and entertaining anecdotes into his talks. He communicated his positions in a straightforward, convincing manner without being didactic or formulaic.[28] One Tar Heel soldier who attended a Vance speech in the spring of 1864 described the governor's style as "decidedly fascinating and novel," though "not marked with that impassioned eloquence and those inspired lighting flashes that dazzle with their sublimity." Nevertheless, the listener found Vance "a great stump speaker" who "reasons well, illustrates better, and carries the sympathies of the crowd with him all the while," leaving them "spell bound with wonder at his great gifts, and tickled to death at the budget of fun he opens and pours out into their delighted ears."[29]

At Wilkesboro, Vance prepared the stage carefully. He brought in the band of his former regiment, the 26th North Carolina, to play stirring numbers for the crowd, including "The Old North State." He hired a reporter, Clinton Stedman from Richmond, to record the speech in shorthand.[30] In the chilly February air, before an audience of 2,000, Vance delivered a brilliantly orchestrated strike. Over the course of the speech, he clearly distinguished himself from Holden and the peace advocates while simultaneously acknowledging the excesses of policies em-anating from Richmond. Vance chose his approach carefully. He warned that a convention aimed at achieving an "honorable peace" would destroy slavery in the state. At the same time, he took pains to recognize the legitimate concerns raised by Holden. There was nothing disingenuous in this. Vance had publicly tangled with President Davis on policy issues throughout the war and vigorously defended his state's autonomy.

Though Vance tipped his hat to Holden and the convention supporters, he also exposed fundamental flaws in their positions by focusing on the incongruous, uncertain, and generally undesirable results of a negotiated peace. In particular, he noted that a breakaway North Carolina could find itself embroiled in new fighting with both the Confederacy and the Union simultaneously. He predicted that many of the state's soldiers serving in Lee's army would remain loyal to the Confederacy. In addition, the state would be subject to the debts and taxes of the Federal government. In short, the resulting economic entanglements and shifting loyalties associated with a separate peace would lead to chaos.[31]

During the Wilkesboro speech, Vance also warned that a negotiated peace could have dire consequences for slavery. He expected the slaves would "be turned loose upon us if we consent to the only terms Mr. Lincoln offers us." He cautioned listeners that their "lands [would be] confiscated and sold to [their] own slaves!"[32] Though he acknowledged that Holden and his ilk hoped to keep slavery intact, he found such expectations dangerously naïve. In his view, negotiations would not restore the status quo prior to the war. To underscore his point, Vance offered a macabre analogy, which drew immense applause: "There is no more possibility of reconstructing the old Union and reinstating things as they were 4 years ago, than exists for you to gather up the scattered bones of your sons who have fallen in this struggle . . . reclothe them with flesh, fill their veins with the blood they have so generously shed, and their lungs with the same breath with which they breathed out their last prayer for their country's triumph and independence."[33] Vance offered a clear alternative to negotiations. "The only way to obtain a continued peace . . . is to fight it out now," he proclaimed. At the same time, he acknowledged concerns about Richmond's overreach and reminded the audience of his frequent opposition to Richmond's policies. Even so, he eagerly acknowledged his preference to engage Davis rather than Lincoln on these issues, explaining, "while we are simmering and frying, and the under side done pretty brown, to look over into the coals and estimate their temperature . . . we might be glad enough to get back into the pan, hot as it is."[34]

The Wilkesboro speech, repeated to large crowds over the next few weeks at Statesville, Salisbury, and other locales, proved a resounding success for Vance and his cause.[35] It publicly solidified the governor's views on the fundamental issues of peace and war. His friends rejoiced. In the *Fayetteville Semi-Weekly Observer*, Hale announced that the speech "lays bare with a master-hand, the dangers of the proposed Convention, as well as those of an unauthorized movement for peace, and the utter impossibility of reconstruction on any terms."[36] The *Greensboro Patriot* believed the address placed Vance "above suspicion and beyond reproach."[37] Others liked it too. The "destructives" on his right flank nodded with approval. Raleigh's *Daily Confederate* called the speech a "wise, logical, and patriotic effort." It applauded Vance's "timely arrival on the field" and concluded, "We have never met with so extraordinary a mélange of qualities as our Governor possesses—converted into a dish of suckatash, there would be rations for any army for an entire campaign."[38] It soon became clear that Vance's messaging had lifted the hopes of ardent Confederates in North Carolina and elsewhere. He had delivered a significant blow to Holden and the peace advocates. As one soldier in Kinston put it, "I never saw a man come down so fast as [Holden] has since Gov. Vance commenced speaking. Everybody is for Gov. Vance again."[39]

"To Secure an Honorable Peace"

Vance's onslaught forced Holden's hand. On March 3, the Raleigh editor officially announced his candidacy for governor. In doing so, he drew the lines sharply, vowing to do everything in his power "to secure an honorable peace" if elected. One of his allies added, "If the people of North Carolina are for perpetual conscriptions, impressments, and seizures to keep up a perpetual, devastating, and exhausting war, let them vote for Governor Vance." With Holden's formal entry into the race, the stakes were high. If he could mount an effective campaign, his victory might threaten the very viability of the Confederacy.[40] But Holden's effort was slow in taking shape. He had difficulty gaining traction, even early in the contest. He was damaged by Vance's speeches at Wilkesboro and elsewhere, which cast doubt on the coherence and efficacy of the peace strategy. The governor successfully stoked concerns about the tangible results of Holden's positions, particularly whether they would keep slavery and the state's sovereignty intact. By failing to clearly define what an "honorable peace" entailed, Holden did not help himself and created an opportunity for his opponent to define the contest.[41]

Some of Holden's campaign problems may have stemmed from his contradictory positions throughout the war. He had been an early advocate of secession, then a conditional Unionist, and then a full supporter of the Confederate cause once the fighting started. Now, his push for negotiations puzzled many and drew skepticism from some in the peace movement.[42] At the same time, ultra-secessionists, such as General Thomas Clingman, believed Holden "was bound by his personal honor to sustain the cause" and could not "abandon the men in the field without the deepest *personal disgrace*."[43]

Holden pressed his plea for peace, but he did so against serious headwinds. His decision to halt publication of his newspaper in response to government threats clearly weakened his efforts. He also declined to campaign actively or even to deliver speeches to the public. Some of his reluctance may have stemmed from the threat of the new habeas corpus law. However, there may have been a more straightforward reason: simply put, Holden was a poor public speaker. Recognizing his own limitations, he apparently saw little advantage in taking to the stump. In late spring, he began to publish his newspaper again. But throughout March and April, with no way to reach the voters, he had been largely defenseless against Vance's onslaught.[44]

"The N.C. Troops . . . Love Gov. Vance"

Vance's performance at Wilkesboro and in other North Carolina counties clearly separated him from his opponent, but his most effective campaigning may have occurred outside his home state. In accordance with plans hatched in December, he visited Lee's army in late March to shore up support in the ranks. Lending an air of spontaneity to the trip, he received several invitations from North Carolina soldiers urging him to travel north and speak to the men. "The N.C. Troops . . . love Gov. Vance as a kind father, and admire him as a fine and able statesmen," gushed one typical letter. "They will not have any one else for Governor."[45]

Vance left Raleigh on March 21 for a ten-day visit to Virginia. When he arrived at the camps of the Army of Northern Virginia, he was greeted by sunny weather. Vance began his speaking tour on Saturday, March 26, at the camp of Junius Daniel's North Carolina brigade near Orange Court House. The event drew many of the army's general officers, including Robert E. Lee, corps commanders Richard Ewell and A. P. Hill, cavalry chief J. E. B. Stuart, and several division commanders. On Monday, he visited the North Carolinians in the Second Corps, who conducted a grand review in the governor's honor. According to a participant in the 2nd North Carolina, the soldiers stood in "line almost as far as the eye could reach, with their arms glistening in the noon-day sun," and then marched with precision, their "bullet-rent flags flying" at the front. In the correspondent's opinion, the Tar Heel soldiers "could not but impress the observer with the magnitude of the power which the old North State wields in this contest for freedom."[46]

Following the parade, the participants repaired to the camp of the 30th North Carolina in Ramseur's brigade, where Vance climbed a newly constructed platform and spoke to the crowd packed "as thick as they could stand." For those following Vance's campaign up to that point, the themes were no doubt familiar. True to his style, he began with some humor. Apologizing for addressing the men as his "fellow soldiers" in a previous speech, he admitted that he had "skulked out of service by being elected to a little office down in North Carolina." He settled on calling the men his "fellow Tarheels." He then proceeded to the substance of his message. He emphasized that peace could be achieved only by fighting for it. He rejected calls for negotiations, listing many of the reasons set out in his Wilkesboro speech. He predicted that neutrality would bring both the Federal government and the Confederacy down on the state and cause the "whole land to become a howling wilderness." He also asserted that the upcoming presidential election in the North held great promise for the Confederacy, for the success of the Northern peace party could end the war.

He closed his remarks by acknowledging the dissatisfaction in North Carolina with the Confederate government, particularly the habeas corpus issue. However, he assured his audience that the people of the state would "not do anything desperate." North Carolinians "sometimes honestly differed from other people in matters of public policy and propriety," he explained, "but her popular heart beat in unison with her soldiers, and her determination was as strong as theirs to fight this war through to victory and independence."[47]

Vance repeated his speech several times. He spoke to Scales's brigade on Thursday, March 31. But a visit to James Lane's brigade on April 3 was canceled due to heavy rain, which started as snow. A disappointed Lane noted that "J. E. B. Stuart followed [Vance] around and seemed to be completely carried away with his speeches, and I understand General Lee on one or two occasions forgot his usual dignity and laughed heartily at his anecdotes."[48] On April 4, the governor spoke before Robert Johnston's brigade in the camps at Taylorsville, near Hanover Junction. According to one thoroughly entertained listener, Vance "commenced with a joke, went on with a joke, joked a little while longer, and then told another joke," but he eventually addressed the serious issues of the peace convention. The listener concluded that Vance "made more friends by that one speech than Holden has made in twelve months through his paper."[49]

Vance's tour of the army was an unmitigated success. He drilled home the themes outlined in his Wilkesboro speech. His wit and charm, coupled with the content of these talks, were devastatingly effective. The visit generated positive stories in the press and many glowing reports in letters home. Lee supposedly remarked that Vance's efforts had been the equivalent of adding 50,000 to the ranks.[50] One soldier-correspondent predicted that nearly every man in his brigade would vote for Vance and that Holden's stock was "considerably below par, and getting worse every day."[51]

With the gubernatorial election only months away, the visit could not have been better timed. Problems remained in North Carolina, including dissatisfaction with Confederate policies and continued Union military control of eastern portions of the state. Yet, beginning with his watershed speech at Wilkesboro, Vance crafted a winning message that resonated with a broad swath of voters. Meanwhile, Confederate military leaders had not abandoned their hopes for further operations against the Federal bases at New Bern, Washington, and Plymouth. Vance's campaign surely stoked optimism that North Carolina would remain steadfastly in the Confederacy. But a clear-cut military victory would also contribute mightily to the cause.

George E. Pickett, CS, Department of Virginia and North Carolina (Courtesy of Library of Congress)

John J. Peck, US, District of North Carolina (Courtesy of Library of Congress)

Robert F. Hoke, CS, commanding Confederate forces at Plymouth (Courtesy of North Carolina Collection, University of North Carolina Library at Chapel Hill)

Innis N. Palmer, US, commanding defenses at New Bern (Courtesy of Library of Congress)

Zebulon B. Vance, North Carolina governor (Courtesy of Library of Congress)

William W. Holden, editor of the *North Carolina Standard* (Courtesy of North Carolina Collection, University of North Carolina Library at Chapel Hill)

James W. Cooke, CS, commanding ironclad *Albemarle* (NH 63719, Photography, Archives Branch, Naval History and Heritage Command, Washington, DC)

Charles W. Flusser, US, commanding Union naval forces at Plymouth (NH 49566, Photography, Archives Branch, Naval History and Heritage Command, Washington, DC)

John Taylor Wood, CS,
commanding Confederate
naval forces during New
Bern expedition (NH 616,
Photography, Archives Branch,
Naval History and Heritage
Command, Washington, DC)

Matt W. Ransom, CS, brigadier
general at New Bern and
Plymouth (Courtesy of Library
of Congress)

Benjamin F. Butler, US, commanding Department of Virginia and North Carolina (Courtesy of Library of Congress)

Henry W. Wessells, US, commanding army forces at Plymouth (Courtesy of Library of Congress)

Wartime view of New Bern looking east from Fort Totten at Union camps. Watercolor by
Edward C. Cabot, 44th Massachusetts (Courtesy of Library of Congress)

New African American recruits march through the New Bern streets passing Broad Street
Church immediately following the failure of Pickett's offensive in early February 1864. A
sketch by "Our Special Artist," F. H. Schell. *Leslie's Illustrated*, February 27, 1864 (Image
supplied by Internet Archive at archive.org)

An undated photograph of the Evans' Mill blockhouse along Brice's Creek south of New Bern. This structure was similar in construction to blockhouses at Beech Grove, Bogue Sound, and other locations. ("Block House, Evans' Mills, NC," MOLLUS-Mass Civil War Photograph Collection, US Army Heritage and Education Center, Carlisle, PA)

The *Albemarle* sinks the *Southfield* at Plymouth, April 19, 1864. From *Battles and Leaders*, Vol. 4 (Image supplied by Internet Archive at archive.org)

The capture of the *Underwriter* by John Taylor Wood's Confederates in the early morning hours of February 2, 1864. *Leslie's Illustrated*, February 27, 1864 (Image supplied by Internet Archive at archive.org)

Sketch of Plymouth in 1864. "The War in North Carolina—Plymouth—From a Sketch by Mr. Von Grief," *Leslie's Illustrated*, May 14, 1864 (Courtesy of North Carolina Collection, University of North Carolina Library at Chapel Hill)

"Plymouth, N.C. 1863" by Merrill G. Wheelock. An artist before the war, Wheelock served as a private in the 44th Massachusetts (Co. F). This scene was painted from the right bank of the Roanoke River looking upstream (west). The white vessel to the right is likely the converted ferry USS *Southfield*. (Courtesy of the North Carolina Museum of Art, Raleigh)

An 1863 sketch of Washington, North Carolina, looking eastward. *Leslie's Illustrated*, May 16, 1863 (Courtesy North Carolina Collection, University of North Carolina Library at Chapel Hill)

USS *Sassacus* ramming the Confederate ironclad *Albemarle* during fighting off Sandy Point at Batchelor's Bay in the Albemarle Sound, May 5, 1864. (Archives Branch, Naval History and Heritage Command, Washington, DC)

CHAPTER THIRTEEN

Ransom's Raid

"Bringing Out the Bacon"

During the cold weather, Confederate soldiers did not remain idle as the political campaigning continued. George Pickett, seeking to boost Confederate commissary stores, planned a raid to gather supplies in the northeastern corner of the state. In correspondence with Richmond officials back in January, he had proposed a jaunt into Pasquotank, Gates, and Perquimans Counties aimed at bringing "out the bacon and provisions so very necessary for us at this present time." The New Bern expedition delayed this raid until late February. Thus, weeks after the New Bern attack, Pickett assigned North Carolina native Matt Ransom to lead a force containing Ransom's own brigade, the recently formed 68th North Carolina, two artillery batteries, and James Dearing's 8th Confederate Cavalry. The expedition would cross ground covered by Edward Wild's African American regiments in December. To reach these counties, which were located in largely Union-controlled territory, Ransom's force would have to march east through a strip of country bordered on the north by the Federal position at Suffolk and on the south by the Chowan River and the Albemarle Sound. In devising the raid, Pickett's goal was not only to obtain provisions; he no doubt hoped to demonstrate that the Confederates could project power into these remote areas.[1]

Most of Ransom's units left their camps at Weldon on Wednesday, February 24, and marched east to Murphy's Station near Franklin, Virginia, just over the border. On Friday, they spent nearly the entire day pulling their wagons and artillery across the Blackwater River on a single ferry. The next day, they reentered North Carolina, marching two dozen miles on sandy roads southeast to Gatesville, where the 68th North Carolina joined the column. On February 29, the units finally reached South Mills in Camden County. There, the foraging began and continued for several days, as detachments moved off in every direction. The men found the

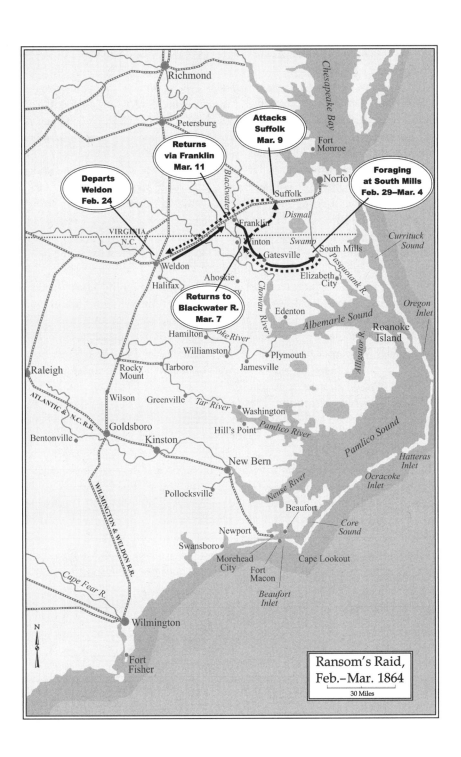

Richmond

Petersburg

**Attacks
Suffolk
Mar. 9**

Fort
Monroe

**Returns
via Franklin
Mar. 11**

Norfolk

**Foraging
at South Mills
Feb. 29–Mar. 4**

Suffolk

Dismal

**Departs
Weldon
Feb. 24**

Blackwater

Franklin

VIRGINIA
N.C.

Winton

Swamp

Gatesville

South Mills

*Currituck
Sound*

Weldon

Ahoskie

Elizabeth
City

Pasquotank R.

Halifax

**Returns to
Blackwater R.
Mar. 7**

Chowan River

Edenton

Albemarle Sound

*Oregon
Inlet*

Hamilton

oke River

Alligator R.

Roanoke
Island

Williamston

Plymouth

Raleigh

Rocky
Mount

Tarboro

Jamesville

ATLANTIC & N.C. R.R.

Wilson

Greenville

Tar River

Washington

Goldsboro

Hill's Point

Pamlico River

Pamlico Sound

*Hatteras
Inlet*

Bentonville

Kinston

New Bern

*Ocracoke
Inlet*

WILMINGTON & WELDON R.R.

Pollocksville

Neuse River

Beaufort

*Core
Sound*

Newport

Swansboro

Morehead
City

Fort
Macon

Cape Lookout

Cape Fear R.

*Beaufort
Inlet*

N

Wilmington

Fort
Fisher

**Ransom's Raid,
Feb.–Mar. 1864**

30 Miles

region rich in stored provisions, particularly pork, and gathered up as many victuals as their wagons could carry.[2]

The Federals did not let the Confederates operate unmolested. From outposts at Ballahock Station and Deep Creek just across the border in Virginia, Yankee cavalry ventured south and tangled with the rebels. At one point, Dearing pushed back a detachment of Federals north along the Dismal Swamp Canal for 12 miles, carrying on a "running fight."[3] However, the Federals did not press the matter further, and Ransom's force continued to scour the countryside.[4] Ransom remained at South Mills for several days, not departing until Friday, March 4, when he headed back west, stopping at Sandy Cross on Saturday. By Monday, the force had returned to the Blackwater River south of Franklin. The next day, Colonel Dearing's cavalry and five infantry companies escorted the wagons, bulging with supplies, back to Weldon.[5] Upon his return, Dearing reported to this wife: "I have been on the tramp constantly ever since I left you with but little rest."[6]

Ransom and his regiments did not accompany Dearing on the return. Instead, the bulk of the force turned northeast into Virginia to prevent any Union forces in the area from pursuing his overstuffed, vulnerable wagon train. On Tuesday, March 8, Ransom headed for Suffolk, passing through the hamlet of Somerton (modern-day Whaleyville). Framed by the Dismal Swamp and the Nansemond River, Suffolk had fallen to Federal troops in 1862 after the Confederates abandoned Norfolk. With its railroad connections, the town offered a convenient base for Federal operations into the rebel interior. John Peck, who commanded the Union garrison there in 1863, considered Suffolk "the key to all the approaches to the mouth of the James River."[7] In 1863, when Confederate forces under James Longstreet besieged the town, Peck's men constructed elaborate defenses.[8] Not everyone agreed with Peck about Suffolk's importance at the time, especially the men assigned to dig these fortifications under his watchful eye. "Though we did not suffer much from the enemy, we did a good deal from General Peck," wrote one of his men. "This fidgety old man kept fortifying and re-fortifying until his soldiers had become regular mud-diggers." According to this critic, "no end of labor and money" had been wasted to "defend a position not worth holding."[9] The grousing of his men aside, Peck was successful in protecting Suffolk from capture.

"We Did Not Take Any Prisoners"

On Wednesday, March 9, Ransom's column, augmented by the 8th North Carolina from Petersburg, collided with the enemy just outside Suffolk. With the 24th and 56th North Carolina leading the way, the rebels encountered members of the 2nd US Colored Cavalry, a recently formed regiment comprised mostly of freedmen from southeastern Virginia.[10] By chance, some of the African American cavalrymen had ventured out that morning on a reconnaissance. A small detachment of Confederate cavalry that was still with Ransom made first contact in a thick fog. The Union horsemen, led by Colonel George Cole, withdrew toward Suffolk, while the Confederate infantry pursued at the double-quick. The North Carolinians struggled through deep sand in the Somerset Road, splashed across a small stream, passed through the town's unoccupied fortifications, and pushed on. It was "a romantic charge—infantry in pursuit of cavalry," recounted one rebel. In town, they continued to engage with the Union horsemen. Confederate cavalry captain Theophilus Barham recalled that the "fighting was sharp," and nearly every member of the small detachment received wounds from bullets or saber cuts. Although he had participated "in many larger engagements," wrote Barham, "this was the closest fighting I saw during the war."[11] According to Union reports, the Federals "whipped the enemy in every charge they made."[12] But Ransom's infantry and artillery soon arrived to push back the horse soldiers. The clash with black troops fueled a malignant determination in Ransom's men. The "southern yell, so peculiar, so stirring, rose above the [cannon's] roar," wrote one attacker, "and on we pressed to engage the inhuman wretches and annihilate, if possible, the dastard foe."[13] As the Confederates entered the streets, white women emerged from their homes waving handkerchiefs, crying, praying, and offering water from buckets and pitchers. Some implored the rebel soldiers to "kill the negroes."[14]

The cavalrymen made a brief stand at the town's far end, firing from houses and bringing up a small howitzer. But Ransom's artillerymen soon unlimbered their guns and opened on the Federals, pushing the horsemen away. The Confederate infantrymen, flagging from their rapid advance into town, could not catch up. "We could see them tumble though, when the Artillery fired," one explained.[15] Appreciating the size of Ransom's force, members of the Union regiment soon withdrew northeast toward Norfolk across swampy ground, halting at a camp near a hamlet known as Bower's Hill.[16] However, several of the horsemen remained in Suffolk, holing up in a house and continuing to fire at the attackers. Any "romantic" aspect of the engagement ended when the Southerners set the house ablaze. "Soon the fire and smoke had its effect," recounted one rebel, "suffocation commenced—one of the infernals leaped from the window to escape the horrible death of burning, a minute more and a dozen bayonets pierced his body." The Confederates shot four more cavalrymen as they tried to escape the inferno.[17]

Other captured Union horsemen suffered a similar fate. In later years, Confederate veterans often took care when recounting the treatment of black prisoners, avoiding any discussion of battlefield atrocities. However, immediately after the Suffolk fighting, there was no such restraint. By their own admission, Ransom's men murdered all their captives. "We did not take any prisoners," boasted one participant to a Charlotte newspaper. "Officers and men were perfectly enthusiastic in killing the 'd—d rascals,' as I heard many call them."[18] John W. Graham, a member of the 56th North Carolina and son of prominent politician William A. Graham, informed his father that his regiment gave "no quarter" to the black troops, for it was "understood amongst us that we take no negro prisoners."[19] Sergeant Thomas Roulhac of the 49th North Carolina wrote that several captives were bayoneted or burned, adding that the "men were perfectly exasperated at the idea of negroes opposed to them & rushed at them like so many devils."[20] After hearing from several participants about the Suffolk fight, Catherine Edmondston noted in her diary: "They took no prisoners & never intending taking any."[21] Accounts of Federal casualties differ. Confederate John W. Graham wrote in a letter to his father that about thirty Union horsemen had been killed, and Theophilus Barham later asserted the number was forty. However, official Union casualty numbers were lower, totaling eight killed and missing, with several wounded. Some of the Union soldiers lost in this fight had been slaves from the area and died close to their former owners' homes. Ransom's command lost about two killed and eight wounded.[22]

The Confederates remained at Suffolk on Wednesday night, gathering the spoils of the victory, which included a small brass howitzer, several horses, and many small arms scattered about by the retreating Federals. At the captured camps outside town, the victors plundered "to their hearts' content." "It was a scene of indescribable confusion—'confusion worse confounded,'" wrote Henry Chambers, where "clothing and implements, paper, books, baker's bread, etc., etc. were handled in regular rampant Rebel fashion."[23] On Thursday, the Union cavalry returned and advanced against the town, only to be driven back by a "few well directed shots" from the artillery, according to one Confederate source.[24] Shortly after noon, Ransom's force withdrew. By the next day, his regiments reached Franklin and entrained there for the return to Weldon.[25]

With the men back in their camps, Confederate officers assessed the expedition's results. The haul was impressive. Ransom's men had gathered nearly 150,000 pounds of bacon from the northeastern counties without any substantial fighting, save for the Suffolk clash. However, with the continued Union control of the North Carolina sounds, it was unclear whether Federal commanders would allow it to occur again. For their part, Union officers focused on the positive aspects of the engagement. Butler, a committed advocate of the black troops, informed Secretary Stanton that the cavalrymen had "behaved with the utmost courage, coolness, and daring. I am perfectly satisfied with my negro cavalry."[26] Reports, however, contained no hint of concern about what Ransom had just achieved. In their correspondence, Union commanders did not delve into the goals behind the Confederate raid or the ease with which Ransom had managed to occupy a large portion of northeastern North Carolina for nearly a week.

Likewise, Union reports made no mention of what had befallen some of the captured cavalrymen. Nevertheless, the prisoner executions at Suffolk reflected an emerging pattern as more black men joined the Union ranks and the Confederates began to encounter them on the battlefield. At Olustee in Florida, Confederate soldiers had murdered black prisoners in February, and about a month after the Suffolk fight, victorious rebels would kill hundreds of black soldiers after combat ended at Fort Pillow in Tennessee. As the number of black regiments grew, so did the frequency with which black soldiers saw combat. Not every battle resulted in black prisoners, nor was every black prisoner killed after being captured. However, several of these engagements resulted in mistreatment and worse. Indeed, the events at Suffolk were not unique and would be repeated elsewhere in 1864.[27]

CHAPTER FOURTEEN

Preparing for the Spring

"The Condition in the South"

One evening in 1885, a freight train crept out of Raleigh along the Seaboard Line headed for Charlotte. A lone sleeping car, carrying only two passengers, joined the line of boxcars pointed west. One of the riders was Joseph Blount Cheshire, the rector of St. Peter's Episcopal Church in Charlotte; the other was Robert F. Hoke, a successful businessman and former Confederate general. With time to kill, the two strangers struck up a conversation. As a child in Tarboro during the 1860s, Cheshire had heard much about Hoke's accomplishments during the war and was eager to engage the veteran on the subject. The former officer, however, showed little interest in recounting those bygone days. This was not surprising, given Hoke's famous reluctance to speak publicly about his war experiences. But it was a long trip, and Cheshire managed to coax the older man into discussing those years of strife. Their talk touched on the 1864 campaign. In laying out the context for those events, Hoke explained, "The condition in the South was growing increasingly difficult," and military officials hoped for additional results after the New Bern expedition. He recalled the supply crisis afflicting Lee's army and noted that eastern North Carolina remained an important source of provisions. Rebel leaders also understood the political benefits that military victories would yield. By Hoke's recollection, William W. Holden had sought to create "a 'Peace at any Price' party," and it "was therefore seen to be of the last importance" that the Confederates seize Union positions in the state that year.[1]

Hoke's discourse with Cheshire was instructive. It revealed how the former general and his fellow veterans would remember their efforts in the spring of 1864. As Thomas Kenan, Hoke's friend and comrade, put it many years later, "The disaffection in some portions of North Carolina against the Confederate government, caused by disappointed persons, was growing to such an extent that it was determined to make an effort to allay it by an attempt to change the military situation."[2]

The New Bern expedition in February did not mark the end of that bid to garner victories. With spring approaching, and with much still to be gained, Confederate officials held fast to their designs for reconquering positions lost to the enemy in 1862.

But as February drifted into March, several factors weighed against the resumption of operations. First, concerned about the impending enemy offensive in Virginia, Robert E. Lee wanted his men back. Even as George Pickett had moved against New Bern in early February, Lee had hoped to consolidate his widely dispersed units. "The approach of spring causes me to consider with anxiety the probable action of the enemy," he admitted.[3] On February 15, he complained that elements of his army, which included Hoke's regiments, were much scattered, and their absence was "deleterious to discipline," "injurious to the service," and "hazardous to the country." As warm weather drew closer, he would repeat his call.[4]

Lee also began to make plans for the spring campaign in Virginia. He considered taking the offensive but harbored no illusions about the ultimate impact of such schemes. "We are not in a condition, and never have been . . . to invade the enemy's country with a prospect of permanent benefit," he conceded. "But we can alarm and embarrass him to some extent, and thus prevent his undertaking anything of magnitude against us."[5] Lee's plans, coupled with his frequent entreaties to Davis, demonstrated that a limited window remained for North Carolina campaigning. For the time being, though, he left Robert Hoke and his brigade at Kinston, still augmented by the 21st Georgia and 43rd North Carolina. Other units remained in the area as well, making up the roughly 13,000-man force of Pickett's Department, stationed at various posts in North Carolina and southern Virginia. These units would not stay for long, however. Many would shift north to help repel Union operations against Richmond once the warm weather arrived.[6]

Confederate leaders still hoped for support from the ironclads. Yet those uncompleted gunboats remained in makeshift naval yards at Halifax and Kinston, and the timing of their deployment was far from clear. During February and March, the rebels engaged in a waiting game as work crews hastened to armor and fit the gunboats and Lee's men looked for signs of a grand Union offensive. The Confederates knew the clock would run out as the warm spring weather brought clear skies and dry roads. At that time, the Army of the Potomac would lunge again, and Lee would need every available man to parry the blow. The Confederate desire for military victories in the Old North State would then bow to the immediate priority: the survival of Lee's army and the protection of the rebel capital.

"The War Spirit Is up in the Army"

During the winter months, George Pickett returned to Petersburg and managed the affairs of his department. Back at Kinston, Robert Hoke remained with his brigade, waiting for another attempt at the Union occupiers. Lee maintained communication with the brigadier, even suggesting that Hoke send his depleted regiments west to hunt for deserters and gather conscripts.[7] Although Hoke chose to remain at Kinston, he enjoyed some recruiting success and managed to replace much of the losses suffered at Rappahannock Station in October. By the end of February, he had increased his brigade to 1,665 officers and men.[8]

Hoke's units settled in at Kinston along with Montgomery Corse's Virginians, who were camped across the Neuse River in full view of the town. The men kept busy drilling and manning picket posts throughout the country, stretching east toward New Bern and Washington. Hoke also put his troops to work suppressing illicit cotton and tobacco trading with the enemy. In mid-February, the unusually mild weather turned bitter cold. Temperatures dropped so low that coffee and water froze on dinner tables.[9] Even after the temperatures moderated, some still found the camps unpleasant. One Virginian, a member of the 17th Infantry, took a dim view of his winter experience, which he spent either drilling or waiting out the rain in his tent. Of the two activities, he preferred the rain, for it allowed him to write letters home.[10] To be sure, other matters occupied the soldiers' time. They served on picket duty and helped strengthen defensive positions, and throughout February, they witnessed a string of prisoner executions. Some also fought off illness, including an outbreak of measles that hit the camps.[11]

As the winter wore on, the men continued to express dissatisfaction with conditions at Kinston. "This is a very low swampy country," wrote Henry Barrow of the 21st North Carolina; the "water is not good & fire wood is very scarce here at this place."[12] A member of the 43rd North Carolina was more direct, calling his camp "doleful & dreary looking," with "nothing but pine thickets & swamps, as far as you can see."[13] A Virginian described Kinston as a "miserable, dilapidated, god-forsaken hole."[14] Even General Corse found the town a difficult post. Writing home to his wife, he confessed, "This dull little place gives me the blues extensively, & I am anxious all the time having the responsibility of this command on me."[15]

Amid this gloom, there were some bright spots, as the winter provided its own diversions. On Tuesday, March 22, a substantial snowstorm blanketed the region. A Fayetteville newspaper noted that the "young townfolks took advantage of the late fall of snow by having *real* sleigh rides . . . a luxury they seldom enjoy."[16] According to a soldier in Kinston, it "stormed awfully, rained, hailed and snowed by turns and the wind blew very hard."[17] As much as 7 inches of the white stuff accumulated in some places—the deepest in five years, by one estimate.[18] The next day, the sun rose and Hoke's men emerged from their quarters, looking for some recreation in the wintry landscape. Leaving their weapons stacked in camp, they ventured across the river, led by their young general, to surprise one of Corse's regiments. As one Virginian recalled, the snowball-wielding Tar Heels arrived "with their band playing and halted in front of our Camp [and] before we knew what they were after they charged us and drove in our camp." Corse's men managed to hold their opponents in check and soon called for reinforcements from another regiment. "We made a yell and charged them and drove them back over the ground they had gained in to a Swamp." Some of the Virginians focused on the leaders, peppering Hoke and three of his staffers with snowballs, then cornering and capturing them. The young general acknowledged that he was "fairly whipped" and returned to his tent cold and soaking.[19]

As the mock battle wound down, the sun rapidly melted the snow, and the men returned to their tents. With spring approaching, the rebels at Kinston were ready for more than snowball fights. They knew Holden and others were agitating for peace and an end to North Carolina's war. "All we wish now in the field is, that all useless men at home may rally to the army—and a hearty and cheerful support from the others," wrote one Tar Heel. "The war spirit is up in the army; and our position now calls for war to the knife and the knife to the hilt."[20]

"A Sea Monster"

In early February, before the snow, Catherine Edmondston reveled in the unusually mild days bathing Halifax County. "Such weather as we have is almost unprecedented," her diary reported, "fine bracing white frosts . . . whilst the middle of the day is mild & serene." Taking advantage of the respite from winter, Edmondston spent several days at Hascosea, one of her family's properties near the Roanoke River. The house, a wood-clad, two-story structure nestled in an oak grove, served as a summer retreat from the larger plantation house, Looking Glass, that stood close by. During that unseasonably warm February, Edmondston visited Hascosea to sort her garden seeds and prune the scuppernong grape vines, which dripped when cut, as if spring had already arrived. But as the soldiers in Kinston discovered, the balmy temperatures did not last. When the weather turned frigid, Edmondston accompanied family members into Halifax on Monday, February 15, to attend to some legal business. Once those matters were concluded, she headed down to the modest navy yard in town to view a local marvel, the unfinished ironclad. "She is now nearly completed," wrote Edmondston. "Engines & Propeller in & will, if the Department at Richmond send on the iron to complete her armour, steam down the river next month." In her opinion, Captain James Cooke, who was supervising the construction effort, had managed to achieve quite a bit in a short time. During her brief tour, she examined the boat's two rifles, which were smaller than she expected.[21]

Edmondston's visit provides a glimpse into the frantic push to complete the ironclads. Early in the war, Confederate leaders had hoped these vessels would tip the balance in the North Carolina sounds. Secretary of the Navy Stephen Mallory had focused limited resources on these unconventional craft, and his plan had borne fruit elsewhere, most famously in the battle between the CSS *Virginia* and the USS *Monitor* in 1862. But on the whole, the ironclad strategy had yielded mixed results, creating alarm among Union commanders but few meaningful victories. In eastern North Carolina, the improvised projects—the *Neuse* at Kinston and the *Albemarle* on the Roanoke River—had crawled along throughout the war, with scarce material (most notably iron), few skilled laborers or experienced sailors, and no advanced facilities to speak of. Indeed, the *Albemarle*'s keel had been set down in a cornfield, and much of its iron plating had been cannibalized from rail lines. As the war stretched into 1864, deployment of the two remaining ironclads seemed more of a lark than a solid military venture.[22]

But the Confederates pressed on. They understood the difference these craft could make. Pickett's failed New Bern expedition highlighted the need for naval power and pushed officials to devote more energy to the boats' completion. Any attack, whether at New Bern, Plymouth, or even Washington, would require the aid of these vessels. By early 1864, the ironclads were nearly ready, and despite their simple design and material limitations, they offered the best hope for a renewed offensive. With spring approaching in Virginia and the window closing for North Carolina operations, the rebels diverted many men and resources to complete the vessels. Before the boats could become more than a theoretical danger, workers needed to finish the hulls and the superstructure and, most importantly, apply the armor.

Iron, however, remained the sticking point. In February, Colonel James Hinton traveled to Halifax to gauge the *Albemarle*'s progress. Once there, he ushered boat-builder Gilbert Elliott down to Wilmington to speed the transportation of iron plates from that point. If the armor could be obtained, Hinton expected the boats could be completed within thirty days.[23] Others pitched in as well. Following the *Underwriter* attack, John Taylor Wood spoke with Secretary Mallory and urged him to do something about the delays.[24] In turn, in early February, Mallory asked the president of the Atlantic and North Carolina Railroad for help in transporting iron from the Atlanta rolling mill to Kinston and Halifax.[25] By the end of the month, Wood reported rapid progress on the vessels and predicted they would "soon be ready for work."[26]

In early March, fourteen loads of iron plate reached Wilmington. However, getting the armor north to Kinston and Halifax proved difficult. The prickly William Lynch, who remained involved with the projects from his desk in Wilmington, complained to Secretary Mallory that the army had tied up the railroad. On March 11, 1864, Lynch griped to Secretary of War James Seddon about inadequate rail capacity. Mallory, who understood the problem, also raised the issue with Seddon directly. He was worried that the Neuse River would drop progressively lower as the summer approached. In the wake of these directives, more material made its way to the construction sites.[27]

Work on the *Albemarle* accelerated. Lieutenant Robert D. Minor visited the Hal-

ifax yard on February 28 and observed, "With the exception of some little connecting work to be completed [the gunboat] may be considered ready." The craft itself
was afloat in the river, its rudder shipped, and its shell room and magazine ready.
Carpenters had already fastened iron to the wooden hull and were bolting plating
on the deck.[28] Five layers of wood and iron formed the *Albemarle*'s casemate. The interior tier consisted of foot-wide yellow pine timbers covered by 5-inch pine planks
and finished with an outer layer of 4-inch oak planks attached vertically. Atop these
wood coverings, the carpenters bolted on two layers of 6-inch-wide iron plates, each
separated by a 2-inch space filled with more wood.[29]

Construction also progressed on the *Neuse* at Kinston. At Robert E. Lee's urging, Hoke contributed greatly to the project, detailing ninety-five carpenters and
mechanics and fifty laborers from his brigade. He expected the craft would be completed by March 1 and noted, "there can be no doubt of success . . . we cannot and
must not stop."[30] In mid-February, Secretary Mallory had sent Lieutenant Minor
to Kinston to supervise the effort. Upon his arrival, Minor found nearly 200 men
working on the vessel, including those assigned by General Hoke.[31] Carpenters
caulked portions of the hull, workers lowered the boiler into the vessel, and as-
semblers fastened two layers of iron "on the forward end of her shield." However,
Minor found no plating on the broadsides or on the stern and predicted the boat
would not be ready until March 18.[32] The Navy Department assigned Lieutenant
Benjamin P. Loyall to command the *Neuse*. With Loyall in charge of the vessel itself,
Minor continued to oversee construction operations. Everyone pitched in. On at
least two occasions, Hoke returned from Richmond carrying his personal trunk
filled with augurs and other tools.[33]

Many hoped for great things from the *Neuse*. In March, a member of the 43rd
North Carolina wrote that the gunboat "is almost finished, and is expected to do
wonders in conjunction with the one on the Roanoke river."[34] However, not everyone was impressed. Some officers, underwhelmed by the construction's progress,
began to call the boat the "Neus'ance." "I am afraid that name will prove but to[o]
appropriate," complained Richard Bacot, who had served on the ironclad *Arkansas*
and participated in the *Underwriter*'s destruction. According to Bacot, neither the
boat's quarters, storerooms, nor "iron fixin's" were ready. He also fretted that the
river was falling about a foot a day, casting doubt on successful operations until rain
reversed the trend. Bacot had choice words for the crew as well, describing them
as "long, lank, 'Tar Heels' (N.C.'s from the Piney woods)," who were "all legs and
arms and while working at the guns their legs get 'tangled' in the tackles and they
are always in the wrong place and in each other's way."[35]

As the last days of March ebbed away, the slow delivery of iron continued to re-
tard progress. Lieutenant Loyall was beside himself. On April 7, he wrote to Minor
about the iron delays, noting a three-week gap between shipments. The frustrated
Loyall explained, "Every time I telegraphed to Lynch he replies, 'Army monopoliz-

ing cars.' It is all exceedingly mortifying to me."[36] As the weeks went by, the water level in the Neuse and Roanoke Rivers became a crucial consideration. At Halifax, Cooke and his men kept an eye on the river, which fluctuated significantly, depending on rainfall. To the south, the Neuse River was unusually low; at only 5 feet deep, it was too shallow for the 6 or 7 feet drawn by the ironclad.[37]

Despite the delays and worries, the Confederates had reason for cheer. They had nearly completed two formidable vessels primed to attack the Union bases at Plymouth and New Bern. It had been a long, frustrating, and imperfect saga. In many ways, the mere fact that these boats had been built at all was nothing short of remarkable. Their very existence stood as a testament to the vision of Stephen Mallory, the persistence of boatbuilder Gilbert Elliott, and the tenacity of officers such as Hoke and Minor, as well the day-to-day work of the gunboat captains, Cooke and Loyall.

The two craft shared a similar design: a flat, armored deck only several inches above the waterline, topped by at iron-plated casemate on the vessel's middle third. Given the exigencies of construction, the designers, engineers, and builders stuck to a simple, straightforward plan. The boats had no complicated turrets, no elaborate ventilation systems, and no iron hulls. The engines, whose precise origins remain murky, may have been borrowed from sawmills or constructed from scratch.[38] On the *Albemarle*, two 200-horsepower engines turned two propeller shafts. Measurements taken by Federal officials after the war revealed that the *Albemarle* was 158 feet long and slightly more than 35 feet in breadth at its widest point. The *Neuse* was similar in configuration but shorter, measuring about 136 feet long. Fully loaded, the *Albemarle* drew 9 feet. The deck had a 1-inch layer of plating, while the casemate, with eight sides sloped at thirty-five degrees, held two layers of 2-inch iron plates. At the bow, the *Albemarle* featured a solid oak prow with 2-inch plating, which served as a ram. The two gun positions inside the casemate had 7 feet of headroom. Thick iron shutters shielded the ports when not in use, and a small "pilothouse" protruded a few feet above the casemate roof, which consisted primarily of iron grating.[39]

Both vessels carried two 6.4-inch Brooke rifled guns, mounted inside the casemate at each end. Each weapon could be run out of one of three portholes. Named for their designer John Mercer Brooke, these guns were the mainstay of the Confederate navy and coastal defense batteries. In Secretary Mallory's view, they were "in strength, accuracy, and range . . . superior to all our guns."[40] They resembled the Federal Parrott rifles in appearance, primarily due to the distinctive iron band around the weapon's chamber, designed to prevent the barrel from bursting during action. With its high velocity and long range, the Brooke rifle posed a dire threat to the Union navy's wooden boats stationed in the North Carolina sounds. The *Albemarle* would later be described as "a sea monster equal in the eyes of friend and foe to the terrible Merrimac." There was little reason to doubt this assessment.[41]

With these two vessels taking shape, the Confederates looked ahead. Hoke, in particular, fully expected to resume the offensive soon. In late March, he assigned a detail under Henry Guion from the 10th North Carolina to help finish the ironclad at Kinston. While his men worked, Guion drafted maps and charts of the New Bern area from his own memory, as well as information gleaned during the recent expedition. On March 19, he drew a sprawling freehand map detailing the roads, rivers, and works surrounding the city and provided the sketch to General Hoke.[42]

"I Have Worked at Shoveling . . . Digging Again the Next Day"

While the Confederates busied themselves with the ironclads, the Union commanders remained alert to the possibility of further enemy operations. Major General John J. Peck, still in command of Union forces in the state, became convinced in February that "Jeff. Davis has decided upon recovering Newbern and the Sounds" and believed the Confederates would follow up on their earlier efforts. Peck and other commanders had known for more than a year that the rebels were building the ironclads—the "rams," as he called them—and expected the vessels would soon support an upcoming attack at New Bern or perhaps Plymouth.[43] Reports to this effect poured in throughout February. One story suggested that the Kinston gunboat would descend the Neuse River after the next heavy rain to aid a renewed assault.[44] Another warned that the Confederates had set the attack date for March 14, the second anniversary of Burnside's victory.[45] Peck also heard that the Southerners were massing 25,000 men for another strike on New Bern. He warned Butler of the danger in a string of dispatches throughout February and March.[46]

In response to these warnings, New Bern buzzed. Private Luther Baldwin of the 15th Connecticut wrote, "Gen. Peck is preparing to receive the rebs . . . every precaution is taken to prevent a surprise & a repetition of the game they played on the *Underwriter*, a few weeks ago."[47] Peck and the commander of the New Bern garrison, Innis Palmer, implemented several measures to improve the defenses. They ordered men to sink old hulks in the Neuse upstream to block the rebel ironclad's passage.[48] They also improved the fortifications, particularly the lines and forts just west of the city along the river, extending the defenses south of Fort Totten after discovering that attacking infantry could cross the marsh there.[49] They enhanced the forts south of the Trent River as well, clearing fields of fire and strengthening the works. In addition to these various measures, Peck and Palmer closed the camps for freed slaves outside the lines and consolidated them on the south bank of the Trent inside the fortifications.[50]

Joining the men in uniform, civilians, both white and black, took up shovels and picks to pile more dirt on the fortifications. The crews expanded the walls and formed new facings for them. Baldwin reported that "all hands" were "at work on a Fort we are building near our barracks, or on guard, or picket, about every other day." He noted, "I have worked at Shoveling, & gone on picket at night, digging again the next day."[51] Whole artillery units left their barracks and posts to join in these efforts, which yielded a new redoubt north of Fort Rowan near the riverbank, a small work mounting one 100-pounder rifle and two 32-pounders sweeping the front. The men worked hard, and details received whiskey rations for their efforts. On the Trent to the south, the engineers traced out an extension of Fort Amory, which allowed Union gunners to cover the river itself as well as approaches to Fort Totten.[52] In addition to these improvements, the garrisons received much-needed reinforcements from the north. The 3rd New York Artillery absorbed nearly 500 recruits in early March, and the entire 16th Connecticut arrived from Norfolk to bolster the force at Plymouth. Peck also traveled to Plymouth to personally inspect the defensive improvements there.[53] The preparations throughout the district bred confidence. "We hear that the rebs say that they will have Newbern by the 21 of March," recalled Baldwin. "We don't see it. If they attempt to take it, they will meet with a warm reception."[54]

Union naval officers also augmented their force in the North Carolina sounds. Lieutenant Commander Flusser, in charge of the gunboats at Plymouth, called for more firepower after the New Bern attack. He understood the continued presence of a large rebel contingent in the state meant that another advance was in the offing.[55] He concluded, "We must also have a large force here and soon," and he warned that the existing collection of gunboats was incapable of defending New Bern, Washington, and Plymouth against a simultaneous attack. In Flusser's view, Plymouth stood out as the easiest position to defend because the enemy could not plant batteries on the marshy banks opposite the town. To him, the small flotillas guarding points other than Plymouth "would prove no match for" the rebel cannon, and successful Confederate efforts would cut off and starve the garrisons. He understood that the introduction of a rebel ironclad to these operations heightened the danger significantly.[56] To aid the boats already in the state, Secretary of the Navy Gideon Welles dispatched the formidable double-ender *Tacony*, carrying two 100-pounder Parrott rifles, four large Dahlgren guns, and several other smaller weapons.[57]

"Forewarned, Forearmed"

Flusser was not the only commander concerned about the rebel gunboats. Peck, in New Bern, had been worried about the threat from these armored craft for a long time.[58] Back in September 1863, he had asked the navy for an ironclad of his own to protect his posts. None was provided. In fact, even in April 1864, there were no armored boats available that could operate effectively in Carolina's shallow waters. "Were our iron-clads, now completed, available for service in the sounds, they could not be sent there," confessed Secretary Welles, "as they draw too much water to cross the Bulkhead at Hatteras. Our light-draught ones will not be completed for some time to come."[59] The absence of a suitable Union ironclad for operations in North Carolina would continue well into 1864.

The Federals turned to other measures. In 1863, Welles and Rear Admiral Lee urged the army to move out and destroy the incomplete rebel ironclads in their yards, or at least obstruct "the river by torpedoes and piles or otherwise, so as to prevent their descent." In response, Stanton referred the matter to his subordinates. In August, Peck took the initiative and began to plan a direct strike against the gunboats before they became operational, but department commander Foster thought the available forces were inadequate. With his limited resources, Peck focused on defense.[60]

At Plymouth, Federal defenders pushed improvements to their works and armament. In late 1863, they moved a 100-pounder gun from Fort Hatteras to cover the Roanoke River upstream of the town. In early 1864, Peck remained concerned that the Confederate army, along with the new gunboats, would deliver devastating blows on his positions.[61] He sank more hulks in the Neuse and ordered similar measures in the Tar River upstream from Washington.[62] The navy prepared as well. In October 1863, with advice from Lee, Flusser began to place obstructions in the Roanoke River and conducted a detailed survey of the various channels and river segments above the town.[63]

Butler, with overall command of Union army forces in North Carolina and southeastern Virginia, seemed to vacillate between indifference and engagement in response to the Confederate threat. He cast doubt on Peck's warnings about Confederate troop strength in the state, chiding that if the Confederates actually had 25,000 men available for an attack on New Bern, they "must be not only ubiquitous but more numerous than the sands of the sea," given reports that Pickett's men were also massing in southeastern Virginia.[64] At times, Butler was equally dismissive of the ironclad threat. In a much-referenced dispatch to Peck drafted on February 20, 1864, he wrote that he did not "believe in the iron-clad."[65] He had made a similar statement to Admiral Lee several days before, and back in the fall, he had expressed "unconcern" for the danger. Butler's various statements led some to conclude that he doubted the ironclad's very existence.[66]

But Butler was not completely blind to the peril. He knew the Confederates had kept troops in the state, though not as many as Peck estimated. He also understood and accepted that the gunboat existed, that it was nearly finished, and that it would likely threaten Plymouth. Although he disagreed with Peck about the magnitude of the risk at hand, he did not discourage Peck from placing obstructions in the river, explaining that it was not his intention "to cripple you or to interfere with your judgment as to means of defense." He also explained in his February 20 letter, "I don't believe in the iron-clad arrangement, and if you cannot deal with her from the point we visited together with your 200-pounder Parrott I shall be very much surprised." Butler suspected that the greater danger lay in a rebel amphibious assault that would land troops via barges above the obstructions, seize the batteries, and open the way for the ironclad. "Forewarned, forearmed," Butler advised. He recommended that commanders station a small, quick steamboat above the obstructions to alert the garrison of such an attack.[67]

Responding to his superior's musings, Peck assured Butler that the ironclad posed a serious threat. "Hitherto it has been a question of iron and time," he correctly explained. However, new reports indicated that iron was in fact arriving to cover the rebel gunboats.[68] Peck told Butler, "Every day and hour brings testimony bearing upon the plan of the Confederate authorities for driving us out of the 'Old North State.'" He knew from informants that Hoke was poised at Kinston with several brigades and that the boat on the Roanoke was nearly done, with "her machinery . . . all in."[69]

Throughout February and March, Union commanders continued to receive troubling reports about the concentration of Confederate troops and progress on the ironclads. In February, rumors arrived that the boat at Kinston remained on the stocks but had already been partially plated. In early March, Davenport gathered from a deserter, a cavalry sergeant, that the vessel was almost ready and would soon float down the Roanoke to attack Plymouth. The man predicted the rebels would send a small diversionary column to New Bern and Washington to fix the forces there and prevent them from reinforcing Plymouth.[70] These warnings set the Plymouth garrison on edge. Some officers hurried their families onto Norfolk-bound steamers.[71]

On March 16, Flusser passed along word from "an old steamboat captain" that the gunboat would descend the river on April 1, plated with two layers of iron. But Flusser held on to the belief that the plating was thin and would be easily penetrated by batteries in the Plymouth defenses.[72] From New Bern, Peck agreed, predicting that the heavy guns in Plymouth's forts would repel or destroy the ironclad.[73] Nevertheless, Flusser continued to prepare for the menace, dropping more old schooners upstream in the Roanoke and attaching mines ("torpedoes") to these obstructions.[74] Near the beginning of April, he heard that the enemy vessel was at Hamilton, ready for service, and that the rebels were busy removing torpedoes and obstructions in the river.[75]

As rumors of the ironclad and the new rebel operations increased, so did Butler's interest in North Carolina. Like Peck months earlier, Butler wanted to go after the gunboats directly. On March 21, 1864, he asked Admiral Lee, "Why cannot we organize a little expedition to burn the iron-clad."[76] He coupled his query with a report that the boat had grounded in the Roanoke 25 miles above Plymouth, and its guns had been removed in an effort to refloat it. The implication of this rumor was clear: the ironclad was stranded and unarmed, perhaps ripe for the picking.[77]

On the same day, Butler advised Peck, "I think if the navy cannot go up with their gunboats and destroy [the ironclad], that you had better organize a little expedition by land. A single regiment of cavalry would do it, and it is only four hours' ride."[78]

Peck pursued the possibility of a raid. He asked his naval counterparts whether the ram could be destroyed and explored whether a force of cavalry would be adequate to do the job. However, without information about which bank of the river the vessel was on, Peck feared a land approach would be risky.[79] Admiral Lee responded enthusiastically to the idea of a raid, agreeing that a project to burn the ironclad "seemed feasible." He directed Flusser to organize the expedition's naval component.[80] But Flusser, who was scrambling to arm his two main gunboats (the *Southfield* and the *Miami*), advised against the raid. He had received intelligence that conflicted with Butler's information, and other reports convinced Flusser that the ironclad remained at Halifax in an unfinished condition and that the Confederates were alert to a possible movement "up country" by Union troops. In Flusser's judgment, Union preparations to meet the gunboat had placed the rebels on guard. Lee agreed, noting that the information behind Butler's suggestion appeared to be "unreliable."[81] Talk of a raid to burn the ironclad ended there, and with it, perhaps the Union's best chance to nullify the threat it posed.[82]

During the first days of April, the focus of Union dispatches shifted from offensive operations to defensive measures aimed at repelling the impending attack.[83] Peck assured Butler that all the subdistrict commanders were ready. The navy also continued to prepare. By the end of March, Admiral Lee had arranged a substantial collection of gunboats to guard against the upcoming offensive.[84] The *Southfield*, *Miami*, and *Whitehead* protected Plymouth; the *Tacony*, *Hetzel*, *Commodore Hull*, and *Ceres* stood off New Bern.[85] Of these various craft, the *Southfield*, *Miami*, and *Tacony* were the most formidable. However, even these prodigious wooden vessels would not fare well in a slugging match against an iron-plated boat.[86]

"Expensive, Insecure"

In the churn of Union efforts during the spring of 1864 to prepare Plymouth, Washington, and other posts, there was much talk of reinforcements, river obstructions, battery construction, and armament. No one, however, seemed to question whether these towns were worth defending in the first place. The issue had been debated in the early months of Union occupation, when General Foster had batted away Admiral Lee's concerns. Into 1863, Lee continued to question the value of holding these posts, believing them to be insecure and expensive to maintain.[87] The small, isolated garrisons at Plymouth and Washington offered tempting targets for the Confederates seeking victories in North Carolina. Their capture would significantly aid rebel supply efforts and increase Confederate morale. Conversely, their loss would have a limited impact on Union military efforts. For instance, Plymouth, which was not connected to a rail line, was a poor location to serve as a supply base for large offensive operations into the interior. In addition, Union positions elsewhere at Roanoke Island, Hatteras Inlet, New Bern, and Morehead City provided Federal forces more than ample locations to continue their control over the region. By 1864, however, Admiral Lee had seemingly resigned himself to the army's arrangement. And in the rapid exchange of messages about the approaching rebel gunboat, no officer in either the army or the navy broached the subject.

Throughout March and into April, Federal commanders in the state focused on anticipating the timing and location of the impending enemy offensive. However, amidst the flurry of reports, directives, and warnings, there was little discussion of overall strategy for the region and the arrangement of Union forces there. Commanders in Washington, DC, and at Fort Monroe focused on the upcoming campaign in Virginia. There is little evidence that Halleck or Grant gave any significant attention to broad matters in North Carolina. Butler continued to engage with Peck on the details of the rebel ironclad but showed no inclination to change the overall Federal approach. Accordingly, the men in the North Carolina bases would sit tight and conduct their routine, minor operations while hoping the Confederates would not attack again.

As they prepared for the Virginia campaign, members of the high command continued to view North Carolina as little more than a troop reservoir. Indeed, on April 2, Grant ordered Butler to "collect all the forces from your command that can be spared from garrison duty." Grant also directed the transfer of 10,000 men from South Carolina to Fort Monroe.[88] Peck knew what Grant's plan meant for the troops at New Bern and other posts. On April 4, he warned Henry Wessells, the overall commander at Plymouth, not to expect more gunboats or troops, for "every thing seems being sent to the Army of the Potomac."[89] Butler, in implementing Grant's instructions, began to siphon troops from Peck's command and ship them north. On April 10, for instance, he ordered Peck to send two batteries north, as well as the 3rd New York Cavalry. More would follow.[90]

By weakening positions in North Carolina to feed operations elsewhere, Federal commanders were calculating that the rebels would not succeed in the Old North State, and if they did, the results would have little impact. To be sure, a Confederate victory there was unlikely to affect the material strength of Union forces. Months before, Halleck had pushed aside Grant's proposal to make North Carolina the focus of Federal operations, given concerns about protecting Washington, DC. The decision to ignore the potential behind Grant's plan would fix the protracted bloody fighting of 1864 to the combat-torn fields and forests of central Virginia. By neglecting North Carolina, the high command seemed to discount or ignore the impact of potential rebel victories there on Confederate morale, Lee's supply situation, and political conditions in the state.

PART FIVE

Hoke's Attack on Plymouth

In April, warmer weather approached and, with it, the certainty of a Union offensive in Virginia. However, Confederate leaders continued to weigh their options for North Carolina, hoping for one last tug at the Federal positions. Robert Hoke and his men remained at Kinston and waited anxiously for work crews to complete the ironclads. Finally, as April wound down, orders arrived for an attack on Plymouth.

CHAPTER FIFTEEN

Plymouth Is the Target

"Another Attempt"

In early March, the *New York Times* reported that a rebel deserter had slipped into the Union lines in Washington with news that the Confederates planned to attack Plymouth.[1] Throughout the first several months of 1864, a storm of rumors pelted Union commanders about an upcoming Confederate offensive. At the Federal bases, anxiety rose and fell with the news of rebel plans. One Union soldier in Plymouth, S. J. Gibson, noted in his diary in late March, "There is some apprehension of an attack at this place but as yet I see no signs of danger."[2] There was not much consistency to the stories, for other potential targets were mentioned as well. The Confederates, it was heard, would hit New Bern or perhaps Washington or maybe Norfolk. Even rebel soldiers could only guess at what would happen. From Kinston, one Tar Heel infantryman wrote in early March, "Every one seems to think that Gen'l Hoke will make another attempt to take Newbern as soon as the boat here and the one at Halifax are completed."[3] As it turned out, the *New York Times* was correct.

The Confederate high command was indeed considering plans to move against Plymouth. By the spring of 1864, a new personality had arrived in Richmond to help coordinate the war effort. President Davis had brought in the quarrelsome Braxton Bragg to be his military adviser. Despite Bragg's recent resignation from the Army of Tennessee and his proclivity for perturbing colleagues, Davis valued the North Carolinian's military expertise.[4] From Richmond, Bragg helped coordinate activities between departments, fielding communications from Robert E. Lee and persistent requests from the various departmental commanders. As part of his new duties, Bragg looked into plans for a resumption of the Confederate offensive in his home state.

With the ironclads nearing completion in early April, Bragg asked Pickett to draft plans for a new offensive against the Federal positions in eastern North Carolina. On April 6, 1864, Pickett responded, presenting a "synopsis of the plan of proposed operations" that identified Plymouth as the target.[5] He proposed to hit the town with three brigades and the completed ironclad. To aid the assault, he recommended that John Taylor Wood descend the Chowan River with a "boat party" to attack the Union vessels at Plymouth and otherwise support the offensive. Pickett's blueprint also included a diversion toward New Bern two days prior to the operation. Following Plymouth's capture, he urged that all available forces combine with both ironclads and proceed to New Bern. Despite Wood's involvement, he viewed the armored gunboats as essential to his plan, stressing that "it might not be wise to attempt" the attack without them.[6] Like the New Bern expedition in February, Pickett's Plymouth operation would allow the Confederates to use the railroad to quickly concentrate force on an isolated enemy base. Once again, the Wilmington and Weldon Railroad would facilitate the rapid transport of scattered units to a central staging area. With adequate secrecy and speed, a sizable force could arrive at the enemy's ramparts with little warning. Furthermore, Pickett's proposed diversion against New Bern would enhance the offensive by sowing doubt about the Confederates' true target.

Bragg sought Robert E. Lee's thoughts on Pickett's plan. Though concerned about Hoke's return to his army, Lee had not followed the events in North Carolina carefully over the last two months, admitting to Davis in late March that he had "heard nothing on the subject recently."[7] Bragg brought the general up to date. On April 11, he informed Lee that President Davis viewed the effort as "an important expedition which may add materially to our sources of supply for the subsistence of your command."[8] While Lee commented favorably on the plan, he also used the opportunity to lobby once again for Hoke's return, suggesting that a brigade from Wilmington or Charleston step in for Hoke's troops.[9] Lee remained deeply concerned about supplying his army and even warned that he might have to withdraw as far south as North Carolina to feed his men.[10] He also conveyed urgency, given the upcoming Federal operations, and recommended that if "anything is to be done in North Carolina it should be done quickly."[11]

"Some Distrust" of Pickett's Adequacy

Although Pickett had drafted the plan to take Plymouth, the high command ultimately declined to put him in charge of the new offensive. On April 12, Bragg approved Pickett's scheme, with one important caveat: Hoke, not Pickett, would lead the attacking force. In removing Pickett from the picture, Richmond officials nudged him into a supporting role, directing him to coordinate demonstrations from Petersburg and Kinston to distract the enemy. In explaining the decision to Pickett, Bragg simply stated that the "conduct of this expedition is intrusted to Brigadier General Hoke, so as not to withdraw you from a supervision of your whole department at this critical time."[12] Though Bragg did not express any particular dissatisfaction with Pickett, it is unlikely that the Virginian perceived the decision as anything but a personal slight. War Department official Robert Kean, relaying gossip heard from General James Kemper, wrote in his diary that the expedition "was planned . . . by Pickett, and the command taken from him, i.e., he was anxious to conduct in person."[13] Relations between Pickett and Bragg would soon deteriorate. Over the coming weeks, Bragg would criticize Pickett for crowding official reports with irrelevant rumors.[14] Demoralized, the increasingly thin-skinned Pickett shot back that the "tone [of Bragg's letter] is as harsh as the inferences to be drawn are unmerited."[15] Later correspondence between Bragg and Secretary of War Seddon suggests that they both held a decidedly dim view of Pickett, and Seddon even expressed "some distrust" about the general's ability to handle his duties.[16] The schism later received attention outside the army. The *Richmond Enquirer*, for instance, accused Bragg of pursuing the Plymouth operation and elevating Hoke at the expense of Petersburg's safety, as well as the reputations of Virginians Barton and Pickett.[17]

Some evidence suggests that, despite his willingness to craft a plan for the expedition, Pickett opposed further advances in North Carolina that spring. According to his wife after the war, the general argued against the Plymouth venture, viewing it as an unnecessary risk, given the impending Federal threat to Richmond and Petersburg. LaSalle Pickett later claimed that her husband raised the matter directly with Robert E. Lee in confidential correspondence. According to her account, Lee stated that he was "in perfect sympathy with your apprehensions."[18] However, no such dispatches have surfaced outside of quotations from Mrs. Pickett's published writings, which historians have treated with immense caution, given her tendency to edit, invent, and embellish.[19] However, her assertion that Pickett and Lee had concerns about the Plymouth expedition is highly plausible. Saddled with the responsibility for both southern Virginia and eastern North Carolina, Pickett harbored long-standing concerns about Petersburg's vulnerability, particularly given Union control of the land bases at Norfolk, Suffolk, and Fort Monroe.[20] In April, a cascade of reports, some of them more credible than others, hinted at a Federal advance along the axis of the James River.[21] For Pickett, this threat may have diminished his enthusiasm for offensive operations in North Carolina.[22] Although his actual views remain murky, there was some reason for concern, for other events threatened to derail the Plymouth venture. Throughout April, warnings abounded that Ambrose Burnside would soon land somewhere on the coast, perhaps in Virginia or North Carolina, and push inland in conjunction with other advances orchestrated by Grant.[23] In addition, as Bragg and Lee reviewed Pickett's plan, Grant was assembling his spring offensive designed to apply simultaneous pressure on Confederate forces at multiple points. Once the fighting commenced in Virginia, the opposing armies would need all the troops they could scrape together.

As the high command wrestled with priorities, Pickett faded out of the 1864

North Carolina campaign. He would remain in Petersburg, contributing to defensive operations there and at Bermuda Hundred in early May. Ultimately, his time as head of the North Carolina Department would bring him few laurels. Certainly, Matt Ransom's foraging raid and Hoke's successful deserter hunt, both of which occurred under his command, had provided some reason for Confederate cheer. However, the low points had mostly blotted out these events. During his tenure, the region had seen Edward Wild's humiliating raid, the failed New Bern offensive, the tragic executions at Kinston, the slow work on the ironclads, and the mushrooming peace movement. Pickett's months in charge of the department had done little to enhance his reputation and, instead, had raised more questions about his capabilities.

"This Expedition Is Intrusted to Brigadier General Hoke"

With Pickett cast aside, Robert Hoke, the rising star, stepped into command. Born in Lincoln County in 1837, he had watched his father run for governor, lose, and pass away a month after the contest. He then attended military school in Kentucky but returned home at age seventeen to run the family business, which involved the manufacture of cotton, paper, iron, and linseed oil.[24] In 1861, at age twenty-four, he joined the 1st North Carolina Infantry, Company K, as a second lieutenant. He distinguished himself at Big Bethel in June of that year, at New Bern in 1862, and in many of the campaigns fought by Lee's army in Virginia. He rose rapidly, attaining the rank of brigadier general in early 1863, a month after the Battle of Fredericksburg. Seriously wounded when a bullet tore through his shoulder at Salem Church during the Chancellorsville campaign, he missed the offensive into Pennsylvania and the fighting at Gettysburg.[25] Nevertheless, he retained a good reputation among his superiors. In recommending him for promotion back in 1862, General Jubal Early wrote that Hoke had "shown himself eminently qualified to command a Brigade, both in camp, on the march, and in action." Early described Hoke as "an officer of great energy and industry, and attends most diligently to his duties on all occasions."[26]

Hoke was calm, intelligent, and likable. His contemporaries left glowing descriptions. One wrote, "Gen. Hoke is nearly six feet in height, stands erect, has dark hair and dark eyes, and is noted as a high-toned Christian gentleman, having been for several years . . . a communicant in the Protestant Episcopal Church . . . he is a pious, praying man."[27] Another acquaintance recalled that he had "very pleasant manners, fine conversational powers, & is very handsome."[28] John Cheshire, who would share the rail journey with the general in 1885, noted that Hoke was kind, humane, modest, and gentle but also "a man of great force and of iron will, quiet in method, but immovable and inexorable in matters of duty."[29] An anonymous officer who served with Hoke in 1864 wrote that he displayed "wonderful tact, force, activity, and an endurance that despises fatigue" and handled "troops with great ease and celerity, and has their unbounded confidence."[30]

As the Confederates set their sights on Plymouth, Hoke played a significant role behind the scenes, just as he had done before the New Bern expedition a few months earlier. According to several accounts, he traveled to Richmond at least twice that spring to confer with officials there. One of those visits occurred in mid-March, and he left Montgomery Corse at Kinston to tend to matters there. Corse fretted that Hoke's trip would deprive him of his "main support & dependence for keeping every thing straight on the outposts."[31] On Sunday, March 13, Hoke attended church in Richmond with a gaggle of other generals.[32] In early April, he traveled to Virginia again and reportedly heard Governor Vance speak to the troops in Lee's army.[33]

On at least one of these trips, most likely the April visit, Hoke met personally with President Davis to discuss North Carolina operations. No contemporaneous records of such a meeting have been found, but Thomas Kenan, a veteran of the 43rd North Carolina and state attorney general after the war, later indicated that President Davis held a "long conference in Richmond" with Hoke about ways to "encourage the people" of North Carolina. Davis asked Hoke "many questions about the different points occupied by the Federal troops, and especially about the feasibility of attacking Plymouth."[34] Another account, an 1894 letter written by an anonymous source (identified only as "Private A. N. V."), reported that Bragg also attended this meeting and produced a complete campaign plan set out in "the minutest details, even to fixing the time of marching, places of encampment and the hour of storming the fortifications of Plymouth," as well as additional plans should the town be taken. After reviewing the program, Hoke identified "some defective combinations" and raised concerns about the plan's prescriptive detail. In response to these comments, Bragg reportedly modified the scheme to give Hoke more discretion. Hoke may have discussed the political situation in his home state as well. According to one North Carolina historian, President Davis asked Hoke what was to be done about peace agitation. Hoke reportedly replied, "Arrest Holden and send him out of the country." Davis rejected the notion out of hand and explained that he was seeking military advice, a statement the historian described as awakening "the enthusiasm of General Hoke."[35] Yet another account of the meeting indicates that President Davis stressed the need for "rapid movement and a prompt attack," given the failure at New Bern. Hoke, in turn, expressed eagerness to lead the expedition and assured the president that "the attack would be made at the first moment possible."[36]

According to some accounts, Hoke asked the president for special authority to ensure unity of command over all the forces involved in the Plymouth campaign—both army and navy. During their conversation, Davis reportedly called for an orderly from the secretary of the navy's office and dictated a letter "placing all the Confederate vessels in that part of North Carolina under" Hoke's direct command and control. In doing so, Davis put an army officer in charge of naval operations in the state. To ensure the directive's secrecy, the president instructed the orderly to make no copy nor enter any record of the document. Hoke returned south with the president's secret in his pocket.[37]

Hoke arrived back in Kinston on April 12.[38] There, he received Bragg's final written orders for the Plymouth attack, which assigned Hoke "special command" of the expedition. The young general shared the news with Henry Guion, who recorded: "Met the Gen'l and he tells me that Pickett has given over the expedition to Plymouth, and he is put in command of it."[39] The force would include Hoke's own brigade at Kinston, Ransom's brigade from Weldon, and Kemper's (Terry's) brigade then at Tarboro, as well as artillery and a cavalry regiment from Kinston. Bragg emphasized the need for speed and secrecy and urged Hoke to coordinate with naval commander James Cooke. If successful at Plymouth, Hoke was to proceed to Washington and New Bern. Bragg's directive avoided specifics and exhorted Hoke to rely on his "well-known activity and energy." It also emphasized the need for "prompt and decided action" and warned that delay would alert the enemy, scuttle the operation, and "make it cost too dearly for you to reap the fruits so confidently expected." Bragg hoped Hoke would set off for Plymouth from Tarboro on April 16 or 17.[40]

"Few Tumbled-Down Houses"

Sited on the Roanoke's south bank just a few miles upriver from the Albemarle Sound, Plymouth had ranked as one of the state's larger ports during the colonial period. It also served as an important source of naval supplies, including masts and spars, shingles, and barrels and casks hewn from the juniper and cypress trees crowding the swampy countryside. However, in the decades prior to the Civil War, the town's population declined, and by the time the war broke out, Plymouth struggled to compete with other inland ports such as New Bern, Washington, and Elizabeth City. Nevertheless, it remained a significant site for commerce, and in 1860, a new customhouse was under construction there.[41]

Plymouth was not a large town. It consisted of eighteen blocks arranged in a rectangle, six blocks long and three deep. Three roads connected it to the outside world. The Washington Road, from the southwest, served as Plymouth's primary link to the state's interior. The Mill Road exited the town south, leading to the farms and swamps dappling the countryside on the Albemarle-Pamlico Peninsula. The Columbia Road headed east toward a small hamlet of the same name in a remote, sparsely populated area south of the Albemarle Sound.

Like New Bern, Plymouth had become a magnet for self-emancipated slaves and Confederate deserters following the Federal victories of 1862.[42] It had also become the target of Confederate attacks. In fact, the town changed hands several times early on, like a "shuttle-cock" in a badminton game, according to one Federal observer.[43] A successful raid by the 17th North Carolina Infantry in December 1862 overran the Federal defenders there and temporarily filled the town with Confederates. During the fight, Union gunboats stationed in the Roanoke River lobbed shells into the streets, igniting several buildings before the Federals eventually regained control of the town.[44]

Battered by months of war, Plymouth became an armed camp that was largely devoid of shops, houses, and public buildings. Union soldiers found the town in a "dilapidated condition," a "mere remnant" of a once "thriving village" consisting of only a "few tumble-down houses that had escaped the flames, two or three brick stores and houses, and the rest a medley of negro shanties." In addition to the soldiers in the Union garrison, the town itself contained about 500 people, mostly refugees. "The whole place had a Rip Van Winkle look," explained Massachusetts soldier Warren Goss, "as though it had composed itself into a long sleep to awake after the era of revolution and rebellion had passed."[45] William H. Stiner, the *New York Herald* reporter who had accompanied Benjamin Butler's November 1863 inspection, noted, "the appearance of the town is dismal indeed," and its occupants had "the sallow tint of fever and ague stamped upon their features."[46] The war sharply divided Washington County and the rest of the region around Plymouth, and the area's mix of social classes, races, and divided loyalties generated sustained tension and much violence.[47]

The US Army had made Plymouth its own. The town served as headquarters for the Union Subdistrict of Albemarle, which encompassed Roanoke Island and other locations around the Albemarle Sound. Command of the subdistrict fell to Brigadier General Henry W. Wessells, a veteran of the Second Seminole and Mexican Wars. A Connecticut native, Wessells served on the Missouri border early in the war but was transferred east, where he commanded a brigade during the Peninsula Campaign and was wounded at Fair Oaks. Throughout 1863, he served at various posts in southeastern Virginia and eastern North Carolina, eventually settling in to command at Plymouth. Though the fifty-five-year-old Wessells rarely donned full military dress and was often mistaken for an enlisted man, he was always "dignified and reserved in demeanor."[48] A Connecticut soldier in the garrison described him as "a fine man of the old school," "a quiet sort of man," and "a very good drill master."[49]

The Plymouth garrison contained a few thousand men, including several infantry regiments, a few cavalry companies, and several batteries. The base furnished a platform from which Union forces could stretch up along the Chowan and Roanoke Rivers, out into the Albemarle Sound, and overland into the state's interior. The town's location also offered a position of natural defensive strength. The Roanoke River covered its northern flank, and the land on the opposite bank was a

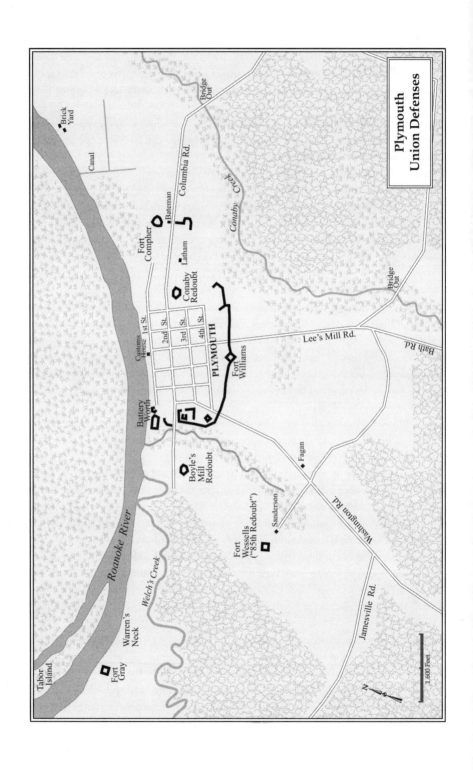

Plymouth
Union Defenses

swampy morass unsuitable for anything but frogs and snakes. To the west and the east, two creeks, Welch and Conaby (often spelled Coneby), framed the town, both running roughly northeast and emptying into the river. More swampland bordered these streams and formed difficult barriers on the town's east and west sides. To the east, the defenders considered the swamps bordering Conaby Creek "almost impassable."[50] With the river and the two creeks blocking most of the approaches, the only open ground lay to the town's south and southwest.

In the face of the Confederate threat, Union army commanders focused on improving the defenses ringing the town. In the fall of 1863, General Peck had recommended improvements to these works "with all dispatch possible."[51] Wessells responded, and by early 1864, the fortifications stretched from the riverbank west of town and formed a ring around Plymouth. The navy also provided protection for the base, though not always with enthusiasm. In 1863, Rear Admiral Lee, who considered Plymouth a "sickly place," strongly recommended that the land defenses be as "complete as practicable" to minimize reliance on naval support.[52] Despite Admiral Lee's concerns, the navy maintained a strong complement of gunboats at the town's waterfront. Well aware of the rebel ironclad threat, they watched, waited, and prepared. They blocked the Roanoke upstream with a line of sunken old boats attached to floating percussion-triggered torpedoes consisting of 60-pound powder kegs. One officer noted equivocally that the arrangement "might do a good deal of damage and might not."[53]

By mid-April, Wessells and Charles Flusser, the thirty-one-year-old lieutenant commander at Plymouth, had filtered through a string of reports from "disconnected sources" and determined that a Confederate strike was imminent. A lot of rumors passed through headquarters at Plymouth. In early April, Wessells learned of Confederate reconnaissance efforts down the Roanoke River.[54] On April 12, Flusser reported that the rebel ironclad was on its way, accompanied by a land force of 11,000 men. With concern mounting, Wessells knew he needed more men. "I do not feel disposed to neglect these warnings," he wrote to Peck on April 13, "and in view of their importance I request a temporary re-enforcement of 5,000 men."[55] The next day, Peck replied that no troops were available for Plymouth's defense. Indeed, in response to a directive from Grant for more men in Virginia, Butler had recently ordered the 3rd New York Cavalry and several batteries north to Virginia. Peck urged Wessells to prepare. "If attacked you must hold on and fight the rebels," he advised, "and I will help you all I can."[56]

From his headquarters at Fort Monroe, Butler remained skeptical about the severity of the Confederate threat. Several days later, he confided to Admiral Lee that he was "not much impressed with the views of Generals Peck and Wessells." Even though Butler believed that various reports had "greatly overestimated" the enemy's strength, he sought additional naval support from Lee. In summing up his guidance for North Carolina, however, he made it clear that there would be little assistance. "You will have to defend the district with your present force," his chief of staff informed Peck. "You will make such disposition of them as will in your judgment best subserve this end."[57] The "present force" in North Carolina was not particularly impressive, though. The entire district held about 10,000 men, spread out over many points.[58]

As the Union forces prepared, one officer was particularly eager to meet the Confederate attack. Charles Flusser had spent much of the war on the region's sounds and rivers. He was born in Annapolis but raised in Kentucky, and his two brothers joined Confederate units at the war's outset. His Southern connections generated whispers of disloyalty, but Flusser remained in the navy and exhibited a steadfast devotion to the United States. Though brave, aggressive, and ambitious, he was not physically imposing. One comrade described him as "a little below medium height, sparsely built, of light complexion, bronzed from exposure," with "a long tawny mustache, the ends of which he sometimes unconsciously pulled while talking."[59] Observers also noted his "large, bright, and expressive" eyes and a visage that broadcast a "strength of character."[60] However, some thought his personality was a little too strong. A Rhode Island veteran recalled that Flusser "seemed to brood over some deep-seated trouble or affliction and" was "courageous to a point of foolhardiness."[61] Behind his back, his subordinates often referred to him as the "Old Man."[62] During Ambrose Burnside's campaign, Flusser commanded the gunboat *Commodore Perry* in actions at Roanoke Island and New Bern. In October 1862, he earned the nickname "Lion-Hearted Flusser" for his aggressive conduct during a sharp fight on the Chowan River near Franklin, Virginia. By the end of that year, he had gained command of all the gunboats in the Albemarle Sound.

From his post at Plymouth aboard the *Miami*, Flusser managed operations with tenacity and imagination. His correspondence with family members revealed an unusually intense yearning for success and an indifference to danger.[63] During his tenure at Plymouth, the rebel ironclad had become Flusser's obsession. He and his colleagues routinely referred to the vessel as the "ram" or the "sheep," in part because they believed the gunboat would never show itself. "Fact is I look on her as peculiarly my own," he confessed. While bedridden with fever for more than a week in March, he had fixed his thoughts on the armored threat. In collaboration with Wessells, Flusser ensured there were adequate guns for his boats and requested "good shot" to penetrate the ram's armor. Digesting the various reports drifting in from upriver, he concluded that the rebel ironclad posed a substantial danger and predicted, "We will have our hands full to whip it." He expected combat with the Confederate vessel to be short and violent. "In fifteen minutes after we get to close quarters," Flusser predicted, "my commission as commander is secured or I am a dead man."[64]

CHAPTER SIXTEEN

The Attack on Plymouth

"A Dirty Black Box"

Shortly after his return to North Carolina, Robert Hoke visited Captain James Cooke and the ironclad on the Roanoke River. A few weeks before, the captain had floated the unfinished vessel downstream from Halifax into deeper water at Hamilton.[1] Leaving his staff in town, Hoke walked alone to the river and found the *Albemarle*, "squat and ugly upon the water, like a dirty black box," tethered to the bank under a slight bluff. Emerging from the casemate, Cooke greeted General Hoke and, assuming that an inspection was at hand, gave him a thorough tour of the work site. The boat's condition did not impress. Only one gun sat on its mounting, half the casemate remained unarmored, and litter sprinkled the deck. Blacksmiths and carpenters crowded the vessel, hurrying back and forth "fixing all sorts of things." At a glance, Hoke could tell the craft was not ready for action, a fact the glum, overworked Cooke candidly acknowledged after the two men went ashore. But regardless of the boat's state, Hoke could wait no longer. Time had run out on the long-suffering project. Reaching into his pocket, he produced President Davis's secret letter that placed him in command of all land and water operations. He then informed Cooke that the Plymouth attack would occur within days and that the *Albemarle* was needed, regardless of its condition. Cooke happily agreed to join the venture, whether his vessel was "ready or not ready."[2]

Hoke's news transformed Cooke, flushing his face and eyes with "battle-fever" and rendering him nearly "out of breath with excitement."[3] The encounter also bolstered Hoke, who had found a kindred spirit in his naval counterpart. Cooke, born in Beaufort in 1812, had entered the US Navy at the age of sixteen. In 1861, he resigned his commission and joined the Confederate cause. During the war, he commanded the gunboat *Ellis* during the fighting at Roanoke Island in 1862. After recovering from wounds suffered during that battle, Cooke was detailed to the construction of the ironclad.[4] Years later, Hoke would tell friends that Cooke "was a splendid fighter" who "loved action and courageous deeds and an opportunity for doing them as much as any man he ever knew." Following the encounter, Hoke returned to Kinston to continue gathering his forces. Back on the riverbank, Cooke placed forges on the deck itself to accelerate the work. He tore down houses in Halifax to obtain "fat pine" for fuel and packed the boat with lard-filled barrels to fire the furnace during combat. Soon, all the squabbling about construction and the fretting about materials would end. The *Albemarle* would cast off and head downstream to its primary target: Plymouth.[5]

Back at Kinston, Hoke hurried to assemble his expeditionary force. His order of battle included three infantry brigades (Hoke's own brigade, led by Colonel John T. Mercer; Matt Ransom's North Carolinians; and Kemper's Virginia brigade under Colonel William Terry), a cavalry regiment commanded by James Dearing, several artillery batteries, and a few companies of the 10th North Carolina (artillery) assigned to serve as engineers and manage the pontoon train.[6] Nearly all these units had fought at New Bern two months before. In fact, they had been in the thick of the action for much of the war, serving in Lee's army during many of the important campaigns in Virginia. Hoke's entire force totaled about 7,000. John Taylor Wood also joined the mission, apparently acting in an advisory role. In conjunction with Hoke's move on Plymouth, Montgomery Corse's Virginians, consistent with George Pickett's original suggestion, would conduct a small demonstration against New Bern to tie down potential Union reinforcements.[7]

The Plymouth operation represented Hoke's first independent combat command. With it, he hoped to turn things around in his home state. His mission to hunt down deserters in the Quaker Belt during the fall of 1863 had allowed him to make decisions and lead men on his own. However, that fall dragnet had not involved the complexity associated with planning, preparing, and executing an assault on a well-defended enemy position, with all the decisions, contingencies, and friction that entailed. By all indications, Hoke had few reservations about moving on Plymouth. He had been privately critical of Pickett's and Barton's performance at New Bern. Now he had the chance to demonstrate that he could do better and reward Robert E. Lee and Jefferson Davis for putting their faith in him.

The strike against Plymouth carried many uncertainties. It is not clear whether Hoke had reliable information about the strength and extent of the Plymouth fortifications. According to one postwar story, Plymouth native William F. Beasley, a lieutenant colonel in the 48th North Carolina, had reconnoitered the town and prepared an accurate sketch of the Union defenses for Hoke, as well as information about the enemy troops manning the works. Whether this account is true or not, Hoke faced other uncertainties about his target. The Union naval presence at the base changed frequently. But perhaps more than anything else, details about the Confederate ironclad remained unclear. The *Albemarle* was still an unfinished, haphazard affair. As one naval officer explained later, the boat's construction, "under all the disadvantages of place and circumstances, was viewed by the community as a chimerical absurdity."[8] Many unknowns remained: the reliability of the boat's engines, the adequacy of its helm and rudder, its ability to clear Union obstructions, and the effectiveness of its crew. Despite these questions, Hoke understood that, in all likelihood, his offensive would not achieve a great deal without the beast. But time was running out. Campaigning in Virginia would soon call his brigade north, eliminating any opportunity for one last pull at the enemy in his home state. Thus, the long weeks of February, March, and April were surely a frustrating period for Hoke as he awaited news of progress.

With his orders in hand, Hoke wasted little time arranging the Plymouth strike, which would be staged from Tarboro, a small town at the terminus of a branch line extending from Rocky Mount. Soon, trains were running in and out of Kinston, shuttling troops to Goldsboro and north.[9] As the soldiers rode the rails, cavalry and horse-drawn wagons traveled to Tarboro by road. On Thursday, April 14, Hoke's brigade left Kinston, while Ransom's moved from Weldon.[10] Terry's brigade, the third principal unit in the attack force, was already in Tarboro, having arrived several weeks earlier after a brief sojourn in Wilmington.[11]

Hoke's entire force began its 45-mile journey to Plymouth on the morning of Friday, April 15. With colors flapping in the breeze and bugles sounding, the units formed "a line some three or four miles long" and marched out of Tarboro as "ladies and citizens cheered" and the regimental bands "played a few choice tunes." The men departed under light marching order, leaving their knapsacks in camp and carrying only one blanket apiece. Terry's Virginians led the way, followed by Ransom's regiments, then Hoke's.[12] By that evening, the column had reached within 2 miles of Hamilton, where Cooke had moored the *Albemarle* several weeks before. Colonel Wood split off to meet with Cooke and let him know that Hoke "intended to take the outer works at Plymouth and then await [the *Albemarle*'s] coming."[13] On Saturday, under a drizzle, the weary men drew their rations, cooked, and filled their haversacks.[14] By 9:00 a.m., they were on the move again, with Ransom's men in front, tramping along good roads and resting for ten minutes every hour. The force passed Williamston, where the 35th North Carolina from Ransom's brigade joined the column. A Baptist clergyman in the town, Cushing Hassell, noted in his diary that three Confederate brigades marched through "with the purpose it was thought of attacking the Yankees at Plymouth."[15] Late on Saturday, a few miles southeast of Williamston at Foster's Mill, Hoke's men stopped, their way blocked by the wide, deep Sweetwater Creek. Hoke called for the pontoon train.[16]

Lieutenant Colonel Henry T. Guion brought his engineers to the head of the column. His three companies from the 10th North Carolina, which would serve as pioneers during the campaign, had endured a hectic few days. Their train had arrived in Tarboro at noon on Friday, but they had difficulty obtaining adequate transportation for their pontoon boats. After some delay, Guion managed to scrape together a few subpar wagon teams. On the march, his men had to drag the wagons by hand to ascend even the slightest inclines. That night, they camped a mere 8 miles from Tarboro. However, on Saturday the sixteenth, the men covered 26 miles and caught up with Hoke's main force at Foster's Mill.

At Sweetwater Creek, Guion found that the crossing presented a challenge. His six pontoons could not cover the stream's width, and he knew a "long night and no rest would be required." Fortunately, he found an abundance of lumber at Foster's Mill to form bridge sleepers and planks. Working late into Saturday evening, he set posts into the muddy bank and laid cap sills across them. These makeshift adjustments, coupled with several pontoons, stretched the bridge across the creek. Hoke's troops began stepping across at 5:30 a.m. on Sunday, the seventeenth. With the column moving on, Guion left about twenty men and two pontoons at Foster's Mill to ferry across commissary and quartermaster stores. The rest of Hoke's force headed east for Plymouth, about 20 miles away. Sunday's march followed a "miserable" time-consuming route over many crossroads.[17] To help Hoke navigate the way, Lieutenant William J. Hardison and a dozen local soldiers served as guides. Late in the afternoon, Hoke's column, moving along the Jamesville Road, reached Welch's Creek, about 4 miles west of Plymouth.[18]

"Any Considerable Force of the Enemy"

As Hoke approached, the Union commanders at Plymouth continued to filter through the rumors emanating from the state's interior. They also sought to strengthen their force. On Saturday, support for the Union garrison arrived in the form of the large gunboat *Tacony*, sent by Peck to augment the *Miami* and the *Southfield*. In dispatching the formidable double-ender to Plymouth, Peck reminded Wessells, "We are under 'bare poles' everywhere in this command," and the *Tacony* was "worth all the other gun-boats" at the New Bern station.[19] However, almost as soon as it arrived at Plymouth, the *Tacony* steamed away. Based on reports that the enemy was headed for Washington and that the rebel ironclad was undergoing repairs at Hamilton, Wessells decided that he did not need the *Tacony* and ordered it off to help in Washington's defense. "I cannot learn that there is any considerable force of the enemy on the river now," he wrote to Peck. "I very much doubt if there is any design of bringing the thing (iron-clad) down."[20] Flusser included a similar note to his superior Henry Davenport, thanking him for the *Tacony* but explaining, "I think General Peck misinterpreted General Wessells' letter. We have no bad scare here yet, and not even a small one for several days."[21] Peck later explained that Flusser and Wessells had "exhibited such confidence in their own ability to hold the place against any force the enemy would in any probability bring that they sent back the *Tacony*."[22] Thus, on the morning of April 17, with Hoke only a few miles away, the large double-ender left the wharf and headed downstream from Plymouth.

The decision to send the *Tacony* away was an odd one, and the explanations in the official correspondence seem jumbled and not entirely logical. For months, Flusser and Wessells had scrambled to prepare their men, digesting an endless string of rumors about an impending Confederate offensive. They struggled to gauge the veracity of reports about the Confederate ironclad—its thickness, armament, draft, and speed. They heard that the *Albemarle* was nearly complete and knew it could attack only one position—theirs. Wessells's concerns over Washington's safety were equally strange. There was no rebel ironclad upstream from Washington; the only such vessel had been burned in the stocks by Potter's raid in 1863. Yet, despite all these considerations, Wessells chose to send the powerful *Tacony* away from Plymouth on the morning of the seventeenth.

Notably, the diary of a New York infantryman stationed at Plymouth placed a different twist on the *Tacony*'s visit. On April 16, 1864, Charlie Mosher of the 85th New York wrote, "The gunboat *Tacoma* [*Tacony*] came in. She mounts 12 guns. Her commander had a dispute as to seniority with Lt. Com. C. W. Flusser of *Miami*. Flusser won out. The *Tacoma* [*Tacony*] put back to New Bern."[23] William Truxtun, the *Tacony*'s skipper, was in fact senior to Flusser.[24] Mosher may have been repeating an unfounded camp rumor, but a curious note from Davenport to Flusser hinted otherwise. In discussing the movements of the *Tacony*, Davenport wrote: "You know full well that I would not send anyone senior to yourself unless I deemed that the exigencies of the service required that I should send some heavy reinforcements to you."[25] However, any dispute between Flusser and Truxtun escaped mention in official reports and correspondence. After leaving Plymouth, Truxtun simply reported that Flusser and Wessells had concluded that the *Tacony*'s "services were not necessary there."[26] Whatever the circumstances of its departure, the *Tacony* steamed away at just the wrong time.

"Prompt and Decided Action"

Amid the shuffling of gunboats and all the rumors, the men in the Plymouth garrison went about their routine. On Saturday evening, following a gloomy, drizzly day, the 16th Connecticut band treated the soldiers to a "fine" concert. The next morning, they were greeted by a "lovely day," with pleasant spring temperatures that climbed into the sixties. The soldiers spent the early hours of April 17 like so many other Sunday mornings in this remote town, which was "about 9 miles from nowhere," as one soldier joked. Officers conducted regimental inspections. Men who were not assigned to the defenses broke ranks to attend their "various places of worship." At Grace Church, the Reverend Amos Billingsley of the 101st Pennsylvania delivered the sermon and, according to one soldier, "preached the text 'Lovest Thou Me?'"[27]

Unknown to the Federals, the Confederates were closing in. Though worn down by two days of marching, the Virginians and North Carolinians pressed forward in anticipation of the coming fight. Hoke's precise plan for Plymouth is unclear. No battle report or official correspondence from the general survives, and it is uncertain whether he in fact prepared any plan. Pickett's original proposal, drafted in early April, provided no tactical details about his recommended attack. In addition, Bragg's orders contained only a general advisement that "prompt and decided action will most probably be crowned with complete success." Against a heavily fortified position backed by powerful gunboats, Bragg understood that the best chance lay in surprise. He warned that a delay would allow Union reinforcements to reach Plymouth and frustrate the attack.[28] To be sure, if Hoke could catch the defenders unawares, he might be able to penetrate the Union line and enter the town. Absent a swift victory, any attack against Plymouth's ramparts would cost his men dearly.

With an incomplete knowledge of what lay ahead, it appears that Hoke largely improvised the Plymouth operation, perhaps aided by William Beasley's map. Anticipating the *Albemarle*'s arrival, he first looked to neutralize Fort Gray, a detached Union position upstream from the town built to fend off Confederate gunboats descending the river. As his column closed in, Hoke detached a separate force under James Dearing to attack the fort. According to one of Dearing's subordinates, the young colonel "acted as chief of staff for Hoke" during the campaign.[29] Breaking off from the main force, Dearing's column, consisting of Terry's Virginia brigade and several guns, including three 20-pounder Parrotts (probably from Blount's and Macon's batteries), turned left off the Jamesville Road and headed north on the Long Acre Road.[30]

The rest of Hoke's force continued east and soon reached Welch's Creek, the final water barrier. There, the rebels found the bridge gone. With Guion's pontoons stuck back at the end of the column, the brigades turned right along the bank of the creek, and officers hurried ahead to look for a suitable crossing.[31] Swerving south along the stream, Ransom's and Mercer's (Hoke's) brigades eventually crossed atop a mill dam and headed over the countryside toward the Washington Road. Later, Guion would lay a bridge at the Jamesville Road crossing, using only one pontoon for the task.[32] On the Washington Road, General Hoke made his headquarters in a house about 3½ miles southwest of town. The cavalry pushed ahead north, and by 4:00 p.m., they reached the junction of the Washington and Jamesville Roads.[33]

At this intersection, the rebel horsemen hit the Union trip wire, a manned outpost referred to by Union soldiers as "Red Top." The rebels captured many of these men and drove in others.[34] Lieutenant Robert Russell of the 12th New York Cavalry rushed a detachment to reinforce the beleaguered troopers, but it too collapsed after a "murderous volley" erupted from the woods in front. The Union cavalrymen retired to Plymouth, taking the wounded Russell with them, as well as several riderless horses.[35] Hoke's brigade pushed ahead, straddling the road while Ransom's men pressed along the right.[36] Skirmishers—some of Ransom's men under Major John W. Graham—advanced within sight of the Plymouth entrenchments and over-ran more Union pickets, capturing nearly a dozen. "The skirmishers on our front are now engaged, and keep up a heavy fire until dark," wrote Graham. A detail of 250 men, led by Colonel Paul Faison, began to erect a new redoubt on the James-ville Road. This allowed the guns to be placed within easy range of Fort Wessells (also called the 85th Redoubt), the detached work west of town.[37]

Hoke's arrival utterly surprised the men manning the Union outposts. Mosher of the 85th New York, returning to camp with a basket of biscuits, encountered a squad of cavalrymen galloping in from their vedette posts with the wounded Lieu-tenant Russell. The horsemen reported that rebels had overwhelmed their position and wounded their commander on the first volley.[38] Other reports of Hoke's ap-pearance soon flooded into Plymouth. From Fort Gray, Captain J. A. Brown hastily wrote that an enemy force of unknown size was "reported to be between the fort and the Jamesville Road," taking apart the roadblock there.[39] Wessells immediately strengthened his infantry outposts and began to load civilians onto transports, all the while looking out for the rebel ironclad. He alerted Flusser that "all is now in readiness, and I am anxious to meet the boat."[40] As the garrison scrambled to pre-pare, a New York infantryman wrote, "Our town [is] in full excitement now. The officers have discovered there is fun ahead. . . . We have been spoiling for a fight here for months. We will have it."[41]

"Courageous and Unterrified"

Hoke had surprised the cavalry outposts, but his advantage ended there. Union commanders had time to alert their units and man their fortifications. As Wessells later noted, "This design [to surprise Plymouth] failed, as our line of skirmishers re-mained steady." When the Union vedettes galloped into town, the garrison readied for an attack.[42] The force there totaled about 2,800 men and included the better part of four regiments (16th Connecticut, 85th New York, and 101st and 103rd Pennsylvania), a few smaller detachments from other units, several artillery units (Companies G and H of the 2nd Massachusetts Heavy Artillery and the 24th New York Independent Battery), some cavalry (Companies A and F of the 12th New York), two companies of the 2nd North Carolina Union Volunteers, and nearly 250 "unattached recruits," many of them African Americans. Flusser's naval force at Plymouth consisted of the large double-enders *Miami* and *Southfield*, as well as several lesser vessels—the *Whitehead*, *Bombshell*, and *Ceres*.[43]

The Union rank and file fell in, carrying their haversacks stuffed with whatever rations they could find. Officers changed out of their parade uniforms and into fatigue dress. As the men rushed to fill the defenses, shells from Confederate guns began to streak through the town. The first round crashed through the guardhouse of the 85th New York, while the second demolished the living quarters of Captain Seneca Allen of Company F of the same regiment. A few rounds hit the 16th Connecticut's camps on the east side of town.[44] Women and children gathered their belongings and hurried aboard the steamer *Massasoit*, which prepared to head for Roanoke Island.[45] The civilians, according to one witness, hurried to the wharf, leaving "behind school-books, school-furniture, house-furniture and much clothing, but they were courageous and unterrified."[46]

Surrounding the town proper, the several redoubts and enclosed forts studded the main line and bristled with guns. Union engineers had sited these works to repel attacks from the land. Most of the trenches and batteries faced east, south, and west.[47] For the most part, the works were open to the river in the rear and had been configured with the expectation that Federal gunboats would shield that quarter. The main line contained several key positions. Battery Worth anchored the town's right flank next to the river with its 200-pound rifled cannon. In addition, a redoubt sat west and outside of the works near the Boyle's Mill Road. To the southwest of town, a detached redoubt known as Fort Wessells, sited between the Washington Road and Welch's Creek, covered the approach from that direction. The largest position was Fort Williams, an enclosed, south-facing earthwork with four 32-pounders and two 6-pound brass cannon; it commanded the center of the line and served as Wessells's headquarters.[48] The left (east) side of the Plymouth defenses was less formidable but contained two stout positions, the Conaby Redoubt and Fort Compher, as well as additional earthworks protecting the approach there. These defenses were not continuous, however, and relied on Conaby Creek, a deep, swamp-bordered stream southeast of town. In this sector, the Union gunboats in the river added firepower that could be trained on an attacking force. Other smaller batteries also stood guard on the perimeter.

The principal regiments manning the garrison had not experienced a particularly eventful war. The 16th Connecticut had participated in the Antietam and Fredericksburg campaigns during 1862 but had spent most of their tour on garrison duty in southeastern Virginia and eastern North Carolina. The 85th New York, 101st Pennsylvania, and 103rd Pennsylvania had all fought in the Peninsula Campaign in 1862 but had then been transferred to eastern North Carolina and Virginia, where they spent all of 1863.[49]

General Wessells spread these troops throughout the fortifications. Fort Wessells contained forty-two men of Company K, 85th New York, and twenty-three from Company H, 2nd Massachusetts Heavy Artillery, all led by Captain Nelson Chapin of New York. Upriver from the town, Company H and part of Company G from the 85th New York held Fort Gray. In Plymouth's main line of defense, Wessells deployed troops to cover all approaches. On the west side of town (the right side of the defenses), Colonel E. H. Fardella of the 85th New York Volunteers had overall command. On the far right, Battery Worth on the riverbank was manned by

Main Federal Forts at Plymouth

Fort Williams

Fort Gray

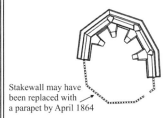

Stakewall may have
been replaced with
a parapet by April 1864

Fort Compher

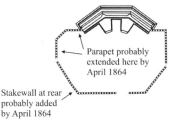

Parapet probably
extended here by
April 1864

Stakewall at rear
probably added
by April 1864

Conaby Redoubt

Battery Worth

Fort Wessells

50 Yards

Based on Federal engineer maps prepared by Felix Vinay of the 85th NY in 1863.
Unless otherwise indicated, the diagrams display the works as they were designed. Expansions or
modifications may have been made later to these forts in the months preceding the battle.
Source: Plan of Plymouth Maps, Felix Vinay Maps, NCOAH

a company of the 16th Connecticut, supported by a pair of companies of the 85th New York on a small knoll overlooking the river. Close by, North Carolina troops from the 2nd NCUV, armed refugees, and new African American recruits held a segment of the defense line, which included another redoubt. Two companies of the 85th New York, along with the 24th New York Independent Battery, occupied the works where the Washington Road crossed the line of fortifications. The 103rd Pennsylvania formed at the center, near Fort Williams, under the command of Colonel Theodore Lehman. On the left, the works held the 16th Connecticut and 101st Pennsylvania, a combined force led by Colonel Francis Beach.[50] To boost their numbers, Union officers emptied the guardhouses of men who had been arrested for infractions that now had little relevance.[51] One New Yorker explained that Wessells's force was so scattered that it "made it a large job for the few men that were left to defend the long line of breastworks and do the whole picket duty."[52]

The African American recruits piling into the trenches were not part of Wessells's formal command. In April 1864, the District of North Carolina contained no black regiments. However, officers from various US Colored Troops (USCT) units commonly conducted recruitment activities in the state. Like New Bern, Plymouth had become, in the words of one Massachusetts soldier, "a general rendezvous for fugitive negroes, who came into our lines by families while escaping from conscription or persecution, and for rebel deserters, who had become lean, hungry, ragged, and dissatisfied with fighting against the Union." As at New Bern, many of the newcomers enlisted in the service and soon found themselves in blue uniforms.[53]

At the time of Hoke's attack, four recruiting officers resided in Plymouth, enlisting freedmen for their respective commands stationed elsewhere: Major William F. Baker of the 10th USCT, Captain Hiram Marvin of the 37th USCT, Lieutenant Richard Bascombe of the 38th USCT, and Lieutenant George French of the 2nd US Colored Cavalry.[54] Additionally, Lieutenant Oliver McNary of the 103rd Pennsylvania, a member of Wessells's staff, served as the garrison's acting "superintendent of negro affairs."[55] The number of black recruits at Plymouth in late April is not clear, and their identities are largely unknown. Wessells later tallied 245 "unattached" recruits, many of whom were undoubtedly USCT volunteers, although there were some new recruits for the 2nd NCUV.[56] Whatever their number, Wessells needed every able-bodied man he could find and did not hesitate to arm the recruits and fold them into the lines. There were other refugees as well. Men drifting into town from the surrounding countryside often brought their families with them, adding a sizable population of dependent women and children. Two Massachusetts women, Sarah Freeman and her daughter Kate, established a school in Plymouth staffed with several volunteer soldiers from the ranks.[57]

"To Hug Mother Earth Very Closely"

Hoke had lost the element of surprise, but he continued to press. Southwest of town along the Washington Road, Mercer and Ransom advanced with their brigades. Under the most optimistic scenario, this Confederate phalanx would crash through the defensive perimeter, rush into town, and capture the position outright, with no aid from the ironclad. At first, things seemed promising for the Confederates. Hoke's men managed to overrun the picket posts. However, General Wessells and his officers poured troops into the fortifications and prevented Hoke from seizing the town quickly. Recognizing the futility of a direct advance, Hoke shifted Mercer's brigade west of the Washington Road, brought Ransom's regiments up on the right to the east, and ordered the guns forward. Details of men moved up to dig artillery emplacements just behind the skirmish line.[58]

While Mercer and Ransom deployed their brigades in front of Plymouth, Dearing threatened Fort Gray, 2 miles upriver, with Terry's brigade and several batteries from Major John Read's 38th Virginia artillery battalion. In targeting this position, Hoke attempted to clear the way for the leviathan. The fort, a square redoubt separated from the town by Welch's Creek, contained a large 100-pounder Parrott rifle as well as two 32-pounder cannon; it occupied a slight rise, mostly surrounded by swamp. A Union drawing of the fort as originally designed in 1863 depicts a work 40 yards square with three gun emplacements facing the river. If the Confederates could capture or neutralize this position, Cooke's vessel would have an open path to Plymouth.[59]

Late on Sunday afternoon, Dearing pushed toward the redoubt with his mixed command. As his men approached from the west, they caught a glimpse of the small fort's walls through the trees.[60] Terry's brigade formed in battle line, with Major George Norton's 1st Virginia deployed as skirmishers and the regiment's left flank touching the riverbank. The infantrymen reached within 900 yards of the fort, with the rebel gun battery several hundred yards behind them. As the skirmishers passed through the woods and into the open, they came across a white object on the ground that appeared to be a discarded flag of truce. But when more such objects were found, the men realized they had stumbled upon several range markers.[61]

The Federal artillery opened fire, making full use of the white swatches to zero in on the attackers. The Confederate guns replied. The crews of the six Napoleons and three 20-pounder Parrott rifles from Blount's and Macon's batteries unlimbered their pieces and began a "heavy cannonade." A thumping roar enveloped the scene. Rebel sharpshooters also leveled fire at the parapet, forcing the Union gunners and officers to take cover. Nevertheless, the Yankees fired back with "great vigor," wounding two men in Blount's battery.[62] The shelling continued until darkness fell. All the while, Terry's Virginians had "to hug mother earth very closely to evade the flying fragments." One of the Confederate shells—the fifth shell, by one count—split the fort's flagstaff, toppling the colors outside the parapet. Later, two defenders managed to retrieve the banner and tie it back onto the stump of the flagpole.[63] Aside from this cosmetic damage, the Confederate bombardment had no apparent effect. After surveying the difficult, marshy ground in front, including the impressive moat and the steep walls, Dearing declined to order an assault.[64]

As the Confederate infantrymen confronted Fort Gray, another threat appeared. One of the Virginia skirmishers, William H. Morgan of the 11th Regiment, peered toward the river past the fort and saw what he took to be a train through the trees. Soon, however, a puff of smoke floated from the object, and a shell wailed over his head.[65] The gun platform turned out to be the small side-wheel steamer *Ceres* churning upriver, under orders from Flusser to make contact with the picket boat *Whitehead* and then continue upriver, looking out for the ironclad. The Confederate gunners trained their Parrott rifles on the *Ceres* and opened a storm of shot.[66] Several found their mark. One smashed a launch, wrecked machinery, and hit the port quarter just above the waterline near the magazine. Another drilled through the port gangway. The projectiles killed fireman William Rose outright and wounded cook Samuel Pascall, who died later. The *Ceres* replied with its two 20-pounder Parrott rifles but made little impact. After running this gauntlet, the *Ceres* met the *Whitehead* and returned to Plymouth, passing by Fort Gray without incident and reaching the wharf at Plymouth.[67] There, the bodies of Rose and Pascall were laid out in the quartermaster's office. Seven others had been wounded, and they were all treated by the *Miami*'s surgeon, Dr. William Mann, with the assistance of Sayres Nichols.[68]

Back at Fort Gray, Dearing's force settled in for the night. On the far left, upriver from the fort, a small group of men from the 1st Virginia ventured into an abandoned "old frame house." When the firing stopped for the evening, the Virginians started a fire and prepared a meal from the eggs, butter, and flour they found in the kitchen. Rebel gunners mistook the bright light emanating from the home for a Union gunboat, and soon shells whistled past. The infantrymen sent word to cease fire, and the episode ended. However, fearing that the rebels would use the house for more than dining, Union gunners destroyed it the next day.[69]

On Sunday evening, Wessells and Hoke took stock as Confederate shells continued to fall on the town. Based on reports from local citizens, the Union general estimated that Hoke's force contained five brigades, two more than the actual number. He also received news that the ironclad had reached Williamston upriver and that the Confederates had shelled Fort Gray. "My men are in good spirits, but we have not enough," he wrote to Peck at New Bern.[70] He also attended to the noncombatants under his charge. Around midnight, the steamer *Massasoit* departed the Plymouth wharf, again carrying officers' families and the town's women, children, and disabled. A veteran later recalled the "hasty farewells . . . the pale faces of the affrighted women and children, and groans of the sick and wounded" as the boat prepared to shove off for Roanoke Island. Flusser paced the transport's deck before it left, seeking to boost the passengers' spirits and saying, "Ladies, I have waited two long years for the rebel ram. The navy will do its duty. We shall sink, destroy or capture it, or find graves in the Roanoke."[71]

In the Confederate lines, Hoke put his men to work digging battery positions. With no sign of Cooke's ironclad, he prepared for his own operations the next day. His focus would be the two Union outer works: Fort Gray and Fort Wessells. Artillery would be his main tool. His train included several heavy 20-pounder Parrott rifles, along with the usual smoothbore 12-pounder Napoleons. His men prepared to put these weapons to good use. Given the unlikely prospect of a successful infantry assault against Plymouth's strong fortifications, Hoke's artillery officers looked to batter the defenses. Dearing had deployed several of these guns against Fort Gray on Sunday afternoon, and they would certainly get more use in the coming days. In the evening, Hoke's infantrymen tried to get some rest. "We lay down in line of battle to sleep," wrote Private Lewis D. Burklow of the 56th North Carolina, "not allowed to have a spark of fire, for we were within sight of the town."[72]

Wessells had survived Sunday's initial attack. Though caught unawares, he had not been unprepared. His troops had responded to the alarm and promptly manned their positions. Thus, instead of sweeping over poorly manned trench lines, Hoke's men had encountered stoutly defended works at all points, backed by the menacing gunboats churning the river. Hoke's initial attempt had failed. Now he would have to settle on a new approach. He determined to seize positions piece by piece, a daunting task made even more so by the *Albemarle*'s absence. He had hoped the ironclad would drive Union gunboats away and turn the tables on Wessells's land forces. However, without Cooke's vessel, the Confederates faced substantial odds.

"We See Your Toes Sticking Out!"

As Hoke approached Plymouth, Montgomery Corse sought to distract Union commanders at New Bern by pushing men down the main approaches to that city. On Sunday morning, the 6th North Carolina Cavalry with two artillery pieces trotted along the Trent Road while Corse's own brigade strode down the Dover Road. At Heath's Mill, where the Trent Road crossed Beaver Creek about 20 miles southeast of Kinston, the 6th North Carolina Cavalry under Colonel George N. Folk tangled with troopers from the 12th New York and advanced well past the picket posts.

During the skirmishing, two Tar Heels, Captain Julius Gash and Lieutenant Stephen J. Brown, found themselves isolated and well ahead of their comrades. Before they could rejoin their command, they spied two men in the bushes near the road and demanded that the strangers show themselves. "Come out of there, I say; and tell us who you are!" one demanded. The other chuckled, "Yes, come out. We know you are in there; we see your toes sticking out!" The comical scene quickly transformed into something more serious when a dozen men in blue uniforms emerged from the shadows and emptied their rifles in the direction of the Confederate pair. Gash and Brown wheeled their mounts and galloped west, miraculously evading the lead zipping past them. Their rebel comrades in the distance responded, sending the regiment's first squadron thundering down the road in support. The Federals, a detachment led by Captain John W. Horn from the 12th New York Cavalry, unleashed a volley while the Confederates reined in their mounts and replied with their own fire. After a few seconds, the New Yorkers broke and fled toward New Bern, leaving one dead and one mortally wounded.[73] The sparring continued on Monday, as Corse's brigade scattered Union pickets back across Bachelor Creek. Ignorant of developments at Plymouth, and fearing a repeat of the February attack, the Federals destroyed the bridge there and manned their blockhouses and fortifications. However, by that afternoon, Peck had connected the dots and realized that Corse's operation was only a feint. On Tuesday morning, April 19, Corse returned to Kinston.[74]

Peck recognized that the rebel movement on New Bern was designed to "draw troops from Plymouth and Washington." Still, he had received no report of the Confederate attack on Plymouth. Forced to decide where to deploy his limited force, he chose to send two transports loaded with 600 men to Washington, where they would join the powerful *Tacony*. Peck had fallen for the Confederate diversion. Hoke and his fellow officers had disseminated a steady stream of false reports and conducted the advance west of New Bern. As a result, Union reinforcements were headed away from Plymouth, to places they were not needed.[75]

CHAPTER SEVENTEEN

Fort Gray and Fort Wessells

"Yankees Let Loose the Dogs of War upon Us"

Early Monday morning, Hoke resumed the offensive on the Union right against Fort Gray, opting against a general assault on Plymouth. Still seeking to neutralize this river battery before the *Albemarle*'s arrival, the Confederates launched an initial probe before the sun rose. For the task, Colonel William Terry picked a limited contingent of about eighty men from Companies C and G of the 11th Virginia, veterans of the Seven Days' battles, Second Manassas, Fredericksburg, and Pickett's charge at Gettysburg. Lieutenants William Morgan and James Franklin, leading the diminutive force, received orders before dawn to "march out in the field in front of the fort to within musket range, open fire and keep down the Yankee gunners" while the Confederate batteries opened on the fort.[1] Spread as skirmishers, the Virginians crept forward in the darkness through a wide, "awful swamp . . . overgrown and filled with all kinds of trees, vines, and cypress knees—and tangled so as to make a complete web, nearly impenetrable." Scratched and bruised from the difficult passage, the men of Company C emerged from the muck as the first rays appeared in the sky and found themselves within a few hundred yards of the fort. Behind them, Company G struggled to catch up.[2]

In the dim light, the Federal defenders spied "a long line of objects but a few rods from the fort" and inching forward. The Northern gunners wasted no time. Immediately, a roar rose as fire sprayed from the parapet. The "Yankees let loose the dogs of war upon us," recalled Lieutenant Morgan, with "all kinds of guns and shot, big and little—shells, grapeshot, canister, and minié balls." The Virginians went to ground immediately. But Morgan, fearing his men were too far from their target, ordered the line to move forward. The skirmishers did so, but soon they knelt down in the grass again and popped away at any target visible in the works. Company G, having finally navigated the swamp, caught up and joined the firefight. The open field offered no cover, and the Union riflemen, aiming from protected loopholes, quickly took a toll, killing and wounding several Virginians. With the skirmishers heavily engaged, the Confederate artillery in the rear opened fire, but much to the skirmishers' dismay, the shells went flying high over the fort, exploding well beyond the target.[3]

The Union men in Fort Gray responded with more than small arms. The gunners there managed to pivot the 100-pounder and point it landward. Installed in the fort to confront the ironclad in the river, the massive weapon now played on the Virginians scattered about the field. However, the huge, solid rounds had no "decided effect" on the infantrymen pressing their bodies into the earth.[4] The rest of the Union garrison, though, delivered "a most terrible fire."[5] At the height of the exchange, some members of the 2nd Massachusetts Heavy Artillery reportedly deserted one of the 32-pounder Parrott guns. As Captain Joseph E. Fiske tried to cajole the shirkers back to their station, some New York infantrymen from Company C (85th Regiment) stepped up and loaded the weapon with "double charges of grape and canister" and added to the devastating small-arms fire.[6] With his command taking casualties and running low on ammunition, Lieutenant Morgan ordered his Virginians to withdraw. The Southerners turned and fell back, recrossing the troublesome swamp and returning to their starting positions. In doing so, they left about half a dozen comrades dead on the field; their bodies were retrieved later that night.[7] The Confederates had killed two men from the 2nd Massachusetts Heavy Artillery and damaged the carriage of one of the 32-pounders in the fort.[8]

The wet, shivering Virginians were furious. One complained that the advance had been a "fool order." The anger was well founded. The flawed plan had thrust a small squad of men into an open killing ground. The damage inflicted on these two companies dwarfed the marginal benefit gained. In the field, exposed to the rifles and cannon of a well-sited and well-designed fortification, the members of the 11th Virginia had no chance. It is doubtful that a larger attacking force would have achieved different results. Word spread that a particular "little lieutenant" had suggested the mission to his superiors. As that officer observed the action, he received a crippling heel wound from a stray round but, according to Morgan, received no "sympathy from any one."[9]

"All Day Fight"

As the 11th Virginia poked at Fort Gray on the morning of Monday, April 18, rebel artillery under Colonel James R. Branch opened "a heavy fire" on Plymouth's main defenses from the cover of gun pits dug the night before.[10] The Union batteries responded, sending shells along the Washington Road. Confronted with this bombardment, the Confederate infantrymen kept their distance, maintaining a 1,000-yard buffer between their temporary positions and the formidable Union fortifications. Mercer's and Ransom's brigades remained well to the southwest, and cavalry guarded the Columbia Road, looking for any danger from that quarter.[11] All along the lines, skirmishing flared throughout the morning and afternoon.[12] "I was out on a skirmish line," scrawled a Connecticut soldier in his diary. "We got drove back to the breastworks. There was very heavy firing from the forts."[13]

During the day, Colonel Paul Faison of the 56th North Carolina, with 250 men, constructed an earthwork at the intersection of the Washington and Jamesville Roads near the woods at the Fagan house. The Southerners deployed three rifled pieces there. The Union gunners in Fort Wessells, the detached work several hundred yards southwest of the main Plymouth defense line, noticed the activity and fired their 32-pounder, wounding some soldiers in Faison's detail. "When a shell from a 32 pounder explodes it kicks up a big dust. You bet," noted Charlie Mosher, a New York private who spent the day observing from the picket line. Unperturbed, the Confederates loaded their guns and sent shells screeching toward the fort. Several rounds found their mark, burrowing into the redoubt's earthen walls but doing no significant damage.[14]

A contest between the skirmishers ensued. In front of Fort Wessells, Union soldiers withdrew from the picket line and took position in front of the fort. Astride the Washington Road, the Federals maintained a strong skirmish line consisting in part of Company F of the 103rd Pennsylvania under Captain John Donaghy and a company from the 85th New York under Lieutenant Stephen Andrews. Hidden behind "bushes, stumps and fallen trees," the men emptied their cartridge boxes at the enemy as the hours passed. "It was an all day fight," recalled Donaghy. Bullets and shells filled the air. The skirmish lines pressed forward, close enough to engage in "some amusing bantering." "The verbal hits" early in the day "were more numerous and telling than were the sanguinary ones," wrote the Pennsylvania captain. Scrambling from post to post, he found that the rebel marksmen recognized his shoulder straps and sword and "saluted" him with a lethal fire. Unhappy with this attention, he donned a private's greatcoat and carried a musket as he made his rounds the rest of the day.[15]

Several times on Monday afternoon, a thin line of Southerners ventured forward toward Fort Wessells but scampered back under a menacing Union fire. On one occasion, a Federal rifleman crawled into the open field in front of the fort, only to be discovered and sent rushing rearward with minié balls zipping around him. There were other small clashes. From his prone position on a low, sandy ridge, Mosher spied a Confederate rifleman hidden behind a large pine at the edge of the woods. Flat on his stomach, he used wood fragments to construct a "cob house" on which to rest his rifle and "banged away" at this solitary foe. His errant shots gave away his position, and soon the rebel returned fire. A private duel ensued, consuming half an hour. One of the Southerner's rounds landed within 8 feet of Mosher. "It was quite sport," recorded the New Yorker, but it finally ended when orders arrived to cease fire.[16]

As the skirmishers exchanged shots and the artillery lobbed shells across the line, Flusser scrambled to organize his gunboats and aid the land forces. He used the battered *Ceres* and the armed transport *Bombshell* to maintain communication with Fort Gray and transfer 100 Parrott rounds there during the day. On one of these trips early on Monday morning, Confederate field guns scored several hits on the *Bombshell* below the waterline, sending it limping back to Plymouth, where its skipper managed to drive it on to the bank before it sank.[17] Aboard the *Miami*, Flusser received a report from a freedman named David Ryan that the *Albemarle* was on its way. That morning, Ryan had passed the ram and its escort at daylight a few miles upstream from Williamston. According to Ryan, the gunboat had been delayed by a branch hanging in the river. Flusser also learned that the *Whitehead* could not get past the Confederate field battery above Fort Gray. To remedy the situation, he directed the boat to avoid the rebel guns by steaming down Ryan's Thoroughfare, a northern offshoot of the Roanoke that rejoined the river downstream from the town.[18]

Late Monday afternoon, Wessells's forces continued to hang on, girded by Flusser's gunboats behind them. Elsewhere, there was little awareness of the fight brewing at Plymouth. Back in New Bern, district commander John Peck, still distracted by Corse's demonstration, remained ignorant of Hoke's attack. In addition, rumors from rebel deserters continued to suggest that an advance would hit Washington, although the actual target remained uncertain. Peck nevertheless appeared unflustered. "Wherever he goes he will get a good fight," he predicted.[19]

"Completely Raked the Whole Top of the Fort Off"

After a day of inconsequential jousting, Hoke focused his attention on Fort Wessells (the 85th Redoubt) on Monday evening. Isolated from the main Federal line, the small fort commanded the open ground southwest of town, including the approach along the Washington Road.[20] Hoke determined to take this work and clear the way to Plymouth's main defenses. The plan was a simple one. The attack would start with a demonstration by Ransom's brigade against the Union center near Fort Williams. Following this diversion, Hoke's brigade would storm Fort Wessells from the left, supported by most of Terry's regiments, which had marched from Fort Gray that morning.[21] Hoke trusted his own Tar Heel brigade to Colonel John T. Mercer, who had orchestrated the successful flanking maneuver at Bachelor Creek on February 1. A West Point graduate, Mercer had served with the 1st US Dragoons in California before the war. He had earned praise for his performance in the Shenandoah Valley in 1862 and at Chancellorsville and Gettysburg in 1863. Despite his drinking and abusive command style, Mercer had won Hoke's respect for his fighting qualities.[22]

The Confederate attack began minutes before sunset with Ransom's feint at the heart of the Plymouth fortifications. His brigade stepped out of the woods east of the Washington Road, with the 24th North Carolina on the right, the 8th and 56th in the center, and the 35th on the left.[23] From the Union lines, a Connecticut officer observed the Tar Heels debouching from the trees "in swarms" and rushing toward the skirmishers "with their usual yell."[24] Four companies of the 56th North Carolina led the way. The Confederate artillery, coordinated by Major John Read, also joined in, opening more than a dozen guns from positions dug the previous night. While most of the pieces fired from the rear, Richard Pegram's battery galloped forward with the infantry and unlimbered in front of the advancing skirmishers. After throwing a few rounds at the Union works, the crews reattached their guns, rolled them forward, unhitched, and fired again.[25] "They planted a battery right in front of us, and blazed away with the greatest rapidity," wrote one Union soldier.[26] Ransom's skirmish line lunged forward several times and pushed the Federal pickets backward, eventually reaching a point where nothing stood between them and the main Union line but tree stumps.[27]

From the first moments of Ransom's advance, news of the movement rippled along the Union line. A sergeant near Captain Donaghy's position yelled, "Captain, they are coming!" "All right, Sergeant!" Donaghy replied. "You know what to do." In the previous months, Union troops had cleared the field in front and, as they had at Fort Gray, placed target markers to help the gunners gauge distance. A brisk fire checked the rebels, and for a short time, the defending skirmishers even nudged forward to a slight rise. But these men soon found themselves outflanked on the left, and Donaghy ordered them back. The adventurous pickets withdrew under the cover of a detachment of black recruits in the main trench line. Their "eager faces looking over their gleaming bayonets made a striking picture," according to Donaghy.[28] Farther on the Union left, "when the ball first opened," Lieutenant Colonel John H. Burnham of the 16th Connecticut ordered the band to form at the breastworks and "play national airs."[29]

Behind the skirmishers, Ransom's main battle line pushed forward.[30] "Steadily our line advances," wrote one attacker, "lying down at every halt, the iron bolts falling thickly in front and rear, and sometimes in the line itself." They pressed the Union skirmishers back and stopped within 800 yards of the main breastworks to avoid "the heavy shower of grape" spraying from the Federal guns.[31] It was a furious bombardment. "I lay flat on the ground and watched the Yankees' cannon as they would fire," recalled one of the Confederates, "and here would come the shell with its streak of fire following it and right over our heads it would burst." The firing continued for three hours.[32]

To the west around Fort Wessells, Union officers feared that Ransom's advance heralded a general assault. The pickets withdrew to the fortifications. New Yorker Charlie Mosher headed rearward from his spot, sprinting through the swampy ground between the fort and the town. Balancing along a chain of logs, Mosher dodged the artillery rounds splashing into the mud around him. "If I had by any means made a misstep or a shell had disabled me, I surely would have been in a fix," he noted. "Those shells chased me clean through the morass."[33]

With the Yankee skirmishers flushed from the front, the Union batteries, including the guns in Fort Wessells and Fort Williams, continued to respond to Ransom's incursion. With months of practice on this ground, the battery crews played on the Confederate positions with "fearful certainty." According to one New Yorker, the gunners' range was so exact "that in some instances a single shot disabled the rebel piece which had invited the salute."[34] The Federals extracted a toll, blowing up a caisson and limber, killing two and wounding seven in the Fayette battery alone.[35] One witness could see men and horses thrown about in the flash of the caisson's explosion.[36]

The gunboats in the river contributed as well. Flusser unshackled the *Miami* and the *Southfield*, which had been lashed together to greet the Confederate ironclad, and repositioned them to provide a better angle over the town. The *Miami* fired 117 rounds, the *Southfield* 200.[37] The large naval shells were particularly impressive to the Confederates. The bombardment "was magnificent," wrote one. "The screaming, hissing shells meeting and passing each other through the sulphurous air, appeared like blazing comets with their burning fuses, and would burst with frightful noise, scattering their fragments as thick as hail."[38] The spectacle had a deadly aspect too. One round landed 150 yards in front of the 8th North Carolina and skipped into the battle line, causing fifteen casualties in a split second.[39] The 56th and 24th North Carolina Regiments alone suffered more than twenty losses from wounds, as well as two lieutenants killed.[40]

While Ransom probed the main works and drew the attention of the Union gunners, Hoke focused on Fort Wessells. The detached, four-sided work was surrounded by a ditch with walls approximately 20 yards long. The garrison contained forty-two men from the 85th New York (Company K) and twenty-three from the 2nd Massachusetts Heavy Artillery who manned a light 32-pounder mounted on a ship carriage and a 6-pounder field piece. As the attack commenced, Major Read rushed a rebel battery into the field south of the work and opened fire on the fort. The Union gunners responded and managed to score a direct hit on a caisson. As darkness fell, Mercer's regiments edged forward, and his sharpshooters crept to the tree line. Behind them, the men formed up, some finding themselves knee-deep in a chilly swamp.[41] The lines stepped forward and began the attack. Leading the advance was a two-regiment front made up of the 21st North Carolina and 21st Georgia—or the "21s," as some called the units collectively.[42] On the heels of the infantry, Graham's battery pounded onto the field, halted within 400 yards of the fort, and unlimbered. The attackers knew the task ahead would be difficult. They marveled at the strength of the work, with its menacing abatis, 10-foot-deep ditch, and 25-foot parapet.[43]

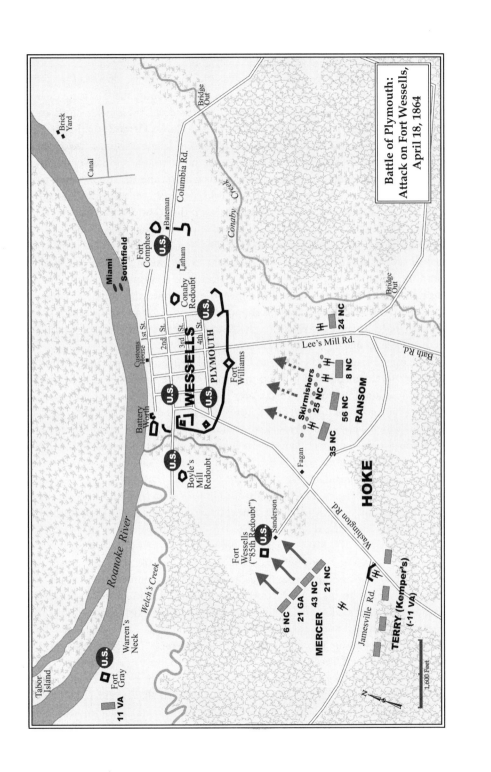

Battle of Plymouth:
Attack on Fort Wessells,
April 18, 1864

Brick Yard

Canal

Columbia Rd.

Conaby Creek

Bridge Out

Bridge Out

24 NC

Lee's Mill Rd.

Bath Rd.

8 NC

Skirmishers

25 NC

RANSOM

56 NC

35 NC

HOKE

Fagan

Washington Rd.

Miami

Southfield

Fort Compher

Bateman

U.S.

Latham

Conaby Redoubt

U.S.

2nd St.

1st St.

3rd St.

4th St.

Customs House

WESSELLS

PLYMOUTH

U.S.

Fort Williams

Battery Worth

U.S.

U.S.

U.S.

Boyle's Mill Redoubt

Roanoke River

Welch's Creek

Fort Wessells ("85th Redoubt")

Sanderson

U.S.

6 NC

21 GA

43 NC

21 NC

MERCER

Jamesville Rd.

TERRY (Kemper's)
(-11 VA)

Tabor Island

Warren's Neck

U.S.

Fort Gray

11 VA

N

1,600 Feet

The defenders prepared to repel the enemy, but in the darkness, confusion took hold. The advancing gray column blended into the shadows. The Massachusetts and New York men peering over the parapet did not identify the Confederate line until it was within 100 yards of the position. Once detected, the attacking formation received a fusillade from the fort but continued to lunge forward. As they neared their target, the Tar Heels sought to break in. But the defenders rained fire on them and tossed hand grenades into their midst; the novel weapons unnerved many of the rebels, causing several to break and run. The abatis and the moat proved even more troublesome. The sharpened apple and cedar tree branches strung together with wire, combined with the deep ditch, brought the advance to a halt.[44]

Still, Mercer's force managed to envelop the fort, although this might not have occurred by design. According to one account, some of the attackers mistakenly drifted several hundred yards past the redoubt in the gloom. As the error became clear, the Union gunners opened on the rear of these wayward men, while Mercer struggled to reverse their course.[45] Another source claimed the flanking maneuver was intentional, with the Georgians slipping by on the west while the North Carolinians passed on the east. Whatever the case, friendly fire soon became a problem as the Confederates fired from all sides toward the fort. Sergeant J. T. Camp of the 21st Georgia recognized the crisis and informed Mercer. However, just as the colonel sorted matters out and ordered the men to reverse and attack, a bullet found him, killing him there on the field. After the battle, Mercer's men would bear his body to Tarboro to be interred at the Episcopal church next to his relative William Dorsey Pender, who had been mortally wounded at Gettysburg only months before. In the heat of the fight, command of the brigade passed to Lieutenant Colonel William Gaston Lewis of the 43rd North Carolina, who was "said to be a good officer" but "not popular in the brigade."[46]

The infantrymen continued the attack. Three or four separate waves sought to claw through the nettlesome abatis. Some Georgians managed to squirm through the obstacles, cross the ditch, and start scaling the rampart. The 21st Georgia's color-bearer, James D. King, received a boost up the fort's wall and planted the regiment's flag there. Soon, though, a Union defender broke the staff in two with a cutlass and hurled King backward as he clutched the banner. The struggle had consumed nearly an hour. With losses mounting and no progress in sight, Lewis abandoned hope of taking the fort by infantry assault.[47] The lieutenant colonel had seen the troops hurl themselves against the fort, to no avail. "The men were falling fast, and I saw we were losing too much," he commented.[48] Directing those at the front to find cover, Lewis pulled the rest of the brigade east to a low bluff lining a narrow swamp between the fort and the town.[49] Small packets of Tar Heels trapped in the ditch or caught in the abatis, about two dozen in all, surrendered and were hauled into the fort. The defenders had suffered relatively few casualties—one killed and eight wounded. Unfortunately, the wounded included "the only competent gunners fit for duty," recalled one officer.[50]

With the infantry thwarted, Lieutenant Colonel Lewis settled on a new approach. "Seeing the difficulty of attacking the fort by assault, I adopted a safer and more certain plan," he later explained. He now sought to obliterate the fort's earthen walls with artillery fire and blast the enemy out at close range.[51] He sent word back for artillery support, and from the south, Major Read's battery readied to open a withering fire. One veteran recalled that Hoke and Dearing ordered some of Terry's Virginians to approach Fort Wessells through the swamps from the west.[52] Infantrymen took position between the redoubt and the town, ensuring Fort Wessells's complete isolation. The rifleman soon began a steady fire of their own.[53]

The Confederate batteries closed in. Members of the Fayette artillery pushed their guns within 100 yards of the fort, an alarmingly close range.[54] More rebel cannon, including at least one 20-pounder, rolled forward and opened fire from a small rise about 250 yards to the south.[55] The lull ended at around 9:30 p.m. when the Southerners unleashed a devastating barrage and the sharpshooters swept the parapet. Percussion shells hit a small structure in the fort, spraying bricks and large splinters and wounding many defenders, including Captain Nelson Chapin, the redoubt's commander. The Confederate projectiles also burrowed into the rampart, "throwing off much earth," breaking the sandbags apart, and destroying the loopholes that protected the Union riflemen.[56] One Virginian in the skirmish line recalled that the "shells completely raked the whole top of the fort off."[57] As Hoke's guns pummeled the position, the Union artillerymen back in the main line sought to relieve the pressure on their comrades. Their ordnance had little impact. The Union gunboats also contributed "dropping their huge 'beer-kegs'" on the rebels, obliterating a caisson from Fayette Artillery. But most of their shots did little good; some even hit their own works, one landing near a Federal magazine.[58]

The rebel shelling silenced the fort. With victory at hand, the gray infantrymen pressed forward, choking the position with a tight grip and demanding surrender.[59] Inside the work, the Union officers, including the mortally wounded Captain Chapin, discussed their fate. The Confederates had firmly wedged themselves between the fort and the town. As First Lieutenant Lucien A. Butts remembered, the "cartridges were nearly expended, only half a dozen grenades were left, our gunners were disabled, the prisoners were a great embarrassment; there were no means of spiking guns or of making signals."[60] Around 11:00 p.m., the officers unanimously concluded that their position was hopeless and agreed to surrender. "Cease firing; the fort surrenders," came the cry from behind the walls. Later, rumors made their way to General Wessells that the redoubt had capitulated under a threat of no quarter. However, Butts, the fort's ranking officer at the time, mentioned no such thing in his report.[61]

Butts and the rest of the prisoners tramped 3 miles to the rear, escorted by a detachment of Henry Guion's command, and were then handed over to the provost marshal. Guion himself stayed behind and occupied Fort Wessells with his battalion, pursuant to Hoke's orders. In the fort, Guion and his men found conditions less than ideal. The breeching on the naval 32-pounder was damaged, and the rampart facing the town had to be "cut away." With ropes and tools, his men shifted the gun positions. When the repair effort attracted Federal fire, Guion's men scrambled to find as many intact sandbags as they could and rapidly piled them up for cover.[62]

Following the fall of Fort Wessells on Monday evening, Hoke sought an immediate end to the battle and dispatched Colonel James Dearing to demand Plymouth's surrender. Escorted by Sergeant William Parrot and Private David Johnston of the 7th Virginia, Dearing approached the Union lines under the moonlight with a "rather dirty white handkerchief tied to a pole." At a picket post, Parrot shouted, "Flag of truce!" The response, "What do you want?" floated back through the night air. Stepping forward, Dearing explained that the commanding Confederate officer sought to communicate with his Federal counterpart.[63] After a half-hour wait, an officer in blue arrived with a reply. It was a short one. General Wessells had declined the offer. The Stars and Stripes continued to fly over Plymouth.[64]

Despite the small victory, Hoke knew there was more fighting to be done. Fort Wessells was an isolated work, easily surrounded and overcome. With its capture, Hoke turned to a much bigger challenge: the town's main defenses. The lines hugging Plymouth's western outskirts were substantial and included a nearly continuous line studded with redoubts, redans, and batteries stretching north to the banks of the Roanoke. Neither the Union right nor the center, anchored by Fort Williams, seemed particularly promising targets for an attack. The left, however, was a different story. The works there were less imposing, consisting of a few unconnected redoubts and trench segments. Union commanders apparently expected that the swampy ground around Conaby Creek, as well as the fire from friendly gunboats, would deter attacks in that sector.

Late on Monday evening, April 18, Hoke began to shift troops for the next day's operation. Some units began to move immediately; others remained in place to get some much-needed sleep. Still wet and cold from slogging through swamps during the day, the men lay down on the battlefield amid "the groans of the wounded & dying."[65] A member of the 43rd North Carolina from Hoke's brigade recalled that his company slept flat on the ground between the fort and the town during the cold, uncomfortable night.[66] Ransom's brigade pulled back from its advanced position in the fields fronting Fort Williams, leaving only a skirmish line there.[67]

Monday evening, the bulk of Plymouth's Union force remained largely untouched, alert, and well supplied. Wessells tried to convey a sense of optimism in his correspondence to Butler, explaining that his men continued to hold the town "effectively sustained" by the gunboats and had weeks of subsistence on hand. However, he was worried about his ammunition supply, especially artillery shells, following the intense exchange over the previous twenty-four hours. "The attack is most rigorously sustained and there is no rest day or night," he reported. He also harbored concerns that his left, the redoubts east of town, was weak "in infantry."[68]

Outside of the town's fortifications, Hoke understood that a key ingredient to success was still missing: the *Albemarle*. He knew Cooke was on the way. But as Monday ended, he must have wondered whether something was amiss. With Fort Gray isolated and Fort Wessells taken, Hoke had run out of easy targets. Now he was forced to turn his attention to Plymouth's hardened shell. Without control of the river, it seemed an impossible task, even with the aid of his heavy field artillery. Anxiety began to creep through the ranks. "Every one wondered at the *Albemarle*'s delay, and prayed for her speedy arrival," wrote one Tar Heel.[69]

CHAPTER EIGHTEEN

The *Albemarle*

"Then or Never"

On Sunday afternoon, as Hoke's force arrived at Plymouth, the *Albemarle* began its journey from Hamilton. A dispatch from Commander James W. Cooke announced, "The C.S.S. Albemarle was placed in Commission this day at 2 o'clock P.M."[1] On Cooke's signal, the ironclad pushed away from shore and pointed down the river. The launch served as a testament to Confederate determination and improvisation. At the same time, the crude construction conditions, the struggle to obtain iron, and the long delays in the project were all indicia of the Confederates' limited industrial and technical capacity. In fact, as the boat glided down the Roanoke, it was still incomplete. Iron plating was missing from significant portions of the casemate. In addition, although two naval officers and twenty seasoned sailors had augmented the crew at the last minute, the boat's complement still included many landsmen entirely ignorant of naval matters. Whether old hands or not, no one had any experience operating this particular vessel. There had been no shakedown cruise to work out its kinks and uncover its eccentricities.[2] In addition, the reliability of its machinery remained unknown. Anticipating mechanical problems and hoping to attach more iron plates during the voyage, Cooke stowed a small forge on board and "turned the battery deck into a machine shop."[3]

As the *Albemarle* slid away from Hamilton, men crowded its decks, fastening plates onto its sides. Trouble arose soon after its departure. At around 10:00 p.m., bolts holding the center shaft's main coupling tore from their housing, stopping the boat dead in the water. With the aid of the onboard forge, the crew repaired the damage within six hours, and the voyage resumed. But soon the rudder head broke off, consuming another four hours. Once under way again, Cooke found it difficult to navigate the unwieldy vessel along the Roanoke's many narrow bends. To keep the ironclad in the channel and avoid grounding on the banks, he took unusual measures, facing the vessel's stern downstream and dragging chains on the river bottom.[4]

As the journey progressed on Monday, April 18, the boat continued to swarm with blacksmiths hovering over the forge and carpenters wielding sledgehammers.[5] The officers also took advantage of the short trip to conduct gunnery practice with the raw crew "under a thousand difficulties." According to one account, Cooke climbed atop the pilothouse and shouted commands as the men practiced with the Brooke rifles. "Drive in spike No. 10!" he bellowed. "On nut below and screw up! In vent and sponge! Load with cartridge. Drive in No. 11, port side—so. On nut and screw up hard! Load with shells—prime!"[6] The ironclad presented a strange sight to civilians who happened to glimpse it winding along the river. One elderly plantation owner later wrote, "I never perceived of something more perfectly ridiculous, than the appearance of the critter as she slowly passed by my landing."[7] But despite all the obstacles, Cooke managed to arrive 3 miles above Plymouth by Monday night, reaching there with the small vessel the *Cotton Plant*. Cooke dropped anchor and gathered information for his attack.[8] The crew cleared the "vessel of 'mechanical' debris" and ferried the forges and other unnecessary equipment ashore. The blacksmiths and carpenters, who would not be needed for the upcoming fight, also disembarked. Despite frantic efforts during the voyage, the gunboat still may have been incompletely clad.[9]

Ready or not, Cooke prepared to steam ahead. His mission was clear enough. He had to engage the Federal vessels and shore batteries at Plymouth. Aside from these basic instructions, though, he was still enveloped by a fog of ignorance. He had heard nothing from Hoke and did not know what stood in his way downriver; the location of Federal obstructions and batteries remained a mystery.[10] To gain a better picture of the challenges ahead, he dispatched one of his lieutenants to probe downriver. Throughout the spring, Union naval personnel had labored to sink old hulks and drive pilings into the channel above the town. Not surprisingly, the officer returned two hours later to report that it was "impossible to pass the obstructions."[11]

But boatbuilder Gilbert Elliott, who accompanied Cooke on the expedition, was not ready to give up. Believing that it was "then or never" for his creation, he sought permission to inspect the obstructions himself. Climbing into a small lifeboat piloted by John Luck and rowed by two experienced seamen, Elliott visited the barrier and took soundings. His findings were encouraging. To Cooke's good fortune, Elliott found a gap where at least 10 feet of water covered the obstacles, just enough to accommodate the *Albemarle*'s draw. Elliott did not stop there. He guided the lifeboat down the river, hugging the north bank in the shadow of the trees draping the shore, floating past Fort Gray at Warren's Neck and the 200-pound battery at Battery Worth. He returned to the ironclad and reported his findings. The attack would proceed.[12]

As Cooke readied his strike, news of the ram's arrival reached Flusser. Shortly after midnight, the *Whitehead* appeared just downstream of the town after passing through Ryan's Thoroughfare. George Barrett, the *Whitehead*'s captain, informed Flusser that the ironclad was steaming downriver accompanied by a smaller vessel.[13] Flusser readied his two main weapons: the *Miami* and the *Southfield*. A converted ferryboat, the *Southfield* carried one 100-pounder Parrott, five 9-inch Dahlgren smoothbores, and one 12-pounder smoothbore.[14] The *Miami* was a large double-ended craft that could move both forward and backward. As a floating barracks, it was roomy and comfortable. It was also heavily armed with four 9-inch Dahlgren guns on each side, a 100-pounder Parrott rifle at the front, and a 9-inch pivot gun aft. However, it was not particularly maneuverable, and its uncooperative handling earned it the nickname "Miasma."[15]

After his men ceased firing on Hoke's forces Monday evening, Flusser ordered them to lash the *Miami* and the *Southfield* together again. He still expected to lure the *Albemarle* into the jaws formed by his two gunboats and pulverize it between two fires. He hoped that, at close range, the monster's iron plates would prove no match for the Union guns.[16] After giving his orders, Flusser scurried to shore and consulted with Wessells, leaving his crew to prepare the gunboats. The *Southfield* came alongside the *Miami* at 1:30 a.m. Earlier in the day, chains had fastened the two vessels together at the stern to create the trap for the ironclad. However, during the lieutenant commander's brief absence in town, Master William Welles, a strong-willed man who "thought that his way was best," decided to reconnect them with hawsers instead. According to one report, when Flusser returned, he asked if the two boats had been secured. Welles supposedly responded in the affirmative. However, due to conflicting accounts, it is not clear whether the boats were in fact fastened together, and if so, how they were connected.[17] Whatever the case, Flusser and his men waited for signs of the Confederate craft. An officer aboard the *Miami* recalled the scene: "The moon was shining. The men were resting at the guns. The officer of the deck took his customary walk up and down. Everything was ready at a moment's notice. Capt. Flusser seated himself on the low edge of the starboard rail . . . on the quarter deck. . . . His face wore the calm yet determined look that usually characterized him."[18] Flusser knew this long-awaited opportunity was near.

Back upriver, an eager Cooke weighed anchor and proceeded downstream at 2:30 a.m. on April 19. In the darkness, the *Albemarle* passed effortlessly over the submerged obstructions and approached its first test: the guns at Fort Gray. Union engineers had sited this work, with its large 100-pounder gun and two 32-pounders, specifically to repel the ram. In the previous months, the men at the fort had attended to gunnery practice and burned off shrubs and bushes on an island upstream to maximize their view of the river. When they were not drilling and firing their weapons, they plowed the nearby land and planted a garden. However, vegetables were far from their minds as they squinted out at the river early Tuesday morning. In the darkness, the men in the fort spotted the ironclad drifting along the far bank and opened fire. But their rounds were ineffective. Later, the fort commander,

Captain Joseph E. Fiske, simply commented, "The Ram passed my fort paying no attention to the firing."[19] Gilbert Elliott, aboard the ironclad, later recalled with satisfaction that "the noise made by the shot and shell as they struck the boat sounded no louder than pebbles thrown against an empty barrel."[20]

With Fort Gray fading behind him, Cooke approached Battery Worth. Manned by members of the 2nd Massachusetts Heavy Artillery under Lieutenant Henry P. Hoppin, that work had also been constructed specifically to contest the ironclad. It was hoped that its 200-pounder rifle would penetrate the gunboat's armor. Strangely, though, in one of the campaign's more curious incidents, the massive siege gun did not fire a single shot at the *Albemarle* as it drifted past, the river a mere 200 yards wide at that point. The reasons for this failure are unclear. One soldier in the Plymouth garrison complained, "It will be a long time before I can forgive those in charge of the heavy guns we had for the express purpose of destroying the monster for allowing her to pass them without firing a shot at her until she was perfectly past them."[21] According to official reports, the *Albemarle* slipped by in the dark "unnoticed," perhaps masked by the trees on the far bank.[22] Another account suggested that Hoppin and his gunners mistook the rebel vessel for one of their own.[23]

A pair of contemporaneous accounts offered yet another explanation for the battery's failure. In a Richmond newspaper a few days later, a correspondent noted that the Confederate craft had glided so close to the fort that "the cowardly cannoneers would not man their guns."[24] A Union soldier's diary was more specific. New Yorker Charlie Mosher, who had manned the skirmish line the previous day, heard that the rebel gunboat had passed so near the battery that the gunners could hear Cooke's crew talking to one another. The gunners trained the big Parrott rifle directly at the ram. The officer in charge of the gun asked, "Number one, are we ready?" The men responded, "Yes." But then the officer in command of the fort (presumably Hoppin), who "had no sand," according to Mosher, refused to utter the command, fearing he would draw the *Albemarle*'s fire.[25] In any event, the ironclad made it safely past the battery.

"Broadside after Broadside"

Around 3:15 a.m., Cooke and his gunboat approached Flusser's small flotilla stationed about half a mile below Plymouth. The tiny *Ceres* arrived abreast of the *Miami* and warned of the *Albemarle*'s imminent arrival. Flusser ordered his two large gunboats to steam forward "as fast as possible and run the ram down." The boat's bells rang, signaling full speed ahead. Within a minute, lookouts spotted the *Albemarle* headed their way, closing rapidly.[26] Below Plymouth, Cooke in turn spied the two Union gunboats—the *Southfield* closest to the south bank, and the *Miami* on its starboard rail. It was 3:45 a.m., according to the *Miami*'s log.[27]

A determined Cooke pressed ahead. He had no intention of relying on finesse or even the firepower of his two rifled guns. Instead, he followed a more direct approach. Running along the river's northern shore, he increased his speed and directed pilot John Luck to steer directly across the river for the two Union craft with the throttles wide open.[28] Showing no sign of stopping or even slowing down, the *Albemarle* reached the Union vessels, brushed the *Miami*'s port bow, "gouging two planks through for nearly 10 feet," and then drove straight into the *Southfield*'s starboard bow.[29] It was no contest. The *Albemarle*'s iron-plated prow sliced right through the Union vessel's hull, penetrating 10 feet through the forward storeroom and into the fire room, then driving "a hole clear through to the boiler."[30] The impact delivered a catastrophic blow to the *Southfield*, which immediately started to sink with much of its crew still inside. The damaged *Southfield* also endangered the *Albemarle*, whose ram had become lodged in its victim. As the Union gunboat descended into the brown water, it began to drag the *Albemarle* down with it. Cooke, recognizing the threat to his craft, ordered his engines reversed in an effort to pull away. But the *Albemarle*'s forward deck continued to dip, and water began pouring into its forward port.[31]

In the wake of this initial collision, a frenetic, confusing series of events occurred that generated various and often conflicting reports from those who were there. With the *Southfield*'s demise a certainty, its crew still sought to deal some damage. From the hurricane deck, which remained above the water, Jack Quinlan and another sailor took charge of the 12-pound howitzer and managed to depress the tube enough to hit the *Albemarle*. According to the story, Quinlan's shot penetrated a porthole and set the *Albemarle* ablaze. However, this was certainly an exaggeration.[32] One Union soldier, watching from the riverbank, recalled that members of the *Southfield*'s crew tried to "throw shells down the smoke pipe of the ram" and hurled "hand torpedoes." Their brave efforts changed nothing. As their boat settled into its grave, much of the *Southfield*'s crew escaped onto the *Miami*.[33]

With his vessel locked with the ruined *Southfield*, Cooke could not work his own guns to any effect. The *Miami*'s crew had no such problem and turned their 100-pounder Parrott and 9-inch Dahlgren on the *Albemarle*.[34] During the first moments of the fight, Charles Flusser personally manned several of the *Miami*'s guns, firing the first three shots at point-blank range.[35] According to one eyewitness aboard the *Miami*, Flusser hopped from gun to gun, firing the 100-pounder first, then the bow gun, and then the port broadside Dahlgren.[36] Surgeon's steward Sayres Nichols recalled that the first round "struck her plumb, but the shot, though solid, produced no more effect, than one of those little torpedoes we have on fourth of Julys."[37] When Flusser reached the third piece on the port side ahead of the hurricane deck, the weapon's captain yelled, "There's a shell, sir, in that gun," revealing that the tube had been charged with an explosive round and not solid shot. Flusser supposedly replied, "Well, it does not matter much. Depress—stand clear, boys."[38]

With that, he yanked the lock string, sending the round jetting toward the ironclad. The projectile, a "10-second" Dahlgren shell, smacked against the *Albemarle*'s casemate and ricocheted back, exploding on board the *Miami*. One large fragment, 4 inches square, tore through Flusser's body and severed his arm. Another shard entered his skull. As he fell with the lanyard still in his hand, he was heard exhorting his men to "sink the ram."[39]

With Flusser dead, the tangled boats drifted toward the river's left bank. The gun crews on the *Miami* continued to fire, mostly with solid shot, which "glanced upward from her slanting sides."[40] They fired "broadside after broadside," hitting the ironclad's metal plating but making "no perceptible indentations." By one account, a few rounds penetrated the metal skin in several places where the plates had not been completely bolted down. But the damage was not fatal.[41]

With the ironclad's guns unable to fire and his boat in danger of slipping beneath the surface, Cooke ordered many of his men onto the top deck and directed them to fire at the *Miami* with pistols and muskets. During this exchange, Cooke lost one crew member. The situation looked grim for Cooke.[42] Soon, however, the *Albemarle* shook loose from the *Southfield*, perhaps because the damaged boat had hit the river bottom and rolled on its side.[43] The ironclad's forward deck bobbed back to the surface like a cork.[44]

The *Miami* drifted away from the sunken *Southfield*, either because the lines connecting the two vessels had become unfastened in the collision or because they had never been joined in the first place.[45] As the *Southfield* settled on the bottom, with its deck poking above the surface, the *Miami* swerved to starboard, exposing its beam to the *Albemarle* and nearly slamming into the riverbank. The *Miami* reversed its engines, and the boat straightened out, but the ironclad now threatened to push forward again. The surviving Union officers, having witnessed the *Southfield*'s rapid destruction, decided it would be "useless to sacrifice the *Miami* in the same way." They understood that standing toe-to-toe with the *Albemarle* would lead to certain destruction, so they steered their vessel downriver to make their escape.[46]

With the armored gunboat once again level on the surface, Cooke's men went back to work and fired the Brooke rifles at the *Miami*, which was now steaming away while maintaining a heavy but ineffective fire. The ironclad's consort, the *Cotton Plant*, also pressed downstream, crowded with sharpshooters who fired at the *Miami*.[47] The *Whitehead* and the *Ceres* soon joined the *Miami*, having "run the gauntlet" past the *Albemarle* while taking several shots from the Brooke rifles.[48] The *Albemarle* did not pursue its quarry. Instead, it took up a position below the town, away from Union batteries, and managed to pluck eight *Southfield* survivors out of the water. Cooke assessed his battle damage and had a few moments to reflect on the victory. Remarkably, the Confederates had gained naval superiority at Plymouth.[49]

"Mournful Cortege"

Once they were safely away from Plymouth, the *Miami*, *Whitehead*, and *Ceres* hove to. With the flags at half mast, the *Miami*'s crew placed Flusser's body in a coffin and transferred it to the *Ceres*, along with the men wounded during the engagement. The small steamer headed for New Bern. Back up the Roanoke River, dozens from the *Southfield* remained missing, and many would be captured.[50] The *Whitehead* steamed back upriver to keep an eye on the *Albemarle* and found it lying below the town next to the sunken hulk of the *Southfield*.[51]

Flusser's funeral took place several days later. On Friday morning, surgeon L. H. Kendall reported from the New Bern hospital that "the coffin is soldered and we are ready for the funeral at anytime you may appoint."[52] At noon on Saturday, April 23, the shops in New Bern closed for the ceremony. Palmer's headquarters announced that every available officer was expected to attend "as a tribute to the memory of this noble man."[53] The storefront of T. L. Merrill & Co. was draped in mourning, and L. L. Merrifield & Co. "displayed a beautiful flag, clad with sable weeds." Detachments from the 17th Massachusetts Infantry and 2nd Massachusetts Heavy Artillery gathered at the navy hospital, and the unit's band formed in the street. Behind the musicians, a hearse drew up carrying the remains of the young lieutenant commander. Behind the casket strode Flusser's comrades, including every available sailor and naval officer from the New Bern station. Army officers from the post joined as well. The pallbearers included the senior commanders in North Carolina, Henry K. Davenport of the navy and Innis Palmer of the army, along with Colonel Thomas Amory. The procession headed to the Episcopal church for a service conducted by chaplain J. Hill Rouse. After the proceedings, the "mournful cortege" resumed its journey, ending at the Army and Navy Burying Ground outside the main defense line near the Neuse River, where Flusser's body was placed in a small ceremonial house there.[54]

Well after the fight, participants and witnesses sought to piece together the engagement's details. Some blamed the *Southfield*'s captain, Lieutenant Charles A. French, for leaving his post prematurely. One Union veteran, Alonzo Cooper, asserted that French abandoned his ship immediately after the collision and leaped aboard the *Miami*, leaving his crew on the *Southfield* to deal with the crisis on their own. Cooper claimed that surviving crew members "were very bitter in their denunciation of . . . French," accusing him of cowardice.[55] However, another witness, Frank Hackett of the *Miami*, concluded that French's decision to steam away had been "prudent and praiseworthy," given that the *Miami* alone was "no match for this ironclad ram."[56]

Immediately after the battle, no one questioned the decisions made by Flusser, who had died a hero's death. The decision to send the *Tacony* to Washington a few days before the battle went largely unmentioned at the time. In addition, no one questioned whether a different tactical approach in confronting the ironclad might have yielded a better result. By placing his two main gunboats together, Flusser created an easy target for the Confederate behemoth and its lethal ram. This left little opportunity for the Union boats to maneuver the heavy, underpowered, and untested craft onto the banks or upstream toward the land batteries. In the days and weeks following the battle, no one engaged in such speculation.

Whatever the "might have beens," the implications of the *Albemarle*'s victory for the Confederate attack on Plymouth were clear. As one New York veteran later explained, this "reverse, and the consequent withdrawal of our naval supports, and the undisturbed occupancy of the river by the rebels, gave a serious phase to the siege, and our capture then seemed to be a question of time and endurance only."[57] Another Union veteran concluded, "The loss of Plymouth was a foregone conclusion" from "the time the rebel ram passed our batteries."[58] General Wessells accurately noted in his report that the wooden gunboats could not contend "with an antagonist so securely mailed." To avoid the *Southfield*'s fate, they prudently steamed away from the rebel monster. With the *Albemarle* just downstream from the Plymouth wharfs, the Confederates forces sought to engulf the town. "This unlooked-for disaster created among the troops a moral effect of the most discouraging character," recalled Wessells.[59]

CHAPTER NINETEEN

Hoke Presses the Advantage

"You Need Not Be Uneasy as to the Result"

The *Albemarle*'s success turned the tables at Plymouth and spelled disaster for the Union garrison there. The unchallenged Confederates now endangered the Federals from the water, a threat not considered by the engineers who had designed the works ringing the town. Isolated from other forces in the district, Wessells could do little more than hunker down and hope reinforcements would arrive and drive the Confederates away. However, the chances for such a rescue were small. Back at New Bern, Peck possessed few units with which to attempt any such operation. Furthermore, any attempt to reach Plymouth by land would take days, and any waterborne effort would have to overcome the ironclad.

News of developments at Plymouth reached the outside world. On Tuesday, April 19, John Taylor Wood sent a coded message to his uncle, President Davis, announcing that Hoke had captured some outer works and Cooke had brought his boat to the fight. According to Wood, Hoke was already looking ahead and was seeking permission to continue against New Bern after Plymouth's capture.[1] The news from Plymouth put Union forces in North Carolina on edge, fueling speculation about Confederate designs.[2] Word of the initial attack did not reach Peck until early Tuesday morning. It arrived in the form of dispatches from both Wessells and Flusser.[3] These notes, drafted on Sunday, April 17, lacked any sense of urgency. "My men are in good spirits," reported Wessells. Flusser also expressed confidence in "success as far as we (the navy) are concerned," and he assured Davenport at New Bern that "you need not be uneasy as to the result."[4] Mindful of weakening the New Bern defenses, Peck nevertheless loaded the transport *Farrow* with infantry bound for Plymouth and urged Butler to help "General Wessells to cope properly with the enemy." With a dig at Butler, who had starved the district of troops, Peck lamented that his total available force in North Carolina was "very small indeed, there being only about 10,150 present for duty."[5]

The events in Plymouth also caught the attention of the Union high command in Washington, DC. On Tuesday, Butler relayed the news to Grant, noting that the garrison in Plymouth remained intact and the rebel ironclad had not appeared.[6] He indulged in some backfilling, too, observing that Peck had a large force and claiming that he had taken only a small number of troops from the state.[7] Grant seemed unperturbed by the events. In two separate dispatches on Tuesday, the lieutenant general expressed confidence that Peck would hold Plymouth with his present force. He also predicted that the rebel operations would be short-lived. Once active campaigning began in Virginia, he expected the Confederates to rush north to reinforce Lee. Grant spoke with authority on this. In a matter of days, he would unleash extensive operations throughout the South. The Army of the Potomac would attack Lee west of Fredericksburg, and Butler's forces would move against Richmond.[8] After weighing the situation in the Old North State, Grant advised that the Plymouth defenders should "hold the place at all hazards, unless it is of no importance to hold," an uncharacteristically vague directive that essentially left the decision to Butler and his subordinates. Grant looked beyond the clash on the Roanoke River and urged Butler to ready transports to bring the Plymouth troops north to Virginia.[9]

On the same day the news about Plymouth reached Fort Monroe, Butler announced an unexpected personnel decision: he was relieving John Peck from command in North Carolina and replacing him with Innis Palmer.[10] The timing was odd, coming in the middle of an enemy offensive against key positions in the district. It surprised and puzzled nearly everyone, especially Peck and Palmer, and the reasons behind the decision were not exactly clear. Nevertheless, at the time, Peck apparently ignored Butler's dismissal. As the alarming news poured in from Plymouth, he continued to manage his district, issuing orders and directing operations as if nothing had happened. Perhaps he believed his abrupt departure would seriously harm Union efforts to repel Hoke's offensive, or maybe he simply refused to believe he had been sacked. Whatever the case, Peck remained in New Bern while a confused Palmer stood by, watching and wondering what to do.[11]

"The Rebs Are before Us, behind Us, and on Each Side of Us"

While Butler shuffled commanders on Tuesday, Hoke and Wessells weighed the changing fortunes on the Plymouth battlefield. On the Union right, the well-armed Federal gunboats no longer glided back and forth behind the town's trench lines and redoubts. In their place, the rebel ironclad loomed downstream, threatening Wessells and his men. The naval results changed Hoke's calculus considerably, opening up key possibilities that did not exist before. With the *Albemarle*'s support, the Confederates could push against the Union flanks without risking enfilade fire from the river. Obstacles remained, though. On the Union right, Battery Worth and a connected series of smaller redoubts barred the way into town, buffered by a narrow, menacing swamp just to the west, separating the main line from Fort Wessells. *Albemarle* or no, the Union right would be difficult to break.

The Union left presented challenges as well. There, Conaby Creek formed a deep, boggy moat neatly shielding the town's eastern half. The Columbia Road, which crossed over the creek, offered the only viable approach to this sector. Apparently encouraged by the creek's natural strength, Union commanders had not constructed a continuous curtain to protect this flank. Instead, only two detached works, the Conaby Redoubt and Fort Compher (sometimes called Fort Comfort), along with several trench segments, covered this front. Although these works provided some protection, the defenders relied mostly on the creek and the Union gunboats. They expected that any attacking force approaching this sector would receive deadly, close-range fire from the craft floating only yards from their right flank. But the *Albemarle*'s arrival deranged Union plans and made this sector an inviting target for the Confederates.

Hoke sought to press his advantage. With news of the *Albemarle*'s victory, he planned a "thorough reconnaissance" of the Union lines on Tuesday. He hoped to hit the sector west of town hard while conducting a demonstration on the Federal left.[12] In line with this plan, he massed most of his troops, including his own North Carolina regiments and Terry's Virginians, to push against the well-formed Union works. Three regiments of Ransom's North Carolina brigade, along with Colonel James Branch's artillery, would remain in support. Ransom himself, with the 24th and 56th North Carolina and some cavalry, received orders to head east of the Lee's Mill Road and make a demonstration on the east side of town.[13]

Early Tuesday, artillery fire, the dominant feature of the Plymouth fighting thus far, resumed in earnest. Guns at Fort Williams and other positions dotting the defense line opened on Hoke's men at dawn. The Confederates replied. To augment the several batteries already ringing the town, Hoke's troops brought the captured guns at Fort Wessells into service. Lieutenant Colonel Henry Guion and his men cleared away debris and prepared for action before daybreak. With orders from Hoke to shell the enemy fortifications, Guion opened a "brisk fire" with the fort's 32- and 6-pounders. Plymouth's defenders responded with sharpshooters and artillery fire. The Confederate gunners in Fort Wessells also "pegged away with good effect" throughout the day at the redoubt just west of town near the Boyle's Mill Road. Similar exchanges were repeated all along the lines. The Confederate cannonade silenced the batteries on the Union right near the river, but the guns in Fort Williams "kept up a slow accurate fire." Back at Fort Wessells, Guion's men continued to man their guns as some shells passed straight over their heads and others plowed into the fort's walls. One projectile killed three horses nearby. Fire from Union sharpshooters hit the gun carriages, and one minié zipped through a cannoneer's clothing. As Guion's gunners in Fort Wessells continued to ply their trade, their captured ordnance began to wear out. When the "feeble breeching" on the 32-pounder broke, they abandoned the piece and continued to fire with the smaller gun until midafternoon.[14]

Fresh from its recent victory, the *Albemarle* joined in, shelling the Union batteries throughout the day from a position just off the south bank downriver. The return fire from Union gunners was ineffective. According to one questionable story, even the 200-pounder gun at Battery Worth had no impact at all, and the rounds glanced off the *Albemarle's* sides "like peas thrown against the round surface of a stove pipe."[15] As the gunboat exchanged fire with the Plymouth defenders, Cooke sent a party ashore to open communications with Hoke. Once again, Gilbert Elliott and the gunboat's pilot volunteered, and after a long, roundabout journey, they managed to make contact with the general and received dispatches for Cooke.[16]

In town on Tuesday, the Federals crouching in the Union fortifications continued to endure Confederate shelling. "Morning comes after a night of terror," wrote Pennsylvanian Samuel J. Gibson in his diary. "The Rebs are before us, behind us, and on each side of us . . . bombardment continues. . . . We are under a galling crossfire all day and all night."[17] Many of the town's defenders "had not slept or cooked rations since the commencement of the attack." Moreover, camps were "completely torn and riddled with bullets, shot, and shell."[18] The officers and men did their best to protect themselves from the new naval threat in their rear. The men received entrenching tools and went to work with a "grim determination," constructing embankments, bombproofs, and traverses facing the river.[19] The enhancements had a haphazard quality. One Pennsylvanian wrote that his company's protection "consisted of a hole in the ground roofed over with beams and thickly covered with earth."[20] But the soldiers expected the structures to help. "The boys have built some very good bombproofs, and the Rebs will have a hard time to get us out of them," wrote Robert Kellogg of the 16th Connecticut.[21] In any case, Wessells believed the covered excavations built on Tuesday helped keep the Union casualties "comparatively slight" during the day.[22]

In the midst of the preparation, a sense of foreboding pervaded the garrison. "There was no doubt now but what we must succumb sooner or later," explained a second lieutenant in the 16th Connecticut.[23] The mood in the works dipped as exhaustion began to take its toll. "Every hour our prospect grew darker and our hopes weaker," wrote one officer, and "we began seriously to think of a march to Richmond, Va., and the registry of our names at her famous Libby Hotel."[24] Nate Lanpheur, who was on commissary duty and delivered rations to members of the 85th New York throughout the ordeal, observed that the men "seemed in good spirits," but "all knew it was only a question of time before we were completely surrounded on the land and the ram had command of the river and could hold it against any force."[25] Another Federal soldier's diary recorded, "Our flag still floats defiantly but we cannot hold out much longer."[26]

A particular fear gripped those several hundred white and black North Carolina volunteers in the Plymouth garrison. Expecting certain death upon capture, some of the black recruits exchanged their Union uniforms for civilian clothes. But despite the danger, many others resolved to hold fast. At some point on Tuesday, a Plymouth citizen, identified only as "Mr. Johnston," visited headquarters to pass along a rumor that Confederates were hunting for the white officers in charge of the black troops. According to this man, Hoke's provost marshal had offered a $10,000 reward for the capture, "dead or alive," of Captain Hiram Marvin and Lieutenant Oliver McNary, two of the Union officers assigned to recruiting duties. On receiving the news, McNary notified Wessells. Earlier in the war, the Confederate government had issued inconsistent instructions about the treatment of black prisoners and their officers, either calling for their summary execution or ordering them to be turned over to state authorities. As events at Suffolk and elsewhere indicated, it was difficult to predict what Confederate soldiers in the field would do to black prisoners. Accordingly, Wessells and his officers took the reports seriously.[27]

Given the rumors about Hoke's bounty, the Federal officers discussed their next steps. In consultation with Marvin and McNary, Wessells recommended that the black recruits and recruiting officers cross over the river that night and head into the swamps. But according to McNary, many of the recruits remained in uniform and refused to leave.[28] Wessells reportedly advised the "Buffaloes" to "take care of themselves as best they could." Some members of the 2nd NCUV knew all too well what had happened at the Kinston gallows in February, so they simply left and headed over the river on Tuesday.[29] Indeed, Confederate cavalry captain Theophilus Barham recalled that "great numbers of people" left the town on Tuesday and headed down the river, though he could not determine "who or what they were."[30]

"It Was Now Ransom's Turn"

As the artillery dueled on Tuesday, the Confederates tested the Union line. From the west, they tried to cross the swampy ravine between the town and Fort Wessells. It did not go well. The advance triggered heavy skirmishing, generating "many casualties" and trapping several men in the mire, where they remained until dark.[31] With efforts stalled on the Union right, Hoke modified his plan and looked to the enemy's left, determined to make a "simultaneous demonstration" on both wings the next day. To effect this, he ordered Brigadier General Matt Ransom's entire brigade east along the Columbia Road to Conaby Creek.[32]

Ransom headed off at noon, and his units began a circuitous march along a tree-covered route that brought them near Conaby Creek at dusk. Skirmishers from

Company E of the 24th North Carolina, led by Captain Barney Lane, crept ahead in the dark along an exposed 500-foot causeway leading to the stream. The Federals had removed the trees on both sides of the road, leaving scant cover. The skirmishers soon discovered Union troops on the north bank. Colonel W. N. Rose, who accompanied Lane, hurried back to report to Ransom.[33] The general, from his field headquarters in a "little hut" to the rear, ordered three guns under Captain Joseph G. Blount to push ahead and go into battery about 800 yards from the bridge. The gunners moved quickly. Rounds were rammed home and lanyards pulled. In no time, muzzles boomed and shells whistled toward Union defenders in the distance. The Yankees at the crossing withdrew from sight in response to the shelling. Ransom's men raced ahead, led by Company E of the 24th North Carolina (the "Lone Star Boys") along with Company A of the 25th North Carolina, all under the command of Captain Lane. But before the troops reached the crossing, the Yankee defenders reappeared.[34]

The Confederates did not shrink back. Colonel Rose, accompanied by an aide to Ransom identified only as Lieutenant Applewhite from Texas, proceeded down the causeway to examine the bridge, joined along the way by Colonel Dearing and Private William Cavanaugh. The small group reached the crossing, where they found the bridge destroyed and the narrow creek too deep to ford. Union troops had burrowed into rifle pits on the opposite shore, "stubbornly refusing to yield the position."[35] They also discovered that Union artillery, two 32-pounders and five 12-pounders, had the range on the crossing.[36] It was clear Ransom would need more men and some luck to get over the creek.

Late in the afternoon, Hoke ordered Guion to take his pontoons and assist Ransom. Guion's men exited Fort Wessells in separate squads to avoid attracting the attention of the watchful Union gunners. They retrieved the pontoons 4 miles to the rear and headed for Conaby Creek. After a 7-mile trip, Guion's detachment approached the crossing at 8:00 p.m. and found Ransom's force there. Captain James L. Manney took a few men forward and cautiously approached the stream to examine its width and looked for any bridge abutments protruding from the muck. The detachment discovered that the abutments were in good shape and that the stream could be spanned using a single boat. Men from the 24th and 35th North Carolina, once again led by Captain Lane, advanced to the creek bank.[37]

According to Guion's journal, his engineers ventured forward and "dashed down at a gallop" along the narrow causeway with a single boat, as well as the balks (wooden stringers connecting the pontoons) and chesses (cross-planks) for the bridge. As the detachment began to unload the wagons, Union skirmishers opened fire. In the chaos, slaves driving the wagons fled, forcing some of Guion's men to step in and hold the mule teams while others pulled off the equipment. The engineers immediately began to ferry Lane's men across in the pontoon boat, and they came into line "as fast as they could get over."[38] Other accounts conflicted with Gu-

ion's, suggesting that Ransom's men crossed in a small boat retrieved from the opposite bank by a brave swimmer who volunteered for the task.[39] In any case, enough
Confederates floated or swam across to push the defenders away. The Yankees fell
back. Guion's engineers then constructed the bridge in less than fifteen minutes,
and Ransom's regiments immediately "double-quicked" across the completed span
and formed on the opposite bank.[40]

With remarkable ease, Ransom had cleared a substantial hurdle on the Union
left. In failing to hold back this Confederate force at Conaby Creek, the Federal
defenders committed a huge error. General Wessells recognized the misstep. "This
disaster is unexplained," he later wrote, "and placed me in a most critical position."
The reasons behind the failure are unclear. No Union report details the incident,
although one accounts suggests the crossing occurred "in the teeth of a sharp and
destructive fire." Confederate accounts indicate the crossing was well manned and
covered by artillery but give no hint of a vigorous defense. In fact, the Confederates
managed to reconnoiter the location at close range, shuffle men across the narrow
stream by pontoon boat (or skiff), and then clear out the positions on the opposite
bank. The crossing stands out as either a marvel of small-unit tactics or a serious
defensive lapse, or perhaps a little of both.[41]

With an entire rebel brigade forming up east of the fortifications, Union officers understood their predicament. Wessells shifted men to bolster the Union left.
Company G of the 16th Connecticut made its way east of town and took a position
near the riverbank, training its rifles on the deck of the *Albemarle* and watching
the gunboat duel with Union batteries under the moonlit sky. The riflemen also
pushed back Confederate cavalry that sought to "procure beef that was in a yard
near by."[42] To the Federals, the detached redoubts on the left suddenly seemed
alarmingly inadequate. As one Pennsylvanian explained later, "These redoubts . . .
were, with the assistance promised from the gunboats in the river, deemed sufficient to defend the place against the attacks from the east."[43] But now with no naval
protection, it was unclear whether these works would hold up.

On Tuesday evening, with the regiments spreading out before the fortifications
on the Union left, Ransom and Hoke coordinated the next day's attack. According
to the plan, Ransom would launch a rocket early in the morning, signaling his advance, and Hoke would conduct a determined attack at the same time. All seemed
ready. However, at 1:00 a.m., Ransom informed Hoke of a change in plans. Ransom
realized that the Conaby Creek crossing had placed his men remarkably close to the
Union line. In fact, Ransom's battle line rested only a few hundred yards from the
enemy. He believed this location offered the greatest possibility for success, and
instead of a "simultaneous demonstration," he concluded that the better approach
was an all-out assault by his brigade at daylight against the Union left, while Hoke
gingerly probed the lines on the right, west of Fort Williams. With Hoke informed

of the new scheme, Ransom gathered his field officers and discussed the details of the revised plan.[44]

While Ransom prepared for the upcoming assault, Hoke again sought to negotiate an end to the contest, according to one account. On Tuesday evening, Colonel Dearing and another officer approached Fort Williams with a flag of truce. When General Wessells refused to talk with them, Hoke rode forward himself, and the two generals held a short conference. As detailed by one story, Wessells claimed that surrender was impossible, and a perturbed Hoke responded, "Then, I understand that you are fighting for your commission and for no other cause. If such is your reply, I have only to compel you to surrender, which I will do if I have to fight to the last man."[45] Hoke left the meeting determined to drive home the assault the next day.

In the darkness, Ransom's infantry advanced into position, his five regiments forming a continuous battle line from the riverbank south to the creek. Skirmishers from the 24th North Carolina, commanded by Captain Cicero Durham and Lieutenant Applewhite, fanned out in front of the regimental lines. Ransom ordered his men to "sleep on their arms," and they huddled under their blankets in clumps of two or three beneath a cool, cloudless sky with "the full moon shedding its soothing beams." Ransom kept his artillery, several batteries from Branch's battalion, on the creek's south side to avoid stirring up the Union gunners. His men prepared for the difficult work ahead. As one correspondent for the *Raleigh Confederate* explained, William Terry's "brigade had fought gallantly at Warren's Neck—Hoke's men had taken Fort Wessell[s] with three guns and 60 prisoners. It was now Ransom's turn."[46] The general and his men would soon get their chance.

CHAPTER TWENTY

The Final Attack at Plymouth

"A Peal of Thunder"

As the moon set below the horizon early Wednesday morning and the dawn's faint glow appeared in the east, signal flares announced the Confederate attack.[1] East of town, Ransom had arranged his five North Carolina regiments as follows, from left to right: 24th, 35th, 8th, 25th, and 56th.[2] At the ends of the line, the 24th straddled the Columbia Road, while the 56th hugged the riverbank. Sharpshooters from Company I of the 56th held the extreme right and maintained contact with the *Albemarle*. Some of Ransom's units were acquainted with the bloody business of assaulting enemy positions. Many members of the 24th, 25th, and 35th North Carolina had hurled themselves against Union lines at Malvern Hill and Antietam in 1862 and understood how difficult it was to press an attack in the face of enemy fire. Ransom's other regiments had seen their share of combat but had not participated in an all-out assault like the one they were about to conduct. Whatever the troops' experience up to that point in the war, the way ahead would not be easy. Three obstacles stood in Ransom's way: Fort Compher, a redoubt on the Union left near the river, with three heavy guns just outside of town and north of the Columbia Road; a pair of trench segments in the middle, which framed the Columbia Road near the James Bateman house; and the Conaby Redoubt, similar in design to Fort Compher, but sited 300 yards to the southwest on the outskirts of town.

Signal rockets streaked into the sky, Ransom's artillery opened on the Union defenses, and the attack began. Stationed behind the infantry, four batteries (Blount's, Pegram's, Marshall's, and Lee's) under Colonel James R. Branch's overall command raced forward at a full gallop and unlimbered on the left of Ransom's line about 1,000 yards from the Federal works. The gray-clad artillerymen served their guns with determination, pouring a destructive fire on the small forts. The *Albemarle*, keeping pace with the advance, fired its two Brooke rifles from the river.[3] "Instantly over our heads," wrote a Connecticut soldier, "came a peal of thunder

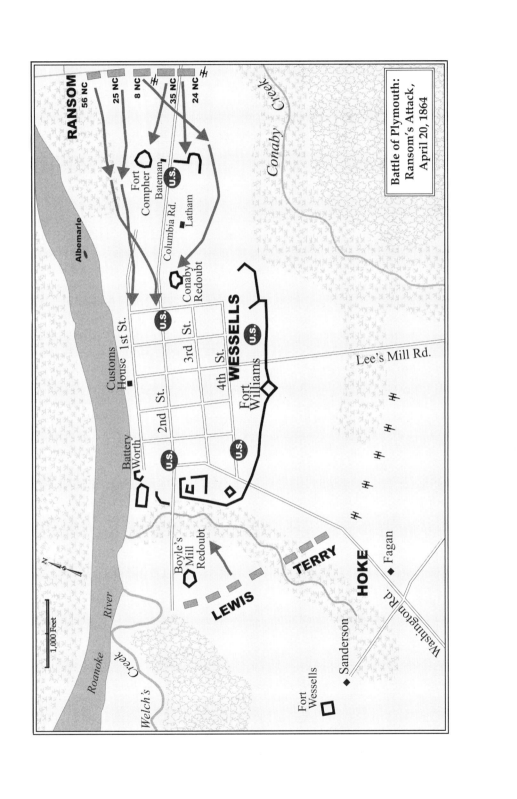

Battle of Plymouth:
Ransom's Attack,
April 20, 1864

RANSOM

56 NC
25 NC
8 NC
35 NC
24 NC

Albemarle

Fort
Compher

Bateman,

U.S.

Latham

Columbia Rd.

Conaby
Redoubt

Conaby Creek

Customs
House   1st St.

U.S.

3rd St.

4th St.

WESSELLS

Fort
Williams

U.S.

Lee's Mill Rd.

2nd St.

Battery
Worth

U.S.

U.S.

Boyle's
Mill
Redoubt

LEWIS

TERRY

HOKE

Fagan

Sanderson

Washington Rd.

Fort
Wessells

Roanoke River

Welch's Creek

N

1,000 Feet

from the ram" and "up rose a curling wreath of smoke, the batteries had opened, and quickly flashed fierce sparks of flame—loud and earth-shaking roars in quick succession."[4] To the south and west of town, Hoke conducted a diversion on the Federal right. There, artillery opened, and Hoke's regiments, led by W. G. Lewis, made a "sham charge." The Union guns paid attention and poured a severe fire from both field and siege pieces.[5]

From their starting line, Ransom's regiments prepared to advance. At about 4:00 a.m., the North Carolina infantrymen, "nearly chilled with cold" from a night spent in the open air, pulled themselves from the ground and took their places in the battle line. Ransom's regiments stretched over more than 1,000 yards of open ground. On the right of his brigade, the general stood up in his stirrups and shouted, "Charge, boys and the place is yours." As the shells howled overhead, Ransom's skirmishers sprang forward, led by Captain Cicero Durham of the 49th North Carolina. Possessing "superior business qualities," Durham had become his regiment's quartermaster earlier in the war, but given his combat leadership skills, he was often tapped when "cool courage and skillful leadership" were needed.[6] The main Confederate line lurched forward, slowly, "dressing on the centre, and halting occasionally" to ensure alignment.[7] James Dearing also accompanied the men, continuing to coordinate matters as Hoke's unofficial chief of staff. One cavalryman recalled that "Dearing, always a splendid figure, being over six feet and mounted on a magnificent bay stallion, led the center well in advance." His seventeen-year-old orderly followed him everywhere on a pony, acting as "perfect foil to him."[8]

The defenders opened fire from the cover of their works. Members of 101st Pennsylvania and the 16th Connecticut, peering over the parapets, snapped shots into the haze. One Connecticut soldier recalled that "lines of men came forth from the woods—the battle had begun."[9] Ordnance serviced by men from the 2nd Massachusetts Heavy Artillery barked out as well. At first, though, the shells sailed over the attacking lines and whistled harmlessly toward the rear. But soon the Union fire began to take its toll. The Bay State gunners "served double shotted with canister" and hurled "disorder and death" into the attacking rebels, knocking gaps in the oncoming regiments.[10] As the attackers got closer, "they suffered very severely, as the ground in front had been surveyed and was staked off with target posts."[11] Ransom's men closed up the gaps in their ranks and kept coming. One anonymous correspondent likened them to "the wildest gust of the tornado as it prostrates the forest, or the mad fire as it dashes through the prairie." The Confederate batteries followed right behind, but only after each gun had fired several rounds. The Lynchburg Artillery, under Captain Joseph Blount, unwittingly deployed near one of the Federal targeting stakes and soon received a withering fire that killed all the battery's horses.[12]

On Ransom's left, the 24th and the 35th North Carolina headed straight for Fort Compher and the earthworks near the Bateman property. South of the road, these works consisted of a parapet and a ditch that ran south about 100 yards and then bent back at a right angle, stretching west about 50 yards.[13] North of the road stood another short curtain. The men of the 24th, who had slept behind a hedgerow, headed straight for Bateman's, while the 35th proceeded toward Fort Compher just to the north. In response to Captain Durham's command, skirmishers from the 24th Regiment's Company E, led once again by Captain Lane, pushed ahead and into a spray of minié balls. Behind them, the regiment's main line stepped forward quietly, its left stretching across the Columbia Road. The rebel yell rang out, and the men surged forward, receiving fire directly from the works as well as enfilading fire from distant Fort Williams. As the infantry advanced, the Confederate artillery aggressively pushed the matter. Richard Pegram's battery rushed ahead and deployed on the left of the attackers and in front, a mere 150 yards from the works.[14]

The Union trenches near the Bateman house fell quickly. Confronted with a heavy fire, the 24th North Carolina rolled ahead against these works. One veteran recalled that "Ransom's main line was up, silent, grim, unbroken, irresistible, firing not a shot." The regiment swept over the position "with scarcely a moment's delay." Daniel King, an orderly sergeant from Company E, scaled the works first and demanded that the occupants surrender. His comrades then spilled over the enemy's line, and "as if every energy had been pent up for the supreme moment, the men gave forth such a yell as only Confederate victors could give."[15] Some of the defenders gave up; others turned and fled into the town a few hundred yards to the rear. The little victory had been quick, but not without cost. Company E, at the tip of the spear, suffered twenty-one casualties. Nevertheless, Ransom's men had taken the first of the three obstacles facing them.[16]

As the 24th North Carolina challenged the works at Bateman's, the 35th North Carolina attacked the next target, Fort Compher (named after Captain Alexander Compher of the 101st Pennsylvania). Union engineers' sketches prepared the year before showed four gun platforms in the work, all facing east or southeast, and a small powder magazine nestled between two of the platforms. The fort most likely contained two 32-pounders and two 12-pounders on April 20. Palisades (stake walls) enclosed the rear, although an earthen parapet may have covered much of the rear by the spring of 1864.[17]

With the aid of some members of the 24th North Carolina, the 35th, led by Colonel J. G. Jones, advanced directly toward Fort Compher. The attackers encountered a stout rampart fronted by a ditch 8 feet deep and 10 feet wide, mounted with at least several heavy guns and crammed with Union soldiers. Three companies of Tar Heels hit the front while other men wrapped around the sides, completely surrounding the redoubt. Colonel Jones reached the parapet first. According to an eyewitness, he "mounted the works, waving his sword and demanding the surrender of the Fort," and subdued its commanding officer. The men of the 35th North Carolina followed their colonel, some "crawling through the port holes and other[s] climbing over the high embankment, to the utter astonishment of the garrison."[18] The Confederates scrambled into the fort, squeezing through any opening they could find. The shocked defenders laid down their arms as the North Carolinians swarmed around them.[19] The 35th North Carolina paid dearly for the victory, losing about 100 killed or wounded. Later, General Ransom would rename the position Fort Jones, in the colonel's honor.[20]

Ransom's men had overcome the first two obstacles. Now the only barrier to Plymouth's interior was the Conaby Redoubt, several hundred yards southwest of Fort Compher. As originally constructed, the redoubt had two gun emplacements facing south and palisades on its flanks, but accounts of the fight suggest the Federals might have added an east-facing parapet. While the 24th and 35th North Carolina seized Fort Compher, the 8th North Carolina attacked the Conaby Redoubt, reaching it in a roundabout fashion. The regiment had begun the attack that morning in the center of Ransom's line, well to the north and east of the redoubt. However, as the assault commenced, several factors sent the regiment swerving south. First, a battery thundered across the regiment's front, deploying ahead and to the left and partially blocking its way forward. In addition, from the right of Ransom's line, the 56th and 25th North Carolina drifted south to avoid boggy ground and crowded the 8th's path. In response, the regiment swerved southwest toward the Conaby Redoubt.[21]

The 8th North Carolina's precise route is not clear, but it likely veered south behind the 35th and 24th North Carolina and approached the Conaby Redoubt from the east. However, a few accounts indicate that it passed north of Fort Compher.[22] As the 8th North Carolina reached within 150 yards of the fort and the rebel artillery support slackened, a rebel yell arose from the line and the Tar Heels rushed ahead, pushing skirmishers before them. Forty-two members of Company G of the 16th Connecticut, who had been flushed away from the skirmish line, crowded into the redoubt with a number of Pennsylvanians from the 101st Regiment as well as forty members of the 24th New York Independent Battery. The defenders opened a heavy fire, cutting the Confederates "down like mown grass." Nevertheless, the men of the 8th North Carolina pressed forward, vaulted into the ditch, and began scaling the walls. The Yankees along the parapet lobbed hand grenades and fired into the advancing line, killing many.[23]

Finding no success in front of the Conaby Redoubt, some of the attackers skirted to their right and sought to break through the palisades in the rear. The Federals there fired through loopholes in the stake wall, hitting some rebels in the head. However, the tenacious North Carolinians clawed atop the wooden pales and thrust their own guns through the loopholes, discharging them into the fort at point-blank range. "Such deadly work could not last long," wrote H. T. J. Ludwig, a Carolina drummer in Company H who would later pen a history of his regiment. More Confederates edged farther to the rear and destroyed the gate there, and the rebels swarmed through the opening. The men in the garrison capitulated, after spiking their guns. This ended the fight, and a yell of "three cheers for North Carolina" rose from the victors.[24] In fifteen minutes, the 8th North Carolina suffered more than 100 casualties, including over two dozen killed. The garrison's losses had been surprisingly small, perhaps only a handful.[25]

As their sister regiments engaged the defenses near the Columbia Road, the 25th and 56th North Carolina on Ransom's right found a wholly different set of obstacles near the river. The 56th, with the sharpshooters of Company I on the extreme flank, initiated the advance at quick time. At the same time, the *Albemarle* slowly steamed up the river, firing all the while. Soon, the order for double time passed along the line, and cheers rent the air. However, the regiment's first challenge was an unusual one. By chance, the advance headed straight for a herd of livestock, apparently part of the Federal meat supply. "Our Reg't is now charged by a drove of Cattle, but we succeed in flanking them," wrote Major John W. Graham immediately after the battle.[26] The men drove the beasts before them "as a living wall between us and the enemy." The 56th and 25th North Carolina then encountered a steep-sided, 6-foot-deep ditch. The cattle refused to accompany the attack any further and filed through the ranks to the rear, but the men managed to navigate the obstacle. Beyond the canal, they encountered a swamp, thick with mud and cypress knees. A member of the 25th remembered that some men "found themselves in a marsh which was so treacherous that some of us sank almost to our waist" in the chilly, briny muck.[27] After battling the cows and the swamps, the regiment emerged at the outskirts of town, having neatly avoided Union defenses. As they tramped ahead, the 56th crossed ahead of the 25th, the latter unit shifting left toward Second Street. The regiments brushed aside defenders forming on the edge of town behind a fence of palings, gathered several hundred prisoners there, and sent them to the rear.[28]

"Driving the Enemy from the Streets, Yards, Houses, Cellars, and Bombproofs"

Ransom had opened the door to Plymouth. His regiments had breached the town's fortifications on the Union left and overrun an entire sector of the garrison's defense line. They had done so in the face of horrific fire and had suffered greatly for it. It had been an impressive, devastatingly effective assault. Now the streets lay wide open before them, and a short march of a few blocks would bring them to the back of Fort Williams and all the other works along the Union line. To the west, outside the defenses, Hoke's and Terry's brigades stood poised to pour in from the opposite end. Confidence was high. However, the regiments would have to do more than simply parade through the town, for much fighting lay ahead.

As Ransom's regiments spilled through the streets and around the houses, a confusing string of events followed. Units became separated in street fighting, and various positions fell haphazardly, one by one. Afterward, participants had difficulty piecing the details together in their letters and memoirs. Buildings in town blocked their views and segmented the battlefield, making it all but impossible for men in one area to know what was going on elsewhere. One Federal soldier recalled that his comrades "fought by squads, by companies and reg'ts without any general commander."[29]

As Ransom's regiments breached the town, General Wessells recognized that a crisis was at hand, and he ordered officers to turn their men rearward, exit the earthworks, and head north into the streets to contest Ransom's attack. From his headquarters at Fort Williams, Wessells directed Colonel Enrico Fardella of the 85th New York to send reinforcements rearward to help the beleaguered Pennsylvania and Connecticut infantrymen straggling back from their captured positions. According to one New Yorker, Companies E and G spilled into the streets "to stay the advancing tide of Confederate troops that now filled them."[30] Captain John Donaghy of the 103rd Pennsylvania also answered the call and pulled his company out of the trenches to join other units in the town.[31] With these Union troops rushing among the houses to meet the onslaught, Ransom's men pushed forward into Plymouth.

The streets channeled the North Carolina regiments westward. On the left of this rebel tide, the 8th North Carolina, fresh from its capture of the Conaby Redoubt, stepped south across Fourth Street and swept inside the main trench line. Emboldened by the promise of victory, the men, acting without orders, attempted to storm Fort Williams, the Federal citadel. Unbowed by deadly fire, many of the Tar Heels piled into the ditch outside the walls, only to realize that their impetuous charge had been a horrible idea. The fort's guns opened on them, and Union defenders along the line added their fire. The Confederates turned tail, and as they pulled away, grape and canister sprayed at their backs.[32] Also on the left, the 35th North Carolina pushed into town and, like the 8th, swung south and ended its movement near Fort Williams, halted by a vicious fusillade and pushed back Adjutant John B. Clapp's Company D of the 16th Connecticut.[33] On Ransom's far right near the river, the 25th North Carolina skirted along First Street (also known as Water Street), making steady progress into town.[34]

At the center of Ransom's advance, the 24th and 56th North Carolina Regiments cut into Plymouth's heart. With Major John Graham at the column's head, the 56th crossed Madison Street and pushed along Second Street. In an open space near the county jail, the regiment spread into battle line. Eight companies headed down Second Street, and several others spilled onto Water Street. As they pressed ahead, they found the defenders secreted behind fences, around corners, and even "under ground in holes."[35] Graham's men charged toward a Union battery that was scrambling to deploy in the center of Second Street. The gunners managed to

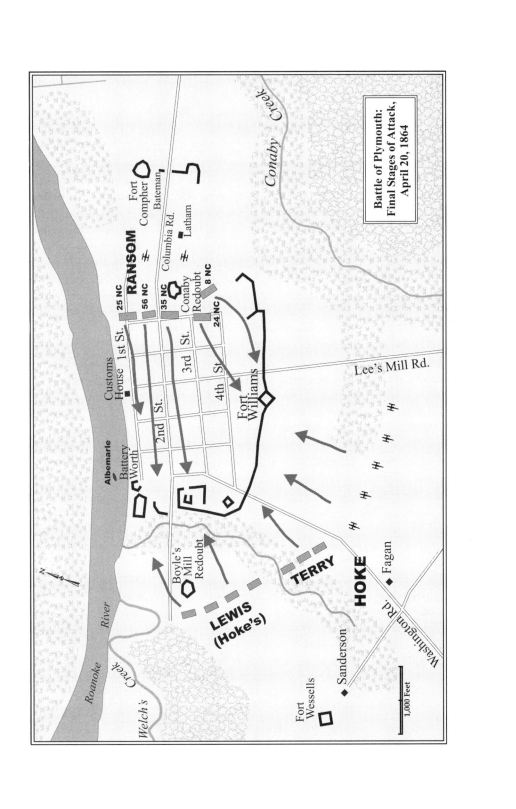

Battle of Plymouth:
Final Stages of Attack,
April 20, 1864

Conaby Creek

Fort
Compher

Bateman

RANSOM

Columbia Rd.

Latham

25 NC

56 NC

35 NC

Conaby
Redoubt

8 NC

24 NC

Customs
House   1st St.

2nd St.

3rd St.

4th St.

Fort
Williams

Lee's Mill Rd.

Albemarle

Battery
Worth

Boyle's
Mill Redoubt

TERRY

LEWIS
(Hoke's)

HOKE

Fagan

Sanderson

Fort
Wessells

Washington Rd.

Roanoke River

Welch's Creek

1,000 Feet

N

fire off a few rounds, but fortunately for the Carolinians, the shells flew high and whistled harmlessly eastward. As the Confederates overran the pieces, one member of the battery managed to commandeer a caisson. However, as he made his escape, friendly fire from Fort Williams hit the limber chest, killing the driver along with the horses.[36]

The 56th North Carolina continued west, with its left still on Second Street and its right on Water Street. The fighting became even more chaotic. "The advance is steadily continued but bullets seem to come from every direction, both from houses and excavations in the ground," wrote one officer. The sustained cross fire from Fort Williams proved deadly, as Captain Ira Sampson's Massachusetts gunners hurled grape and case shot down the streets and into the rebel units pouring through town.[37] The 56th North Carolina passed through lots and yards between Water and Second Streets. During its advance, the regiment drove the "enemy from the streets, yards, houses, cellars, and bombproofs," which they exited "like a colony of prairie puppies, or ground hogs on the 2d of February." The regiment eventually reached the rear of an open work on the west end of town.[38]

The 24th North Carolina's advance was similar. After sweeping over the works at Bateman's, the regiment proceeded west along Second and Third Streets. Just outside of the town's street grid, the unit formed into line and carefully forged ahead down Second and Third, clearing the Federals from yards and houses. A Union battery at the western end of town, most likely commanded by Captain Lester Cady (24th New York Independent Battery), opened a rapid fire down the street, blunting the advance. Other defenders fought just as tenaciously, firing out of windows and from behind fences. It was slow work for the rebels. However, within an hour, the Tar Heels had pushed many of the defenders southwest into Fort Williams.[39]

Ransom's advance demoralized the Federals who rushed from their trenches and into the streets to stem the rebel attack. Captain John Donaghy, who formed his company of Pennsylvanians along a drainage ditch, recalled that "the rebels were pouring on us a severe fire from buildings and from behind any object that would conceal them." "We saw but few of them," he continued, "though the whizzing balls and the white smoke from their weapons told us of their presence." As Donaghy stood with his men, a bullet pierced his thigh and dropped into his boot. He limped south along the street and back into the works, leaving a sergeant in command of his company. The detachment remained, but it accomplished little and suffered much. The Federals soon withdrew to Fort Williams, carrying their casualties. One of them, the mortally wounded Benjamin Mortimer, met Donaghy in the bombproof and remarked, "Oh, Captain! Why did you take us out there?"[40]

Another effort by a company from the 85th New York met with a similar result. Rushing into town, the New Yorkers encountered one of Ransom's regiments "on a grand charge up the street." "We were so close to them we could look into their eyes," remembered Charlie Mosher, a member of the detachment. The outnumbered company promptly turned and fled back to the trenches. From the relative cover of the works, these Federals had better luck firing at the rebels swarming the town. Mosher wrote, "It was like shooting into a flock of black birds. Mighty good shooting for a while."[41]

Brushing the defenders aside, the Confederates pushed on. The 56th and 24th North Carolina outpaced the other regiments, tramping all the way through Plymouth and reaching the town's western edge at Monroe Street.[42] At the end of Second and Third Streets stood a large entrenched camp that contained a west-facing redan, its rear open to Ransom's approaching men. The 24th, still advancing along Second and Third Streets, first confronted the rear of this camp while fire from Fort Williams threatened from the south. The 56th North Carolina on the right flank pressed along Second Street and overran the battery, commanded by Captain Lester Cady, which had been sending a raking fire down the street throughout the fight.[43]

The small work and entrenched camp at the town's western edge were manned by members of the 103rd Pennsylvania.[44] Resistance ended quickly. With the appearance of Ransom's force from behind, the Pennsylvanians "threw down their arms and raised the white flag." Captain Joseph Lockhart of the 56th North Carolina received the formal surrender of the demoralized group. The rebels quickly took advantage of the captured position. As one member of the 24th North Carolina recounted immediately after the battle, "Both regiments poured into the camp, and throwing down their foul guns and empty cartridge boxes took the clean, well filled ones which were lying about, and pressed on through the tents on the western side of the camp."[45]

The Confederates on Ransom's right near the river made good progress.[46] At around 9:00 a.m., Colonel Paul Faison, commander of the 56th North Carolina, reached Battery Worth and found it full of Union troops. The Confederates soon forced them to surrender when, with the aid of the ever-present Colonel Dearing, members of the 56th North Carolina rolled several captured guns forward and opened on the rear of the battery. Lieutenant Alonzo Cooper, a New Yorker in charge of Battery Worth at the time, recalled that the shots hit the "slat door" at the back of the work, disturbingly close to the powder magazine. Cooper's men, unable to train the fort's massive gun on the attackers, fired their carbines at the Confederates instead. However, Cooper and his fellow officers concluded that further resistance was useless.[47] Soon, a bayonet adorned with a white handkerchief poked above the parapet. A jubilant Dearing rushed across the moat ahead of the men and "jumped on the big gun as if he were going to spike it." Sergeant A. R. Carver, close behind, accepted the surrender of a Union officer (perhaps Cooper) and became the owner of his sword and pistol. Major John Graham of the 56th North Carolina herded 300 prisoners, including members of Companies B and E of the 2nd North Carolina Union Volunteers, into the ravine west of the battery.[48]

The capture of Battery Worth and other works in Plymouth's northwest sector near the river isolated Fort Williams and other positions along the Union line. With Ransom pushing from the east and Hoke's men pressing from the west, the Confederates had the remaining defenders completely surrounded. Major Graham climbed atop the redan at the end of Second Street and waved the 56th's flag at Hoke's regiments lined up across the swampy ravine to the west.[49] Stymied by the strong works and muddy ravine earlier, Hoke's brigade, still under Colonel W. G. Lewis's command, had made no progress. But now that the way was clear, they sloshed through the swamp and along the causeway on the Boyle's Mill Road, where the small redoubt had apparently been silenced earlier when a shell entered its magazine, and joined Ransom's triumphant men in town. Once the junction with Hoke's brigade was secured, the 56th North Carolina proceeded south along the ravine outside the trench line while the 24th tracked inside, sweeping up defenders as they went.[50]

The victory was nearly complete. However, as the Confederates swarmed through the town around midmorning, the main Federal strongpoint remained unconquered.[51] "Fort Williams was the only obstacle to our complete success," scribbled Henry Guion in his journal.[52] Many Union soldiers crowded into the citadel and into some portions of the adjacent works. The Federals continued to resist, even though Confederate fire pinned many behind the ramparts and curtains. Even General Wessells pitched in, pulling off his coat and tossing grenades over the fort's parapet.[53]

Hoke gathered his officers to discuss the next move. Colonel Lewis argued that an assault against Fort Williams was unnecessary. Others concurred, and just as they had done at Fort Wessells two days earlier, the Confederates resolved to bring their guns forward and demolish the enemy defenses with shot and shell while suppressing the men inside with small-arms fire. Sharpshooters deployed throughout the town "to overlook [the fort's] interior from the windows and tops of the nearest houses."[54] The rebel riflemen plugged away at any sign of movement above the fort's walls and prevented the Federals from serving their guns. Artillery crews in butternut and gray rolled their guns within close range and pounded the fort from nearly every direction. The *Albemarle* lobbed its huge 90-pound shells at the position as well.[55] The bombardment was withering. Fort Williams shook with the impact, and the defenders huddled into whatever cover they could find. As Wessells explained later, "No man could live at the guns."[56]

"Indiscriminate Slaughter Was Intimated"

Sensing victory, Hoke again demanded surrender. He mounted his "old black" horse and met General Wessells outside Fort Williams for the parley. Rebel soldiers crowded the meeting, straining to hear every word. The gaggle of witnesses generated many conflicting accounts of the negotiations. However, most agreed that Hoke demanded surrender and warned that his men would give no quarter in the ensuing assault should the Union commander refuse the offer.[57] According to Wessells, a "courteous and soldierlike" Hoke made it clear that "indiscriminate slaughter was intimated" should the Federals continue to fight. Nonetheless, Wessells refused to surrender and returned to the fort to prepare for more combat.[58] One Connecticut veteran claimed that Hoke warned, "I will fill your citadel full of iron! I will compel your surrender if I have to fight to the last man!"[59] According to another account, which trickled into New Bern later and was not corroborated by others, Wessells refused to surrender because Hoke would not agree to treat "the negroes and North Carolina soldiers" as "prisoners of war."[60]

According to Captain Donaghy, who was nursing his wounded thigh in works adjacent to the fort, Federal officers expressed surprise that Wessells chose to continue the fight.[61] Following Wessells's refusal, Hoke reportedly turned in his saddle and said, "Captain Graham, bring your battery into position."[62] Guion placed howitzers in an enclosed work near Fort Williams to be used as mortars that would rain destruction on the defenders. Combat resumed, and the Confederate guns commenced a "furious bombardment." "The cannonading was perfectly awful," recalled Samuel Grosvenor of the 16th Connecticut.[63] In the fort, Captain Sampson observed rebel shells arriving from "8 or 10 different" locations, including the Conaby Redoubt, Fort Wessells, the *Albemarle*, and a six-gun battery planted directly in front of the fort.[64] The *Albemarle*, stationed off Battery Worth, sent its rounds streaking across town into, and sometimes over, Fort Williams. Rebel shot thumped into every side and literally "trimmed the top of the fort," according to one witness.[65] Confederate fire also engulfed the defenders. "Fragments of shells sought almost every interior angle of the work, the whole extent of the parapet was swept by musketry, and men were killed and wounded on the banquette slope," wrote a New Yorker.[66] John William Wynne of the 1st Virginia noted that the "cannonading is furious & terrible, but grand to even sublime."[67]

The end soon arrived. But, like parts of the battle itself, the finale's details are murky, the subject of conflicting accounts. One Confederate witness claimed that, during the bombardment, members of the 24th North Carolina crept close to the fort and found a position from which to enfilade the men inside. In response to this fire, hundreds of unarmed defenders rushed from the sally port and surrendered. As this occurred, "a shell burst directly on the magazine, and when the smoke cleared away," the US flag floated "rapidly down to the ground," and the Confederates swarmed into the fort.[68] However, according to Captain Donaghy, members of the 101st Pennsylvania and 16th Connecticut simply emerged from cover and surrendered, led by Colonel Burnham waving a white handkerchief fastened to his sword. Then Captain James F. Mackey of the 103rd Pennsylvania, which was crammed in the lines just outside the fort, risked his life to enter the work, find Wessells, and urge him to surrender. It was at that point, Donaghy explained, that "an enlisted man from within the fort mounted the parapet and waved as a flag of truce a white woolen shirt fastened to a musket," and the garrison flag descended. Wessells, in his official report written months later, simply stated, "In compliance with the earnest desire of every officer I consented to hoist a white flag, and at 10 a.m. of April 20 I had the mortification of surrendering my post to the enemy with all it contained."[69]

The Confederates rejoiced. "One long, wild, prolonged shout, went up from our army, and never was a flag of truce more eagerly and heartily greeted during the war," remembered a veteran of the 43rd North Carolina.[70] The victors swarmed into the fort, and the vanquished collected whatever belongings they could find and prepared for captivity. The color guard of the 16th Connecticut burned the regiment's colors.[71] Standard-bearers in the 85th New York ripped their flags into strips and distributed the pieces among the officers and several men.[72]

Accounts generally describe a gentlemanly exchange between the twenty-six-year-old Hoke and the fifty-five-year-old Wessells. The latter offered his sword, which Hoke refused, uttering words about the defenders' bravery. Hoke then said, "After such a gallant defense you can bear the fortune of war without self-reproach."[73] Another version depicts a not-so-humble Hoke. As chronicled by a Union veteran, Hoke boasted to a mortified Wessells, "General, this is the proudest day of my life." In any case, there was no prolonged discussion, as Wessells and his staff were led away immediately.[74]

Despite the fall of Fort Williams, pockets of Federal resistance remained in and around Plymouth. Remarkably, these detachments held out for several hours throughout Wednesday morning and into the afternoon. As one Union veteran noted, the "unusual and surprising character of the siege and capture of Plymouth was the isolation of several portions of the Federal force throughout the contest and the persistent, determined resistance of each and every portion of it." For Union veterans, the tenacity of this resistance sounded a positive note in an otherwise disastrous day. According to one, each isolated squad "fought upon its own responsibility, with unflinching courage and determination," even after all hope was gone.[75]

One such force held the southwest corner of the Union works, near Harriet Toodle's house. There, Colonel Enrico Fardella, with a few remnants of the 85th New York, continued to man a small, isolated sliver of the works. During the fighting that morning, a portion of Fardella's command attempted to reinforce Fort Williams. However, rebels swarming through the streets and around the trench line scooped up this squad. Strangely, the rest of Fardella's men remained untouched for several hours following Fort Williams's fall. By 2:00 in the afternoon, his band understood that the end was near and held a meeting to discuss whether to leave their cover and charge the enemy. His fellow officers rightly objected, understanding that such an attempt would be certain suicide. With that, the colonel and his men emerged from their position and surrendered.[76]

Upriver at Warren's Neck, the US flag continued to fly over Fort Gray. The men there had successfully repelled every Confederate attack since Sunday. Wednesday morning, as Ransom's men swept through Plymouth, Fort Gray's occupants could hear the combat raging in the streets. But late in the morning, the firing ceased, and the rebel yell rose up from the east. Afterward, a small boat appeared in the river carrying Colonel Dearing and a Union officer. The 11th Virginia, which had remained at Warren's Neck since Monday, marched into the fort victorious. Some of the captured Federals commended the Virginians for their courage during Monday's attack. With Fort Gray's capitulation, the Battle of Plymouth was over.[77]

In the midst of the exultation, Hoke assessed the damage to his command. His men had paid a dear price for victory. Reports vary, but the Confederates probably lost more than 80 killed and 550 wounded; the majority of these, more than 400, came from Ransom's brigade. Most of these losses occurred during the harrowing attack against the Union left that morning. Ransom's ranks, exposed to short-range artillery and musket fire, eventually overwhelmed the redoubts and works there. Hoke's own brigade suffered about 30 killed and about 100 wounded, a reflection of their work at Fort Wessells on April 18 and against the town's inner line on the last day. The Virginians of Terry's brigade, who played mostly a supporting role (with the exception of the ill-advised probe against Fort Gray on Monday morning), suffered 5 killed and 45 wounded. The names of the dead and wounded filled the North Carolina and Virginia newspapers over the next several days.[78]

By contrast, the Union garrison weathered the fight with comparatively light losses. "Our casualties are not heavy," wrote Samuel Gibson of the 103rd Pennsylvania.[79] The 16th Connecticut, which faced the teeth of Ransom's attack, lost only 1 killed and 12 wounded. The entire garrison suffered about 30 killed and 200 wounded and missing. All the rest were captured. Records at the New Bern National Cemetery show the reinterment of approximately 30 who were killed in action or died from wounds suffered at Plymouth. These results stand as a testament to the virtue of fighting behind fortifications.[80] The Confederates also captured many black recruits and civilians in Plymouth. In a list of captured "material," a rebel correspondent mentioned "about 600 negroes . . . about 100 men, the balance women and children—not many men who were soldiers."[81] Similarly, John W. Graham of the 56th North Carolina informed his father that Hoke's force captured "a large number of horses and negroes, probably 300 of the former, and 700 of the latter."[82]

After the fight, the victors surveyed their prize. The scars of battle were evident all around, as shell and bullet holes pocked buildings throughout town. "All over the streets were the wounded and dead lying, and dead horses and big puddles of blood here and there, the most affecting scene I ever saw," wrote one soldier.[83] The trench lines and redoubts bore the gashes of heavy artillery fire. Members of the 43rd North Carolina took time to visit the house of Charles Latham, which stood south of the Columbia Road only a few hundred feet in front of Fort Compher. One Tar Heel recalled that the "splendid residence . . . was perforated by balls, while one or two of the enemy lay dead in the yard."[84] During the attack, some citizens had huddled in the basement of the house. When a shell smashed through a window, one brave occupant hurled the round outside into the yard. After the battle, Confederate and Union dead were laid outside as Latham himself searched among the bodies for family members.[85] The Confederates also inspected the newly captured fortifications. Guion and Lewis visited Fort Gray on Warren's Neck and decided to dismantle the work and transfer the guns in town "to consolidate our small force as much as possible." They would also build a permanent bridge over Welch's Creek, trace out a complete line of entrenchments around the town, and take up the pontoon bridge over Conaby Creek.[86]

"Everything That One Could Wish to Eat"

As the victorious Confederates flooded the town, they participated in less serious activities as well. Flushed with triumph, officers allowed their men unfettered access to the garrison's stores and property. The soldiers stacked their muskets in the streets and went foraging. They emptied their haversacks of "old corn-dodgers and pieces of rancid bacon" and filled them with delicacies. Plymouth's culinary riches astonished the hungry soldiers. One Virginian reported gleefully, "For two hours, we . . . got everything that one could wish to eat, candies, cakes, preserves, pickles & all kinds of confectionaries, plenty of ham, cheese, coffee, tea, crackers, in fact everything that is good to eat."[87] In a letter to his family, Captain William Clopton of the Fayette Artillery reported that the scene was "almost indescribable" as the stores became "the prey of the victors." The captain and his men soon had access to "every imaginable luxury. Fruits hermetically sealed and everything in the eating line that the New York markets can afford grace our table daily." Clopton also marveled at the Federal accommodations in Plymouth. "These rascals were fixed up as if they expected to live here the balance of their mortal lives."[88] One soldier mistook a box of chocolates for soap. Others broke mirrors for pieces of "looking glass," and some men pilfered piano wire to hang their tin cups in camp. The Southerners found more than food and lodging. Artillery colonel James R. Branch, who had headed the tribunal for the Kinston hangings, secured too much "commissary whiskey" and broke his leg "attempting circus tricks on a battery horse"—an embarrassing accident that his hometown newspaper covered up.[89]

In addition to satisfying their immediate hunger and thirst, the soldiers found that victory fulfilled one of Robert E. Lee's primary goals. Plymouth contained an astounding amount of supplies. In a letter to a Lynchburg paper, one soldier listed a bonanza of captured rations, including "10,000 barrels of flour, 180,000 pounds of fine sugar cured canvassed hams, 500 barrels of molasses, 700 barrels of ground coffee, 3000 sacks of green coffee, 1500 barrels of white, yellow and brown sugar, 1000 sacks of Liverpool salt, a large amount of rice, soap, peas, vinegar, and many other articles of subsistence." In addition, there were 1,000 horses and plenty of forage.[90] Guion's men filled three pontoon boats with the spoils. When Hoke learned of this, he remarked, "Well, they deserve it."[91] A Raleigh newspaper received another list of captured goods, which included "a large quantity of coal, a splendid machine shop, 12 forges, any amount of tools, 40 pieces artillery, 25 wagons and teams, some 200 fine horses, a good supply of medicines, a large supply of ammunition, the best fortifications in the State and the key to a wealthy country."[92]

Following the soldiers' bacchanalia, ample supplies remained for shipment to Lee's army in Virginia. Editors of the *Petersburg Register*, witnessing the largesse rolling through their city, thanked the "Yankee Commissary Department of the State of North Carolina." The first train clattered through the Cockade City bulging with barrels and boxes of supplies valued at $1 million, with more trains on the way.[93] Word spread that the quantity of supplies surpassed expectations and included "enough to feed a large army for many months to come." Indeed, the Federal supplies stockpiled at Plymouth—and, perhaps more important, the surrounding farmlands and fisheries opened by the campaign—would greatly aid Lee's army over the coming months.[94]

"The Whole Brutal Transaction"

But more than plunder occupied the rebels. Some of them participated in an altogether different endeavor: hunting down and, in some cases, killing black soldiers. Soon after Plymouth's fall, disturbing accounts emanated from both sides. A letter published in the *Raleigh Daily Confederate* several days after Hoke's victory stated that, early on Wednesday morning, "a large body, perhaps six hundred negroes and buffaloes came out of the Garrett fort [Fort Williams] and made for the nearest point of Peacock swamp. Three companies of cavalry and one of infantry were hunting them there all day, and nearly all were killed. I suppose no prisoners were taken there."[95] In a note home on April 24, Captain Clopton wrote, "I forgot to mention that several hundred negroes & negro officers attempted to escape when the town fell but were pursued & all most the last one of them killed—the woods are full of them."[96] North Carolina resident Rebecca P. Davis wrote a few weeks after the battle, "Several persons say they saw Mary Newell's Alfred at Plymouth. They say he begged to be sent to his mother, but was shot, as all negroes were who were dressed in Yankee uniforms, so I have heard."[97]

Over the next weeks and months, similar stories multiplied, appearing in newspapers, letters home, and veterans' reminiscences.[98] The most graphic account came from the affidavit of an African American soldier who identified himself as Samuel Johnson of the 2nd Union Colored Cavalry. Although his name does not appear in regimental records, he claimed to be in Plymouth aiding Lieutenant George French with recruiting efforts, and he shared his harrowing account with Benjamin Butler's staff outside Richmond in July 1864. According to Johnson, over the course of several days, the Confederates at Plymouth killed "all" the black men in blue uniforms by hanging them in the woods, stripping and shooting them on the riverbank, braining them with musket butts, and dragging them through the town with ropes around their necks.[99]

Many Union soldiers relayed similar stories, although they often differed as to timing, scope, and other details.[100] Wessells made no mention of such events in his report, although some lower-ranking Union officers later confirmed that a massacre had occurred. First Lieutenant Isaiah Conley of the 101st Pennsylvania, who escaped from captivity after Plymouth, reported to his hometown paper "the massacre of more than two hundred colored prisoners by the rebels." According to the paper, Conley "saw the squads of rebel soldiers as they severally returned from shooting the negroes, and heard them state how many each shot."[101] In addition, First Lieutenant Alonzo Cooper of the 12th New York Cavalry witnessed the execution of black soldiers "drawn up in line at the breastwork." He continued, "This I plainly saw from where we were held under guard, not over five hundred yards distance. There were but few who saw this piece of atrocity, but my attention was attracted to it and I watched the whole brutal transaction."[102]

In the following weeks, Confederate officials disputed the accounts, and after the war, rebel veterans denied such events ever occurred. In responding to Samuel Johnson's affidavit, Confederate Robert Ould, in charge of prisoner matters, called Johnson's statements "a villainous lie, and badly told at that."[103] Confederate newspapers also offered vehement denials.[104] Long after the war, one North Carolina writer stated, "The authors of these charges are mistaken. Many negroes and native North Carolinian Union soldiers were killed but they were attempting to make their escape, when by the laws of war—the victors are justified in shooting even unarmed men."[105] Others made similar arguments. A Confederate cavalryman wrote several decades later that he saw no one killed "who promptly obeyed the order to halt."[106] Decades after the war, even some Union veterans expressed doubt that any large massacre had occurred.[107]

To be sure, some accounts conflicted, and others were questionable. For instance, in some cases, estimates of the number of victims exceeded the total number of black soldiers and civilians likely to have been present in Plymouth at the time. Other reports came from unreliable thirdhand accounts. Unlike similar incidents at Fort Pillow and the Crater, the Federal government never conducted an official investigation. In Washington, DC, the reports were greeted with incredulity. President Lincoln's attorney general, Edward Bates, recorded that the cabinet found the "horrid story" unbelievable. "For the sake of humanity, I hope this is not true," wrote Bates.[108] The conflicting reports and opinions regarding the postbattle incidents at Plymouth remained a subject of debate after the war.

In 1995, historians Weymouth Jordan and Gerald Thomas published an extensive study of the killing of blacks at Plymouth. The pair combed through mounds of diaries, correspondence, newspapers, and official records. Based on this examination, the authors concluded that murders had in fact occurred. According to their research, "at some point" prior to the surrender, about 500 black soldiers and civilians, as well as about 50 white North Carolina Union soldiers, attempted to escape the works and reach the swamps. Infantry and cavalry opened fire on those who "refused to halt or were too terrified to do so." The fugitives who made it to the swamps were pursued by the rebels. In Jordan and Thomas's view, the Confederates took most of the civilians and "Buffaloes" alive, but some of the black troops found "in uniform were summarily executed." The pair also speculated that some black troops were executed three or four days after the surrender, perhaps on the Plymouth docks. In the authors' estimation, the total number of blacks massacred (in uniform or otherwise) after the surrender or when asking for "quarter or mercy" amounted to at least 50.[109]

The events at Plymouth were not unique. Throughout the war, Confederate policy on dealing with captured black soldiers lacked clarity. In 1862, Secretary of War James Seddon informed Confederate commanders that slaves "in flagrant rebellion are subject to death by the laws of every slave-holding State" and that "summary execution must therefore be inflicted on those taken." In other directives, however, Richmond officials declared that captured black prisoners were to be treated as runaway slaves and handed over to state officials to be dealt with under state law.[110] Whatever the official Confederate policy, many Confederate soldiers chose to take matters into their own hands when encountering captured black soldiers on the battlefield. The events at Plymouth fit an emerging pattern. Confederate soldiers had killed black prisoners at Olustee in Florida in February and at Fort Pillow in Tennessee in early April. Ransom's men, by their own admission, had shot captured black soldiers only weeks before at Suffolk, during their engagement with African American cavalry. Confederates would do so again at the Crater outside Petersburg in July and at Saltville, Virginia, in October. Smaller, lesser-known incidents would also occur outside Richmond.[111]

At Plymouth, there is no evidence that Robert Hoke or other officers played a direct role. In unsubstantiated reports, General Peck indicated that, during negotiations with Wessells prior to surrender, Hoke refused to treat black and white North Carolina soldiers as "prisoners of war."[112] However, nothing has indicated that Hoke, Dearing, Ransom, or any other high-ranking officers ordered the execution of black prisoners.[113] But the lack of any direct connection does not absolve these men from the taint of events at Plymouth. They may not have ordered the killings, but it is difficult to believe these events occurred without their knowledge. In addition, there is no indication that any Confederate soldiers under Hoke's command were punished or even investigated for these acts.[114]

Following the battle, the Confederates corralled the surviving black soldiers and civilians and sent most, if not all, of them back into slavery. A report relayed to a Petersburg paper indicated that 300 or 400 black civilians "who had been taken from their legal owners, were re-captured at Plymouth." According to the story, General Hoke had confined an unidentified Union lieutenant who had commanded black troops with the captured black women and children. The officer, it reported, presented "a most abject, hang-dog appearance, and has requested to be sent off with the other prisoners of war, but as he preferred the company of negroes previous to the capture of Plymouth, General Hoke has determined not to separate him from them now."[115]

Confederate officials, not wishing to arouse Northern ire, largely concealed the disposition of the surviving black recruits captured at Plymouth. A day after the town fell, Braxton Bragg in Richmond advised Governor Vance to take custody of the black prisoners and return them to their "respective owners" in North Carolina, should such people be identified. From all over the region, slave owners flocked to Plymouth to claim their former slaves, as well as horses and equipment seized by Union forces there.[116] Bragg directed Vance to retain the other prisoners—those enslaved in other states or otherwise unclaimed—until President Davis weighed in. He also asked Vance to avoid "any publicity," keep any reference to black prisoners out of the newspapers, and prevent "all complications with the military authorities of the United States in regard to the disposition which will be made of this class of prisoners."[117] Eventually, Confederate officials sent many of the prisoners who were unclaimed by their former owners to work on the fortifications in Wilmington.[118]

The 166 white soldiers serving in Companies B and E of the 2nd North Carolina Union Volunteers (the "Buffaloes") also faced peril at the hands of their rebel captors. Nine died in action during the battle. Nearly 60 managed to escape, either before Plymouth's surrender or when General Wessells and their officers, Captains Calvin Hoggard and Littleton Johnson, urged them to leave town because their safety could not be ensured. Many swam across the Roanoke River and tramped through the swamps north into Bertie County. Following the Kinston hangings, officers of these men in blue were "fearful that it would not be possible for them to be protected or receive the same [treatment] in case of capture that the other troops received."[119] Connecticut veteran Warren Goss recalled that many fled across the river before the surrender. "On those who were not thus fortunate, fell all the concentrated rage and hatred of the rebels," he wrote.[120]

In the battle's aftermath, Hoke's men made a concerted effort to locate these men and eventually managed to identify at least eight Buffaloes who had formerly served in Confederate units. According to Lieutenant Conley of the 101st Pennsylvania, the Confederates formed the prisoners into two ranks and marched them past rows of rebel Tar Heels. Similarly, local citizens were tasked with identifying Buffaloes as well as the black soldiers' officers. Lieutenant Colonel Oliver McNary escaped detection when a local woman, Miss Norkum, deliberately ignored him in the lineup, refusing to betray him to a Confederate officer.[121] One Pennsylvanian recalled that when the enemy searched for deserters in his regiment, one of these men "stood at my elbow and was passed and repassed by his cousin, yet not recognized."[122] Lieutenant Conley indicated that five or six men were pulled from the line, but most escaped detection.[123] Those identified as formerly enlisted in rebel units were executed soon afterward. According to Goss, the men were "strung up to the limb of trees by the roadside . . . without even the ceremony of a drum-head court martial."[124] The rest of the Buffaloes, about forty, headed to Andersonville prison in Georgia, many of them dying there. Still others remain unaccounted for. According to one veteran, many clothed themselves in the uniforms of dead artillerists and managed to avoid discovery. Some assumed the identities of soldiers from other units.[125]

In the days following the surrender, the victors marched the Union prisoners out of town.[126] The officers, including General Wessells, his adjutant general, two aides, and fourteen others, arrived in Richmond a week later. Wessells was eventually exchanged. However, for many of these captives, the road ahead would be a tragic one. On April 27, nearly 700 prisoners passed through Goldsboro, looking like an "impudent set of well-dressed vagabonds, full of insolence and impertinence," according to one rebel witness.[127] The enlisted men headed into the interior, most of them destined for the misery of Andersonville. As one veteran wrote:

> The evening of April 30, 1864, the moon shone bright, and the soft winds of spring fanned the foot-sore and weary Union prisoners from Plymouth as they passed through the gates and into the grim stockade of the rebel prison at Andersonville. Home, friends, and country were now shut out from those brave men in all but memory. Through three years of hardships and dangers, thoughts of the home-coming time had cheered them in camp and inspired them in battle. The history of that charnel-house at Andersonville can never be painted in words that express the reality.[128]

The Union soldiers captured in the town and sent south into confinement earned the sobriquet "Plymouth Pilgrims." Those who survived the ordeal would record their experiences in many speeches, articles, and books.[129] The accounts detailed the misery, deprivation, and death in the Confederate prison, as well as the heroic escapes, which were often aided along the way by slaves.[130]

CHAPTER TWENTY-ONE

Confederate Victory at Plymouth

"Remarkably Well Planned and Executed"

For Hoke's men, it had been an astounding victory, a success that would prove to be one of the last unmitigated Confederate triumphs. It had not been easy. The Plymouth defenses were strong, the garrison stout and well armed. Successful attacks against well-fortified positions had been a rarity during the war. However, Robert Hoke managed to overcome the odds. He exercised care in picking points to attack. He also demonstrated flexibility in taking advantage of opportunities as they arose and improvising his moves. On the first day, he probed Fort Gray for weaknesses and found none. On the second night, he identified the vulnerability of the detached Fort Wessells and conducted a well-orchestrated assault. Through an effective diversion and the use of an overwhelming artillery barrage, Hoke managed to capture this position without significant casualties. On the third day, he wisely refrained from throwing his men against the strength of the main Federal line and showed patience in deploying Ransom's brigade on the Union left. And when Ransom managed to get his men over Conaby Creek, Hoke approved Ransom's proposal to unleash a devastating assault that cracked through the Federal perimeter on the fourth morning. At the end, Hoke prudently relied once again on artillery in finishing off Fort Williams.

But Hoke's ultimate success might not have occurred without two key events. First, joint-service cooperation was vital to victory. To be sure, the success of the *Albemarle* stood out as the fulcrum of Plymouth's demise. By clearing the river of Union naval support, Commander James Cooke eliminated a vital component of Plymouth's defense and immediately rendered the fortifications vulnerable to fire from the rear. The combined operation, coordinated ably between Cooke and Hoke, paved the way for Plymouth's fall. Cooke received his well-deserved share of the credit. In addition to the dramatic accounts appearing in newspapers and letters home, the Confederate Congress issued a resolution thanking the captain for his contribution to the victory.[1] Second, and perhaps just as important, Ransom's crossing at Conaby Creek on the night of April 19 exposed Plymouth's left flank. Without opening this door, Ransom's men would have sat on the sidelines Wednesday morning, while Hoke's and Terry's brigades attacked into the teeth of the Union defenses west of Fort Williams.[2]

Word of the victory immediately generated recognition for Hoke and others involved with the operation. On April 21, 1864, Hoke wrote to Bragg, announcing: "I have stormed and carried this place."[3] John Taylor Wood, who joined Hoke on the expedition, sent word to Richmond the same day, proclaiming, "Heaven has crowned our efforts with success. General Hoke has captured this point with 1,600 prisoners, 25 pieces of artillery, and navy cooperation."[4] Hoke receive substantial praise. Lieutenant Colonel William G. Lewis, who commanded the young general's brigade during the battle, later remarked that Hoke was "always ready to attack the enemy, a good strategist, cool, brave, full of enthusiasm, and remarkable in infusing enthusiasm and dash in the troops of his command." At Plymouth, Lewis noted that Hoke's operation "was remarkably well planned and executed," and the *Fayetteville Weekly Observer* proclaimed that Hoke "may well rank with the ablest division commanders of the service."[5] There were also calls for Hoke's promotion. "We hope Mr. Davis will remember the 'Old Tar State,' the victory of Plymouth, and Gen. Hoke," pleaded the editors of the *Daily Progress* in Raleigh.[6]

Official recognition did not take long. The Confederate government showered praise, reflecting the victory's positive impact on officials in Richmond. President Davis was delighted. According to John Beauchamp Jones in the War Department, the victory had "a wonderful effect in the President's mind."[7] On Saturday, April 23, 1864, Davis wrote Hoke: "Accept my thanks and congratulations for the brilliant success which has attended your attack and capture of Plymouth. You are promoted to be a major-general from that date."[8] Davis's decision made Hoke the youngest major general in the Confederate service. Several days later, Robert E. Lee, writing from his headquarters in the field, expressed approval of the promotion but regretted losing Hoke from his army, unless, as Lee put it, "he can be sent to me with a division." The Confederate Congress and the North Carolina legislature followed with resolutions honoring Hoke.[9]

Other officers in Hoke's force received attention. James Dearing won promotion to brigadier general, earning plaudits for his dashing style, "great skill and bravery."[10] "Col. Dearing of the cavalry," argued the *Fayetteville Weekly Observer*, "is worthy of notice . . . his services were valuable."[11] Indeed, Dearing was everywhere, leading both artillery and cavalry units and acting as Hoke's de facto chief of staff. He commanded the artillery at Fort Gray on the first day, operated against Fort Wessells on the second night, conveyed the request for surrender that evening, helped with the crossing at Conaby Creek on Tuesday night, and was in the thick of the street fighting on the last day.

Matt Ransom also garnered well-deserved praise for his crushing attack on the Union left on Wednesday morning. "His military genius comprehended the situation, and he was master of it," stated the *Fayetteville Weekly Observer*.[12] His assault truly broke the back of the Union defense. Colonel John Taylor Wood reportedly called it "one of the most brilliant charges [he] ever knew." He noted, "not a man faltered [and] all vied with each other to see who could plant their flag first on the walls." In Wood's view, Ransom "acted very well and bravely."[13] In turn, Ransom commended his men's performance. "I am safe, my brigade greatly distinguished itself," he telegraphed his wife soon after the battle. In a subsequent letter, he elaborated: "I must tell you my brigade has immortalized itself. The charge and the storming of the forts was the noblest thing of the war. I wish you could have seen it."[14]

"Glorious News"

The victory gave Confederate North Carolina a rare reason to celebrate. From her plantation near Halifax, Catherine Edmondston rejoiced at the "news of a gallant & glorious success of our arms here in our own borders."[15] Charlotte's *Western Democrat* similarly hailed the "glorious news."[16] The victory resonated beyond the state, boosting morale in Richmond and elsewhere. "The fight is ours and we have taken Plymouth," wrote Dearing to his wife in Richmond.[17] Upon hearing the news, Robert E. Lee wrote: "I am profoundly grateful to the Giver of all Victory for our success in North Carolina. I trust it may continue, and that the end may be as favorable as the beginning."[18]

In addition to the captured prisoners and piles of supplies, the result freed a significant portion of the state from Union occupation. Hoke and Cooke's achievement also opened the path to eastern North Carolina and the other Federal bases there. On the water, Cooke's ironclad challenged Union control throughout the sounds and rivers, effectively blocked Federal access to the Chowan River and points northeast, and stood poised to take the fight to the rest of North Carolina's waters. The *Richmond Daily Dispatch* predicted the gunboat "could initiate a Grand ball on the amber hued waters of the Pamlico." The paper forecast that the Union boats would comport themselves like "a school of fat, delicate panfish" after "discovering a shark in their midst busily engaged and gulping them down."[19]

Although the Southern press sensed more opportunities ahead, it understood that the Plymouth triumph had yielded benefits of its own. "Taking of that town is an event highly cheering, and in its self of great importance," wrote the editors of the *Daily Dispatch*.[20] A contributor to a Charlotte paper reported that the results "rejoiced the people" throughout the region. He recognized that the victory had "free[d] an immense section of the country . . . abounding as it does in valuable fisheries," bacon, and crops. And he noted that the ironclad would protect the fisheries of the Chowan and Roanoke from Union gunboats and ensure control over the counties of Tyrrell, Washington, Martin, Bertie, Hertford, Gates, Chowan, Perquimans, Camden, and Currituck.[21]

The capture of Plymouth was a Tar Heel victory. For the most part, North Carolina troops and leaders won the battle. Two of the three brigades hailed from that state, and so did most of the principal commanders: Hoke, Ransom, Lewis, and Cooke. This fact certainly raised the morale of the state's Confederate population and aided Governor Vance's reelection efforts. As the editors of the *Daily Progress* in Raleigh noted, the victory sent "a thrill of joy throughout the Confederacy" and was "especially gratifying to North Carolinians, because it was won by North Carolina troops, led by a North Carolina general."[22] Other newspapers recognized the victory's importance. "General Hoke has struck a most effective blow for the redemption of his native State," wrote the *Petersburg Express*.[23] Confederate citizens celebrated as well. "How thankful we should be to God for this signal triumph!" announced Catherine Edmondston. "Plymouth has been a thorn in our side & the garrison there a perpetual uneasiness to us."[24]

However, friction persisted even amid the jubilation. The *Fayetteville Semi-Weekly Observer* noted that, despite ongoing complaints about Virginia's dominance in the army, newspapers in that state had outpaced their Carolina counterparts in covering the campaign. The Fayetteville editors complained bitterly that Virginia papers had provided the most informative coverage. North Carolina papers contained few detailed accounts, letters, and casualty reports at first, although that would change in the coming days. Nevertheless, the editors groused that "this silence about great events which ought to be known, is not modesty—it is a criminal indifference to the truth of history and to the feeling of friends."[25]

The Plymouth victory also fueled more acrimony between the political factions in the state. The *Fayetteville Weekly Observer* predicted that Hoke would "drive the enemy from Eastern North Carolina and obliterate the last vestige of Holdenism."[26] It singled out Holden's *Standard* for its anemic coverage of Plymouth: "Twenty lines devoted to the most important battle that was ever fought in North Carolina . . . and that by a North Carolina paper!"[27] The pro-Vance press also criticized Holden for printing articles critical of Hoke's recent arrests of anti-Confederate citizens. They accused Holden and his editors of denigrating Hoke in the middle of an important military campaign, when Confederate leaders needed unqualified support.[28]

A happy Governor Zebulon Vance heard the reports of victory a day after Plymouth's capitulation. On Thursday, April 21, he visited Fayetteville, home of his close ally E. J. Hale, editor of the *Fayetteville Observer*. The governor was greeted at the town limits by a group of citizens who gave him the news. In a short speech, he touched on the election, criticized Holden's positions, and closed by noting the success of Hoke's expedition. Hale's newspaper added that the "signal and important victory" had electrified the country, and it observed that Hoke had conducted the operation "with such prudence and secrecy that it was almost as little known in the Confederacy as it was to the enemy." The editors also claimed that the achievement had "rescued a North Carolina town from the presence and outrages of a malignant enemy."[29] Vance received a note from Braxton Bragg congratulating him on the victory "under the leadership of the young North Carolinian, Brigadier-General Hoke. May we have many more such to refer to hereafter as part of the history of the campaign of 1864."[30]

"Plymouth Is Lost by This Time"

For Union commanders, Plymouth's loss led to confusion and blame. To the officers in the garrison itself, the defeat marked the low point of their careers. With most of them headed to prison in Richmond to await exchange, news of the disaster was slow to reach other Federal posts. By Wednesday, as the final Confederate assault crushed Wessells's defenses, John Peck received word of the gunboat fight from Commander Davenport.[31] "There is no doubt but that Plymouth is lost by this time," Peck informed Butler, "and the ram will probably come down to Roanoke Island, Washington, and New Berne."[32] However, official confirmation of the final result took time.[33] It was not until Friday, April 22, that definitive reports of Plymouth's fall arrived in New Bern. Over the weekend, the ominous tidings finally made it to the high command in the north.[34]

The finger-pointing began. Benjamin Butler, sitting in his headquarters in Virginia, confidently diagnosed the defeat's causes with little firsthand knowledge. "Plymouth really fell because the theory of its defense presupposed an occupation of the river by our gun-boats, which would cover our flanks," he explained to Halleck. "When the naval force was driven out by the rebel ram then her fire flanked our defenses instead of our fire enfilading the enemy."[35] His bombast aside, the Massachusetts lawyer was largely correct. The Plymouth defenses proved inadequate to neutralize the ironclad once it gained control of the river. However, a string of additional missteps led up to that unfortunate event. Over the previous year, Union leaders had failed to destroy the boat before it deployed. In addition, the land batteries at Plymouth were insufficient, either by design or through poor leadership, to impede the *Albemarle*. Moreover, the naval force at the station was too weak, underscoring Flusser's (and Wessells's) error in turning the powerful *Tacony* away. This unfortunate decision never received much attention after the fight. Finally, the inept defense at the Conaby Creek crossing and the weak fortifications on Plymouth's eastern side doomed the garrison.

In his note to Halleck, Butler unwisely went after the navy. Showcasing one of his less attractive traits, he taunted navy commanders for expressing "the most unbounded confidence in" their ability to hold the river.[36] He also saved some venom for his own subordinate. In a separate dispatch to Palmer at New Bern, Butler, though claiming he did not wish "to prejudge," insinuated that Wessells had not prepared adequately for the attack.[37]

Butler's criticism of the navy triggered a swift reaction. On April 24, Rear Admiral Lee, still in charge of all naval operations in North Carolina and Virginia, heard the statement directly from Butler as the two planned the upcoming operations against Richmond. Butler's aspersions greatly displeased Lee, who immediately complained to Secretary Welles. "Nothing can be more ungenerous and unjust than to make the Navy responsible for the occupation or surrender of this fortified town," he fumed.[38] In his diary, the secretary predicted the navy would receive blame for the "disasters," being "merely auxiliary to the army."[39] In Lee's opinion, the navy had nothing to do with Plymouth's land defenses. Furthermore, it was Butler who had discounted the ironclad's threat over the last year, and it was Butler who had insisted that Plymouth was adequately supplied and manned. The admiral also accurately recalled that, on more than one occasion, he had questioned the wisdom of maintaining multiple detached posts throughout the sounds.[40]

"As Soon as Your Health Will Allow"

As Butler angered his navy colleagues, the bizarre command situation persisted at New Bern. Peck, relieved by Butler on Tuesday, April 19, continued to exercise control over the North Carolina District while his subordinate and successor, Innis Palmer, waited to assume command. Immediately following the Plymouth disaster, Peck poured much of his energy into defending his decisions over the past few months. On Thursday, the day news of the garrison's fall reached New Bern, he sent a lengthy letter to Butler, defending his efforts to counter the Confederates.[41] All the while, he clung to his post, despite Butler's order issued a few days before.

On Saturday, April 23, an assuredly confused Palmer notified Butler that Peck continued to exercise command. On that day, Palmer met with Peck, expecting to commence his tenure as chief of the North Carolina District. But instead of handing over command, Peck held out, hoping that contrary orders would arrive from Fort Monroe.[42] Butler finally ended the drama by telling Peck he was needed in the North for a new assignment. "While I have no doubt that Gen. Palmer will be glad of your advice and assistance in the emergency in which he finds himself placed," Butler explained, "I wish . . . you will report yourself here for light duty." Over the next day or so, Butler and his staff corresponded directly with Palmer.[43]

Peck was livid with Butler's decision. In a letter that escaped publication in the official records, Peck complained that Butler had induced him to remain in North Carolina the previous fall, providing "many reasons and considerations of a confidential character which can hardly have escaped your memory."[44] Indeed, upon Butler's arrival in November 1863, the two had discussed changes in the departmental structure that would give Peck separate command. Specifically, in a private letter written in November 1863, Peck had encouraged Butler to take charge of the "Middle Department" (New Jersey, Pennsylvania, Delaware, and parts of Maryland) and combine it with Butler's Virginia responsibilities, leaving North Carolina to Peck's independent oversight. "Now Gen.," wrote Peck, "suppose you secure the Middle and give me N.C. You can do this from your influence at Court, if it meets your approbation." While it appears that the proposal went nowhere, these discussions and Butler's assurances had convinced Peck to remain in North Carolina.[45] In light of their earlier discussions, Peck was miffed that Butler had dismissed him, particularly in the midst of a large Confederate offensive. "In the face of the enemy I am relieved without consultation or explanation," wrote Peck. "This strange procedure is calculated to injure me in public estimation and must be construed into a disapproval of my administration."[46]

Later, Butler would point to Peck's infirmity as the main reason for his removal, urging the older officer to report to Fort Monroe for light duty "as soon as your health will allow you."[47] Peck had, in fact, suffered serious, long-lasting injuries at Suffolk in 1863 after a jarring fall from his horse. The doctor who had diagnosed the general with paralysis of the right arm concluded that Peck "was in danger [of] being permanently disabled by it." The physician urged him to take leave and recover.[48] However, Butler did not refer specifically to these injuries in his communication relieving the general. He assured Peck that the decision had been made before the Confederate attack and "in no manner implies any censure upon your action or disapproval of your administration."[49]

Despite these soothing words, other evidence betrays Butler's unhappiness with Peck, particularly with respect to his efforts to arm and deploy former slaves. Indeed, communication from Butler's headquarters to Peck's replacement, Palmer, strongly hints at deeper concerns. In a long note written upon Peck's removal, Butler's aide, J. R. Shaffer, suggested that Peck had generated discord or at least dysfunction within the district and had performed poorly in recruiting and arming black soldiers and attending to black refugees.[50] Consistent with Shaffer's intimation, evidence suggests that Peck did not aggressively pursue the recruitment and employment of emancipated slaves. When Peck took control of the North Carolina District from John Foster in August 1863, he transferred black regiments out of the state and notably slowed new recruitment.[51] His half-hearted efforts in dealing with black recruits and laborers did not go unnoticed by his subordinates. Vermonter Colonel Edward Ripley, in charge of the Newport Barracks, wrote home that Peck was "opposed to the employment of the negro, and . . . will not approve requisitions to feed or pay them." Contrary to army policy, Peck prohibited Ripley from compensating freedmen for their labor on fortifications, a decision overruled by Butler when he visited Ripley's post.[52] This was not the only time Peck demonstrated little enthusiasm for this aspect of the Union war effort. A few days before the attack on Plymouth, he drafted a report for Butler on recruitment in North Carolina in which he complained about various regimental recruiting officers throughout his district operating without "proper authority" and with a general "lack of organization and unity of action." Peck also griped that the recruits received too much clothing, ignoring the destitute condition of most of the escaped slaves who arrived in the Union camps. He also warned that aggressive recruitment had corralled the young ("weak, puny, scrofulous") as well as others who were "utterly incapacitated by old age."[53]

Peck may have had the best of intentions in expressing his concerns about recruitment efforts. And it does not appear that his superiors had previously reprimanded him for poor performance in this area. But his gloomy April missive, coupled with his reputation, may have convinced Butler that it was time for a change. Early in the war, Butler, a prewar Democrat, had become a steadfast advocate for African American troops. Once he took charge of the Virginia and North Carolina Department, the abrasive general encouraged the aggressive recruitment of black troops and eagerly supported operations involving them, including Edward Wild's raid in December 1863. Peck's lukewarm approach stood at odds with Butler's program and, for that matter, with the administration's policies.

Following Butler's orders on April 19, the confusion at New Bern continued for several days. Finally, on April 25, Peck issued long-winded orders transferring command to Palmer, who simultaneously issued a short announcement assuming his new position.[54] Even in submitting his resignation, Peck managed to annoy. While complimenting his men, he stated that his troops "have been in the field since the outbreak of the revolution." His word choice inflamed Butler. "What revolution do you mean?" he quipped. "The revolution of our ancestors against England? . . . It is not usual for officers in the United States to style the rebellion a revolution."[55]

On the same day Palmer assumed command, Peck prepared an exhaustive report defending his decisions and attempting to deflect blame for the Plymouth debacle back on Butler. Liberally quoting from his dispatches over the previous year, Peck laboriously cataloged the decisions he had made, the poor guidance Butler had furnished, and the impact of all these factors on Plymouth's fate. He sought to prove that he had taken prudent steps to protect Plymouth, that he had warned Butler of the impending danger, and that he had supported Wessells and Flusser in preparing for the ironclads.[56]

And so ended Peck's tenure in command of the North Carolina District. The drama behind his transfer and Butler's apparent dissatisfaction went largely unnoticed. In discussing the change, the editors of the *New Berne Times* did not mention Peck's flagging health or any other reason for his departure. Instead, they commended him, noting that he had served with "too much zeal and devotion" to leave without recognition. A *New York Times* correspondent praised the general for his prescience in improving the fortifications and his "efficiency and success" in managing the district. "His apprehensions of danger were always rational and timely," continued the reporter, "and had the means been granted him, we should have been enlarging rather than contracting our lines in the old North State."[57] On May 1, Peck and his staff gathered on the New Bern wharf and boarded the *Ellen S. Terry*. Palmer was there to see him off. In July, with his health "restored," Peck would take on a new assignment in the Department of the East in New York City.[58]

"No Use of Our Holding Washington or Plymouth"

For his part, Ulysses S. Grant analyzed matters with an eye to the upcoming Virginia campaign. The lieutenant general understood that success in Virginia would erase the sting of any reverses in North Carolina. On April 22, before news of Plymouth's fall, he warned Butler not to let the enemy's movement interrupt plans in Virginia. He also recommended that commanders in North Carolina abandon Plymouth and Washington rather than waste so many men defending such places. In doing so, Grant repeated what navy commanders—namely, Admiral Lee—had been recommending for some time.[59] Later that day, the lieutenant general echoed this recommendation to Halleck. "It appears to me there is no use of our holding Washington or Plymouth," he wrote. "It would be better to have the forces necessary to garrison those two places added to General Butler's column of attack, which, if successful, will give back to us not only the coast, but probably most of the state." Grant also recognized the costs of giving up these posts, noting that evacuation would compromise those who had maintained their loyalty to the Union "in full faith."[60]

In response to Grant's request, Halleck raised concerns. Harkening back to the Blockade Strategy Board's deliberations in 1861, he explained that Union occupation of these coastal towns, including New Bern, Washington, and Plymouth, eliminated the need to blockade the coast. Halleck also recalled decisions made in 1863 to maintain men at the North Carolina positions because, in the view of army and navy officers, the region's abandonment would "be extremely injurious to our cause in North Carolina, fatal to Union men who had accepted our protection, and destructive to our flotilla in the sounds." Accordingly, Halleck and other Union officials had decided to retain forces at these posts, despite the need for reinforcements elsewhere. Now, with Grant seeking to change matters, Halleck stuck with this previous recommendation.[61]

In an article published two decades after the war, Grant recalled that New Bern needed to be held because it "was a port into which blockade-runners could enter."[62] He did not have the same view of Washington and Plymouth, at least by his recollection. In his memoirs, he wrote that those two towns "had been occupied by Federal troops before I took command of the armies, and I knew the Executive would be reluctant to abandon them, and therefore explained my views; but before my views were carried out the rebels captured the garrison at Plymouth."[63] However, no record of such a discussion with administration officials appears in Grant's papers, and his postwar assertion seems inconsistent with his April 19, 1864, dispatch to Butler directing him "to hold [Plymouth] at all hazards, unless it is of no importance to hold."[64] In his postwar memoirs, Butler made a similar (unsubstantiated) claim, asserting that he had recommended the abandonment of Plymouth and Washington after his November 1863 inspection, judging those posts "useless."[65]

As news of Plymouth's loss eventually reached the Union high command and the Confederates threatened other North Carolina posts, Grant kept his focus on the upcoming spring offensive. In Virginia, he would soon order different forces to move against Lee's army west of Fredericksburg and against rail connections at Lynchburg. In addition, Butler would steam up the James River to threaten Richmond and Petersburg. Grant hoped to kick off the operations in early May, only a few days after the disappointing news from Plymouth had trickled in. With the logistical gears whirring, he understood that the impending Virginia offensive would soon force the Confederates to rush all available troops north, thus nullifying Hoke's campaign. In the meantime, he ordered his commanders in North Carolina to shore up and concentrate their defenses and, most of all, to ensure New Bern's safety. However, despite Plymouth's capture, he did not direct Washington's evacuation—at least not yet.

Confederate leaders faced their own calculus. Following Hoke's victory, they had to decide whether to continue the North Carolina offensive or to reel Hoke and his men back to Virginia. Robert E. Lee, though quick to praise Hoke's achievement, was ready to bring his army back up to strength. Now, with Plymouth captured and a storm forming over Virginia, he repeated his call. On April 23 and again on the April 29, he asked President Davis to return Hoke's brigade, complaining that the division was "much weakened by their absence."[66] However, he no doubt understood that additional victories in the state would benefit the Confederate cause. New Bern's capture would secure tons of supplies, eliminate a key Union base on the coast, and boost the morale of the state's voters. Furthermore, Confederate citizens yearned for more victories. C. L. Burgwin of Mecklenburg County captured the feelings of many in a letter to Secretary of War James Seddon days after the Plymouth triumph. Burgwin urged Confederate officials to devote more troops to the state and argued that the "moral and political effect" of complete victory against Union forces there would be "incalculable" and would immediately impact the New York gold market.[67]

To be sure, Hoke's campaign was incomplete, and the Confederates expected more. "Hoke and Ransom, with the aid from their brethren from the other States, have restored to their mother her lost treasure; and all that is needed is but a few spare days to finish up the job," cheered the *Fayetteville Weekly Observer*.[68] Now, Washington and New Bern beckoned Hoke's column. However, the young general's success, standing by itself, gave Tar Heels ample reason to celebrate. To Confederate leaders in the Old North State, Plymouth furnished a moment of glory in an otherwise grim war. Now they hoped for more and understood that conditions were ripening for a larger victory under Hoke's command. The *Albemarle* had proved a devastating weapon. The *Neuse* at Kinston was ready to launch. The Federal bases at Washington and New Bern remained tempting targets. With his task force still intact, Hoke pointed his column south.

PART SIX

Back to New Bern

Hoke's offensive did not end at Plymouth. With Grant forming his plans for the spring and anxiety among Confederates growing in Virginia, Hoke resumed operations in his home state. Success against the Federal positions at Washington and New Bern would complete his triumph, gain large quantities of supply, and boost morale. At New Bern and other posts, Union commanders knew what was coming and scrambled to avoid further setbacks.

CHAPTER TWENTY-TWO

Washington

"Picked Up in Detail"

On Monday, April 25, Hoke began the final lunge to retake eastern North Carolina for the Confederate cause. A long line of well-fed, well-rested men swung out of Plymouth, followed by artillery battery limbers, caissons, and supply wagons filled to the brim. The column headed for its next target, the town of Washington on the Pamlico River. By evening, Hoke's troops had traveled 10 miles west to the hamlet of Jamesville. Early the next day, they resumed the march, heading south on dry roads and kicking up "almost unendurable" dust.[1] Late in the afternoon, Hoke's lead elements reached Washington's outskirts, halted outside the Union fortifications there, and formed into battle line.[2]

As Hoke departed from Plymouth, a new Confederate commander, P. G. T. Beauregard, arrived in Weldon to supervise affairs in North Carolina. The Louisianan's appearance bumped George Pickett to a lesser post at Petersburg. From the first days of the war, Beauregard had occupied an elevated position in the Confederate hierarchy. He had captured Fort Sumter, commanded forces at Manassas, and led an army in the west. According to historian T. Harry Williams, Beauregard was the "South's first paladin," and a "vague air of romance . . . trailed after him wherever he went." Despite his reputation, Beauregard did not always shine. In planning campaigns, he sometimes dreamed up wildly ambitious schemes that had little chance of success. He suffered battlefield reverses as well, particularly at Shiloh and Corinth. He also had a tendency to cross President Davis, a characteristic that probably damaged his military career more than anything else.[3] By late 1863, he found himself orchestrating Charleston Harbor's defense—an important assignment, but certainly not the prestigious field command sought by generals of his stature. In 1864, personal setbacks afflicted Beauregard. His wife died in March, and he battled a chronic throat ailment. Worn down, he sought a leave of absence. In April, however, with Grant preparing the Union war machine for a comprehensive offensive throughout the South, Jefferson Davis needed the Creole's skills and, setting aside any personal animus, placed him in charge of the North Carolina Department.

Beauregard arrived at his new post in Weldon at 5:30 a.m. on Friday, April 22. He assumed command in a fog of ignorance. In one of his first communications with officials in Richmond, he requested a "pocket map" of North Carolina.[4] He also sought guidance on defining the scope of his authority. "General Beauregard has received no order defining his command . . . [and] desires to know how many troops he will have," wrote an aide sent from Richmond to assist him.[5] Over the next few days, the general attempted to put things in order. He had brought two aides with him to Weldon and expected three more to follow from Charleston. He also requested another half dozen individuals by name from Richmond to round out his staff.[6]

Beauregard arrived as the Confederate high command was discussing what should be done in the state. Despite the Louisianan's arrival at Weldon, Hoke's ongoing operations remained under Braxton Bragg's direct supervision. The Plymouth victory had opened a large region to commissary agents and provided the political boost needed by Governor Vance. However, with trouble stirring in Virginia, some questioned the prudence of maintaining significant numbers of men in the Old North State. Beauregard shared this unease and, like Pickett before him, wondered about ongoing operations. The Louisianan believed the focus on North Carolina was misplaced and worried that a continued offensive was not "judicious." He feared it would create "an untimely division" of his new command and frustrate his ability to concentrate forces to meet a Federal attack. Despite Beauregard's misgivings, Richmond officials still seemed willing to support Hoke's efforts.[7]

But Hoke's path forward was not a clear one. Several days after Plymouth's capture, disappointing news cast a cloud over his campaign. On April 22, in response to orders from Richmond, the unfinished *Neuse* had been launched at Kinston. The spectacular success of the *Albemarle* just days earlier generated high hopes for this ironclad.[8] At first, the gunboat glided easily out of a pocket of deep water in downtown Kinston known as the "cat hole." But once the craft got out in the river, the crew found barely enough water "for us to cross the obstructions."[9] A mere 300 yards from its launching point, the vessel shuddered to a stop, its keel firmly wedged in a sandbar. It looked as if it would remain that way, at least until the river rose.[10] The next day, April 23, Montgomery Corse telegraphed the bad news to Beauregard, who relayed the message to Richmond.[11] The setback at Kinston did not deter Hoke, though. He pushed ahead.

Hoke's arrival outside Washington came as no surprise to the defenders there. Union army and navy leaders in the state understood that the Confederates were not finished. With the pressure mounting, the Federals took measures to protect their bases. In New Bern, Innis Palmer ordered his men to sink more obstructions

in the Neuse River above the city to fend off the Kinston ironclad.[12] He kept his officers and men on alert as he struggled to adequately man his works while contending
with more requests from Butler to transfer troops north to support the campaign in
Virginia. Indeed, even though troops continued to steam northward, Butler sought
at least four more regiments as Hoke's rebels remained on the march. Eventually,
the transfers would leave Palmer with only half the men Peck had commanded in
early February when Pickett had first attacked.[13]

The Federal navy also prepared. Rear Admiral Samuel Phillips Lee informed
Secretary Gideon Welles that an "attack by land and water upon New Berne is ap-
prehended." Lee sent additional vessels south from Virginia.[14] Assistant Secretary of
the Navy Gustavus Fox continued to look for some way to get an ironclad over the
Hatteras bar and into the North Carolina sounds.[15] From New Bern, Commander
Henry Davenport ordered the *Tacony* to Roanoke Island to protect that post "at
all hazards" against the *Albemarle*.[16] Naval commanders also gathered information
about the gunboat and prepared for more close action. "The ironclad, from all
accounts, is very much like the first *Merrimack*," reported the *Tacony*'s skipper, William Truxtun, from Roanoke Island. "With a very long and very sharp submerged
prow . . . it will require a large force to properly blockade the various mouths of the
Roanoke River." Truxtun warned that, without a strong flotilla in the Albemarle
Sound, vessels engaging the ironclad "will only be sacrificed to no purpose" and will
encourage the enemy.[17]

In response to Hoke's continued threat, Palmer sought to consolidate his
forces. Specifically, he looked to evacuate Washington to free troops for Butler
in Virginia as well as for New Bern's defense. He sketched out his priorities in an
April 25 dispatch to Butler from New Bern: "I consider it necessary only to hold
this place, the line of railroad from here to Morehead, Hatteras Inlet, and Roanoke Island," he explained. With Plymouth and Washington no longer competing
for Union resources, Palmer thought his command would be "as well, if not better,
off than we were before." In his view, Plymouth and Washington had only served
to protect black and white refugees and prevent small rebel boats from operating
in the sounds. In place of the army posts there, Palmer recommended that the navy
simply bottle up the Tar and Roanoke Rivers. In making these recommendations,
Palmer echoed what Admiral Lee and other naval commanders had been saying
all along.[18]

Palmer's proposal also matched Grant's thinking. Indeed, the lieutenant general
continued to believe that Washington was not worth holding. On Sunday, April 24,
after rumors of Plymouth's fall reached the War Department, Grant recommended
against trying to recapture the post, and he considered evacuating Washington.[19]
With Plymouth firmly in rebel hands, he revisited the matter the next day and
communicated a firm directive to Halleck. "I want General Butler to hold New
Berne at all hazards," he wrote, "but would prefer him to remove everything from

Washington to having our little forces in North Carolina picked up in detail, or to being forced to abandon our offensive operations to defend them."[20]

On Tuesday, April 26, as Hoke's brigades shook out into line before Washington, Grant's orders passed through Butler and then Palmer. By 11:00 p.m., they reached Edward Harland, the brigadier general in charge of the town.[21] In relaying the directive to Harland, Palmer wrote, "A very delicate duty is assigned to you: it is no less than the evacuation of Washington." Unaware of Hoke's arrival, Palmer ordered Harland to pull out with speed and secrecy, taking all the guns, ordnance, and supplies with him. He also cautioned that no property "of any description" should be destroyed. He recommended that the evacuation begin with the 1st North Carolina (Union) Regiment, no doubt fearing what would happen should the Buffaloes fall into Confederate hands. He also ordered Harland to evacuate refugees, both black and white. Palmer explained that Washington was "of no strategic importance" and "not worth the expense which is required to hold it."[22] He asked Harland to send a signal that evening, confirming that Washington was still in Union hands and could receive transports from New Bern for the evacuation. Several hours later, the gunners at Washington dutifully fired three times from their large 64-pounders, a noise distinctly heard at headquarters in New Bern 30 miles away.[23]

The news of Hoke's arrival outside Washington reached New Bern the next day. Palmer and Davenport immediately sent support in the form of the *Commodore Barney*, an armed ferryboat, and the transport *Valley City*, along with many other small vessels to carry material away from the beleaguered town. From New Bern, Palmer could hear the rumble of Hoke's artillery. "I feel very anxious to know what is going on there," he wrote to Harland.[24] The men in the ranks at Washington worried too, particularly the North Carolinians in Federal uniforms.[25]

"Waste No Time before Washington"

Washington, sited on the north bank of the Pamlico River, resembled Plymouth in several ways. The orderly street grid, which roughly matched Plymouth's in size and shape, bracketed "many old-fashioned, pleasant houses with fine gardens of ornamental shrubs and trees." William Stiner, the *New York Herald* reporter who had visited there with Benjamin Butler the previous fall, wrote that Washington contained a "number of fine houses, shaded by luxuriant trees." He described one home in particular, the Grist mansion, as a "magnificent building" surrounded by serpentine walks and a "beautiful arbor of evergreens."[26] A Union soldier stationed in Washington earlier in the war found the town to be "very neat and pretty."[27]

Like at Plymouth, the fortifications at Washington formed a semicircle that stretched around the town and was anchored at both ends on the banks of the Pamlico. Swamps on the eastern side added to the position's strength. The defenses contained several blockhouses and redoubts. At the line's apex north of the town

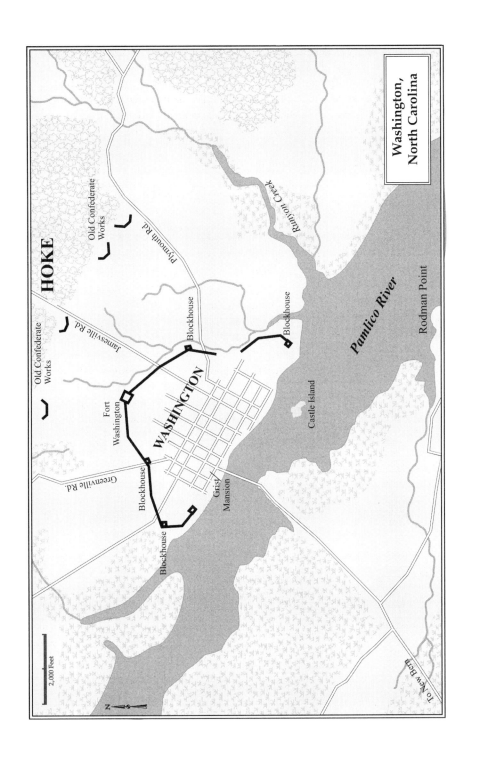

Washington,
North Carolina

stood the most substantial work, Fort Washington, which contained eight guns, including four 32-pounders. Like at Plymouth, Union gunboats at anchor off the town's wharf provided vital communications with New Bern and heavy firepower for the garrison. Unlike the geography at Plymouth, however, a bridge connected downtown Washington to the south bank of the Pamlico and roads south. Across the river, smaller works protected the approaches from that direction. When Hoke brought his regiments to the town's outskirts, many of his men undoubtedly stared at the Union defenses and recalled the costly attacks at Plymouth only days before.[28]

Faced with the strong fortifications and the dangerous, unchallenged gunboats, Hoke weighed whether to attack Washington or bypass the town and proceed directly to the bigger prize: New Bern. Cooke's *Albemarle* was still refitting at Plymouth, and without such naval support, the Federal defense at Washington looked formidable. Given the benefits already yielded by the Plymouth victory, the potentially high costs of an attack on Washington may have seemed prohibitive to the young general. But before making a decision, he pressed his men forward to test the town's defenses.

To Hoke's men, the works looked anything but inviting. "It was a perfect hornet's nest," wrote a Confederate battery commander.[29] Nevertheless, the men pushed ahead. General William G. Lewis, at the tip of the column, drove the Union pickets back into their fortifications. He soon discovered that the town's defenders, like those at Plymouth, had fixed their guns to hit targets set up about a mile and a half from their works. Lewis approached one such bull's-eye and found that the Union gunners had figured the range "too well to make it comfortable." He quickly withdrew to a safer spot.[30]

The Union cannon played on other targets as well. Some rebel units took positions on the low hills surrounding the town. On Wednesday, the 43rd North Carolina advanced to a "semi-circular ridge" that had held a "beautiful farm" before the war and afforded a good view of the town. Like Lewis, these Confederates attracted unwelcome attention and soon realized they had debouched into a killing ground. "The remarkable accuracy with which they threw their shells, was satisfactory evidence that they have been well drilled," recalled one Confederate. The rebels immediately burrowed in, using whatever means they could find—shovels, bayonets, even shingles. With their rifle pits dug, they hugged the ground. One lieutenant unwisely took a position under a small persimmon tree that happened to prop up one of the Yankee targets. When he raised his head to get his bearings, a gun flashed from a mile away, and a missile "cut the tree off about 3 feet from the ground." Such shelling continued throughout the day, trapping men in their shallow ditches under a bright sun.[31] For most of Hoke's men, however, the time spent in front of Washington was not particularly eventful. A member of the 6th North Carolina explained, "The troops lay in the woods all day Wednesday except a strong advance guard who skirmished . . . all day long."[32]

Indeed, there was some fighting. Sometime on Wednesday, a small Union squad made a demonstration against Hoke's position and captured four Confederates who, according to one account, "were at the time visiting outside the lines, and were happily enjoying a 'recess' at a female school." The scouting party of about forty men from the 17th Massachusetts was led by Captain George W. Graham, a hard fighter who usually commanded a company in the 1st North Carolina (Union). Graham's detachment left the works to confront the Confederate center, most likely against members of the 8th North Carolina. The Bay Staters crept forward and encountered rebel pickets in a line of woods, triggering a lively exchange of fire.[33]

From the Union works, officers and men witnessed the fight. In one duel visible from the ramparts, Private William Crofts of Company C tangled with a lone rebel skirmisher. Both combatants ducked and dodged behind tree stumps, then leveled their rifles and fired. The rebel was the better marksman. As his comrades looked on, the unlucky Crofts "rolled over a corpse, with a bullet in his brain." Another Massachusetts man, Joseph Keefe of Company H, also fell dead, and a few others were wounded. Captain Graham did not wait for the bugle to sound "recall." He ordered his men to fall back, and on reaching the works, he assured General Harland that Hoke's force ringed the town.[34]

Lieutenant Colonel Henry T. Guion, still with Hoke's force, had brought his pontoon train to Washington on Wednesday morning and parked his wagons in a field about 3 miles north of town. Leaving his men to rest after the march, he rode to the front and joined Captain John A. Cooper, one of General Hoke's aides, for a little scouting. The pair steered their mounts along a skirt of woods between the road and the river east of town and soon could make out the Union works plainly in the distance. Unfortunately for Guion, the men in the fortifications could see him as well, and two rounds of case shot sprayed in his direction, the deadly fragments falling about 250 yards short. Guion and Cooper guided their horses back into the trees, "secreted" them there, and resumed their "investigation on foot." It is unlikely they discovered anything new, given the Confederate operations conducted over the same ground during D. H. Hill's short siege in 1863.[35]

On their return, Guion and Cooper met with Hoke. His troops had been in front of Washington for only a few hours, but the general had already decided to leave. Hoke had concluded that the town's defenses were too heavy to assault, and the gunboats in the river were largely invulnerable. Unless he could coax the garrison into surrendering without a fight, he resolved to bypass the town and go on to New Bern. Summing things up, he told Guion they would "waste no time before Washington."[36] Hoke had apparently concluded that the town was simply not worth the effort. New Bern, with its prime location and logistical riches, offered a much better target.[37] Hoke may have approached Washington only to divert and unsettle the Union commanders. Some of his officers said as much later. "The demonstration on Washington was only a feint," reported battery commander William Clopton.[38] In the end, the Confederate appearance at Washington did not amount to much. One soldier aptly noted, "We did a very little fighting there, made a big show, and finally evacuated."[39] Hoke prepared to pack up his trains and march his men west toward Greenville.[40]

At 9:00 p.m. on Wednesday, April 27, Guion received orders to move out. As a Union band in the fortifications played some "excellent music," Hoke's forces began to slip away, with Guion and his men leading the column.[41] The night march led to confusion and some harrowing moments, particularly when Guion mistakenly turned onto a road headed straight for the Washington defenses. However, officers sorted out the situation, and the column, pelted by a spring rain, made its way to Greenville, stopping 5 miles beyond that town the next afternoon. General Hoke arrived soon after dark in a buggy, and after taking supper with Guion, he proceeded south to plan his next move: an assault against the Union stronghold at New Bern.[42]

"The Town Was Doomed"

Hoke's departure did not halt the Union evacuation of Washington. With orders in hand to quit the town, Harland sought to remove everyone and everything by Saturday, April 30, as suggested by Palmer. The town's garrison consisted of the 21st Connecticut, the 58th Pennsylvania, several companies of the 1st North Carolina, a detachment of the 15th Connecticut, and some members from the 17th Massachusetts—about 500 men in all. Harland's force also included two companies each from the 12th New York Cavalry and 5th Rhode Island Artillery. The soldiers at Washington sensed an end to Federal control of the town. "A feeling of gloom pervaded the ranks of the defenders, for it became more and more evident from day to day, that the town was doomed," recalled one veteran.[43]

Like the Plymouth garrison, Washington contained a number of Buffaloes, African American recruits, and refugees. Consistent with Palmer's orders, Harland first attended to members of the 1st North Carolina, getting the Buffaloes and their families aboard the *Thomas Collyer* at dusk on Wednesday, April 27.[44] The same day, he sent 3,000 freed people downstream about 5 miles to Hill's Point on the south bank of the Pamlico. Transports then took the refugees to New Bern, a process that continued throughout the day and night and into Thursday. In addition, boats arrived on Wednesday with orders for Harland to load the 58th Pennsylvania and 21st Connecticut aboard and send them not to Palmer in New Bern but north to Fort Monroe, to support Butler's upcoming offensive in Virginia.[45] However, with Hoke still threatening Washington, Harland hesitated to empty the earthworks too quickly and chose to delay the departure of the two regiments until 7:00 p.m. Thursday. The same day, the 23rd New York Light Artillery, three cavalry companies, and twelve wagons left and headed south overland to New Bern, arriving at Fort Anderson the next morning.[46]

From New Bern, Palmer closely monitored the evacuation's progress. On Thursday, April 28, he received confirmation that Hoke's force had appeared outside the town. To speed matters, he sent every available boat from New Bern, including several towed schooners, to ferry the Buffaloes and black refugees to safety. At Washington, one Union officer in the provost marshal's office wrote that the "poor negroes are flying for protection in every direction" in anticipation of the town's occupation by the rebels.[47] With Davenport's cooperation, Palmer continued to direct naval support Harland's way from a "good supply of gunboats, large and small." Harland prepared to send two recently arrived vessels, the *Rucker* and *Thomas Collyer*, back to New Bern "as soon as they can be unloaded." "The families of the North Carolinians," wrote Palmer to Harland on Thursday, "which I fancy was one of your principal troubles, are fortunately now out of your way."[48] Not every civilian chose to leave Washington, however. According to a correspondent with the *New York Times*, several families remained, apparently "pleased at the prospective termination of 'Yankee rule.'"[49]

At New Bern, the thousands of refugees arriving from Washington were not ignored. The influx of these people—black and white, old and young—significantly added to the population already living in that community and elsewhere on the Trent's south bank. The "wretchedness" of these people "beggars description," reported the *New Berne Times*. "It is a great pity that something cannot be done for these poor white loyalists as well as the contrabands," the paper continued. "There is abundant room for the charity of the government and the public."[50] The men of the 1st North Carolina brought their families with them—200 women and 100 children, by one report. Concerned for their safety, Palmer ordered these people to Morehead City.[51]

"Blackens the Fair Fame of the Army of North Carolina"

By Thursday, April 28, Union discipline in Washington began to unravel as the defending force shrank by the hour. With the provost guard from the 58th Pennsylvania and 21st Connecticut preparing to leave, a vacuum of authority formed downtown. A trickle of thefts began on Wednesday afternoon and soon evolved into full-blown pillaging. The bad actors did not discriminate. They hit army supplies, sutler establishments, private shops, and private homes. "Gangs of men patrolled the city," reported a subsequent board of investigation, "breaking into houses and wantonly destroying such goods as they could not carry away"; they insulted the "occupants and owners" who sought in vain to protect their property.[52] Men broke into Berry's General Store, Mill's Jewelry, the Masonic Lodge, and the Odd Fellows

Hall, as well as other buildings and shops. At Berry's, clerk Samuel Hubbard managed to distract the liquor-seeking thieves with a few boxes of cigars.[53] "I saw soldiers and sailors running about the streets, trying stores that were locked and looking into those that were open," recalled one witness. "I heard one of the soldiers or sailors tell another . . . where they had got a box of cigars."[54]

Hampered by the evacuation effort, Harland struggled to end the chaos. When the provost guard departed with the 58th Pennsylvania and 21st Connecticut, Harland tagged Captain Roland R. West of the 12th New York Cavalry and one his companies to step in. These men did not perform well. "The provost guard of Cavalry appeared to be perfectly useless," complained a bitter Harland later. After the horsemen departed for New Bern on Thursday, Harland detailed members of the 17th Massachusetts to take their place. He also put company commanders on notice that they would be held responsible for any misdeeds perpetrated by their men.[55] Out in the fortifications, the officers kept their men close at hand. When word of the pillaging reached Lieutenant Colonel Samuel Tolles of the 15th Connecticut, he immediately clamped down, conducting roll call every hour for the remainder of the day and tracking down the few absentees. Officers in the 17th Massachusetts took similar measures.[56] The problems continued, though. In some cases, there was no one to hold the captured looters, and some miscreants escaped altogether. Afterward, investigators could not pin the misdeeds on any particular unit.[57]

The pillaging eventually subsided, mostly because little valuable property and few soldiers remained. By Thursday evening, the only units left were portions of the 15th Connecticut, 17th Massachusetts, and 5th Rhode Island Artillery. Harland posted the 17th Massachusetts in the works on the west side and the 15th Connecticut on the right. On Friday, the evacuation continued. That night, Harland himself boarded a boat for New Bern, leaving twenty-six-year-old Colonel Joseph McChesney in charge of the final mop-up on Saturday morning. The reasons for Harland's early departure are unclear. In hindsight, the decision was a poor one.[58]

Events on Saturday would further tarnish the Union evacuation of Washington. That morning, as the last troops gathered on the wharf to embark for New Bern, a fire broke out downtown in stables formerly used by the 12th New York Cavalry.[59] As the flames spread, Colonel McChesney delayed his departure and sought to subdue the blaze. When conventional means failed, he attempted to contain the fire by destroying adjacent buildings. His men packed at least two houses with gunpowder and leveled them with huge explosions. However, a strong wind carried the flames beyond the lots. Soon, the fire fanned out along Main Street as Union officers and soldiers scrambled to get ahead of the conflagration. Eventually, the flames diminished and, according to McChesney, stayed "confined to certain limits."[60]

The fire's cause remained elusive well after the ashes cooled. An investigating board was "unable to come to any satisfactory conclusion as to the guilty parties."[61] Witnesses' testimony pointed to several possibilities. Some recalled that men from two companies of the 5th Rhode Island, nearly all of them drunk, had loitered downtown Friday night and into Saturday morning, raising suspicions.[62] However, some citizens claimed that local secessionists had ignited the flames. One informant told Captain Joseph R. Simonds of the 17th Massachusetts that rebel sympathizers had done so "to throw disgrace upon Union soldiers."[63] Others made similar allegations directly to McChesney, and the colonel tended to credit such reports. In fact, he had found several buildings packed with combustibles and "prepared for burning." One of his aides even claimed he had seen a local man attempting to start a fire in the buildings.[64] Other accounts, however, pointed to a Union officer as the disaster's source. Both Harland and McChesney were told that Captain Richard T. Renshaw of the steamer *Louisiana* had announced his intention to burn the town. Some citizens heard the same story. An alarmed McChesney assigned men to shadow Renshaw to ensure he did no such thing. No one, it appears, witnessed the captain doing anything untoward, and ultimately, the culprits' identities were never firmly ascertained.[65]

Mindful of Renshaw's threat, Harland also ordered his men to refrain from burning the bridge across the Pamlico, save for its draw.[66] But contrary to Harland's wishes, Captain Renshaw ordered Edwin McKeever, the *Louisiana*'s acting ensign, to torch the span. McKeever promptly set about this task with five men and an ample supply of tar. The flames soon spread across the bridge and toward the town, igniting some buildings with the help of a fresh breeze.[67] During the subsequent investigation, Renshaw escaped censure, and the matter was batted aside. The board was unable to determine whether Colonel McChesney's "instructions were carelessly given, incorrectly transmitted, or misapprehended, or willfully disregarded."[68]

To make matters worse, the smoke from the fire suggested a Union withdrawal to watching rebels. The Federals understood this and worried that the Confederates would pounce. Southern pickets on the outer lines could be seen galloping rearward after the fire started. With time growing short, McChesney ordered all his men back to the wharf, and they departed, leaving the town of Washington to the Confederates.[69]

Back in New Bern, Harland received high marks for managing "the evacuation with skill and deliberation becoming a brave and humane soldier."[70] However, the pillaging and the fire would eventually draw significant criticism. Palmer, clearly embarrassed by the incident, publicly asserted that men in Washington had "been guilty of an outrage against humanity, which brings the blush of shame to the cheek of every true man and soldier." Apparently unaware of the details, Palmer singled out the 17th Massachusetts and 15th Connecticut as the units responsible for the act that "now blackens the fair fame of the Army of North Carolina."[71] Palmer's finger-pointing drew fire from politicians in Washington, DC, who stepped forward to defend the honor of troops from their home states. Eventually, the investigating board managed to spread the blame widely, concluding that "none of the troops in

Washington on the 28th of April last can reasonably claim to escape a share of the shame and odium which the history of those few days has justly caused."[72]

Palmer and his officers made no secret that Washington had been abandoned to consolidate resources in the state. After his arrival in New Bern, Harland was overheard saying that he could have held "the place against any force the enemy could send." However, he now concluded that Washington's defense was "impracticable," given the departure of so many men north to reinforce Butler in Virginia. The press endorsed the decision to abandon the town. Echoing the argument made by Admiral Lee throughout the war, a *New York Times* correspondent assured Northern readers that Washington had no special military value, especially in light of events developing in Virginia. Instead, the writer noted, other locations such as Roanoke Island, Hatteras, New Bern, and Beaufort furnished the "keys to the possession of Eastern North Carolina."[73]

On Sunday, May 1, word reached Hoke outside Greenville that the Federals had left Washington and that James Dearing's cavalry was pursuing stragglers overland to New Bern. Hoke was eager to take advantage of this mostly bloodless conquest. In forwarding the news to Bragg in Richmond, he urged officials to hurry commissary agents into Hyde County to gather "corn and bacon" along the banks of the Pamlico Sound.[74] Hoke also occupied the town itself, sending the 6th North Carolina, the 3rd Virginia, one battery, and some cavalry to fill the fortifications. In Washington, these men found some relieved Confederate sympathizers amid the debris of the conflagration. A soldier in the 6th North Carolina wrote that the fire had threatened to consume everything, but a fortuitous change in wind direction had limited the destruction to a quarter of the downtown area.[75]

The civilians in Washington remained on edge. On May 2, days after the fire, a Union gunboat appeared in the river and sent a shell into town. This empty gesture did not injure anyone but succeeded in terrifying the citizens there.[76] Despite this distraction, the people of Washington continued to focus on the fire's aftermath. One resident reported that about half the town had been "burnt up," and she observed that it would have been entirely "consumed but the women turned out and worked like men." According to this correspondent, the Union soldiers had destroyed all the pumps, forcing citizens to lug water from the river to fight the blaze. "I never saw women in gear before," she explained. "We buckled it on that day, and have kept it on ever since." The Yankee evacuation and the fire had other impacts as well. "It is nothing now to see the most refined ladies going to the pump," she wrote, "for all have their own to do now—there is not a negro to be had." The fire destroyed the Presbyterian, Methodist, and Catholic churches. It also caused the death of a resident named Winnie Balance, who had rushed across the street toward her burning house to retrieve something and "was enveloped by the flames from both sides." Another civilian, Frank Havens, received severe burns when Colonel McChesney's men detonated a house to prevent the fire's spread.[77]

"The Expedition of General Hoke"

With Washington in their hands, the Confederates looked south to New Bern. But time was running short. At Weldon, Beauregard had become increasingly concerned about the manpower commitment in North Carolina.[78] With the enemy's spring offensive brewing in Virginia, Beauregard wanted to wrap things up in the Old North State and prepare to repel a rumored attack on Petersburg. On April 25, he asked Bragg whether it was "prudent" to leave forces scattered throughout North Carolina and whether New Bern's capture was worth the "great risk incurred."[79] The Louisianan would later reflect that Hoke's continued operations made the "immediate concentration [of his troops] at any threatened point very difficult, if not impossible." Moreover, in his view, Hoke's operations would have a limited impact on the enemy.[80]

Despite Beauregard's reservations, Richmond officials continued to support Hoke's push against New Bern. In an April 26 message to Beauregard, Bragg explained that a victory "will enable us to concentrate a formidable force to meet Burnside," who was rumored to be gathering his corps for a strike in North Carolina. Three days later, he underscored the directive by passing along Jefferson Davis's own words on the subject. The president continued to see promise in the operation, stating that the "capture of Newbern, and possession of the Sound by our vessels . . . will relieve the necessity for guarding the whole line of railroad as proposed." Davis also urged that the campaign be executed with "all vigor."[81]

Almost as soon as these statements reached Beauregard, Richmond's enthusiasm began to wane, and dispatches traveling southward along the telegraph became more equivocal. Only a day after President Davis's enthusiastic endorsement, rumors about impending Federal movements in Virginia peppered the Confederate War Department, and officials there looked to speed up Hoke's efforts. Anxiety rose. Robert E. Lee, who only days before had expressed support for the North Carolina operation, issued another urgent request for the return of his troops to his army.[82] On April 30, Braxton Bragg, writing to Adjutant and Inspector General Samuel Cooper, explained that he wanted "to urge the expedition of General Hoke to an issue at once, so that his force may join General Lee."[83] Cooper went even further, directing an aide to "telegraph General Beauregard to send up Hoke's force if there should be no prospect of an attack" on New Bern.[84] However, the final communication from Richmond to Beauregard simply stated, "If there is no prospect of an attack on New Berne by General Hoke, order his force on also."[85]

Therefore, despite growing doubts, the message was still clear: an attack on New Bern would be carried out. Given the directives from Richmond, Beauregard did not hold back his support for the offensive. Though he had no formal authority over Hoke's operation, he supported and encouraged the young general, leaning in to the task and helping Hoke with whatever was needed. As Hoke's force left

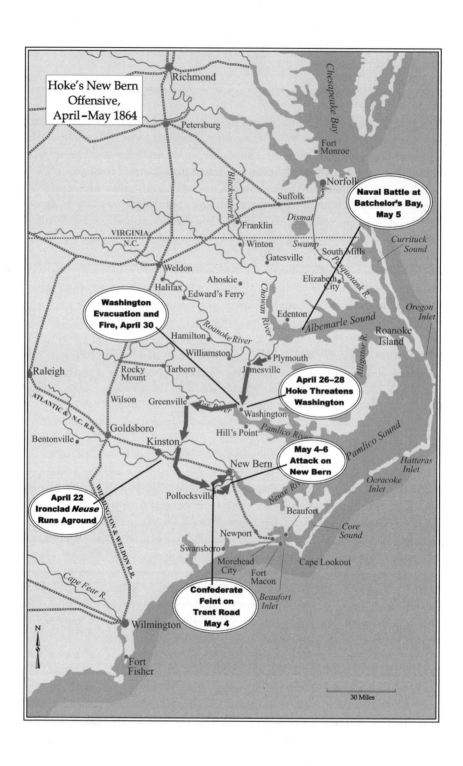

Hoke's New Bern
Offensive,
April–May 1864

Richmond

Petersburg

Chesapeake Bay

Fort
Monroe

Norfolk

Suffolk

Blackwater R.

Franklin

Dismal

**Naval Battle at
Batchelor's Bay,
May 5**

VIRGINIA
N.C.

Winton

Swamp

South Mills

*Currituck
Sound*

Gatesville

Weldon

Ahoskie

Pasquotank R.

Elizabeth
City

Halifax

Edward's Ferry

Chowan River

*Oregon
Inlet*

Edenton

Albemarle Sound

Roanoke
Island

**Washington
Evacuation and
Fire, April 30**

Hamilton

Roanoke River

Williamston

Plymouth

Raleigh

Rocky
Mount

Tarboro

Jamesville

Alligator R.

**April 26–28
Hoke Threatens
Washington**

Wilson

Greenville

Tar River

Washington

*ATLANTIC &
N.C. R.R.*

Goldsboro

Hill's Point

Pamlico River

Pamlico Sound

Bentonville

Kinston

**May 4–6
Attack on
New Bern**

*Hatteras
Inlet*

New Bern

*Ocracoke
Inlet*

**April 22
Ironclad *Neuse*
Runs Aground**

WILMINGTON & WELDON R.R.

Pollocksville

Neuse River

Beaufort

*Core
Sound*

Newport

Cape Fear R.

Swansboro

Morehead
City

Fort
Macon

Cape Lookout

**Confederate
Feint on
Trent Road
May 4**

*Beaufort
Inlet*

N

Wilmington

Fort
Fisher

30 Miles

Washington and headed south, Beauregard hopped aboard a train for Kinston to discuss the matter in person with the young Tar Heel.[86]

As Hoke and Beauregard prepared, Confederate officers in North Carolina hoped the ironclads would join the offensive. "If both our gun boats get in the Neuse safe and sound, I think Newbern will fall," wrote Brigadier James Martin from Plymouth in late April.[87] But only a few days later, it was unclear whether there would be any naval support at all. Just south of Kinston, the gunboat *Neuse* remained stuck in the river, and no amount of cajoling had managed to lift it off. Reports even hinted that the boat would break its back in the shallows should the water level continue to drop.[88] This was a bitter pill for all involved. Similar in design and function to the *Albemarle*, the *Neuse* presented a formidable threat to the wooden Union gunboats at New Bern. But with the river continuing to drop, the vessel was nothing but a toothless hulk, stranded miles upstream from its intended target. Union commanders sighed in relief upon hearing the news.[89] The Confederates were devastated. "It does seem hard to be sorely disappointed after expecting so much," wrote one of the boat's officers.[90]

There was still hope for the *Albemarle*, though. In the first days of May, James Cooke remained at Plymouth with his gunboat, which was still very much afloat. Following the Plymouth victory, he had conducted a short expedition into the Albemarle Sound and then up the Alligator River to escort captured vessels and supplies. During the sortie, enemy vessels backed off from the ironclad. "There was four yankee gun boats lying in Edenton bay," wrote one soldier stationed at Plymouth, "and as soon as they saw her they" ran for Roanoke Island.[91] On his return, Cooke conjured up larger plans and prepared his craft and crew. On May 2, James Martin, writing from his Plymouth headquarters, informed his wife that the *Albemarle* would be ready in two or three days to assist in the New Bern attack and then move against Roanoke Island and Hatteras.[92] To begin the campaign, Cooke planned to enter the Albemarle Sound, drive out the Federal navy, and steam for New Bern.[93]

"Deliverance of This Portion of the Good Old N[orth] State"

On Sunday, May 1, a warm, pleasant day in Kinston, Confederate commanders began to plan the campaign's next phase.[94] Beauregard, recently arrived from Weldon, met with Lieutenant Colonel Guion, the forty-three-year-old New Bern native, engineer, and Hoke confidant. During this preliminary discussion, which Hoke did not attend, Guion pulled out the detailed map of New Bern he had drafted after Pickett's failed expedition.[95] The two officers went to work, discussing New Bern's challenges in depth. Guion was impressed with Beauregard, jotting in his journal that he was "struck with the clearness of his perception—the pains he took to investigate and make himself acquainted with the minutiae. His pleasant manner of doing business." The two wrapped up their talk and planned to meet the next day with Hoke to discuss the operation further.[96]

On the same day, most likely after his meeting with Guion, Beauregard prepared a remarkably detailed plan for the upcoming operation. His blueprint included several prongs. First, cavalry and infantry would cut the railroad at Croatan Station south of New Bern, isolating the city from the coast. Second, an infantry force would conduct a demonstration at Bachelor Creek from the west, and a small cavalry detachment would block the Clermont Bridge on the Trent to the south, preventing reinforcements from supporting the city. Third, the main attacking force would approach along the Trent River's south bank, much like Barton's effort in February. However, instead of pushing to Brice's Creek, as Barton had done, this force would recross the Trent west of New Bern along a hastily built pontoon bridge and get behind Bachelor Creek. The main force would then march north, reaching the Neuse, and attack the main New Bern works (the Fort Totten line) from the west. On top of these broad approaches, Beauregard's plan bent down into a surprising level of detail. For instance, it contained information about the size and location of Union troops and delved into the number of artillery pieces to be aimed at each face of the fortifications.

Despite Beauregard's thought and effort, his memorandum was confusing and typically unrealistic in several respects. In particular, he failed to explain how the main thrust would overwhelm Fort Totten and the other works in the main line, defenses that were universally acknowledged to be practically unassailable. The plan appeared to rely greatly on the *Albemarle*, apparently buttressed by the assumption that the gunboat would make such a grand assault possible. Beauregard expected a lot from the ironclad. He hoped Cooke's beast would destroy the Union vessels, burn the Trent River railroad bridge, and cut off New Bern from reinforcements. But without the support of Cooke's guns, Beauregard feared the "sacrifice of life must be very great." The chances of an isolated infantry attack against the city's well-constructed moats and ramparts seemed slim.[97]

On the evening of May 2, Hoke joined Beauregard and Guion to discuss the plan. It was a collaborative exchange. Beauregard may have harbored misgivings about the campaign as a whole, yet he offered nothing but enthusiastic support to Hoke. The young commander, in turn, actively sought Beauregard's counsel. In fact, several days before, Hoke had even offered to hand over command of the operation to Beauregard. The senior officer had declined, explaining that, since the endeavor had been "organized by the War Department and placed directly under your charge, I am not at liberty to interfere in these arrangements." However, the Louisianan emphasized that he would "be most happy to give you all the advice and assistance in my power." He also assigned his chief engineer, Colonel David B. Harris, to report to Hoke and aid him throughout the operation.[98]

During the meeting, the officers discussed the plans at length, including Beauregard's idea to throw the main column across the Trent behind the Federal outer line. Hoke and Guion questioned this approach. By this time, the two understood that the ironclads might not make it to New Bern, and without naval support, an attacking column would find itself dangerously exposed against the Fort Totten line. Bending to their concerns, Beauregard agreed to toss away the suggestion, and the three decided to direct the main column south of the Trent and conduct the attack that "Barton was ordered to make" in February.[99] Hoke still planned to make a demonstration west of New Bern, near Bachelor Creek. With the consultation complete, Beauregard prepared to return to his Weldon headquarters. On his way back, he wired Richmond with news of the expedition, indicating that Hoke would proceed with "utmost dispatch" and complete the operation within four or five days.[100]

On Tuesday, May 3, good news arrived from Plymouth. Commander Robert Pinkney, newly in charge of Confederate naval affairs in North Carolina, relayed a message from Cooke: the ironclad had done "a great deal better than he had expected [on its recent cruise], and will cooperate. Will be around on Thursday."[101] Based on these reports, Hoke noted that the *Albemarle* "can stand the sound, and will be with us" in the upcoming attack.[102] Though this was welcome news, Hoke may have hedged his bets. Some evidence suggests he also collected marines and rowboats to attempt a repeat of John Taylor Wood's expedition against the *Underwriter*.[103]

For the New Bern attack, Hoke gathered the three triumphant brigades from Plymouth, along with several other units. Although no official report survives, Hoke's force apparently consisted of five brigades, including his own (North Carolina regiments commanded by William G. Lewis), Matt Ransom's (North Carolina), Montgomery Corse's (Virginia), William Terry's (Virginia), and William S. "Live Oak" Walker's (South Carolina—Evan's brigade). In addition, he had Colonel John D. Whitford's 67th North Carolina Infantry Regiment; several cavalry regiments, including the 3rd and 6th North Carolina and Dearing's unit; and several artillery batteries, including Major John Read's 38th Virginia Battalion.[104] Some regiments did not join their brigades for the operation. For example, the 3rd Virginia, from Terry's brigade, remained at Washington. In addition, only two regiments from Walker's brigade (the 22nd and 26th South Carolina) joined the expedition. Many of Hoke's units had stayed in Greenville through May 2 and arrived outside Kinston that evening.[105]

With the men rested and plans in place, Hoke's column readied to step off for New Bern. Hoke began his advance nearly a week after abandoning his position outside Washington. The reasons for this delay are unclear, but they may have had something to do with news about the ironclads and an attempt to gather marines and boats.[106] In any case, New Bern's capture would crown an already successful campaign. The victories at Plymouth and Washington had opened a wide portion of the state to the Confederate commissary. The meat, fish, and grain harvested from the counties surrounding these locations would greatly aid the Confederate forces in the coming fight in Virginia. Success also brightened the state's political situation. With the election three months off, these battlefield victories lifted Governor Vance, who had already helped his own cause through vigorous campaigning. But more was expected. James Evans of the 6th North Carolina captured the hopes of many when he wrote home, "many prayers which have been offered in the past 2 yrs for Deliverance of this Portion of the good old N. State from the hands of our ruthless Foe are now being answered."[107]

CHAPTER TWENTY-THREE
New Bern, May 1864

"To Drive In the Enemy's Pickets"

The march on New Bern began early Tuesday morning, May 3.[1] Hoke's troops formed up outside their bivouacs northeast of Kinston and snaked south. Shortly after dawn, the lead units crossed the Neuse River on a bridge laid over sixteen pontoons, assembled the night before by Lieutenant Colonel Henry Guion's pioneers. At "Becton old field," a spot about 8 miles downstream from Kinston, Guion's men had graded the road on the south bank to ease the way for wagons and artillery caissons.[2] Hoke's force lurched across. The column, with its cavalry regiments, infantry brigades, artillery batteries, ambulances, and supply wagons, stretched out for several miles and took hours to pass over the river. In fact, the last wagons did not roll over the bridge until the afternoon. The pioneers then disassembled the crossing; packed the pontoons, balks, and chesses; and hurried to catch up, toiling all night over wagon-churned roads.

Late that night, as the pioneers struggled along, an encouraging message arrived from Hoke: "Cook[e] has got out. Hurry up." When the news passed along the line, "the boys made the 'welkin ring' with their cheers," recalled Guion.[3] The next morning, the bridge builders caught up with Hoke's little army and, after only three hours rest, resumed the march, this time, at the head of the column. By late afternoon, after trudging south all day in the heat and the dust, the men reached the Trent River's north bank near Pollocksville, about a dozen miles west of New Bern. At this spot, they prepared to cross and swing south of the city, using the same route (the Pollocksville, or Trenton, Road) Barton had followed three months before.[4]

As most of Hoke's force steered for New Bern's back door, Lieutenant Colonel William G. Lewis conducted the planned diversion to the west with Hoke's brigade, the 67th North Carolina Regiment, some cavalry, and a few cannon. Breaking off from Hoke's column, Lewis turned northeast along the Trent Road and approached the city's outer defense line with instructions from Hoke "to drive in the enemy's pickets, bombard . . . the earth-works of the enemy on a creek about six miles from New Berne, and then fall back to Pollocksville on the Trent."[5] It was hoped that Lewis's feint would draw the enemy's attention westward, away from Hoke's main force hooking around New Bern. After 5:00 p.m., Lewis's troops reached the enemy's outer pickets at Deep Gully, a small stream nestled in a narrow depression. From the outpost there known as Pine Tree, a Union signal officer wired the news back to Palmer's headquarters in New Bern. The bluecoats prepared to greet the enemy.[6]

Craven County native John H. Whitford, commander of the unattached 67th North Carolina, opened the fighting personally, firing at the Union pickets while three cavalrymen crouched behind and handed him their loaded rifles. Soon, twenty sharpshooters led by Lieutenant John Guion joined him. The riflemen inched forward and unleashed a volley at the enemy position. Although strong entrenchments covered Deep Gully, only a small force of Federal cavalrymen occupied them, merely three companies, by one estimate. The blue vedettes did not hold their ground and "at once incontinently took to flight, and no candidate for Governor ever 'went tearing' down the road with more fury," wrote one Confederate.[7]

By 6:00 p.m., Lewis had overrun Deep Gully.[8] The gray sharpshooters pursued their prey along the Trent Road for about 2 miles and found more Union troops in trenches beyond Rocky Run.[9] The defending force there was more substantial, consisting of Colonel James Savage's 12th New York Cavalry, along with two companies of infantry. The New Yorkers guessed the rebel force in their front "consisted of two companies of cavalry, about 150 infantry, and two 10-pounder Parrott guns." Apparently, Lewis kept most of his men out of sight.[10]

Colonel Savage had little interest in withdrawing from Rocky Run. He pushed out pickets several hundred yards to the west of his position. As the enemy approached, his howitzers opened up, and his men raised their rifles. But the Confederates halted, and the fighting ended there. Reporting the action to General Palmer in New Bern, Savage predicted the rebels would not resume their effort. He was correct. Lewis withdrew most of his men to join Hoke's column south of the Trent, leaving only the 21st Georgia under Major Thomas Glover at Deep Gully.[11]

Lewis had accomplished his mission. He had threatened New Bern from the west and drawn the defenders' attention away from Hoke. In his wake, Savage and other Union officers strained to divine Hoke's intentions and, in particular, determine whether the action on the Trent Road signaled a minor demonstration or a major attack. Along Bachelor Creek to the north, where Hoke had attacked in February, Colonel Peter Claassen of the 132nd New York monitored reports flooding into his headquarters and prepared.[12] That evening, Giles Ward, General Palmer's aide, rode out from New Bern to assist Savage and press out with cavalry the next morning. However, they would find only Glover's Georgians in front, hunkered down beyond Deep Gully.[13]

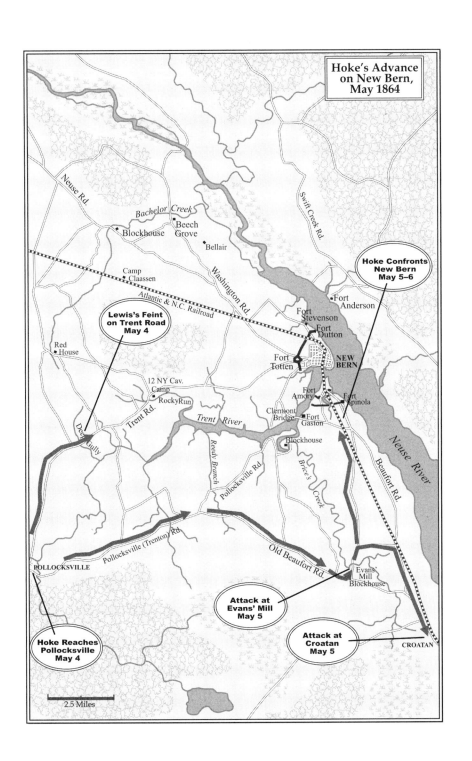

Hoke's Advance
on New Bern,
May 1864

Neuse Rd.

Bachelor Creek
Blockhouse
Beech Grove
Bellair

Swift Creek Rd.

Camp Claassen

Atlantic & N.C. Railroad

Washington Rd.

Hoke Confronts
New Bern
May 5–6

Fort Anderson
Fort Stevenson
Fort Dutton

Lewis's Feint
on Trent Road
May 4

Red House

Fort Totten

NEW BERN

12 NY Cav. Camp
RockyRun

Fort Amory
Fort Spinola

Clermont Bridge
Fort Gaston

Deep Gully

Trent Rd.

Trent River

Blockhouse

Neuse River

Reedy Branch

Pollocksville Rd.

Brice's Creek

Beaufort Rd.

Pollocksville (Trenton) Rd.

Old Beaufort Rd.

POLLOCKSVILLE

Evans' Mill Blockhouse

Hoke Reaches
Pollocksville
May 4

Attack at
Evans' Mill
May 5

Attack at
Croatan
May 5

CROATAN

2.5 Miles

The Confederates' appearance on the Trent Road came as no shock to New Bern's defenders. Palmer had been keeping an eye toward the west since Plymouth's capture two weeks before. A detailed intelligence report, gleaned from the interrogation of a straggler from the 6th North Carolina, accurately noted that the Confederates were headed to take New Bern. The prisoner also reported that the ironclad *Albemarle* was undergoing repairs.[14] With Hoke bearing down on this principal base, General Palmer worried about the size of his defending force and concluded he could "not afford to march out and give them battle." Instead, he resolved to man the defenses and await developments. Following Lewis's demonstration, Palmer expected more.[15]

Hoke would not disappoint. As Lewis threatened, the bulk of Hoke's force was well on its way to New Bern, swinging south of the Trent River. On Wednesday afternoon (May 4), Hoke split his column into two sections. Corse's and Walker's brigades crossed the Trent upstream from Pollocksville, while the balance of the command, including Ransom's and Terry's brigades, crossed at Pollocksville itself. At Hoke's urging, Henry Guion brought his pioneers forward and found a suitable bridging spot, with an "excellent abutment on the opposite bank." By 9:00, a nine-pontoon bridge connected the Trent's banks. An impressed Hoke congratulated the pioneers' endurance and efficiency over the past twenty-four hours. During supper with Guion, the young general exuded optimism and appeared "very sanguine of success" in the upcoming attack.[16]

South of the Trent River, the Confederate column continued east along the Pollocksville Road. James Dearing's cavalry led the way. Back at Pollocksville, Guion left the bridge in place but brought three additional pontoons with him to cover the streams ahead. When Guion expressed concern about his men's fatigue and lack of sleep, Hoke replied, "Tomorrow will be an easy march and I hope the last hard one for some time to come."[17] However, the general was wrong, at least partially, for the men found the road in terrible condition, and Guion's pioneers were once again pressed into service. Nevertheless, Hoke's command made progress, and by early Thursday, the front of his column approached its first target: Brice's Creek, south of New Bern.[18]

"Had the Expedition Not Started I Would Say It Should Not Go"

By happenstance, Hoke's movement on Wednesday, May 4, coincided with the opening of Grant's massive operation in Virginia. On that day, George Meade's Army of the Potomac crossed the Rapidan River and triggered bloody fighting in the Wilderness west of Fredericksburg. In addition, Benjamin Butler loaded his men into transports and steamed up the James River toward Richmond. With the rebel capital threatened from two directions, the crisis that had loomed for weeks now engulfed the Confederate high command, and in an instant, New Bern's capture ceased to be a priority. Hoke's expedition, which tied up thousands in North Carolina, had to end.

At 4:00 p.m. on Wednesday, General Beauregard in Weldon received a telegram from President Davis, stating that "unless New Berne can be captured by *coup de main* the attempt must be abandoned, and the troops returned with all possible dispatch to unite in operations in North Virginia. There is not an hour to lose. Had the expedition not started I would say it would not go." Davis urged Beauregard to arrange troop transport to Richmond "with the greatest dispatch."[19] The Louisianan, who had consistently advised against the operation since his arrival at Weldon in late April, scribbled the words "I had told you so" on Davis's telegram.[20]

Beauregard acted immediately. He sent his trusted staffer, Lieutenant Alexander R. Chisholm, to New Bern with Davis's telegram in hand, along with orders for Hoke to return part of his force to Kinston immediately. As Chisholm raced south, Hoke's window to achieve success at New Bern shrank to a matter of hours.[21] Following the president's instructions, Beauregard directed Hoke to send back most of his troops "as rapidly as practicable" by rail from Kinston and Goldsboro. Those units unable to cram onto the railcars would march to Goldsboro; others would head to Weldon, also on foot. However, Davis's message contained enough ambiguity to allow Hoke to make one last lunge at New Bern. Beauregard did not order Hoke to halt the entire offensive immediately. Specifically, he told Hoke to keep Corse's and Walker's brigades and the 6th North Carolina Cavalry and explained, "The attack on Newbern is to be resumed as soon as the *Albemarle* can reach Newbern, or the one on the Neuse can be sent down."[22]

"Rapidly, without Fear, and in Considerable Force"

As of Thursday, May 5, Hoke remained ignorant of developments in Richmond and continued his advance. That morning, his brigades approached Brice's Creek, seeking advantage where Barton had failed months before.[23] Unlike Barton, Hoke had no plans to attack directly near the Trent River, where the creek's twisting channel was wide and deep and the guns of Fort Gaston swept the approach. Instead of marching straight toward those hazards on the Pollocksville Road, he forked southeast onto the Old Beaufort Road and headed for a different crossing upstream at Evans' Mill, where Brice's Creek was narrower.

General Dearing led the cavalry to Evans' Mill and drove in the pickets early Thursday morning.[24] Across the stream, a single company of Union cavalry armed with one artillery piece defended a blockhouse and attached entrenchments. Curiously, these defenders were Federal soldiers from North Carolina—Buffaloes—much like the men captured at Beech Grove months before. Why they had been assigned to this exposed position is unclear. However, these soldiers were members of Company L of the 1st North Carolina (Union), a hard-bitten lot of mounted infantry-men led by the fearless, malevolent Captain George W. Graham. The captain, a "brave, but . . . bad man" from New York, had a reputation as a tough brawler who bullied subordinates and even commanding officers and "left a trail of misery and desolation behind him" when left to his own devices.[25] In 1863, Graham and his men had participated in Edward Potter's raid, which had destroyed the ironclad in Tarboro. Graham had recently received a commendation from General Peck for another successful excursion against Greenville in March. At Washington, during Hoke's probe there only days earlier, he had commanded the detachment of Massa-chusetts men in the skirmishing north of town. His command, Company L, would steadily gain respect and admiration for its performance during raids and battles in the coming months.[26]

The Evans' Mill blockhouse and entrenchments stood on a slightly elevated spot overlooking the creek, "well suited to enable a small band to hold in check a larger force for the purposes of delay." However, Graham and his company would have no real opportunity for glory. As the head of the column arrived within range of the blockhouse, Hoke and his staff reined up and personally reconnoitered the posi-tion. This gaggle of officers did not escape the attention of the Federals across the creek. Soon, a puff of smoke appeared in the distance, and a 12-pound ball whirred over their heads. Hoke ordered Colonel John A. Baker, commander of the 3rd North Carolina Cavalry, to dismount his men and send them ahead as skirmish-ers. Baker's men encountered a nearly "impassable bog" and then edged around the flanks, seeking to suppress any sharpshooters. In addition, Captain James D. Cummings unlimbered two Napoleons in a clearing a few hundred yards from the Union position and opened a threatening fire.[27]

Graham's men fired a few more shots from their lone gun, but seeing they had no hope of holding on, they soon fled. The Confederates swarmed around the blockhouse and found one Union soldier dead with a bullet through his skull.[28] The engagement had consumed "fifteen or twenty minutes." Hoke's show of force had been overwhelming, and Captain Graham had wisely chosen to withdraw, en-suring that the Kinston hangings would not be repeated. Colonel Baker's cavalry-men moved in, seized the position, and ransacked the blockhouse, which contained "a considerable amount of commissary stores." The triumphant rebels gathered up whatever valuables they could find and resumed their advance.[29]

While Baker captured the Evans' Mill blockhouse, Dearing, along with five com-panies of the 6th North Carolina Cavalry under Colonel G. N. Folk, trotted south to Croatan Station, a Union post protected by a small fort about a dozen miles south of New Bern on the railroad. If successful, this foray, hatched by Beauregard, Hoke, and Guion a few days earlier, would block reinforcements from reaching New Bern along the railroad and complicate any Federal retreat from the city.[30] Before reaching the station, Dearing encountered a train rolling south toward Morehead

City. However, swampy ground hindered the cavalrymen, and the train escaped. The men had to settle for prying up rails, burning some ties, and cutting telegraph wires.[31] Most of Dearing's force did not linger and pressed on to Croatan, one of many similar positions in the region's network of blockhouses and earthworks that protected the rail and telegraph line against guerrilla attacks and ensured reliable communications between New Bern and Morehead City. Company A of the 5th Rhode Island Heavy Artillery under Captain John A. Aigan occupied the post.[32]

When the Confederate cavalry approached Croatan at around 7:00 a.m. and tore down a blockade stacked across the road, a freedwoman rushed into Captain Aigan's camp and alerted the Rhode Islanders of the threat. The captain initially dismissed the warning, but after more refugees arrived with similar reports, he mounted his horse to take a look for himself. North of the fort, he stumbled into a squad of twenty Confederates, but before the cavalrymen could seize him, Aigan wheeled his mount and galloped back to his command. At the fort, the defenders readied their weapons and hastily gathered water and rations. All the while, Colonel Folk's rebels pressed forward. It looked to be a repeat of the capture at Evans' Mill.[33]

It was. The Confederates drove on "rapidly, without fear, and in considerable force."[34] The defenders responded with their muskets and a small 6-pounder howitzer, the position's only ordnance. The first Union shell skipped into the cavalry column, decapitating a horse. The show of resistance halted the Confederates, who filed into the woods and completely surrounded the position. The defenders maintained a vigorous fire, which overheated the howitzer and the muskets. Silas Stepp, a member of the 6th North Carolina, recalled that "several shells struck close to me the nearest about 8 or 10 feet." Stepp and his comrades replied in kind, unleashing an impressive fire, some of it from sharpshooters perched in the trees.[35]

The pop of rifled muskets and the solitary boom of the howitzer continued for half an hour. Dearing, assuming the Yankees had endured enough, sought a truce, and Aigan emerged to talk things over. Demanding the position's surrender, Dearing warned his adversary, in a tone more "emphatic than polite," that the artillery would soon advance and completely reduce the work. But Aigan refused to give up. While Dearing hurried north to retrieve artillery from Hoke's main force and make good on his threat, Aigan returned to the fort. On the way, he discovered that the Confederates had ventured forward into better positions during the truce. Back under cover, the Rhode Islander consulted with his officers and concluded that further resistance was useless. Before Dearing's additional firepower arrived, the captain and his men surrendered the position to Colonel Folk, handing over fifty-nine prisoners in the bargain.[36]

The casualties at Croatan were light, given the amount of lead exchanged. The Federal defenders suffered only one wounded, and according to one account, the Confederates lost none. In the fight's aftermath, Aigan extracted an agreement that two black cooks with his Rhode Island company would "be treated with humanity." According to Private Stepp, the Union soldiers wanted to ensure that these men were "not abused" by the Confederates, a demand no doubt shaped by recent reports of executions at Plymouth and Fort Pillow. Aigan also managed to ensure that all the men would be allowed to retain two sets of clothes, which would help them during their captivity in Southern prisons. The Tar Heel horsemen led the captured men north along the railroad back to Hoke's position, where the Southerners were cooking chickens and waiting for orders to advance on the Union fortifications. The prisoners would spend the night in the captured blockhouse at Evans' Mill before marching into the Confederate interior the next day, on their way to prison.[37]

Hoke's initial operations on Thursday morning produced an unblemished success. By taking Evans' Mill and Croatan, he firmly severed New Bern's overland communication with the coast. Now, with the afternoon hours burning, he steered his brigades north, using the railroad as a guide, toward the prize of New Bern, less than 5 miles away.

"New Berne Will Be Defended at All Hazards"

As news of Hoke's appearance south of the Trent River reached New Bern, Palmer prepared for a fight. The New Yorker understood that the Confederates had severed his communications with Morehead City and that the *Albemarle* might appear in the river at any moment. Confronted with these threats, he sought to project confidence and downplay the significance of the Confederate operation. "I still think it is merely a raid on the railroad, and even if we are cut off for a few days we can hold our own," he informed his naval counterpart Captain Melancton Smith, who had recently replaced Henry Davenport as the chief naval officer in the North Carolina sounds. Palmer expected the Confederate offensive to be short-lived and guessed that the rebels were already streaming north to Virginia.[38] The *New Berne Times* noted Palmer's confidence and was pleased "to learn that a most determined spirit exists at Head Quarters—that New Berne will be defended at all hazards and to the last extremity."[39] But that confidence was not universal. One Massachusetts veteran later recalled that the men's lack of conviction that the lightly manned city would hold. "It was evident enough, that New Berne was doomed," he wrote, even though Union commanders had a "general determination to make a defence" and had "no thought of surrender."[40]

Whatever the expectations, the Union troops scrambled to repel Hoke. Official returns compiled only a few days earlier tallied about 4,000 men in the New Bern defenses. This total included units that had been there for months, such as the 132nd and 99th New York, as well as troops newly arrived from the town of Washington, among them portions of the 15th Connecticut, 5th Rhode Island Heavy Artillery, and 1st North Carolina (Union).[41] With Hoke threatening, Palmer canvassed New Bern to fill the fortifications, gathering every able-bodied person, as well as some who were not so able, including a convalescent battalion formed from hospital patients.

In the outer fortifications and picket lines, the soldiers prepared for a rebel assault. Savage's 12th New York Cavalry and Claassen's 132nd New York Infantry continued to guard the approaches along Bachelor Creek. On Thursday morning, Giles Ward and Colonel Savage had advanced west with four cavalry squadrons and two guns. That little foray ended at 10:00 a.m. without any fighting, and Ward return to New Bern to report to Palmer.[42]

The Union defenders also readied themselves south of the Trent River, the sector now targeted by Hoke. The works on this front, including Forts Gaston, Spinola, and Amory, were well manned, abundantly armed, and amply supplied. The forts themselves and their connecting curtains faced south, looking out over a broad plain bifurcated by a small stream known as Scott's (or Greenspring) Creek. The fortifications were substantial. Fort Gaston boasted seven 32-pounders, four long and three short; Fort Amory contained three long 32-pounders; and Fort Spinola held eight 32-pounders, including two rifles.[43] The works covered all approaches. On the Union right, Fort Gaston protected the Clermont (County) bridge, the Brice's Creek crossing near the Trent River, and open ground to the south. On the left, on the banks of the Neuse, Fort Spinola could pour shot and shell on the railroad line as well as the rail bridge. Fort Amory, in the center, added to the firepower.[44] The trench segments connecting the forts did not offer the "strongest" cover, according to one veteran, but they were certainly sturdy enough to protect the infantry manning them, mostly members of the 17th Massachusetts.[45] The impressive array of parapets and ditches bred confidence. "We will give them a hard one if they come here," wrote artillerist William Hoyle of the 23rd New York.[46]

As Palmer prepared, Hoke advanced and personally examined the fortifications in his front; he may have been slightly wounded in the process. Nevertheless, he brought his troops forward. Following Dearing's lead on Thursday morning, the infantry brigades crossed the creek at Evans' Mill and turned north toward New Bern.[47] The men edged forward under tree cover and established a position more than a mile south of the Federal fortifications.[48] To the east, they looked for battery positions near the Neuse, where Confederate works had stood in 1862, and began digging earthworks to protect their gun positions.[49] The 1st Virginia Regiment, in Terry's brigade, formed in battle line on a farm south of the Union works, also near the Neuse. Members of Corse's brigade placed their right flank on the riverbank. During the day, the rebels pushed out skirmishers and halted. They could see the buildings and homes of New Bern across the Trent. The Virginians remained there, serving as pickets throughout the day.[50]

The Union commanders did not wait for Hoke to attack. At 10:00 a.m., Colonel Thomas Amory, a Boston native and commander of the 17th Massachusetts, clattered over the Trent River with an artillery section and a cavalry escort. That morning, in New Bern, Amory's wife struggled through the last stages of labor with their fourth child, a daughter. After ensuring that Captain Graham's Buffaloes had safely reached the fortifications after their scrape at Evans' Mill, Amory drove his small force out into the open to a position outside the works, about 1,000 yards south of the bridge. The gun crews unlimbered at the edge of the woods there and began lobbing shells in Hoke's direction, seeking to draw Confederate fire and reveal rebel positions.[51] Observers from the Union parapets in the rear feared the enemy might "burst from those woods any moment and either kill or capture the little party." A captain in the 17th Massachusetts asked a nearby major for permission to head out and protect Amory. The major refused, citing the absence of positive orders. Ultimately, there was no need for such support. The rebels declined Amory's bait, and after an hour of firing, he withdrew.[52]

Following Amory's withdrawal, a new source of Federal firepower arrived in the form of the railroad monitor. Ward, fresh from the cavalry action on the Trent Road that morning, boarded the rolling ironclad in New Bern.[53] The "musket-proof" car, with its two Wiard guns, chugged out of the city across the Trent bridge and began tossing shells at the Confederates. The forts on the monitor's flanks added their guns to the din. According to one witness, "a spirited duel ensued, lasting for about an hour." The guns of Fort Gaston, at the Clermont bridge, added a particularly dangerous fire, having an advantageous angle on Hoke's position.[54] The ordnance in Fort Spinola, handled by Company B of the 5th Rhode Island Heavy Artillery, contributed fire to the contest.[55] From the parapet at Fort Spinola, a group of spectators watched the duel, including General Palmer and dozens of other officers, along with a *New York Herald* reporter.[56]

The Union pieces mostly targeted a six-gun battery commanded by Lieutenant Halcott P. Jones, which included at least two 20-pounders and was supported by Walker's South Carolina regiments. Jones attempted to engage the rail monitor, but the Union's Wiard guns replied from behind the thick iron plating and silenced the Confederate gunners four separate times, by Ward's count.[57] However, Ward was having a "hard time," by his own admission, and at around 4:00, Palmer sent two gunboats down the river to help, augmenting the fire from the rail and land batteries.[58] One of these vessels, the *Commodore Barney*, bobbed in the river off Hoke's right flank and hurled rounds into the woods for an hour, expending eighty-three 9-inch and nineteen 100-pound shells.[59] A staff officer from one of Corse's regiments noted, "here our forces endured a terrific shelling . . . for several hours." But some Southerners scoffed at the "total inefficiency of these monsters," which, in their view, did little damage, despite the duration of the bombardment.[60]

By 5:00, Ward pulled the railroad monitor back across the Trent into New Bern after firing 250 rounds and emptying its magazine.[61] Whether at the hands of the gunboats, the rail guns, or the batteries, Union fire caused about twenty casualties.[62]

One shell landed among a group of men, killing four and wounding three. Henry Guion, advancing to the front with one of his officers, encountered the remains of one of these poor soldiers, nearly atomized by the explosion. A horrified Guion found "the man's entrails draped across tree limbs thirty feet overhead." When alerted to the gruesome spectacle, Hoke ordered the man's immediate burial.[63]

During Thursday's artillery contest, Hoke considered his next move. He personally reconnoitered the defenses and "pronounced them 'pretty strong.'"[64] Undaunted, he developed his plan for an attack the next day.[65] No report from Hoke survived, so his precise plan is not clear. According to one account, his men prepared to place a pontoon bridge in the Trent River parallel to the bank after capturing the works there; then, in a sudden move, they would swing it across to the New Bern side under the protection of the guns. However, it is unknown where the bridge would deposit the troops and what they would do once they landed. Whatever his scheme, Hoke projected optimism.[66] The general told Guion his services would not be required that evening but emphasized that Guion would be sorely needed the next day. In his notebook, Guion jotted, "To morrow, aye to morrow; how much depends upon that simple word that never comes." He hoped to "have our heavy pieces in position, to drive their gunboats from our presence, to charge them from their lurking places."[67]

Given the forts, the trenches, the rail gun, and the gunboats, the approach to New Bern would be difficult for the Confederates. Nevertheless, Hoke seemed content. Perhaps he was counting on Cooke and his ironclad. During the shelling on Thursday, his men could hear the faint booms of the *Albemarle*'s guns drifting through the air from the north.[68] The rebels hoped the distant rumbling signaled good news. While Hoke challenged the New Bern works on Thursday, he surely kept one eye out on the water for signs of the metal beast.

"The Red Flashes of New Broadsides"

The *Albemarle* was, in fact, on its way. In the days following the battle at Plymouth, James Cooke had become satisfied of two things: his vessel could handle a trip to New Bern, and the enemy would not put up substantial resistance on the way. Cooke had restocked his coal, ammunition, and supplies. His men had completed the hurried repairs. During a test run into the Albemarle Sound, Union vessels had scattered before him, suggesting there was no appetite to challenge the ironclad. At noon on Thursday, May 5, as Hoke's batteries tangled with the railroad monitor and the gunboats at New Bern, Cooke shoved off from the Plymouth shoreline and piloted the *Albemarle* down the Roanoke, accompanied by the salvaged *Bombshell*, which served as the ironclad's tender, and the *Cotton Plant*, which was carrying troops.[69]

As Cooke entered the Albemarle Sound, he looked out from the small pilothouse atop the casemate and spied several small vessels 10 miles away across a "glassy sheet of water" under a "dazzling sunshine." These dots on the horizon were Union picket boats laying "torpedoes" across the channel in an effort to contain the ironclad. With the *Albemarle* and its consorts closing in, the small Union craft turned east in retreat. The fastest of the lot, the *Ida May*, raced to warn heavier vessels stationed at Roanoke Island. With the way apparently clear, Cooke forged ahead, expecting clear waters. However, after a 16-mile chase of the picket boats, several large Union double-enders, along with a collection of smaller vessels, steamed into view on the eastern horizon. Cooke and his crew immediately understood that trouble lay ahead.[70]

The larger Union vessels, the double-enders *Mattabesett*, *Sassacus*, *Wyalusing*, and *Miami*, each carried about a dozen guns and could throw an extraordinary amount of metal. In fact, these vessels were superior to the small ironclad in nearly all respects, including length and breadth, speed, armament, and crew. However, they all had one critical deficiency: they were made of wood. The navy had been unable to bring an ironclad into the North Carolina sounds. Given this key disadvantage, Captain Melancton Smith and his officers sought to repel the rebel vessel with sheer numbers. The Union flotilla swarmed up the sound toward Cooke's vessel. The crews, responding to signals that "the ram is out" and orders to "get under way," cleared the decks for action and lurched forward at full steam. From the deck of the 205-foot *Sassacus*, an observer "discerned a glistening speck upon the water beyond our retiring vessels, with two other dark hulls hovering near, which we knew to be the ram accompanied by her consorts."[71]

Cooke, knowing he could not outrun this force, signaled his two support boats back to Plymouth. The *Cotton Plant* managed to break off and head back up the sound, avoiding danger. The *Bombshell*, however, perhaps owing to some confusion, remained with the *Albemarle* as the combatants continued their collision course. Around 4:00 p.m., in a section of the sound known as Batchelor's Bay near a spit of land called Sandy Point, the Union gunboats approached the ironclad in two columns half a mile apart. In the southern line, the *Mattabesett*, *Sassacus*, *Wyalusing*, and *Whitehead* formed in file approaching the *Albemarle*'s port; to the north, the *Miami*, *Commodore Hull*, and *Ceres* advanced toward Cooke's starboard bow. The vessels closed rapidly.[72]

At around 4:40 p.m., the first shot of the contest rocketed from the *Albemarle*'s forward Brooke gun, smacking into the *Mattabesett*'s launch, scattering splinters and debris across its deck, and wounding five men. The Union vessels replied, discharging their broadsides as they passed the ironclad. One of these shots proved a lucky one, managing to crack off a nearly 2-foot fragment from the stern Brooke rifle. Although it was still operable, the damage most likely affected the piece's accuracy, leaving Cooke with only one fully functioning gun. The *Albemarle* did not receive all the attention. In the fight's opening moments, the two lead Union dou-

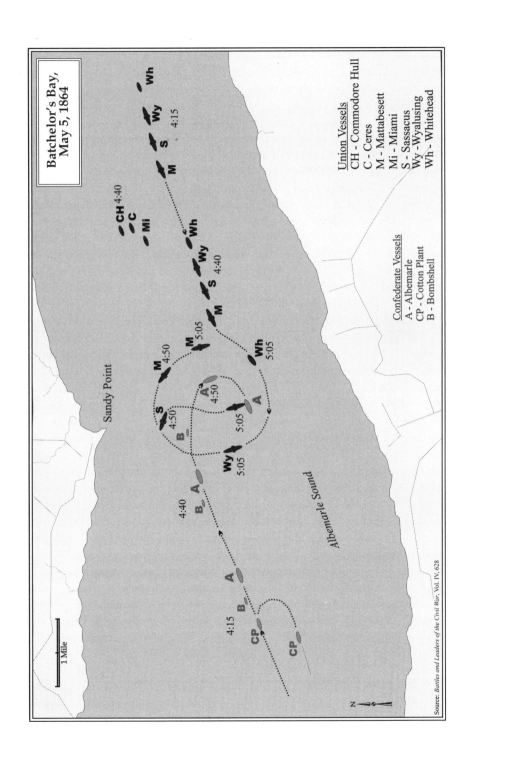

Batchelor's Bay,
May 5, 1864

1 Mile

Sandy Point

CH 4:40
C
Mi

Wh
Wy
S   4:15
M

Wh
Wy
S   4:40
M

M   4:50
S   5:05
4:50   Wh   5:05
B
A   5:05
A   4:50
Wy
5:05

4:40
A
B

4:15
B   A
CP
CP

Albemarle Sound

N

Union Vessels
CH - Commodore Hull
C - Ceres
M - Mattabesett
Mi - Miami
S - Sassacus
Wy - Wyalusing
Wh - Whitehead

Confederate Vessels
A - Albemarle
CP - Cotton Plant
B - Bombshell

Source: Battles and Leaders of the Civil War, Vol. IV, 628

ble-enders, the *Mattabesett* and the *Sassacus*, singled out the diminutive *Bombshell* and hulled it in three places with well-placed shots. With water pouring in and the crew frantic to plug the holes, the small boat struck its colors and anchored, exiting the fight.[73]

After its first pass along the *Albemarle's* port side, the *Sassacus's* pilot pushed his helm starboard and began a wide, 180-degree arc. Simultaneously, the *Albemarle* swept to starboard, executing a similar turn. These maneuvers resulted in the *Sassacus's* bow pointing at the *Albemarle's* starboard quarter. From the Union vessel, Commander Francis Roe saw an opportunity to ram the ironclad and shouted, "Lay her course for the junction of the casemate and the hull!"[74] Roe poured on the steam, the side-wheels spun faster, and the double-ender headed straight for the rebel monster. Within moments, the *Sassacus* crashed into the ironclad. Water washed over the *Albemarle's* deck and shield, igniting confusion and panic among the Confederate crew. "Most of the men left their station and ran around," recalled seaman John Patrick. "Captain Cooke was standing in the hatch and was knocked down. He looked kinder scared like."[75]

The two boats locked in an embrace, and for some time, neither crew could train a weapon for a clean shot. The Union vessel, with its higher deck, towered over the smaller, squat ironclad. The *Albemarle's* Brooke rifles had no angle, and the gunners in the *Sassacus* could not depress their Parrotts or Dahlgrens sufficiently to hit their target. Soon, though, the standoff ended when the *Albemarle* slowly twisted away with no fatal damage and managed to send two shells at point-blank range into its foe. The first shell, discharged from the damaged aft gun, hit the *Sassacus's* starboard side, passing through the yeoman's storeroom and the berth deck and exiting the opposite side into the river. A second round followed immediately, this one from the forward battery. It entered the starboard side diagonally and was much more destructive, slicing through planking, "smashing the dispensary . . . passing through the forward coal bunker," piercing clear through the starboard boiler and the engine room, and then "through the steerage and wardroom bulkheads, smashing doors and furniture," crashing into an oak stanchion, and lodging in one of the starboard staterooms.[76]

Fighting steamships of the nineteenth century contained many sources of danger. Among these, the large boilers, so vital to the ship's propulsion, were often the primary cause of death and injury following a catastrophic malfunction or battle damage. At Batchelor's Bay, the second Brooke round that plowed through the *Sassacus's* boiler proved devastating. Immediately, high-pressure steam escaped from the punctured boiler with a piercing scream, drowning out the sound of the guns for a moment. The deadly cloud enveloped men in the fire room, and soon the steam's shrill pitch was replaced by the cries of scalded and blinded crewmen. The hot gas decimated the men, "killing some, stifling some, and rendering all movement for a time impossible."[77] On deck, a shaken correspondent watched as the injured "frantically rushed up from below, with their shriveled flesh hanging in shreds upon their tortured limbs." In all, the incident caused twenty casualties, including six fatalities.[78]

Amid the grisly chaos, the *Sassacus*'s crewmen struggled to land a blow of their own. However, in depressing their guns to reach the *Albemarle*'s deck, they damaged the screws of the large Parrott rifles. When they finally managed to hit the rebel craft, the heavy iron shot simply splintered on the *Albemarle*'s metal plates.[79] The loss of steam from the starboard boiler caused the Union ship to shift drastically to port, and soon word passed among the crew that it was sinking. Although the boat remained afloat, the damage left the massive craft ineffective, and after breaking away from the ironclad, it drifted off, wrapped in a cloud. On shore, a local citizen noted, "The hold of the largest steamer issued a thick column of smoke, which increased as the cloud of powder smoke was flown away." The steam pouring from the *Sassacus* led Cooke to believe that he had sunk "one of their most formidable boats." Some of the Union commanders suspected the same.[80]

The fight was not over, though. In fact, it dragged on for three hours. During much of the combat, the Union vessels surrounded the *Albemarle* at a respectful distance. The onshore witness wrote that the large gunboats "kept up their solemn waltz," while the smaller boats edged nearer to the fight. All the while, the vessels "vomited forth their shell and solid-shot at irregular and frequent intervals." From time to time, a thick white cloud shrouded all the vessels. "Then," continued the civilian, "the soft South wind would lift the curtain just in time to disclose the red flashes of new broadsides from the enemy, or the jet of lurid fire which proceeded one of the sonorous, metallic voices of the iron monster."[81]

Consistent with plans drawn up before the engagement, Union commanders employed all manner of devices and maneuvers to sink the *Albemarle*. Union crews tried to foul its propellers with nets and lines, lob grenades onto its decks, and toss satchels of powder into its smokestack. They attempted to ram the ironclad and tried to drive torpedoes into its side.[82] None of these schemes worked, however. In the process, the Union gunboats fired more than 500 rounds, keeping the dozens of gun captains, loaders, spongers, tacklemen, and powder monkeys busy firing the guns. Despite the huge amount of iron expended, the Federal boats failed to land a lethal blow. In fact, most of the rounds, whether shell or solid shot, simply shattered on the *Albemarle*'s iron plates, spraying fragments harmlessly into the air or, as an observer aboard the *Mattabesett* noted, bounding "from her armor like rubber balls."[83]

There were a few injuries aboard the rebel vessel, none of them serious. Still, several rounds managed to do some harm to Cooke's boat. Twenty-five shots cracked iron plates, seven rounds dislodged plates, a few penetrated the underlying wood, and others hit open ports. One loosened iron plate hung over the bow and dragged in the water, counteracting the effect of the rudder and severely hampering the ability to steer the boat. In addition, several rounds pierced the smokestack, leaving huge holes. This damage caused more than an aesthetic concern, for without a fully intact funnel, the draw and therefore the fire would not create sufficient steam. As a result, the *Albemarle* was in danger of going dead in the water. This ended the fight for Cooke, and he eventually turned back for Plymouth. To maintain headway, he ordered his crew to use "bacon, lard, and other combustible material" as fuel, which would burn well under the circumstances.[84] Overcoming the various challenges, the crew managed to coax the ironclad back into Plymouth without further harm. The Union gunboats did not give chase, and the battle ended. The *Albemarle* had held its own against tremendous odds. Back in Plymouth, rumors abounded that it had sunk several Union gunboats. Although this was untrue, the contest's results once again underscored the wisdom exhibited by Confederate Secretary of the Navy Stephen Mallory. By focusing resources on building the ironclads, he managed to give his naval commanders a fighting chance against heavy odds. The fight also highlighted the folly of Union planners in failing to develop and deploy an ironclad in the shallow Carolina sounds.[85]

The *Albemarle*, built under exigent circumstances with limited resources, awed Federal commanders with its performance. Captain Melancton Smith found the ram "very formidable . . . fast for that class of vessel, making from 6 to 7 knots, turns quickly, and is armed with heavy guns." Smith, a native of Long Island and grandson of a continental congressman, also noted that shots fired at the *Albemarle* would strike "upon the casemates and hull, flying upward and falling in the water without having had any perceptible effect upon the vessel."[86] Francis A. Roe, commander of the *Sassacus*, added that "the *Albemarle* is more formidable than the *Merrimack* or *Atlanta*, for our solid 100-pounder rifle shot flew into splinters upon her iron plates."[87]

Such observations obscured an unpleasant fact for Cooke and his men. Even though the gunboat survived the engagement and received praise from friend and foe, it failed in its mission. The May 5 fight off Sandy Point, which came to be known as the Battle of Batchelor's Bay, prevented the ironclad from reaching New Bern. As one Union correspondent put it, the engagement left "us the undisputed control of the Sound, and by her defeat saving Newbern, and doubtless the Department of North Carolina, from being lost to our Government."[88] In fact, it was a tremendous victory for the Union navy, one that would garner well-deserved attention in official reports and the press. The war would give Union naval commanders few opportunities to test their vessels and crews in the chaotic violence of close action with enemy craft. At Batchelor's Bay on May 5, the Federal sailors stationed in North Carolina's brackish rivers and sounds made the most of it. The gunboat commanders and their crews demonstrated that, with adequate numbers, tenacity, and luck, wooden vessels could match the Confederate ironclads. It had been a close call, though. Cooke's crew had demonstrated equal bravery and resolve. A couple of fortuitous bolts from the *Albemarle* could have turned the tables. Ultimately, though, instead of steaming out to help Hoke recapture the key Union base at New Bern, Cooke and his men found themselves and their vessel bottled up at Plymouth.[89]

"Send Forward Everything Available as Fast as Practicable"

On Thursday afternoon, as the *Albemarle* jousted and Hoke's guns dueled, Bragg intensified his requests for troops. With Richmond in danger, Bragg's communications reflected an unprecedented urgency. Men were needed from every station. Bragg directed Beauregard to empty the troops from newly won Plymouth and Washington, save for half a regiment at each town. In relaying the directive to William Whiting in Wilmington, Beauregard explained that the "order now is, to send forward everything available as fast as practicable." At Weldon, the Louisianan prepared another note to Hoke, calling all forces "forthwith" to Goldsboro to await rail transport. Time had completely run out on Hoke's New Bern assault and, with it, the entire Confederate campaign to regain North Carolina.[90]

Throughout Thursday, Hoke remained ignorant of the crisis building in Virginia. However, that changed by evening. As Henry Guion returned to his camp from the front lines at dark, he passed Lieutenant Alexander Chisholm of General Beauregard's staff. Chisholm, whose presence was unexpected, was looking for General Hoke. Sensing that something was afoot, Guion pulled Chisholm aside and whispered, "[If] you bring orders for us to fall back, tell me." The lieutenant simply replied, "I judge so," and proceeded to deliver the news to Hoke. Chisholm was not the only messenger to arrive that evening. A string of exhausted couriers appeared at Hoke's field headquarters, carrying urgent dispatches and passing along Beauregard's entreaties. Poised to launch his attack within hours, Hoke learned that his time was up. Resigned to this fact, he prepared his brigades for departure. Before leaving, though, he would try one last audacious gambit to take the Federal base.[91]

On Friday morning, the railroad monitor rolled out of New Bern to engage Hoke's batteries once again. However, before the first shell could be fired, a flag of truce emerged from the tree line in the distance beyond the Federal works.[92] Major John P. W. Read, the artillery battalion commander, stepped forward. Captain I. M. Potter of the 5th Rhode Island Heavy Artillery emerged from the Union works to receive him. Giles Ward alighted from the monitor to participate in the discussion. One Rhode Islander remembered that Read spoke in a "boastful manner," saying that his force included several infantry brigades, along with artillery and cavalry.[93] According to Ward, Read sought a personal conference with Palmer. When this was refused, the rebel major delivered Hoke's surrender demand directly to Ward. "I laughed in his face. I could not help it," Ward recounted a few days later. Nevertheless, he left the field to convey the message to Palmer in New Bern.[94] While

Read waited for a response, he "talked pleasantly" with the Union officers there but, gazing across the Trent, predicted he would "have supper in the Gaston House tonight." In response, Warren Haines of the 17th Massachusetts quipped, "Have it hot or cold, Major?"[95]

Back in New Bern, Ward and Palmer discussed the Confederates' demand. The general summarily refused the "impudent" request, believing Hoke's move to be a "mere *ruse de guerre*, and hardly worth the effort."[96] Palmer explained that the "delicate jest was duly appreciated . . . but . . . he must leave in one-half hour, or we should fire upon him."[97] Three hours after the flag first appeared, Ward delivered Palmer's emphatic refusal. The Union commander gave the rebels thirty minutes before the monitor would begin pounding their lines again. Soon, some of Hoke's batteries opened in earnest, and a general exchange occurred for a time, including "considerable shelling" from the gunboats in the river. But the firing soon ceased, and the Union defenders discovered that Hoke's main force had departed and was headed back to Kinston. The Federals cautiously rolled their guns forward toward the Confederate lines. When Ward reached the position held by the rebel battery the day before, he found no sign of the Confederates. The operation was over, and with it the Confederate campaign in North Carolina. Surely, Hoke never seriously expected the Federals to surrender, and his demand may have been a ruse to allow him to withdraw his troops without pursuit or counterattack. In any case, by refusing Hoke's demand, Palmer had won at New Bern.[98]

On Friday afternoon, Captain George Graham and his North Carolina Unionists returned to their camp at the Evans' Mill blockhouse. Graham confirmed what others suspected: Hoke's force was in full retreat. His men had fired at the gray column disappearing in the distance but did nothing more. "We have given them some shells, and I think they are satisfied," wrote one officer describing Graham's efforts.[99] Union soldiers, examining Hoke's former position, found "a large number of freshly made graves behind in the woods where we had shelled him."[100] As Hoke's column swung back west on the other side of New Bern, the picket posts along the Bachelor Creek line remained on alert. On Friday, reports of possible rebel movements flooded Claassen's headquarters. However, the feared attack turned out to be nothing more than a "cavalry scare." Claassen was not pleased with the lack of composure demonstrated by his outpost. "These false alarms from your command are very mortifying, and I am surprised that you take action upon idle rumors," Claassen chastised the officer responsible for these alarms.[101]

"No Doubt of Its Success"

As Hoke withdrew his men, Beauregard continued to pelt him with dispatches demanding a halt to the New Bern operation and a return to Kinston. "Hurry forward your troops as rapidly as possible," he urged. Later, he directed Hoke to march his men to Goldsboro to board trains to Petersburg. He assured officials in Richmond that "every effort is being made to transport the troops as rapidly as possible."[102] For the Confederates, the journey back to Kinston was not a pleasant one. The Virginians on the picket line south of the New Bern defenses were some of the last to leave and marched deep into the night, "going through water and mud; it being pitch dark, the men kept shooting their guns off to see the way." They reached Kinston on May 8.[103] Hoke arrived in Petersburg on May 10, and his troops followed, arriving in time to participate in the Bermuda Hundred Campaign and the brutal fighting to come in Virginia.[104]

Looking back on their lunge at New Bern, Hoke and his men took satisfaction in knowing they had pushed farther than Barton in February, a comparison that drew attention from observers. In 1901, one regimental historian recalled that Hoke had "captured the block house on Brice's creek that General Barton thought such a Gibraltar last February, and took fifty prisoners."[105] Sixty years later, historian John G. Barrett, in his authoritative survey of the war in North Carolina, also commented favorably on Hoke's May effort compared with Barton's February attempt. Such contrasts were not entirely fair. For one, Hoke did not capture the same blockhouse Barton had targeted. In February, Barton approached Brice's Creek near the banks of the Trent, where the creek was impossibly deep and prohibitively wide. He dispatched his cavalry south toward Evans' Mill and Croatan but chose to keep his main force near the Trent River. In his report, Barton observed, "It still remained practicable to make a detour by Evans' Mill, to cross Brice's Creek, but this route would have brought me in front of the same and other fortifications." Certainly, Hoke did well to march south to the headwaters of Brice's Creek and cross there. He also cut the railroad and telegraph lines into the city. However, as Barton predicted, Hoke's new position along the railroad simply put him in front of the forts and trench lines crowning the right bank of the Trent. Accordingly, despite the praise directed Hoke's way, it is not clear what he really accomplished.[106]

Inevitably, participants and others questioned whether Hoke could have taken the works south of the Trent River and then stormed New Bern. Hoke later stated that he had "no doubt of its success," and the "recall [back to Virginia] was one of the greatest disappointments I ever had." Robert Graham, regimental historian for the 56th North Carolina, wrote that the "spirit of the troops assured success."[107] Another writer attached to the 67th North Carolina believed victory was "almost a certainty."[108] However, an anonymous correspondent for the *Daily Conservative* offered a more balanced assessment only a few days after the operation. He noted that the question of whether New Bern could have been captured "is much discussed by outsiders" and concluded: "We cannot really say. The troops *know* they could, but we don't." He also observed that, with the *Albemarle*, "we think the Yankees would have been 'dug out'"; without it, though, he judged "the attempt was very properly not made, and there the matter must rest so far as our opinion is concerned."[109]

Indeed, without naval support, Hoke's troops would have been highly vulnerable to the guns and men filling the fortifications on the south bank of the Trent, not to mention the Union gunboats standing by in the river. In addition, it is not clear what other options were available to Hoke. Any effort to deposit troops across the Trent via a pontoon bridge or boats south of town, as apparently planned for May 6, would have been equally unpromising. Such a move would have simply deposited his men outside of the Fort Totten line, an uncommonly strong position. Whether or not New Bern could have been taken, the final results detract little from Hoke's energy and enterprise. He led a remarkable campaign in his native state, one that would bring a host of benefits to the Confederate cause. However, with the withdrawal from New Bern on May 6, the Confederate offensive and resurgence in North Carolina ended.

The Confederate Resurgence Considered

"Into the Jaws of Death and the Mouth of Hell"

On June 1, 1864, men of the 8th North Carolina took up a hasty position at the end of their brigade's battle line near swampy ground about a mile west from a remote Virginia crossroads known locally as Old Cold Harbor. Peering over makeshift works, the men spied a cloud of blue uniforms spilling through the trees in the distance. "Here they are, as thick as they can be!" sang out a staff officer. The brigade's commander, Thomas Clingman, could see the tightly packed mass headed his way. From outside the trench line, Tar Heel pickets sprinted back into the line, and a silence briefly enveloped the scene. Soon, though, the Yankees crashed into the regiment's "front, flank, and rear," leading with their bayonets and pouring over the works. Deafening bursts of rifle fire filled the air.

The confusing swirl of combat followed. Some of the defenders broke, some gave up, and others rallied and counterattacked. The lines shifted back and forth nearly half a dozen times. "Truly we had marched into the jaws of death and the mouth of hell," recalled a New Yorker. The North Carolinians eventually regained their position and exchanged a murderous fire with a Vermont regiment, "each line face to face, standing (falling) about three rods apart, and the leaden hail flying thick and fast, among and around each line, thinning and felling many brave soldiers." When the shooting stopped, General Clingman found that the Union "dead were much thicker than I have ever seen them on any battle field."[1]

The 8th North Carolina, which had done so well when attached to Hoke's Plymouth expedition, would earn no laurels for the June 1 fight at Cold Harbor. In fact, the entire brigade would draw criticism from a Richmond paper for giving way in the face of the attack. Seeking to correct the record, Clingman complained publicly about the "great injustice" of such barbs, to no avail. The vicious melee on June 1 would be typical of the weeks to come, a period of sustained violence. To the Tar

Heels fighting in Virginia that summer, the little river town of Plymouth must have seemed far away.[2]

Immediately following the North Carolina campaign, the Plymouth victors found themselves spread out all over Virginia. Like the 8th North Carolina, many others who had fought under Robert Hoke in the Old North State headed for Bermuda Hundred in May, Cold Harbor in June, and eventually into the lines outside Richmond and Petersburg. Few results would match their triumphs in the spring of 1864 in their home state. In fact, for many, Plymouth would represent their last taste of battlefield victory, and that success would stand out as the largest, most significant Confederate military accomplishment on North Carolina soil.

The Plymouth operation offered a model of planning and execution. The Confederates concentrated their strength where it could have the largest impact, and they used their interior lines, particularly the railroad, to rapidly gather forces while shielding their preparations from the enemy. They conducted effective diversions outside New Bern, confusing Union commanders. At Plymouth, Hoke developed and orchestrated his movements to bring his forces to bear on the vulnerable points in the Union defense line. He also improvised and adjusted to changing conditions. He avoided useless attacks, did not press unsuccessful ones, conducted assaults where he enjoyed a clear advantage, and used artillery to devastating effect. He waited for the ironclad to arrive before throwing his most powerful punch. To be sure, the Confederate victory was a limited one. As Hoke's men boarded their trains for Virginia, the main Federal base at New Bern remained firmly in Union hands, a fact few Confederates emphasized when summing up the operation's results. However, in a year that would see few rebel successes, the events in North Carolina provided a welcome tonic to anxious Confederates.

Plymouth also represented a rare example of a successful Confederate joint-service operation. Though rebel leaders managed to deploy several ironclads and other vessels during the war, they never used them in conjunction with land forces to such devastating effect. Difficulties related to timing, command disagreements, miscommunications, and interservice rivalries generally plagued such combined efforts. But these problems did not arise at Plymouth. The successful coordination there may have had something to do with the simplicity of the plan. Indeed, there was little to coordinate. Hoke directed Cooke to steam downriver and engage the enemy gunboats guarding the town. With the infantry and artillery investing the works beginning on Sunday, April 17, the precise timing of Cooke's arrival was not particularly important. Remarkably, the unfinished and untested vessel managed to navigate the Roanoke River, defeat the opposing craft, and then turn the tide by blanketing Plymouth with fire as Ransom and Hoke delivered the coup de grace. After the ironclad's victory, coordination between Cooke and Hoke allowed the gunboat to lay fire on the town's exposed defenses, particularly the citadel of Fort Williams. Again, such cooperation was not complicated. Cooke simply needed to find a suitable anchorage from which to shell the lines, and ultimately, the *Albemarle* made a substantial difference.[3]

Confederate partisans celebrated Hoke's conquests at Plymouth and Washington. The North Carolina newspapers brimmed with accolades for the newly minted major general. The results achieved by Hoke were impressive. However, many of the details behind his performance remain shrouded in fog. Hoke did not help clarify matters. It seems he did not prepare an official battle report, and in later years, he wrote no memoirs and gave no speeches. Little of Hoke's official correspondence survives. In fact, most of the information about his activities during the campaign comes from scattered anecdotes in the letters, diaries, and recollections of his men, officers, and acquaintances. Thus, it is difficult to compose a clear, comprehensive picture of Hoke's actions and deliberations.

Nevertheless, the portrait of Hoke that emerges is one of competence, clear thinking, and resolve. By all accounts, he planned matters thoroughly and acted decisively. He remained flexible, taking advantage of opportunities when they materialized. He exercised firm command of his force during the fighting and effectively delegated to his subordinates, capable officers such as James Dearing and Matt Ransom. One strains to find a critical word from his men about his performance. His meteoric rise at such a young age and his triumph at Plymouth made him a hero in his home state.

Hoke's popularity may have benefited from the ongoing rivalry between North Carolina and its neighbor to the north. He had gained success where Pickett of Virginia had failed, a fact not lost on Hoke's fellow Tar Heels. The campaign's results, however, did not defuse the long-simmering tension between the two states. In June, a quarrel broke out between editors of the *Richmond Enquirer* and the *Wilmington Journal* over the performance of Virginia and North Carolina commanders during the New Bern and Plymouth operations.[4] The *Enquirer* insinuated a sinister aspect to Bragg's orchestration of the Plymouth offensive, writing that "while Barton and Pickett fell, Hoke rose. One general promoted, two relieved. Plymouth was recaptured, but Petersburg was offered in exchange."[5]

After his return to Virginia, Hoke's ascent slowed considerably. As the Richmond-Petersburg campaign ground on through 1864 and into 1865, he failed to achieve additional notoriety.[6] A poor performance at Cold Harbor on June 1, a failed attack outside Petersburg on June 24, and a disastrous counterattack at Fort Harrison on September 30 generated a string of complaints and criticisms.[7] Unlike at Plymouth, Hoke was not in overall command of these later operations. He either shared responsibility with fellow officers or served in a subordinate role. In August, Josiah Gorgas remarked in his diary that Hoke had "not maintained his reputation" after Plymouth.[8] Following an unsuccessful assault outside Richmond on October 7, fellow officers flung angry complaints at the young major general, accusing Hoke of failing to push his troops to attack and relieve enemy pressure on another division.[9] A particularly incendiary and questionable account of the battle appeared in the *Charleston Mercury* and was reprinted in a Raleigh paper. It claimed that, during the fight, Hoke had confided to a fellow officer that "he would fight no more."[10] North Carolina papers quickly dismissed the rumor, and the matter faded away. Throughout the fall, Hoke would continue to command, steering his troops outside Richmond.[11] In December, he returned to his home state with his division. He fought at Fort Fisher in January 1865 and later led his men against Sherman's juggernaut, which overran the state in the last two months of the war.

"I Am Making a Crop of Corn"

According to a well-worn story, a group of former Confederate soldiers traveling in the countryside shortly after the war spied a familiar figure plowing a field. The party waited for the farmer to steer his team in their direction. One of group then called out, "Isn't that General Hoke?" "Yes," came the reply. "Why, General! What are you doing? Why are you plowing in the field?" the veteran asked. "I am making a crop of corn," he responded. "I think it is a better business than killing Yankees."[12] The encounter, whether apocryphal or not, is emblematic of Hoke's postwar career. After the conflict, he retreated into private life and became a model of modesty and restraint. He turned down requests to run for office. He refused to attend reunions or events commemorating the Confederate cause. He rarely discussed his wartime experiences and consistently declined to share his recollections publicly. In fact, it was not until the turn of the century, when he was in his sixties, that he began to discuss his memories with fellow veterans.[13]

However, the same cannot be said of many of his comrades. Like former Confederates everywhere, Tar Heel veterans eagerly produced their own accounts of the war. They shared their stories at meetings, at ceremonies, and in books and articles, celebrating their accomplishments, recounting their battlefield deeds, and mourning their comrades. As the war faded further into memory, these aging men produced more and more material. In North Carolina, several efforts helped capture the recollections of the former Confederates. In the 1870s, Stephen D. Pool, a veteran of the North Carolina campaign, edited *Our Living and Our Dead*, a New Bern–based journal filled with war reminiscences and Southern literature. During the 1890s, veteran Walter Clark, the chief justice of the state supreme court, published a multivolume compilation of North Carolina regimental histories, covering campaigns and battles in minute detail. In addition, former soldiers routinely published accounts of combat and camp life in newspapers. In some cases, they revisited old controversies.[14] As for the Confederate campaign of 1864, stories often extolled the high points of the operations at Plymouth, Washington, and New Bern. The Plymouth victory emerged as a shining example of Confederate pluck and bravery. Events such as the destruction of the *Underwriter* and the *Albemarle*'s success received repeated treatment in books and articles.[15]

"It Cost Something to Be Loyal to the Union"

The darker aspects of the Confederates' 1864 offensive, such as the first New Bern expedition, the Kinston hangings, and the prisoner executions at Plymouth, received less attention. To be sure, the Kinston hangings attracted interest in the North as Federal officials sought to determine what happened and who was responsible. George Pickett's decisions drew scrutiny in the form of investigations and congressional inquiries in the years immediately after the war. But once President Johnson's wide-ranging amnesty proclamation shielded Pickett, the issue slipped away and received little attention until the end of the twentieth century.

Similarly, the battlefield executions at Plymouth did not generate much interest.[16] In the absence of army and congressional investigations, the events faded away, bubbling up only occasionally. For instance, a few years after the war, in an editorial attacking the conduct of ex-Confederates, William Holden's newspaper identified Robert Hoke as the man "who ordered the murder of colored Union soldiers at Plymouth, and who was the terror of the Union men of the West." The incident received only occasional mention in various Federal reminiscences and denials in a few accounts from Confederate veterans. But such attention was uncommon.[17]

Whatever Hoke's virtues as a battlefield leader, the murder of black prisoners by men under his command tainted his achievements. While there is no evidence that Hoke directed or otherwise encouraged these offenses, there is also no indication that he conducted an inquiry into the incidents or punished those involved. Further, when asked about the killings by a Union veteran after the war, Hoke did not respond.[18] At Plymouth, he was in charge of all the Confederate units and thus shouldered ultimate responsibility. As one Massachusetts veteran later concluded, the treatment of prisoners at Plymouth "will always remain as a black spot on his record."[19]

Eventually, the killings at Plymouth and similar events at Fort Pillow, Olustee, and the Crater became part of the history of African American units in the Union army. Historians have cited various reasons for the mistreatment and murder of black prisoners by Confederate forces: racial hatred, the humiliation of fighting men they viewed as inherently inferior, the desire to decrease enlistments, the need to demoralize the enemy, and base "feral-rage."[20] Furthermore, many white Southerners harbored a deep and long-standing fear of slave insurrection in North Carolina and elsewhere, anxiety no doubt magnified by the Emancipation Proclamation, the formation of black units, and Edward Wild's raid. Certainly, each Confederate participant had his own reasons and motivations. Thus, it is likely that multiple factors motivated each soldier, making it difficult, if not impossible, to pinpoint the reasons behind these incidents. However, it is doubtful that such killings were simply the product of impromptu battlefield passions. By their own admission, units involved in the Plymouth killings had participated in similar acts only weeks before at Suffolk. One officer confirmed in a March 1864 letter home that the men in Ransom's brigade had resolved to "take no negro prisoners" and followed a no-quarter policy against black troops.[21] It appears that at least some of Hoke's men carried this understanding into the Plymouth fight and acted accordingly. However, the number of Confederates who participated, the number of Union soldiers killed, and the extent to which Confederate commanders were involved will likely never be known.

Other aspects of the campaign went largely ignored as well. Little mention was made after the war of the thousands of native North Carolinians, both white and black, who fought for the Union army. Many individuals who remained loyal to the United States throughout the conflict found themselves the target of scorn and worse. After the war, ex-Confederates and their supporters—constituting the large majority of white citizens—ostracized Unionists, threatening their livelihoods and sometimes their lives. As one Union officer remarked, "It cost something to be loyal to the Union . . . we have thought that the Northern people, too little appreciated the suffering borne by the Union men and women, in localities where secession was the prevailing sentiment."[22] In the war narrative assembled by the ex-Confederate majority in the postwar years, the North Carolina Unionists and other opponents of the Confederate government were largely missing. However, in recent decades, the service and sacrifice of the state's Union soldiers and loyal citizens have received more attention. Scholars and public history sites have delved into the contributions of white Unionists, African Americans, and other Confederate detractors during the conflict. It is through this broader lens that the impact of the Confederate resurgence can be viewed.[23]

"Reverses in North Carolina Are Bad at This Time"

The Confederate victory at Plymouth delivered a stinging defeat to Union forces. The Federals lost two towns they had heavily fortified and held for much of the war. Furthermore, most of the 4,000 men captured at Plymouth later perished in Southern prisons. Those Union losses in North Carolina were preventable. Federal commanders were well aware of the Confederate threat during the spring of 1864 and understood the danger posed by the ironclads. In the end, though, they failed to take the steps necessary to prevent Plymouth's fall. The campaign revealed a damaging complacency and a host of missteps by Union leaders. Federal officers up and down the chain of command demonstrated limited interest in aggressively countering the Confederate threat in early 1864. In addition, there were several tactical mistakes during the Plymouth campaign. For reasons that are still unclear, Flusser and Wessells unwisely turned back the powerful gunboat *Tacony* on the very day Hoke arrived at Plymouth. The land batteries in and around the town failed to stop or even impede the *Albemarle*, suggesting significant flaws in their design or operation. Finally, the failure to stop Ransom's column at Conaby Creek on April 19 opened the door to the defenses east of the Federal perimeter. This, coupled with the failure to stop the *Albemarle*, doomed the Union garrison.

Details of the Plymouth fight aside, Union leaders implemented a muddled strategy for defending their posts and generally neglected the advantages afforded by their early, impressive gains in the state. Union leaders understood the implications of the defeat. "Reverses in North Carolina are bad at this time," confided Secretary of the Navy Gideon Welles to his diary following the Plymouth defeat.[24] Throughout Pickett's and Hoke's efforts in 1864, Union commanders opted against an active defense and demonstrated little aggression in confronting Confederate forces, particularly the ironclads. They did not take full advantage of the mobility afforded by their control of the sounds and rivers connecting their fortified enclaves. In February and again in April, Peck and Palmer kept their troops frozen in the bases. For months, Federal army and navy leaders were aware that the ironclads were incubating not far from Union bases. Yet they did not hunt down these craft in their stocks or find a way to bring their own armored vessels into the sounds. Their failure to seek out and destroy the nascent rebel ironclads is particularly puzzling. Even Benjamin Butler, who sometimes seemed to dismiss the threat, urged his subordinates to head out and burn the vessels in March. The navy, particularly Admiral Lee, supported such a mission. But the will to undertake the operation did not exist. If Butler, Peck, Wessells, Flusser, Davenport, and other Union commanders had aggressively searched for and destroyed the *Albemarle*, the Confederate victory at Plymouth probably would not have occurred.

Despite all these considerations, there was one positive note for the Union side following Plymouth's loss. At the campaign's conclusion, the unsung Union commanders held on and retained control of their most vital base: New Bern. In February, Innis Palmer stood his ground there, and he did the same in May. He did not panic; he did not abandon the post. In addition, navy commanders Henry Davenport and Melancton Smith helped contain the rebel offensive, checking the *Albemarle* at Batchelor's Bay on May 5 and virtually assuring there would be no more Confederate gains.

"No Action"

Beyond the tactical details, the overall Federal approach to defending the various posts in the state raises questions as well. For much of the war, the army leaders Foster, Butler, Peck, and Palmer drove the strategy in eastern North Carolina, while the navy supported the garrisons, conducted raids up the rivers, and weighed in on strategy and policy. Officers and officials in both services had been debating dispositions in the state since 1862. Rear Admiral Phillips Lee warned about the vulnerability of the detached garrisons, particularly at Plymouth and Washington. Army commanders, especially John Foster, pushed back, emphasizing the importance of those locations for deploying troops and countering enemy supply efforts. In hindsight, Admiral Lee's warning proved prescient. Throughout 1862, 1863, and into 1864, Union officials in the North Carolina District struggled to find enough men to adequately defend these posts.

In the spring of 1864, Benjamin Butler was largely focused on his own plans in Virginia. However, in ordering Wild's raid, he demonstrated a willingness to conduct modest operations in North Carolina. Later, in his memoirs, he recalled his own recommendation in the fall of 1863 to abandon Plymouth and Washington, accusing administration officials of taking "no action."[25] Butler may have held such a view, but no evidence of that recommendation has surfaced. Furthermore, his communications do not shed much light on his overall vision for the region; nor is there much evidence of engaged leadership on Butler's part during his tenure as department head. In fact, after his initial inspection tour of the garrisons in November 1863, Butler never visited them again.[26]

Union officials higher on the chain of command were even less helpful in guiding the defense of positions in North Carolina. As Hoke hammered Plymouth's defenses in late April, Grant weighed in and pronounced the small towns not worth protecting. Like Butler, Grant would later remember recommending withdrawal from Plymouth and Washington prior to the Confederate offensive.[27] However, like Butler's claim, no evidence has emerged to support this. Ultimately, the Union high command did not devote adequate attention or resources, whether in the form of additional troops, gunboats, or ironclads, to ensure that the Union bases would hold. Even as Hoke's columns threatened Plymouth and Washington, Butler, following orders from Grant, siphoned men north to support the spring offensive in Virginia. Union commanders simply focused their attention elsewhere, particularly on the upcoming operations against Richmond and Robert E. Lee's army. In this mix of competing military needs in multiple regions, such prioritization was inevitable, and positions in North Carolina were sacrificed to increase the chances for greater gains elsewhere.

Union leaders also largely ignored the offensive possibilities offered by their position in the state. Indeed, throughout 1863 and for much of 1864, they treated North Carolina as a place to recruit and station troops and rarely showed an inclination to use their foothold there to substantial advantage. With relatively secure bases on the rivers and sounds, as well as ocean ports at Beaufort and Morehead City, the ground gained by Burnside in 1862 offered an ideal means to cut into the Confederacy's trunk and sever Virginia from the other Southern states. In particular, the Atlantic and North Carolina Railroad, which began at Morehead City, provided a solid line of advance into the heart of the state and threatened the vital Wilmington and Weldon Railroad.

On two occasions in 1862, following Ambrose Burnside's success, Union commanders and administration officials pursued big plans for the state. First, Burnside nearly launched an attack against Goldsboro in the summer, but the operation was halted before it began in order to feed troops into Virginia for McClellan's Peninsula Campaign. Second, near the end of that year, Foster planned a large army-navy venture against Wilmington, but that offensive never went off, mostly due to problems with the expedition's naval component. Many of Foster's men were then shunted south to support operations at Charleston Harbor throughout 1863. Later, Foster would recommend another operation in North Carolina, but he could gain no traction with Henry Halleck, who preferred to concentrate troops in Virginia to protect Washington, DC. Thus, in the wake of Burnside's 1862 campaign, Union forces in eastern North Carolina limited their activities to minor raids against points in the interior. Despite the promise offered by these hard-won positions, Union officials chose to focus their energy on other fronts.[28]

In January 1864, Grant's proposal to conduct a massive expedition from Suffolk and into North Carolina held promise. If successful, it would have cut supplies to Lee at a key moment before the spring campaign, severed Virginia from the rest of the Confederacy, and neutralized or eliminated one of the only significant rebel ports remaining. Grant's effort also would have wreaked havoc on the lines of supply and communication in North Carolina.[29] But Halleck blocked the operation, again fearing for the capital's safety. In addition, Butler, the department commander from late 1863 into 1864, focused on opportunities in Virginia. By opting not to strike North Carolina in 1864, the Union high command handed the initiative to the Confederates.

Beyond military considerations, the fall of Plymouth and Washington dealt a demoralizing blow to Union supporters in the state. Many soldiers captured at Plymouth would suffer and perish at Andersonville and elsewhere, and Union troops at the remaining North Carolina bases would face other problems. The rebel victories also struck fear into Buffaloes and the black troops, and the Kinston hangings and prisoner killings at Plymouth provided a strong hint of what would happen should the Confederates win another victory. Indeed, officers in the Buffalo units reported plunging morale as Hoke advanced toward New Bern. The Confederate offensive also impacted noncombatants aligned with the Union cause. Confederate control of Washington and Plymouth eliminated havens for fugitive slaves in the region, a fact well understood by Union commanders.[30]

"Commissariat Has of Late Been Much Improved"

To many Confederates, the military offensive in North Carolina stood out as a significant success that may have helped prolong the war by boosting supplies for Lee's army and aiding Governor Zebulon Vance's reelection. Newspapers, letters, and official reports all suggest that the effort fulfilled the goals privately articulated by Lee in January. To be sure, observers at the time noted that the Plymouth and New Bern attacks reduced the Confederate supply crisis, aided Vance's political fortunes, and improved morale among the secessionist citizenry.

The offensive generated tangible results for Confederate supply. In addition to providing access to the Union stores at the Plymouth garrison, the operation opened up the rich countryside on the Albemarle-Pamlico Peninsula and in the northeastern counties. The Subsistence (Commissary) Department benefited greatly. The Confederate army's supply situation improved at just the right time, during the grueling Overland Campaign in May and the harried fighting at Petersburg in June. The bonanza continued for several months. In the days following the Plymouth victory, railcars rolled north crammed with arms, ammunition, and equipment destined for rebel quartermasters. Captured stores made their way north to feed beleaguered troops. In addition, the fisheries in the rivers upstream from Plymouth and Washington, thick with herring and shad, were available to the Confederates once again. Hoke and Beauregard took immediate measures to resume fishing operations. Likewise, Beauregard urged Richmond officials "to get out the large quantities of pork in Hyde Co."[31] The Confederate gains allowed commissary agents to scour the countryside for meat, grain, and other foodstuffs.

The potential gains from Hoke's victories were large. According to the 1860 agricultural census, the eleven counties surrounding Plymouth and Washington, including counties north of the Albemarle Sound, produced roughly 10 to 15 percent of the state's cattle, pork, corn, and beans.[32] Although several years of war had certainly diminished such production, these counties yielded substantial supplies for the Confederate cause.

The precise amount of supplies generated in the months following Hoke's victories is not clear, especially given the lack of comprehensive Confederate commissary records. However, the information available from newspaper reports and subsistence officials suggests that the supplies gained from both the Federals and the surrounding countryside had a substantial impact. Back in November 1863, Governor Vance estimated that the Union presence at Winton on the Chowan River deprived Confederate commissary agents and thus Lee's soldiers of "four or five million pounds of pork" available in the northeastern counties.[33] Furthermore, in the days following Hoke's victories, reports of the bounty made their way into the papers. The *Memphis Daily Appeal* wrote that the "reclaimed districts of North Carolina are furnishing large quantities of nice bacon."[34] In June, a report noted that the "commissariat has of late been much improved," greatly influencing the soldiers' morale. The "captures at Plymouth," coupled with cargoes run through the blockade, "have placed such a store of bacon at the disposal of the authorities that each man now daily receives a ration of half a pound, within four ounces of the regulations' allowance."[35] Most notably. though, correspondence from Confederate supply officials clearly revealed that eastern North Carolina provided much for the army in 1864. In the fall, Lieutenant Colonel Frank G. Ruffin in Richmond identified the region around Plymouth as "the area from which we now draw a very considerable proportion of our supplies."[36]

"Steadfast Adherence to Our Cause"

The campaign also had a significant political impact. It delighted Governor Vance, who was fighting for his political life in the gubernatorial election. In a proclamation issued to the legislature in mid-May, he highlighted "the very splendid success of the opening of the campaign in our State, resulting in the re-capture of the towns of Plymouth and Washington, and the rescue of a considerable portion of our territory from the enemy." Hoke and Cooke, "two distinguished sons of North-Carolina," received special mention from the governor. He also welcomed those citizens "rescued from the enemy" and thanked them for "their steadfast adherence to our cause under the tyranny and oppression of our foe."[37] Vance applauded the "very great loyalty and patriotism of that whole portion of the state within or contiguous to the enemy lines, which has been alike subjected to his blandishments and his ravages."[38]

In the wake of the Plymouth victory, Vance continued his vigorous reelection campaign. In addition to his pivotal visit to Lee's army, he crisscrossed North Carolina, not hesitating to visit towns where sentiment for Holden was strong. In speeches delivered to enthusiastic crowds, he followed the strategy first deployed in Wilkes County in February, expressing firm support for the war while acknowledging the excesses of Confederate policy. The governor also attacked his opponent. He criticized the newspaper editor for refusing to debate, for changing his position on the war, and for advocating peace negotiations at the expense of an independent Confederacy.[39] By highlighting the uncertainties and ambiguities of Holden's position, Vance gained much-needed traction with the electorate. He also managed to define Holden in the public eye and successfully painted the contest as a question of "Lincoln or no Lincoln."[40] This was unfair but effective. Holden and many of his allies were by no means Lincoln supporters. The editor made it clear that he supported slavery and that he sought negotiations with the Federals because he considered it the best means to ensure the institution's survival.[41] He also insisted that he had no desire for the state to act alone.[42] Nevertheless, Vance managed to define Holden and his supporters as a danger to the Confederacy.[43]

With his campaign dead in the water, Holden accused Vance and his administration of corruption. It had little effect. Then, in July, Holden suffered a serious blow when a pro-Vance newspaper revealed the existence of the Heroes of America (also known as the Red Strings), a clandestine group of North Carolinians loyal to the Union and bent on defeating the Confederacy. On June 18, 1864, the *Daily Confederate* claimed that the group's goal was "political; and every member of the order is expected to vote for Mr. Holden—who, though not a member, is a beneficiary of the organization."[44] Holden sought to distance himself from the Red Strings, but the rumors and innuendo surely damaged him and his cause.[45]

Vigorous campaigning and Confederate military successes contributed to Vance's electoral advantage, but other factors helped too. Various Confederate measures, including Hoke's deserter hunt and the suspension of habeas corpus, no doubt chilled Holden's supporters. Holden himself temporarily shut down his most important weapon, his newspaper, in response to fears generated by the legislation. David L. Swain, a Vance ally and the college president at Chapel Hill, remarked in a letter to the governor that the suspension had "paralyzed and stupefied the public mind" and "inaugurated a reign of terror," causing men to speak "sparingly, cautiously, warily."[46]

Electoral abuses occurred as well. In the army, some officers directed their men to vote for Vance, threatening to deny passes, furloughs, and medical care to those who did not toe the party line. On Election Day, reports circulated that provost guards and other officials coerced men into voting for Vance or impeded Holden supporters from casting their votes at all.[47] In addition, many men exempted from army service owed their status to Vance and his subordinates, and the threat of losing their positions kept their allegiance to the governor firm. The same held true for public officials, including judges and militia officers who owed their positions to Vance. At the polls, Vance voters received ballots printed on yellow paper at many stations, which allowed electoral officials to easily identify Holden supporters. In addition, the governor sent troops to guard polling places in the Quaker Belt.[48]

When the election finally took place late in the summer, it was not close. The voting itself was conducted in two stages: one for the army, and a subsequent one for civilians. The soldiers cast their ballots in late July and handed Vance a prodigious lead: 13,209 to 1,824. The lopsided results from the army were reported in the state's newspapers several days before the civilian vote.[49] On August 4, Vance won the nonmilitary vote as well: 44,664 to Holden's 12,608.[50] Vance's win spread joy among Confederate supporters. They knew the result was a blow to opponents of the Confederate cause. The *Daily Confederate* captured the mood of many when it proclaimed that Vance's win "must strike every true man with the highest gratification—not as a party triumph, but as a thorough vindication, of the patriotism and loyalty of the people of Carolina."[51]

"My Work Is Done, but Yours Is Not"

The extent to which Confederate military operations aided Vance's reelection and helped quell the peace movement is difficult to estimate. The battlefield gains at Plymouth and elsewhere were not the only factors assisting Vance. The governor's excellent campaigning, Holden's poor performance, the repression of Unionists, and military successes elsewhere surely impacted the elections results. However, the effort and resources invested in the military offensive in North Carolina certainly heartened beleaguered Confederate supporters. The first attack on New Bern in February, though ultimately unsuccessful, demonstrated that the Confederate high command was willing to commit resources and take risks to achieve gains in the state. And the Plymouth victory, the first substantial rebel triumph in North Carolina, boosted spirits and helped keep the state in the war.

The impact of the military campaign on political affairs is difficult to gauge with any precision, but it was clear enough to participants and observers at the time. It was widely understood that the goal behind the operation was to address the disaffection with the Confederate government "by an attempt to change the military situation," as one participant put it.[52] Confederates reveled in the victory. "Let the sons and daughters of the Old North State rejoice, for the day of redemption is at hand," cheered the *Daily Confederate* in late April.[53] The editors of the *Fayetteville Weekly Observer* predicted that Hoke would "drive the enemy from Eastern North Carolina and obliterate the last vestige of Holdenism in the State."[54] William Pettigrew, a plantation owner from Washington County outside of Plymouth, urged voters to remember the sacrifices made during the campaign, stating, "The gallant soldier who, wrapped in his blanket, rests in the bed of glory beneath the turf of the battlefield seems to whisper my work is done, but yours is not."[55] After Washington's capture, the *Daily Confederate* in Raleigh added: "This is indeed a day of rejoicing for North Carolina. Let the stout-hearted and valiant men rejoice in the fulfillment of their confident expectation; the weak-kneed and the 'hope-it-may-be so's,' gather courage from this bright harbinger of still brighter days; and the craven, yankee-hearted croaker and disloyalist read and learn the doom that but surely awaits them; for the day of our redemption most assuredly draweth nigh."[56] Northern observers also weighed in. "It is generally believed in the interior," noted a Pittsburgh paper, "that the fall of Plymouth and the evacuation of Washington will enable Gov. Vance, the secession candidate, to secure his re-election."[57]

"Who Have Preached Liberty and Independence with Their Lying Tongues"

The Confederate gains from the 1864 North Carolina campaign did not last. The *Albemarle*'s failure at Batchelor's Bay on May 5 and the withdrawal of Hoke's forces from the state brought an end to the string of Confederate victories. Later that year, Union forces struck back. In October at the Plymouth wharf, a small Union launch led by intrepid Commander William B. Cushing slipped past rebel sentry boats in the dark and planted a lethal torpedo in the *Albemarle's* side as it sat quietly at its moorings. Following this daring caper, a Union flotilla enveloped Plymouth and flushed the Confederates out of the town, reversing Hoke's triumph. Though Cushing's bold exploit was noteworthy, it was lost in a swarm of other, much larger Union victories at Atlanta, Mobile Bay, and the Shenandoah Valley.[58]

In late 1864, Confederate fortunes rapidly declined at nearly all points. Within a matter of days after Federal troops recaptured Plymouth, Lincoln won reelection, ensuring the war's vigorous, unimpeded prosecution and largely sealing the Confederacy's fate. The next year, William T. Sherman delivered the coup de grace for Confederate North Carolina when his men boiled up from the south and rolled over threadbare defenders in a series of lopsided engagements. Sherman's campaign culminated in the rebel surrender at the Bennett place near Durham on April 26, 1865.

After the war, formal Confederate control of the state ceased, but the political and social divisions so prevalent during the armed conflict endured. Holden, in charge of the postwar Republican Party, became North Carolina's provisional governor, displacing Vance and other Confederate nationalists. With the support of the Federal government, Holden sought to steer the state through the early years of Reconstruction. His bitterness toward former Confederate leaders remained. He pulled no punches in criticizing Vance and others over their actions during the war. In 1868, his *Weekly Standard* railed at former rebels "who have shot and hung conscripts—who have whipped women and put their thumbs under the fence, or justified or ordered it—who have run down panting deserters with bloodhounds . . . who have preached Liberty and Independence with their lying tongues, and illustrated it with bucking, gagging, the torture, handcuffs, starvation and murder!"[59] Under the new political order, Holden did more than hurl words. He supported black political rights and enacted reforms that drew intense opposition from many former Confederates. When the Ku Klux Klan conducted a campaign of sustained terror against black citizens, Holden took drastic action to halt the atrocities, going so far as to deny habeas corpus to those accused of fomenting the violence. Ex-Confederates and their allies resisted Holden's efforts and fought back in the legislature, eventually managing to impeach the governor and remove him from office. As Reconstruction stuttered, the old order and its policies took hold once again. By 1876, Vance had returned to the governor's mansion in Raleigh and he and other former Confederates would continue to exercise power in the state for decades to come.

When Robert E. Lee and other Confederate planners envisioned the North Carolina campaign back in early January 1864, they had specific goals in mind. The dire supply situation, the Union military presence, and the growing cries for peace in the Old North State posed genuine threats to the Confederate war effort and to the survival of the Confederate cause itself. The events of the summer—Grant and Lee's epic campaign in Virginia and Sherman's steady march toward Atlanta—would largely swallow the memory of the Plymouth and New Bern battles for most. But throughout the campaigns and battles to come in 1864, Confederates on the home front held on to the tangible results of Plymouth and Washington.

The Confederate efforts in North Carolina in early 1864 would not rank among the Civil War's largest or most decisive military operations. However, the victories there aided the Confederacy. Confronted with huge manpower odds and material disadvantages, the rebels assembled and executed a remarkable campaign—a "very splendid success," in Vance's words—that may have helped keep North Carolina in the war.[60] Plymouth's capture and the occupation of Washington yielded large quantities of supplies that substantially aided Lee's troops in Virginia. The gains also helped buoy Confederate morale in North Carolina and elsewhere, as the principal rebel armies prepared for a crucial summer of campaigning. Furthermore, the success fueled Governor Vance as he fought for reelection and strove to keep his state in the Confederacy. Beyond the marches, battles, supplies captured, and ground gained, the Confederate military resurgence of 1864 also impacted African Americans seeking their freedom, loyal Unionists struggling against Confederate rule, and other civilians hoping to navigate the war's dangers. In the end, the results of these engagements reverberated well beyond the confines of the towns and waterways in which they were fought.

Acknowledgments

Many hours of solitary research, writing, and rewriting dominate any book project. In the end, however, the best part of the whole thing is the time spent with generous, knowledgeable people who pitch in to help out. I have many people to thank for pushing this book along. First, I am happy to note that the manuscript was carefully reviewed by Dickie Newsome, a retired surgeon who grew up in Hertford County, North Carolina, and happens to be my father. He went through the draft line by line, furnishing his observations and sharing his knowledge about the region that was his boyhood home. In addition, Bob Rogers, professor emeritus at Hampden-Sydney College and my father-in-law, graciously reviewed several chapters and kindly offered helpful suggestions and corrections.

This project began with a suggestion from veteran historian Bryce Suderow, who also provided his candid views on the manuscript and raised several important issues. The manuscript also benefited from the help of several historians who shared their knowledge of Civil War North Carolina and kindly read all or part of early drafts, including Wade Sokolosky, coauthor of two excellent books on Sherman's campaign in 1865; Gerald Thomas, author of several books on Bertie County as well as the definitive study on the Plymouth massacre; Mosby expert and New Bern resident Horace Mewborn; Eric Lindblade, author of the definitive study on the Battle of Newport Barracks; Jimmy Hardison, an expert on the Battle of Plymouth; William Marvel, who has written many thoughtful, original books on the conflict; and Mark Bradley, author of several excellent titles about North Carolina during the Civil War and Reconstruction. Others helped as well, including my friends and coeditors on *Civil War Talks: Further Reminiscences of George S. Bernard and His Fellow Veterans*; John Selby, author of *Meade: The Price of Command, 1863–1865*; and John Horn, author of *The Siege of Petersburg: The Battles for the Weldon Railroad, August 1864* and *The Petersburg Regiment in the Civil War*. Historian Sharon McDonald also shared her thoughts about Grant's "Suffolk" plan as well as Union strategy along the mid-Atlantic coast. Judkin Browning, James Burke, Joe Mobley, and Barton

Myers kindly answered research questions and helped locate documents. Catherine Shreve and Steven Wade gathered research from various repositories in North Carolina.

I would also like to thank several archivists, historians, and collectors who went out of their way to gather material for the project and provide suggestions and encouragement: David Bennett and Elizabeth Freier (Port O'Plymouth Museum), Bryan Cheeseboro and Paul Harrison (National Archives and Records Administration), Matthew Turi and Elizabeth Shulman (Southern Historical Collection, University of North Carolina), Dominique Dery and Ashley Young (Duke University), Lee Sherrill (late author of an excellent study of the 21st North Carolina), Sierra Dixon (Connecticut Historical Society), Adrienne Serra (Virginia Tech), H. Paul Cojeen (my friendly neighbor and distinguished naval architect), Sandra Fox and Timothy Bostic (Naval History and Heritage Command), John Coski (American Civil War Museum), John Hennessey (National Park Service), John McClure (Virginia Historical Society), Damon Talbot (Maryland Historical Society), Susan Lintelmann (US Military Academy Library), Vann Evans (North Carolina State Archives), Jim Hodges (New Bern Historical Society), Timothy Engels (Brown University), Morris Bass (North Carolina Department of Cultural Resources), Patrick McCullough of New Bern, who shared maps from his personal collection, David Silkenat (University of Edinburgh), Chandra Manning (Georgetown University), Steve Alvin, Celia Niepold Slater, and Doug Cooke. Chris Meekins of the North Carolina State Archives and author of a study on Elizabeth City during the Civil War provided several suggestions throughout the process and shared his transcriptions of letters from the Thomas Pittman Papers. I would also like to thank the staff at the University Press of Kansas, including Joyce Harrison, who provided enthusiastic support for the project early on; Larisa Martin, who guided the manuscript through production; and copyeditor Linda Lotz, who did fantastic work helping to transform my manuscript into a book. Once again, many thanks to all, and as always, any mistakes in this book are my own.

Finally, I would like to thank Margot, Jake, and Silas for all their support and patience.

New Bern Order of Battle, February 1–3, 1864

Union

Brigadier General Innis N. Palmer (Major General General John Peck on leave)

New Bern Defenses

> 17th Massachusetts Infantry, 92nd New York Infantry, 99th New York Infantry, 132nd New York Infantry, 19th Wisconsin Infantry (9 companies), 12th New York Cavalry (8 companies), 3rd New York Light Artillery, 5th Rhode Island Heavy Artillery (7 companies), 2nd Massachusetts Heavy Artillery
> USS *Underwriter*, USS *Lockwood*, USS *Commodore Hull*

Subdistrict of Beaufort

Colonel James Jourdan
> Beaufort–2nd North Carolina Union Volunteers (detachment); 158th New York Infantry, Companies B, D, and E
> Newport Barracks–Colonel Valentine G. Barney (Colonel Edward H. Ripley on leave): 9th Vermont Infantry; 19th Wisconsin Infantry, Company F (en route to New Bern on February 2); 2nd Massachusetts Heavy Artillery, Company D, Captain Russell H. Conwell; 5th Rhode Island Heavy Artillery; Mix's New York Cavalry (3rd New York), Companies A and B

Confederate

Major General George E. Pickett

Brigadier General Seth Barton's Column

Kemper's Brigade, Colonel William Terry
1st, 3rd, 7th, 11th, and 24th Virginia Infantry
Ransom's Brigade, Brigadier General Matt Ransom
24th, 25th, 35th, and 49th North Carolina Infantry
Barton's Brigade, Colonel William R. Aylett
9th, 14th, 38th, 53rd, and 56th Virginia Infantry
12 pieces of artillery (8 rifled pieces) (units not specified)
3rd North Carolina Cavalry, Colonel John A. Baker (7 companies); 62nd Georgia Cavalry, Lieutenant Colonel John T. Kennedy (5 companies)

Colonel James Dearing's Column

Montgomery Corse's Brigade (2 regiments): 15th Virginia Infantry, 17th Virginia
67th North Carolina Infantry, Colonel John N. Whitford
300 cavalrymen (units not specified)

Brigadier General Robert F. Hoke's Column

Corse's Brigade (3 regiments): 18th, 29th, and 30th Virginia Infantry
Ransom's Brigade (1 regiment): 56th North Carolina Infantry
Hoke's Brigade: 6th, 21st, 43rd, 54th, and 57th North Carolina Infantry; 21st Georgia Infantry
Clingman's Brigade (2 regiments): 8th and 51st North Carolina
Read's (38th Virginia) Battalion, Major John P. W. Read: Fauquier Artillery, Richmond Fayette Artillery (Macon's Battery), Lynchburg Artillery (Blount's Battery), Richmond Hampden Artillery

Brigadier General James G. Martin's Column (from Wilmington)

17th North Carolina Infantry; 42nd North Carolina Infantry; 3rd Battalion North Carolina Light Artillery, Company A; 5th North Carolina Cavalry, Company E; 5th South Carolina Cavalry, Company K; Staunton Hill Artillery

Plymouth Order of Battle, April 17–20, 1864

Union

Brigadier General Henry W. Wessells
2nd North Carolina Union Volunteers (2 companies), 101st Pennsylvania Infantry, 103rd Pennsylvania Infantry, 16th Connecticut Infantry, 85th New York Infantry, 3rd Pennsylvania Heavy Artillery (small detachment), 2nd Massachusetts Heavy Artillery (2 companies), 24th New York Independent Battery, 12th New York Cavalry (2 companies)
New recruits and recruiting detachments: 10th US Colored Troops, 37th US Colored Troops, 38th US Colored Troops; 2nd US Colored Cavalry
Bombshell and *Dolly* (US Army), USS *Miami*, USS *Southfield*, USS *Ceres*, USS *Massasoit*, USS *Whitehead*

Confederate

Brigadier General Robert F. Hoke
Because Confederate commanders prepared no reports detailing the forces at Plymouth, there is no complete official list of Confederate units there. The information below comes from correspondence and other accounts, including casualty returns prepared by Hoke's chief surgeon Isaac S. Tanner. The identity of the artillery units in the Confederate force is not clear.

Hoke's Brigade, Colonel John T. Mercer

6th, 21st, and 43rd North Carolina Infantry; 21st Georgia Infantry
(54th and 57th North Carolina Infantry did not join the expedition)

Ransom's Brigade, Brigadier General Matt Ransom

8th (from Clingman) 24th, 25th, 35th, and 56th North Carolina Infantry (49th North Carolina Infantry was on picket duty on the Chowan River)

Kemper's Brigade, Colonel William Terry

1st, 3rd, 7th, 11th, and 24th Virginia Infantry

Dearing's Battalion, Colonel James Dearing (also acted as Hoke's chief of staff)

8th Confederate Cavalry, Virginia Horse Artillery (Edward Graham's Petersburg Horse Artillery)
10th Regiment North Carolina State Troops, Companies B, G, and H, Lieutenant Colonel Henry T. Guion

Branch's (Coit's) Battalion, Colonel James R. Branch

Bradford's Missisippi Battery, Petersburg Battery (Graham), R. Pegram's Artillery

Read's (38th Virginia) Battalion, Major John P. W. Read

Fauquier Artillery, Richmond Fayette Artillery (Macon's), Lynchburg Artillery (Blount's)
Montgomery True Blues (Lee), Wilmington Artillery (Miller; Company E, 10th North Carolina)
CSS *Albemarle*, CSS *Cotton Plant*

APPENDIX C

Plymouth Casualty Estimates

Union

Unit	Killed	Wounded	Missing	POW	Total
16th Connecticut	1	11	0	434	446
2nd Massachusetts					
Heavy Artillery	3	14	0	273	290
12th New York Cavalry	2	4	12	118	136
85th New York	6	5	2	376	389
24th New York Light					
Independent Battery	1	0	12	109	122
3rd Pennsylvania					
Heavy Artillery	0	0	8	8	16
101st Pennsylvania	8	24	0	429	461
103rd Pennsylvania	6	10	2	463	481
2nd North Carolina					
Union Volunteers	9	—	101*	56	166
Unattached recruits	Unknown	Unknown	Unknown	Unknown	245
Total	36	68	137	2,266	2,752

*Includes men who escaped and were otherwise unaccounted for (from Jordan and Thomas, "Massacre at Plymouth," 171).

Confederate

Unit	Killed	Wounded	Total
Kemper's (Terry's) Brigade	5	45	50
1st Virginia Infantry	0	6	6
7th Virginia Infantry	0	7	7
11th Virginia Infantry	4	13	17
24th Virginia Infantry	1	19	20
Hoke's (Mercer-Lewis's) Brigade	31	107	138
6th North Carolina Infantry	3	35	38
21st North Carolina Infantry	14	35	49
43rd North Carolina Infantry	4	13	17
21st Georgia Infantry	10	24	34
Ransom's Brigade	48	400	448
24th North Carolina Infantry	13	88	101
25th North Carolina Infantry	3	20	23
35th North Carolina Infantry	20	88	108
56th North Carolina Infantry	5	84	89
8th North Carolina Infantry	7	120	127
Cavalry (Dearing)	Unknown	Unknown	Unknown
Artillery (multiple batteries)	2	45	47
Total (Hoke's entire command)	86	597	683

Note: As is often the case, the various sources for Plymouth casualties offer conflicting totals. Accordingly, the numbers here should be treated as estimates only. Sources consulted for Union casualties include the American Civil War Database (drawn from service records from the National Archives and other sources) and Wessells report, ORA 33:301. Confederate sources include Tanner, "Report of Killed and Wounded, Plymouth, North Carolina"; Clark, *Histories of the Several Regiments*, 3:348; *Daily Confederate*, April 30 and May 2, 1864 (Hoke's casualties), May 5, 1864 (Ransom's casualties); *Charlotte Observer*, November 24, 1901; *Charlotte Western Democrat*, May 3, 1864; Adjutant General's Roll of Honor Scrapbook (various undated newspaper clippings containing casualty reports), NCOAH; and Jordan and Thomas, "Massacre at Plymouth," 171 (2nd NCUV).

The casualty report for Hoke's command prepared by surgeon Isaac S. Tanner provides the following numbers (which are slightly lower than those cited in other reports): Kemper's (Terry's) Brigade, 45 wounded and 5 killed (no 3rd Virginia casualties); Hoke's Brigade, 105 wounded and 33 killed; Ransom's Brigade, 269 wounded and 42 killed; various artillery batteries, 35 wounded and 2 killed; no numbers were given for cavalry units. Tanner's report also contains detailed information about the injuries suffered by each soldier listed. General Wessells's official report includes a table showing 2,834 total Union losses at Plymouth, but it does not break down that total in terms of killed, wounded, missing, and captured.

Notes

Abbreviations

BOI	Board of Investigation, "Convened to Investigate the Facts and Circumstances Connected with the Burning of Certain Portions of the Town of Washington, N.C., and the Pillage of that Place during the Late Evacuation"
CHS	Connecticut Historical Society
DMRL	David M. Rubenstein Rare Book and Manuscript Library, Duke University
ECU	Joyner Library, East Carolina University
LOC	Library of Congress
NARA	National Archives and Records Administration
NCOAH	North Carolina Office of Archives and History
NHHC	Naval History and Heritage Command
NYSMM	New York State Military Museum
ORA	US War Department, *The War of the Rebellion: A Compilation of the Official Records of the Union and Confederate Armies*, series 1 (unless otherwise noted)
ORN	US Navy Department, *Official Records of the Union and Confederate Navies in the War of the Rebellion*, series 1 (unless otherwise noted)
RG	Record Group
SHC	Southern Historical Collection
SLNC	State Library of North Carolina
UNC	University of North Carolina
VHS	Virginia Historical Society

Preface

1. Diary of John Witherspoon (captain, 24th Michigan, 1st Army Corps), January 2, 1864, Burton Historical Collection, Detroit Public Library.

2. Lee to Davis, January 2, 1864, *ORA* 33:1061.

Chapter 1. Taking the Coast

1. Crumpler, *Speech on Federal Relations*, January 10, 1861; *Fayetteville Weekly Observer*, July 14, 1862. In 1887, 1,500 people would attend the unveiling of a monument over Crumpler's grave site in Rockford, North Carolina. *People's Press*, July 7, 1887.

2. Yearns and Barrett, *North Carolina Civil War Documentary*, 7–9.

3. See Crofts, *Reluctant Confederates*, 37; Myers, *Rebels against the Confederacy*, 16–21; Brown, "North Carolinian Ambivalence," 9. See also Kennedy, *Agriculture of the United States in 1860*, 104–111 (agricultural production by county); Moore, *Old North State at War*, 6 (population tables by county).

4. Browning, *Shifting Loyalties*, 23–25 (discussion of Beaufort and Carteret Counties).

5. Yearns and Barrett, *North Carolina Civil War Documentary*, 4–5.

6. Crofts, *Reluctant Confederates*, 104–105. See also Browning, *Shifting Loyalties*, 23, 27; Myers, *Rebels against the Confederacy*, 16–21.

7. Barrett, *Civil War in North Carolina*, 10.

8. Dowd, *Life of Zebulon B. Vance*, 442; Battle, *Memories of an Old-Time Tar Heel*, 168–169.

9. Battle, *Memories of an Old-Time Tar Heel*, 168–169; Myers, *Rebels against the Confederacy*, 11, 119.

10. Yearns and Barrett, *North Carolina Civil War Documentary*, 125; Barrett, *Civil War in North Carolina*, 18–29; Hill, "North Carolina," 6–11.

11. Lee, *Recollections and Letters of General Robert E. Lee*, 62.

12. Hatteras, Roanoke Island, and Ocracoke Island were accessible only by water. Historically, Ocracoke Inlet had served as the primary entry point for shipping to the interior waters. However, a powerful hurricane in 1846 carved a new inlet in the barrier island south of Cape Hatteras, which soon became the preferred point of ingress serving the North Carolina sounds. See Pilkey, *North Carolina Shore and Its Barrier Islands*, 160–161.

13. ORN 12:198–201. See also memorandum, July 16, 1861, Blockade Strategy Board Minutes, ON Subject File, RG 45, NARA. Board members were Professor Alexander Dallas Bache, head of the US Coast Survey; John G. Barnard, the army's chief engineer; and Captains Charles H. Davis and Samuel Francis Dupont, both of the navy.

14. Sauers, *Burnside Expedition in North Carolina*, 17–20; Welles to Stringham, August 9, 1861, ORN 6:70; Barrett, *Civil War in North Carolina*, 35, 46.

15. Board to Welles, September 2, 1861, and Board to Fox, September 12, 1861, Blockade Strategy Board Minutes, ON Subject File, RG 45, NARA.

16. McClellan to Burnside, January 7, 1862, ORA 9:352–353. See also Reed, *Combined Operations in the Civil War*, 39–43; Sauers, *Burnside Expedition in North Carolina*, 115–118.

17. Browning, *From Cape Charles to Cape Fear*, 21–27; Myers, *Executing Daniel Bright*, 37 (importance of Roanoke Island to the Union). The victory at Roanoke Island opened the way for Union forces in the Albemarle Sound. Soon after, Union vessels under Commander Stephen C. Rowan engaged and neutralized a tiny Confederate naval force, the "Mosquito Fleet," operating in the Albemarle Sound near Elizabeth City, thus leading to Union incursions against Winton, Plymouth, and other towns. Myers, *Executing Daniel Bright*, 41.

18. Sauers, *Burnside Expedition in North Carolina*, 261–308; Hoke report, ORA 9:260.

19. At first, the Fort Macon defenders appeared to weather the attack. But Union officers had familiarized themselves with the installation and targeted its weak points. The fire began to take its toll on the guns crowning Fort Macon's parapet, and after bolts from Union Parrott guns cracked the ceiling of one of the fort's magazines, the rebel commander surrendered. Sauers, *Burnside Expedition in North Carolina*, 313–340; Branch, *Fort Macon*.

20. Browning, *From Cape Charles to Cape Fear*, 34.

21. Barrett, *Civil War in North Carolina*, 124–125.

22. In April 1862, Brigadier General Jesse Reno led an unsuccessful raid to destroy the lock on the Dismal Swamp canal at South Mills and block Confederate ironclads descending from Norfolk. However, on May 10, the Confederates abandoned Norfolk, effectively removing any immediate rebel naval threat. Sauers, *Burnside Expedition in North Carolina*, 377–407; Parramore, "Burning of Winton in 1862."

23. Tucker, *Zeb Vance*, 130.

24. Evans, *Confederate Military History*, 4:44.

25. Tucker, *Zeb Vance*, 130.

26. Lee to Randolph, October 25, 1862, ORA 19(2):681.

27. For a positive portrayal of Burnside's career that goes against the conventional grain, see Marvel, *Burnside*.

28. Fox to Goldsborough, February 24, 1862, ORN 6:664; Kennedy, *Agriculture of the United States in 1860*.

29. Rowan to Du Pont, April 14, 1862, in Hayes, *Samuel Francis Du Pont*, 5.

30. Sauers, *Burnside Expedition in North Carolina*, 443–445. On June 28, 1862, President Lincoln wrote to Burnside directly: "I think you had better go, with any re-enforcements you can spare, to General McClellan." ORA 9:404. For discussions of McClellan's plan, see McClellan to Burnside, January 7, 1862, ORA 9:352–353; Reed, *Combined Operations in the Civil War*, 39–43; Sauers, *Burnside Expedition in North Carolina*, 115–118; Skaggs, "A Thorn, Not a Dagger."

31. Abstract of return of the Department of North Carolina, July 1862, ORA 9:414.

32. Barrett, *Civil War in North Carolina*, 131.

33. Ibid.; Flusser report, ORA 7:556; *News and Observer*, June 11, 1909 (Plymouth attack).

34. In the 1850s, Stanly moved to California, where he unsuccessfully ran for governor on the Republican ticket. Within days of his appointment, he warned Secretary of War Edwin Stanton against setting abolition as a war aim. Stanly to Stanton, June 12, 1862 (quoting a letter written to Stanton May 31, 1862), ORA 9:400.

35. Barrett, *Civil War in North Carolina*, 128. One New York cavalryman described the governor as the slave "hunter whom our Southern Kentucky President has sent down here to insult us." Sauers, *Burnside Expedition in North Carolina*, 414–440. The *Richmond Whig* and the *Winston Sentinel* referred to Stanly as a "traitor." See *Weekly Standard*, July 2 and 16, 1862; Hamilton, *Reconstruction in North Carolina*, 88–95.

36. See, generally, Current, *Lincoln's Loyalists*. The notion of recruiting North Carolinians first appeared in a letter to Lincoln shortly after the capture of Hatteras. In response, the

president voiced skepticism at first, scrawling on the back of the recommendation, "if arms were in the hands of a Union regiment in N.C. they probably would not remain in their hands long." Lincoln to Cameron, August 31, 1861, in Basler, *Collected Works of Abraham Lincoln*, 4:504. Soon afterward, however, Colonel Rush C. Hawkins, stationed in North Carolina, repeated the suggestion, and the president revised his position. Hawkins soon gathered about sixty white locals for duty at Hatteras. Lincoln to Scott, September 16, 1861, ORA 4:613.

37. Burnside to Stanton, May 5, 1862, ORA 9:385.

38. Moore, *Old North State at War*, 63.

39. J. G. Foster, Return of 18th Army Corps, ORA 7:533. For an extensive discussion of the Buffaloes, see Browning, "'Littled Souled Mercenaries'? The Buffaloes of Eastern North Carolina," 337.

40. Mallory report, April 26, 1861, ORN 2:53; Mallory to Conrad, May 10, 1861, ibid., 69; Luraghi, *History of the Confederate Navy*, 55–69 (construction of ironclads).

41. See, generally, Elliott, *Ironclad of the Roanoke*; *Albemarle*, ZC File, NHHC. Plans for the Halifax ironclad were drafted by John L. Porter, chief constructor for the Confederate navy.

42. In November, with a force of 5,000, Foster conducted a large raid into the region west of Plymouth, freeing many slaves and destroying much property. See ORA 18:20–23.

43. Foster to Halleck, December 10, 1862, ORA 18:476; Lee to Fox, December 2, 1862, ORN 8:245. Admiral Lee summarized Foster's plan: "General Foster proposes to march from New Berne and cut the railroad at or about Goldsboro; thence either to go to Tarboro and destroy the gunboats, or return to New Berne, which I prefer . . . and thence to march to Wilmington."

44. Browning, *From Cape Charles to Cape Fear*, 91; French, *Two Wars*, 154.

45. Foster to Halleck, December 23, 1862, ORA 18:489–490.

46. Ibid.

47. Halleck to Dix, December 24, 1862, ORA 18:490.

48. See Lee to Welles, December 26, 1862, ORN 8:320–321 (referencing Lee's discussions with Foster).

49. Lee to Foster, December 28, 1862, ORN 8:328; Welles to Lee, January 13, 1863, ibid., 420.

50. Lee to Sands, December 21, 1862, ORN 8:318; Fox, *Confidential Correspondence of Gustavus Vasa Fox*, 1:128; Welles, *Diary of Gideon Welles*, 1:216, 2:127 (arguing that Wilmington was more important than Richmond). Welles would later express support for action against Wilmington. See also Browning, *From Cape Charles to Cape Fear*, 281; Fonveille, "Closing down the Kingdom," 101; Reed, *Combined Operations in the Civil War*, 271–275.

51. Foster to Halleck, February 2, 1863, ORA 18:533.

52. See Reed, *Combined Operations in the Civil War*, 271–278.

53. Evans, *Confederate Military History*, 4:151; Lee to Longstreet, March 30, 1863, ORA 18:907; Longstreet to Lee, March 30, 1863, ibid., 950–951.

54. Barrett, *Civil War in North Carolina*, 151, quoting D. H. Hill to J. Longstreet, February 25, 1863, D. H. Hill Papers, Library of Virginia; Hill report, ORA 18:188–189.

55. Gardner, *Record of the Service of the Forty-Fourth Massachusetts*, 187.

56. Lee to D. H. Hill, May 25, 1863, ORA 18:1071.

57. See Foster's report about Potter's raid, ORA 27(2):963–965; Potter report, ibid., 965.

58. *Wilmington Journal*, July 30, 1863. This *Wilmington Journal* account refers to "Company I" of the 1st NCUV. However, Northern sources make it clear that the unit was Company L, commanded by George W. Graham. See *Philadelphia Inquirer*, July 29, 1863; Clarkson report, ORA 27(2):971.

59. Halleck to Palmer, April 14, 1863, ORA 18:612; Halleck to Foster, May 9, 1863, ibid., 711.

Chapter 2. Liberation, Discontent, and the Friends of Peace

1. Colyer, *Report of the Services Rendered by the Freed People to the United States Army*, 26–29.

2. The raids and skirmishes flaring across the region scarred the surrounding countryside. A Connecticut soldier writing home in January 1863 noted "the ruin devastation and utter abandonment of villages, plantations and farms, which but a short time ago was peopled, fenced, and stocked." W. A. Willoughby to His Wife, January 22, 1863, William Henry Noble Papers, DMRL.

3. See Brown, "North Carolinian Ambivalence," 10–11.

4. In March 1862, revised articles of war criminalized Federal soldiers' efforts to aid the return of slaves to their masters. In addition, the First and Second Confiscation Acts passed in 1861 and 1862 facilitated wide-scale emancipation. Colyer, *Report of the Services Rendered by the Freed People to the United States Army*, 5.

5. See, generally, Oakes, *Freedom National.*

6. Proclamation Made to the People of North Carolina, February 16, 1862, ORA 9:363–364.

7. General Orders No. 2, March 12, 1862, ORA 9:369; Burnside to Stanton, March 27, 1862, ibid., 373.

8. Colyer, *Report of the Services Rendered by the Freed People to the United States Army*, 34.

9. Chapin, *Memorandum and Journal of Samuel Chapin*, 27.

10. Browning, *Shifting Loyalties*, 88; Franklin, *Free Negro in North Carolina*, 18.

11. W. H. Doherty to Abraham Lincoln, May 13, 1862, Abraham Lincoln Papers, LOC.

12. Browning, "Bringing Light to Our Land," 1–17.

13. *Daily Progress*, January 28, 1864.

14. Cecelski, *Fire of Freedom*, 66; Silkenat, *Driven from Home*, 63–65.

15. Durrill, *War of Another Kind*, 5; Myers, *Executing Daniel Bright*, 41–48. In commenting on conditions at Elizabeth City in May 1862, Charles Flusser of the navy noted the absence of Confederate troops in the area and pegged the blame for any Unionist persecution on "the work of evil-minded citizens." He planned to "subject those citizens to summary punishment." Flusser to Mayor of Elizabeth City, May 18, 1862, ORA, navy series 1, 7:385.

16. Durrill, *War of Another Kind*, 5.

17. Myers, *Execution of Daniel Bright*, 6–7; Myers, *Rebels against the Confederacy*, 57.

18. Browning, *Shifting Loyalties*, 3.

19. Jno. Peebles to Z. Vance, October 31, 1862, in Johnston, *Papers of Zebulon Baird Vance*, 1:286; Silkenat, *Driven from Home*, 63–65.

20. Clingman to Hill, August 7, 1862, ORA 9:476–477. Clingman reported that about a third of the state's slaves were east of the Wilmington and Weldon Railroad.

21. Durrill, *War of Another Kind*, 6.

22. Browning, *Shifting Loyalties*, 166.

23. Durrill, *War of Another Kind*, 121.

24. W. A. Willoughby (10th Connecticut) to His Wife, January 22, 1863, Noble Papers.

25. Browning, *Shifting Loyalties*, 166.

26. Haines, *Letters from the Forty-Fourth Regiment M.V.M.*, 39.

27. *Impeachment Investigation*, 732; Hamilton, *Reconstruction in North Carolina*, 94.

28. *Weekly Standard*, October 8, 1862. Another paper added that the proclamation showed what Lincoln would do "with the South if he had her in his power, and it also shows that we did not withdraw from his government a day too early." *Western Democrat*, January 13, 1863.

29. See Levin, *Remembering the Battle of the Crater*, 25–26.

30. Mobley, *"War Governor of the South,"* 90.

31. Pool to Vance, July 25, 1863, in Mobley, *Papers of Zebulon Baird Vance*, 2:222.

32. Mobley, *"War Governor of the South,"* 85–90.

33. Edmondston, *Journal of a Secesh Lady*, 16.

34. Lincoln to J. Conklin, August 26, 1863, ORA, series 3, 3:733; Mobley, *"War Governor of the South,"* 98.

35. Browning, *Shifting Loyalties*, 97–98.

36. W. A. Willoughby to His Wife, January 22, 1863, Noble Papers.

37. Derby, *Bearing Arms in the Twenty-Seventh Massachusetts*, 167–169.

38. Andrew to Stanton, April 1, 1863, ORA, series 3, 3:109–110.

39. Vincent to Wild, April 13, 1863, ORA, series 3, 3:122.

40. Cecelski, *Fire of Freedom*, 66; Silkenat, *Driven from Home*, 63–65.

41. Derby, *Bearing Arms in the Twenty-Seventh Massachusetts*, 192.

42. Smith, *Autobiography of James L. Smith*, 123.

43. See Reid, *Freedom for Themselves*, 42; Bardolph, "Inconstant Rebels," 163–189.

44. Proclamation from Vance, January 26, 1863, ORA 18(1):860–861; *Tarboro Southerner*, May 23, 1863.

45. Robert E. Lee to Jefferson Davis, August 17, 1863, ORA 29(2):649–650; Hess, *Pickett's Charge*, 361 (some desertion stemmed from post-Gettysburg demoralization).

46. Vance to Seddon, August 26, 1863, ORA 34(2):676. See also Mobley, *Papers of Zebulon Baird Vance*, 2:255.

47. Vance to Seddon, September 3, 1863, ORA, series 4, 2:787 (Vance complaining about men from other states serving in Confederate posts in North Carolina); Lee to Seddon, April 18, 1863, ORA 18:998; Lee to Imboden, August 17, 1863, ORA 29(2):650–651. Lee asked James Longstreet to send either Robert Hoke or Stephen Ramseur to their native state. Hoke got the nod.

48. Barrett, *Civil War in North Carolina*, 192; Cooper to Seddon, October 3, 1863, *ORA* 29(2):729; Auman, *Civil War in the North Carolina Quaker Belt*, 103–125. For a detailed account of this operation, see Sherrill, *21st North Carolina Infantry*, 279–288. On September 8, 1863, General Hoke, writing from High Point, requested that Vance send Colonel Faison and cavalry from Raleigh. Telegram, Hoke to Vance, September 8, 1863, Governor's Papers 1863 (NCAH-8609), Zebulon Vance Papers, NCOAH, and Zebulon Vance Papers (microfilm ed.), LOC.

49. See Vance to Hoke, September 7, 1863, in Mobley, *Papers of Zebulon Baird Vance*, 2:267.

50. *Weekly Standard*, January 20, 1864, December 23, 1863.

51. James Cordill et al. to Vance, January 25, 1864, Vance Papers, LOC; Inscoe and McKinney, *Heart of Confederate Appalachia*, 127.

52. *ORA* 29(1):930.

53. Lee to Hoke, November 12, 1863, *ORA* 29(2):833 (Hoke's losses "3 killed, 19 wounded, and 906 missing"). On November 11, 1863, Hoke asked Vance, "What is reliable concerning my brigade?" Telegram, Hoke to Vance, November 11, 1863, Vance Papers, LOC.

54. Lee to Seddon, October 30 and November 4, 1863, *ORA* 29(2):806–807, 820.

55. See Myers, *Rebels against the Confederacy*, 62–65; Browning, *Shifting Loyalties*, 48–50 (Craven County examples); Bynum, *Long Shadow of the Civil War*, 19–53 (Confederate resistance by women in the Quaker Belt).

56. See Myers, *Rebels against the Confederacy*, 62–65; Inscoe and McKinney, *Heart of Confederate Appalachia*, 139–165.

57. *Weekly Standard*, June 24, 1863.

58. Myers, *Rebels against the Confederacy*; Delaney, "Charles Henry Foster and the Unionists of Eastern North Carolina," 352; Browning and Smith, *Letters from a North Carolina Unionist*.

59. Although Holden clearly advocated for slavery's retention, other peace advocates did not insist on it and in fact pushed for Reconstruction. See Yearns and Barrett, *North Carolina Civil War Documentary*, 296; Harris, *William Woods Holden*, 132.

60. *Weekly Standard*, January 20, 1864.

61. *Daily Progress*, July 15, 1863. Some claimed that John Pennington advocated slavery's abolition. See *Weekly State Journal*, January 12, 1864.

62. *Weekly Standard*, August 19, 1863.

63. *Weekly Standard*, August 12, 1863 (reporting on public meetings in Johnston, Wayne, and Yadkin Counties). For Holden's denial, see *Standard*, July 13, 1864. For more on the Heroes of America, see Auman, *Civil War in the North Carolina Quaker Belt*, 143–146; Auman and Scarborough, "Heroes of America"; Hamilton, "Heroes of America"; Myers, *Rebels against the Confederacy*, 114–120.

64. McPherson, *Battle Cry of Freedom*, 698.

65. Harris, *William Woods Holden*, 143.

66. Vance to Davis, July 26, 1863, *ORA* 51(2):740; Davis to Vance, July 24, 1863, ibid., 739.

67. Hill to Seddon, June 3, 1864, ORA 18:1092; Hess, *Pickett's Charge*, 361 (quoting John Thomas Jones to father, August 17, 1863, Jones Family Papers, SHC, UNC); Harris, *William Woods Holden*, 138.

68. Barrett, *Civil War in North Carolina*, 195–196.

69. Harris, *William Woods Holden*, 138.

70. McKinney, *Zeb Vance*, x.

71. Letter from "Hornet," *Fayetteville Weekly Observer*, April 11, 1864.

72. Historian Joe Mobley brought Vance's statement regarding slavery to light. See Mobley, "Zebulon Vance," 434, 454.

73. Guelzo, *Gettysburg*, 24. Early in the war, the Virginia press made an effort to defuse such concerns. For instance: "North Carolina has done her whole duty to the cause, and without bragging about it." *Raleigh Weekly Standard* (quoting the *Richmond Whig*), July 2, 1862.

74. Guelzo, *Gettysburg*, 24. Virginia had forty-three regiments; North Carolina, forty-four.

75. Hamlin, *Old Bald Head*, 133.

76. *Richmond Enquirer*, July 23, 1863.

77. *Raleigh Register*, July 26, 1863 (reprinted in the *Richmond Enquirer*, July 28, 1863).

78. See Reardon, *Pickett's Charge in History and Memory*, 59–61; Hess, *Pickett's Charge*, 360.

79. Lee to Seddon, September 9, 1863, ORA 29(2):723–724.

80. ORA 29(1):5. The North Carolina and Virginia departments had been combined a few months earlier.

81. Oakes, *Freedom National*, 91–92.

82. Butler to Wife, July 28, 1862, in Butler, *Private and Official Correspondence*, 2:115.

83. See Hearn, *When the Devil Came down to Dixie*.

84. Butler, *Autobiography and Personal Reminiscences*, 617; Mrs. Butler to Mrs. Heard, November 27, 1863, in Butler, *Private and Official Correspondence*, 3:163.

85. *New York Herald*, December 2, 1863.

86. Sarah Butler to Harriet Heard, November 27, 1863, in Butler, *Private and Official Correspondence*, 3:164. The author found no mention of Butler's recommendation to abandon Little Washington and Plymouth in the published official records, Butler's published correspondence, or Butler's unpublished correspondence and letter books in the Library of Congress.

87. *New York Times*, January 9, 1864. The Virginia raid, carried out in Princess Anne County, was conducted by Colonel Alonzo Draper. Wild report, ORA 29(1):916. Wild's force included troops from the 2nd NCCV, the 1st USCT, and portions of the 1st NCCV and 5th USCT.

88. *Fayetteville Semi-Weekly Observer*, January 18, 1864.

89. Butler to Stanton, December 31, 1863, ORA 29(2):595.

90. Pickett to Griffin, December 15, 1863, ORA 29(2):874. For recent accounts of Wild's raid, see Myers, "A More Rigorous Style of Warfare"; Casstevens, *Edward A. Wild and the African Brigade*.

91. Wild to Elliott, December 17, 1863, ORA, series 2, 6:847; Hinton to Butler, January 15, 1863, ibid.

92. *New York Times*, January 9, 1864.

93. Wild report, *ORA* 29(1):912.

94. *New York Times*, January 9, 1864. Ray's obituary in *New York Times*, March 5, 1864, identified him as Tewksbury.

95. *New York Times*, January 9, 1864.

96. Pickett to Cooper, December 15, 1863, *ORA* 29(2):873.

97. Wild to Elliott, December 17, 1863, *ORA*, series 2, 6:847; Butler to Hinton, January 27, 1864, ibid., 883.

98. *Daily State Journal*, December 31, 1863. See also *Charlotte Democrat*, February 2, 1864, for reports of Union troops forcing loyalty oaths on locals and unpunished crimes committed by free blacks.

99. *Fayetteville Semi-Weekly Observer*, January 18, 1864 (excerpt from the *Richmond Examiner*).

100. Butler to Stanton, December 31, 1863, *ORA* 29(2):595–597 (also in Mobley, "War Governor of the South," 93; Myers, *Executing Daniel Bright*, 105); Myers, *Executing Daniel Bright*, 18–19; Mobley, "War Governor of the South," 93; statement of W. J. Munden, *ORA*, series 2, 6:1129–1130.

101. Vance to Ould, December 29, 1863, *ORA*, series 2, 6:776–777.

102. Vance was not alone in his complaints. In the latter part of 1863, Georgia governor Joseph Brown emerged as a vocal critic of Richmond's policies, but like Vance, Brown remained a firm supporter of the war. See Vance to Davis, July 26, 1863, *ORA* 51(2):740.

103. Vance to Seddon, December 21, 1863, *ORA*, series 4, 2:1061.

104. Seddon to Adjutant General, December 25, 1863, *ORA*, series 4, 2:1062.

105. Jones, *Rebel War Clerk's Diary*, 2:119.

106. Vance to Seddon, December 29, 1863, *ORA*, series 4, 2:1072.

107. Seddon to Vance, January 11, 1864, in Mobley, *Papers of Zebulon Baird Vance*, 3:38–39; S. P. Moore, Surgeon-General, to Sec. of War (second endorsement to Vance's December 31, 1863, letter), *ORA*, series 4, 2:1067.

108. Vance to Davis, December 30, 1863, *ORA* 51(2):807.

109. Vance to W. Graham, January 1, 1864, in Mobley, *Papers of Zebulon Baird Vance*, 3:5; Vance to D. Swain, January 2, 1964, ibid., 7–8.

110. Davis to Vance, January 8, 1864, in Davis, *Papers of Jefferson Davis*, 158–161.

111. Woodward, *Mary Chesnut's Civil War*, 527 (January 4, 1864, entry).

112. Mobley, "War Governor of the South," 111–112.

113. See *Daily Conservative*, May 27, 1864.

114. Montgomery, "Relations between the Confederate States Government and the Government of North Carolina," 54.

Chapter 3. Lee's Design for North Carolina

1. R. E. Lee to his wife, April 19, 1863, in Dowdey and Manarin, *Wartime Papers of Lee*, 438.

2. Jones, *Rebel War Clerk's Diary*, 2:114, 118.

3. Rafuse, *Robert E. Lee and the Fall of the Confederacy*, 129–131; Grimsley, "Surviving Military Revolution."

4. Younger, *Inside the Confederate Government*, 119.

5. Jones, *Rebel War Clerk's Diary*, 2:314. Georgia authorities complained about payment for sugar seized by the commissary general. In addition, administration officials urged Lee to use the Subsistence Bureau to impress supplies. The general pushed back, arguing that such measures should be carried out by the War Department, not by officers and their combat units. Impressment, he warned, would encourage "concealment and waste" and deter farmers from "producing full and proper crops." Lee to Seddon, November 19 and 20, 1863, ORA 29(2):837–839; Northrop to Lee, November 22, 1863, ibid., 843; Lee to Northrop, December 7, 1863, ibid., 862; Lee to Kemper, January 29, 1864, in Dowdey and Manarin, *Wartime Papers of Lee*, 663.

6. Lawton to Lee, October 12, 1863, ORA 29(2):784–785. In November, the government put contracts in motion to import 3 million pounds of bacon. Goff, *Confederate Supply*, 177; Wise, *Lifeline of the Confederacy*, 145. Railroad administrators cannibalized secondary roads to provide iron for the overburdened principal lines. Freeman, *R. E. Lee*, 3:248–249.

7. S. B. French, December 8, 1863, ORA, series 4, 2:960.

8. Lawton to Lee, October 12, 1863, ORA 29(2):784–785; Lee to Lawton, January 30, 1864, ORA 33:1131–1132.

9. Lee to Northrop, January 5, 1864, ORA 33:1064–1065. See also Lee to Jones, January 5, 1864, ibid., 1065–1066.

10. Lee to Davis, January 11, 1864, ORA 33:1076–1080 (including detailed tables of recent meat shipments). A week later, Lee wrote to Lawton again about the shortage of shoes and blankets, a problem that had caused "much suffering" and impaired efficiency in his army. Lee to Lawton, January 18, 1864, ibid., 1093. Lee's wife, from her wheelchair in Richmond, marshaled her daughters to knit socks for the troops. Lee to his wife, October 28, 1863, March 19, 1864, in Dowdey and Manarin, *Wartime Papers of Lee*, 616, 680.

11. Lee to Northrop, January 5, 1864, ORA 33:1064–1065. Lee also groused that the Army of Northern Virginia was apparently the only one forced to reduce rations.

12. Freeman, *R. E. Lee*, 3:252. Lee also looked to his own men to conduct raids and collect foodstuffs from areas under the enemy's control. See Lee to Early, December 22, 1863, ORA 29(2):889.

13. Lee to Seddon, January 22, 1864, ORA 33:1113–1114; Lee to Stuart, December 27, 1863, ORA 29(2):892 (reporting increases in the Army of the Potomac).

14. Lee concluded his letter to Davis with a postscript about his efforts to address the supply situation elsewhere and his fear that no meat would be available for further operations. Lee to Davis, January 2, 1864, ORA 33:1061. Lee recommended two brigades for the operation: Seth Barton's, which was already at Kinston and attached to Pickett's department, and an additional brigade from his own army. Ibid.

15. Lee to Pickett, January 20, 1864, ORA 33:1102–1103. Lee predicted the expedition would have "the happiest effect" on the people in North Carolina. Rumors in late De-

cember warned of substantial Union operations in North Carolina, and news of Wild's raid stirred anxiety in Virginia. George E. Pickett, still in charge of the Department of North Carolina, recommended that all slaves in areas under Union control "be brought back within our lines," and on December 31, he warned of a raid planned against Suffolk. Pickett to Cooper, December 15 and 31, 1863, *ORA* 29(2):872, 897. From Wilmington, William Whiting, who frequently requested more troops, continued to warn Richmond about impending enemy attacks against his post. Whiting to Cooper, December 21 and 28, 1863, ibid., 887–888, 892.

16. The source of Lee's information about New Bern is unclear. Later, it was rumored that Brigadier General Seth Barton, stationed near Kinston the previous fall, had reported that New Bern was "slenderly garrisoned," Union forces had become "careless," and the "fortifications were of an uneven, trifling character." Edward Cook Barnes to Mother, February 9, 1864, Barnes Family Papers, University of Virginia. One postwar account suggests in passing that President Davis's aide John Taylor Wood visited Lee's headquarters and suggested the attack. *Daily Journal*, April 7, 1887. Lee himself indicated he received information from Hoke. Lee to Pickett, January 20, 1864, *ORA* 33:1102.

17. Lee to Davis, January 2, 1864, *ORA* 33:1061.

18. Bishir, *North Carolina Architecture*, 84.

19. Cecelski, *Fire of Freedom*, 64–65.

20. Browning, *Shifting Loyalties*, 17.

21. Lee to Davis, January 2, 1864, *ORA* 33:1061.

22. Moore, *Rebellion Record*, 8:361. In January, a Raleigh paper noted that the counties along the Albemarle Sound near Plymouth and Roanoke Island constituted "a rich country . . . one of the most important sources of meat supplies that is now accessible to our armies." *Daily State Journal*, January 19, 1864.

23. Letter from "Roanoke," *Weekly State Journal*, January 12, 1864; *Wilmington Journal*, January 7, 1864.

24. Ruffin to Seddon, February 8, 1864, *ORA*, series 4, 3:88.

25. The Raleigh and Gaston line also connected the Carolina interior to Weldon. Burke, *Wilmington & Weldon Railroad*, 125–126.

26. See Black, *Railroads of the Confederacy*.

27. Pickett to Cooper, January 6, 1864, *ORA* 33:1067–1068.

28. Lee to Pickett, January 20, 1864, *ORA* 33:1102.

29. *Charleston Mercury*, February 19, 1864 (reprint from the *Richmond Dispatch*, February 10, 1864).

30. *Semi-Weekly Messenger*, May 16, 1905.

31. Evans, *Confederate Military History*, 4:219.

32. Davis to Lee, January 4, 1864, *ORA* 33:1064.

33. Union Jack, "Cutting out the *Underwriter*," 215; *Richmond Dispatch*, March 13, 1898.

34. Davis to Wood, January 6, 1864, scrapbook, John Taylor Wood Papers, SHC, UNC.

35. Elliott, *Ironclad of the Roanoke*, 119.

36. Hinds, *Hunt for the Albemarle*, 92. See also Burke, *Wilmington & Weldon Railroad*.

37. Cooke to Vance, January 21, 1863, Vance Letter Book, Zebulon Vance Papers, NCOAH.

38. Mallory to Lynch, February 13, 1863, *ORA* 18:875; Price, "North Carolina Railroads during the Civil War," 298–309; Hinds, *Hunt for the Albemarle*, 92. By December 1863, Lynch informed Governor Vance that he had sent 435,000 pounds of "old rails" to Atlanta and 125,000 pounds to Richmond, and the plates had begun to arrive. Elliott, *Ironclad of the Roanoke*, 148.

39. Lynch to Vance, October 21, 1863, Vance Papers, NCOAH, and Zebulon Vance Papers (microfilm ed.), LOC.

40. Elliott, "Career of the Ram *Albemarle*," 419; Elliott, *Ironclad of the Roanoke*, 116.

41. Vance to Mallory, November 28, 1863, in Mobley, *Papers of Zebulon Baird Vance*, 2:330. Lynch also mandated the vessel's launch before the holes for its propeller shafts had been bored through the hull, causing more complications. Hinds, *Hunt for the Albemarle*, 106–107; Cooke to Vance, January 28, 1864, and Elliott to Vance, January 27, 1864, Vance Papers, NCOAH and LOC.

42. Edmondston, *Journal of Secesh Lady*, 482. The dissatisfaction with Lynch increased. In November 1863, Vance complained directly to Mallory. Vance to Mallory, November 28, 1863, in Mobley, *Papers of Zebulon Baird Vance*, 2:330. With copies of Vance's letter to Mallory in hand, Lynch responded by simultaneously seeking to "preserve harmony" among all parties involved and maintaining his harsh criticism of Elliott's efforts on the ironclad. Mallory tried to smooth over matters and expressed support for Lynch, but the problems remained. Lynch to Vance, December 4, 1863, and Mallory to Vance, December 11, 1863, in Mobley, *Papers of Zebulon Baird Vance*, 2:336, 339–341.

43. Still, "Career of the Ironclad 'Neuse,'" 5.

44. Elliott, "Career of the Ram *Albemarle*," 420–421.

45. Vouchers paid in early 1864 reveal that the boat's steam engines had been hauled aboard in late 1863. Elliott, *Ironclad of the Roanoke*, 138–139 (citing Halifax Yard, Confederate Subject File, Microfilm M-1901, RG 45, NARA). Postwar accounts differ on the source of the engines; one suggests they came from a sawmill. See *Commonwealth*, May 13, 1897. Wilson, *Ironclads in Action*, 1:107, says the engines were obtained from the Tredegar Works in Richmond.

46. Union Jack, "Cutting out the *Underwriter*," 215.

47. Ransom to Pickett, December 30, 1863, *ORA* 29(2):895; returns for Pickett's command, December 31, 1863, ibid., 906–907; Cooper, third endorsement, January 8, 1864, *ORA* 33:1070.

48. Jones, *Rebel War Clerk's Diary*, 2:131.

49. Pickett found himself competing for resources with William Whiting, the Wilmington commander. In response to Whiting's request, the War Department announced in early January the transfer of Thomas Clingman's North Carolina brigade from Virginia to Wilmington. Returns, *ORA* 29(2):907; Whiting to Cooper, January 4 and 6, 1864, *ORA* 33:1064, 1069.

50. The issue involved the transfer of Thomas Clingman's North Carolina brigade.

During the exchange, Pickett noted that Clingman was "quite anxious not to go back" to the state. Pickett to Cooper, January 8, 1864, ORA 33:1073. For more on this controversy between Whiting and Pickett, see Pickett to Cooper, January 6, 1864, ibid., 1067–1068; Barton to Pickett, January 5, 1864, ibid., 1068–1069; Whiting to Cooper, January 4, 1864, ibid., 1064 ("J. D. Endorsement"); J. A. S. endorsement, January 8, 1864, ibid., 1068; Cooper to Pickett, January 8, 1864, ibid., 1072.

51. Cooper to Pickett, January 9, 1864, ORA 33:1074.

52. Lee, "Fourth Endorsement," January 12, 1864, ORA 33:1070. After a confusing exchange of dispatches, Secretary Seddon eventually ordered Kemper's brigade to "Wilmington or such other point as General Whiting may indicate." Seddon to Pickett, January 16, 1864, ORA 33:1092; Pickett to Cooper, January 14, 1864, ibid., 1090–1092.

53. Lee to Dear Mary, January 15, 1864, in Dowdey and Manarin, *Wartime Papers of Lee*, 652.

Chapter 4. Grant's Suffolk Plan

1. Halleck to Grant, January 8, 1864, ORA 32(2):40–42.

2. Simon, *Papers of Ulysses S. Grant*, 10:40–41.

3. Sumner, *Diary of Cyrus B. Comstock*, 252 (January 18, 1864). A draft of Grant's plan, probably penned by Comstock and Smith, was sold at auction in 1950. See *Autograph Letters Manuscripts and Documents*, 124.

4. Grant to Halleck, January 19, 1864, ORA 33:394–395. For further analysis of Grant's raiding strategy, see Beringer et al., *Why the South Lost the Civil War*, 309–317; Hattaway and Jones, *How the North Won*, 501–515; Jones, *Civil War Command and Strategy*, 181–186.

5. Grant to Halleck, January 19, 1864, ORA 33:394–395.

6. John Foster, who had made ambitious plans for North Carolina in 1862, recommended a different approach (one he had recommended to Halleck earlier), urging Grant to ascend the James River and capture Petersburg before proceeding south into North Carolina. Major General George Thomas, then in Chattanooga but a native of southeastern Virginia, recommended that the proposed expedition begin at Smithfield, Virginia, and head to Raleigh via Sussex Court-House and Hicksford, near the North Carolina border, thus avoiding several difficult crossings. Foster to Halleck, February 24, 1864, ORA 31(1):285–286; Foster to Halleck, February 26, 1864, ORA 33:602–604; Thomas to Grant, January 30, 1864, ORA 32(2):264; Foster to Halleck, October 8, 1863, ORA 29(2):267.

7. Halleck to Grant, February 17, 1864, ORA 32(2):411–413. Halleck had used nearly identical language in a dispatch to Edwin Stanton in 1862, related to matters in Tennessee. Halleck to Stanton, April 26, 1862, ORA 10(2):128–129 ("we are now at the enemy's throat, and cannot release our great grasp to pare his toe nails").

8. Halleck to Grant, February 17, 1864, ORA 32(2):411–413.

9. See Browning, *From Cape Charles to Cape Fear*, 97.

10. Lee to Foster, April 17, 1863, ORN 9:688–689; Lee to Welles, May 1, 1863, ibid., 689–690.

11. Foster to Lee, April 22, 1863, ORA 18:247–249.

12. See Lee to Foster, April 17 and May 1, 1863, ORN 9:688–690. See also Boynton, *History of the Navy during the Rebellion*, 2:495.

13. Ensminger to My Dear, January 11, 1863, in Ensminger, *Letters to Lanah*, 16. A Vermonter stationed there described it as "about the size of Rutland . . . a beautiful place, decidedly the prettiest Southern town I have seen." Ripley, *Vermont General*, 163. Bachelor Creek, the spelling that appears on modern maps, is used in this study, rather than the common nineteenth-century variations such as Bachelder's, Batchelders, or Batchelor's.

14. Chapin, *Memorandum and Journal of Samuel Chapin*, 117.

15. Merrill, *Records of the 24th Independent Battery*, 193.

16. Palmer to Foster, February 19, 1864, ORA 33:577; Hess, *Field Armies and Fortifications in the Civil War*, 203–204.

17. *New York Herald*, December 2, 1863, in describing Butler's inspection of North Carolina, noted that "a fine bridge . . . spans the Trent, over which not only the railroad crosses, but it has been widened so as to accommodate the immense hauling of wood and stores."

18. Moore, *Rebellion Record*, 8:358.

19. Chapin, *Memorandum and Journal of Samuel Chapin*, 66–67.

20. Derby, *Bearing Arms in the Twenty-Seventh Massachusetts*, 106–107; Burlingame, *History of the Fifth Regiment of Rhode Island Heavy Artillery*, 181.

21. Brown, *Signal Corps*, 423–424; *New York Herald*, December 2, 1863; Plum, *Military Telegraph during the Civil War*, 2:33; Knox to Stager, Signal Department, District of N.C., May 12, 1864, RG 393, NARA.

22. Fox, *Confidential Correspondence of Gustavus Vasa Fox*, 2:225–226.

23. Hoehling, *Thunder at Hampton Roads*, 6.

24. Lee to Welles, August 17, 1863, ORN 9:162; Roberts, *Now for the Contest*, 143–155; Welles to Stanton, September 17, 1863, ORN 9:202; Tucker, *Civil War Naval Encyclopedia*, 1:338.

In September 1863, Secretary of the Navy Welles raised the issue of ironclads with Secretary of War Edwin Stanton, warning that wooden boats could not compete with ironclads. At least one shallow-draft ironclad, the *Keokuk*, was in operation well before 1864. An unusual vessel with a turtle-back shape and partially armored sides, the *Keokuk* was severely damaged in February 1863 off Hatteras Inlet on its way to support operations off Charleston. It was destroyed several weeks later in action against Fort Sumter's guns.

25. Letter from Hand, June 16, 1863, and Dix to Halleck, June 18, 1863, Letters Received by the Adjutant General, 1861–1870, RG 94, NARA.

26. Denny, *Wearing the Blue in the Twenty-Fifth Mass. Volunteer Infantry*, 248.

27. See Reid, *Freedom for Themselves*, 46.

28. Hazard Stevens to O. B. Ireland, April 29, 1863, Ireland Papers, DMRL; Gordon, *Broken Regiment*, 304 n. 96.

29. Peck report, ORA 33:288; Hall and Hall, *Cayuga in the Field*, 193.

30. Peck to Foster, August 20, 1863, ORA 29(2):81. In August 1863, Peck also learned from Admiral Lee about reduced naval support in his department and expressed concern

that enemy batteries placed across the Neuse "would make this position very uncomfort-able." Peck improved the water-facing side of Fort Spinola south of the Trent and constructed a work on the point across the river. Peck to Foster, August 25, 1863, ibid., 100–101.

Chapter 5. On to New Bern

1. Lee to Davis, January 20, 1864, ORA 33:1101–1102.

2. Lee to Pickett, January 20, 1864, ORA 33:1102–1103.

3. Hamilton, "General Robert F. Hoke and His Military Career," Robert F. Hoke Papers, SHC, UNC.

4. For Hoke's 1862 tour of New Bern defenses, see Clark, *Histories of the Several Regiments*, 1:8. University of North Carolina historian J. G. de Roulhac Hamilton wrote in his 1919 state history: "Acting upon a plan of General Robert F. Hoke, whom he called into consulta-tion, an attack on New Bern was undertaken." Hamilton, *History of North Carolina*, 23–24. In a speech given in the 1950s, Hamilton asserted that Hoke, concerned about dissatisfaction in North Carolina, submitted to Lee "a carefully prepared plan" for New Bern's capture that "was approved most heartily and authorized." Hamilton, "General Robert F. Hoke and His Military Career," Robert F. Hoke Papers.

5. Lee to Pickett, January 20, 1864, ORA 33:1102. Lee's report indicated that Hoke had "recently returned from a visit to that country, and it is mainly upon his information that my opinion has been formed."

6. Hamilton, *History of North Carolina*, 23. Several accounts point to Hoke's role in plan-ning the operation. See Clara Boyd to "Mrs. Carter," February 23, 1864, David Miller Carter Papers, SHC, UNC ("Gen. Hoke was the . . . spirit of the expedition and the secret was admirably kept"); recollections of Thomas Kenan, *Farmer and the Mechanic*, May 16, 1905; account by Victor S. Bryant, *Farmer and the Mechanic*, February 4, 1913; recollections of "Private A. N. V.," *Evening Visitor*, March 6, 1894. Lee's own January 20 dispatch appears to reveal Hoke's involvement. Discussing the importance of Wood's naval effort, Lee wrote, "it was by aid from the water that I expected Hoke to be mainly assisted." By mentioning Hoke's name instead of Pickett's, Lee may have revealed much about the young general's intended role. Lee to Davis, January 20, 1864, ORA 33:1101–1102.

7. Lee to Pickett, January 20, 1864, ORA 33:1101–1102; Pickett to His Wife, February 1864, Arthur Crew Inman Papers, John Hay Library, Brown University. Lee directed Whit-ing at Wilmington to send troops stationed north of Cape Fear to threaten "the enemy's positions at Morehead City." Lee to Whiting, January 20, 1864, ORA 33:1103.

8. Lee wrote to Quartermaster A. R. Lawton, telling him to arrange for the transfer of Hoke's brigade from Gordonsville through Richmond to Petersburg. Lee to Lawton, January 20, 1864, ORA 33:1104.

9. The guns and ammunition would travel from Richmond and Petersburg by railroad, while the horses would move "by the common route." Lee to Pickett, January 20, 1864, ORA 33:1102–1103; Lee to Whiting, January 20, 1864, ibid., 1103 (directing Whiting to send troops to Morehead).

10. Lee to Pickett, January 20, 1864, ORA 33:1102–1103.

11. Pickett report, ORA 33:93. Colonel Wood and his party arrived at Kinston on Saturday night and proceeded down the river on Sunday.

12. Lee to Wood, January 20, 1864, ORA 33:1104.

13. Lee to Davis, January 20, 1864, ORA 33:1101–1102.

14. Lee to Whiting, January 20, 1864, ORA 33:1103.

15. Lee to Hoke, January 20, 1864, ORA 33:1103–1104. Lee directed Hoke to "take some convenient position" in the state to gather recruits for his depleted regiments after completing the "business" at New Bern.

16. Lee to Pickett, January 20, 1864, ORA 33:1102–1103.

17. *Daily State Journal*, January 16, 1864. The article pointed to Fred and Ruben White as the "ringleaders of this lawless band of desperados," who had been uncanny in their ability to surprise and capture Confederate pickets.

18. Smith, "Recollections of Capt. John G. Smith," 295. See a similar account by Smith in *Wilmington Morning Star*, June 10, 1914.

19. Portions of Smith's account, prepared decades after the war, were no doubt embellished or simply distorted by a hazy memory. Smith, "Recollections of Capt. John G. Smith," 295.

20. Reminiscences of William G. Morton in *Times Dispatch*, April 6, 1913. His charges included a "Mrs. Taylor" looking for her wounded son in Union-controlled Washington, as well as two Raleigh women headed for New Jersey, where they were part owners of a piano business.

21. Barton report, ORA 33:97–100.

22. Martin report, ORA 33:84–86; *Charlotte Democrat*, February 23, 1864 (letter reprinted from the *Wilmington Journal*).

23. Hoke report, ORA 33:95–97. Montgomery Corse and three of his Virginia regiments had spent a frigid January in Tennessee, supporting James Longstreet's unsuccessful operations there against Ambrose Burnside. Returns for December 31, 1863, ORA 29(2):908; Cooper to Longstreet, January 20, 1864, ORA 32(2):579 (Corse's brigade "needed for an emergency"); Longstreet to Cooper, January 21, 1864, ibid., 597 (regarding Corse's move),

24. The expedition included Major John Read's 38th Battalion of artillery. His batteries departed from Petersburg for North Carolina. The battalion, which numbered about 300 men and officers, included the Richmond Fayette Artillery, Caskie's (Hampden) Battery, Stribling's (Fauquier) Battery, and Blount's (Lynchburg) Battery. *Richmond Dispatch*, March 28, 1897; Gaines, "Fayette Artillery," 288; February 1864 returns for Department of North Carolina, ORA 33:1201; Hoke report, ibid., 95–97.

25. The Georgia regiment had been assigned to Hoke's brigade earlier in the war. When he visited the regiment's camp to deliver the news, "loud, lusty cheers rent the air when we found that we were off for a frolic with 'Our Bob.'" Thomas, *History of the Doles-Cook Brigade*, 358; W. J. Pfohl to C. T. Pfohl, February 9, 1864, Christian Thomas Pfohl Papers, SHC, UNC.

26. The six infantry brigades gathering at Kinston totaled about 10,000 men. Hoke's brigade contained about 1,200. Of the four Hoke regiments, only the 21st North Carolina

retained adequate strength in January. Sherrill, *21st North Carolina Infantry*, 290 n. 13 (citing monthly report of Hoke's brigade, December 9, 1863, entry 118, box 1, RG 109, NARA). December inspection reports tallied the following numbers present for duty: Terry's brigade, 1,256 men and 98 officers; Barton's brigade, 1,300 men and 84 officers; Corse's brigade, 1,324 men and 95 officers; Clingman's brigade, 1,930 men and 145 officers; Ransom's entire brigade (not all of which was included in the expedition), 2,589 men and 152 officers; 67th North Carolina (Whitford), 512 men and 26 officers. Returns for Department of North Carolina, December 31, 1863 (10,931 men present for duty in the entire department), *ORA* 33:1201–1203 and 29(2):904–908. Official records for Wilmington suggest that Martin brought about 2,000 men from his brigade on the expedition. Those men, coupled with cavalry and artillery, probably increased his total by several hundred. See January 1864 returns, *ORA* 33:1138; February 1864 returns (2,700 total effectives in brigade—not all regiments participated in the expedition), ibid., 1202; Barney report (estimating Martin's force at 1,700), ibid., 81. Union reports estimated Pickett's force at 15,000 men, and this number is often repeated in accounts of the expedition. See Palmer report, *ORA* 33:53; Peck report, ibid., 60.

27. Jones, *Rebel War Clerk's Diary*, 2:133.

28. Hoke report, *ORA* 33:95–97.

29. A displeased Barton, who reportedly referred to his men as "rags and thiefs," turned out the entire brigade in late December for an inspection that uncovered an array of stolen goods. James Booker to Chloe Unity Blair, January 1, 1864 (the soldiers don't like "the N.C. nor the N.C. don't like the Va. soldiers"), John and James Booker Collection, Library of Virginia. See also Gregory, *53rd Virginia Infantry*, 68.

30. Barton report, *ORA* 33:97–100.

31. W. J. Pfohl to C. T. Pfohl, February 9, 1864, Pfohl Papers.

32. J. Randall to Darling Kate, January 30, 1864, James Ryder Randall Papers, SHC, UNC.

33. A. W. Mangum to his sister, February 1, 1864, A. W. Mangum Papers, SHC, UNC.

34. See *Daily Progress*, January 30, 1864; *Fayetteville Observer*, February 1, 1864.

35. At some point, General Martin traveled from Wilmington to confer with Hoke about the upcoming operation. Martin report, *ORA* 33:84–86.

36. Hoke report, *ORA* 33:95–97; letter from A. H. P., *Daily Dispatch*, February 8, 1864.

37. Barton report, *ORA* 33:97–100; Hoke report, ibid., 95–97; letter from A. H. P., *Daily Dispatch*, February 8, 1864; Gregory, *53rd Virginia Infantry*, 48.

38. Roulhac, "Forty-Ninth Regiment," 135; Barton report, *ORA* 33:97–100; Barnes to "Dear Mother," February 9, 1864, Edward Cook Barnes Papers, University of Virginia.

39. Hoke report, *ORA* 33:95–97; *Public Ledger*, February 20, 1873; Pickett report, *ORA* 33:92–94.

40. Wallace, *3rd Virginia Infantry*, 56; Warfield, *Manassas to Appomattox*, 139.

41. Pickett report, *ORA* 33:92–94. Corse's regiments arrived in Kinston on Saturday. Hoke report, *ORA* 33:95–97; Ludwig, "Eighth Regiment," 396; Krick, *30th Virginia Infantry* (Corse regiment); Gaines, "Fayette Artillery," 288; Clingman report, *ORA* 33:101–102; letter from A. H. P., *Daily Dispatch*, February 8, 1864; Paris diary, January 30, 1864, John Paris

Papers, SHC, UNC. The 8th North Carolina from Clingman's brigade arrived by rail during the morning.

42. It is unclear why Pickett (or perhaps Hoke) chose to split up Corse's brigade between Hoke's and Dearing's columns, but the decision may have reflected the need to balance the columns' strength. Corse personally accompanied Hoke's column. A veteran of the Mexican War and an Alexandria, Virginia, native, Corse was a "good man and a brave officer," according to one description. He led a brigade in Lee's army for most of the war and managed to avoid distinguishing himself by either stunning success or catastrophic failure. His men had several good-natured nicknames for him, including "Old Puss in the Boots," "Old Grand Dad," and "Jack-of-Clubs." Burrell, *History of Prince Edward County, Virginia*, 145; Manarin, *15th Virginia Infantry*, 54–55.

43. Hoke report, ORA 33:95–97; Clingman report, ibid., 101–102.

44. Henry T. Guion journal, William Hoke Papers, SHC, UNC; Roe, *Fifth Regiment Massachusetts*, 234; Gaines, "Fayette Artillery," 288.

45. Pickett report, ORA 33:92–94. Pickett apparently shared the plans with his wife, writing, "I enclose Marse Robert's letter of the 22nd in regard to my proposed plans." Pickett to His Wife, January 22, 1864, Arthur Crew Inman Papers, John Hay Library, Brown University. Pickett's reference to Lee's orders (and the fact that he shared them with his wife) was omitted from his published letters. See Pickett, *Heart of a Soldier*, 162.

46. Testimony of W. G. Lewis, in US Congress, *Murder of Union Soldiers in North Carolina*, 75.

47. During the New Bern operation, Pickett's wife stayed with the family of Brigadier General Matt W. Ransom on their plantation, Verona, on the Roanoke River near Weldon. Pickett, *What Happened to Me*, 135; Marlow, *Matt W. Ransom*, 85.

48. Raphael Jacob Moses autobiography, 1892, SHC, UNC.

49. Pickett, *Heart of a Soldier*, 3.

50. Sorrel, *Recollections of a Confederate Staff Officer*, 54.

51. See Coleman, *Pig War*.

52. Gordon, *General George E. Pickett*, 118–119; Gordon, "Let the People See the Old Life as It Was."

53. *Daily Progress*, September 19, 1863; *Progress-Index*, August 6, 1961 (reminiscences of G. E. Stowers). The Picketts lived in the Gilliam residence at Petersburg.

54. See Robertson, *Back Door to Richmond*, 44–46.

55. Morgan, *Personal Reminiscences of the War*, 178. Morgan was in the 11th Virginia.

56. Diary of Captain Henry A. Chambers, January 31, 1864, Henry A. Chambers Papers, SHC, UNC.

57. *Raleigh Daily Confederate*, February 13, 1864 (reprinted from the *Richmond Sentinel*).

58. *Wilmington Journal*, February 18, 1864; *Tarboro Southerner*, June 11, 1864.

59. Hoke report, ORA 33:95–97; Guion journal.

60. Members of the 56th North Carolina filtered out in advance. Graham, "Fifty-Sixth Regiment," 333; letter from "D" (43rd North Carolina), *Charlotte Democrat*, February 23, 1864; letter from A. H. P., *Daily Dispatch*, February 8, 1864; Hoke report, ORA 33:95–97.

61. Gaines, "Fayette Artillery," 288.

62. Letter from A. H. P., *Daily Dispatch*, February 8, 1864; department returns, January 31, 1864, ORA 33:484–485.

63. Palmer, General Orders No. 12, ORA 33:425.

64. Warner, *Generals in Blue*, 357–358.

65. Returns from January 31, 1864 (3,518 officers and men present for duty), ORA 33:485; Hall and Hall, *Cayuga in the Field*, 193.

66. Whiting to Cooper, January 24, 1864, ORA 33:1119; Humphreys to Cullum, January 24, 1864, ibid., 406 (intelligence that Barton's and Hunton's brigades had passed through Petersburg); Palmer to Davis, January 29, 1864, ibid., 23 (Hoke's mission was to round up deserters).

67. Moore, *Rebellion Record*, 8:358; *New York Times*, February 3, 1864.

68. In January, the 103rd Pennsylvania conducted two expeditions into Hertford County, destroying large quantities of pork, sugar, and salt. On January 29, soldiers from Plymouth ventured up the Cashie River to Windsor, where they descended on a rebel camp and captured horses, mules, wagons, clothing, and ammunition. Palmer to Davis, January 29, 1864, ORA 33:23; Griffin to Vance, February 4, 1864 (Unionist sentiment in Bertie County), Zebulon Vance Papers (microfilm ed.), LOC; Griffin report, ORA 33:107; Dickey, *History of the 103d Regiment*, 103. See also Foster to Denny, January 19, 1864, Foster to Palmer, January 21, 1864, and Palmer to Davis, January 29, 1864, Letters Sent, New Bern Sub-District, Records of Subdistricts, RG 393, NARA.

Chapter 6. Bachelor Creek

1. *Newburgh Journal*, undated clipping, Civil War Newspaper Clipping Collection, 132nd Infantry, NYSMM.

2. Chapin, *Memorandum and Journal of Samuel Chapin*, 90–97.

3. "The Battle of Bachelor's Creek," undated newspaper clipping, Civil War Era Scrapbook, ECU.

4. Chapin, *Memorandum and Journal of Samuel Chapin*, 90–97.

5. Williams, "Fifty-Fourth Regiment," 274; John Paris diary, February 1, 1864, John Paris Papers, SHC, UNC (Paris claims the march began at 2:00 a.m.); account of Bohemian, *Daily Dispatch*, February 12, 1864.

6. Hoke report, ORA 33:95–97; "Sketch of the Life of W. G. Lewis," SLNC; letter from "D" (43rd North Carolina), *Charlotte Democrat*, February 23, 1864; Pickett report, ORA 33:92–94; letter from A. H. P., *Daily Dispatch*, February 8, 1864.

7. Hoke report, ORA 33:95–97; Thomas Stephen Kenan, "Sketch of the Forty-Third Regiment, North Carolina Troops," 10, SLNC; Sherrill, *21st North Carolina Infantry*, 298; account of Frank Salter (12th New York Cavalry), *Dakota County Herald*, October 23, 1913. In 1864, the Neuse Road crossed Bachelor Creek at a spot several hundred yards north (and downstream) of the location where modern-day State Route 55 crosses the creek. See Newbern Quadrangle Map, US Geological Survey, 1901.

8. "Sketch of the Life of W. G. Lewis"; Kenan, "Sketch of the Forty-Third Regiment, North Carolina Troops," 10.

9. Letter from "D," *Charlotte Democrat*, February 23, 1864.

10. Beyer and Keydel, *Deeds of Valor*, 1:307; Smith report, ORA 33:73–76.

11. Hall and Hall, *Cayuga in the Field*, 194.

12. *Annual Report of the State Historian of the State of New York*, 2:121.

13. *Baltimore Sun*, February 8, 1864.

14. Dispatch 944 (4:00 p.m.), Bachelor Creek Signal Station, Army and District of North Carolina, RG 393, NARA.

15. Smith report, ORA 33:73–76.

16. "Headquarters Out Post, 132d N.Y. Infantry," letter from "E. A. J." dated February 10, 1864, *Newburgh Journal*, Civil War Newspaper Clipping Collection, NYSMM.

17. Entry for "Haring, A. P.," New York Civil War Muster Roll Abstracts, 1861–1900, New York State Archives; Whittemore, *History of Montclair Township, State of New Jersey*, 291–293.

18. "The Battle of Bachelor's Creek," Civil War Era Scrapbook, ECU; Palmer to Davis, February 20, 1864, ORA 33:57–59; *Dakota County Herald*, October 23, 1913.

19. Whittemore, *History of Montclair Township, State of New Jersey*, 291–293.

20. Beyer and Keydel, *Deeds of Valor*, 1:307.

21. "The Battle of Bachelor's Creek," Civil War Era Scrapbook, ECU; Whittemore, *History of Montclair Township, State of New Jersey*, 291–293.

22. "Headquarters Out Post, 132d N.Y. Infantry," *Newburgh Journal*, Civil War Newspaper Clipping Collection, NYSMM.

23. Gaines, "Fayette Artillery," 288; Smith report, ORA 33:73–76.

24. According to one account, the gunners could not manage to depress their pieces sufficiently to hit the target. Letter from "D," *Charlotte Democrat*, February 23, 1864.

25. Henry T. Guion journal, William Hoke Papers, SHC, UNC.

26. "The Battle of Bachelor's Creek," Civil War Era Scrapbook, ECU.

27. Letter from A. H. P., *Daily Dispatch*, February 8, 1864; W. J. Pfohl to C. T. Pfohl, February 9, 1864, Christian Thomas Pfohl Papers, SHC, UNC; Hoke report, ORA 33:95–97.

28. Burgwyn, "Clingman's Brigade," 486.

29. Ludwig, "Eighth Regiment," 396–397; Burgwyn, "Clingman's Brigade," 486; Evans, *Confederate Military History*, 4:732. In March, Major General Whiting at Wilmington named one of the Oak Island batteries after Colonel Shaw, who commanded at Roanoke Island.

30. Letter from "D," *Charlotte Democrat*, February 23, 1864. As Shaw's body was borne to the rear, Lieutenant Colonel James Whitson assumed command of the regiment. Clingman report, ORA 33:101–102 (stating that Shaw was within 200 or 300 yards of the creek); Guion journal (stating that Shaw was killed at 4:00 a.m. about 600 yards from the bridge).

31. *New York Times*, January 1, 1897.

32. Unidentified newspaper clipping, Civil War Newspaper Clipping Collection, NYSMM.

33. Claassen to Foster, February 8, 1864, ORA 33:62–67; Salter account, *Dakota County Herald*, October 23, 1913. Claassen directed Captain Charles G. Smith to take men to Har-

ing. Company D was led by Captain Thomas B. Green. One of the company's officers, Lieutenant Cornelius Cusick, was a Tuscarora chief. Smith report, ORA 33:73–76; "The Battle of Bachelor's Creek," Civil War Era Scrapbook, ECU.

34. Upon his arrival at Haring's position, Honstain assumed command. Claassen to Foster, February 8, 1864, ORA 33:62–67; Smith report, ibid., 73–76; "The Battle of Bachelor's Creek," Civil War Era Scrapbook, ECU.

35. "Headquarters Out Post, 132d N.Y. Infantry," *Newburgh Journal*, Civil War Newspaper Clipping Collection, NYSMM. A 1901 article published in *Everybody's Magazine* contains significant detail about Haring's stand. However, based on a comparison with other sources, it seems likely that it was significantly embellished. Hovey, "How Haring Held the Bridge," 233.

36. Hall and Hall, *Cayuga in the Field*, 193.

37. In New Bern itself, crews from the 5th Rhode Island Heavy Artillery, led by Colonel Henry T. Sisson, and the 2nd Massachusetts Heavy Artillery, commanded by Major Samuel C. Oliver, manned the guns. The 17th Massachusetts stood to arms in the works south of the Trent. Kirwan, *Memorial History of the Seventeenth Regiment*, 11; Headley, *Massachusetts in the Rebellion*, 245.

38. Kirwan, *Memorial History of the Seventeenth Regiment*, 196–198.

39. *New York Times*, February 9, 1864; Moore, *Rebellion Record*, 8:358. See also Simpson to Wilson, February 4, 1864, 3:10 p.m., ORA 33:512. Palmer also wrote to Edward Harland, the commander at Washington, and urged him to organize the unarmed black men at that post. Palmer to Harland, February 2, 1864, Letters Sent, New Bern Sub-District, Records of Subdistricts, RG 393, NARA.

40. Palmer to Claassen, February 1, 1864, ORA 33:496.

41. Merrill report, ORA 33:47–48.

42. Private Robert B. Vanderhoef operated the telegraph and transmitted Claassen's messages with "promptness and correctness" throughout the morning. Another telegraph operator on the Bachelor Creek line, D. C. McGaughey, a natural daredevil, found his post overrun by the Confederate advance early in the morning and continued to transmit until his line was cut. He then slipped through the rebel lines and reached New Bern that day. Plum, *Military Telegraph during the Civil War*, 2:34.

43. Palmer to Davis, February 20, 1864, ORA 33:57–59.

44. Brown, *Signal Corps*, 423–425 (includes a signal station photograph); Merrill report, ORA 33:47.

45. Claassen to Foster, February 8, 1864, ORA 33:62–67.

46. At 6:35 a.m., Colonel Claassen ordered Savage to get his command ready, cover the Trent Road out toward Deep Gully, and send a full troop and howitzers north to help the 132nd New York. Savage sent "strong patrols" along the Trent River, including Tar Landing, Lime Kiln Landing, and Bear Grass Landing. See Savage report, 12th New York Cavalry, ORA 33:69–71; Claassen to Foster, February 8, 1864, ibid., 62–67.

47. Claassen to Foster, February 8, 1864, ORA 33:62–67. Captain David Bailey of the 99th New York was the ranking officer at the Beech Grove post, but this was apparently unknown to Claassen at the time.

48. Various Claassen dispatches, ORA 33:68; Smith report, ibid., 73–76.

49. Palmer to Davis, February 20, 1864, ORA 33:57–59; Claassen to Foster, February 8, 1864, ibid., 62–67; Smith report, ibid., 73–76; *Annual Report of the State Historian of the State of New York*, 2:121.

50. Some of Smith's force, led by Lieutenant William Wells, ventured forward to find the enemy, creeping toward Rigdon Richardson's house. Under the circumstances, the ground should have been crawling with rebels. But Wells found nothing in the darkness and went back across the small stream. Smith then recoiled his small force and was eventually pushed back by Corse's Confederates. For details of Smith's efforts, see Smith report, ORA 33:73–76; "The Battle of Bachelor's Creek," Civil War Era Scrapbook, ECU; Guion journal; Pickett report, ORA 33:92–94.

51. Letter from A. H. P., *Daily Dispatch*, February 8, 1864.

52. Hoke report, ORA 33:95–97; Guion journal. There are conflicting accounts as to the location of the flank crossing. A few suggest the Confederates crossed upstream (to the south) of the brigade. See Moore, *Rebellion Record*, 8:358; Paris diary, Paris Papers. In the author's opinion, shared by others who have considered the issue, Mercer's crossing was downstream (north) of the bridge. See Sherrill, *21st North Carolina Infantry*, 298–299.

53. Letter from "D," *Charlotte Democrat*, February 23, 1864.

54. At Bull Run in 1861, Mercer drew criticism for endangering the men under his command. During the Peninsula Campaign, his drinking led to his arrest. Thomas, *History of the Doles-Cook Brigade*, 349; Allardice, *Confederate Colonels*, 279.

55. W. J. Pfohl to C. T. Pfohl, February 9, 1864, Pfohl Papers.

56. Thomas, *History of the Doles-Cook Brigade*, 358; Guion journal (stating that the crossing was made between 7:00 and 8:00 a.m.); Salter account, *Dakota County Herald*, October 23, 1913.

57. Letter from A. H. P., *Daily Dispatch*, February 8, 1864.

58. Thomas, *History of the Doles-Cook Brigade*, 358; Guion journal.

59. "Sketch of the Life of W. G. Lewis"; "Another 'Old" Confederate," 171; letter from "D," *Charlotte Democrat*, February 23, 1864.

60. Hoke report, ORA 33:95–97.

61. Gaines, "Fayette Artillery," 288.

62. Letter from A. H. P., *Charlotte Democrat*, February 16, 1864 (from the *Richmond Dispatch*).

63. "Sketch of the Life of W. G. Lewis"; Paris diary, Paris Papers; Salter account, *Dakota County Herald*, October 23, 1913.

64. Ibid.; "The Battle of Bachelor's Creek," Civil War Era Scrapbook, ECU.

65. "Headquarters Out Post, 132d N.Y. Infantry," *Newburgh Journal*, Civil War Newspaper Clipping Collection, NYSMM.

66. Letter from "D," *Charlotte Democrat*, February 23, 1864.

67. "The Battle of Bachelor's Creek," Civil War Era Scrapbook, ECU.

68. Gaines, "Fayette Artillery," 288.

69. Letter from A. H. P., *Daily Dispatch*, February 8, 1864.

70. Letter from "D," *Charlotte Democrat*, February 23, 1864.

71. Claassen to Foster, February 8, 1864, ORA 33:62–67.

72. Claassen dispatch, February 1, 1864, ORA 33:68.

73. Claassen to Foster, February 8, 1864, ORA 33:62–67.

74. Kirwan, *Memorial History of the Seventeenth Regiment*, 197.

75. Claassen to Foster, February 8, 1864, ORA 33:62–67; Moore, *Rebellion Record*, 8:358. Moore says that Fellows arrived at around 8:00 a.m. Battery K was commanded by Captain James Angel.

76. Hall and Hall, *Cayuga in the Field*, 194; "The Battle of Bachelor's Creek," Civil War Era Scrapbook, ECU.

77. Claassen dispatch, February 1, 1864, 9:20 a.m., ORA 33:69.

78. Smith report, ORA 33:73–76.

79. *New York Times*, February 9, 1864: "Coming up to the One Hundred and Thirty-second, in an open space, the whole force was immediately formed in line of battle. The enemy also drew up in line at the same time resting his wings on either side so as to flank our forces, thus compelling another retreat, which was made in good order, firing as they retired through the woods." See also Smith report, ORA 33:73–76.

80. Whittemore, *History of Montclair Township, State of New Jersey*, 291–293.

81. Hall and Hall, *Cayuga in the Field*, 194; "Headquarters Out Post, 132nd N.Y. Infantry," *Newburgh Journal*, Civil War Newspaper Clipping Collection, NYSMM. A member of the 21st North Carolina noted that the Union line "was easily routed," but Union forces "attempted to make another stand." W. J. Pfohl to C. T. Pfohl, February 9, 1864, Pfohl Papers.

82. "The Battle of Bachelor's Creek," Civil War Era Scrapbook, ECU (includes a sketch showing battle lines arranged at "Ipoc's Farm"); Smith report, ORA 33:73–76 (noting a "vastly superior force").

83. Moore, *Rebellion Record*, 8:358; Smith report, ORA 33:73–76.

84. Hoke report, ORA 33:95–97. One rebel artillery officer wrote that the "enemy are now flying in every direction." Guion journal.

85. Guion journal; letter from A. H. P., *Daily Dispatch*, February 8, 1864.

86. *Daily Progress*, February 25, 1864; Pickett report, ORA 33:92–94.

87. Letter from A. H. P., *Daily Dispatch*, February 8, 1864.

88. W. I. Clopton to "Dear Mother," February 17, 1864, Clopton Family Papers, DMRL.

89. Hall and Hall, *Cayuga in the Field*, 194.

90. Palmer to Davis, February 20, 1864, ORA 33:57–59; Gaines, "Fayette Artillery," 288.

91. Years later, one Southern veteran credited Fellows's capture to the Fayette Artillery. Gaines, "Fayette Artillery," 288. For accounts of the withdrawal, see Claassen to Foster, February 8, 1864, ORA 33:62–67; Headley, *Massachusetts in the Rebellion*, 245; Kirwan, *Memorial History of the Seventeenth Regiment*, 198. In his February 8 report, Claassen confessed, with a measure of melodrama, that "the order to lower the colors was the only one which caused a choking sensation in me."

92. Claassen to Palmer, February 1, 1864, ORA 33:68. Claassen requested the second train at 8:25 a.m.

93. Gardner, *Record of the Service of the Forty-Fourth Massachusetts*, 200–201.

94. Wiard guns were a rarity on the Civil War battlefield. Records suggest that fewer than 100 were ever produced. Wiard, *Wiard's System of Field Artillery*, 15.

95. "The Battle of Bachelor's Creek," Civil War Era Scrapbook, ECU. Union records (ORA 33:825) indicate that the Wiard guns on the monitor were 6-inch. However, other sources clarify that they were the 6-pound version. Gardner, *Record of the Service of the Forty-Fourth Massachusetts*, 200.

96. Claassen to Foster, February 8, 1864, ORA 33:62–67. Colonel Claassen did not miss the opportunity to note that the artillerists "managed to throw some shells around myself."

97. Hoke report, ORA 33:95–97.

98. "Sketch of the Life of W. G. Lewis."

99. A member of the 21st North Carolina wrote that his unit followed the fleeing Unionists, but "on a retreat they were too fast for us." W. J. Pfohl to C. T. Pfohl, February 9, 1864, Pfohl Papers.

100. Kenan, "Sketch of the Forty-Third Regiment, North Carolina Troops," 11.

101. Clingman report, ORA 33:101–102.

102. Hall and Hall, *Cayuga in the Field*, 194.

103. Hoke and Guion believed five minutes would have made the difference. A few days after the battle, William J. Pfohl of the 21st North Carolina wrote, "We were only a few minutes too late to capture the train." W. J. Pfohl to C. T. Pfohl, February 9, 1864, Pfohl Papers; Guion journal.

104. Burgwyn, "Clingman's Brigade," 487.

105. Gaines, "Fayette Artillery," 288.

106. Ibid.; "Sketch of the Life of W. G. Lewis."

107. Burgwyn, *A Captain's War*, 119.

108. Letter from "D," *Charlotte Democrat*, February 23, 1864.

109. Hall and Hall, *Cayuga in the Field*, 194; Claassen to Foster, February 8, 1864, ORA 33:62–67. According to most accounts, Hoke's men simply failed to reach the train in time. However, veteran artillerist E. W. Gaines argued that the train never would have reached New Bern if the officer in command had "permitted one or two of the guns to have taken up position in the road, where a fair sweep could have been had." Gaines, "Fayette Artillery," 288.

110. Claassen reached New Bern at about 1:00 p.m. "The Battle of Bachelor's Creek," Civil War Era Scrapbook, ECU; Smith report, ORA 33:73–76; Claassen to Foster, February 8, 1864, ibid., 62–67; "Headquarters Out Post, 132d N.Y. Infantry," *Newburgh Journal*, Civil War Newspaper Clipping Collection, NYSMM.

111. The Georgians from Hoke's brigade had pressed forward after storming the Neuse Road blockhouse and, moving 2 or 3 miles beyond the Neuse Road bridge heading southeast, stumbled along the railroad. Kimbrough stepped forward and, through a "grand bluff," convinced the Union men to capitulate. Thomas, *History of the Doles-Cook Brigade*, 358; Ellis to his wife, February 6, 1864, Josiah Robert Peele Ellis Papers, ECU (stating that they "took a good many prisoners and horses and some artillery and negroes").

112. Claassen communicated with Savage throughout the morning. Savage report, *ORA* 33:69–71.

113. Ibid. According to one account, some of Savage's men charged at the rebels "and through them" to reach safety. Moore, *Rebellion Record*, 8:358. Once they were inside the fortifications, Savage immediately sent men back out to collect troops from the 99th New York who were reportedly still at the Red House outpost. In commenting on the events of February 1, a New Yorker stated that "the 12th New York Cavalry disgraced themselves." However, there is little evidence of this. Diary of Orlando P. Benson, 92nd New York, *Courier and Freeman*, February 4, 1925,

114. Hoke report, *ORA* 33:95–97.

115. Claassen to Foster, February 8, 1864, *ORA* 33:62–67.

116. Kirwan, *Memorial History of the Seventeenth Regiment*, 198.

117. Hall and Hall, *Cayuga in the Field*, 194–195.

118. Claassen to Foster, February 8, 1864, *ORA* 33:62–67. Claassen sent his acting quartermaster, Lieutenant Arnold Zenette, on the same mission, but Zennette was killed on the way.

119. Merrill report, *ORA* 33:47–48; Claassen to Foster, February 8, 1864, ibid., 62–67. Claassen acknowledged that he should have been more aggressive in communicating with Beech Grove.

Chapter 7. Fort Anderson and Brice's Creek

1. Pickett to Seddon, January 12, 1864, *ORA* 33:1083 (recommending Dearing for promotion); February 1864 returns for Department of North Carolina, ibid., 1201; T. G. Barham, war record, 21, Fredericksburg and Spotsylvania National Military Park.

2. Pickett report, *ORA* 33:92–94.

3. Palmer to Foster, February 19, 1864, *ORA* 33:576–577; Wallace, *3rd Virginia Infantry*, 56.

4. Palmer to Foster, February 19, 1864, *ORA* 33:577; Hess, *Field Armies and Fortifications in the Civil War*, 203–204.

5. Letter from Bohemian, *Daily Dispatch*, February 12, 1864.

6. Account of George Gift, *Public Ledger*, February 20, 1873.

7. Seth Barton Records, Unfiled Papers and Slips Belonging in Confederate Compiled Service Records, RG 109, NARA; Lee to Pickett, January 20, 1864, *ORA* 33:1102–1103. The Pollocksville, or Trenton, Road is labeled Island Creek Road on modern maps. For the purposes of this study, it is referred to as the Pollocksville Road to avoid confusion with the Trent Road, an entirely different road north that led into New Bern from the west, north of the Trent River.

8. Pickett report, *ORA* 33:92–94; Barton report, ibid., 97–99.

9. Diary of Captain Henry A. Chambers, January 24, 1864, Henry A. Chambers Papers, SHC, UNC.

10. Clarke to Mary Bayard Clarke, February 7, 1864, in Clarke, *Live Your Own Life*, 163;

Barnes to "Dear Mother," February 9, 1864, Edward Cook Barnes Papers, University of Virginia; Chambers diary, February 1, 1864.

11. Chambers diary, February 1, 1864. Barton's cavalry failed to cut the railroad and telegraph to Morehead City. Pickett report, *ORA* 33:92–94; Barton report, ibid., 97–99.

12. Chambers diary, February 1, 1864; letter from "R," *Wilmington Journal*, February 18, 1864.

13. Chambers diary, February 1, 1864.

14. Barnes to "Dear Mother," February 9, 1864, Barnes Papers; Chambers diary, February 1, 1864.

15. Lee to Pickett, January 20, 1864, *ORA* 33:1102.

16. Barton report, *ORA* 33:97–99; Lee to Pickett, January 20, 1864, ibid., 1102–1103; Aylett to Cooper, June 30, 1864, William R. Aylett Service Record, RG 109, NARA.

17. Barton report, *ORA* 33:97–99.

18. Chambers diary, February 1, 1864; Roulhac, "Forty-Ninth Regiment," 135. The skirmishers advanced toward the Federal positions under Captain Cicero Durham, the regiment's quartermaster. Barnes to "Dear Mother," February 9, 1864, Barnes Papers.

19. Letter from "R," *Wilmington Journal*, February 18, 1864.

20. Ibid.; Barton report, *ORA* 33:97–99.

21. Barnes to "Dear Mother," February 9, 1864, Barnes Papers.

22. Hall and Hall, *Cayuga in the Field*, 195. Amory, an 1851 graduate of West Point, had served in the 7th US Infantry before the war.

23. Chambers diary, February 1, 1864; Barton report, *ORA* 33:97–99.

24. Palmer to Davis, February 20, 1864, *ORA* 33:57–59; Hall and Hall, *Cayuga in the Field*, 195; letter from "R," *Wilmington Journal*, February 18, 1864.

25. In the 24th North Carolina, Colonel William J. Clarke lost one man killed from his regiment and three wounded, including Lieutenant Alexander Long. Clarke to Mary Bayard Clarke, February 7, 1864, in Clarke, *Live Your Own Life*, 163; Barton report, *ORA* 33:97–99.

26. Barton report, *ORA* 33:97–99.

27. Ibid.

28. Ibid.

29. Pickett recalled later that the men had "hardly pursued" the enemy because they were "much worn by the long night's march." Pickett report, *ORA* 33:92–94.

30. Palmer to Davis, February 20, 1864, *ORA* 33:57–59.

31. Letter from Bohemian, *Daily Dispatch*, February 12, 1864.

32. W. J. Pfohl to C. T. Pfohl, February 9, 1864, Christian Thomas Pfohl Papers, SHC, UNC.

33. Hoke report, *ORA* 33:95–97.

34. Clingman report, *ORA* 33:101–102; Burgwyn, *A Captain's War*, 119; Burgwyn, "Clingman's Brigade," 486.

35. Clingman report, *ORA* 33:101–102. Clingman was pleased with his brigade's conduct, noting it had "performed the movements ordered with as much coolness and precision as I ever saw them when on drill."

36. Letter from Bohemian, *Daily Dispatch,* February 12, 1864; Palmer to Davis, February 20, 1864, ORA 33:57–59.

37. Hall and Hall, *Cayuga in the Field,* 195.

38. Moore, *Rebellion Record,* 8:359.

39. Judson to Sisson, February 15, 1864, Letters Sent, New Bern Sub-District, Records of Subdistricts, RG 393, NARA. Not a single company from the three black regiments formed in New Bern over the past year occupied the city at the time of Hoke's attack. The 1st NCCV, which would soon be redesignated the 35th USCT, had recently left New Bern for service in Florida and would take part in the fighting at Olustee several weeks later. The 2nd NCCV was stationed at Norfolk and Portsmouth, and most of the 3rd NCCV was doing service there as well. Dyer, *Compendium of the War of the Rebellion,* 2:1472, 1720–1730.

40. Palmer to James, February 5, 1864, Letters Sent, New Bern Sub-District, Records of Subdistricts, RG 393, NARA.

41. James, *Annual Report of the Superintendent of Negro Affairs in North Carolina, 1864,* 7.

42. *New York Times,* February 9, 1864.

43. Jourdan report, ORA 33:77–81; letter from Sergeant B., *Brooklyn Daily Eagle,* February 11, 1864; Jourdan to Barney, February 1, 1864, ORA 33:496; Palmer to Jourdan, February 1, 1864, ibid. Jourdan also moved 100 men from Fort Macon to Beaufort and Morehead City to increase his numbers. Captain Nehemiah Fuller, of the 2nd Massachusetts Heavy Artillery, took command at Beaufort and distributed arms to citizens there.

44. *New York Times,* February 11, 1864.

45. Burlingame, *History of the Fifth Regiment of Rhode Island Heavy Artillery,* 189.

46. Palmer to Davis, February 1, 1864, 8:00 p.m., ORA 33:49.

47. Derby, *Bearing Arms in the Twenty-Seventh Massachusetts,* 106–107, 233.

48. Letter from Bohemian, *Daily Dispatch,* February 12, 1864.

49. Henry T. Guion journal, William Hoke Papers, SHC, UNC.

50. Bohemian, *War Songs of the South.* In addition to his work for the *Daily Dispatch,* Shepardson wrote for the *Mobile Advertiser and Register* under the name "Evelyn."

51. For a lengthy sketch of Shepardson's reporting, see Wilcox, "William G. Shepardson," 276.

52. Letter from Bohemian, *Daily Dispatch,* February 12, 1864.

53. Pickett to His Wife, February 1864, Arthur Crew Inman Papers, John Hay Library, Brown University.

54. Pickett report, ORA 33:92–94.

55. Hall and Hall, *Cayuga in the Field,* 196.

56. *Daily Progress,* February 4, 1864.

57. *Weekly Standard,* February 10, 1864. A telegram to Governor Vance from Goldsboro on February 3 stated: "Yesterday at twelve (12) o'clock Gen. Pickett within two (2) miles of Newbern ready to make the attack. Genl Hoke has captured three hundred (300) prisoners. Nothing further. All goes well." E. Warren to Vance, February 3, 1864, Zebulon Vance Papers, NCOAH, and Zebulon Vance Papers (microfilm ed.), LOC.

Chapter 8. The Underwriter

1. G. Gift to Ellen Shackleford, February 7, 1864, George Gift Papers, SHC, UNC.

2. John Taylor Wood diary, April 13, 1861, John Taylor Wood Papers, SHC, UNC.

3. Quarstein, CSS Virginia, 76–77. One of Wood's biographers suggests that the New Bern raid was, in fact, Wood's brainchild and that he shared the idea with Davis during afternoon horseback rides in the autumn of 1863. Shingleton, John Taylor Wood, 90. However, the letters between Lee and Davis, as well as the diary of Lee's aide, indicate that it was Lee's idea. Taylor to Saunders, February 2, 1864, in Tower, Lee's Adjutant, 115.

4. Shingleton, John Taylor Wood, 62–71. In the winter of 1863, Wood toured Wilmington and Charleston.

5. See Daily Dispatch, September 2, 1863.

6. Wood to Gift, January 25, 1864, ORN 9:450.

7. Several years after the war, Gift wrote of Whiting: "Poor fellow, he did us a deal of harm; and as he was killed at Fort Fisher, and had to be killed, I have often regretted that his time was put off to so late a day." Account by Gift, Public Ledger, February 18, 1873. In fact, Whiting died two months after being wounded at Fort Fisher on January 15, 1865.

8. G. Gift to Ellen Shackleford, February 7, 1864, Gift Papers.

9. Public Ledger, February 18, 1873; account of W. F. Clayton, New Berne Weekly Journal, August 16, 1904.

10. Account of Reid Whitford, New Berne Weekly Journal, August 16, 1904; Loyall, "Capture of the Underwriter," 325–333 (the article first appeared in the Virginia-Pilot, April 30, 1899).

11. Loyall, "Capture of the Underwriter," 325–333.

12. Conrad, "Capture of the USS Underwriter," 93–100.

13. G. Gift to Ellen Shackleford, February 7, 1864, Gift Papers; Loyall, "Capture of the Underwriter," 325–333; Public Ledger, February 18 and 19, 1873.

14. Loyall, "Capture of the Underwriter," 325–333. Loyall's printed account identifies the word as "Sumpter," but this is likely a typographical error.

15. Charleston Mercury, February 19, 1864 (reprint of Bohemian's account from the Daily Dispatch).

16. Conrad, "Capture of the USS Underwriter," 93–100.

17. G. Gift to Ellen Shackleford, February 7, 1864, Gift Papers. Loyall says they shoved off at 4:00 p.m. See Loyall, "Capture of the Underwriter," 325–333; Public Ledger, February 18 and 19, 1873.

18. G. Gift to Ellen Shackleford, February 7, 1864, Gift Papers; Public Ledger, February 18, 1873; Loyall, "Capture of the Underwriter," 325–333; Conrad, "Capture of the USS Underwriter," 93–100.

19. Loyall, "Capture of the Underwriter," 325–333; Public Ledger, February 18, 1873.

20. Conrad, "Capture of the USS Underwriter," 93–100.

21. Clayton account, New Berne Weekly Journal, August 16, 1904.

22. G. Gift to Ellen Shackleford, February 7, 1864, Gift Papers; Charleston Mercury, Febru-

ary 19, 1864 (reprint from the *Daily Dispatch*); Loyall, "Capture of the *Underwriter*," 325–333; Clayton account, *New Berne Weekly Journal*, August 16, 1904.

23. *Charleston Mercury*, February 19, 1864 (reprint from the *Daily Dispatch*); Conrad, "Capture of the USS *Underwriter*," 93–100.

24. Loyall, "Capture of the *Underwriter*," 325–333.

25. Conrad, "Capture of the USS *Underwriter*," 93–100; *Daily Dispatch*, February 12, 1864.

26. G. Gift to Ellen Shackleford, February 7, 1864, Gift Papers; *Public Ledger*, February 18, 1873.

27. G. Gift to Ellen Shackleford, February 7, 1864, Gift Papers; Whitford account, *New Berne Weekly Journal*, August 16, 1904.

28. Wood report, *ORN* 9:453–454.

29. Loyall, "Capture of the *Underwriter*," 325–333.

30. Wood report, *ORN* 9:453–454.

31. *Charleston Mercury*, February 19, 1864 (reprint of Bohemian's story from the *Daily Dispatch*); *ORN*, series 2, 1:228 (*Underwriter*'s armament); Davenport to Lee, February 17, 1864, *ORN* 9:443–444. Earlier in the war, the *Underwriter* had carried an 80-pounder rifle, which was switched out for an 8-inch smoothbore in 1863.

32. Davenport to Lee, January 31, 1864, *ORN* 9:423; Palmer to Davis, February 2, 1864, *ORA* 33:49–50.

33. Graves report, *ORN* 9:441–442.

34. At 1:00 a.m., Giles Ward, from General Palmer's staff, took the *Underwriter*'s gig, along with a few crew members, and embarked on a reconnaissance upriver. *Richmond Whig*, February 26, 1864 (excerpt from the *New York Times*); Burlingame, *History of the Fifth Regiment of Rhode Island Heavy Artillery*, 192; Barnes report, *ORN* 9:458 (mentions Foster's Wharf). Gift estimated the *Underwriter* lay about 200 yards from Fort Stevenson and 600 to 800 yards from Dearing's fort. *Public Ledger*, February 18, 1873.

35. Clayton account, *New Berne Weekly Journal*, August 16, 1904.

36. Union Jack, "Cutting out the *Underwriter*," 215.

37. Whitford account, *New Berne Weekly Journal*, August 16, 1904.

38. Lee to Pickett, January 20, 1864, *ORA* 33:1102.

39. G. Gift to Ellen Shackleford, February 2, 1864, Gift Papers.

40. *Daily Dispatch*, February 12, 1864. It is not clear how Shepardson (aka Bohemian) managed to move freely between Wood's command and Pickett's headquarters without detection by Union lookouts.

41. Loyall, "Capture of the *Underwriter*," 325–333; *Public Ledger*, February 19, 1873.

42. Clayton account, *New Berne Weekly Journal*, August 16, 1904; *Public Ledger*, February 19, 1873.

43. G. Gift to Ellen Shackleford, February 7, 1864, Gift Papers.

44. *Richmond Whig*, February 26, 1864 (excerpt from the *New York Times*); Allen report, February 2, 1864, *ORN* 9:441.

45. *Daily Dispatch*, February 12, 1864; Loyall, "Capture of the *Underwriter*," 325–333; *Public Ledger*, February 19, 1873.

46. G. Gift to Ellen Shackleford, February 7, 1864, Gift Papers; *Charleston Mercury*, February 19, 1864 (reprint from the *Daily Dispatch*).

47. *Richmond Whig*, February 26, 1864 (excerpt from the *New York Times*); G. Gift to Ellen Shackleford, February 7, 1864, Gift Papers.

48. *Public Ledger*, February 19, 1873; Allen report, ORN 9:441.

49. Conrad, "Capture of the USS *Underwriter*," 93–100.

50. *Daily Dispatch*, February 12, 1864.

51. Conrad, "Capture of the USS *Underwriter*," 93–100; Clayton account, *New Berne Weekly Journal*, August 16, 1904.

52. *Daily Dispatch*, February 12, 1864; Clayton account, *New Berne Weekly Journal*, August 16, 1904; Loyall, "Capture of the *Underwriter*," 325–333; account of Thomas Scharf, *Pulaski Citizen*, February 12, 1874; account of Shepardson, *Daily Dispatch*, February 10, 1864; Scharf, *History of the Confederate States Navy*, 397–400 (Scharf lifted some of Shepardson's wartime reporting).

53. Conrad, "Capture of the USS *Underwriter*," 93–100.

54. *Daily Dispatch*, February 12, 1864. These boats were led by Lieutenants Hoge, Kerr, Porcher, Gardner, Rody, and Wilkinson.

55. Davenport to Lee, February 17, 1864, ORN 9:443–444.

56. Clayton account, *New Berne Weekly Journal*, August 16, 1904; *Public Ledger*, February 19, 1873; *Charleston Mercury*, February 19, 1864 (reprint from the *Daily Dispatch*); Loyall, "Capture of the *Underwriter*," 325–333.

57. Loyall, "Capture of the *Underwriter*," 325–333; Conrad, "Capture of the USS *Underwriter*," 93–100.

58. *National Tribune*, June 7, 1894.

59. *Daily Dispatch*, February 12, 1864; Loyall, "Capture of the *Underwriter*," 325–333; G. Gift to Ellen Shackleford, February 7, 1864, Gift Papers; *Public Ledger*, February 19, 1873.

60. Loyall, "Capture of the *Underwriter*," 325–333.

61. *Public Ledger*, February 19, 1873; Allen report, ORN 9:441.

62. Conrad, "Capture of the USS *Underwriter*," 93–100.

63. G. Gift to Ellen Shackleford, February. 7, 1864, Gift Papers.

64. Conrad, "Capture of the USS *Underwriter*," 93–100; *Boston Post*, February 11, 1864.

65. *Public Ledger*, February 19, 1873; *Daily Dispatch*, February 12, 1864.

66. Conrad, "Capture of the USS *Underwriter*," 93–100.

67. Loyall, "Capture of the *Underwriter*," 325–333; *Public Ledger*, February 19, 1873; Conrad, "Capture of the USS *Underwriter*," 93–100.

68. *Public Ledger*, February 19, 1873. Steam was not a problem. Gift wrote, "She was lying with banked fires, and consequently ready to move at a moment's warning."

69. Conrad, "Capture of the USS *Underwriter*," 93–100; Loyall, "Capture of the *Underwriter*," 325–333.

70. The *Underwriter* was fired on by guns from Fort Stevenson and artillery at the old fair grounds. Fort Stevenson was about a quarter mile from where the *Underwriter* was moored. Whitford account, *New Berne Weekly Journal*, August 16, 1904; *National Tribune*, June 7, 1894.

71. Hall and Hall, *Cayuga in the Field*, 196; Burlingame, *History of the Fifth Regiment of Rhode Island Heavy Artillery*, 193.

72. Clayton account, *New Berne Weekly Journal*, August 16, 1904; Allen report, *ORN* 9:441; account of Loyall, *Virginia-Pilot*, April 30, 1899; Conrad, "Capture of the USS *Underwriter*," 93–100; Edward Burgess Peirce to John Peirce, February 1863 [1864], Edward Burgess Peirce Letters, 1862–1871, Massachusetts Historical Society.

73. Conrad, "Capture of the USS *Underwriter*," 93–100; Loyall, "Capture of the *Underwriter*," 325–333; *Virginia-Pilot*, April 30, 1899; *Charleston Mercury*, February 19, 1864 (reprint from the *Daily Dispatch*); Clayton account, *New Berne Weekly Journal*, August 16, 1904; G. Gift to Ellen Shackleford, February 7, 1864, Gift Papers; *Boston Post*, February 11, 1864; Allen report, *ORN* 9:441.

74. Edgar Allen would receive a promotion for this feat. *Boston Post*, February 11, 1864. See also Allen report, *ORN* 9:441.

75. *Charleston Mercury*, February 19, 1864 (reprint from the *Daily Dispatch*); *Virginia-Pilot*, April 30, 1899; *Public Ledger*, February 19, 1873 (Gift reported that Wood joined Hoge); G. Gift to Ellen Shackleford, February 7, 1864, Gift Papers.

76. Conrad, "Capture of the USS *Underwriter*," 93–100.

77. W. J. Pfohl to C. T. Pfohl, February 9, 1864, Christian Thomas Pfohl Papers, SHC, UNC.

78. Hall and Hall, *Cayuga in the Field*, 196.

79. *Virginia-Pilot*, April 30, 1899; Conrad, "Capture of the USS *Underwriter*," 93–100; Clayton account, *New Berne Weekly Journal*, August 16, 1904 (two officers and seven men killed). Engineer Gill died there and was buried on the property of Mrs. S. Nelson. Account of George B. Colbert, *New Berne Weekly Journal*, August 16, 1904; *Virginia-Pilot*, April 30, 1899. Immediately after the fight, Gift put the losses at four killed and eight wounded, while the *Underwriter* crew lost eight killed, four wounded, and twenty-five prisoners. G. Gift to Ellen Shackleford, February 2, 1864, Gift Papers; Davenport report, March 1, 1864, *ORN* 9:446 (Union estimates).

80. G. Gift to Ellen Shackleford, February 2, 1864, Gift Papers; *Public Ledger*, February 20, 1873.

81. *Public Ledger*, February 20, 1873.

82. G. Gift to Ellen Shackleford, February 7, 1864, Gift Papers; *Public Ledger*, February 20, 1873.

83. *Public Ledger*, February 19, 1873. Back in Petersburg the next week, Dearing reciprocated Gift's gesture.

84. Palmer to Davis, February 2, 1864, *ORA* 33:49–50.

85. *Public Ledger*, February 20, 1873; Davenport to Lee, February 7, 1864, *ORN* 9:468. Later examination found that the *Underwriter*'s hull was damaged beyond salvage. However, the boiler was eventually extracted from the wreck and sat on the New Bern wharf for many years. Lee to Welles, March 25, 1864, *ORN* 9:449; Whitford account, *New Berne Weekly Journal*, August 16, 1904.

86. A memorandum issued two weeks later by Commander Foxhall Parker, in charge of

the Potomac Flotilla, warned crews not to "allow boats to come alongside after sunset until their character and business are known," and it set out detailed protocols for night encounters. Foxhall Parker, "Instructions Regarding Boats at Night," February 12, 1864, Area File of the Naval Collection, 1775–1910, Area 7, RG 24, NARA. Naval officials worried that the *Underwriter*'s signal book had been seized, but there is no evidence this occurred. Davenport to Lee, February 8, 1864, *ORN* 9:440.

87. Palmer to Davis, February 2, 1864, ORA 33:49–50; Palmer to Davis, February 7, 1864, ibid., 56.

88. *New York Times*, February 9 and 29, 1864.

89. Moore, *Rebellion Record*, 8:360 (alleging that Westervelt's disloyalty caused the *Underwriter*'s demise); *Daily Dispatch*, February 12, 1864 (alleging that captured Union officers accused Westervelt of cowardice); Lee to Welles, February 15, 1864, ORN 9:443 (promising to conduct a court of inquiry). Apparently, no one on the Union side knew the details of Westervelt's daring escape attempt and his quick death until well after the war, when George Gift recounted the events. *Public Ledger*, February 19, 1873.

90. *Columbian Register*, March 12, 1864; *New York Tribune*, March 7, 1864; Davenport to Lee, February 25, 1864, ORN 9:446; Davenport to Lee, February 28, 1864, ibid., 445.

91. In addition to Westervelt, others killed in the fight included John Fealy, a fireman; James Ryan, a landsman; John H. Belderman, an ordinary seaman; and Alfred Banks, a captain's boy. Union officials learned from the newspapers that dozens of crew members were in rebel hands. Davenport to Lee, March 1, 1864, ORN 9:444; list of men "saved" from the *Underwriter*, ibid., 448.

92. Barnes report, ORN 9:458.

93. G. Gift to Ellen Shackleford, February 7, 1864, Gift Papers; *Daily Dispatch*, February 12, 1864.

94. Clayton account, *New Berne Weekly Journal*, August 16, 1904.

Chapter 9. Beech Grove and Newport Barracks

1. Bell, *11th Virginia Infantry*, 44.

2. Gaines, "Fayette Artillery." During one foray at a nearby plantation, lucky foragers discovered a large cigar full of silver, handfuls of "quarters, dimes, and shining dollars." *Daily Progress*, February 17, 1864.

3. J. R. P. Ellis to Betty, February 6, 1864, Josiah Robert Peele Ellis Papers, 1863–1864, ECU.

4. Palmer to Davis, February 3, 1864, 8:00 p.m., ORA 33:52–53.

5. Hall and Hall, *Cayuga in the Field*, 197; Burlingame, *History of the Fifth Regiment of Rhode Island Heavy Artillery*, 190, 194 (account of firing a 32-pounder and shell from an 8-inch Columbiad hitting a mounted Confederate).

6. Burlingame, *History of the Fifth Regiment of Rhode Island Heavy Artillery*, 189.

7. Palmer to Davis, February 2, 1864, ORA 33:49–50.

8. Palmer to Davis, February 20, 1864, ORA 33:57–59.

9. See Kirwan, *Memorial History of the Seventeenth Regiment.* Greenhalge, a Harvard graduate, had volunteered for civil service after being rejected by the army for health reasons.

10. Diary of Captain Henry A. Chambers, February 1, 1864, Henry A. Chambers Papers, SHC, UNC.

11. Roulhac, "Forty-Ninth Regiment." See also reminiscences of W. A. Day (49th North Carolina), *Landmark,* January 2, 1934.

12. Hall and Hall, *Cayuga in the Field,* 197.

13. Pickett report, ORA 33:92–94.

14. Henry T. Guion journal, William Hoke Papers, SHC, UNC; Pickett report, ORA 33:92–94; Burgwyn, *A Captain's War,* 120. The column moved south along the Savanna Road past an old racetrack and on to the Trent Road at the Blackledge Plantation. Here, Hoke arrayed the bulk of his brigade in battle line, blocking the Trent Road and anchoring Pickett's right flank near the Trent River.

15, Chambers diary, February 1, 1864; Pickett report, ORA 33:92–94; Barton report, ibid., 97–99.

16. Palmer report, ORA 33:53. Union reports claim that some members of the garrison escaped the Confederate net, but their numbers are unclear.

17. US Congress, *Murder of Union Soldiers in North Carolina,* 57.

18. Hall and Hall, *Cayuga in the Field,* 197–198.

19. Giles F. Ward to his father, February 3, 1864, Giles F. Ward Papers, DMRL; Budington, *Memorial of Giles F. Ward, Jr.,* 21–22.

20. Winan report, ORA 33:71–73. Back in New Bern, Palmer's headquarters had been informed that Ward had been dispatched to take the men from Beech Grove away. Foster to Fellows, February 1, 1864, Records of Armies, RG 393, NARA.

21. Guion journal; Graham, "Fifty-Sixth Regiment," 333.

22. Ibid.; Smith, "Recollections of Capt. John G. Smith." Smith, writing decades later, made the unlikely claim that the 8th and 19th Georgia Cavalry conducted the operation.

23. Gaines, "Fayette Artillery"; *Daily Dispatch,* March 28, 1897. After Lieutenant Kirby's capture, friends forwarded money and clothing to him through an exchanged prisoner. When the rebel absconded with the money, General Pickett reportedly reimbursed Kirby and, in turn, General Butler reimbursed Pickett. Lieutenant Kirby managed to escape captivity that spring. *New Berne Times,* April 30, 1864. The Bellair house still stands today.

24. Claassen report, ORA 33:63; Palmer report, ibid., 53.

25. Palmer report, ORA 33:53; Gaines, "Fayette Artillery."

26. Graham, "Fifty-Sixth Regiment," 334; Hoke report, ORA 33:97.

27. W. I. Clopton to "Dear Mother," February 17, 1864, Clopton Family Papers, DMRL; Gaines, "Fayette Artillery"; Hall and Hall, *Cayuga in the Field,* 197–198. The captured guns would serve the rebellion until Appomattox, where "they were spiked and cut down."

28. See Smith, "Recollections of Capt. John G. Smith," 295.

29. Hall and Hall, *Cayuga in the Field,* 197–198, discusses the destination of prisoners: officers were sent to Libby Prison, and enlisted men went to Belle Isle and then Andersonville, where most died.

30. See Barton to Martin, January 31, 1864, ORA 33:87 ("I am afraid you will not reach the point designated by P[ickett] at the time we expected"). For a full account of the Newport Barracks battle, see Lindblade, *Fight as Long as Possible*.

31. *Charlotte Democrat*, February 23, 1864.

32. Martin report, ORA 33:84–86; *Charlotte Democrat*, February 23, 1864 (letter reprinted from the *Wilmington Journal*); January Wilmington returns, ORA 33:1138; February Wilmington returns, ibid., 1202; Barney report, ibid., 81 (estimating Martin's force at 1,700).

33. Martin report, ORA 33:84–86.

34. Elliott, "Martin's Brigade—Hoke's Division," 189; Martin to Barton, February 1, 1864, 8:00 a.m., ORA 33:87; Martin report, ibid., 84–86; *Charlotte Democrat*, February 23, 1864 (letter reprinted from the *Wilmington Journal*). Swansboro is the modern spelling. It was usually spelled Swansborough during the war.

35. Martin report, ORA 33:84–86.

36. *Brooklyn Daily Eagle*, November 2, 1910 (stating that Jourdan may have been born in Northern Ireland); *New York Times*, November 2, 1910 (stating that Jourdan was born in New Jersey).

37. See Davenport report, ORN 9:468 (noting that a steamer was headed for Beaufort from New Bern via Core Sound).

38. Morehead City, a relatively new village consisting of about fifteen to twenty houses on Bogue Sound, formed the eastern terminus of the Atlantic and North Carolina Railroad. The 1860 census tallied Morehead's population at 165 whites, 4 free blacks, and 147 slaves. Branch, "Lost Carolina City"; Phinney, *Adventures of an Army Nurse in Two Wars*, 137.

39. Branch, "Lost Carolina City."

40. Chapin, *Memorandum and Journal of Samuel Chapin*, 23. For more soldier descriptions of the Newport environs, see Wickman, *"We Are Coming Father Abra'am,"* 259–261.

41. Like the forces at New Bern and Plymouth, Jourdan's command had been busy conducting raids in the previous weeks. On Monday, February 1, two companies of the 9th Vermont and two cavalry companies returned from an expedition to Onslow County. Letter from Sergeant B. (158th New York), *Brooklyn Daily Eagle*, February 11, 1864.

42. Palmer report, ORA 33:58; Jourdan report, ibid., 77–81; letter from Sergeant B., *Brooklyn Daily Eagle*, February 11, 1864; Palmer to Jourdan, February 1, 1864, ORA 33:496.

43. Martin report, ORA 33:84–86; *Wilmington Journal*, February 11, 1864.

44. Letter from Soldat, *Wilmington Journal*, February 18, 1864; *Carolina Watchman*, March 7, 1864.

45. John L. Swain diary, February 12, 1864, John L. Swain Papers, SHC, UNC.

46. Gale's Creek is sometimes spelled Gales' or Gales Creek. Martin claimed to have killed or captured the entire post there. However, this does not appear to be accurate. Another Confederate account recalled that the entire post, about twenty-five to thirty cavalrymen, had "retreated as fast as their horses would carry them." Swain diary, February 12, 1864; *Wilmington Journal*, February 11, 1864; Benedict, *Vermont in the Civil War*, 2:227; Martin report, ORA 33:84–86. Muse apparently died just as his blow landed on a Federal.

47. Jourdan report, ORA 33:77–81; Benedict, *Vermont in the Civil War*, 2:227; letter from Horace (9th Vermont), *Lamoille Newsdealer*, February 24, 1864.

48. *Wilmington Journal*, February 11, 1864; Martin report, ORA 33:84–86. Both sources state that Martin overran two blockhouses, a smaller one and the larger Bogue Sound blockhouse.

49. Benedict, *Vermont in the Civil War*, 2:228; *Wilmington Journal*, February 11, 1864; letter from Horace, *Lamoille Newsdealer*, February 24, 1864.

50. Martin report, ORA 33:84–86; letter from Horace, *Lamoille Newsdealer*, February 24, 1864; *Green Mountain Freeman*, February 23, 1864.

51. Jourdan report, ORA 33:77–81; Martin report, ibid., 84–86; Benedict, *Vermont in the Civil War*, 2:228; *Wilmington Journal*, February 11, 1864.

52. *Wilmington Journal*, February 11, 1864; Palmer to Davis, February 20, 1864, ORA 33:57–59. A company of the 19th Wisconsin (Company F) was at Newport Barracks on January 31 (ORA 33:485). However, it appears that on February 2 the company was marching to the New Bern fortifications, and only one member of the regiment, George Neumann, was at Newport Barracks drawing rations. See Smith, "Siege and Capture of Plymouth," 581.

53. Benedict, *Vermont in the Civil War*, 2:227. Colonel Jourdan had been reluctant to approve Ripley's trip to Fort Monroe. See Edward Ripley Service Record, Compiled Service Records of Volunteer Union Soldiers, RG 94, NARA; telegram, Jourdan to Ripley, January 29, 1864, ibid.; Jourdan report, ORA 33:77–81. Union commanders prepared other outposts along the rail line for the onslaught. At New Bern, Palmer ordered the men at Croatan and Havelock to "spike, bury, or conceal" their guns, destroy excess ammunition, and withdraw to New Bern. Palmer to Johnson, February 2, 1864, 9:40 a.m., ORA 33:502.

54. Jourdan report, ORA 33:77–81.

55. Benedict, *Vermont in the Civil War*, 2:228; Barney report, ORA 33:81–82.

56. V. Barney to M. Barney, February 5 and 12, 1864, Valentine G. Barney Correspondence, University of Vermont Libraries; Chapin, *Memorandum and Journal of Samuel Chapin*, 23. The Union fort south of the Newport River is generally referred to today as Fort Benjamin (or occasionally Fort Ripley). However, it appears that those names were not used in 1864.

57. Ripley, *Vermont General*, 168.

58. Benedict, *Vermont in the Civil War*, 2:228–229; Barney report, ORA 33:81–82. Barney's correspondence mentions that the enemy approached the fort from the rear, rendering the defenses "of little account." However, the meaning of this statement is unclear, as there is no indication that the fort was sited to protect only against threats from the north. V. Barney to M. Barney, February 5 and 12, 1864, Barney Correspondence. In March, Barney would write that fortifications there had been vastly improved after the February attack. "We have got a breast work thrown up all around us and any amount of slashing done to prevent all advance of Cavalry or Artillery upon us." V. Barney to M. Barney, March 6, 1864, ibid.

59. *Wilmington Journal*, February 11 and 18, 1864.

60. Martin report, ORA 33:84–86.

61. Letter from Soldat, *Wilmington Journal*, February 18, 1864.

62. Benedict, *Vermont in the Civil War*, 2:229.

63. Martin report, ORA 33:84–86.

64. Letter from Soldat, *Wilmington Journal*, February 18, 1864; *Wilmington Journal*, February 11, 1864.

65. Jourdan report, ORA 33:77–81.

66. Benedict, *Vermont in the Civil War*, 2:229.

67. William A. James to Lydia D. James, February 9, 1864, William A. James Papers, DMRL.

68. V. Barney to M. Barney, February 5 and 12, 1864, Barney Correspondence.

69. Letter from Soldat, *Wilmington Journal*, February 18, 1864; Jourdan report, ORA 33:77–81.

70. Benedict, *Vermont in the Civil War*, 2:229.

71. Swain diary, February 12, 1864.

72. Writing home a few days after the battle, Lieutenant Colonel Barney explained that the "enemy came to our rear, which gave us no chance to use our Guns in the Fort." V. Barney to M. Barney, February 5, 1864, Barney Correspondence; *Wilmington Journal*, February 11, 1864.

73. Letter from Horace, *Lamoille Newsdealer*, February 24, 1864.

74. Jourdan report, ORA 33:77–81. Vermont veterans later asserted that the Massachusetts artillerymen fled to New Bern and reported the 9th Vermont cut off and captured. Benedict, *Vermont in the Civil War*, 2:229.

75. Martin report, ORA 33:84–86.

76. *Wilmington Journal*, February 18, 1864.

77. Erastus Jewett Medal of Honor File (R&P 296635), RG 94, NARA. Jewett was discharged on November 21, 1864, so that he could tend to family business following his father's death. Benedict, *Vermont in the Civil War*, 2:229; Jones, *Story of American Heroism*, 373.

78. Phinney, *Adventures of an Army Nurse in Two Wars*, 137. Phinney also mentioned the 19th Wisconsin (Company F), but it appears that the unit left for New Bern earlier that day.

79. Barney report, ORA 33:81–82, Martin report, ibid., 84–86; Jourdan report, ibid., 77–81.

80. Jourdan report, ORA 33:77–81; V. Barney to M. Barney, February 9, 1864, Barney Correspondence.

81. Martin report, ORA 33:84–86. Martin later burned the trestle because, in the absence of news from New Bern, he sought to protect his command. However, Martin left the road bridge intact.

82. Benedict, *Vermont in the Civil War*, 2: 229.

83. Martin report, ORA 33:84–86; *Wilmington Journal*, February 11, 1864.

84. William A. James to Lydia D. James, February 9, 1864, James Papers.

85. Letter from Soldat, *Wilmington Journal*, February 18, 1864; William A. James to Lydia D. James, February 9, 1864, James Papers.

86. *Wilmington Journal*, February 18, 1864; Martin report, ORA 33:84–86.

87. Clara Boyd to "Mrs. Carter," February 23, 1864, David Miller Carter Papers, SHC, UNC.

88. *Wilmington Journal*, February 18, 1864.

89. Whiting report, ORA 33:82–83.

90. The account of one Vermont veteran indicated that, had "the fort at the barracks and the redoubt north of the river been held by the heavy artillery stationed in them, a final stand might now have been made under the cover of their guns." Benedict, *Vermont in the Civil War*, 2:229.

91. General Orders No. 61, May 20, 1864, Russell Conwell Service Record, RG 92, NARA.

92. V. Barney to M. Barney, March 14, 1864, Barney Correspondence. See Pohoresky, "Legend of Johnnie Ring." Conwell would later claim he rejoined the army after his dismissal and served on General James B. McPherson's staff.

93. *Wilmington Journal*, February 18, 1864.

94. Phinney, *Adventures of an Army Nurse in Two Wars*, 134.

95. Jourdan report, ORA 33:77–81; George Lillie to Sarah Stevens, February 12, 1864, George C. Lillie Correspondence, Vermont Historical Society.

96. V. Barney to M. Barney, February 5 and 9, 1864, Barney Correspondence.

97. Wilbur, *Early History of Vermont*, 4:255; V. Barney to M. Barney, February 5 and 9, 1864, Barney Correspondence; Barney report, ORA 33:81–82. Jourdan's reported losses—four killed, eleven wounded, and sixty-two missing—did not match Martin's estimate. Jourdan report, ORA 33:77–81. In addition, Martin's force ignited the magazine, spiked three guns, disabled their carriages, cut the flagstaff, and burned the railroad bridge. One rumor indicated the captured rations greatly aided Martin's men, who had been living off of corn, peanuts, and sweet potatoes. Dove to Lee, February 6, 1864, ORN 9:466.

98. Martin report, ORA 33:84–86.

99. Letter from Sergeant B., *Brooklyn Daily Eagle*, February 11, 1864 (the provost general was H. T. P. Mayo); Jourdan report, ORA 33:77–81.

100. Stationed in Bogue Sound were the *Nansemond*, an armed side-wheel steamer with one 30-pounder and two 24-pounder guns under Commander Benjamin Dove, and a smaller boat. Jourdan later thanked Dove for lending the gunboats *Nansemond*, *Mercedita*, and *Emma*. Jourdan report, ORA 33:77–81; Dove report, ORN 9:455.

101. Phinney, *Adventures of an Army Nurse in Two Wars*, 134.

Chapter 10. Decisions at New Bern

1. Henry T. Guion journal, William Hoke Papers, SHC, UNC.

2. Burgwyn, "Clingman's Brigade," 487–488.

3. Reminiscences of W. A. Day (49th North Carolina), *Landmark*, January 2, 1934.

4. Pickett report, ORA 33:92–94. The trains continued to run to New Bern until Martin captured Newport Barracks on Tuesday afternoon.

5. Barton report, ORA 33:97–99.

6. Guion journal.

7. Palmer to Davis, February 20, 1864, *ORA* 33:57–59; diary of Orlando P. Benson (92nd New York), *Courier and Freeman*, February 4, 1925.

8. Colonel Henry Sisson, commander of the 5th Rhode Island Heavy Artillery, wrote, "Well, well, if they serenade us by day with shell, and with music at night, we must not be outdone in gallantry." Burlingame, *History of the Fifth Regiment of Rhode Island Heavy Artillery*, 190; Kirwan, *Memorial History of the Seventeenth Regiment*, 201.

9. The units with Pickett west of New Bern began their withdrawal early on the morning of Wednesday, February 3. John Paris diary, February 3, 1864, John Paris Papers, SHC, UNC (the march began at 2:00 a.m.). The column halted on Wednesday after crossing Core Creek. Guion journal; Clingman report, *ORA* 33:101–102 (withdrawal at 1:00 a.m.). Some men remained outside New Bern until Wednesday afternoon and did not reach Kinston until Friday afternoon. W. J. Pfohl to C. T. Pfohl, February 9, 1864, Christian Thomas Pfohl Papers, SHC, UNC; Burgwyn, *A Captain's War*, 220.

10. Wallace, *3rd Virginia Infantry*, 56; Day reminiscences, *Landmark*, January 2, 1934.

11. Diary of Captain Henry A. Chambers, February 3, 1864, Henry A. Chambers Papers, SHC, UNC. Out of rations, Barton's hungry men pilfered sweet potatoes from farms along the way.

12. J. L. Stuart to Mary A. Harper, February 5, 1864, J. L. Stuart Papers, DMRL.

13. *Wilmington Journal*, February 18, 1864 (reprinting a letter from "R." to the *Petersburg Express*).

14. Johnston, *Story of a Confederate Boy in the Civil War*, 237: "We silently folded our tents and stole away, floundering all night long through the swamps and mud, crossing the Trent a little after dawn." *Wilmington Journal*, February 18, 1864 (letter from "R." to the *Petersburg Express*); Roulhac, "Forty-Ninth Regiment," 133.

15. *Wilmington Journal*, February 18, 1864 (letter from "R." to the *Petersburg Express*); Chambers diary, February 5, 1864; letter from A. H. P., *Daily Dispatch*, February 8, 1864. Barton's men arrived at Kinston at 4:00 on Thursday afternoon.

16. Account of Gift, *Public Ledger*, February 19, 1873; Conrad, "Capture of the USS *Underwriter*," 93–100; G. Gift to Ellen Shackleford, February 7, 1864, George Gift Papers, SHC, UNC.

17. Whiting report, *ORA* 33:84; Martin report and enclosure, ibid., 84–88; Jourdan report, ibid., 77–81; Barney report, ibid., 81–82; Jeffords report, ibid., 90–92 (details of Jeffords's withdrawal); Conrad, "Capture of the USS *Underwriter*," 93–100. Federal reports repeatedly discussed the presence of rebel forces in the area for several days after Martin departed Newport Barracks. Colonel Robert J. Jeffords burned the deserted barracks at Havelock and found a spiked brass 6-pounder rifled gun. At Evans' Mill, he found the bridge over Brice's Creek dismantled, a cannon sitting in the road, and dead horses littering the ground.

18. Writing from Morehead City on Friday, February 5, Lieutenant Colonel Barney confessed that he and his men were worn out, having failed to sleep "except by seconds" since Monday. V. Barney to M. Barney, February 5, 1864, Valentine G. Barney Correspondence, University of Vermont Libraries.

19. Phinney, *Adventures of an Army Nurse in Two Wars,* 135.

20. Jourdan report, ORA 33:77–81 (Federal cavalry found enemy camps 11 miles away); Benedict, *Vermont in the Civil War,* 2:232.

21. On February 6 and 7, the Federals responded to various reports of Confederate cavalry in the region. There was much shifting of Colonel Jourdan's forces out of Morehead City in response to the threats. See Judson to Amory, February 6, 1864, Letters Sent, New Bern Sub-District, Records of Subdistricts, RG 393, NARA; Jourdan report, ORA 33:77–81.

22. Palmer to Davis, February 7, 1864, ORA 33:54–57; Palmer to Davis, February 20, 1864, ibid., 57–59.

23. On Tuesday evening, February 2, Innis Palmer assured Benjamin Butler that there had been "no material change" at New Bern since Monday. Palmer to Davis, February 2, 1864, ORA 33:49–50; Judson to Davis, February 2, 1864, ibid., 52. Over the course of their correspondence, Butler and Palmer disagreed on the estimates of rebel strength outside New Bern. Butler, in fact, underestimated the force. In any case, Butler sent the 400 men of the 21st Connecticut to reinforce Morehead City. Butler to Halleck, February 3, 1864, ORA 33:506; Butler to Halleck and Stanton, February 3, 1864, ibid. Palmer also alerted his district's navy and army commanders, claiming that the city would hold as long as the "fortifications are worth a cent." Palmer to Davenport and Flusser, February 2, 1864, ORA 33:501; Barnes report, ORN 9:458.

24. The gunboats *Southfield* and *Whitehead,* along with the 15th Connecticut, left Plymouth and steamed to New Bern. Wessells also sent the *Miami* to the garrison at Washington. Wessells to Palmer, February 3, 1864, ORA 33:51; Palmer to Davis, February 4, 1864, 3:15 p.m., ibid., 54; Davenport report, ORN 9:468 (specifying that the steamer was headed for Beaufort from New Bern via Core Sound); Palmer to Davis, February 3, 1864, 8:00 p.m., ORA 33:52–53 (reporting continuing threats to his communications); Palmer to Davis, February 20, 1864, ibid., 57–59.

25. Butler to Halleck, February 3, 1864, ORA 33:506; note from Union agents, January 30, 1864, ibid., 520. To the north, Butler believed Lee had stationed only 20,000 men behind the Rappahannock River. Butler had discussed his proposed raid on Richmond with Halleck in a face-to-face conversation several days before. Butler's sources suggested that Richmond's defenses were bare.

26. See Halleck to Butler, February 5, 1864, 9:30 a.m., ORA 33:518–519; Butler to Halleck, February 3, 1864, ibid., 506; Halleck to Sedgwick, February 3, 1864, 6:00 p.m., ibid., 502; Butler to Sedgwick, February 3, 1864, 6:00 p.m., ibid.; Sedgwick to Butler, February 4, 1864, 4:00 p.m., ibid., 512–513; Butler to Sedgwick, February 4, 1864, 4:35 p.m., ibid., 513.

27. Sedgwick to Halleck, February 5, 1864, 1:45 p.m., ORA 33:514; Sedgwick's order to his corps commanders (army circular), ibid.

28. Union and Confederate reports, ORA 33:114–141; Sedgwick to Halleck, February 7, 1864, noon, ibid., 532.

29. See Butler report, ORA 33:143–144. Brigadier General I. J. Wistar, in command of the raid on Richmond, found four batteries of artillery and three infantry regiments barring the way.

30. Claassen, return of casualties (9 killed, 15 wounded, 302 captured), ORA 33:69.

31. *New York Times*, February 11, 1864; Giles F. Ward to his Father, February 3, 1864, Giles F. Ward Papers, DMRL.

32. Palmer to Davis, February 7, 1864, ORA 33:54–55; Foster to Wessells, February 5, 1864, ibid., 54 (discussing disagreements with Butler about the strength of the Confederate force).

33. See Judson to Savage, February 8, 1864, Letters Sent, New Bern Sub-District, Records of Subdistricts, RG 393, NARA.

34. General Orders No. 12, ORA 33:61.

35. Palmer to Davis, February 7, 1864, ORA 33:54–55 (listing the regiments represented by deserters and prisoners); Palmer to Davis, February 20, 1864, ibid., 57–59.

36. *Newburgh Journal* (undated clipping), Civil War Newspaper Clipping Collection, 132nd Infantry, NYSMM.

37. Palmer to Davis, February 7, 1864, ORA 33:54–55. Peck also passed on reports from Wessells at Plymouth that "a formidable expedition was preparing near Halifax, with boats, for the opening of the Roanoke." Peck to Davis, February 10, 1864, ibid., 60–61.

38. *Leslie's Illustrated*, February 27, 1864.

39. Smith report, ORA 33:73–76.

40. Beyer and Keydel, *Deeds of Valor*, 1:307; Claassen to Foster, February 8, 1864, ORA 33:62–67; circular from Colonel Claassen, February 6, 1864, Abram Haring Medal of Honor File, RG 94, NARA.

41. Moore, *Rebellion Record*, 8:360; account of Frank Salter, *Dakota County Herald*, October 23, 1913 (stating that Haring's defense gave time for reinforcements to move from Morehead City to New Bern). On February 7, 1864, the *New York Times* noted that, on reflection, it was clear that all would have been lost had Haring faltered.

42. A. Haring to T. Vincent, June 13, 1890, Abram Haring Medal of Honor File, RG 94, NARA. Haring referred to the Medal of Merit instead of the Medal of Honor.

43. *Medal of Honor, 1863–1968*.

44. *Salina Daily Republican*, June 11, 1897 (reprint from the *New York Sun*).

45. Hovey, "How Haring Held the Bridge," 233.

46. Claassen to Foster, February 8, 1864, ORA 33:62–67. Claassen sought compensation for his men who had left their personal belongings in camp.

47. Claassen to Thomas, February 15, 1864, ORA 33:61–62.

48. *New York Times*, January 1, 1897. In September 1864, Claassen faced a court-martial unrelated to the Bachelor Creek fight, but he continued to command his troops until the end of the war. Palmer to Smith, November 16, 1864, Letters Received by the Adjutant General, 1861–1870, RG 94, NARA.

49. Palmer to Davis, February 20, 1864, ORA 33:57–59; Smith report, ibid., 73–76 (Smith praised Hitchcock, Green, Haring Cusick, Gearing, Ryan, Wells, Jones, Hallenbac, Ludlum, and Zenette).

50. Palmer to Davis, February 7, 1864, ORA 33:54–56.

51. Kirwan, *Memorial History of the Seventeenth Regiment*, 198. The rebels shipped the men captured with Fellows to Andersonville prison.

52. *New York Times*, February 21, 1864. The article also contains a full list of casualties from the 132nd New York.

53. Flusser to his mother, February 13, 1864, Charles W. Flusser ZB File, NHHC; Moore, *Rebellion Record*, 8:360.

54. Peck to Butler, February 9, 1864, ORA 33:60.

55. Letter from Bohemian, *Daily Dispatch*, February 12, 1864.

56. Peck to Butler, February 9, 1864, ORA 33:60.

57. Lee to Welles, February 4, 1864, ORN 9:457–458.

58. Lee to Welles, February 11, 1864, ORN 9:477; Blake report, ibid., 477–478.

59. *New York Times*, February 11, 1864.

60. *New York Tribune*, March 7, 1864.

61. Lee to Hoke, February 11, 1864, ORA 33:1160–1161.

62. W. Taylor to "Betty," February 2, 1864, in Tower, *Lee's Adjutant*, 115. Although the letter is dated February 2, Taylor wrote these specific lines on the sixth.

63. *Daily Progress*, February 8, 1864; *Staunton Spectator*, February 9, 1864.

64. *Charlotte Democrat*, February 9, 1864 (reprinting a letter from D. K. McRae to the *Raleigh Confederate*). Echoing this optimism about victory at New Bern, many soldiers felt they had achieved something worthwhile, despite the failure to capture the Federal base. "The enemy have been driven panic stricken from encampments," wrote McRae. William J. Clarke, commander of the 24th North Carolina from Ransom's brigade, wrote home to say, "We have rendered very efficient service and undergone great hardship during the past week." He vowed the Confederates would take "the place yet." Clarke, *Live Your Own Life*, 162–164.

65. Pickett report, ORA 33:92–94.

66. J. L. Stuart to Mary A. Harper, February 5, 1864, Stuart Papers; Chambers diary, February 3 and 5, 1864.

67. W. R. Burwell to his brother, March 10, 1864, Edmund Burwell Papers, SHC, UNC; "Headquarters Out Post, 132d N.Y. Infantry," *Newburgh Journal*, Civil War Newspaper Clipping Collection, NYSMM.

68. W. I. Clopton to "Dear Mother," February 17, 1864, Clopton Family Papers, DMRL. Not everyone enjoyed the spoils. A Virginian in Terry's brigade who marched with Barton's column expressed bitterness that Hoke's men had collected "clothes, [and] rations of every kind" from the Union camps west of New Bern, whereas he and his comrades had little to eat and obtained "no yankee goods." Barnes to "Dear Mother," February 9, 1864, Edward Cook Barnes Papers, University of Virginia.

69. *Daily Progress*, February 8, 1864.

70. *Nashville Daily Union*, March 5, 1864 (attributing the story to the *Petersburg Register*).

71. Pickett, *Heart of a Soldier*, 121; Pickett to His Wife, February 1864, Arthur Crew Inman Papers, John Hay Library, Brown University.

72. Pickett report, ORA 33:92–94.

73. *Daily Confederate*, February 13, 1864 (article reprinted from the *Richmond Sentinel*).

74. "To sum up," the editors continued, "the expedition marched from Kinston, captured a Yankee outpost consisting of two or three hundred Yankees and negroes, camp equipage,

&c., and destroyed one gunboat, and marched back again." *Weekly Standard*, February 10, 1864 (excerpt from the *Wilmington Journal*).

75. *Wilmington Journal*, February 11, 1864.

76. Pickett report, ORA 33:92–94; Pickett to His Wife, February 1864, Inman Papers.

77. Criticism of Barton went beyond his decision to hold back on February 1. Edward Cook Barnes, from the 3rd Virginia, suggested that Barton himself had initially recommended the operation and had informed Pickett that New Bern "was very slenderly garrisoned," the enemy careless, and the fortifications of "trifling character." Barnes to "Dear Mother," February 9, 1864, Barnes Papers.

78. Chambers diary, February 7, 1864.

79. Thomas Roulhac (49th North Carolina, in Ransom's brigade) concluded that the artillery duel "resulted in nothing." Roulhac, "Forty-Ninth Regiment," 135. Virginian Hodijah Lincoln Meade expected future efforts to be more successful, as long as Barton was not there to "embarrass" the operations. Hodijah Lincoln Meade to his brother, February 21, 1864, Meade Family Letters, VHS.

80. Denny, *Wearing the Blue in the Twenty-Fifth Mass.*, 252; W. J. Pfohl to C. T. Pfohl, February 9, 1864, Pfohl Papers (rumor that Palmer planned to capitulate); Roulhac, "Forty-Ninth Regiment," 135 (rumor that Palmer planned to surrender).

81. J. L. Stuart to Mother, February 5, 1864, Stuart Papers. Another soldier-correspondent informed the *Petersburg Express* that the contemplated attack "was not very popular." *Wilmington Journal*, February 18, 1864 (letter from "R." to the *Petersburg Express*).

82. *Daily Progress*, February 9, 1864.

83. *Wilmington Journal*, February 18, 1864 (letter from "R." to the *Petersburg Express*).

84. W. I. Clopton to "Dear Mother," February 17, 1864, Clopton Family Papers. After the war, a veteran of Ransom's brigade recalled that Union guns were aimed at the Trent River bridge "to take it with grape and canister" and concluded it would have been "folly" for Barton to attempt the crossing. Day reminiscences, *Landmark*, January 2, 1934.

85. Barton complained about Pickett's allegations. Lee agreed with Barton and believed the brigadier was entitled to a court of inquiry. Barton report, ORA 33:97–99 (Lee endorsement, March 3, 1864). On March 5, 1864, Samuel Cooper's office issued Special Orders No. 54 (ORA 33:100), appointing a court of inquiry to meet in Richmond on March 10 to examine Barton's alleged failure at New Bern. The court's detail included Major General Samuel Jones, Major General Arnold Elzey, Brigadier General J. R. Cooke, and Major L. R. Page. On March 12, 1864, the tribunal requested a copy of Lee's orders to Pickett for the New Bern expedition. See Gordon McCabe to Walter Taylor, March 12, 1864, Seth Barton Service Record, RG 109, NARA.

86. According to one camp rumor, Pickett gathered opinions from the various brigade commanders and "was satisfied" with what he learned. Barnes to "Dear Mother," February 9, 1864, Barnes Papers. However, no official records corroborate such a story, and results of the formal inquiry have not come to light. A few months later, Barton would face more charges, this time from General Matt Ransom. The case was caught up in bureaucratic machinery until the end of the war. See Ransom endorsement, May 19, 1864, ORA

37(2):220–221; Barton to Cooper, November 24, 1864, ibid., 230; Clark to Kean, March 20, 1865, ibid., 235.

87. Thomas Roulhac wrote that it "is now well ascertained" that "New Bern could have been taken in a short time and without any considerable loss, if any vigorous pressing had been undertaken by our troops on either side of the river." Roulhac, "Forty-Ninth Regiment," 135. Barton survived the conflict to become a well-known chemist.

88. Guion journal.

89. *Daily Confederate*, February 13, 1864 (soldier's letter to the *Richmond Sentinel*). Raleigh's *Weekly Standard* echoed these various assessments and concluded that the enemy works were strong and the sacrifice involved in taking the brigade would have been too great. *Weekly Standard*, February 10, 1864; *Daily Confederate*, February 13, 1864 (article reprinted from the *Richmond Sentinel*).

90. Pickett, *Heart of a Soldier*, 120–122.

91. Letter from Bohemian, *Daily Dispatch,* February 12, 1864.

92. *Western Reserve Chronicle*, March 9, 1864.

93. Palmer to Davis, February 20, 1864, ORA 33:57–59.

94. Barton report, ORA 33:97–99; Lee to Pickett, January 20, 1864, ibid., 1102; Hoke report, 1862, ORA 9:260. Crossing the wagon bridge at Fort Gaston would merely deposit troops outside the Fort Totten line.

95. *New York Herald*, December 2, 1863 (description of Butler's North Carolina inspection).

96. Conrad, "Capture of the USS *Underwriter*"; Union Jack, "Cutting out the *Underwriter*."

97. Guion journal.

98. Palmer to Davis, February 20, 1864, ORA 33:57–59; *Newburgh Journal* (undated clipping), Civil War Newspaper Clipping Collection, NYSMM; Denny, *Wearing the Blue in the Twenty-Fifth Mass.*, 252.

99. Pickett report, ORA 33:92–94.

100. Over the years, the issue of Hoke and Lee's role received little scrutiny in discussions of the expedition's results. It was understood in North Carolina at the time and by historians later that Hoke played a significant role in the operation's planning. Instead of considering the results, the focus remained on Hoke's role in developing the plans for the February operation. One North Carolina historian even suggested that the operation was hatched when the president specifically solicited Hoke's views. Samuel A. Ashe, a Civil War veteran, newspaper editor, historian, and legislator, wrote in his massive *History of North Carolina* that President Davis sent for Hoke and asked the young officer what was to be done with the "unfavorable political conditions in the State." However, considering additional postwar accounts, it appears that Ashe intended to refer to a different meeting with Davis that occurred later in April 1864 and addressed operations in North Carolina at the time, not the initial New Bern expedition. See Hoke's recollections as relayed by Thomas Kenan, *Farmer and the Mechanic*, May 16, 1905; anonymous recollections of "Private A. N. V.," *Evening Visitor*, March 6, 1894; account of Victor S. Bryant, *Farmer and the Mechanic*, February 4, 1913.

101. W. Taylor to "Betty," February 2, 1864, in Tower, *Lee's Adjutant*, 115.

102. *Charlotte Democrat*, February 9, 1864 (D. K. McRae's letter to the *Raleigh Confederate*). A member of Corse's brigade complained about the lack of credit his brigade received in Pickett's report. *Daily Progress*, February 25, 1864 ("more than one half of the prisoners and nearly all the horses captured, were taken by this brigade").

103. W. R. Burwell to his brother, March 10, 1864, Burwell Papers.

104. *Charlotte News*, July 4, 1912.

105. Guion journal.

106. Hoke report, ORA 33:95–97.

107. W. J. Pfohl to C. T. Pfohl, February 9, 1864, Pfohl Papers.

108. Ibid.

109. Clara Boyd to "Mrs. Carter," February 23, 1864, Carter Papers; Meade to his brother, February 21, 1864, Meade Family Letters.

110. Palmer to Davis, February 7, 1864, ORA 33:54–55.

111. Pickett report, ORA 33:92–94.

Chapter 11. The Kinston Hangings

1. Blunt King testimony, in US Congress, *Murder of Union Soldiers in North Carolina*, 80. For recent scholarship on the Kinston hangings, see Collins, "War Crime or Justice?"; Gordon, "'In Time of War,'" 48; Patterson, *Justice or Atrocity*.

2. King testimony, in *Murder of Union Soldiers in North Carolina*, 80. Haskett and Jones were members of Henry Guion's regiment, the 10th North Carolina, which was redesignated the 1st North Carolina Artillery. For information on their desertion, see Compiled Service Records, 1st Artillery (10th State Troops) North Carolina, RG 109, NARA.

3. Confederate States of America, Headquarters [of Major George E. Pickett], Department [of] North Carolina, General Order No. 6, Camp on Dover Road, February 3, 1864.

4. Derby, *Bearing Arms in the Twenty-Seventh Massachusetts*, 235.

5. Some of the men deserted from the 40th, 41st, and 61st North Carolina. See Davis, "Kinston Hangings," New Hanover County Public Library, Wilmington, NC.

6. The Confederate Partisan Ranger Act, which was not passed until 1862, stated that men in partisan ranger units were to be "regularly received into the service." However, not all the commanders and men on the ground in North Carolina understood this. In postwar testimony, Confederate general James Martin recalled that the men were considered enlisted for "local service" only, at least until the units were consolidated into regiments later in the war. See General Orders No. 30, April 28, 1862, ORA, series 4, 1:1094–1098; Confederate States of America, *Articles of War*. See also McKnight and Myers, *Guerrilla Hunters*, 15; Board report, in *Murder of Union Soldiers in North Carolina*, 57; James Martin testimony, ibid., 84 (units organized under "Local Service Law" of 1861).

7. John Neathery testimony, in *Murder of Union Soldiers in North Carolina*, 62.

8. Ripley, *Vermont General*, 168.

9. Neathery testimony, in *Murder of Union Soldiers in North Carolina*, 63.

10. George Quinn testimony, ibid., 79.

11. Zebulon Vance testimony, ibid., 72.

12. Others left the 66th when the regiment received orders to move from Kinston to Wilmington. Martin testimony, ibid., 85.

13. Board report, ibid., 57; Neathery testimony, ibid., 62; Vance testimony, ibid., 72.

14. W. J. Pfohl to C.T. Pfohl, February 9, 1864, Christian Thomas Pfohl Papers, SHC, UNC; H. W. Barrow to C. T. Pfohl, February 17, 1864, ibid.

15. "But what makes it more charming," Kennon concluded, "'tis filled with the first young ladies of the state—refugees from Nuburn + other places now in possession of the Enemy." Henry Kennon to "Truthful Cousin," June 9, 1863, Henry Thomas Kennon Papers, NCOAH.

16. Gordon, "'In Time of War,'" 48.

17. To Tar Heel editors, the portrait, reprinted in a Richmond paper, was considered another slight against North Carolina by its unfriendly neighbors. *Tarboro Southerner*, January 17, 1863 (excerpt from the *Charleston Courier*).

18. John Hughes testimony (Hoke's quartermaster), in *Murder of Union Soldiers in North Carolina*, 70–71; Quinn testimony, ibid., 78; Confederate States of America, General Order No. 6, February 3, 1864; William I. Clopton to "Mother & Sisters," February 8, 1864, Clopton Family Papers, DMRL.

19. Confederate States of America, General Order No. 6, February 3, 1864, 7–8.

20. *Wilmington Journal*, April 28, 1864 (reprinted from the *North Carolina Presbyterian*, April 13, 1864).

21. King testimony, in *Murder of Union Soldiers in North Carolina*, 79.

22. Henry T. Guion journal, William Hoke Papers, SHC, UNC.

23. *Western Democrat*, February 23, 1864.

24. Polk to "My Dear Sallie," February 13, 1864, Leonidas Polk Papers, SHC, UNC.

25. Jesse Summerlin testimony, in *Murder of Union Soldiers in North Carolina*, 28; Gaines, "Fayette Artillery," 296. One letter indicates that the five prisoners were executed on Sunday, February 14, 1864. See J. R. P. Ellis to Betty, February 15, 1864, Josiah Robert Peele Ellis Papers, 1863–1864, ECU.

26. Drury Lacy testimony, in *Murder of Union Soldiers in North Carolina*, 80–83.

27. Samuel McDonald Tate testimony, ibid., 68–69.

28. Paris account, *Wilmington Journal*, April 28, 1864.

29. *Western Democrat*, February 23, 1864.

30. Paris account, *Wilmington Journal*, April 28, 1864,

31. Burwell to brother, March 10, 1864, Edmund Burwell Papers, SHC, UNC.

32. W. D. Carr to Mack, February 22, 1864, Herman W. Taylor Collection, NCOAH. See also *Daily Confederate*, February 26, 1864 (reporting that William Hill and Elijah Kellum were executed).

33. Nancy Jones testimony, in *Murder of Union Soldiers in North Carolina*, 31.

34. Bryan McCallan testimony, ibid., 26.

35. *New York Daily Tribune*, March 7, 1864.

36. *New Berne Times*, March 9, 1864.

37. *New York Times*, March 11, 1864. See also *Raftsman's Journal*, March 16, 1864; *Liberator*, March 26, 1864; *Evening Star*, March 11, 1864. The hangings received some coverage in North Carolina papers. A report of the first execution appeared in the *Fayetteville Weekly Observer* on February 8, 1864. In addition, on April 13, 1864, the *North Carolina Presbyterian* published a lengthy account from a regimental chaplain that was widely reprinted throughout the state; see, for example, *Wilmington Journal*, April 28, 1864. Northern accounts of the prisoners' conduct at the executions differed. According to one report, the prisoners "scornfully spurned all overtures of concession" and "fearlessly proclaimed their readiness to die for their country." *New York Times*, March 11, 1864 (the article claims to quote the March 6, 1864, edition of the *Raleigh Confederate*, but no such article has been found). The March 9, 1864, edition of the *New Berne Times* agreed, stating, "We hear that they met their fate like gallant men, without a murmur."

38. Ripley to Peck, April 22, 1864, ORA 33:948–949.

39. *New Berne Times*, March 9, 1864. In Foster's view, a "rebel army is never de jure in the field . . . and a subject or a citizen abandoning it and resuming his true allegiance is not a deserter."

40. In January and February, the 1st and 2nd NCUV added nearly 200 men to their muster rolls. However, in March and April, the new enlistments plummeted to fewer than 20. Moore, *Old North State at War*, 63 (Union enlistment by date and regiment); *New York Times*, March 11, 1864 (reporting that recruiting had not been hurt).

41. Butler, *Autobiography and Personal Reminiscences*, 619.

42. Neathery testimony, in *Murder of Union Soldiers in North Carolina*, 62.

43. Quinn testimony, ibid., 79.

44. *North Carolina Presbyterian*, April 13, 1864.

45. Polk scrap, February 13, 1864, Polk Papers.

46. *Weekly Confederate*, February 17, 1864; *Daily Progress*, April 19, 1864.

47. Barney, *Oxford Encyclopedia of the Civil War*, 98.

48. Lee to Seddon, April 18, 1863, ORA 18:998.

49. Lee to Seddon, October 30, 1863, ORA 29(2):806–807.

50. See Lee to President Davis, April 13, 1864, in Freeman, *Lee's Dispatches*, 154–158.

51. Peck to Pickett, February 11, 1864, ORA 33:866–867. Peck's letter passed through the picket lines the next day, carried by First Lieutenant C. R. Stirling under a flag of truce. Peck to Barton, February 12, 1864, Army and District of North Carolina, RG 393, NARA.

52. Pickett to Peck, February 16, 1864, ORA 33:866–867.

53. Ibid., 867–868. For an analysis of other incidents involving captured black troops, see Urwin, *Black Flag over Dixie*; Burkhardt, *Confederate Rage, Yankee Wrath*.

54. Peck to Pickett, February 13, 1864, ORA 33:867.

55. Peck to Pickett, February 20, 1864, ORA 33:868–869; Butler to Peck, February 17, 1864, ibid., 869.

56. Pickett to Peck, February 17, 1864 (enclosure no. 4), ORA 33:868 (Pickett misspelled

"desserts"). The enclosure read: "List of prisoners captured before New Berne and executed at Kinston, N.C., as deserters from the Confederate Army: David Jones, J. L. Haskett, John L. Stanly, Lewis Bryan, Mitchell Busick, William Irving, Amos Armyette, John J. Beck, William Haddick, Jesse Summerlin, Andrew J. Britteau, William Jones, Lewis Freeman, Calvin Hoffman, Stephen Jones, Joseph Brock, Lewis Taylor, Charles Cuthrell, William H. Daughtry, John Freeman, Elijah Kellum, William J. Hill."

57. Butler to Peck, February 17, 1864, *ORA* 33:569.

58. Peck to Pickett, February 27, 1864, *ORA* 33:869–870.

59. Butler to Ould, March 3, 1864, *ORA*, series 2, 6:1006. No record of a response from the Confederate authorities has been found.

60. Butler to Grant, April 14, 1864, *ORA* 33:865.

61. See Grant to Johnston, February 26, 1864, *ORA*, series 2, 6:991. See also Lonn, *Desertion during the Civil War*, 214.

62. Grant to Johnston, February 26, 1864, *ORA*, series 2, 6:991.

63. Pickett to Johnson, June 1, 1865, in US Congress, *Rebel General Pickett*, 7.

64. Note to file from Stanton, June 19, 1865, ibid.

65. Arguably, all these men had entered Confederate service when they joined the irregular units. These units fell under the Confederate Partisan Ranger Act, which explicitly stated that such men were in the regular service. However, testimony indicated that many of the men had originally been brought into "local service" only. General Orders No. 30, April 28, 1862, *ORA*, series 4, 1:1094–1098; Confederate States of America, *Articles of War*; Board report, in *Murder of Union Soldiers in North Carolina*, 57; Martin testimony, ibid., 84.

66. Report of Board of Inquiry, March 29, 1866, in *Murder of Union Soldiers in North Carolina*, 59. The board was unable to identify the officers presiding over the tribunal. Documents would later reveal at least two members: the aforementioned Captain James R. Branch, who headed the proceeding, and Lieutenant William I. Clopton of the Fayette Artillery. Confederate States of America, General Order No. 6, February 3, 1864; William I. Clopton to "Mother & Sisters," February 8, 1864, Clopton Family Papers. One account, written fifty years after the war, claimed a "Captain Richardson" of the 8th Georgia Cavalry served as the judge advocate. Smith, "Recollections of Capt. John G. Smith," 295. In addition, Montgomery Corse's son claimed Corse served as president of the court-martial. However, this may have been a separate proceeding. Biography of General Montgomery D. Corse by his son Montgomery B. Corse, Montgomery B. Corse Papers, Lloyd House, Alexandria Library, Alexandria, VA.

67. Pickett to Grant, March 12, 1866, in US Congress, *Rebel General Pickett*, 7.

68. Simon, *Papers of Ulysses S. Grant*, 16:121–122.

69. Grant to Johnson, March 16, 1866 (endorsement on Pickett's letter to Grant), US Congress, *Rebel General Pickett*, 9.

70. In response to congressional inquiries about the Kinston hangings, Johnson submitted a stack of reports and correspondence gathered by the War Department in 1866. But Secretary Stanton suggested that recent Supreme Court deliberations had cast doubt on further inquiry. Stanton to Johnson, December 10, 1866, in US Congress, *Rebel General Pickett*, 3.

President Johnson's submittal garnered interest in the press. See *New York Times*, December 12, 1864; *Newbern Weekly Journal of Commerce*, December 18, 1864.

71. During President Johnson's impeachment hearings, Grant batted away questions about his involvement in Pickett's case, claiming he had never, "under any circumstances, signed a recommendation for [Pickett's] pardon." *Impeachment Investigation*, 830–831. In doing so, he ignored his earlier "clemency" recommendation that President Johnson had provided to Congress in December 1866. Grant to Johnson, March 16, 1866 (endorsement on Pickett's letter to Grant), in US Congress, *Rebel General Pickett*, 9.

72. Hawkins, *Account of the Assassination of Loyal Citizens of North Carolina*, 21.

73. Savage, *Loyal Element in North Carolina*.

74. Lee to Pickett, January 20, 1864, ORA 33:1102–1103.

Chapter 12. The Politics of Peace

1. For scholarship on Vance and the 1864 election, see Auman, *Civil War in the North Carolina Quaker Belt*; Manning, "Order of Nature Would Be Reversed," 109–110; Yates, "Governor Vance and the Peace Movement," pt. 2; Mobley, "Zebulon Vance"; Mobley, *"War Governor of the South"*; McKinney, *Zeb Vance*.

2. Vance to Hale, February 4, 1864, in Mobley, *Papers of Zebulon Baird Vance*, 3:88.

3. Zebulon B. Vance, January 28, 1863, ibid., 2:359.

4. See Vance to Alexander Collie, February 8, 1864, and Vance to Theodore Andreae, February 11, 1864, ibid., 3:91–92, 101–103. Vance took great personal interest in the blockade-runner enterprise, leading his friend E. J. Hale to question the fixation. Vance to E. J. Hale, February 11, 1864, ibid., 3:102–104. See also McKinney, *Zeb Vance*, 281.

5. See Whiting to Davis, February 25, 1864, ORA 33:1198 ("many writs are being sued out under the authority of Judge Pearson").

6. Davis to Congress, February 3, 1864, ORA, series 4, 3:67–70.

7. *Journal of the Congress of the Confederate States of America*, 6:805; General Orders No. 31, March 10, 1864, ORA, series 4, 3:203–204.

8. *Weekly Standard*, January 20, 1864.

9. Holden to Calvin Cowles, March 18, 1864, in Raper and Mitchell, *Papers of William Woods Holden*, 1:154.

10. Vance to Davis, February 9, 1864, in Mobley, *Papers of Zebulon Baird Vance*, 3:93–95.

11. Ibid.

12. Davis to Vance, February 29, 1864, ibid., 122–125.

13. Ibid.

14. Vance to Seddon, March 5, 1864; Vance to Davis, March 17, 1864; and Davis to Vance, March 26, 1864, ibid., 132–133, 151–153, 158–160.

15. In early March, Vance wrote to Davis again, this time sending a conciliatory note to smooth the president's ruffled feathers, but also cataloging many specific examples to support his earlier allegations. Vance to Davis, March 9, 1864; and Davis to Vance, March 31, 1864, ibid., 140–144, 161–163. See also Yates, "Governor Vance and the Peace Movement," pt. 2, 93.

16. Harris, *William Woods Holden*, 141; Auman, *Civil War in the North Carolina Quaker Belt*, 130–132.

17. One column in the *Weekly Standard*, penned by "Observer" in late January, pleaded with Vance to call a convention and send commissioners to other states to ensure "the safety and preservation of the country and its institutions." *Weekly Standard*, January 20, 1864.

18. The similarity between Holden's views and those of the Northern Copperheads has been largely ignored. However, in his study of the peace movement in North Carolina's Quaker Belt, William Auman notes this connection, arguing that the similarities between Holden and pro-slavery Northerners were well understood in North Carolina at the time. See Auman, *Civil War in the North Carolina Quaker Belt*.

19. Vance to Hale, December 30, 1863, in Mobley, *Papers of Zebulon Baird Vance*, 2:359.

20. Vance to Swain, January 2, 1864, ibid., 3:7–8; Vance to Hale, February 11, 1864, ibid., 102–104 (expressing Vance's ongoing concern about Holden).

21. Manning, "Order of Nature Would Be Reversed," 109–110.

22. Christopher Hackett to John C. Hackett and Family, January 15, 1864, John C. Hackett Papers, DMRL.

23. "The Sentiments of Soldiers," *Weekly Standard*, September 2, 1863. See also Manning, "Order of Nature Would Be Reversed"; Yates, "Governor Vance and the Peace Movement," pt. 2.

24. Hyman to Vance, February 17, 1864, in Mobley, *Papers of Zebulon Baird Vance*, 3:109; McKinney, *Zeb Vance*, 207.

25. Vance to Hale, December 21, 1863, in Mobley, *Papers of Zebulon Baird Vance*, 2:346–347.

26. Gilmer to Vance, January 5, 1864, ibid., 3:16–18.

27. Vance to Hale, February 11, 1864, ibid., 102–104.

28. McKinney, *Zeb Vance*, xii.

29. Letter from "Hornet," *Fayetteville Weekly Observer*, April 11, 1864.

30. McKinney, *Zeb Vance*, 207–208.

31. *Daily Conservative*, April 16, 1864.

32. Ibid.

33. *Semi-Weekly Standard* (Raleigh, NC), March 3, 1864 (speech of Governor Vance).

34. *Daily Conservative*, April 16, 1864.

35. *Fayetteville Semi-Weekly Observer*, February 29, 1864; *Iredell Express*, March 3, 1864 (Statesville speech).

36. *Fayetteville Semi-Weekly Observer*, March 3, 1864. The *Observer* estimated that 2,000 attended the Statesville speech.

37. *Daily Progress*, March 5, 1864 (quoting the *Greensboro Patriot*).

38. *Daily Confederate*, March 2, 1864. See also *Weekly Standard*, April 6, 1864 (reprinting excerpts from the *Daily Confederate*, March 16, 1864); McKinney, *Zeb Vance*, 213–214.

39. Johnston, "Confederate Letters of Ruffin Barnes," 75–99.

40. *Weekly Progress*, June 14, 1864.

41. For more on Holden and the election, see Harris, *William Woods Holden*; Raper, "William W. Holden and the Peace Movement in North Carolina"; Folk, *W. W. Holden*.

42. See Auman, *Civil War in the North Carolina Quaker Belt*, 141.

43. Clingman to Vance, February 18, 1864, in Mobley, *Papers of Zebulon Baird Vance*, 3:111–113.

44. McKinney, *Zeb Vance*, 211; Harris, *William Woods Holden*, 146.

45. See *Fayetteville Semi-Weekly Observer*, March 27, 1864.

46. Letter from "G.," *Daily Confederate*, April 4, 1864. See also *Charlotte Democrat*, April 5, 1864; Tower, *Lee's Adjutant*, 143.

47. Letter from "G.," *Daily Confederate*, April 4, 1864; Warren, *Doctor's Experiences in Three Continents*, 314–318. Vance's speech was followed by short remarks from Generals Early, Steuart, and Rhodes.

48. Lane, "Glimpses of Army Life in 1864," 407–408.

49. Letter from "Hornet," *Fayetteville Weekly Observer*, April 11, 1864.

50. Warren, *Doctor's Experiences in Three Continents*, 316. For more on Lee's relationship with Vance, see Williams, "The General and the Governor," 108–132.

51. Letter from "G.," *Daily Confederate*, April 4, 1864.

Chapter 13. Ransom's Raid

1. Pickett to Seddon, January 12, 1864, ORA 33:1083; Thomas, *Divided Allegiances*, 50.

2. John Graham to William Graham, March 3, 1864, in Williams, *Papers of William Alexander Graham*, 6:39–44. Ransom's brigade contained the 8th, 24th, 25th, 49th, and 56th North Carolina Regiments.

3. T. G. Barham, war record, 20, Fredericksburg and Spotsylvania National Military Park.

4. Heckman and Smith reports, ORA 33:225–227; Clark, *Histories of the Several Regiments*, 3:335 (56th North Carolina), 2:280 (24th North Carolina). "Ransom's whole command went on a raid."

5. John Graham to William Graham, March 3, 1864.

6. Dearing to his wife, March 8, 1864, James Dearing Papers, VHS.

7. Peck report, May 5, 1863, ORA 18:275.

8. For more information on the 1863 Suffolk Campaign, see Wills, *War Hits Home*; Cormier, *Siege of Suffolk*.

9. Blakeslee, *History of the Sixteenth Connecticut Volunteers*, 34.

10. John Graham to William Graham, March 3, 1864. The 2nd US Colored Cavalry was led by Colonel George W. Cole.

11. Barham, war record, 20–21.

12. Heckman report, ORA 33:238–239.

13. *Evening Bulletin*, March 18, 1864.

14. John Graham to William Graham, March 3, 1864, 43.

15. Ibid., 44. See also account of W. A. Day (49th North Carolina), *Statesville Record*, January 2, 1934.

16. *Pittsburgh Daily Commercial*, March 15, 1864; Heckman report, ORA 33:238–239.

17. *Evening Bulletin*, March 18, 1864; Rose, "Twenty-Fourth Regiment," 279–283; *Hartford*

Courant, March 15, 1864 (reporting that Colonel Pond shot a Confederate cavalry officer). One Southern account claimed that the Union soldiers in the house refused to surrender; one was killed after he left the burning house, firing at the Confederates, and three more died in the flames. *Richmond Dispatch*, March 14, 1864.

18. *Evening Bulletin*, March 18, 1864.

19. John Graham to William Graham, March 3, 1864, 43.

20. Roulhac letter, March 13, 1864, Ruffin, Roulhac, and Hamilton Family Papers, SHC, UNC.

21. Edmondston, *Journal of a Secesh Lady*, 547 (April 18, 1864, entry).

22. Heckman report, ORA 33:238; Cole report, ibid., 239 (containing revised casualty numbers that were lower than Heckman's); John Graham to William Graham, March 3, 1864; Barham, war record, 20. See also *New Berne Times*, March 23, 1864 (reporting twenty-nine Union killed, wounded, and missing); *Daily Journal*, March 15, 1864; *Hartford Courant*, March 15, 1864 (reporting about twenty Union killed, wounded, and missing).

23. Diary of Henry A. Chambers, Henry A. Chambers Papers, SHC, UNC.

24. *Evening Bulletin*, March 18, 1864.

25. John Graham to William Graham, March 3, 1864, 41. For further details regarding the Suffolk engagement, see Wills, *War Hits Home*, 213–219.

26. Ibid.; Butler, Heckman, and Cole reports, ORA 33:237–238.

27. For a recent study of Fort Pillow, see Wills, *River Was Dyed with Blood*. For an overview of battlefield atrocities, see Urwin, *Black Flag over Dixie*; Burkhardt, *Confederate Rage, Yankee Wrath*.

Chapter 14. Preparing for the Spring

1. Cheshire, *Nonnulla*, 145.

2. *Charlotte Observer*, May 14, 1905.

3. Lee to Davis, February 3, 1864, ORA 33:1144.

4. Lee to Elzey, February 15, 1864, ORA 33:1175.

5. Lee to Davis, February 3, 1864, ORA 33:1144.

6. Abstract of return for Department of North Carolina, February 1864, ORA 33:1202; biography of General Montgomery D. Corse by his son Montgomery B. Corse, Montgomery B. Corse Papers, Lloyd House, Alexandria Library, Alexandria, VA; General Orders, ORA 33:1232 (Corse at Kinston); Lawton to Ransom, February 17, 1864, ibid., 1200 (Ransom at Weldon). Following the New Bern operation, the forces in Pickett's department, excluding Hoke's brigade, included Montgomery Corse's Virginians (1,688 men and officers in late February) stationed with Hoke at Kinston; Matt Ransom's North Carolinians (more than 3,000) spread over the state, with their commander based in Weldon; and Thomas Clingman's North Carolina brigade (2,100). Abstract of return for Department of North Carolina, February 1864, ORA 33:1202.

7. Lee to Hoke, February 11, 1864, ORA 33:1160.

8. Abstract of return for Department of North Carolina, February 1864, ORA 33:1202 (includes attached 21st Georgia and 43rd North Carolina).

9. Letter from "Alpha" (3rd North Carolina Cavalry), *Weekly Intelligencer*, March 29, 1864; *Daily Journal*, March 28, 1864; Ward to "Dear Mother," February 18, 1864, Giles F. Ward Papers, DMRL; Fiske, *War Letters of Capt. Fiske*, 48.

10. George to Dearest Friend, March 27, 1864, Aurelia Hooper Papers, DMRL.

11. Henry Barrow to Christian, February 17, 1864, Christian Thomas Pfohl Papers, SHC, UNC ("Camp is a hard place to have measles").

12. Ibid.; Reeves reminiscences and letter, February 23, 1864, Edward Payson Reeves Papers, SHC, UNC.

13. Burwell to Brother, March 10, 1864, Edmund Burwell Papers, SHC, UNC.

14. Barnes to "Dear Mother," March 24, 1864, Edward Cook Barnes Papers, University of Virginia.

15. Corse to His Wife, March 9, 1864, Corse Papers.

16. *Weekly Intelligencer*, March 29, 1864. The men found the Neuse River an excellent source of "very fine fish." Henry Barrow to Christian, February 17, 1864, Pfohl Papers.

17. George F. Fisher to Mother, March 23, 1864, George F. Fisher Letters, Wood Family Collection, High Point, NC.

18. *Greensboro Patriot*, March 24, 1864; *Charlotte Democrat*, March 29, 1864.

19. George to Dearest Friend, March 27, 1864, Hooper Papers (various misspellings corrected). The day witnessed more than one snowball fight. A newly arrived member of the 21st North Carolina wrote that he "went into his first battle today." George F. Fisher to Mother, March 23, 1864, Fisher Letters.

20. *Weekly Intelligencer*, March 29, 1864.

21. Edmondston, *Journal of a Secesh Lady*, xxxvii, 524–526.

22. See Elliott, "Career of the Ram *Albemarle*," 420–427.

23. Elliott, *Ironclad of the Roanoke*, 148. In addition to the *Albemarle*, Elliott had constructed a floating battery to defend the Roanoke's upper reaches.

24. Robert D. Minor to wife, February 11, 1864, Minor Family Papers, VHS.

25. Elliott, *Ironclad of the Roanoke*, 149.

26. Wood to Jones, February 26, 1864, *ORN* 9:800–801.

27. Lynch to Mallory, March 8, 1864, *ORN* 9:803; Mallory to Seddon, March 11, 1864, ibid., 802–803.

28. Minor to Mallory, February 28, 1864, in *Civil War Naval Chronology*, 4:24. See also Hinds, *Hunt for the Albemarle*, 162.

29. Elliott, *Ironclad of the Roanoke*, 155–157.

30. Hoke report, *ORA* 33:95–97; Lee to Hoke, February 11, 1864, ibid., 1160–1161. Among others, Henry Guion and his men drove hard to finish the *Neuse*. "I furnish good ship carpenters—the navy keep[s] the workmen waiting for material," Guion wrote. Henry T. Guion journal (entry for March 18–28, 1864), William Hoke Papers, SHC, UNC.

31. Robert D. Minor to Stephen R. Mallory, February 16, 1864, Minor Family Papers; W. R. Burwell to his brother, March 10, 1864, Burwell Papers. Burwell indicated that members of the 43rd North Carolina were detailed to work on the project.

32. Minor to Lynch, February 16, 1864, in *Civil War Naval Chronology*, 4:20–21; Robert D. Minor to Stephen R. Mallory, February 16, 1864, Minor Family Papers.

33. By March 9, Loyall reported that the two Brooke rifle guns had been mounted in the vessel and that the "first course of iron" was complete. *Commonwealth*, May 13, 1897.

34. R. T. Burwell letter, March 19, 1864, Burwell Papers.

35. Richard H. Bacot to "Sis," March 19, 1864, Richard H. Bacot Papers, NCOAH. Lieutenant Loyall also had a low opinion of the boat's complement. "The ignorance and greenness of my conscripts is inconceivable," he grumbled. Benjamin P. Loyall to Robert D. Minor, March 9, 1864, Minor Family Papers.

36. Benjamin P. Loyall to Robert D. Minor, April 7, 1864, Minor Family Papers.

37. Robert D. Minor to Stephen R. Mallory, February 16, 1864, Minor Family Papers; Minor to Lynch, February 16, 1864, in *Civil War Naval Chronology*, 4:20–21. In March, heavy rains produced freshets along the Roanoke River. Despite the rains, the rivers remained a concern. Edmondston, *Journal of a Secesh Lady*, 545.

38. See *Commonwealth*, May 13, 1897. See also Wilson, *Ironclads in Action*, 1:107 (reporting that engines were obtained from Tredegar Works in Richmond).

39. Elliott, *Ironclad of the Roanoke*, 159.

40. Mallory to Bulloch, April 30, 1862, *ORN*, series 2, 2:186–187.

41. Article by Geo. L. Kilmer, *Girard Press*, November 14, 1889.

42. H. T. Guion, "Map of New Bern and the Country Adjacent—from Memory," DMRL.

43. Peck report, *ORA* 33:290. See Flusser to Lee, August 21, 1864, *ORN* 9:175; Behm to Lee, September 8, 1863, ibid., 194.

44. Peck to Butler, February 13, 1864, *ORA* 33:557–558.

45. Ripley to William, March 1, 1864, in Ripley, *Vermont General*, 196.

46. See Peck to Butler, February 29 and March 4, 1864, *ORA* 33:634–635, 642.

47. Letter from Luther M. Baldwin, March 6, 1864, Nettleton-Baldwin Papers, DMRL.

48. Peck to Butler, February 13, 1864, *ORA* 33:557–558. See also Claassen to Foster, February 13, 1864, ibid., 558; Lee to Butler, February 20, 1864, *ORN* 9:498.

49. Peck to Palmer, March 3, 1864, Army and District of North Carolina, RG 393, NARA.

50. Judson dispatch to 5th Rhode Island commander, February 15, 1864, Letters Sent, New Bern Sub-District, Records of Subdistricts, RG 393, NARA. Lumber from the huts in the camp outside Fort Totten was sent to Roanoke Island.

51. Baldwin letter, March 6, 1864, Nettleton-Baldwin Papers; Edward Burgess Peirce to Mother, March 3, 1864, Edward Burgess Peirce Letters, 1862–1871, Massachusetts Historical Society.

52. See Judson to Strong, February 13, 1864, Letters Sent, New Bern Sub-District, Records of Subdistricts, RG 393, NARA; Peck to Palmer, February 21, 1864, Army and District of North Carolina, RG 393, NARA; Peck report, *ORA* 33:293.

53. Hall and Hall, *Cayuga in the Field*, 198; Baldwin letter, March 6, 1864, Nettleton-Baldwin Papers; Peck to Butler, February 13, 1864, *ORA* 33:557–558. See also Claassen to Foster, February 13, 1864, ibid., 558.

54. Letter from Luther M. Baldwin, February 28, 1864, Nettleton-Baldwin Papers.

55. Some rumors suggested the Confederates would attack New Bern; others hinted at Washington. Henry Wessells, at Plymouth, heard that the Confederates were forming at Halifax to regain the Roanoke River. Peck to Davis, February 10, 1864, *ORA* 33:61.

56. Flusser to S. P. Lee, February 5, 1864, *ORN* 9:463–464.

57. Welles to Lee, February 5, 1864, *ORN* 9:462; Lee to Welles, March 4, 1864, ibid., 524; USS *Tacony*, ZC File, NHHC.

58. See Peck to Foster, September 10, 1863, *ORA* 29(2):164–165.

59. Welles to Stanton, September 17, 1863, *ORN* 9:202.

60. Ibid.; Lee to Welles, August 17, 1863, *ORN* 9:162.

61. Peck report, *ORA* 33:289–293; Peck to Foster, August 17, 1863, *ORA* 29(2):63–64.

62. Peck to Butler, February 18, 1864, *ORA* 33:573.

63. Lee to Flusser, October 3, 1864, *ORN* 9:227. See also Flusser to Lee, October 31, 1864, ibid., 255 (discussing various approaches open to the ironclad).

64. Butler to Peck, March 5, 1864, *ORA* 33:645.

65. Butler to Peck, February 20, 1864, *ORA* 33:580.

66. Butler to Lee, February 17, 1864, *ORN* 9:491 ("I do not much believe in the 'ram,' either in the Roanoke or the Neuse"); Lee to Welles, November 24, 1863, ibid., 325 (reporting Butler's visit to Plymouth); Hinds, *Hunt for the Albemarle*, 115; Browning, *From Cape Charles to Cape Fear*, 102.

67. Butler to Peck, February 20, 1864, *ORA* 33:580.

68. Peck to Butler, February 23, 1864, *ORA* 33:589.

69. Peck to Butler, February 24, 1864, *ORA* 33:593; Peck report, ibid., 289–293. Peck received similar news about the *Neuse* at Kinston on February 29. Peck to Butler, February 29, 1864, ibid., 634–635.

70. Peck report, *ORA* 33:289–293; Flusser to S. P. Lee, February 5, 1864, *ORN* 9:463–464; Flusser to Davenport, March 6, 1864, ibid., 535. On February 26, Admiral Lee heard that a large shipment of iron was headed from Wilmington to Halifax to plate the ironclad on the Roanoke. Lee to Welles, February 26, 1864, ibid., 507.

71. Hinds, *Hunt for the Albemarle*, 121.

72. Flusser to Lee, March 16, 1864, *ORN* 9:552.

73. Peck to Wessells, March 20, 1864, *ORA* 33:707.

74. Flusser to Lee, March 18, 1864, *ORN* 9:555–556.

75. Flusser to Davenport, March 24, 1864, *ORN* 9:562.

76. Butler to Lee, March 21, 1864, *ORA* 33:711.

77. Lee to Flusser, March 22, 1864, *ORN* 9:560.

78. Butler to Peck, March 21, 1864, *ORA* 33:711.

79. Peck to Butler, March 25, 1864, *ORA* 33:740.

80. Lee to Butler, March 22, 1864, *ORN* 9:559–560.

81. Flusser concluded, "beyond possibility of doubt . . . the whole affair was a fabrication." Flusser had observed the man at Plymouth and suspected him of being a rebel agent or at least highly untrustworthy. Flusser to Lee, March 30, 1864, *ORN* 9:577; Lee to Flusser,

April 4, 1864, ibid., 584–585; Flusser to Lee, March 27, 1864, ibid., 569; Flusser to Davenport, March 24, 1864, ibid., 562.

82. See Peck to Butler, March 26, 1864, *ORA* 33:748.

83. More news trickled into Plymouth about the ironclad. See Flusser to Lee, March 27, 1864, *ORN* 9:569 (report that the iron was 6 to 10 inches thick; rebel officer claimed the attack would occur on New Bern and Plymouth simultaneously). Peck had also heard rumors of Confederate movement. See Peck to Wessells, March 20, 1864, Army and District of North Carolina, RG 393, NARA; Peck to Wessells and Peck to Butler, March 29, 1864, *ORA* 33:769 (Confederates would attack when the rivers were high enough).

84. Union commanders scrambled to replace the damaged 100-pounder rifle from the *Southfield* after receiving new reports that the ironclads' armor was 4½ inches thick, not the 3 inches understood before. See Peck to Butler, March 26, 1864, *ORA* 33:748; Peck to Davenport, March 26, 1864, ibid., 749; Peck to Wessells, March 29, 1864, ibid., 768; Lee to Welles, March 22, 1864, *ORN* 9:560 (100-pounder and 9-inch headed to Plymouth).

85. Lee to Welles, March 4, 1864, *ORN* 9:524.

86. Davenport to Lee, March 25, 1864, *ORN* 9:569.

87. Lee to Foster, April 17, 1863, *ORN* 9:688–689.

88. Grant to Butler, April 2, 1864, *ORA* 33:794–795; Grant to Burnside, April 5, 1864, ibid., 808.

89. Peck to Wessells, April 4, 1864, Army and District of North Carolina, RG 393, NARA.

90. Davis to Peck, April 10, 1864, *ORA* 33:837–838.

Chapter 15. Plymouth Is the Target

1. *New York Times*, March 11, 1864.

2. Samuel J. Gibson diary, March 25, 1864, LOC. Henry Tilton, a New York artillery officer, wrote home in late March: "Gen'l Wessells has been expecting an attack on this place but I guess it has all blown over now." H. Tilton to "My Dear Mother," March 24, 1864, Tilton Family Papers, LOC. Pennsylvania lieutenant Isaiah Conley wrote, "The much talked of Rebel ram has not made its appearance and my opinion is that it will not." Conley to "My Dear Wife," April 7, 1864, Isaiah Conley, Civil War Correspondence, Special Collections, Virginia Polytechnic Institute and State University. See also Meade to Halleck, March 17, 1864, *ORN* 9:553 (rumored move against Norfolk).

3. W. R. Burwell to Brother, March 10, 1864, Edmund Burwell Papers, SHC, UNC.

4. General Orders No. 23, February 24, 1864, *ORA* 33:1196.

5. George E. Pickett to Braxton Bragg, April 6, 1864, Charles S. Venable Papers, SHC, UNC. Pickett's plan does not appear in the official records, but a copy resides in the papers of Charles S. Venable, a member of Robert E. Lee's staff. Specifically, Pickett recommended that the attack column include Ransom's and Kemper's (Terry's) brigades, as well as another brigade drawn from Virginia (Pickett suggested Eppa Hunton's from his own division). He also included James Dearing's cavalry and four artillery batteries as part of the plan.

6. George E. Pickett to Braxton Bragg, April 6, 1864, Venable Papers. For the diversion, Pickett pointed to Corse's and Hoke's brigades and a detachment from Wilmington.

7. On March 30, Lee once again raised the return of his troops with President Davis, explaining that he had held back his requests, hoping "the object of his visit to North Carolina may it be accomplished." Lee to Davis, March 30, 1864, ORA 33:1244; Lee to Bragg, April 7, 1864, ibid., 1265.

8. Bragg to Lee, April 11, 1864, ORA 51(2):855.

9. Lee to Pickett, April 11, 1864, ORA 33:1273.

10. Lee to Davis, April 12, 1864, ORA 33:1275.

11. Lee to Bragg, April 13, 1864, ORA 33:1279.

12. Bragg to Pickett, April 12, 1864, ORA 51(2):857.

13. Younger, *Inside the Confederate Government*, 145.

14. Bragg to Pickett, April 16, 1864, ORA 51(2):863–864.

15. Pickett to Bragg, April 17, 1864, ORA 51(2):865.

16. Gordon, *General George E. Pickett*, 138 (citing Seddon to Bragg, May 7, 1864, Braxton Bragg Papers, DMRL).

17. *Richmond Enquirer*, May 27, 1864.

18. Pickett, *Pickett and His Men*, 338–339.

19. See Gordon, "Let the People See the Old Life," 170–184; Gordon, *General George E. Pickett*, 1–5.

20. Pickett to Cooper, November 7, 1863, ORA 29(2):827; Harrison, *Pickett's Men*, 123.

21. See Lee to Davis, April 15, 1864, ORA 33:1282.

22. See Robertson, *Back Door to Richmond*, 44–46.

23. See Lee to Davis, April 2, 1864, ORA 33:1254; Whiting to Pickett, April 10, 1864, ibid., 1271.

24. *Fayetteville Weekly Observer*, December 30, 1909. See also article by Fred Olds, *Pinehurst Outlook*, January 29, 1916 (with extensive quotes from Hoke).

25. *Evening Bulletin*, June 17, 1863 (Hoke's convalescence).

26. Speech by Hamilton, "General Robert F. Hoke and His Military Career," Robert Hoke Papers, SHC, UNC.

27. Adjutant General's Roll of Honor Scrapbook, NCOAH.

28. Auman, *Civil War in the North Carolina Quaker Belt*, 110 (citing Mary to "My dearest Rufus," September 9, 1863, Rufus L. Patterson Papers, SHC, UNC).

29. Cheshire, *Nonnulla*, 150.

30. Hamilton speech, "General Robert F. Hoke and His Military Career"; See also Barefoot, *General Robert F. Hoke*.

31. Corse to His Wife, March 9, 1864, Montgomery B. Corse Papers, Lloyd House, Alexandria Library, Alexandria, VA. "Genl Hoke is ordered to Rich'd which will deprive me of my main support & dependence for keeping every thing straight on the outposts, I think will go on right until he returns, which I am in hopes will be in a few days."

32. Woodward, *Mary Chesnut's Civil War*, 586.

33. John Paris diary, April 12, 1864, John Paris Papers, SHC, UNC; Stedman, "Address of Mr. Stedman, of North Carolina," 74–75.

34. *News and Observer*, May 14, 1905. See also *Farmer and the Mechanic*, May 16, 1905; *Charlotte Observer*, May 26, 1907. Hoke would occasionally discuss his memories with friends and acquaintances, and at least once, late in his life, he sat for a brief interview with Fred A. Olds. A transcript appeared in the *Charlotte Observer*, November 26, 1905.

35. Recollections of "Private A. N. V.," *Evening Visitor*, March 6, 1894; Ashe, *History of North Carolina*, 2:863 (Hoke recommended Holden's arrest).

36. Cheshire, *Nonnulla*, 146.

37. Account of Fred A. Olds, *Charlotte Observer*, May 26, 1907; account of Fred Olds, *Western Sentinel*, March 14, 1919; Cheshire, *Nonnulla*, 145; *Charlotte Observer*, May 14, 1905 ("An order was also issued by the Navy Department placing Captain Cooke . . . under Hoke's direction").

38. Paris diary, April 12, 1864, Paris Papers.

39. Guion's journal entry is dated April 11 but was originally written as April 12 (Guion crossed out the "2"), so it is possible this communication actually occurred on the twelfth—the day Bragg sent instructions to Pickett assigning the operation to Hoke. Henry T. Guion journal, William Hoke Papers, SHC, UNC.

40. Bragg to Hoke, April 12, 1864, ORA 51(2):857–858. Bragg also gave instructions to Ransom.

41. Edward L. Conn, "Plymouth," *News and Observer*, June 11, 1909.

42. Goss, *Soldier's Story of His Captivity*, 55.

43. James, *Annual Report of the Superintendent of Negro Affairs in North Carolina*, 34.

44. Durrill, *War of Another Kind*, 177 (citing H. B. Short to William Pettigrew, May 19, 1863, Pettigrew Papers, SHC, UNC).

45. Goss, *Soldier's Story of His Captivity*, 55.

46. *New York Herald*, December 2, 1863 (description of Butler's North Carolina inspection).

47. See Durrill, *War of Another Kind*; James, *Annual Report of the Superintendent of Negro Affairs in North Carolina*, 34; Reed, *History of the 101st Regiment*, 123.

48. Dickey, *History of the 103d Regiment*, 271–272.

49. Samuel Grosvenor diary, April 20, 1864, CHS.

50. *Richmond Examiner*, April 24, 1864; Reed, *History of the 101st Regiment*, 123.

51. Peck to Lee, November 13, 1863, ORN 9:302.

52. Lee to Foster, May 1, 1863, ORN 9:689–690. See also Boynton, *History of the Navy during the Rebellion*, 2:495. After visiting the town in August 1863, Admiral Lee concluded that it was "strongly fortified." Lee to Welles, August 17, 1863, ORN 9:162.

53. Fiske, *War Letters of Capt. Fiske*, 54. Fiske ventured upriver and recorded his impressions: "a gloomy place you can scarcely imagine. For miles there is nothing but almost impenetrable swamps full of the cypress covered with moss."

54. Peck to Butler, April 7, 1864, Army and District of North Carolina, RG 393, NARA.

55. Wessells to Judson, April 13, 1864, ORA 33:281; Flusser to Lee, April 12, 1864, ORN 9:609–610.

56. Peck to Wessells, April 15, 1864, ORA 33:877.

57. Butler to Lee, April 17, 1864, ORA 33:895; Shaffer to Peck, April 17, 1864, ibid., 895–896.

58. Peck to Butler, April 19, 1864, ORA 33:281–282. Returns from New Bern in early April had identified about 5,000 men manning the various fortifications around the city. Palmer to Judson, April 8, 1864, ibid., 824–826.

59. Hackett, *Flusser and the Albemarle*, 5.

60. Stewart, "Lion-Hearted Flusser."

61. Allen, *Forty-Six Months with the Fourth R.I. Volunteers*, 59.

62. Hackett, *Flusser and the Albemarle*, 5.

63. Stewart, "Lion-Hearted Flusser," 311–312 (letter transcripts appended to the article).

64. Flusser to "My Dear Fan," April 12, 1864, Charles W. Flusser ZB File, NHHC; Stewart, "Lion-Hearted Flusser," 311–312.

Chapter 16. The Attack on Plymouth

1. Scharf, *History of the Confederate States Navy*, 409.

2. Fred A. Olds, *Charlotte Observer*, May 26, 1907; Cheshire, *Nonnulla*, 148.

3. Cheshire, *Nonnulla*, 148.

4. For details of Cooke's life and career, see "James Wallace Cooke Biographical Sketch, 1898," SHC, UNC.

5. Olds, *Charlotte Observer*, May 26, 1907. The date of Hoke's visit with Cooke is not clear, and accounts differ. For instance, Confederate veteran and historian J. Thomas Scharf says Hoke ordered Cooke to prepare as early as three weeks before the Plymouth operation. See Scharf, *History of the Confederate States Navy*, 404. Cooke's wife recalled after the war that Hoke visited on April 17, surely too late. Hinds, *Hunt for the Albemarle*, 141 (citing transcription of Cooke's papers from a private collection). John Maffitt, who did not accompany Cooke but commanded the *Albemarle* later, claimed that Hoke visited Cooke on two occasions: once several weeks before the operation, and again "some days" before the attack. Given the timing of Pickett's plan (submitted to Bragg on April 6), Hoke's journey to Virginia (early April), Bragg's orders to Hoke (April 12), and Hoke's announcement to Henry Guion that Pickett had handed the operation over to him (April 12), it appears that Hoke visited Cooke on April 12 or 13. Cheshire and Olds, who spoke with Hoke after the war, suggest that Hoke gave Cooke his orders only about a week before the operation. Olds's account places that meeting at Halifax. By some accounts, Cooke had moved the *Albemarle* to Hamilton in late March, although as of April 1, invoices for the project were still being processed through Halifax. Cheshire, *Nonnulla*, 147; Olds, *Charlotte Observer*, May 26, 1907; Scharf, *History of the Confederate States Navy*, 409; *Daily Review*, June 28 and 29, 1877; "Appropriation of Iron Clads," April 1, 1864, Subject File of Confederate States Navy, 1861–1865, RG 109, M1901, NARA.

6. Hoke's brigade at Plymouth consisted of the 6th, 21st, and 43rd North Carolina, augmented by the 21st Georgia (the 54th and 57th North Carolina did not join the expedition). Ransom's brigade included the 24th, 25th, 35th, and 56th North Carolina, as well as the 8th North Carolina from Clingman's brigade (the 49th North Carolina of Ransom's brigade was stationed on picket duty along the Chowan at the time). Kemper's Virginia brigade included the 1st, 3rd, 7th, 11th, and 24th Virginia. John W. Graham to William A. Graham, April 24, 1864, in Williams, *Papers of William Alexander Graham*, 6:68–77; *Charlotte Observer*, November 24, 1901; *Richmond Examiner*, May 3, 1864; Sherrill, *21st North Carolina Infantry*, 316. The cavalry apparently included several companies of the 8th Confederate Cavalry (Dearing's regiment); one account, which may be in error, also mentions the 7th Confederate Cavalry. Clark, *Histories of the Several Regiments*, 4:83. See also Jordan and Thomas, "Massacre at Plymouth," 133 (which claims the 8th Confederate Cavalry was at Plymouth).

7. Graham, "Fifty-Sixth Regiment," 337; Barnes to "Charlie," April 30, 1864, Barnes Family Papers, University of Virginia; Iobst and Manarin, *Bloody Sixth*, 190; Manarin and Jordan, *North Carolina Troops*, 14:49.

8. Maffitt, "Reminiscences of the Confederate Navy," 502–505; *Roanoke Beacon*, July 13, 1903. The story claimed Beasley's map was so accurate that it accounted for every piece of Federal artillery save two.

9. See *Squires and Bennett, Through the Years in Norfolk*, 126.

10. Graham, "Fifty-Sixth Regiment," 337. As Hoke rushed his troops out of town, he was briefly delayed by rumors that Corse was fighting west of New Bern.

11. Loehr, *War History of the Old First Virginia*, 42; Johnston, *Story of a Confederate Boy in the Civil War*, 242. In Wilmington, Terry's men had enjoyed a steady diet of oysters and crabs.

12. *Daily Journal*, May 16, 1864; William Beavans, diary and letters, SHC, UNC; Elliott, *Southern Soldier Boy*, 13; Iobst and Manarin, *Bloody Sixth*, 190.

13. *Charlotte Observer*, May 26, 1907.

14. Letter from Burklow, *Wilmington Journal*, May 19, 1864.

15. Cushing Biggs Hassell Papers, SHC, UNC; *Polkton Ansonian*, July 12 and 19, 1876.

16. John Graham to William Graham, April 24, 1864, 6:71. Sweetwater Creek was about 6 feet deep.

17. Henry T. Guion journal, William Hoke Papers, SHC, UNC.

18. William A. Biggs to his sister, May 3, 1864, Asa Biggs Papers, DMRL; Guion journal.

19. Peck to Wessells, April 15, 1864, ORA 33:877; Wessells to Judson, April 13, 1864, ibid., 281; Outwater to Harland, April 18, 1864, ibid., 905–906 (*Tacony* was "the largest and one of the most valuable of her class").

20. Wessells report, ORA 33:296–300; Peck to Butler, April 25, 1864, ibid., 287–293 (quoting Wessells's dispatch); Flusser, May 13, 1863, ORN 9:20.

21. Flusser to Davenport, April 18, 1864, Area File of the Naval Collection, 1775–1910, Area 7, January–June 1864, RG 45, M625, NARA.

22. Peck to Butler, April 21, 1864, ORA 33:285. They even returned some reinforcements sent to the Plymouth post. Peck report, ibid., 288.

23. Mahood, *Charlie Mosher's Civil War*, 193. Mosher mistakenly referred to the vessel as the *Tacoma*. The Union navy had no such vessel at the time, but the USS *Tahoma* was serving in Florida. See Mooney, *Dictionary of American Naval Fighting Ships*, vol. 3.

24. Truxtun became a lieutenant commander on July 16, 1862, the same day Flusser achieved that rank. However, the elder Truxtun had entered service as a midshipman in 1841, giving him more time in service than Flusser. See Callahan, *List of Officers*. See also Navy Pension Applications, 1861–1910, RG 15, M1279, NARA.

25. Davenport to Flusser, April 19, 1864, ORN 9:662.

26. Davenport to Lee, April 19, 1864, ORN 9:663.

27. Croffut, *Military and Civil History of Connecticut*, 486; Mahood, *Charlie Mosher's Civil War*, 193; Gordon, *Broken Regiment*, 119 (quoting J. Leander Chapin to Gilbert Chapin, Chapin Papers, CHS); Kellogg, *Life and Death in Rebel Prisons*, 25; USS *Ceres* log, RG 24, NARA; diary of Sergeant Major Robert Hale Kellogg, vol. 3, CHS.

28. Bragg to Hoke, April 12, 1864, ORA 51(2):857–858.

29. T. G. Barham, war record, 21, Fredericksburg and Spotsylvania National Military Park.

30. *Daily Dispatch*, May 2, 1864.

31. Guion journal.

32. John Graham to William Graham, April 24, 1864, 6:71; Guion journal.

33. According to local Plymouth historian Jimmy Hardison, the house that served as Hoke's headquarters was located on the Washington Road near present-day Morrattock Road. See also Sherrill, *21st North Carolina Infantry*, 495–496 n. 15. Sherrill's discussion includes an extensive comparison of the modern-day road network.

34. Account of Major J. W. Graham, *Charlotte Observer*, November 24, 1901; Kellogg diary, vol. 3. Graham's account from the *Charlotte Observer* was also published in Clark, *Histories of the Several Regiments*, 5:175.

35. Wessells report, ORA 33:296; Donaghy, *Army Experience of Capt. John Donaghy*, 147.

36. John Graham to William Graham, April 24, 1864, 6:68–77.

37. Graham, "Fifty-Sixth Regiment," 337; Kellogg, *Life and Death in Rebel Prisons*, 25; John Graham to William Graham, April 24, 1864, 6:74; *Fayetteville Weekly Observer*, May 9, 1864; Graham account, *Charlotte Observer*, November 24, 1901.

38. Mahood, *Charlie Mosher's Civil War*, 193.

39. Brown to Captain A. S. Stewart, April 17, 1864, Area File of the Naval Collection, 1775–1910, Area 7, January–June 1864, RG 45, M625, NARA.

40. Wessells report, ORA 33:296–300; Wessells to Flusser, April 17, 1864, Area File of the Naval Collection, 1775–1910, Area 7, January–June 1864, RG 45, M625, NARA.

41. Mahood, *Charlie Mosher's Civil War*, 193.

42. Wessells report, ORA 33:296–300; Kellogg, *Life and Death in Rebel Prisons*, 25.

43. Wessells report, ORA 33:297.

44. Smith, "Siege and Capture of Plymouth," 328; Kellogg diary, vol. 3.

45. Kellogg, *Life and Death in Rebel Prisons*, 25.

46. James, *Annual Report of the Superintendent of Negro Affairs in North Carolina*, 35.

47. The Plymouth street grid is not laid out in a strict north-south, east-west orientation. For instance, Lee's Mill Road, which became Washington Street in town, was situated north-northwest rather than true north. For ease of description, the narrative generally uses the cardinal points of the compass to describe the location of positions and the direction of troop movements.

48. Dickey, *History of the 103d Regiment*, 76; Hess, *Field Armies and Fortifications in the Civil War*, 302–304. Fort Williams was named after Brigadier General Thomas Williams, killed at Baton Rouge in 1862. General Orders No. 60, ORA 18:644.

49. The core of Plymouth's garrison came from portions of four regiments: 16th Connecticut (400 men), 101st Pennsylvania (300 men), 103rd Pennsylvania (400 men), and 85th New York (450 men). Smith, "Siege and Capture of Plymouth," 328.

50. Ibid.; Reed, *History of the 101st Regiment*, 129.

51. Donaghy, *Army Experience of Capt. John Donaghy*, 148.

52. Diary of First Sergeant Oliver W. Gates, Company F, 16th Connecticut, CHS.

53. Goss, *Soldier's Story of His Captivity*, 55.

54. Jordan and Thomas, "Massacre at Plymouth," 154. See also William F. Baker Service Record, RG 94, M1821, NARA. Several other members of the 10th USCT were part of Baker's recruiting detachment at Plymouth.

55. McNary, "What I Saw and Did Inside and Outside of Rebel Prisons," 26.

56. See Wessells report, ORA 33:296–300; Peck to Davis, April 14, 1864, ibid., 870. Evidence from earlier in the year revealed that recruiting had yielded mixed results. Edmund Blount to Foster, February 9, 1864, 2nd North Carolina Regiment, RG 94, M401, reel 10, NARA. Captain Marvin specifically stated that he had about forty recruits at the time. Jordan and Thomas, "Massacre at Plymouth," 45.

57. James, *Annual Report of the Superintendent of Negro Affairs in North Carolina*, 35. See also Gordon, *Broken Regiment*, 122–123; Smith, "Siege and Capture of Plymouth," 324 (100 black recruits).

58. John Graham to William Graham, April 24, 1864, notes that the 56th North Carolina was assigned to construct breastworks.

59. Fiske, *War Letters of Capt. Fiske*, 48–52. The parapet in the drawings contains no embrasures, suggesting that the guns were placed "en barbette," to fire over the wall. These Federal maps, which provided detailed views, measurements, and elevations of each major Federal work at Plymouth, were prepared by First Lieutenant Felix Vinay of the 85th New York, most likely in the spring of 1863. Vinay, "Plan of Plymouth, N.C. Its Fortifications and Environs," NCOAH. See also Wessells to Hoffman, May 17, 1863, ORA 18:721–722 (describing the progress of initial construction efforts on various fortifications at Plymouth).

60. Barnes to "Charlie," April 30, 1864, Barnes Family Papers.

61. Reeves diary, Reeves Papers; *Fayetteville Weekly Observer*, May 9, 1864.

62. Hodijah Lincoln Meade letter, April 29, 1864, Meade Family Letters, VHS; *Fayetteville Weekly Observer*, May 2, 1864 (specifically mentions the 20-pounder Parrotts).

63. Reeves diary, Reeves Papers; Smith, "Siege and Capture of Plymouth," 331–332; Fiske, *War Letters of Capt. Fiske*, 57.

64. *Fayetteville Weekly Observer*, May 9, 1864.

65. Morgan, *Personal Reminiscences of the War*, 181–185.

66. Reeves diary, Edward Payson Reeves Papers, SHC, UNC.

67. Pursell report, ORN 9:644–646; Foster report, ibid., 635; USS *Ceres* log, RG 24, NARA; Nichols, "Fighting in North Carolina Waters," 75–84.

68. Nichols, "Fighting in North Carolina Waters," 75–84. Nichols fainted during the commotion. Mann "amputated one arm, two fingers, took out several balls and dressed the other wounds very skillfully."

69. Loehr, *War History of the Old First Virginia*, 43–44.

70. Wessells report, ORA 33:295; Kellogg diary, vol. 3.

71. Merrill, *Records of the 24th Independent Battery*, 213; "Fall of Plymouth North Carolina," Nate Lanpheur Papers, DMRL.

72. Letter from Burklow, *Wilmington Journal*, May 19, 1864. Plymouth historian Jimmy Hardison has confirmed through fieldwork that Hoke's batteries included 20-pounder Parrott guns. The Port o' Plymouth Museum has one of the 20-pound shells unearthed by Hardison on display. See also *Burlington Free Press*, April 28, 1864; *Daily Dispatch*, April 23 and May 2, 1864; Wessells report, ORA 33:296–300.

73. *Wadesboro, North Carolina, Argus*, April 28, 1864; *Daily Progress*, April 21, 1864; Savage report, ORA 33:277.

74. *Charlotte Democrat*, April 26, 1864; *Philadelphia Inquirer*, May 5, 1864 (reporting that Corse's brigade marched to within 15 miles of New Bern and then marched back); Claassen to Palmer, April 19, 1864, ORA 33:917–918.

75. Outwater to Harland, April 18, 1864, ORA 33:905–906; Peck report, ibid., 288–294.

Chapter 17. Fort Gray and Fort Wessells

1. Morgan, *Personal Reminiscences of the War*, 182–186 (orders from Colonel Kirkwood Otey).

2. Barnes to "Charlie," April 30, 1864, Barnes Family Papers, University of Virginia; Morgan, *Personal Reminiscences of the War*, 182–186.

3. Morgan, *Personal Reminiscences of the War*, 182–186.

4. Wessells report, ORA 33:296–300.

5. Barnes to "Charlie," April 30, 1864, Barnes Family Papers.

6. Smith, "Siege and Capture of Plymouth," 331–332.

7. Morgan, *Personal Reminiscences of the War*, 182–186.

8. Wessells to Judson, April 18, 1864, General Correspondence, Benjamin F. Butler Papers, LOC.

9. Barnes to "Charlie," April 30, 1864, Barnes Family Papers; Morgan, *Personal Reminiscences of the War*, 182–186.

10. *Fayetteville Weekly Observer*, May 9, 1864.

11. Account of Major J. W. Graham, *Charlotte Observer*, November 24, 1901.

12. Wessells report, ORA 33:296–300.

13. Mahlon D. Cushman diary, April 18, 1864, SHC, UNC.

14. Graham, "Fifty-Sixth Regiment," 333; Graham account, *Charlotte Observer*, November 24, 1901; Mahood, *Charlie Mosher's Civil War*, 195; Butts report, ORA 33:301–303; Smith, "Siege and Capture of Plymouth," 329.

15. Donaghy, *Army Experience of Capt. John Donaghy*, 148–150; Reed, *History of the 101st Regiment*, 129.

16. Mahood, *Charlie Mosher's Civil War*, 195.

17. Wessells report, ORA 33:296–300; Flusser dispatches, ORN 9:636–637; *Ceres* log, ibid., 771–773.

18. Over the previous months, Flusser's men had constructed a "blockade" of driven pilings at the mouth of Ryan's Thoroughfare to prevent the rebel ironclad from using that route. To allow the *Whitehead* to get through, Flusser sent the *Ceres* to remove the obstructions, even though this raised the risk that Cooke's ironclad would pass as well. Flusser to Lee, March 27, 1864, ORN 9:569; Charles W. Flusser ZB File, NHHC. The *Ceres* spent much of Monday afternoon at the mouth of Ryan's Thoroughfare. At 7:00 p.m., the *Ceres* squeezed through the blockade to ensure that enough pilings had been removed and then headed back to Plymouth via the Cashie. *Ceres* log, ORN 9:771–773.

19. Peck to Butler, April 18, 1864, ORA 33:281–282; Outwater to Harland, April 18, 1864, ibid., 905–906.

20. Graham, "Fifty-Sixth Regiment," 333.

21. The 11th Virginia remained at Fort Gray on Monday. John William Wynne to Dear Father, April 24, 1864, Wynne Family Papers, VHS; account of Jacob Brown (101st Pennsylvania), *National Tribune*, October 3, 1889.

22. Thomas, *History of the Doles-Cook Brigade*, 349; Allardice, *Confederate Colonels*, 279; Mercer obituary, *Richmond Enquirer*, April 29, 1864; *Memphis Daily Appeal*, May 4, 1864.

23. Graham account, *Charlotte Observer*, November 24, 1901.

24. Sergeant Major Robert Hale Kellogg, diary, vol. 3, April 18, 1864, CHS.

25. *Daily Dispatch*, May 2, 1864; Mahood, *Charlie Mosher's Civil War*, 195; Ludwig, "Eighth Regiment," 399–404 (claiming that guns were fired from within 300 yards of the enemy works); *Fayetteville Weekly Observer*, May 9, 1864.

26. Kellogg diary, vol. 3, April 18, 1864.

27. *Daily Dispatch*, May 2, 1864; Graham account, *Charlotte Observer*, November 24, 1901.

28. Graham account, *Charlotte Observer*, November 24, 1901; Donaghy, *Army Experience of Capt. John Donaghy*, 140.

29. Kellogg diary, vol. 3, April 18, 1864.

30. Burklow letter, *Wilmington Journal*, May 19, 1864.

31. Graham account, *Charlotte Observer*, November 24, 1901.

32. Burklow letter, *Wilmington Journal*, May 19, 1864.

33. Mahood, *Charlie Mosher's Civil War*, 195.

34. Merrill, *Records of the 24th Independent Battery*, 213–217.

35. William Clopton to "Mother & Sisters," April 24, 1864, Clopton Family Papers, DMRL.

36. Reed, *History of the 101st Regiment*, 131.

37. Mahood, *Charlie Mosher's Civil War*, 195; Welles report, *ORN* 9:640; Nichols, "Fighting in North Carolina Waters," 80–81.

38. *Charlotte Observer*, November 24, 1901; *Fayetteville Weekly Observer*, May 9, 1864.

39. Wessells report, *ORA* 33:296–300; Ludwig, "Eighth Regiment," 399.

40. Graham account, *Charlotte Observer*, November 24, 1901. Lieutenant C. R. Wilson, Company D, 56th North Carolina, and Lieutenant Wilkins, 24th North Carolina, were both killed.

41. Vinay, "Plan of Plymouth" maps, "Eighty Fifth Redoubt," NCOAH; Butts report, *ORA* 33:301; *Polkton Ansonian*, July 12, 1876.

42. Camp, "History of the Twenty-First Georgia Regiment," 360.

43. *Polkton Ansonian*, July 12, 1876; *Tarboro Southerner*, April 30, 1864; Butts report, *ORA* 33:301.

44. *Tarboro Southerner*, April 30, 1864; Butts report, *ORA* 33:301; "Sketch of the Sixth Regiment," SLNC; *National Tribune*, August 1, 1889; Camp, "History of the Twenty-First Georgia Regiment," 360; *Polkton Ansonian*, July 12, 1876. A group of sharpshooters from the 43rd North Carolina cleared some of the abatis, making a passage for the attackers. *Polkton Ansonian*, July 12 and 19, 1876.

45. *Tarboro Southerner*, April 30, 1864.

46. Camp, "History of the Twenty-First Georgia Regiment," 360; S. C. James letter, May 5, 1864, Christian Thomas Pfohl Papers, SHC, UNC.

47. Butts report, *ORA* 33:301; Camp, "History of the Twenty-First Georgia Regiment," 360; John William Wynne to Dear Father, April 24, 1864, Wynne Family Papers; S. C. James letter, May 5, 1864, Pfohl Papers.

48. "Sketch of the Life of W. G. Lewis," SLNC.

49. *Tarboro Southerner*, April 30, 1864; Butts report, *ORA* 33:301.

50. Butts report, *ORA* 33:301.

51. "Sketch of the Life of W. G. Lewis."

52. *Tarboro Southerner*, April 30, 1864; *Roanoke Beacon*, July 26, 1895. Dearing asked "Dr. Shackleford to bring all the ambulances in the battalion, along with the Fayette Artillery."

53. Loehr, *War History of the Old First Virginia*, 43; John William Wynne to Dear Father, April 24, 1864, Wynne Family Papers; "Another 'Old' Confederate," 171 (members of the 43rd North Carolina took a position "between the fort and town to prevent reinforcements," and the men pressed to the ground to avoid the "shell and grapeshot" from the gunboats and forts).

54. William Clopton to "Mother & Sisters," April 24, 1864, Clopton Family Papers; Butts report, *ORA* 33:301; John William Wynne to Dear Father, April 24, 1864, Wynne Family Papers.

55. Historian Jimmy Hardison found spent 20-pound shells in the swamps north of the Fort Wessells site, in line with the location of Confederate batteries, confirming that the rebels used 20-pounder Parrott rifles during the fight.

56. Butts report, *ORA* 33:301; Smith, "Siege and Capture of Plymouth," 329.

57. Loehr, *War History of the Old First Virginia*, 44; *Roanoke Beacon*, July 26, 1895.

58. Butts report, *ORA* 33:301; *Roanoke Beacon*, July 26, 1895.

59. *Tarboro Southerner*, April 30, 1864.

60. Butts report, ORA 33:301.

61. Henry T. Guion journal, William Hoke Papers, SHC, UNC; Wessells report, ORA 33:298; *Roanoke Beacon*, July 26, 1895.

62. Guion journal.

63. Johnston, *Four Years a Soldier*, 297.

64. Wessells report, ORA 33:298; John William Wynne to Dear Father, April 24, 1864, Wynne Family Papers; Johnston, *Story of a Confederate Boy in the Civil War*, 242.

65. John William Wynne to Dear Father, April 24, 1864, Wynne Family Papers.

66. "Another 'Old' Confederate," 171.

67. Graham account, *Charlotte Observer*, November 24, 1901.

68. Wessells to Judson, April 18, 1864, General Correspondence, Butler Papers. This letter was not published in the official records.

69. *Daily Dispatch*, May 2, 1864.

Chapter 18. The Albemarle

1. James W. Cooke, April 17, 1864, CSS *Albemarle* ZC File, NHHC.

2. Cooke report, ORN 9:656–658; Maffitt, "Reminiscences of the Confederate Navy," 502–505; Jonathon N. Maffitt, C.S.N., to Davis at Wilmington, August 17, 1874, George Davis Papers, DMRL ("Before the Albemarle was completely clad—the spires of Plymouth hove in sight"); account of Major J. W. Graham, *Charlotte Observer*, November 24, 1901. Graham claimed the *Cora* carried the new men.

3. Maffitt to Davis, August 17, 1864, George Davis Papers.

4. Cooke report, ORN 9:656–658; Elliott, "Career of the Ram *Albemarle*," 420–427.

5. Jonathon Maffitt, who was not present but commanded the *Albemarle* later, surely heard firsthand accounts from the officers and crew. He noted that Cooke "worked day and night on the passage, with a perseverance and energy that was truly marvelous." Maffitt to Davis, August 17, 1874, George Davis Papers.

6. Maffitt, "Reminiscences of the Confederate Navy," 502–505; Elliott, "Career of the Ram *Albemarle*," 420–427; Maffitt to Davis, August 17, 1874, George Davis Papers.

7. *Daily Review*, June 29, 1877.

8. Cooke report, ORN 9:656–658.

9. Maffitt, "Reminiscences of the Confederate Navy," 502–505. See also *Charlotte Democrat*, October 8, 1880; Maffitt to Davis, August 17, 1874, George Davis Papers.

10. Cooke report, ORN 9:656–658.

11. Elliott, "Career of the Ram *Albemarle*," 420–427; Maffitt, "Reminiscences of the Confederate Navy," 502–505.

12. Ibid.

13. *Whitehead* and *Miami* logs, Records of the Bureau of Naval Personnel, RG 24, NARA.

14. USS *Southfield* ZC File, NHHC. According to naval records, two 9-inch Dahlgrens were put on the *Southfield* on April 20, 1864.

15. Hackett, *Flusser and the Albemarle*, 3. Hackett recalled that the *Miami* ran better with its stern leading.

16. Cooke report, *ORN* 9:656–658.

17. Nichols, "Fighting in North Carolina Waters," 80–81; Welles report, *ORN* 9:640. The log of the *Whitehead* states that the two vessels were fastened together with chains. *Whitehead* and *Miami* logs, Records of the Bureau of Naval Personnel, RG 24, NARA.

18. Hackett, *Flusser and the Albemarle*, 14.

19. Fiske, *War Letters of Capt. Fiske*, 57.

20. Elliott, "Career of the Ram *Albemarle*," 420–427. Elliott claims that Cooke, in his haste, slipped his anchor. Cooke's official report, written soon after the battle, states that the *Albemarle* weighed anchor before leaving.

21. Diary of First Sergeant Oliver W. Gates, Company F, 16th Connecticut, CHS.

22. Wessells report, *ORA* 33:298. Another account indicates that darkness prevented the lookout in the battery from seeing the *Albemarle*. Cooper, *In and out of Rebel Prisons*, 20.

23. Morgan, *Personal Reminiscences of the War*, 188; Donaghy, *Army Experience of Capt. John Donaghy*, 151. According to Donaghy, Lieutenant Hoppin mistook the ironclad for the Union vessel *Dolly*.

24. *Richmond Enquirer*, April 24, 1864.

25. Mahood, *Charlie Mosher's Civil War*, 196–197; Hackett, *Deck and Field*. Hackett, aboard the *Miami*, recalled that the *Albemarle* "slipped by the water-battery without a shot being fired at her."

26. Welles report, *ORN* 9:640; *Whitehead* log, Records of the Bureau of Naval Personnel, RG 24, NARA.

27. *Miami* log, Records of the Bureau of Naval Personnel, RG 24, NARA. It is unclear whether the two Union gunboats were connected as Flusser intended. An officer aboard the *Southfield* reported that his boat "was ordered alongside [the *Miami*] to relash at once, but before the coupling was completed the ram made her appearance." Other accounts suggest that the crew managed to reconnect the two boats. Lieutenant Charles A. French, commander of the *Southfield*, offered contradictory statements about whether the two vessels were fastened. In one dispatch, he stated that the pair "had just been refastened" with the rebel ironclad attacked. French preliminary report, April 19, 1864, 6:30 a.m., *ORN* 9:638. But in his full report, he stated that the ram appeared "before the coupling was completed." French report, April 21, 1864, ibid., 642. The *Miami*'s log indicates that at 1:30 a.m., the *Southfield* "came along side and commenced making fast."

28. Pursell report (surgeon of the *Southfield*), *ORN* 9:645: "About 3 a.m. on Tuesday, the 19th, the ram dropped down along the left bank . . . and then near ran obliquely across into the starboard bow of the Southfield." In an article published in 1888, Gilbert Elliott wrote that Cooke "ran the ram close to the southern shore." Elliott, "Career of the Ram *Albemarle*," 423. However, several contemporaneous accounts, including Union reports (such as Pursell's, quoted above), clearly indicate that the *Albemarle* steamed along the opposite shore.

29. Welles report, *ORN* 9:640.

30. Hackett report, *ORN* 9:638; French report, ibid., 642.

31. Cooke report, *ORN* 9:656–658; Hackett, *Flusser and the Albemarle*.

32. Mahood, *Charlie Mosher's Civil War*, 196–197.

33. Merrill, *Records of the 24th Independent Battery*, 227–228; French report, *ORN* 9:641–642.

34. Welles report, *ORN* 9:639–640.

35. Ibid.

36. Account of "X.Y.," *Nashville Daily Union*, May 7, 1864.

37. Nichols, "Fighting in North Carolina Waters," 80–81.

38. Account of "X.Y.," *Nashville Daily Union*, May 7, 1864; Hackett, *Flusser and the Albemarle*; Hackett to Stewart, March 2, 1900, Charles W. Flusser ZB File, NHHC. Various sources provide different, sometimes contradictory, accounts of the timing of Flusser's death and the events related to it. Many of these accounts appeared long after the war, and the contemporaneous official reports are short on details. In describing the circumstances of Flusser's death, the author relied on, among other things, an anonymous account by a *Miami* crew member ("X.Y.") prepared on April 19, immediately after the battle, and carried aboard the *Massasoit* on its way to Roanoke Island. The letter appeared in the *Nashville Daily Union*, May 7, 1864. A shorter version appeared in the *Pittsburgh Daily Commercial*, May 2, 1864.

39. Welles report, *ORN* 9:639–640; *Miami* log, Records of the Bureau of Naval Personnel, RG 24, NARA; Elliott, "Career of the Ram *Albemarle*," 420–427; account of "X.Y.," *Nashville Daily Union*, May 7, 1864. At least one source asserts that the shell that killed Flusser had been loaded into the gun by mistake. See Cooper, *In and out of Rebel Prisons*, 21. The explosion also fatally wounded Acting Ensign Thomas Hargis and injured several engineers. Hackett, *Flusser and the Albemarle*. Several sources, including official reports, state that Flusser died during the first few minutes of the engagement. According to the *Miami*'s log, the time of Flusser's death was 4:15 a.m., half an hour after the engagement began and twenty minutes after the *Southfield* sank.

40. French preliminary report, *ORN* 9:638.

41. Graham account, *Charlotte Observer*, November 24, 1901.

42. Cooke report, *ORN* 9:656–658.

43. Elliott, "Career of the Ram *Albemarle*," 420–427; Stewart, "Lion-Hearted Flusser," 296; Graham account, *Charlotte Observer*, November 24, 1901.

44. Cooke report, *ORN* 9:656–658; account of "X.Y.," *Nashville Daily Union*, May 7, 1864. The *Miami*'s log states that the *Southfield* sank at 3:55 a.m., ten minutes after the engagement commenced. *Miami* log, Records of the Bureau of Naval Personnel, RG 24, NARA. At some point during the fight, Captain French transferred to the *Miami*.

45. According to the assistant surgeon aboard the *Miami*, the impact parted the hawsers connecting the two vessels "like so much yarn." This seems unlikely, given the strength of the lines used in the service. It seems more likely that, as French suggested in one of his reports, the two vessels were not fastened at all. Nichols believed the lines would not have separated if Welles had bound the vessels with chains instead of hawsers. Nichols, "Fighting in North Carolina Waters," 80–81.

46. Hackett report, *ORN* 9:638; Welles report, ibid., 640.

47. *Miami* log, Records of the Bureau of Naval Personnel, RG 24, NARA. The log contains the improbable statement that the *Cotton Plant* bore 200 sharpshooters.

48. Account of "X.Y.," *Nashville Daily Union*, May 7, 1864.

49. Cooke report, ORN 9:656–658.

50. See Wm. B. Newman to Prof. J. R. Soley, May 15, 1888 (includes "List of Officers and Men of the U.S.S. *Southfield* Taken Prisoner after the Sinking of the Vessel at Plymouth, N.C., April 19, 1864"), RG 24, NARA.

51. Account of "X.Y.," *Nashville Daily Union*, May 7, 1864.

52. Kendall to Davenport, April 22, 1864, Charles W. Flusser ZB File, NHHC.

53. J. A. Judson, "Funeral of Captain Flusser," April 22, 1864, Charles W. Flusser ZB File, NHHC.

54. *New Berne Times*, April 27, 1864. In 1868, Flusser's body was reburied at the US Naval Academy in Annapolis, MD.

55. Cooper, *In and out of Rebel Prisons*, 21. According to Cooper, French ordered the *Miami*'s crew to sever the hawsers joining the two vessels and then steered the *Miami* away from the fight. There is no basis for these accusations in the official reports or other correspondence.

56. Hackett, *Flusser and the Albemarle*, 16; Davenport to M. Smith, May 4, 1864, Charles A. French ZB File, NHHC (stating that French "always maintained a reputation, for courage, &c., creditable to himself and the service").

57. Merrill, *Records of the 24th Independent Battery*, 215.

58. Goss, *Soldier's Story of His Captivity*, 59.

59. Wessells report, ORA 33:296–299: "Hitherto every hardship and exposure had been met with cheerfulness and confidence."

Chapter 19. Hoke Presses the Advantage

1. Wood to Davis, April 19, 1864, ORA 51(2):867.

2. See Judson to Stewart, April 19, 1864, Letters Sent, New Bern Sub-District, Records of Subdistricts, RG 393, NARA; Claassen to Palmer, April 19, 1864, 10:20 a.m., ORA 33:917. Claassen believed Washington was the Confederates' true focus.

3. Peck to Butler, April 19, 1864, ORA 33:281–282.

4. See Wessells to Davis, April 17, 1864, ORA 33:295–296; Flusser to Davenport, April 17, 1864, ORN 9:634–635.

5. Peck to Butler, April 19, 1864, ORA 33:281–282. Peck had begun reinforcing his outposts before word arrived from Plymouth. See Peck to Amory, April 19, 1864, Letters Sent, New Bern Sub-District, Records of Subdistricts, RG 393, NARA (discussing the possibility of sending men from the 19th Wisconsin to Plymouth).

6. Butler to Grant, April 19, 1864, ORA 33:278.

7. Butler, *Private and Official Correspondence*, 4:97.

8. Grant to Butler, April 19, 1864, ORA 33:914.

9. Grant to Butler, April 19, 1864, in Butler, *Private and Official Correspondence*, 4:95–96. See also Simon, *Papers of Ulysses S. Grant*, 10:356.

10. Special Orders No. 109, ORA 33:916.

11. Palmer to Butler, April 23, 1864, ORA 33:959–960.

12. *Fayetteville Weekly Observer*, May 9, 1864.

13. *Charlotte Observer*, November 24, 1901. Hoke's brigade was on the left and Terry's on the right.

14. Henry T. Guion journal, William Hoke Papers, SHC, UNC; *Daily Confederate*, May 3, 1864.

15. Cooper, *In and out of Rebel Prisons*, 24. The account seems unlikely, given the weight of the round. Indeed, the ineffectiveness of the big gun may have had more to do with the redoubt's configuration than anything else. Union drawings of the position suggest that the location of the battery's downstream embrasure limited the gun's field of fire, making it difficult to hit any vessel hugging the south bank below the town. Vinay, "Plan of Plymouth," map 1, NCOAH.

16. Cooke report, ORN 9:656–658. Elliott rowed down to the river away from the town, ascending a "creek in the rear of Plymouth distant from the boat by water about 12 miles." On their way down, the boat crew drew the attention of Alonzo Cooper of the 12th New York Cavalry, who had been dispatched downriver to a place called Stewart's Hill to search for rebel parties. But Cooper was too late, arriving just in time to see Elliott's small craft pulling away along the north shore. Cooper, *In and out of Rebel Prisons*, 24.

17. Diary of Samuel J. Gibson, April 19, 1864, LOC.

18. Diary of First Sergeant Oliver W. Gates, Company F, 16th Connecticut, CHS.

19. Mahood, *Charlie Mosher's Civil War*, 197; diary of Sergeant Major Robert Hale Kellogg, vol. 3, April 18, 1864, CHS.

20. Donaghy, *Army Experience of Capt. John Donaghy*, 151.

21. Kellogg diary, vol. 3, April 18, 1864.

22. Wessells report, ORA 33:296–300.

23. Blakeslee, *History of the Sixteenth Connecticut Volunteers*, 57.

24. Kellogg, *Life and Death in Rebel Prisons*, 31.

25. "Fall of Plymouth North Carolina," Nate Lanpheur Papers, DMRL.

26. Gibson diary, April 19, 1864.

27. See Berlin, *Freedom*, 567–70; Manning, *What This Cruel War Was Over*, 160–162.

28. McNary, "What I Saw and Did Inside and Outside of Rebel Prisons," 26.

29. Hedrick letter, May 8, 1864, in Browning and Smith, *Letters from a North Carolina Unionist*, 205; Ball, *Escape from Dixie*, 29.

30. T. G. Barham, war record, 22, Fredericksburg and Spotsylvania National Military Park.

31. Blakeslee, *History of the Sixteenth Connecticut Volunteers*, 57; Wessells report, ORA 33:296–299.

32. *Charlotte Observer*, November 24, 1901.

33. *Daily Dispatch*, May 2, 1864; *Fayetteville Weekly Observer*, May 9, 1864; letter from W. N. Rose Jr., *Smithfield Herald*, April 19, 1901.

34. *Daily Dispatch*, May 2, 1864.

35. Rose, "Twenty-Fourth Regiment," 279–283; Rose letter, *Smithfield Herald*, April 19, 1901; *Fayetteville Weekly Observer*, May 9, 1864. Apparently, the redoubt near the Boyle's Mill Road did not offer much resistance, if any, to Hoke's advance on Tuesday. Two accounts suggest that the work may have been destroyed during the battle when its magazine was hit by a shell, although the timing of its destruction is unclear. Graham, "Fifty-Sixth Regiment," 345; *Daily Confederate*, May 3, 1864.

36. *Daily Dispatch*, May 2, 1864.

37. Guion journal.

38. Ibid.

39. A regimental history of the 24th North Carolina indicated that the men with James Dearing spied a small boat across the stream, near some defenders huddled behind works only 40 yards from the bank. Dearing saw promise in the boat, and William Cavanaugh volunteered to retrieve it, jumping in to accomplish the task. *Fayetteville Weekly Observer*, May 9, 1864; Rose, "Twenty-Fourth Regiment," 279–283; Rose letter, *Smithfield Herald*, April 19, 1901.

40. Guion journal. Ransom's regiments were across and in battle line by 8:00. *Daily Dispatch*, May 2, 1864.

41. Wessells report, ORA 33:296–300; Reed, *History of the 101st Regiment*, 133.

42. Blakeslee, *History of the Sixteenth Connecticut Volunteers*, 57; *Fayetteville Weekly Observer*, May 9, 1864 (reprinting an account from the *Richmond Examiner*).

43. Account of George H. Slaybaugh (101st Pennsylvania), *National Tribune*, August 22, 1889.

44. Graham account, *Charlotte Observer*, November 24, 1901; John W. Graham to William A. Graham, April 24, 1864, in Williams, *Papers of William Alexander Graham*, 6:68–77; *Fayetteville Weekly Observer*, May 9, 1864 (account from the *Richmond Examiner*, stating that Ransom informed Hoke at 1:00 a.m. about the decision to conduct an assault).

45. Account of George King (11th Virginia), *Daily Conservative*, April 28, 1864. The precise timing of this exchange between Hoke and Wessells is not clear, but it probably occurred on Tuesday evening.

46. Blakeslee, *History of the Sixteenth Connecticut Volunteers*, 57; *Daily Dispatch*, May 2, 1864 (undated excerpt from the *Raleigh Confederate*); *Fayetteville Weekly Observer*, May 9, 1864.

Chapter 20. The Final Attack at Plymouth

1. Ludwig, "Eighth Regiment," 400.

2. At least one account reverses the position of the 8th and 35th in the battle line. Graham, "Fifty-Sixth Regiment," 333.

3. Account by J. W. Graham, *Charlotte Observer*, November 24, 1901; letter from "R," *Fayetteville Weekly Observer*, May 9, 1864.

4. Blakeslee, *History of the Sixteenth Connecticut Volunteers,* 57.

5. Graham account, *Charlotte Observer,* November 24, 1901; "Sketch of the Life of W. G. Lewis," SLNC.

6. Moore, "Ransom's Brigade," 363–366; Cicero Durham Service Record, RG 109, NARA. Cicero Durham would be dead in less than a month, killed in fighting at Drewry's Bluff.

7. John W. Graham to William A. Graham, April 24, 1864, in Williams, *Papers of William Alexander Graham,* 6:68–77; letter from "R," *Fayetteville Weekly Observer,* May 9, 1864; "Lone Star" account, *Daily Confederate,* April 30, 1864; Graham account, *Charlotte Observer,* November 24, 1901.

8. T. G. Barham, war record, 23, Fredericksburg and Spotsylvania National Military Park. Barham identifies Dearing's orderly as "Tom McKenny."

9. Blakeslee, *History of the Sixteenth Connecticut Volunteers,* 57.

10. Graham account, *Charlotte Observer,* November 24, 1901; Reed, *History of the 101st Regiment,* 133.

11. Undated clipping from *Petersburg Express,* Adjutant General's Roll of Honor Scrapbook, NCOAH.

12. Letter from "R," *Fayetteville Weekly Observer,* May 9, 1864; Hodijah Lincoln Meade to Lottie, April 29, 1864, Meade Family Letters, VHS; account of Blount, in Hewett, *Supplement to the Official Records,* pt. 2, 72:666; clipping, Adjutant General's Roll of Honor Scrapbook, NCOAH.

13. The angle of the work south of the Columbia Road near the Bateman house contained an irregular bastion, although it is not clear whether the platforms there mounted a gun at the time of the battle. See Vinay, "Plan of Plymouth," map 3, NCOAH. The Vinay map depicting the works south of the Columbia Road was labeled "Coneby Redoubt," but most participants in the April 1864 battle did not refer to the work by that name. See also Wessells to Hoffman, May 17, 1863, ORA 18:721–722 (describing construction efforts on various fortifications in Plymouth).

14. Rose, "Twenty-Fourth Regiment," 279–283; Moore, "Ransom's Brigade," 363–366; letter from "R," *Fayetteville Weekly Observer,* May 9, 1864.

15. Moore, "Ransom's Brigade," 363–366; account of Edward G. Moore (24th North Carolina), *Commonwealth,* February 28, 1901.

16. Rose, "Twenty-Fourth Regiment," 279–283; "Lone Star" account, *Daily Confederate,* April 30, 1864.

17. Vinay, "Plan of Plymouth," map 2 ("Fort Compher"), NCOAH; *Roanoke Beacon,* April 22, 2015 (describing Fort Compher's ordnance; information also appears on historical markers in Plymouth).

18. *North Carolina Argus,* May 5, 1864; *Fayetteville Semi-Weekly Observer,* April 28, 1864.

19. Burgwyn, "Thirty-Fifth Regiment," 616–619.

20. Graham account, *Charlotte Observer,* November 24, 1901; *Fayetteville Observer,* May 9, 1864. Jones died at Petersburg on June 17, 1864.

21. Vinay, "Plan of Plymouth," drawing 6, NCOAH. This Vinay drawing identifies the

work as "Wessells" and the "101st Redoubt," and it labels the work on the Bateman property as the "Coneby Redoubt." However, the former is generally referred to as the Conaby Redoubt in both Confederate and Union accounts. Perhaps the works were renamed after the maps were prepared. See Graham, "Fifty-Sixth Regiment," 344; Reed, *History of the 101st Regiment*, 126. Ludwig, "Eighth Regiment," 400; *Fayetteville Observer*, May 9, 1864.

22. A widely reproduced battle map drawn in 1901 by Captain Robert D. Graham of the 56th North Carolina depicts the 8th North Carolina skirting north of Fort Compher and then heading southwest toward the Conaby Redoubt. Graham, "Fifty-Sixth Regiment," 344. However, a separate analysis of the attack prepared by John W. Graham, also in 1901, suggests that the regiment may have veered left (south) behind the 35th and 24th Regiments and approached the Conaby Redoubt from due east, moving south of and parallel with the Columbia Road. Graham account, *Charlotte Observer*, November 24, 1901. This suggestion—that the 8th advanced left and south—seems to offer the most plausible scenario, given that (1) a battery, according to regimental historian Ludwig, unlimbered "in front (on the left of) the regiment," blocking the way forward; (2) the space north of Fort Compher looks too narrow to allow three regiments to pass simultaneously; and (3) it seems unlikely that the 8th would have passed behind Fort Compher and the Bateman works in the midst of the fighting there.

23. Blakeslee, *History of the Sixteenth Connecticut Volunteers*, 59; *Daily Confederate*, April 30, 1864 (list of casualties for Ransom's brigade).

24. Ludwig, "Eighth Regiment," 400.

25. Blakeslee, *History of the Sixteenth Connecticut Volunteers*, 59 (noting only one man wounded); *Daily Confederate*, April 30, 1864 (list of casualties for Ransom's brigade).

26. John Graham to William Graham, April 24, 1864, 6:68–77.

27. Graham, "Fifty-Sixth Regiment," 340; John Graham to William Graham, April 24, 1864, 6:68–77; "Reminiscences: Pinckney Rayburn Young 25th North Carolina Infantry, Company I," NCOAH.

28. Graham account, *Charlotte Observer*, November 24, 1901; Graham, "Fifty-Sixth Regiment," 340; letter from "R," *Fayetteville Weekly Observer*, May 9, 1864.

29. John Graham to William Graham, April 24, 1864, 6:76; "Fall of Plymouth North Carolina," Nate Lanpheur Papers, DMRL.

30. Smith, "Siege and Capture of Plymouth," 337.

31. Reed, *History of the 101st Regiment*, 133; Donaghy, *Army Experience of Capt. John Donaghy*, 152.

32. Ludwig, "Eighth Regiment," 401–402; diary of Ira Sampson, SHC, UNC.

33. Graham, "Fifty-Sixth Regiment," 342; diary of Sergeant Major Robert Hale Kellogg, vol. 3, April 20, 1864, CHS.

34. Graham account, *Charlotte Observer*, November 24, 1901; Wright, "Capture of Plymouth, N.C.," 200.

35. John Graham to William Graham, April 24, 1864, 6:76.

36. Graham, "Fifty-Sixth Regiment," 340. Another account suggests that a sergeant destroyed the limber. John Graham to William Graham, April 24, 1864, 6:76.

37. Graham, "Capture of Plymouth," 189; Graham account, *Charlotte Observer*, November 24, 1901; Sampson diary.

38. Graham, "Fifty-Sixth Regiment," 342.

39. Graham account, *Charlotte Observer*, November 24, 1901; "Lone Star" account, *Daily Confederate*, April 30, 1864.

40. Donaghy, *Army Experience of Capt. John Donaghy*, 41.

41. Mahood, *Charlie Mosher's Civil War*, 198.

42. Graham account, *Charlotte Observer*, November 24, 1901; Graham, "Fifty-Sixth Regiment," 340.

43. *Daily Confederate*, April 30, 1864; Graham, "Fifty-Sixth Regiment," 340; Graham account, *Charlotte Observer*, November 24, 1901.

44. Graham, "Fifty-Sixth Regiment," 340; Graham account, *Charlotte Observer*, November 24, 1901; *Daily Confederate*, April 30, 1864.

45. *Daily Confederate*, April 30, 1864.

46. According to some accounts, Company I of the 56th, under Captain Lawson Harrill, captured Battery Worth, at least temporarily, early that morning. Harrill and his company had pushed along the corridor between Water Street and the river well ahead of the other units. Around sunrise, they had supposedly advanced far ahead of Ransom's regiments, reached the end of the street, and arrived at Battery Worth, which sat near the river. Harrill and his men fired into the redoubt's open rear door. The twenty gunners inside surrendered immediately, leaving their 200-pound cannon intact. Graham, "Fifty-Sixth Regiment," 340–344; Graham account, *Charlotte Observer*, November 24, 1901; Harrill, *Reminiscences*, 18–20.

One Union account calls Harrill's story into question. Lieutenant Alonzo Cooper of the 12th New York Cavalry was temporarily in charge of Wessells's small cavalry detachment and had been ordered the night before to protect Battery Worth. In his detailed reminiscences, Cooper makes no mention of Harrill's attack and claims that he remained in Battery Worth for much of the morning. Cooper, *In and out of Rebel Prisons*, 28–29. It is difficult to reconcile Harrill's claim that he captured Battery Worth early in the morning with Cooper's recollection that he remained in the fort until the final artillery-assisted assault by Colonel Faison and the 56th North Carolina. Perhaps other Federals filled the work after Harrill moved on, or perhaps Cooper was in the entrenched camp when Harrill approached the battery. Whatever occurred, it is clear that well after sunrise, Union soldiers continued to man Battery Worth. Graham, "Fifty-Sixth Regiment," 344.

47. Cooper, *In and out of Rebel Prisons*, 28–29.

48. Graham, "Fifty-Sixth Regiment," 344; Cooper, *In and out of Rebel Prisons*, 28–29; "Lone Star" account, *Daily Confederate*, April 30, 1864; Graham account, *Charlotte Observer*, November 24, 1901. Battery Worth is referred to as "Fort Hal" in some accounts.

49. Graham, "Fifty-Sixth Regiment," 340.

50. Graham account, *Charlotte Observer*, November 24, 1901; Graham, "Fifty-Sixth Regiment," 340–345. The fate of the Boyle's Mill redoubt is unclear. According to one account immediately after the battle, "some say it was blown up by the garrison, and some that it was

exploded by a shell from Fort Sanderson [Wessells], fired by our men." *Daily Confederate*, May 3, 1864.

51. "Sketch of the Life of W. G. Lewis," SLNC; Sampson diary. Sampson's report says Fort Williams became isolated at 9:30 a.m.

52. Henry T. Guion journal, William Hoke Papers, SHC, UNC.

53. *Sunbury American*, May 7, 1864.

54. Graham, "Fifty-Sixth Regiment," 342.

55. John Graham to William Graham, April 24, 1864, 6:76.

56. Wessells report, ORA 33:299.

57. Graham account, *Charlotte Observer*, November 24, 1901; "Lone Star" account, *Daily Confederate*, April 30, 1864; diary of Ira E. Forbes, Civil War Manuscripts Collection, Yale University.

58. Wessells report, ORA 33:296–299.

59. Blakeslee, *History of the Sixteenth Connecticut Volunteers*, 57.

60. Peck to Butler, April 22, 1864, ORA 33:286–287. A few accounts suggest that the first parley, refused by Wessells, came from Generals Ransom and Dearing. *Fayetteville Weekly Observer*, May 9, 1864; Burgwyn, "Thirty-Fifth Regiment," 616–619.

61. Donaghy, *Army Experience of Capt. John Donaghy*, 153–156. Some accounts indicate that Hoke's threat of no quarter convinced Wessells to surrender on the spot; others state that the Confederates demanded surrender several different times; and still others suggest that Wessells refused the demand and the flag came down only after more fighting. According to at least one account, soldiers in the fort hauled down the flag without Wessells's permission. See Blakeslee, *History of the Sixteenth Connecticut Volunteers*, 57; Guion journal; *Fayetteville Weekly Observer*, May 9, 1864; Kellogg, *Life and Death in Rebel Prisons*, 25–26.

62. *Polkton Ansonian*, July 19, 1876. Graham's battery, commanded by Captain Edward Graham, was also known as the Petersburg Virginia Artillery. See *Brooklyn Daily Eagle*, April 28, 1864 (reprinting a *Petersburg Express* article confirming that Pegram's and Graham's batteries took part at Plymouth).

63. Donaghy, *Army Experience of Capt. John Donaghy*, 153–156; diary of Samuel Grosvenor, April 20, 1864, CHS.

64. Guion journal (Guion says there were two parleys); Sampson diary.

65. *Polkton Ansonian*, July 19, 1876. Plymouth historian Jimmy Hardison found rounds from the *Albemarle* south of the fort in a location that proves the ironclad fired from a position near Battery Worth.

66. Smith, "Siege and Capture of Plymouth," 337.

67. John William Wynne to his father, April 24, 1864, Wynne Family Papers, VHS.

68. "Lone Star" account, *Daily Confederate*, April 30, 1864; *Roanoke Beacon*, August 2, 1895.

69. Wessells report, ORA 33:296–299; *New Berne Times*, June 1, 1864; Donaghy, *Army Experience of Capt. John Donaghy*, 153–156.

70. *Polkton Ansonian*, July 19, 1876.

71. *New Berne Times*, June 1, 1864.

72. Mahood, *Charlie Mosher's Civil War*, 198.

73. See Graham, "Fifty-Sixth Regiment," 345.

74. Reed, *History of the 101st Regiment*, 135; Wessells report, *ORA* 33:296–299.

75. Smith, "Siege and Capture of Plymouth," 342.

76. Ibid.

77. Morgan, *Personal Reminiscences of the War*, 186.

78. Several inconsistent casualty totals appeared in newspapers after the battle. Hoke's chief surgeon, Isaac Tanner, compiled a list of the names of those killed and wounded in infantry and artillery units; he also detailed the wounds suffered by each man. Tanner's totals are lower than those from other sources. See Jordan and Thomas, "Massacre at Plymouth," 146; *Daily Confederate*, April 30 and May 2, 1864 (Hoke's casualties), May 5, 1864 (Ransom's casualties); *Charlotte Observer*, November 24, 1901; *Western Democrat*, May 3, 1864; undated clippings, Adjutant General's Roll of Honor Scrapbook, NCOAH; Tanner, "Report of Killed and Wounded," Ellen S. Brockenbrough Library, Museum of the Confederacy. No list of casualties from Dearing's command has been found, but a postwar account states, "There were quite a number killed and wounded we were truly glad to see it no worse." Kennedy and Parker, "Seventy-Fifth Regiment," 83.

79. Diary of Samuel Gibson, LOC; Kennedy and Parker, "Seventy-Fifth Regiment," 83; Jordan and Thomas, "Massacre at Plymouth," 133 (claiming the 8th Confederate Cavalry was at Plymouth).

80. Blakeslee, *History of the Sixteenth Connecticut Volunteers*, 61; research conducted at New Bern National Cemetery by Edward Boots Jr., Civil War Plymouth Pilgrims Descendants Society (http://cwppds.org/). See also appendix C.

81. *Fayetteville Observer*, May 5, 1864 (reprinted from the *Raleigh Confederate*). See also Johnston, *Four Years a Soldier*, 301 (claiming that 700 African Americans were captured).

82. John Graham to William Graham, April 24, 1864, 6:69; George W. Love to his sister, April 24, 1864, Matthew N. Love Papers, DMRL. Matthew Love, from the 25th North Carolina, estimated there were about 500 black prisoners, 330 of which were soldiers.

83. Letter from Burklow, *Wilmington Journal*, May 19, 1864.

84. *Polkton Ansonian*, July 19, 1876.

85. See *Historic Washington County*.

86. Guion journal.

87. John William Wynne to his father, April 24, 1864, Wynne Family Papers; Loehr, *War History of the Old First Virginia*, 44.

88. William I. Clopton to his mother and sisters, April 24, 1864, Clopton Family Papers, DMRL.

89. *Roanoke Beacon*, August 2, 1895; Barham, war record, 24. According to the Petersburg newspapers, Colonel Branch broke his leg in a fall from his horse during the battle. However, Barham's memoir clearly states otherwise. *Brooklyn Daily Eagle*, April 28, 1864 (reprinting a *Petersburg Express* article).

90. *Abingdon Virginian*, May 6, 1864 (story relayed from a member of the 11th Virginia; reprinting a letter to the *Lynchburg Republican*).

91. Guion journal.

92. *Daily Confederate*, May 3, 1864.

93. *Daily Conservative*, May 11, 1864 (citing the *Petersburg Register*).

94. *Confederate Union*, May 10, 1864; Ruffin to Northrop, November 4, 1864, ORA, series 4, 3:784.

95. *Daily Confederate*, May 3, 1864.

96. William I. Clopton to his mother and sisters, April 24, 1864, Clopton Family Papers.

97. Jimerson, *Private Civil War*, 115 (quoting Rebecca P. Davis to Burwell Davis, May 9, 1864, Rebecca P. Davis Papers, SHC, UNC).

98. See Palmer to Butler, April 23, 1864, ORA 33:959; *New Berne Times*, May 7, 1864; diary of First Sergeant Oliver W. Gates, Company F, 16th Connecticut, CHS ("showed the Negroes no mercy but shot them down in cold blood"); *Emporia News*, May 7, 1864 ("negroes found in uniform were also shot"); Luther M. Baldwin letter, April 23, 1864, Nettleton-Baldwin Papers, DMRL ("wholesale murder of negroes").

99. Butler to Grant, enclosure, Samuel Johnson affidavit, July 11, 1864, ORA, series 2, 7:459–460. No "Samuel Johnson, Company D" appears on the rolls of the 2nd US Colored Cavalry, raising doubts about the reliability of the Johnson affidavit. A review of the 2nd USCC regimental books at the National Archives and at Duke University failed to shed light on the issue. See US Army 2nd Colored Cavalry Regiment Orders and Morning Reports, 1864–1866, DMRL; Records Relating to Volunteers and Volunteer Organizations, RG 94, NARA. The man identified as Samuel Johnson in the ORA was illiterate, and his affidavit was taken in the field outside Richmond by Butler's intelligence officers, John I. Davenport and John Cassels (the provost marshal). The affiant correctly identified Sergeant French as the regiment's recruiting officer at Plymouth, an obscure fact. He also correctly identified two of the Confederate regiments at Plymouth (6th and 8th North Carolina). It is possible that Cassells, who wrote down the account, mistook the affiant's name. See Records of 2nd Union Colored Cavalry, RG 94, M1817, NARA.

100. McNary, "What I Saw and Did Inside and Outside of Rebel Prisons," 26 ("immediately after our men surrendered, the Rebel soldiers commenced firing on the negroes, shooting them down, old and young, wherever they found them; some ran for the timber and were pursued by Dearing's Cavalry and shot as they ran"); Goss, *Soldier's Story of His Captivity*, 61 ("Every negro found with United States equipments, or uniforms, was [we were told by the rebel guard] shot without mercy"). For other accounts, see Donaghy, *Army Experience of Capt. John Donaghy*, 153–156; George Robbins, "Some Recollections," 31, CHS (cited by Gordon, *Broken Regiment*, 139); Blakeslee, *History of the Sixteenth Connecticut Volunteers*, 62–72; account of Robert Black (103rd Pennsylvania), *National Tribune*, May 1, 1884 (black soldiers "shot down like so many cattle"); account of F. Van Vleit (2nd Massachusetts Heavy Artillery), *National Tribune*, May 22, 1884 ("will always remain as a black spot on [Hoke's] record"); Merrill, *Records of the 24th Independent Battery*, 217; *Vermont Transcript*, April 29, 1864; Fiske, "Involuntary Journey through the Confederacy," 514; recollections of Thomas Crossley (16th Connecticut), *Citizen* (Honesdale, PA), May 30, 1913. Another account that made its way into a Missouri paper indicated that the black prisoners were stripped and executed. See *Smoky Hill and Republican Union*, May 7, 1864.

101. *Bedford Inquirer*, December 2, 1864; Reed, *History of the 101st Regiment*, 81. Notably, Conley omitted the incident from a lengthy account of his experience as a prisoner of war. Harmon and Hazlehurst, "Captain Isaiah Conley's Escape," 85.

102. Cooper, *In and out of Rebel Prisons*, 34.

103. R. Ould endorsement, July 16, 1864, *ORA*, series 2, 7:468–469.

104. *Daily Confederate*, May 2, 1864. A Richmond newspaper discounted the stories in the Northern press but asserted that "if Gen. Hoke had butchered the whole garrison in the assault after a refusal to surrender, it would have been perfectly proper under the laws of war." *Daily Dispatch*, April 30, 1864.

105. Article by Fred A. Olds, *Twin-City Daily Sentinel*, July 28, 1922; Dickey, *History of the 103d Regiment*, 270.

106. Kennedy and Parker, "Seventy-Fifth Regiment," 83.

107. Dickey, *History of the 103d Regiment*, 269–270; *Day*, September 4, 1907.

108. Beale, *Diary of Edward Bates*, 361.

109. Jordan and Thomas, "Massacre at Plymouth," 190–192. Jordan and Thomas provide the following estimates of black troops and civilians killed at Plymouth: "no more than ten" murdered on the day of the surrender, perhaps fifteen executed on April 23 or April 24, forty killed as "they fled the battlefield," and about forty killed in the swamps. Given the uncertain circumstances, they estimate that at least fifty were murdered after the surrender or when asking for "quarter or mercy." In assigning blame for the bloodshed, the authors point to Matt Ransom's brigade and James Dearing's cavalrymen. Jordan and Thomas's study necessarily contains many assumptions, for as the authors readily acknowledge, their work rests on "many qualified deductions, informed speculations, and conditional conclusions." No comprehensive records confirm the size of Plymouth's black population or clearly identify the fate of all these people after the battle.

110. Seddon to Beauregard, November 30, 1862, *ORA*, series 2, 4:954; General Orders No. 111 (President Jefferson Davis), ibid., 5:795–797.

111. See McPherson, *Battle Cry of Freedom*, 793; Urwin, *Black Flag over Dixie*; Burkhardt, *Confederate Rage, Yankee Wrath*; Newsome, *Richmond Must Fall*, 77, 93.

112. Peck to Butler, April 22, 1864, *ORA* 33:287. A few accounts suggest that the first parley, refused by Wessells, came from Generals Ransom and Dearing. *Fayetteville Weekly Observer*, May 9, 1864; Burgwyn, "Thirty-Fifth Regiment," 616–619. A Union officer later recalled that Wessells took Hoke's statements as "a threat of a repetition of the Fort Pillow massacre," which had occurred more than a week earlier in Tennessee. Cooper, *In and out of Rebel Prisons*, 30. However, it is unclear whether news of Fort Pillow had reached the Plymouth garrison by April 20. Reports of the Fort Pillow killings began to appear in eastern newspapers on April 16, 1864. See *Evening Star*, April 16, 1864; *New York Times*, April 16, 1864.

113. Jordan and Thomas found no evidence "that General Hoke ordered or encouraged a massacre." Jordan and Thomas, "Massacre at Plymouth," 181.

114. Lieutenant Oliver McNary, a member of Wessells's staff and acting superintendent of Negro affairs at Plymouth, wrote that the events would "remain a disgrace to the Confederate authorities and a reproach to General Hoke and General Ransom for all time." Accord-

ing to McNary, Hoke specifically asked Wessells to reveal the whereabouts of men like Major Hiram Marvin, who, in Hoke's view, were "stealing and drilling negroes." McNary, "What I Saw and Did Inside and Outside of Rebel Prisons," 26.

115. *Staunton Spectator*, May 10, 1864 (quoting the *Petersburg Express*).

116. One claimed that he found his carriage among General Wessells's personal effects. *Memphis Daily Appeal*, May 9, 1864 (citing the *Richmond Examiner*). And the books of a prominent local citizen, Charles Pettigrew, were reportedly found in the hands of a Union chaplain. *Carolina Watchman*, August 23, 1864; Bragg to Vance, April 21, 1864, ORA, series 2, 7:78.

117. Bragg to Vance, April 21, 1864, ORA, series 2, 7:78. The identities of the captured black recruits are not known, mostly because no roster of recruits at the Plymouth recruiting station survives. These men had not joined their commands, all of which were stationed elsewhere.

118. Beauregard to Vance, April 23, 1864, in Mobley, *Papers of Zebulon Baird Vance*, 3:185.

119. Peck to Judson, April 8, 1864, and Peck to Foster, March 28, 1864, Letters Sent, New Bern Sub-District, Records of Subdistricts, RG 393, NARA. Service records indicate that Captain Oscar Eastmond of the 1st North Carolina Union Volunteers was captured at Plymouth while on "detached service" there (perhaps recruiting). Compiled Service Records of Volunteer Union Soldiers Who Served in Organizations from the State of North Carolina, RG 94, NARA. See also Thomas, *Divided Allegiances*, 127–128 (analyzing pension files for North Carolina Union soldiers from Bertie County).

120. Goss, *Soldier's Story of His Captivity*, 61. One editorial marveled at the courage and loyalty of the North Carolina Unionists, despite the grave threat posed by the Confederate offensive. *New Berne Times*, May 14, 1864.

121. McNary, "What I Saw and Did Inside and Outside of Rebel Prisons," 26.

122. Black account, *National Tribune*, May 1, 1884.

123. Harmon and Hazlehurst, "Captain Isaiah Conley's Escape," 85.

124. Jordan and Thomas, "Massacre at Plymouth," 170–172 (detailed analysis of the Buffaloes' fate); Goss, *Soldier's Story of His Captivity*, 61; *Emporia News*, May 7, 1864 (Buffaloes "were taken out and shot by the enemy after our forces had surrendered").

125. Mahood, *Charlie Mosher's Civil War*, 205. Lieutenant George French, the recruiting officer for the 2nd US Colored Cavalry, assumed another man's name and regiment. This was "not an unusual thing among captured officers of colored troops for fear of maltreatment at the hands of the enemy," according to a note in his widow's pension record. French died at Andersonville in August 1864. Case Files of Approved Pension Applications of Widows and Other Dependents of Civil War Veterans, ca. 1861–1910, RG 15, NARA.

126. As prisoners, most of the Union soldiers could not share their stories immediately after the battle. General Wessells eventually drafted a report when he was released later that summer. Lieutenant Lucien Butts, the surviving commander of Fort Wessells, would not submit an official report until April 1, 1865. Butts report, ORA 33:301. The regimental books, presumably lost, destroyed, or captured during the battle, are not extant in the holdings at the National Archives.

127. *Fayetteville Weekly Observer*, May 2, 1864.

128. Smith, "Siege and Capture of Plymouth," 343.

129. For accounts of the experiences of Union prisoners after their capture at Plymouth, see Goss, *Soldier's Story of His Captivity*, 61; Donaghy, *Army Experience of Capt. John Donaghy*, 153–156; Robbins, "Some Recollections," 31, CHS (cited by Gordon, *Broken Regiment*, 139); Blakeslee, *History of the Sixteenth Connecticut Volunteers*, 62–72; Black account, *National Tribune*, May 1, 1884; Van Vleit account, *National Tribune*, May 22, 1884; Merrill, *Records of the 24th Independent Battery*, 217; *Vermont Transcript*, April 29, 1864; Fiske, "Involuntary Journey through the Confederacy," 514.

130. After the war, regimental associations for the 85th New York, 101st Pennsylvania, 103rd Pennsylvania, and 16th Connecticut met to trade stories about the battle and captivity.

Chapter 21. Confederate Victory at Plymouth

1. Resolution of thanks by Confederate Congress, May 17, 1864, ORN 9:658.

2. A geographically and tactically analogous situation had existed at New Bern in February, but there, Barton had failed to unlock the crossing at Brice's Creek, and the Confederate offensive, unaided by an ironclad, had ended with different results.

3. Hoke to Bragg, April 21, 1864, and Pickett to Bragg, April 20, 1864, ORA 51(2):870, 869.

4. Wood to Davis, April 21, 1864, ORN 9:658.

5. "Sketch of the Life of W. G. Lewis," SLNC; *Fayetteville Weekly Observer*, May 9, 1864; *Confederate Union*, May 3, 1864 (reprinting an article from the *Goldsboro State Journal*, April 22, 1864, praising Hoke).

6. *Daily Progress*, April 23, 1864.

7. Jones, *Rebel War Clerk's Diary*, 2:191.

8. Davis to Hoke, April 23, 1864, ORA 51(2):874.

9. Lee to Davis, April 28, 1864, ORA 33:1320–1321.

10. Morgan, *Personal Reminiscences of the War*, 189–190.

11. *Fayetteville Weekly Observer*, May 9, 1864.

12. Ibid.

13. John W. Broadnax to Thomas Ruffin, April 22, 1864, in Hamilton, *Papers of Thomas Ruffin*, 3:384.

14. Burgwyn, *Address on the Military and Civil Services of General Matt. W. Ransom*, 26.

15. Edmondston, *Journal of a Secesh Lady*, 550.

16. *Western Democrat*, April 26, 1864.

17. Dearing to his wife, April 20, 1864, James Dearing Papers, VHS.

18. Lee to Bragg, April 22, 1864, ORA 33:1303.

19. *Daily Dispatch*, April 22, 1864.

20. Ibid.

21. *Western Democrat*, May 3, 1864; *Memphis Daily Appeal*, April 27, 1864.

22. *Daily Progress*, April 23, 1864.

23. *Brooklyn Daily Eagle,* April 28, 1864 (reprinting an article from the *Petersburg Express*).

24. Edmondston, *Journal of a Secesh Lady,* 551.

25. *Fayetteville Semi-Weekly Observer,* April 28, 1864.

26. *Fayetteville Weekly Observer,* May 9, 1864.

27. *Fayetteville Semi-Weekly Observer,* May 16, 1864.

28. *Daily Confederate,* April 25, 1864.

29. *Fayetteville Weekly Observer,* April 25, 1864.

30. Bragg to Vance, April 21, 1864, ORA 51(2):870. On April 23, Colonel William Clark of the 24th North Carolina sent the governor the Union flag that had flown over one of the first forts captured on April 20, probably Fort Compher. Clark to Vance, April 23, 1864, Zebulon Vance Papers, NCOAH.

31. Davenport to Peck, April 20, 1864, ORN 9:666.

32. Peck to Butler, April 20, 1864, ORA 33:283–284.

33. By Thursday, April 21, Fort Monroe had received news of the naval battle and the *Albemarle's* victory against the Union gunboats, as well as specifics about that fight from the surgeon of the *Miami* the next morning. Butler to Fox, April 21, 1864, and Butler to Fox, April 21, 1864 (received 3:00 a.m., April 22), ORA 33:278, 279.

34. S. P. Lee to Welles, April 24, 1864, ORA 33:967; Butler to Halleck, April 24, 1864, ibid., 279–280; Grant to Butler, April 24, 1864, ibid., 967.

35. Butler to Halleck, April 24, 1864, ORA 33:279–280.

36. Ibid.

37. Butler to Palmer, April 24, 1864, ORA 33:968–969.

38. Lee to Welles, April 24, 1864, ORN 9:688.

39. Welles, *Diary of Gideon Welles,* 2:17.

40. Lee to Welles, April 24, 1864, ORN 9:688; Fox to Ericsson, April 21 and 22, 1864, ibid., 667, 683; Fox to Butler, April 23, 1864, ibid., 686 (indicating that the monitor *Onondaga* was ordered to North Carolina and would make "short work" of the ram).

41. Peck admitted that Corse's feint at New Bern had deceived him into thinking that Washington was the Confederate target. He also noted that he had sent the *Tacony* to Plymouth, but both Wessells and Flusser had sent it back. Peck to Butler, April 21, 1864, ORA 33:284.

42. Palmer to Shaffer, April 23, 1864, ORA 33:960–961.

43. Butler to Peck, April 24, 1864, John James Peck Papers, US Military Academy Library.

44. Peck to Butler, April 24, 1864, General Correspondence, Benjamin F. Butler Papers, LOC.

45. Peck to Butler, November 23, 1863, General Correspondence, Butler Papers (this letter, with its discussion of Peck and Butler's scheming, was never published). Peck and Butler also conducted a private conference at the end of Butler's November inspection. Article by Stiner, *New York Herald,* December 2, 1863.

46. Peck to Butler, April 24, 1864, General Correspondence, Butler Papers.

47. Butler to Peck, April 24, 1864, Peck Papers.

48. Dix to Halleck, June 18, 1863, Letters Received by the Adjutant General, 1861–1870,

RG 94, NARA. Peck applied for several weeks leave in December as a result. On April 23, 1863, Peck forwarded the statement of army physician D. W. Hand, who had diagnosed Peck with a "severe neurologic affliction of the hip and side," to Butler. Peck to Butler, April 23, 1864, General Correspondence, Butler Papers.

49. Butler to Peck, May 3, 1864, *ORA* 33:294 (quoted in Peck's report).

50. Shaffer to Palmer, April 19, 1864, *ORA* 33:915–916. Specifically, Shaffer urged Palmer to rapidly restore "harmony among the various officials, and a speedy return to the good will and co-operation that can alone render their labor effective." Shaffer also urged Palmer to eliminate questions "between quartermaster's department and recruiting officers" and to employ a "competent assistant" to take charge of all matters involving "the contrabands." Finally, he directed the new district commander to improve the district's recruiting stations and to better attend to recruits' families.

51. Reid, *Freedom for Themselves*, 46–50, 160–161.

52. Ripley, *Vermont General*, 168–169.

53. See Peck to Davis, April 14, 1864, *ORA* 33:870. On the poor recruitment efforts, see also Peck to Judson, April 8, 1864, and Peck to Foster, March 28, 1864, Letters Sent, New Bern Sub-District, Records of Subdistricts, RG 393, NARA.

54. General Orders No. 70 and General Orders No. 1, April 25, 1864, *ORA* 33:981 (announcing Peck's departure).

55. Butler to Peck, April 27, 1864, *ORA* 33:1002. It was not the first time Peck had referred to the rebellion as a "revolution." See Peck to Butler, April 12, 1864, Army and District of North Carolina, RG 393, NARA ("General Pickett of the revolutionary Army").

56. Peck to Butler, April 25, 1864, *ORA* 33:287–293.

57. *New Berne Times*, April 30, 1864; *New York Times*, April 29, 1864.

58. *New Berne Times*, May 4 and July 20, 1864.

59. Grant to Butler, April 22, 1864, *ORA* 33:946.

60. Grant to Halleck, April 22, 1864, *ORA* 33:947.

61. Halleck to Grant, April 24, 1864, *ORA* 33:966. Halleck reported that consultation with Butler, as requested by Grant, "would not change my judgment." See also Du Pont to Welles, July 16, 1861, *ORN* 12:198–201; Reports of the Blockade Strategy Board, Subject File, RG 45, NARA.

62. Grant, "Preparing for the Campaigns of '64," 108.

63. Grant, *Personal Memoirs*, 2:138.

64. Butler, *Private and Official Correspondence*, 4:95–96.

65. Contemporary correspondence and war records, as well as Butler's papers in the Library of Congress, provide no evidence of such a suggestion. However, as discussed earlier, a letter from Sarah Butler to her sister states that the posts were not worth holding. Mrs. Butler to Mrs. Heard, November 27, 1863, in Butler, *Private and Official Correspondence*, 3:163. Butler visited New Bern, Beaufort, Washington, Plymouth, Roanoke Island, and Hatteras. See also Butler, *Autobiography and Personal Reminiscences*, 617 (where he states that the occupation was "useless"); Peck to Wessells, November 14, 1863, *ORA* 29(2):456–457 (discussing Butler's visit to Plymouth); Lee to Welles, April 24, 1864, *ORN* 9:688 ("Gen-

eral Butler told me at Plymouth last fall that . . . the fortifications ought to be sufficient to hold the place").

66. Lee to Davis, April 23, 1864, ORA 33:1306–1307.

67. Burgwin to Seddon, April 23, 1864, ORA 33:1308.

68. *Fayetteville Semi-Weekly Observer*, May 12, 1864.

Chapter 22. Washington

1. *Polkton Ansonian*, July 26, 1876. Hoke's column passed James Martin's brigade headed to garrison Plymouth.

2. Graham, "Fifty-Sixth Regiment," 349.

3. Williams, *Napoleon in Gray*, 1, 51, 199.

4. Beauregard to Bragg, April 22, 1864, ORA 51(2):872. Beauregard already had a large map of North Carolina at Weldon.

5. David Urquhart to Bragg, April 22, 1864, ORA 51(2):872.

6. Beauregard to Bragg, April 23, 1864, P. G. T. Beauregard Papers, LOC.

7. Beauregard, "Drury's Bluff and Petersburg," 246; Burgwyn, *Address on the Military and Civil Services of General Matt. W. Ransom* (rumor that Burnside would attack North Carolina again).

8. Robert Minor had directed work crews to construct four camels (external flotation tanks) to help the ironclad float over shallow portions of the river. The camels, if they were used at all, were not adequate. Robert D. Minor to Stephen R. Mallory, February 16, 1864, Minor Family Papers, VHS; Minor to Lynch, February 16, 1864, in *Civil War Naval Chronology*, 4:20–21.

9. R. H. Bacot letter, April 28, 1864, Richard H. Bacot Papers, NCOAH.

10. Diary of James B. Jones, April 22, 1864, Jones Family Papers, SHC, UNC.

11. Beauregard to Bragg, April 23, 1864, ORA 51(2):874.

12. Palmer to Shaffer, April 23, 1864, ORA 33:960. However, as late as April 28, Butler reported that things were "all quiet" at New Bern and Washington, and he expected no "further demonstration." Butler to Grant, April 27 and 28, 1864, ORA 33:1000, 1009.

13. Palmer to Stanton, May 15, 1864, ORA 36(2):808.

14. Lee to Welles, April 21, 1864, ORA 33:938–939; Lee to Williams, April 21, 1864, ORN 9:667–668; Butler to Fox, April 22, 1864, ibid., 650–651; Butler to "Admiral" [Rear Admiral Lee], n.d., Consolidated Department of Virginia and North Carolina, RG 393, NARA (stating that Butler did not plan to send more troops to North Carolina).

15. Lee to Welles, April 24, 1864, ORN 9:688; Fox to Ericsson, April 21 and 22, 1864, ibid., 667, 683. See also Fox to Butler, April 23, 1864, ibid., 686 (indicating that the monitor *Onondaga* had been ordered to North Carolina and would make "short work" of the ram).

16. Davenport to Truxtun, April 20, 1864, ORN 9:665.

17. Truxtun to Davenport, April 21, 1864, ORN 9:671–672.

18. Palmer to Butler, April 25, 1864, ORA 33:979; Grant to Halleck, April 22, 1864, ibid., 947; Palmer to Stanton, May 15, 1864, ORA 36(2):808.

19. Butler to Grant, April 24, 1864, ORA 33:967.

20. Grant to Halleck, April 25, 1864, ORA 33:979. Butler expressed a similar view in guidance to New Bern, notifying Palmer that Washington had no strategic importance and "never should have been garrisoned." Butler to Palmer, April 24, 1864, ibid., 968.

21. Halleck to Butler, April 26, 1864, ORA 33:990.

22. Palmer to Harland, April 26, 1864, ORA 33:990–991.

23. *New York Times*, April 29, 1864; Kirwan, *Memorial History of the Seventeenth Regiment,* 206.

24. Palmer to Harland, April 27, 1864, ORA 33:1011; Judson to Davenport, April 27, 1864, Army and District of North Carolina, RG 393, NARA; Palmer to Davenport, April 28, 1864, ORA 33:1011.

25. Palmer to Butler, April 23, 1864, ORA 33:959–960.

26. *New York Herald*, December 2, 1863.

27. Gardner, *Record of the Service of the Forty-Fourth Massachusetts,* 110.

28. *New York Herald*, December 2, 1863; Hess, *Field Armies and Fortifications in the Civil War*, 205–206.

29. Elliott, *Southern Soldier Boy*, 16 (the 56th North Carolina arrived in Washington at 10:00 a.m. on April 27); William I. Clopton to his mother and sisters, May 1, 1864, Clopton Family Papers, DMRL.

30. "Sketch of the Life of W. G. Lewis," SLNC; Barrow, "Civil War Letters," 68–85.

31. *Polkton Ansonian*, July 26, 1876; Graham, "Fifty-Sixth Regiment," 349.

32. "Statement of Rebel Straggler Picked up in Front of Washington, N.C. Thursday, Apr 28—Examined by Col Dutton," General Correspondence, Benjamin F. Butler Papers, LOC.

33. *Daily Progress*, May 3, 1864.

34. Kirwan, *Memorial History of the Seventeenth Regiment,* 206. The bodies of the two dead Massachusetts men were retrieved the next day and buried in the town. See Simonds testimony, BOI; Ludwig, "Eighth Regiment," 402.

35. Henry T. Guion journal, William Hoke Papers, SHC, UNC.

36. Beauregard to Bragg, April 28, 1864, 9:20 a.m., ORA 51(2):880; Guion journal.

37. Guion journal.

38. William I. Clopton to his mother and sisters, May 1, 1864, Clopton Family Papers.

39. William H. Jackson to "Friend George," May 5, 1864, George A. Root Papers, DMRL.

40. One Confederate remembered that "we skirmished with the yanks 2 days finding [their] works very strong and well protected by gunboats and the yanks preparing to fall back, so we fell back to give them a chance to a get a way." S. D. Newsome to J. B. Jones, June 27, 1864, Jones Family Papers.

41. *Polkton Ansonian*, July 26, 1876.

42. Guion journal.

43. Kirwan, *Memorial History of the Seventeenth Regiment,* 206.

44. Harland testimony, BOI.

45. Ibid.

46. Palmer to Davis, April 29, 1864, ORA 33:1021; Harland testimony, BOI; *New York Times*, April 29, 1864.

47. "Washington, N.C., April 28, '64, I have just time to forward you a few words." Military History–Civil War Collection, Eastern NC Online Collection, ECU. Palmer anticipated that the freed people would prove an asset in New Bern but confessed that the white North Carolina soldiers would be "a great drag upon us at such a time as this." Palmer to Davis, April 28, 1864, ORA 33:1010.

48. Palmer to Harland, April 28, 1864, ORA 33:1011–1012.

49. *New York Times*, April 29, 1864.

50. *New Berne Times*, May 4, 1864. This article put the number of Washington refugees at 25,000, which was surely a gross exaggeration.

51. Judson to Davenport, April 28, 1864, Army and District of North Carolina, RG 393, NARA. Palmer also sent hospital patients to Morehead City.

52. Circular Orders, May 30, 1864, ORA 33:311.

53. Hubbard testimony, BOI.

54. Harland testimony, BOI.

55. Ibid.

56. Tolles and Simond testimony, BOI.

57. Pratt testimony, BOI.

58. Circular Orders, May 30, 1864, ORA 33:311; Simond and Tolles testimony, BOI.

59. E. R. Middlebrook testimony, BOI.

60. McChesney testimony, BOI.

61. Circular Orders, May 30, 1864, ORA 33:311.

62. Simonds and Bishop testimony, BOI. Lieutenant Bishop, of the 15th Connecticut, saw a Rhode Islander leaving the burning building.

63. Simonds testimony, BOI.

64. McChesney testimony, BOI. "Some secessionists were setting the town on fire for the purpose of throwing a stigma on the troops." Gaylord testimony, BOI.

65. Bishop testimony, BOI.

66. Harland testimony, BOI.

67. McKeever testimony, BOI.

68. Circular Orders, May 30, 1864, ORA 33:311.

69. McChesney testimony, BOI.

70. *New York Times*, April 29, 1864.

71. General Orders No. 5, May 3, 1864, ORA 33:310.

72. Circular Orders, May 30, 1864, ORA 33:311.

73. *New York Times*, April 29, 1864.

74. Hoke to Bragg, May 1, 1864, ORA 36(2):940.

75. John Walker to his father, May 3, 1864, John K. Walker Papers, DMRL. See also Iobst and Manarin, *Bloody Sixth*, 199.

76. John Walker to his father, May 3, 1864, Walker Papers.

77. *Daily Dispatch*, May 23, 1864; Loy and Worthy, *Washington and the Pamlico*, 50; *Fayetteville Semi-Weekly Observer*, May 12, 1864 (extract of a letter from "a lady from Washington, N.C.").

78. See Davis to Wood, April 21, 1864, *ORA* 51(2):870 ("General Bragg has communicated with General Hoke on the subject"); Beauregard to Bragg, April 22, 1864, ibid., 872.

79. Beauregard to Bragg, April 25, 1864, *ORA* 51(2):876.

80. Beauregard, "Defense of Drewry's Bluff," 195.

81. Roman, *Military Operations of General Beauregard*, 2:197.

82. Organization, April 29, 1864, *ORA* 33:1236; Lee to Bragg, April 22, 1864, ibid., 1303 (asking for Hoke's return).

83. Bragg to Cooper, April 30, 1864, *ORA* 33:1329.

84. Cooper to Rieley, April 30, 1864, *ORA* 33:1330.

85. Bragg to Cooper, April 30, 1864, *ORA* 33:1329.

86. Beauregard to Bragg, April 29, 1864, *ORA* 51(2):880. For instance, on April 28, Beauregard informed Richmond that Hoke had left Plymouth three days before. Beauregard to Bragg, April 28, 1864, ibid., 879; Beauregard to Bragg, April 29, 1864, 9:20 a.m., ibid., 880.

87. Martin to his wife, April 28, 1864, Starke-Marchant-Martin Papers, SHC, UNC.

88. Beauregard to Bragg, April 24, 1864, *ORN* 9:808.

89. Palmer to Davis, April 29, 1864, *ORA* 33:1021 (report from a Kinston refugee that the *Neuse* was aground).

90. R. H. Bacot letter, April 28, 1864, Bacot Papers.

91. Eli Peal to Luvester Peal, May 1, 1864, Eli Peal Papers, NCOAH; Martin to his wife, May 2, 1864, Starke-Marchant-Martin Papers. Cooke heard rumors that Washington had evacuated over fear of the ironclad.

92. Martin to his wife, May 2, 1864, Starke-Marchant-Martin Papers.

93. See Elliott, *Ironclad of the Roanoke*, 192–194; Hoke to Walker, May 3, 1864, *ORA* 33:294. The dispatch, apparently captured, was quoted in Peck to Butler, May 23, 1864, ibid.

94. William I. Clopton to his mother and sisters, May 1, 1864, Clopton Family Papers.

95. Jones diary, Jones Family Papers. Beauregard left Weldon for Kinston on the evening of April 29. Beauregard to Bragg, April 29, 1864, *ORA* 51(2):880; Guion, "Map of New Bern and the Country Adjacent—From Memory," DMRL.

96. Guion journal.

97. Beauregard to Hoke, May 1, 1864, *ORA* 51(2):882–885; Beauregard to Bragg, May 1, 1864, in Roman, *Military Operations of General Beauregard*, 2:544. In addition, Guion convinced Beauregard to abandon plans to send James Dearing and his cavalry south to Newport Barracks and instead have him seize the Union outpost at Croatan, which was closer to New Bern and would keep Dearing in better contact with Hoke's force. Guion journal.

98. Beauregard to Hoke, April 29, 1864, Beauregard Papers; Guion journal.

99. Guion journal.

100. Jones diary, May 3, 1864, Jones Family Papers; Beauregard to Bragg, May 3, 1864, *ORA* 51(2):886.

101. Minor to Hoke, May 3, 1864, *ORN* 9:811.

102. Hoke to Walker, May 3, 1864, *ORA* 33:294.

103. In correspondence, Hoke identified Robert D. Minor as "commanding the boat

party" and asked him to accompany his party on the expedition. Hoke to Minor, May 3, 1864, *ORN* 9:811.

104. No official report or correspondence reveals the details of Hoke's order of battle for the New Bern expedition. However, various sources provide hints of the units involved. For instance, according to one soldier, Hoke commanded at the time "5 brigades of infy, namely his own, Genl Ransoms, Corse's, Kemper's [Terry's] & Evans, & in addition, two or three regiments of Cavalry, and a large amount of field artillery. I supposed in all about ten thousand strong." S. C. James letter, May 5, 1864, Christian Thomas Pfohl Papers, SHC, UNC. See also Hewett, *Supplement to the Official Records*, pt. 2, 71:547 (Record of Events, 18th Virginia, Company A), 65:188 (Record of Events, 24th Virginia).

105. Stone, *Wandering to Glory*, 169. One postwar account indicates that Barton's brigade also joined the expedition. Elliott, *Southern Soldier Boy*, 16. However, this does not appear to be correct. See Hewett, *Supplement to the Official Records*, pt. 2, vol. 71 (Records of Events for Barton's Regiments); Trask, *9th Virginia Infantry*, 31; Wise, *Seventeenth Virginia Infantry*, 170; Warfield, *Manassas to Appomattox*, 140; Graham, "Fifty-Sixth Regiment," 349. Walker, a Mississippian who had served in the regular army before the war, was supposed to join the main column at Pollocksville, south of the Trent River, and build a bridge over Mill Creek. Hoke to Walker, May 3, 1864, *ORA* 33:294. Beauregard had tapped Walker to take charge of the Kinston Military District just two days before. General Orders No. 5, ibid., 1329. One observer in Kinston described Walker as a "thorough soldier" with "a prepossessing, pleasant face, and withal an unassuming, frank gentleman." Letter from "Van," *Daily Progress*, May 3, 1864.

106. One regimental historian recalled that his unit waited in Greenville from April 29 through May 2 for "the arrival of the Confederate marines and pontoons from Richmond." Graham, "Fifty-Sixth Regiment," 349. See also Hewett, *Supplement to the Official Records*, pt. 2, 70:515.

107. James Evans Jr. to James Evans Sr., May 3, 1864, Evans Papers, SHC, UNC.

Chapter 23. New Bern, May 1864

1. Sources conflict on the start date for Hoke's march on New Bern. Weighing these sources and considering the timing of subsequent events, it appears that Hoke's column left its camps outside Kinston on the morning of Tuesday, May 3. See Hoke to Walker, May 3, 1864, *ORA* 33:294 (captured dispatch from Hoke suggesting he planned to leave on May 4); Henry T. Guion journal, William Hoke Papers, SHC, UNC (stating that the column left on May 3); Beauregard to Cooper, May 3, 1864, *ORA* 51(2):886 (stating that Hoke left on May 2); Hewett, *Supplement to the Official Records*, pt. 2, 71:515, 547, 613 (stating that he left on May 3). William Beavans of the 43rd North Carolina wrote in his diary that his unit did not leave Greenville until May 2 and crossed pontoons on May 3, arriving at Deep Gully on May 4. Diary of William Beavans, May 1, 2, and 3, 1864, SHC, UNC.

2. *Fayetteville Weekly Observer*, March 5, 1884.

3. Guion journal.

4. *Daily Conservative*, May 11, 1864.

5. "Sketch of the Life of W. G. Lewis," SLNC.

6. Ibid.; memorandum by signal operator, May 4, 1864, ORA 36(2):402.

7. S. C. James letter, May 5, 1864, Christian Thomas Pfohl Papers, SHC, UNC; *Fayette-ville Semi-Weekly Observer*, May 12, 1864.

8. Savage to Pratt, May 4, 1864, ORA 36(2):395.

9. *Fayetteville Semi-Weekly Observer*, May 12, 1864; *Polkton Ansonian*, July 12, 1876; *Daily Conservative*, May 11, 1864.

10. Palmer report, ORA 36(2):3; Savage to Pratt, May 4, 1864, ibid., 397.

11. Savage to Palmer, May 4, 1864, ORA 36(2):397; *Polkton Ansonian*, July 12, 1876.

12. Claassen to Savage, May 4, 1864, ORA 36(2):396.

13. Budington, *Memorial of Giles F. Ward, Jr.*, 68.

14. "Statement of Rebel Straggler Picked up in Front of Washington, N.C. Thursday, Apr 28—Examined by Col Dutton," General Correspondence, Benjamin F. Butler Papers, LOC.

15. Palmer to Davis, April 29, 1864, ORA 33:1021.

16. Guion journal.

17. Ibid.

18. *Polkton Ansonian*, July 12, 1876.

19. Davis to Beauregard, May 4, 1864, ORA 51(2):888–889.

20. Davis to Beauregard, May 4, 1864, in Roman, *Military Operations of General Beaure-gard*, 2:547; Davis, *Papers of Jefferson Davis*, 388.

21. Ibid.

22. Beauregard to Hoke, May 4, 1864, P. G. T. Beauregard Papers, LOC.

23. By the afternoon, Lewis's brigade reached Brice's Creek. The roads were dry and dusty, and there was little water for the men. *Daily Conservative*, May 11, 1864.

24. Ibid.; McChesney to Amory, May 5, 1864, 9:30 a.m., ORA 36(2):436.

25. Failey to Potter, May 5, 1864, 11:00 a.m., ORA 36(2):437 ("do not fire on the company coming from Evans' Mill"); Amory to Harland, May 5, 1864, 11:20 a.m., ibid. ("Captain Graham from Evans' Mills reports"); Kirwan, *Memorial History of the Seventeenth Regiment*, 239 (unflattering description of Graham).

26. General Orders No. 49, April 1, 1864, George W. Graham Service Record, RG 94, NARA. See also Crabtree, *Not a Soldier*.

27. *Fayetteville Semi-Weekly Observer*, May 12, 1864. Cummings's guns were part of Colonel Joseph B. Starr's artillery battalion (13th North Carolina). A few of Corse's regiments, in-cluding the 18th, participated as well. Hewett, *Supplement to the Official Records*, pt. 2, 71:547.

28. *Daily Conservative*, May 11, 1864.

29. *Fayetteville Semi-Weekly Observer*, May 12, 1864; Hewett, *Supplement to the Official Re-cords*, pt. 2, 71:515.

30. Beauregard to Hoke, May 1, 1864, ORA 51(2):882–884.

31. *Daily Conservative*, May 11, 1864; Silas Stepp to his wife, May 7, 1864, Silas H. Stepp Civil War Letters, D. H. Ramsey Library, UNC at Asheville.

32. *Daily Conservative*, May 11, 1864. Some accounts indicated that a blockhouse guarded

the position. However, one participant corrected the record in a short letter to the *Daily Confederate*, May 14, 1864. See also Kennedy and Parker, "Seventy-Fifth Regiment," 83 (detachment of 300 cavalrymen approached Croatan on a different, more difficult route than Dearing).

33. Burlingame, *History of the Fifth Regiment of Rhode Island Heavy Artillery*, 208; *Daily Conservative*, May 11, 1864.

34. Burlingame, *History of the Fifth Regiment of Rhode Island Heavy Artillery*, 209.

35. Silas Stepp to his wife, May 7, 1864, Stepp Civil War Letters; Burlingame, *History of the Fifth Regiment of Rhode Island Heavy Artillery*, 205–212.

36. Burlingame, *History of the Fifth Regiment of Rhode Island Heavy Artillery*, 205–212; Sisson report, ORA 36(2):5; *Daily Conservative*, May 11, 1864.

37. Burlingame, *History of the Fifth Regiment of Rhode Island Heavy Artillery*, 214; Silas Stepp to his wife, May 7, 1864, Stepp Civil War Letters (stating there were no casualties).

38. Palmer to Smith, May 5, 1864, ORA 36(2):432–433.

39. *New Berne Times*, May 4, 1864.

40. Denny, *Wearing the Blue in the Twenty-Fifth Mass.*, 254–255.

41. Returns for the Department of Virginia and North Carolina, April 30, 1864, ORA 33:1053.

42. Budington, *Memorial of Giles F. Ward, Jr.*, 68–70. The 21st Georgia still occupied the Trent Road beyond Deep Gully. Geraty to Claassen, May 5, 1864, ORA 36(2):436.

43. Palmer to Judson, April 8, 1864, ORA 33:824–826.

44. Kirwan, *Memorial History of the Seventeenth Regiment*, 208; Denny, *Wearing the Blue in the Twenty-Fifth Mass.*, 254.

45. Kirwan, *Memorial History of the Seventeenth Regiment*, 208.

46. W. Hoyle to Sarah Cornell, May 5, 1864, Sarah Cornell Papers, DMRL.

47. *Daily Conservative*, May 11, 1864; *Daily Confederate*, May 11, 1864. After the war, a veteran who claimed he had been with Hoke "when he was wounded in the arm at New Bern" described some details of the incident. However, the veteran did not identify whether the wound occurred in 1862, in February 1864, or in May 1864. Camp, "'Tarheels' to 'Yaller-Hammers,'" 59; Barefoot, *General Robert F. Hoke*, 164 (stating the incident occurred in May 1864).

48. Palmer to Jourdan, May 5, 1864, ORA 36(2):433.

49. Denny, *Wearing the Blue in the Twenty-Fifth Mass.*, 254; Ripley, *Vermont General*, 212–213; Hall and Hall, *Cayuga in the Field*, 199–200.

50. Loehr, *War History of the Old First Virginia*, 45 (referring to the Confederate battle line being formed on "Colonel Hill's farm"); Hewett, *Supplement to the Official Records*, pt. 2, 71:515.

51. Kirwan, *Memorial History of the Seventeenth Regiment*, 208; Failey to Potter, May 5, 1864, 11:00 a.m., ORA 36(2):437 ("do not fire on the company coming from Evans' Mill").

52. Kirwan, *Memorial History of the Seventeenth Regiment*, 209. Amory and his wife would die in a yellow fever epidemic in October. His bravery on May 5 was praised by his men in their regimental history.

53. Budington, *Memorial of Giles F. Ward, Jr.*, 70.

54. *Daily Conservative*, May 11, 1864; Ward to "Dearest Sister," May 10, 1864, Giles F. Ward Papers, DMRL.

55. Burlingame, *History of the Fifth Regiment of Rhode Island Heavy Artillery*, 205–212. Company B was led by Captain I. M. Potter.

56. Ward to "Dearest Sister," May 10, 1864, Ward Papers. The *New York Herald* reporter was most likely George H. Hart.

57. Graham, "Fifty-Sixth Regiment," 349; Budington, *Memorial of Giles F. Ward, Jr.*, 70.

58. Burlingame, *History of the Fifth Regiment of Rhode Island Heavy Artillery*, 205–212; Ward to "Dearest Sister," May 10, 1864, Ward Papers.

59. Hall and Hall, *Cayuga in the Field*, 199–200; Williams to Davenport, May 5, 1864, ORN 9:730.

60. *Fayetteville Semi-Weekly Observer*, May 12, 1864; Hewett, *Supplement to the Official Records*, pt. 2, 72:118.

61. Budington, *Memorial of Giles F. Ward, Jr.*, 70.

62. *Fayetteville Semi-Weekly Observer*, May 12, 1864 (five killed, thirteen wounded).

63. Guion journal.

64. *Daily Conservative*, May 11, 1864.

65. *Fayetteville Semi-Weekly Observer*, May 12, 1864.

66. Graham, "Fifty-Sixth Regiment," 349.

67. Guion journal.

68. *Fayetteville Semi-Weekly Observer*, May 12, 1864 ("heavy firing in the Sound was distinctly heard by us").

69. Cooke report, ORN 9:770; statement of John B. Patrick, ibid., 768–769; Elliott, *Ironclad of the Roanoke*, 189–190. According to the postwar reminiscences of John N. Maffitt, the purpose of Cooke's sortie was to escort the *Cotton Plant* to the Alligator River. Maffitt, "Reminiscences of the Confederate Navy," 504. However, based on contemporaneous correspondence, including dispatches between Hoke and naval commanders, the plan was clearly for Cooke to join the attack on New Bern. See Martin to his wife, May 5, 1864, Stark-Marchant-Martin Papers, SHC, UNC ("The ironclad . . . left here . . . today . . . to join in the attack on Newbern"); Hoke to Minor, May 3, 1864, ORN 9:811 (the ironclad had done "a great deal better than he had expected [on its recent cruise], and will cooperate. Will be around on Thursday"); Hoke to Walker, May 3, 1864, ORA 33:294 (the *Albemarle* "can stand the sound, and will be with us").

70. Cooke report, ORN 9:770–771; *New York Times*, May 30, 1864.

71. *New York Times*, May 30, 1864.

72. Cooke report, ORN 9:770–771.

73. Ibid.

74. Holden, "The 'Albemarle' and the 'Sassacus,'" 628.

75. Statement of John B. Patrick, ORN 9:968–970.

76. *Sassacus* log, ORN 9:745.

77. Roe and Holden reports, ORN 9:739–741.

78. *New York Times*, May 30, 1864; Roe and Holden reports, ORN 9:739–741.

79. Rode reports, ORN 9:737–740.

80. Account of "H. A. S.," *Daily Confederate*, May 16, 1864.

81. Ibid.

82. Smith instructions, ORN 9:735–736. Another undated, more detailed plan was drafted by Commander W. H. Macomb several months later. Macomb, "Plan of Attack on the Albemarle," Area File of the Naval Collection, 1775–1910, Area 7, RG 24, NARA.

83. *New York Times*, May 30, 1864.

84. According to notes prepared by the *Albemarle*'s acting gunner, Hugh McDonald, the ironclad fired only twenty-seven times (twenty-one shells and six solid rounds). However, given the length of the fight and Union reports of multiple rounds fired by the *Albemarle*, this figure does not seem credible. Elliott, *Ironclad of the Roanoke*, 211 (citing McDonald's report in the private collection of Charles V. Peery, Charleston, SC); statement of John Patrick, ORN 9:969 (no serious injuries).

85. J. G. Sills to "My Dear," May 6, 1864, R. V. Howell Papers, NCOAH; *Confederate Union*, May 24, 1864 ("The *Albemarle* sunk three of their largest steamers besides damaging three or four more").

86. Smith report, ORN 9:934.

87. Roe report, ORN 9:939.

88. *New York Times*, May 30, 1864.

89. For more information on the Battle of Batchelor's Bay, see Elliott, *Ironclad of the Roanoke*; various official reports, ORN 9:733–794.

90. Bragg to Beauregard, May 5, 1864, and Beauregard to Hoke, May 5, 1864, in Roman, *Military Operations of General Beauregard*, 2:547.

91. Guion journal. The *Daily Conservative*, May 11, 1864, wrote: "We will only mention that Col. Guion and his engineer and pontoon corps did much, and did it quickly and well, and deserve more praise than we propose to give them."

92. Budington, *Memorial of Giles F. Ward, Jr.*, 70.

93. Burlingame, *History of the Fifth Regiment of Rhode Island Heavy Artillery*, 205–212.

94. Budington, *Memorial of Giles F. Ward, Jr.*, 71; Ward to "Dearest Sister," May 10, 1864, Ward Papers.

95. Kirwan, *Memorial History of the Seventeenth Regiment*, 210.

96. Budington, *Memorial of Giles F. Ward, Jr.*, 71; Palmer to Stanton, May 15, 1864, ORA 36(2):808.

97. Palmer report, May 7, 1864, ORA 36(2):3–4.

98. Denny, *Wearing the Blue in the Twenty-Fifth Mass.*, 255; Budington, *Memorial of Giles F. Ward, Jr.*, 71; Hewett, *Supplement to the Official Records*, pt. 2, 71:515.

99. McChesney to Armory, May 6, 1864, 5:15 p.m., ORA 36(2):479.

100. Hall and Hall, *Cayuga in the Field*, 199–200; Rose, "Twenty-Fourth Regiment," 269 (24th North Carolina captured fifty prisoners and lost two killed).

101. Claassen to McNary, May 6, 1864, 1:35 p.m., ORA 36(2):478.

102. Roman, *Military Operations of General Beauregard*, 2:550; Beauregard to Cooper, May 6, 1864, ORA 36(2):964.

103. Loehr, *War History of the Old First Virginia*, 45.

104. Roman, *Military Operations of General Beauregard*, 2:554.

105. Graham, "Fifty-Sixth Regiment," 349; Barrett, *Civil War in North Carolina*, 224. See also Barefoot, *General Robert F. Hoke*.

106. Barton report, ORA 33:97–99.

107. Graham, "Fifty-Sixth Regiment," 350.

108. Clark, *Histories of the Several Regiments*, 2:619; *Daily Confederate*, May 5, 1864. Accounts in the press expressed confidence that Hoke could have taken New Bern, given more time. See *Weekly Confederate*, May 18, 1864.

109. *Daily Conservative*, May 11, 1864.

Conclusion

1. Rhea, *Cold Harbor*, 244–246 (citing Alonzo Ansden manuscript, William O. Bourne Papers, LOC, and George R. Imler diary, Company E, 138th Pennsylvania, LOC); Ludwig, "Eighth Regiment," 402–404.

2. *Wilmington Journal*, June 9, 1864 (Clingman letter, "Injustice to a Brigade," excerpted from the *Richmond Dispatch*).

3. After the spring offensive, Cooke took command of the Halifax station, where he oversaw operations in the area, including those at Plymouth. Captain John N. Maffitt had command of the *Albemarle*. In the fall of 1864, Cooke's health broke down, but he continued at his post until the end of the war. He died in 1869. Hinds, *Hunt for the Albemarle*, 197–199.

4. *Wilmington Journal*, June 2, 1864.

5. *Richmond Enquirer*, May 27, 1864. See Patterson, *Justice or Atrocity*, 92 (Union officer attitudes toward Pickett after Appomattox).

6. Barefoot, *General Robert F. Hoke*, 212.

7. For discussions of Hoke's performance, see Freeman, *R. E. Lee*, 3:509–510, 592–593; Freeman, *Lee's Lieutenants*, 3:592–593; Sommers, *Richmond Redeemed*, 116; Newsome, *Richmond Must Fall*, 70–72; Manarin, *Henrico County*, 2:741, 844 n. 345. For defense of Hoke's actions, see Barefoot, *General Robert F. Hoke*, 229–231; Manarin and Jordan, *North Carolina Troops*, 14:648–650.

8. Gorgas, *Journals of Josiah Gorgas*, 131.

9. See Hagood, *Memoirs of the War of Secession*, 309; Field, "Campaign of 1864 and 1865," 558.

10. *Raleigh Daily Confederate*, October 21, 1864 (quoting the *Daily Conservative* and *Charleston Mercury*).

11. *Raleigh Daily Confederate*, October 25, 1864.

12. See Cheshire, *Nonnulla*, 149; *Charlotte News*, July 4, 1912; undated newspaper clipping, Robert F. Hoke Papers, SHC, UNC.

13. *Charlotte Observer*, June 22, 1896; interview with Fred Olds, *Orphan's Friend and Masonic Journal*, March 7, 1919. See also *Farmer and the Mechanic*, May 16, 1905; account of Thomas Kenan, *Charlotte Observer*, May 26, 1907. According to one rumor, Robert E. Lee had tapped Hoke as his successor in the war's last year. North Carolinians gravitated to the account, and it appears Hoke confirmed the story to his friends and family. Account of Victor S. Bryant, *Farmer and the Mechanic*, February 4, 1913. However, some veterans and later historians doubted the story. See Freeman, *R. E. Lee*, 3:379.

14. The conflict over Gettysburg between the Tar Heels and Virginians consumed more than its share of ink. Reardon, *Pickett's Charge in History and Memory*, 59–61.

15. See Loyall, "Capture of the *Underwriter*," 325–333 (the article first appeared in the *Virginia-Pilot*, April 30, 1899); Conrad, "Capture of the USS *Underwriter*," 93–100; account of W. F. Clayton, *New Berne Weekly Journal*, August 16, 1904; Elliott, "Career of the Ram *Albemarle*," 420–427.

16. Article by Fred A. Olds, *Twin-City Daily Sentinel*, July 28, 1922. See Urwin, *Black Flag over Dixie*; Burkhardt, *Confederate Rage, Yankee Wrath*; Levin, *Remembering the Battle of the Crater*.

17. *Weekly Standard*, February 12, 1866, August 28, 1867.

18. Reed, *History of the 101st Regiment*, 138.

19. Account of F. Van Vleit (2nd Massachusetts Heavy Artillery), *National Tribune*, May 22, 1884.

20. See Glatthaar, *Forged in Battle*, 155–156; Trudeau, *Like Men of War*, 273; Jimerson, *Private Civil War*, 111–115; Mitchell, *Civil War Soldiers*, 175; Urwin, *Black Flag over Dixie*, 7; Burkhardt, *Confederate Rage, Yankee Wrath*, 4–5. Confederate veterans provided other explanations of these events. For example, after members of his unit killed black prisoners following an October 27, 1864, engagement, one South Carolinian explained why more prisoners had not been murdered: "Few among even the roughest of our soldiers can be found who, much as they may approve and justify the act [of killing black prisoners] in theory, have hearts sufficiently hardened to enable them, in cold blood, to shoot down a defenseless man." *Daily South Carolinian*, November 4, 1864.

21. John Graham to William Graham, March 3, 1864, in Williams, *Papers of William Alexander Graham*, 6:43.

22. Denny, *Wearing the Blue in the Twenty-Fifth Mass.*, 227.

23. See Browning, *Shifting Loyalties*; Myers, *Rebels against the Confederacy*; Auman, *Civil War in the North Carolina Quaker Belt*; Durrill, *War of Another Kind*; Escott, *North Carolina in the Era of the Civil War*; Click, *Time Full of Trial*; Cecelski, *Fire of Freedom*; Myers, *Executing Daniel Bright*; Reid, *Freedom for Themselves*; Cecelski, *Waterman's Song*; Manning, *Troubled Refuge*.

24. Welles, *Diary of Gideon Welles*, 2:17 (April 25, 1864, entry).

25. Butler, *Autobiography and Personal Reminiscences*, 617.

26. Peck to Butler, April 24, 1864, General Correspondence, Benjamin F. Butler Papers, LOC.

27. Grant, "Preparing for the Campaigns of '64," 108.

28. See Halleck to Palmer, April 14, 1863, ORA 18:612; Halleck to Foster, May 9, 1863, ibid., 711; Hattaway and Jones, *How the North Won*, 511–512.

29. As McClellan had recognized in 1862, long-term possession of the rail line would have imposed significant logistical burdens. However, the benefits of such a move, which would have isolated Virginia, may have outweighed the costs. See McClellan to Burnside, January 7, 1862, ORA 9:352–353; Skaggs, "A Thorn, Not a Dagger" (arguing "Goldsboro was too inland to be sustained by waterborne shipping"). For a different view, see Reed, *Combined Operations in the Civil War*, 33–46.

30. Palmer to Davis, April 28, 1864, ORA 33:1010; Ripley to Peck, April 22, 1864, ibid., 948–949.

31. *Daily Confederate*, May 3, 1864; Beauregard to Cooper, May 3, 1864, ORA 51(2):886. Hoke requested that an unnamed Raleigh man "take charge of the fisheries" at Washington.

32. Based on numbers from the 1860 agricultural census, the counties of Beaufort, Bertie, Camden, Chowan, Currituck, Hertford, Hyde, Martin, Perquimans, Pitt, Tyrrel, and Washington accounted for approximately 9 percent of the state's total meat value, 13 percent of its cattle, 11 percent of its pork, 16 percent of its corn, and 16 percent of its peas and beans. Although production was no doubt reduced in 1864, these numbers provide a general picture of the region's capacity. Kennedy, *Agriculture of the United States in 1860*, 104–111.

33. Vance to Seddon, November 10, 1863, ORA 29(2):831. However, many farms in this war-torn region may have had little to offer by this time in the war.

34. *Memphis Daily Appeal*, May 9, 1864.

35. *Western Democrat*, June 21, 1864.

36. Ruffin to Northrop, November 4, 1864, ORA, series 4, 3:784.

37. Spelman, *Executive and Legislative Documents*, 19–20.

38. *Wilmington Journal*, May 26, 1864.

39. Governor Vance also took a more personal, antagonistic approach, ridiculing Holden's uncourageous response to the mob attack on the *Weekly Standard*'s office the previous fall. McKinney, *Zeb Vance*, 218; *Fayetteville Observer*, April 25, 1864.

40. North Carolina Literary and Historical Association, *Proceedings and Addresses of the Annual Session*, 62.

41. *Weekly Standard*, January 20, 1864. As the *Daily Progress* declared the previous year (July 15, 1863): "We favor peace because we believe that peace now would save slavery, while we very much fear that a prolongation of the war will obliterate the last vestige of it."

42. *Weekly Standard*, June 22, 1864. See also Harris, *William Woods Holden*, 148–149.

43. See Mobley, "War Governor of the South," 119–123; Harris, *William Woods Holden*, 146–148; McKinney, *Zeb Vance*, 223. As part of his campaign, Vance established a newspaper, the *Conservative*, to broadcast his position.

44. *Daily Confederate*, June 18, 1864. The paper also informed readers that Heroes of America was a "secret criminal organization" established to "cause and facilitate desertion, to weaken our army and produce the occasion for negotiation on the basis of submission to the enemy." Vance's own paper raised the issue a few weeks later, detailing the group's activities

and appending a letter from the Reverend O. Churchill of Chatham County, containing a confession of sorts about his involvement with the organization. *Daily Conservative*, July 2, 1864.

45. Evidence excavated by historian Barton Myers reveals that some of Holden's close associates were active members. In his extensive examination of North Carolina Unionist cases in the Southern Claims Commission archives, Myers discovered that James W. Buck, a Red String, served as Holden's bodyguard in 1863. Myers, *Rebels against the Confederacy*, 116–117. For more information on the preelection stories about the Heroes of America and Holden, see *Daily Confederate*, June 18, 1864; *North Carolina Standard*, July 1, 1864; *Daily Conservative*, July 2 (Churchill letter) and 18, 1864; Auman and Scarborough, "The Heroes of America in Civil War North Carolina," 327–363.

46. Swain to Vance, September 28, 1864, Zebulon Vance Papers, NCOAH.

47. See *Daily Progress*, May 3, July 30, and August 3, 1864.

48. Auman, *Civil War in the North Carolina Quaker Belt*, 150.

49. See *Daily Conservative*, July 30, 1864; *Weekly Confederate*, July 27, 1864.

50. McKinney, *Zeb Vance*, 229.

51. *Daily Confederate*, August 6, 1864.

52. *Semi-Weekly Messenger*, May 16, 1905. See also Evans, *Confederate Military History*, 4:219. "General Hoke has struck a most effective blow for the redemption of his native State," wrote the *Petersburg Express*. *Brooklyn Daily Eagle*, April 28, 1864 (reprinting an article from the *Petersburg Express*).

53. Letter from "Lone Star," *Daily Confederate*, April 30, 1864. See also editorial, *Albany Patriot*, May 12, 1864.

54. *Fayetteville Weekly Observer*, May 9, 1864.

55. William S. Pettigrew, speech at Williamston, July 12, 1864, Pettigrew Papers, SHC, UNC (quoted in Durrill, *War of Another Kind*, 210).

56. *Daily Confederate*, May 3, 1864. See also *Weekly Confederate*, July 20, 1864.

57. *Pittsburgh Gazette*, May 5, 1864. Historians have also pointed out the 1864 offensive's beneficial impact on the rebel cause. Wayne Durrill, in his study of Washington County during the war, writes that the "victory created a symbol—the immense number of Confederate dead—around which North Carolina secessionists could rally the faint hearted and draw them away from the peace movement." Durrill, *War of Another Kind*, 210. Zebulon Vance's biographer concluded that the "victory helped to shore up morale throughout the state" and "would be particularly helpful to Zeb's campaign." McKinney, *Zeb Vance*, 215.

58. *New York Times*, November 13, 1864 (account of Plymouth's recapture).

59. *Weekly Standard*, February 12 and August 28, 1868.

60. Spelman, *Executive and Legislative Documents*, 19–20.

Bibliography

Newspapers

Albany Patriot
Baltimore Sun
Bedford Inquirer
Boston Post
Brooklyn (NY) Daily Eagle
Burlington Free Press
Carolina Watchman (Salisbury, NC)
Charleston Mercury
Charlotte (NC) Democrat
Charlotte (NC) Observer
Citizen (Honesdale, PA)
Columbian Register
Commonwealth (Scotland Neck, NC)
Confederate Union (Milledgeville, GA)
Courier and Freeman (Potsdam, NY)
Daily Confederate (Raleigh, NC)
Daily Conservative (Raleigh, NC)
Daily Dispatch (Richmond, VA)
Daily Journal (Wilmington, NC)
Daily Progress (Raleigh, NC)
Daily Review (Wilmington, NC)
Daily South Carolinian (Columbia)
Daily State Journal (Raleigh, NC)
Dakota County Herald
Day (New London, CT)
Emporia (KS) News

Evening Bulletin (Charlotte, NC)
Evening Star (Washington, DC)
Evening Visitor (Raleigh, NC)
Farmer and the Mechanic
Fayetteville (NC) Semi-Weekly Observer
Fayetteville (NC) Weekly Observer
Girard (KS) Press
Green Mountain Freeman (Montpelier, VT)
Greensboro Patriot
Hartford (CT) Courant
Iredell Express (Statesville, NC)
Lamoille (VT) Newsdealer
Landmark (Statesville, NC)
Leslie's Illustrated
Liberator (Boston)
Memphis (TN) Daily Appeal
Nashville (TN) Daily Union
National Tribune
New Berne (NC) Times
New Berne (NC) Weekly Journal
News and Observer
New York Daily Tribune
New York Herald
New York Times
New York Tribune
North Carolina Presbyterian (Fayetteville)
North Carolina Standard (Raleigh)
Orphan's Friend and Masonic Journal
People's Press (Winston-Salem, NC)
Petersburg (VA) Express
Philadelphia Inquirer
Pinehurst Outlook
Pittsburgh Daily Commercial
Polkton (NC) Ansonian
Progress-Index (Petersburg, VA)
Public Ledger (Memphis, TN)
Raftsman's Journal (Clearfield, PA)
Raleigh (NC) Daily Confederate
Raleigh (NC) Weekly Standard
Richmond Dispatch
Richmond Enquirer
Richmond Examiner

Richmond Whig
Roanoke Beacon
Salina Daily Republican
Semi-Weekly Messenger (Wilmington, NC)
Smithfield (NC) Herald
Smoky Hill and Republican Union (Junction City, MO)
Standard (North Carolina Standard) (Raleigh)
Staunton Spectator
Sunbury American
Tarboro (NC) Southerner
Times Dispatch (Richmond, VA)
Twin-City Daily Sentinel (Winston-Salem, NC)
Vermont Transcript
Virginia-Pilot
Wadesboro, North Carolina, Argus
Weekly Confederate
Weekly Intelligencer (Fayetteville, NC)
Weekly Standard (Raleigh, NC)
Weekly State Journal
Western Democrat (Charlotte, NC)
Western Reserve Chronicle (Warren, OH)
Wilmington (NC) Journal
Wilmington (NC) Morning Star

Archival Sources

Adjutant General's Roll of Honor Scrapbook. North Carolina Office of Archives and History.
Bacot, Richard H. Papers. North Carolina Office of Archives and History.
Barham, T. G. War record. Fredericksburg and Spotsylvania National Military Park.
Barnes, Edward Cook. Papers. University of Virginia.
Barnes Family Papers. University of Virginia.
Barney, Valentine G. Correspondence. University of Vermont Libraries.
Beauregard, P. G. T. Papers. Library of Congress.
Beavans, William. Diary and Letters. Southern Historical Collection, University of North Carolina.
Biggs, Asa. Papers. David M. Rubenstein Rare Book and Manuscript Library, Duke University.
Board of Investigation. "Convened to Investigate the Facts and Circumstances Connected with the Burning of Certain Portions of the Town of Washington, N.C., and the Pillage of that Place during the Late Evacuation." Palmer to Thomas, May 31, 1864, Letters Received by the Adjutant General, 1861–1870, Record Group 94, National Archives and Records Administration.

Booker, John and James. Collection. Library of Virginia.

Bragg, Braxton. Papers. David M. Rubenstein Rare Book and Manuscript Library, Duke University.

Burwell, Edmund. Papers. Southern Historical Collection, University of North Carolina.

Butler, Benjamin F. Papers. Library of Congress.

Carter, David Miller. Papers. Southern Historical Collection, University of North Carolina.

Chambers, Henry A. Papers. Southern Historical Collection, University of North Carolina.

Chesson Papers. North Carolina Office of Archives and History.

Civil War Era Scrapbook. Joyner Library, East Carolina University.

Civil War Newspaper Clipping Collection. New York State Military Museum.

Clopton Family Papers. David M. Rubenstein Rare Book and Manuscript Library, Duke University.

Conley, Isaiah. Civil War Correspondence. Special Collections, Virginia Polytechnic Institute and State University.

Cornell, Sarah. Papers. David M. Rubenstein Rare Book and Manuscript Library, Duke University.

Corse, Montgomery B. Papers. Lloyd House, Alexandria Library, Alexandria, VA.

Cushman, Mahlon D. Diary, 1864. Southern Historical Collection, University of North Carolina.

Davis, George. Papers. David M. Rubenstein Rare Book and Manuscript Library, Duke University.

Davis, J. Kenneth. "Kinston Hangings." New Hanover County Public Library, Wilmington, NC.

Davis, Rebecca P. Papers. Southern Historical Collection, University of North Carolina.

Dearing, James. Papers. Virginia Historical Society.

Ellis, Josiah Robert Peele. Papers. Joyner Library, East Carolina University.

Evans Papers. Southern Historical Collection, University of North Carolina.

Fisher, George F. Letters. Wood Family Collection, High Point, NC.

Forbes, Ira E. Diary. Civil War Manuscripts Collection, Yale University.

Gates, First Sergeant Oliver W. Diary. Connecticut Historical Society.

Gibson, Samuel J. Diary. Library of Congress.

Gift, George. Papers. Southern Historical Collection, University of North Carolina.

Grosvenor, Samuel. Diary. Connecticut Historical Society.

Guion, Henry T. Journal. William Hoke Papers. Southern Historical Collection, University of North Carolina.

Guion, Henry T. "Map of New Bern and the Country Adjacent—from Memory." David M. Rubenstein Rare Book and Manuscript Library, Duke University.

Hackett, John C. Papers. David M. Rubenstein Rare Book and Manuscript Library, Duke University.

Hamilton, J. G. de Roulhac. "General Robert F. Hoke and His Military Career." Robert F. Hoke Papers, Southern Historical Collection, University of North Carolina.

Hassell, Cushing Biggs. Papers. Southern Historical Collection, University of North Carolina.

Historical Data System's American Civil War Research Database. civilwardata.com.

Hoke, Robert F. Papers. Southern Historical Collection, University of North Carolina.

Hoke, William. Papers. Southern Historical Collection, University of North Carolina.

Hooper, Aurelia. Papers. David M. Rubenstein Rare Book and Manuscript Library, Duke University.

Howell, R. V. Papers. North Carolina Office of Archives and History.

Imler, Private George R. 1864 Pocket Diary. Library of Congress.

Inman, Arthur Crew. Papers. John Hay Library, Brown University.

Ireland Papers. David M. Rubenstein Rare Book and Manuscript Library, Duke University.

James, William A. Papers. David M. Rubenstein Rare Book and Manuscript Library, Duke University.

"James Wallace Cooke Biographical Sketch, 1898." Southern Historical Collection, University of North Carolina.

Jones Family Papers. Southern Historical Collection, University of North Carolina.

Kellogg, Sergeant Major Robert Hale. Diary. Connecticut Historical Society.

Kenan, Thomas Stephen. "Sketch of the Forty-Third Regiment, North Carolina Troops." State Library of North Carolina.

Kennon, Henry Thomas. Papers. North Carolina Office of Archives and History.

Lanpheur, Nate. Papers. David M. Rubenstein Rare Book and Manuscript Library, Duke University.

Laughlin, Reynolds. Papers. Civil War Miscellaneous Collection, US Military History Institute.

Lillie, George C. Correspondence. Vermont Historical Society.

Lincoln, Abraham. Papers. Library of Congress.

Love, Matthew N. Papers. David M. Rubenstein Rare Book and Manuscript Library, Duke University.

Mangum, A. W. Papers. Southern Historical Collection, University of North Carolina.

Meade Family Letters. Virginia Historical Society.

Military History–Civil War Collection. Joyner Library, East Carolina University, Eastern NC Online Collection.

Minor Family Papers. Virginia Historical Society.

Moses, Raphael Jacob. Autobiography, 1892. Southern Historical Collection, University of North Carolina.

National Archives and Records Administration:
    Record Group 15, Records of the Veterans Administration, M1279
    Record Group 24, Records of the Bureau of Naval Personnel (United States Navy)
    Record Group 45, Naval Records Collection of the Office of Naval Records and Library
    Record Group 94, Records of the Office of the Adjutant General, 1780s–1917
    Record Group 109, War Department Collection of Confederate Records
    Record Group 393, Consolidated Department of Virginia and North Carolina

Nettleton-Baldwin Papers. David M. Rubenstein Rare Book and Manuscript Library, Duke University.

New York Civil War Muster Roll Abstracts, 1861–1900. New York State Archives.

Noble, William Henry. Papers. David M. Rubenstein Rare Book and Manuscript Library, Duke University.

Paris, John. Papers. Southern Historical Collection, University of North Carolina.

Patterson, Rufus L. Papers. Southern Historical Collection, University of North Carolina.

Peal, Eli. Papers. North Carolina Office of Archives and History.

Peck, John James. Papers. US Military Academy Library.

Peirce, Edward Burgess. Letters, 1862–1871. Massachusetts Historical Society.

Pettigrew Papers. Southern Historical Collection, University of North Carolina.

Pfohl, Christian Thomas. Papers. Southern Historical Collection, University of North Carolina.

Pittman, Thomas M. Papers. North Carolina Office of Archives and History.

Polk, Leonidas. Papers. Southern Historical Collection, University of North Carolina.

Randall, James Ryder. Papers. Southern Historical Collection, University of North Carolina.

Reeves, Edward Payson. Papers. Southern Historical Collection, University of North Carolina.

"Reminiscences: Pinckney Rayburn Young 25th North Carolina Infantry, Company I." North Carolina Office of Archives and History.

Root, George A. Papers, David M. Rubenstein Rare Book and Manuscript Library, Duke University.

Ruffin, Roulhac, and Hamilton Family Papers. Southern Historical Collection, University of North Carolina.

Sampson, Ira. Diary. Southern Historical Collection, University of North Carolina.

Shaw, Francis M. Diary. Civil War Miscellaneous Collection, US Military History Institute.

"Sketch of the Life of W. G. Lewis." State Library of North Carolina.

"Sketch of the Sixth Regiment." NC State Troops (Infantry). State Library of North Carolina.

Starke-Marchant-Martin Papers. Southern Historical Collection, University of North Carolina.

Stepp, Silas H. Civil War Letters. D. H. Ramsey Library, University of North Carolina at Asheville.

Stuart, J. L. Papers. David M. Rubenstein Rare Book and Manuscript Library, Duke University.

Swain, John L. Papers. Southern Historical Collection, University of North Carolina.

Tanner, Isaac S. "Report of Killed and Wounded, Plymouth, North Carolina, April 18th, 19th, and 20th, 1864." Ellen S. Brockenbrough Library, Museum of the Confederacy, Richmond, VA.

Taylor, Herman W. Collection. North Carolina Office of Archives and History.

Tilton Family Papers. Library of Congress.

US Army 2nd Colored Cavalry Regiment Orders and Morning Reports, 1864–1866. David M. Rubenstein Rare Book and Manuscript Library, Duke University.

Vance, Zebulon. Papers. North Carolina Office of Archives and History.

Vance, Zebulon. Papers (microfilm edition). Library of Congress.

Venable, Charles S. Papers. Southern Historical Collection, University of North Carolina.

Vernon, Howell. Collections. North Carolina Office of Archives and History.

Vinay, Felix. Map. "Plan of Plymouth, N.C. Its Fortifications and Environs." North Carolina Office of Archives and History.

Walker, John K. Papers. David M. Rubenstein Rare Book and Manuscript Library, Duke University.

Ward, Giles F. Papers. David M. Rubenstein Rare Book and Manuscript Library, Duke University.

Whitford, John. Papers. North Carolina Office of Archives and History.

Witherspoon, John. 1864 Diary. Burton Historical Collection, Detroit Public Library.

Wood, John Taylor. Papers. Southern Historical Collection, University of North Carolina.

Wox, Lucius. Papers. Civil War Miscellaneous Collection, US Military History Institute.

Wynne Family Papers. Virginia Historical Society.

ZC and ZB Files. Navy Department Library, Naval History and Heritage Command.

Books, Articles, and Theses

Allardice, Bruce S. *Confederate Colonels: A Biographical Register*. Columbia: University of Missouri Press, 2008.

Allen, George H. *Forty-Six Months with the Fourth R.I. Volunteers: In the War of 1861 to 1865*. Providence, RI: J. A. & R. A. Reid, 1887.

Annual Report of the State Historian of the State of New York. Vol. 2. Albany, NY: Wynkoop Hallenbeck Crawford, 1897.

"Another 'Old' Confederate." *Confederate Veteran* 11 (1903).

Ashe, Samuel A'Court. *History of North Carolina*. Vol. 2. *From 1783 to 1925*. Raleigh, NC: Edwards & Broughton, 1925.

Auman, William. *Civil War in the North Carolina Quaker Belt*. Jefferson, NC: McFarland, 2014.

Auman, William, and David D. Scarborough. "The Heroes of America in Civil War North Carolina." *North Carolina Historical Review* 58 (October 1981).

Autograph Letters Manuscripts and Documents, Selections from the Collection, Formed by the Late Oliver R. Barrett. New York: Parke-Bernet Galleries, 1950.

Ball, John. *Escape from Dixie: The Experiences of Lt. John Lafler, 85th NY Civil War POW*. Williamsville, NY: Goldstar Enterprises, 1996.

Bardolph, Richard. "Inconstant Rebels: Desertion of North Carolina Troops in the Civil War." *North Carolina Historical Review* 41 (1964).

Barefoot, Daniel. *General Robert F. Hoke: Lee's Modest Warrior*. Winston-Salem, NC: John F. Blair, 1996.

Barney, William L. *The Oxford Encyclopedia of the Civil War*. New York: Oxford University Press, 2011.

Barrett, John. *The Civil War in North Carolina*. Chapel Hill: University of North Carolina Press, 1963.

Barrow, Henry W. "Civil War Letters of Henry W. Barrow to John W. Fries." *North Carolina Historical Review* 34 (January 1957).

Basler, Roy P., ed. *The Collected Works of Abraham Lincoln.* 9 vols. New Brunswick, NJ: Rutgers University Press, 1953–1955.

Battle, Kemp P. *Memories of an Old-Time Tar Heel.* Chapel Hill: University of North Carolina Press, 1945.

Beale, Howard K., ed. *The Diary of Edward Bates, 1859–1866.* Washington, DC: US Government Printing Office, 1933.

Beauregard, P. G. T. "The Defense of Drewry's Bluff." In vol. 4 of *Battles and Leaders of the Civil War.* New York: Century, 1888.

———. "Drury's Bluff and Petersburg." *North American Review,* March 1887.

Bell, Robert T. *11th Virginia Infantry.* Lynchburg, VA: H. E. Howard, 1985.

Benedict, G. G. *Vermont in the Civil War: A History of the Part Taken by the Vermont Soldiers and Sailors in the War for the Union, 1861–5.* Vol. 2. Burlington, VT: Higginson Book Co., 1888.

Beringer, Richard E., Herman Hattaway, Archer Jones, and William N. Still Jr. *Why the South Lost the Civil War.* Athens: University of Georgia Press, 1986.

Berlin, Ira. *Freedom, the Black Military Experience: A Documentary History of Emancipation 1861–1867.* Series 2. New York: Cambridge University Press, 1982.

Beyer, W. F., and O. bF. Keydel, eds. *Deeds of Valor.* Vol. 1. Detroit, MI: Perrin Keydel, 1907.

Bishir, Catherine W. *North Carolina Architecture.* Chapel Hill: University of North Carolina Press, 2005.

Black, Robert. *The Railroads of the Confederacy.* Chapel Hill: University of North Carolina Press, 1998.

Blakeslee, Bernard F. *History of the Sixteenth Connecticut Volunteers.* Hartford, CT: Case, Lockwood & Brainard, 1875.

Bohemian. *War Songs of the South.* Richmond, VA: West & Johnston, 1862.

Boynton, Charles Brandon. *The History of the Navy during the Rebellion.* Vol. 2. New York: D. Appleton. 1867–1868.

Branch, Paul. *Fort Macon: A History.* Charleston, SC: Nautical & Aviation Publishing Co. of America, 1999.

———. "The Lost Carolina City." *Ramparts* 16, 1 (Spring 2009).

Brown, David. "North Carolinian Ambivalence: Rethinking Loyalty and Disaffection in the Civil War Piedmont." In *North Carolinians in the Era of Civil War and Reconstruction,* ed. Paul D. Escott. Chapel Hill: University of North Carolina Press, 2008.

Brown, Derrick S. "Foster Must Build Forts: The Failure of Union Offensive Strategy in Eastern North Carolina, 1862–1863." M.A. thesis, University of North Carolina–Wilmington, 2010.

Brown, Joseph Willard. *The Signal Corps, U.S.A. in the War of the Rebellion.* Boston: US Veteran Signal Corps Association, 1896.

Browning, Judkin. "'Bringing Light to Our Land . . . When She Was Dark as Night': Northerners, Freedpeople, and Education during Military Occupation in North Carolina, 1862–1865." *American Nineteenth Century History* 9, 1 (March 2008).

——. *From Cape Charles to Cape Fear: The North Atlantic Blockading Squadron during the Civil War*. Tuscaloosa: University of Alabama Press, 2003.

——. "'Littled Souled Mercenaries'? The Buffaloes of Eastern North Carolina during the Civil War." *North Carolina Historical Review* 67, 3 (July 2000).

——. *Shifting Loyalties: The Union Occupation of Eastern North Carolina*. Chapel Hill: University of North Carolina Press, 2011.

Browning, Judkin, and Michael Thomas Smith, eds. *Letters from a North Carolina Unionist: The Civil War Letters of John A. Hedrick, 1862–1865*. Raleigh: North Carolina Division of Archives and History, 2001.

Budington, William Ives. *A Memorial of Giles F. Ward, Jr: Late First Lieut. Twelfth N.Y. Cavalry*. New York: A. D. F. Randolph, 1866.

Burgwyn, William H. S. *An Address on the Military and Civil Services of General Matt. W. Ransom*. Raleigh, NC: n.p., 1907.

——. *A Captain's War: The Letters and Diaries of William H. S. Burgwyn 1861–1865*. Shippensburg, PA: White Mane Publishing, 1993.

——. "Clingman's Brigade." In vol. 4 of *Histories of the Several Regiments and Battalions from North Carolina in the Great War 1861–5*, ed. Walter Clark. Goldsboro, NC: Nash Brothers, 1901.

——. "Thirty-Fifth Regiment." In vol. 4 of *Histories of the Several Regiments and Battalions from North Carolina in the Great War 1861–5*, ed. Walter Clark. Goldsboro, NC: Nash Brothers, 1901.

Burke, James C. *Wilmington & Weldon Railroad in the Civil War*. Jefferson, NC: McFarland, 2012.

Burkhardt, George. *Confederate Rage, Yankee Wrath: No Quarter in the Civil War*. Carbondale: Southern Illinois University Press, 2007.

Burlingame, John K. *History of the Fifth Regiment of Rhode Island Heavy Artillery: During Three Years and a Half of Service in North Carolina. January 1862–June 1865*. Providence, RI: Snow & Farnham, 1892.

Burrell, Charles Edward. *A History of Prince Edward County, Virginia: From Its Formation in 1753, to the Present*. Richmond, VA: Williams, 1922.

Butler, Benjamin F. *Autobiography and Personal Reminiscences of Major-General Benj. F. Butler: Butler's Book*. Boston: A. M. Thayer, 1892.

——. *Private and Official Correspondence of Gen. Benjamin F. Butler: During the Period of the Civil War*. 5 vols. Norwood, MA: Plimpton Press, 1917.

Bynum, Victoria E. *The Long Shadow of the Civil War: Southern Dissent and Its Legacies*. Chapel Hill: University of North Carolina Press, 2010.

Callahan, Edward. *List of Officers of the Navy of the United States and of the Marine Corps, from 1775 to 1900*. New York: Hammersly, 1901.

Camp, Charles D. "History of the Twenty-First Georgia Regiment." In Henry Walter Thomas, *History of the Doles-Cook Brigade of Northern Virginia, C.S.A.* Atlanta: Franklin, 1903.

Camp, Henry L. Wyatt. "'Tarheels' to 'Yaller- Hammers.'" *Confederate Veteran* 21 (1913).

Casstevens, Frances H. *Edward A. Wild and the African Brigade in the Civil War*. Jefferson, NC: McFarland, 2005.

Cecelski, David S. *The Fire of Freedom: Abraham Galloway & the Slaves' Civil War*. Chapel Hill: University of North Carolina Press, 2012.

———. *The Waterman's Song: Slavery and Freedom in Maritime North Carolina*. Chapel Hill: University of North Carolina Press, 2011.

Chapin, Samuel. *Memorandum and Journal of Samuel Chapin of South Wilbraham, Massachusetts, Company I, 46th Regt. M.V.M.* N.p.: The Society, 1987.

Cheshire, Joseph B. *Nonnulla*. Chapel Hill: University of North Carolina Press, 1930.

Civil War Naval Chronology, 1861–1865. 6 vols. Washington, DC: US Naval History Division, 1971.

Clark, Walter, ed. *Histories of the Several Regiments and Battalions from North Carolina in the Great War 1861–5*. 5 vols. Goldsboro, NC: Nash Brothers, 1901.

Clarke, Mary Bayard. *Live Your Own Life: The Family Papers of Mary Bayard Clarke, 1854–1886*. Columbia: University of South Carolina Press, 2003.

Click, Patricia. *Time Full of Trial: The Roanoke Island Freedmen's Colony, 1862–1867*. Chapel Hill: University of North Carolina Press, 2000.

Coleman, E. C. *The Pig War: The Most Perfect War in History*. Stroud, UK: History Press, 2013.

Collins, Donald. "War Crime or Justice? General George Pickett and the Mass Execution of Deserters in Civil War Kinston, North Carolina." In *The Art of Command in the Civil War*, ed. Steven Woodworth. Lincoln: University of Nebraska Press, 1988.

Colyer, Vincent. *Report of the Services Rendered by the Freed People to the United States Army: In North Carolina, in the Spring of 1862, after the Battle of Newbern*. New York: Vincent Colyer, 1864.

Confederate States of America, Headquarters [of Major George E. Pickett], Department [of] North Carolina. General Order No. 6, Camp on Dover Road, February 3, 1864. Petersburg, VA: n.p., 1864.

Confederate States of America, War Department. *Articles of War, for the Government of the Army of the Confederate States*. Montgomery, AL: Barrett, Wimbish, 1861.

Conrad, Daniel. "Capture of the USS *Underwriter*, in the Neuse River, off Newbern, N.C., February, 1864." *Southern Historical Society Papers* 19 (January 1891).

Cooper, Alonzo. *In and out of Rebel Prisons*. Oswego, NY: Oliphant, 1888.

Cormier, Steven A. *The Siege of Suffolk: The Forgotten Campaign April 11–May 4, 1863*. 2nd ed. Lynchburg, VA: H. E. Howard, 1989.

Cornish, Dudley Taylor, and Virginia Jeans Laas. *Lincoln's Lee: The Life of Samuel Phillips Lee, United States Navy, 1812–1897*. Lawrence: University Press of Kansas, 1986.

Crabtree, Heidi. *Not a Soldier, but a Scoundrel: The Lives and Deaths of George W. Graham*. Orange, CA: Blue Rose Press, 2015.

Croffut, William Augustus. *The Military and Civil History of Connecticut during the War of 1861–65*. New York: Ledyard Bill, 1868.

Crofts, Daniel W. *Reluctant Confederates: Upper South Unionists in the Secession Crisis*. Chapel Hill: University of North Carolina Press, 2014.

Crumpler, Thomas N. *Speech on Federal Relations, Delivered in the House of Commons*. Raleigh, NC: Printed at the Office of the *Raleigh Register*, 1861.

Current, Richard Nelson. *Lincoln's Loyalists: Union Soldiers from the Confederacy.* Boston: Northeastern University Press, 1992.

Davis, Jefferson. *The Papers of Jefferson Davis: October 1863–August 1864.* Baton Rouge: Louisiana State University Press, 1999.

Delaney, Norman C. "Charles Henry Foster and the Unionists of Eastern North Carolina." *North Carolina Historical Review* 37 (July 1960).

Denny, Joseph Waldo. *Wearing the Blue in the Twenty-Fifth Mass. Volunteer Infantry: With Burnside's Coast Division, 18th Army Corps, and Army of the James.* Worcester, MA: Putnam & Davis, 1879.

Derby, William P. *Bearing Arms in the Twenty-Seventh Massachusetts Regiment of Volunteers Infantry during the Civil War, 1861–1865.* Boston: Wright & Power, 1883.

Dickey, Luther. *History of the 103d Regiment, Pennsylvania Veteran Volunteer Infantry, 1861–1865.* N.p.: L. S. Dickey, 1910.

Donaghy, John. *Army Experience of Capt. John Donaghy, 103d Penn'a Vols. 1861–1864.* De Land, FL: E. O. Painter, 1926.

Dowd, Clement. *Life of Zebulon B. Vance.* Raleigh, NC: Observer Printing & Publishing House, 1897.

Dowdey, Clifford, and Louis H. Manarin, eds. *The Wartime Papers of R. E. Lee.* Boston: Little, Brown, 1961.

Durrill, Wayne K. *War of Another Kind: A Southern Community in the Great Rebellion.* New York: Oxford University Press, 1990.

Dyer, Frederick. *A Compendium of the War of the Rebellion.* Vol. 2. Dayton, OH: Morningside, 1979.

Edmondston, Catherine A. *Journal of a Secesh Lady: The Diary of Catherine Ann Devereux Edmondston, 1860–1866.* Raleigh, NC: Division of Archives & History, Department of Cultural Resources, 1979.

Elliott, C. G. "Martin's Brigade—Hoke's Division, 1863–64." *Southern Historical Society Papers* 23, (January–December 1895).

Elliott, Gilbert. "The Career of the Ram *Albemarle.*" *Century Magazine* 36 (1888).

Elliott, James Carson. *The Southern Soldier Boy: A Thousand Shots for the Confederacy.* Raleigh, NC: Edwards & Broughton, 1907.

Elliott, Robert G. *Ironclad of the Roanoke: Gilbert Elliott's Albemarle.* Shippensburg, PA: White Mane, 2005.

Ensminger, Samuel. *Letters to Lanah: A Series of Civil War Letters Written by Samuel Ensminger.* N.p., 1986.

Escott, Paul D., ed. *North Carolinians in the Era of the Civil War and Reconstruction.* Chapel Hill: University of North Carolina Press, 2008.

Evans, Clement A. *Confederate Military History: A Library of Confederate States History.* Vol. 4. Atlanta: Confederate, 1899.

Field, C. W. "Campaign of 1864 and 1865. Narrative of Major-General C.W. Field." *Southern Historical Society Papers* 14 (January–December 1886).

Fiske, Joseph E. "An Involuntary Journey through the Confederacy." In *Civil War Papers Read before the Commandery of the State of Massachusetts, Military Order of the Loyal Legion of the United States.* Boston: F. H. Gilson, 1900.

——. *War Letters of Capt. Fiske.* Wellesley, MA: Magus Press, 1900.

Folk, Edgar E. *W. W. Holden: A Political Biography.* Winston-Salem, NC: John F. Blair, 1982.

Fonveille, Chris E., Jr. "Closing down the Kingdom: Union Combined Operations against Wilmington." In *Union Combined Operations in the Civil War,* ed. Craig Symonds. New York: Fordham University Press, 2010.

Fox, Gustavas. *Confidential Correspondence of Gustavus Vasa Fox, Assistant Secretary of the Navy, 1861–1865.* 2 vols. New York: De Vinne Press, 1918.

Franklin, John Hope. *The Free Negro in North Carolina, 1790–1860.* Chapel Hill: University of North Carolina Press, 2002.

Freeman, Douglas Southall. *Lee's Lieutenants.* 3 vols. New York: Charles Scribner's Sons, 1945.

——. *R. E. Lee: A Biography.* 4 vols. New York: Charles Scribner's Sons, 1934.

——, ed. *Lee's Dispatches: Unpublished Letters of General Robert E. Lee.* New York: G. P. Putnam & Sons, 1957.

French, S. G. *Two Wars: An Autobiography of General Samuel G. French.* Nashville, TN: Confederate Veteran, 1901.

Gaines, E. W. "Fayette Artillery: The Movement on New Berne Thirty-Three Years Ago; a Richmond Battery's Part." *Southern Historical Society Papers* 25 (1897).

Gallagher, Gary, and Allan Nolan, eds. *The Myth of the Lost Cause and Civil War History.* Bloomington: Indiana University Press, 2000.

Gardner, James Brown. *Record of the Service of the Forty-Fourth Massachusetts Volunteer Militia in North Carolina, August 1862 to May 1863.* Boston: privately printed, 1887.

Glasgow, William M. *Northern Virginia's Own: The 17th Virginia Regiment, Confederate States Army.* Alexandria, VA: Gobill Press, 1989.

Glatthaar, Joseph T. *Forged in Battle: The Civil War Alliance of Black Soldiers and White Officers.* Baton Rouge: Louisiana State University Press, 1990.

Goff, Richard D. *Confederate Supply.* Durham, NC: Duke University Press, 1969.

Gordon, Lesley. *A Broken Regiment: The 16th Connecticut's Civil War.* Baton Rouge: Louisiana State University Press, 2014.

——. *General George E. Pickett in Life and Legend.* Chapel Hill: University of North Carolina Press, 2001.

——. "'In Time of War': Unionists, Hanged in Kinston, North Carolina, February 1864." In *Guerrillas, Unionists, and Violence on the Confederate Home Front,* ed. Daniel E. Sutherland. Fayetteville: University of Arkansas Press, 1999.

——. "Let the People See the Old Life as It Was: LaSalle Corbell Pickett and the Myth of the Lost Cause." In *The Myth of the Lost Cause and Civil War History,* ed. Gary Gallagher and Allan Nolan. Bloomington: Indiana University Press, 2000.

Gorgas, Josiah. *The Journals of Josiah Gorgas, 1857–1878.* Tuscaloosa: University of Alabama Press, 1995.

Goss, Lee Warren. *The Soldier's Story of His Captivity at Andersonville, Belle Isle, and Other Rebel Prisons*. Bedford, MA: Lee & Shepard, 1867.

Graham, John. "The Capture of Plymouth." In vol. 5 of *Histories of the Several Regiments and Battalions from North Carolina in the Great War 1861–5*, ed. Walter Clark. Goldsboro, NC: Nash Brothers, 1901.

Graham, Robert D. "Fifty-Sixth Regiment." In vol. 3 of *Histories of the Several Regiments and Battalions from North Carolina in the Great War 1861–5*, ed. Walter Clark. Goldsboro, NC: Nash Brothers, 1901.

Grant, Ulysses S. *Personal Memoirs of U. S. Grant*. 2 vols. New York: C. L. Webster, 1886.

———. "Preparing for the Campaigns of '64." In vol. 3 of *Battles and Leaders of the Civil War*. New York: Century, 1884.

Gregory, G. Howard. *53rd Virginia Infantry and 5th Battalion Virginia Infantry*. Lynchburg, VA: H. E. Howard, 1999.

Grimsley, Mark. *The Hard Hand of War: Union Military Policy toward Southern Civilians, 1861–1865*. Cambridge: Cambridge University Press, 1995.

———. "Surviving Military Revolution: The U.S. Civil War." In *The Dynamics of Military Revolution, 1300–2050*, ed. MacGregor Knox. New York: Cambridge University Press, 2001.

Guelzo, Allen C. *Gettysburg: The Last Invasion*. New York: Alfred A. Knopf, 2013.

Hackett, Frank W. *Deck and Field*. Washington, DC: W. H. Lowdermilk, 1909.

———. *Flusser and the Albemarle*. Washington, DC: n.p., 1899.

Hagood, Johnson. *Memoirs of the War of Secession from the Original Manuscripts of Johnson Hagood*. Columbia, SC: State Co., 1910.

Haines, Zenas T. *Letters from the Forty-Fourth Regiment M.V.M.: A Record of the Experience of the Nine Months' Regiment in the Department of North Carolina in 1862–1863*. Boston: Herald Job Officer, 1863.

Hall, Henry, and James Hall. *Cayuga in the Field: A Record of the 19th N.Y. Volunteers, All the Batteries of the 3d New York Artillery, and 75th New York Volunteers*. Auburn, NY: n.p., 1873.

Hamilton, J. G. de Roulhac. "The Heroes of America." In vol. 11 of *Publications of the Southern History Association*, ed. Coliwether Meriwether. Washington, DC: Southern History Association, 1907.

———. *History of North Carolina: North Carolina since 1860*. Chicago: Lewis, 1919.

———. *Reconstruction in North Carolina*. New York: Columbia University Press, 1914.

———, ed. *The Papers of Thomas Ruffin*. Vol. 3. Raleigh: North Carolina Historical Commission, 1902.

Hamlin, Percy. *Old Bald Head (General R. S. Ewell): The Portrait of a Soldier*. Strasburg, VA: Shenandoah, 1940.

Harmon, George D., and Edith Blackburn Hazlehurst. "Captain Isaiah Conley's Escape from a Southern Prison, 1864." *Western Pennsylvania Historical Magazine* 47, 2 (April 1964).

Harrill, Lawson. *Reminiscences, 1861–1865: General M. W. Ransom's Brigade*. Statesville, NC: Brady, 1910.

Harris, William C. *William Woods Holden: Firebrand of North Carolina Politics*. Baton Rouge: Louisiana State University Press, 1987.

Harrison, Walter. *Pickett's Men: A Fragment of War History.* New York: D. Van Nostrand, 1870.

Hattaway, Herman, and Richard E. Beringer. *Jefferson Davis, Confederate President.* Lawrence: University Press of Kansas, 2002.

Hattaway, Herman, and Archer Jones. *How the North Won: A Military History of the Civil War.* Champaign: University of Illinois Press, 1991.

Hawkins, Rush. *An Account of the Assassination of Loyal Citizens of North Carolina, for Having Served in the Union Army: Which Took Place at Kingston in the Months of February and March, 1864.* New York: J. H. Folan, 1897.

Hayes, John D., ed. *Samuel Francis Du Pont: A Selection from His Civil War Letters.* Vol. 2. Ithaca, NY: Cornell University Press, 1969.

Headley, Phineas Camp. *Massachusetts in the Rebellion: A Record of the Historical Position of the Commonwealth, and the Services of the Leading Statesmen, the Military, the Colleges, and the People, in the Civil War of 1861–65.* Boston: Walker, Fuller, 1866.

Hearn, Chester G. *When the Devil Came down to Dixie: Ben Butler in New Orleans.* Baton Rouge: Louisiana State University Press, 2000.

Hess, Earl J. *Field Armies and Fortifications in the Civil War: The Eastern Campaigns, 1861–1864.* Chapel Hill: University of North Carolina Press, 2005.

———. *Pickett's Charge–The Last Attack at Gettysburg.* Chapel Hill: University of North Carolina Press, 2001.

Hewett, Janet B., et al. *Supplement to the Official Records of the Union and Confederate Armies.* 100 vols. Wilmington, NC: Broadfoot, 1994–1997.

Hill, D. H., Jr. "North Carolina." In vol. 4 of *Confederate Military History: A Library of Confederate States History,* ed. Clement A. Evans (Atlanta: Confederate, 1899).

Hinds, John W. *The Hunt for the Albemarle: Anatomy of a Gunboat War.* Shippensburg, PA: Burd Street Press, 2001.

Historic Washington County. Plymouth, NC: Washington County Historical Society, 1980.

Hoehling, Adolph. *Thunder at Hampton Roads.* New York: Da Capo Press, 1991.

Holden, Edgar. "The 'Albemarle' and the 'Sassacus.'" In vol. 4 of *Battles and Leaders of the Civil War.* New York: Century, 1888.

Hovey, Carl. "How Haring Held the Bridge." *Everybody's Magazine* 4 (1901).

Humphreys, Andrew. *From Gettysburg to the Rapidan: The Army of the Potomac, July, 1863, to April, 1864.* New York: Charles Scribner's Sons, 1883.

Impeachment Investigation: Testimony Taken before the Judiciary Committee of the House of Representatives in the Investigation of the Charges against Andrew Johnson. 39th Cong., 2nd sess.; 40th Cong., 1st sess. Washington, DC: US Government Printing Office, 1867.

Inscoe, John D., and Gordon B. McKinney. *The Heart of Confederate Appalachia: Western North Carolina in the Civil War.* Chapel Hill: University of North Carolina Press, 2000.

Iobst, Richard W., and Louis H. Manarin. *The Bloody Sixth: The Sixth North Carolina Regiment Confederate States of America.* Gaithersburg, MD: Butternut Press, 1987.

James, Horace. *Annual Report of the Superintendent of Negro Affairs in North Carolina, 1864.* Boston: W. F. Brown, 1865.

Jimerson, Randall C. *The Private Civil War: Popular Thought during the Sectional Conflict.* Baton Rouge: Louisiana State University Press, 1988.

Johnston, David E. *Four Years a Soldier.* Princeton, WV: privately printed, 1887.

———. *The Story of a Confederate Boy in the Civil War.* Portland, OR: Glass & Prudhomme, 1914.

Johnston, Frontis, ed. *The Papers of Zebulon Baird Vance.* Vol. 1. Raleigh, NC: State Department of Archives and History, 1963.

Johnston, Hugh Bucker, Jr. "The Confederate Letters of Ruffin Barnes of Wilson County." *North Carolina Historical Review* 31, 1 (January 1954).

Jones, Archer. *Civil War Command and Strategy: The Process of Victory and Defeat.* New York: Free Press, 1992.

Jones, John B. *A Rebel War Clerk's Diary at the Confederate States Capital.* 2 vols. Philadelphia: J. B. Lippincott, 1866.

Jones, J. W. *The Story of American Heroism: Thrilling Narratives of Personal Adventures during the Great Civil War as Told by the Medal Winners and Roll of Honor Men.* Springfield, OH: J. W. Jones, 1895.

Jordan, Weymouth T., Jr., and Gerald W. Thomas. "Massacre at Plymouth: April 20, 1864." *North Carolina Historical Review* 72, 2 (April 1995).

Journal of the Congress of the Confederate States of America, 1861–1865. Vol. 6. Washington, DC: US Government Printing Office, 1905.

Kellogg, Robert Hale. *Life and Death in Rebel Prisons.* Hartford, CT: L. Stebbins, 1865.

Kennedy, John T., and W. F. Parker. "Seventy-Fifth Regiment." In vol. 4 of *Histories of the Several Regiments and Battalions from North Carolina in the Great War 1861–5,* ed. Walter Clark. Goldsboro, NC: Nash Brothers, 1901.

Kennedy, Joseph C. G. *Agriculture of the United States in 1860: Compiled from the Original Returns of the Eighth Census, under the Direction of the Secretary of the Interior.* Washington, DC: US Government Printing Office, 1864.

Kirwan, Thomas. *Memorial History of the Seventeenth Regiment, Massachusetts Volunteer Infantry (Old and New Organizations) in the Civil War from 1861–1865.* N.p.: Committee on History, 1911.

Krick, Robert K. *30th Virginia Infantry.* Lynchburg, VA: H. E. Howard, 1983.

Lane, James H. "Glimpses of Army Life in 1864." *Southern Historical Society Papers* 18 (1890).

Lee, Robert E. *Recollections and Letters of General Robert E. Lee.* New York: Doubleday, 1904.

Levin, Kevin. *Remembering the Battle of the Crater: War as Murder.* Lexington: University Press of Kentucky, 2012.

Lindblade, Eric. *Fight as Long as Possible: The Battle of Newport Barracks, North Carolina, February 2, 1864.* Gettysburg, PA: Ten Roads Publishing, 2010.

Loehr, Charles T. *War History of the Old First Virginia Infantry Regiment, Army of Northern Virginia.* Richmond, VA: Ellis Jones, 1884.

Lonn, Ella. *Desertion during the Civil War.* New York: Century, 1928.

Loy, Ursula Fogleman, and Pauline Marion Worthy, eds. *Washington and the Pamlico.* Beaufort County, NC: Washington–Beaufort County Bicentennial Commission, 1976.

Loyall, B. P. "Capture of the *Underwriter*, New Bern, 2 February 1864." In vol. 5 of *Histories of the Several Regiments and Battalions from North Carolina in the Great War, 1861–5*, ed. Walter Clark. Goldsboro, NC: Nash Brothers, 1901.

Ludwig, H. T. J. "Eighth Regiment." In vol. 1 of *Histories of the Several Regiments and Battalions from North Carolina in the Great War, 1861–5*, ed. Walter Clark. Goldsboro, NC: Nash Brothers, 1901.

Luraghi, Raimondo. *A History of the Confederate Navy*. Annapolis, MD: Naval Institute Press, 1996.

Maffitt, John N. "Reminiscences of the Confederate Navy." In *The United Service: A Monthly Review of Military and Naval Affairs*. Vol. 3. Philadelphia: L. R. Hamersly, 1880.

Mahood, Wayne. *Charlie Mosher's Civil War: From Fair Oaks to Andersonville with the Plymouth Pilgrims (85th N.Y. Infantry)*. Hightstown, NJ: Longstreet House, 1994.

Manarin, Louis H. *15th Virginia Infantry*. Lynchburg, VA: H. E. Howard, 1990.

——. *Henrico County: Field of Honor*. 2 vols. Henrico County, VA: Henrico County, 2005.

Manarin, Louis H., and Weymouth T. Jordan, comps. *North Carolina Troops, 1861–1865: A Roster*. 18 vols. to date. Raleigh, NC: Division of Archives and History, Department of Cultural Resources, 1966–.

Manning, Chandra. "'The Order of Nature Would Be Reversed': Slavery and the North Carolina Gubernatorial Election of 1864." In *North Carolinians in the Era of the Civil War and Reconstruction*, ed. Paul D. Escott. Chapel Hill: University of North Carolina Press, 2008.

——. *Troubled Refuge: Struggling for Freedom in the Civil War*. New York: Alfred A. Knopf, 2016.

——. *What This Cruel War Was Over: Soldiers, Slavery, and the Civil War*. New York: Vintage, 2008.

Marlow, Clayton Charles. *Matt W. Ransom: Confederate General from North Carolina*. Jefferson, NC: McFarland, 1996.

Marvel, William. *Burnside*. Chapel Hill: University of North Carolina Press, 2000.

McKinney, Gordon B. *Zeb Vance: North Carolina's Civil War Governor and Gilded Age Political Leader*. Chapel Hill: University of North Carolina Press, 2004.

McKnight, Brian D., and Barton A. Myers, eds. *The Guerrilla Hunters: Irregular Conflicts during the Civil War*. Baton Rouge: Louisiana State University Press, 2017.

McNary, Oliver R. "What I Saw and Did Inside and Outside of Rebel Prisons." In *War Talks in Kansas: A Series of Papers Read before the Kansas Commandery of the Military Order of the Loyal Legion of the United States*. 1906. Reprint, Wilmington, NC: Broadfoot, 1992.

McPherson, James. *Battle Cry of Freedom: The Civil War Era*. New York: Oxford University Press, 1988.

Medal of Honor, 1863–1968. Washington, DC: US Government Printing Office, 1968.

Meekins, Chris. *Elizabeth City, North Carolina, and the Civil War: A History of Battle and Occupation*. Charleston, SC: History Press, 2007.

Merrill, Julian Whedon. *Records of the 24th Independent Battery, N.Y. Light Artillery, U.S.V.* Ladies Cemetery Association of Perry, NY, 1870.

Mitchell, Reid. *Civil War Soldiers*. New York: Penguin Books, 1988.

Mobley, Joe A. *"War Governor of the South": North Carolina's Zeb Vance in the Confederacy.* Gainesville: University Press of Florida, 2005.

———. "Zebulon Vance: A Confederate Nationalist in the North Carolina Gubernatorial Election of 1864." *North Carolina Historical Review* 77, 4 (October 2000).

———, ed. *The Papers of Zebulon Baird Vance.* Vol. 2, *1863*. Raleigh, NC: Division of Archives and History, 1995.

———, ed. *The Papers of Zebulon Baird Vance.* Vol. 3, *1864–1865*. Raleigh: North Carolina Office of Archives and History, 2013.

Montgomery, Walter. "Relations between the Confederate States Government and the Government of North Carolina." In *Proceedings and Addresses of the Annual Session of the State Literary and Historical Association of North Carolina.* Raleigh: State Literary and Historical Association of North Carolina, 1906.

Mooney, James. *Dictionary of American Naval Fighting Ships.* Vol. 3. Washington, DC: US Government Printing Office, 1981.

Moore, Edwin G. "Ransom's Brigade." *Southern Historical Society Papers* 36 (1908).

Moore, Frank, ed. *The Rebellion Record, a Diary of American Events: With Documents, Narratives, Illustrative Incidents, Poetry, Etc.* Vol. 8. New York: D. Van Nostrand, 1865.

Moore, Mark A. *The Old North State at War: The North Carolina Civil War Atlas.* Raleigh: North Carolina Department of Cultural Resources, 2015.

Moore, Robert H. *The Richmond Fayette, Hampden, Thomas, and Blount's Lynchburg Artillery.* Lynchburg, VA: H. E. Howard, 1991.

Morgan, William Henry. *Personal Reminiscences of the War of 1861–5: In Camp–en Bivouac–on the March–on Picket–on the Skirmish Line–on the Battlefield–and in Prison.* Lynchburg, VA: J. P. Bell, 1911.

Moss, Juanita P. *Battle of Plymouth, North Carolina (April 17–20, 1864): The Last Confederate Victory.* Westminster, MD: Heritage Books, 2003.

Myers, Barton A. *Executing Daniel Bright: Race, Loyalty, and Guerrilla Violence in a Coastal Carolina Community, 1861–1865.* Baton Rouge: Louisiana State University Press, 2009.

———. "A More Rigorous Style of Warfare: Wild's Raid, Guerrilla Violence, and Negotiated Neutrality in Northeastern North Carolina." In *North Carolinians in the Era of the Civil War and Reconstruction,* ed. Paul D. Escott. Chapel Hill: University of North Carolina Press, 2008.

———. *Rebels against the Confederacy: North Carolina's Unionists.* New York: Cambridge University Press, 2014.

Newsome, Hampton. *Richmond Must Fall: The Richmond-Petersburg Campaign, October 1864.* Kent, OH: Kent State University Press, 2013.

Nichols, Roy F. "Fighting in North Carolina Waters." *North Carolina Historical Review* 40 (January 1963).

North Carolina Literary and Historical Association. *Proceedings and Addresses of the Annual Session of the State Literary and Historical Association of North Carolina.* Raleigh: State Literary and Historical Association of North Carolina, 1906.

Oakes, James. *Freedom National: The Destruction of Slavery in the United States, 1861–1865*. New York: W. W. Norton, 2013.

Parramore, Thomas C. "The Burning of Winton in 1862." *North Carolina Historical Review* 39 (Winter 1962).

Patterson, Gerard. *Justice or Atrocity: Gen. George Pickett and the Kinston, N.C. Hangings*. Gettysburg, PA: Thomas Publications, 2000.

Phinney, Mary. *Adventures of an Army Nurse in Two Wars: Ed. from the Diary and Correspondence of Mary Phinney, Baroness von Olnhausen*. Boston: Little, Brown, 1903.

Pickett, LaSalle Corbell. *The Heart of a Soldier: As Revealed in the Intimate Letters of Genl. George E. Pickett, C.S.A.* New York: Seth Moyle, 1913.

———. *Pickett and His Men*. Atlanta: Foote & Davies, 1899.

———. *What Happened to Me*. New York: Brentano's, 1917.

Pilkey, Orrin. *The North Carolina Shore and Its Barrier Islands: Restless Ribbons of Sand*. Durham, NC: Duke University Press, 1998.

Plum, William R. *The Military Telegraph during the Civil War in the United States*. Vol. 2. Chicago: Jackson McClurg, 1882.

Pohoresky, William. "The Legend of Johnnie Ring." *Civil War Times* 41, 7 (February 2003).

Price, Charles L. "North Carolina Railroads during the Civil War." *Civil War History* 7, 3 (September 1961).

Quarstein, John V. *The CSS Virginia: Sink before Surrender*. Charleston, SC: History Press, 2012.

Rafuse, Ethan. *Robert E. Lee and the Fall of the Confederacy, 1863–1865*. Lanham, MD: Rowman & Littlefield, 2009.

Raper, Horace W. "William W. Holden and the Peace Movement in North Carolina." *North Carolina Historical Review* 31, 4 (October 1954).

———. *William W. Holden: North Carolina's Political Enigma*. Chapel Hill: University of North Carolina Press, 1985.

Raper, Horace W., and Thorton W. Mitchell, eds. *The Papers of William Woods Holden: 1841–1868*. Vol. 1. Raleigh: North Carolina Department of Cultural Resources, 2000.

Reardon, Carol. *Pickett's Charge in History and Memory*. Chapel Hill: University of North Carolina Press, 1997.

Reed, John A. *History of the 101st Regiment, Pennsylvania Veteran Volunteer Infantry 1861–1865*. Chicago: L. S. Dickey, 1910.

Reed, Rowena. *Combined Operations in the Civil War*. Annapolis, MD: Naval Institute Press, 1978.

Reid, Richard M. *Freedom for Themselves: North Carolina's Black Soldiers in the Civil War Era*. Chapel Hill: University of North Carolina Press, 2008.

Rhea, Gordon C. *Cold Harbor: Grant and Lee, May 26–June 3, 1864*. Baton Rouge: Louisiana State University Press, 2000.

Ripley, Edward Hastings. *Vermont General: The Unusual War Experiences of Edward Hastings Ripley, 1862–1865*. New York: Devon-Adair, 1960.

Roberts, A. Sellew. "The Peace Movement in North Carolina." *Mississippi Valley Historical Review* 11, 2 (September 1924).

Roberts, William H. *Now for the Contest: Coastal & Oceanic Naval Operations in the Civil War*. Lincoln: University of Nebraska Press, 2004.

Robertson, William Glenn. *Back Door to Richmond: The Bermuda Hundred Campaign, April–June 1864*. Newark: University of Delaware Press, 1987.

Roe, Alfred S. *The Fifth Regiment Massachusetts Volunteer Infantry in Its Three Tours of Duty 1861, 1862–'63, 1864*. Boston: Fifth Regiment Veteran Association, 1911.

Roman, Alfred. *The Military Operations of General Beauregard*. New York: Da Capo Press, 1884.

Rose, W. N. "Twenty-Fourth Regiment." In vol. 2 of *Histories of the Several Regiments and Battalions from North Carolina in the Great War 1861–5*, ed. Walter Clark. Goldsboro, NC: Nash Brothers, 1901.

Roulhac, Thomas R. "Forty-Ninth Regiment." In vol. 3 of *Histories of the Several Regiments and Battalions from North Carolina in the Great War 1861–5*, ed. Walter Clark. Goldsboro, NC: Nash Brothers, 1901.

Sauers, Richard. *The Burnside Expedition in North Carolina*. Dayton, OH: Morningside House, 1996.

Savage, James W. *The Loyal Element in North Carolina during the War*. Omaha, NE: n.p., 1886.

Scharf, J. Thomas. *History of the Confederate States Navy from Its Organization to the Surrender of Its Last Vessel*. New York: Rogers & Sherwood, 1887.

Sherrill, Lee W., Jr. *The 21st North Carolina Infantry: A Civil War History, with a Roster of Officers*. Jefferson, NC: McFarland, 2015.

Shingleton, Royce Gordon. *John Taylor Wood: Sea Ghost of the Confederacy*. Athens: University of Georgia Press, 1979.

Silkenat, David. *Driven from Home: North Carolina's Civil War Refugee Crisis*. Athens: University of Georgia Press, 2016.

Simon, John Y., ed. *The Papers of Ulysses S. Grant*. 31 vols. Carbondale: Southern Illinois University Press, 1967–2008.

Skaggs, David C. "A Thorn, Not a Dagger: Strategic Implications of Ambrose Burnside's North Carolina Campaign." In *Union Combined Operations in the Civil War*, ed. Craig Symonds. New York: Fordham University Press, 2010.

Skoch, George. *Mine Run: A Campaign of Lost Opportunities October 21, 1863–May 1, 1864*. Lynchburg, VA: H. E. Howard, 1987.

Smith, James L. *Autobiography of James L. Smith*. Norwich, CT: Press of the Bulletin Company, 1881.

Smith, John G. "Recollections of Capt. John G. Smith, 8th Ga. Cavalry, as to a Trip as a Spy in Newbern, N.C., February, 1864." *Carolina and the Southern Cross* 2, 1 (April 1914).

Smith, William A. "The Siege and Capture of Plymouth." In *Personal Recollections of the War of the Rebellion: Addresses Delivered before the New York Commandery of the Loyal Legion of the Soldiers' and Citizens' Album of Biographical Record [of Wisconsin] Containing Personal Sketches of Army Men and Citizens Prominent in Loyalty to the Union*. Vol. 1. Chicago: Grand Army Publishing, 1888.

Sommers, Richard. *Richmond Redeemed: The Siege at Petersburg*. Garden City, NY: Doubleday, 1981.

Sorrel, Moxley G. *Recollections of a Confederate Staff Officer.* New York: Neale, 1905.

Spelman, John. *Executive and Legislative Documents.* Raleigh, NC: John Spelman, 1863-1864.

Squires, Turin, and M. E. Bennett. *Through the Years in Norfolk.* Norfolk, VA: Printcraft Press, 1936.

Stedman, Charles M. "Address of Mr. Stedman, of North Carolina." In *Statue of Zebulon Baird Vance.* Washington DC: US Government Printing Office, 1917.

Stewart, Charles. "Lion-Hearted Flusser: A Naval Hero of the Civil War." *Naval Institute Proceedings* 31, 2 (June 1905).

Still, William N. "The Career of the Ironclad 'Neuse.'" *North Carolina Historical Review* 13 (1966).

Stone, Dewitt Boyd, Jr. *Wandering to Glory: Confederate Veterans Remember Evans' Brigade.* Columbia: University of South Carolina Press, 2002.

Sumner, Merlin E., ed. *The Diary of Cyrus B. Comstock.* Dayton, OH: Morningside Press, 1987.

Taylor, Michael. *Cry Is War, War, War.* Dayton OH: Morningside Press, 1994.

Thomas, Gerald W. *Divided Allegiances: Bertie County during the Civil War.* Raleigh: North Carolina Division of Archives and History, 1996.

Thomas, Henry Walter. *History of the Doles-Cook Brigade of Northern Virginia, C.S.A.* Atlanta: Franklin, 1903.

Tower, Lockwood, ed. *Lee's Adjutant: The Wartime Letters of Colonel Walter Herron Taylor, 1862-1865.* Columbia: University of South Carolina Press, 1995.

Trask, Benjamin. *9th Virginia Infantry.* Lynchburg, VA: H. E. Howard, 1984.

Trudeau, Andre. *Like Men of War: Black Troops in the Civil War, 1862-1865.* Boston: Little, Brown, 1998.

Tucker, Glenn. *Zeb Vance: Champion of Personal Freedom.* New York: Bobbs-Merrill, 1965.

Tucker, Spencer, ed. *The Civil War Naval Encyclopedia.* Vol. 1. Santa Barbara, CA: ABC-CLIO, 2011.

Union Jack. "Cutting out the *Underwriter*. A Brilliant Exploit in a Southern Harbor." *Blue and Gray* 2 (July-December 1893).

United States, 1883-1891. Vol. 1. New York: New York Commandery of the Military Order of the Loyal Legion of the United States, 1891.

Urwin, Gregory. *Black Flag over Dixie: Racial Atrocities and Reprisals in the Civil War.* Carbondale: Southern Illinois University Press, 2005.

US Congress, House. *Murder of Union Soldiers in North Carolina.* Executive Document No. 98, serial 1263, 34th Cong., 2nd sess., 1866.

——. *Rebel General Pickett.* Executive Document No. 11, 39th Cong., 2nd sess., 1866.

US Navy Department. *Official Records of the Union and Confederate Navies in the War of the Rebellion.* 30 vols. Washington, DC: US Government Printing Office, 1894-1922.

US War Department. *War of the Rebellion: A Compilation of the Official Records of the Union and Confederate Armies.* 129 vols. Washington, DC: US Government Printing Office, 1881-1901.

Wallace, Lee. *3rd Virginia Infantry.* Lynchburg, VA: H. E. Howard, 1996.

Warfield, Edgar. *Manassas to Appomattox: The Civil War Memoirs of Pvt. Edgar Warfield 17th Virginia Infantry.* McLean, VA: EPM Publications, 1996.

Warner, Ezra J. *Generals in Blue: Lives of the Union Commanders.* Baton Rouge: Louisiana State University Press, 1964.

Warren, Edward. *A Doctor's Experiences in Three Continents.* Baltimore: Cushings & Bailey, 1885.

Welles, Gideon. *Diary of Gideon Welles: Secretary of the Navy Under Lincoln and Johnson.* 2 vols. Boston: Houghton Mifflin, 1911.

West, Richard S. *Lincoln's Scapegoat General: A Life of Benjamin F. Butler, 1881–1893.* Boston: Houghton Mifflin, 1965.

White, James Edward. *New Bern and the Civil War.* Charleston, SC: History Press, 2018.

Whittemore, Henry. *History of Montclair Township, State of New Jersey.* Montclair, NJ: Unigraphic, 1894.

Wiard, Norman. *Wiard's System of Field Artillery.* New York: Holman, 1863.

Wickman, Don. *"We Are Coming Father Abra'am": The History of the 9th Vermont Volunteer Infantry, 1862–1865.* Lynchburg, VA: Schroeder Publications, 2005.

Wilbur, Lafayette. *Early History of Vermont.* Vol. 4. Jericho, VT: Roscoe Printing House, 1903.

Wilcox, Carol. "William G. Shepardson: Swashbuckling Journalist of the Chesapeake." In *Knights of the Quill: Confederate Correspondents and Their Civil War Reporting,* ed. Patricia McNeely, Debra Reddin Van Tuyll, and Henry H. Schulte. West Lafayette, IN: Purdue University Press, 2010.

Williams, J. Marshall. "Fifty-Fourth Regiment." In vol. 3 of *Histories of the Several Regiments and Battalions from North Carolina in the Great War 1861–5,* ed. Walter Clark. Goldsboro, NC: Nash Brothers, 1901.

Williams, Max R. "The General and the Governor: Robert E. Lee and Zebulon B. Vance." In *Audacity Personified: The Generalship of Robert E. Lee,* ed. Peter S. Carmichael. Baton Rouge: Louisiana State University Press, 2004.

———, ed. *The Papers of William Alexander Graham.* Vol. 6. Raleigh: North Carolina Department of Cultural Resources, 1976.

Williams, T. Harry. *Lincoln and His Generals.* New York: Alfred A. Knopf, 1952.

Wills, Brian S. *The River Was Dyed with Blood: Nathan Bedford Forrest and Fort Pillow.* Norman: University of Oklahoma Press, 2014.

———. *The War Hits Home: The Civil War in Southeastern Virginia.* Charlottesville: University of Virginia Press, 2001.

Wilson, Herbert Wrigley. *Ironclads in Action: A Sketch of Naval Warfare from 1855 to 1895.* Vol. 1. Boston: Little, Brown, 1896.

Wilson, James Grant, ed. *Personal Recollections of the War of the Rebellion: Addresses Delivered before the New York Commandery of the Loyal Legion of the United States.* New York: New York Commandery of the Loyal Legion of the United States, 1891.

Wise, George. *Seventeenth Virginia Infantry.* Baltimore: Kelley, Piet, 1870.

Wise, Stephen R. *Lifeline of the Confederacy: Blockade Running during the Civil War.* Columbia: University of South Carolina Press, 1991.

Woodward, C. Vann, ed. *Mary Chesnut's Civil War.* New Haven, CT: Yale University Press, 1981.

Wright, E. A. "Capture of Plymouth, N.C." *Confederate Veteran* 24 (1916).

Yates, Richard E. "Governor Vance and the Peace Movement." 2 parts. *North Carolina Historical Review* 17, 1 (January 1940) and 17, 2 (April 1940).

Yearns, W. Buck, and John G. Barrett. *North Carolina Civil War Documentary.* Chapel Hill: University of North Carolina Press, 2002.

Younger, Edward, ed. *Inside the Confederate Government: The Diary of Robert Hill Garlick Kean.* New York: Oxford University Press, 1957.

Index

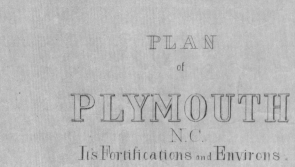

PLAN
of
PLYMOUTH
N.C.
Its Fortifications and Environs.

Scale
416.66 Feet to the Inch.

LIEUT. F. VINAY, 85TH R.N.Y. VOL².

R O A N O